ZON
18F

UNDERSTANDING CONSUMER BEHAVIOR

THE IRWIN SERIES IN MARKETING (Gilbert A. Churchill, Jr., Consulting Editor; University of Wisconsin)

UNDERSTANDING CONSUMER BEHAVIOR

J. PAUL PETER
University of Wisconsin, Madison

JERRY C. OLSON
Pennsylvania State University

IRWIN
Burr Ridge, Illinois
Boston, Massachusetts
Sydney, Australia

▷ **Rose and Angie**

▷ **Becky, Matt, and Seth**

Senior sponsoring editor: *Stephen M. Patterson*
Managing development editor: *Eleanore Snow*
Project editor: *Jean Lou Hess*
Production manager: *Diane Palmer*
Interior designer: *Maureen McCutcheon*
Cover designer: *Jeanne M. Rivera*
Art coordinator: *Mark Malloy*
Cover illustrator: *Francis Livingston*
Photo research coordinator: *Patricia A. Seefelt*
Photo researcher: Michael J. Hruby
Compositor: *Weimer Graphics, Inc.*
Typeface: *9/12 Helvetica*
Printer: *Von Hoffmann Press*

Library of Congress Cataloging-in-Publication Data

Peter, J. Paul
    Understanding consumer behavior / J. Paul Peter, Jerry C. Olson.
  1st ed.
     p. cm.—(The Irwin series in marketing)
  Includes bibliographical references and indexes.
  ISBN 0-256-12278-4
  1. Consumer behavior—United States—Case studies. I. Olson,
Jerry C. (Jerry Corrie), date II. Title. III. Series. 93–13484
  HF5415.33.U6P48 1994
  658.8'342—dc20

Printed in the United States of America
1 2 3 4 5 6 7 8 9 0 VH 0 9 8 7 6 5 4 3

Preface

Consumer behavior is an exciting, dynamic field critically important to the success of business firms and nonprofit organizations. *Understanding Consumer Behavior* captures the many fascinating aspects of consumer behavior while presenting an integrated, coherent approach to the study of consumer behavior. The text reflects the life-long involvement of the Authors with consumer behavior research.

In recent years, managers have become aware that satisfying consumers is the best way to develop and maintain a successful organization, a fact marketers have long recognized. Even managers is such areas as engineering and production are emphasizing consumer satisfaction. Many successful firms encourage everyone in the organization to put the consumer first when developing strategies.

Managers who want to satisfy consumers need an in-depth understanding of those consumers. *Understanding Consumer Behavior* identifies the essential elements of consumer behavior and provides the knowledge and skills to analyze the reasons for consumers' behavior. The text also shows how understanding consumers can be used to develop effective marketing strategies.

Unlike other texts that present students with many complex models, *Understanding Consumer Behavior* is based on a simple model for analyzing consumers, called the Wheel of Consumer Analysis. This model provides a conceptual framework for thinking about consumer behavior issues and is used throughout the text to focus students' attention on the key elements in consumer analysis. It also provides the organizing framework for the text. Section One provides an overview of the field of consumer behavior, introduces the Wheel of Consumer Analysis framework for analyzing consumers, and discusses how marketers use consumer analysis in segmenting markets and designing marketing strategies. The three remaining sections of the text concern the three elements of the Wheel of Consumer Analysis. Section Two focuses on affect and cognition, the feelings and thoughts consumers have about such things as products, advertisements, and stores. Section Three discusses behavior, the overt actions of consumers as they engage in marketing exchanges with organizations. Section Four examines the many factors in the physical and social environment that influence how consumers think, feel, and behave. Overall, the text produces a comprehensive, interesting, and highly readable treatment of the essential elements of consumer behavior analysis and application.

NEW AND UNIQUE CONCEPTS

Compared to other texts, *Understanding Consumer Behavior* includes more unique material useful in understanding consumers.

Understanding Consumer Behavior is organized around the simple Wheel of Consumer Analysis, which is a big advantage over other texts. After reading *Understanding Consumer*

Behavior, students will know a simple framework they can use in virtually any consumer analysis situation to develop more effective understanding of consumers and better marketing strategies.

Understanding Consumer Behavior has a superior treatment of affect, showing clearly its relationship to cognition, and the implications of considering how affect and cognition influence each other. Peter and Olson were the first to include detailed coverage of consumers' product knowledge, means-end chains, and associative networks of knowledge (now included in many other texts). Means-end chains are used throughout the text to analyze consumer/product relationships. *Understanding Consumer Behavior* has superior coverage of involvement, attention and comprehension, and attitudes, while clearly showing the marketing implications of these concepts.

Understanding Consumer Behavior offers a realistic treatment of consumer decision making as a part of the larger problem-solving process. Students learn that consumers make other decisions during problem solving besides brand choice. The chapter on communications includes new concepts such as narrative or drama advertising and the MECCAS model, which uses means-end chains to design effective advertising strategies.

Understanding Consumer Behavior is distinctive among texts in its detailed attention to the centrally important concept of behavior (four chapters) and how to analyze and influence consumers' behaviors.

The chapter on the physical environment is exceptional and includes a detailed treatment of situations that clearly describes this important concept. *Understanding Consumer Behavior* contains a new chapter on culture providing a unique and compelling framework for understanding culture and developing clear marketing implications. The chapter on subcultures presents original material concerning acculturation and covers ethnic, gender, income, gay subcultures.

SPECIAL PEDAGOGY

Understanding Consumer Behavior contains a variety of pedagogical aids to enhance student learning and enjoyment of the course.

▷ **Learning objectives.** Listed at the beginning of each chapter are several learning objectives that direct students to important knowledge and skills they should acquire in studying the chapter.

▷ **Summaries focusing on learning objectives.** To help students focus on the key material, each chapter closes with a summary that provides concise responses, based on the chapter concepts, for each of the learning objectives.

▷ **Chapter introductory examples.** Each chapter opens with an example of a real-world marketing situation that generates student interest in the concepts presented in the chapter.

▷ **Consumer Perspectives.** Each chapter contains several longer examples called Consumer Perspectives that describe how marketers use consumer analysis to develop marketing strategies. The CPs are set off in color to distinguish them from the text material. Each CP is referenced in the text so students easily grasp its relevance.

▷ **Real-world examples and photographs.** *Understanding Consumer Behavior* is replete with real-life examples illustrating the concepts discussed. Full-color photographs and ads provide visual examples and increase student interest.

▷ **Marketing implications.** Implications of consumer analysis for designing marketing strategies are incorporated into the text material. In addition, most chapters include separate sections titled "Marketing Implications" that provide in-depth discussion of the marketing applications of chapter concepts.

▷ **Key terms and concepts.** Important terms and concepts are listed at the end of each chapter and are highlighted in boldfaced type within the chapter text.

▷ **Review and discussion questions.** End-of-chapter review and discussion questions emphasize the understanding and application of chapter material to strategic marketing issues. The questions can be used for written assignments, in-class discussions, essay exam questions, or for student self-study.

▷ **Cases.** Each section of the text concludes with a set of short discussion cases that focus on consumer analysis issues facing well-known companies. The cases include several questions to focus student thinking on key issues of consumer analysis. The case questions also can be used for written assignments or in-class discussion.

▷ **References.** References are provided for text material and frequently include additional references students can use for more detailed study of selected topics.

▷ **Glossary.** The text includes a glossary of key consumer behavior terms and concepts as a reference source for students during the course and in their future careers. Many of the glossary definitions were previously prepared by the Authors for the American Marketing Association's *Dictionary of Marketing Terms.*

▷ **Writing style and clarity.** *Understanding Consumer Behavior* is written in an engaging, relaxed style, using simple sentence structure and minimal jargon. The presentation of concepts is straightforward and is accompanied by definitions and immediate examples to help students grasp both the concept and its application.

▷ **Design.** The large size, use of full-color, inviting design, and easy-to-use layout enhance student interest and comprehension.

The text contains several excellent instructional aids:

INSTRUCTIONAL AIDS

▷ **Instructor's Manual.** This comprehensive Manual, prepared entirely by the Authors, includes a wealth of useful information and suggestions for teaching each of the chapters. Reviewers have applauded both the quantity and the quality of the material contained in the Instructor's Manual, and have called it the best in the discipline. For each chapter, the Manual provides teaching objectives, teaching suggestions, additional topics not covered in the text, materials for mini-lectures, examples not found in the text, and suggested projects to be completed outside of class. The Manual also includes notes and answers to the review and discussion questions, notes on the cases, and a guide to the transparency masters.

▷ **Manual of Tests and CompuTest.** The Manual of Tests consists of approximately 100 multiple-choice and essay questions per chapter. Rationales are given for the answers to the more difficult multiple-choice questions. The test questions are also available in computerized form.

▷ **Transparency Acetates.** A set of about 50 acetates consisting of important exhibits from the text as well as ads not found in the text is available to adopters. Several of these transparencies are in full color.

▷ **Video Package.** Approximately 2 hours of video examples are offered free of charge to adopters. Each segment is approximately 15 minutes in length and can be shown in its entirety or in shorter parts to illustrate particular points about consumer behavior and marketing strategy. Also included is a Video Instructor's Manual prepared by the Authors.

ACKNOWLEDGMENTS

We are indebted to the many people who contributed to the development of this book. First, we thank our students, past and present, for their contributions to our understanding of consumer behavior and the educational process. Second, we thank Gilbert A Churchill, Jr.,

Irwin Consulting Editor; Steve Patterson, Senior Sponsoring Editor; Eleanore Snow, Irwin Managing Development Editor; and Jean Lou Hess, Irwin Project Editor, along with the Irwin Production, Art, and Design staffs for their efforts, insights, and patience in the development of *Understanding Consumer Behavior*. Third, we thank our reviewers for their excellent comments and suggestions: Barbara C. Coleman, Augusta College; Lawrence J. Marks, Kent State University; Amy Rummel, Alfred University; David Strutton, University of Southwestern Louisiana; and Gail Tom, California State University–Sacramento.

Fourth, we thank the survey respondents whose comments were most helpful as we shaped the structure of the text:

Amy B. Rummel *Alfred University*
Paul F. Sable *Allentown College*
Kathy Lacher *Auburn University*
Barbara Coleman *Augusta College*
Katrin Harich *CSU—Fullerton*
Eric Arnould *CSU—Long Beach*
Wanda Fujimoto *Central Washington University*
Rajshekhar Javalgi *Cleveland State University*
Sylvia Clark *College of Staten Island*
Ellen Brown *Davenport College, MI*
Mel Prince *Fordham University*
Richard Nordstrom *Fresno State*
Geng Cui *Hampton University, VA*
Benny Barak *Hofstra University*
Elaine Sherman *Hofstra University*
Lawrence Marks *Kent State University*
Scott W. Burton *Louisiana State University*
Carolyn Predmore *Manhattan College*

Dr. Conniue Bauer *Marquette University*
Steve Lysonski *Marquette University*
Deanna Mader *Marshall University*
Lakshami Thumuluri *Miami University*
Myrtle Cooper *Midlands Tech*
Jack Jacoby *New York University*
Oliver Niehouse *New York University*
Neil Broughton *Niagara Community College*
Roxanne Stell *Northern Arizona University*
Lynn Langmeyer *Northern Kentucky University*
Alan R. Wiman *Rider College*
Edward H. Bonfield *Rider College*
Diane Parents *SUNY—Fredonia*
C. Michael Schaninger *SUNY—Albany*
Mary Ann Stutts *Southwest Texas State University*
Janet Diainno *St. Mary's University*
Barbara Oates *Texas A&I University*

David Prensky *Trenton State College*
Judy Siguaw *UNC—Wilmington*
Ed Cerny *USC—Coastal Carolina*
Thomas Gunter *USC–Spartanburg*
Trudy Kehret—Ward *University of California-Berkeley*
Mary Lou Roberts *University of Massachusetts—Boston*
Jo Ann Asquith *University of MIchigan—Flint*
Kenneth Baker *University of New Mexico*
David H. Strutton *University of Southwestern Louisiana*
Clare Comm *University of Massachusetts—Lowell*
Jhinuk Chowdhury *University of North Texas*
Sharon E. Beatty *University of Alabama—Tuscaloosa*
Nancy Ridgway *University of Colorado—Boulder*
Terrell Williams *Western Washington University*
Fred B. Kraft *Wichita State University*

We also thank the many researchers and teachers in marketing who have contributed to our thinking about consumer behavior and how it can best be taught to future managers. Finally, we thank our families, especially our wives, Rose Peter and Becky Olson, for their encouragement and patience during this project.

J. Paul Peter
Jerry C. Olson

Brief
Contents

Table of Contents

UNDERSTANDING CONSUMER BEHAVIOR

CONSUMER BEHAVIOR OVERVIEW

CHAPTERS IN THIS SECTION

▶ 1. Introduction to Consumer Behavior

▶ 2. The Wheel of Consumer Analysis: A Framework for Understanding Consumers

▶ 3. Using Consumer Analysis: Market Segmentation and the Marketing Mix

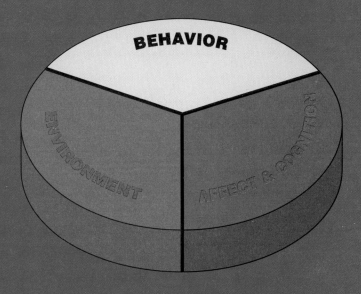

1

Introduction to Consumer Behavior

LEARNING OBJECTIVES

After completing this chapter, you should be able to:

▶ 1. Explain the marketing concept.

▶ 2. Cite three reasons why companies today are changing to serve consumers better.

▶ 3. Define consumer behavior.

▶ 4. Explain three points emphasized in the definition of consumer behavior.

▶ 5. Explain why three major groups are interested in consumer behavior.

▶ 6. List five elements of a marketing strategy for which knowledge of consumer behavior can help make better decisions.

THE LONG LIFE OF THE GRATEFUL DEAD

One of the most successful operations in popular music is the rock 'n' roll group the Grateful Dead—it understands its consumers and gives them what they want. The Dead pioneered such innovations as mail order tickets, recorded telephone messages about performances, and special locations at shows to allow fans (known as "tapeheads") to record the performance, something other rock groups actively discourage.

The group changes its offerings every show to give variety to consumers going to more than one concert. It also offers concerts that run almost twice as long as those of its competition but at no more cost. This market-sensitive approach has allowed the Grateful Dead to be successful for nearly 30 years. In fact, in one recent year, the band sold $29 million worth of tickets to 63 North American shows, fourth among rock stars for that year. In sum, the Grateful Dead succeeds because it understands its consumers and implements strategies to serve them.

APPLYING THE MARKETING CONCEPT

In the 1990s more organizations have recognized that satisfying consumers with quality products and offering superior service is the foundation for success in highly competitive markets.

Marketers have long argued that the marketing concept is the appropriate philosophy for conducting business. Simply stated, the **marketing concept** suggests that to be more profitable an organization must satisfy consumer needs and wants. To implement the marketing concept, organizations must understand and stay close to their customers to provide products and services consumers will purchase.

For many years, U.S. firms have not fully understood the marketing concept. All too often, even firms that accept the marketing concept in principle do not recognize its implementation requires an organization to make dramatic changes in its approach to doing business. In general, these firms have viewed implementation of the marketing concept as a marketing task only, certainly not a comprehensive strategy the entire organization has to buy into. While these companies may carry out marketing and consumer research, they seldom use this research as the basis for designing an entire organizational strategy.

Today, many of the world's most successful companies have designed their entire organizations to serve and stay close to consumers.[1] These companies are committed to developing quality products and services and selling them at a price that gives consumers high value. In these successful companies, not only the marketing department, but also

---

CONSUMER PERSPECTIVE

▶1.1

Staying close to customers

A number of leading U.S. companies owe their success and profitability to designing the organization to stay close to customers. Below are a few examples.

Harley-Davidson, Inc.

By the early 1980s, Japanese motorcycle manufacturers dominated the U.S. market. The Japanese bikes were more sophisticated, of better quality, and cheaper than Harleys. Harley-Davidson was days away from filing for bankruptcy by the end of 1985. When the company found refinancing, it continued to work hard to improve the quality of its motorcycles through better design, encouraging employees to become more committed to quality, working with dealers, and interacting continually with consumers to get feedback on its products and ideas for improvements. By 1990, Harley-Davidson dominated the super-heavyweight motorcycle market with a market share of over 62 percent.

Monroe Auto Equipment

In the past decade, nine companies from Japan and Europe stormed the U.S. market for shock absorbers and struts—under-the-body parts that give cars a smooth ride. Monroe Auto Equipment recognized that to survive in this mature market, it had to improve the quality of its products and reduce costs. Since 1986, productivity in its 36 plants has increased 26 percent, annual sales have increased 70 percent to $900 million, and profits have increased 20 percent. In the $1.5 billion-a-year market, Monroe sells more than half of all the replacement shocks and close to one third of those put on new cars. Monroe learned how to build better quality products by studying Japanese methods. It focuses on having zero defects, which satisfies both organizational and consumer buyers.

Nike

While there are many strong competitors in the sports shoe market, Nike is at the top. In 1990, sales jumped 31 percent over 1989, to $2.2 billion, about $75 million

design, engineering, production, human resources, finance, and other departments focus on doing their jobs in ways that enhance the value of their products to consumers. Some firms find they can improve product quality and reduce costs at the same time, and they encourage employees throughout the company to seek ways to do this. Others first determine what consumers want and how much they are willing to pay for a product, and then they design, produce, and market the best-quality product they can for the price consumers are willing to pay. Consumer Perspective 1.1 discusses four companies that owe their success, if not their survival, to their focus on customers.

What accounts for the changes companies are making to serve consumers better? There are likely three major reasons.

First, the dramatic success of Japanese companies such as Toyota and Sony, which focus on providing value-laden products, has spurred other companies to focus on the consumer. During the 1960s and 70s, many U.S. companies could sell almost anything they could produce. Consumers accepted U.S. products and services as being as good as could be expected. Yet as American consumers discovered the superior quality and lower prices of many Japanese products, they saw that some U.S. products offered inferior value, and they shifted to purchasing foreign-made goods. Faced with this flight of sales, many U.S. companies had to redesign their organizations to serve consumers so they could survive and compete in both U.S. and world markets.

Value-laden products

higher than arch rival Reebok International. Nike's profits were $243 million compared to $177 million for Reebok. Nike sells over 800 models for about 25 sports. It makes three lines of basketball shoes, each expressing what Nike calls a different attitude. The Air Jordan (retail price $125) is for consumers who want to follow in the footsteps of the Chicago Bulls superstar. The Flight (up to $115) is for players who value the lightest Nikes, while the Force (up to $150) incorporates the latest designs, such as a custom air bladder for consumers who want a snug fit. The company updates its shoes at least every six months to tempt new customers to lace on a new pair before last year's wears out. By carefully segmenting the market, introducing frequent innovations and style changes, and continual research to develop the most effective and stylish athletic shoes, Nike offers quality products that consumers want.

Wal-Mart

Sam Walton, founder of Wal-Mart, had a simple idea on how to be a successful retailer: be an agent for consumers; find out what they want, and sell it to them for the lowest possible price. To do so effectively, Wal-Mart has developed a corporate culture that focuses on consumers. The company has a sophisticated computerized warehouse and inventory system that carefully tracks sales and relays sales data to manufacturers to ensure stores remain well stocked with high-demand merchandise. Wal-Mart bargains hard with manufacturers to get the lowest possible price and keeps overhead low—in fact, the lowest in the industry. Wal-Mart stays close to customers. Is it any wonder that in 1991 it became the number one retailer in the United States with sales of over $32 billion?

Sources: *Wisconsin State Journal*, "Business Rev Charges Harley after Long Slump," John Kekis, June 1, 1991; *Northwest Compass Reading Magazine*, "Harley Davidson's Long Marriage of Mechanics and Art," Christopher Boehme, November 1991; "Smart Moves by Quality Champs," Erik Caloneus, and "Is Wal-Mart Unstoppable, Bill Saporito, *Fortune*, © 1991 Time Inc. All rights reserved.

Marketing research firms such as this one can help marketers understand and stay close to consumers.

BETA RESEARCH LEAVES A NOTICEABLE RING.

Improved quality of marketing research

The second major reason for a shift to focusing on consumers is a dramatic increase in the quality of consumer and marketing research. In the past, firms often had no detailed information on people who bought and used their products. While they may have commissioned research to investigate new product concepts and to try to understand consumers, often this research was not ongoing and did not identify the firm's actual customers. Today, computer technology and scanner and other data sources make it possible for firms to know who their customers are and how marketing strategy and strategy changes affect them. Both manufacturers and retailers now have ways to track consumer reactions to new products and services and to evaluate marketing strategies more effectively than ever before. Thus, companies are now in a better position to implement the marketing concept. Consumer Perspective 1.2 (see page 8) provides several examples of segmented mailing lists that offer companies information about specific types of consumers.

Development of consumer behavior research and theory

A third reason for today's increased emphasis on consumers is the development of consumer behavior as a field of study. In the past, marketers had some useful views of consumer behavior to work from; but both the number and the sophistication of theories, concepts, and models to describe and understand consumer behavior have grown dramatically in recent years. Although there is no consensus on what theories or approaches to understanding consumers are best, marketers today have a greater variety of useful ideas for understanding consumers than they once did.

In sum, many successful companies recognize the importance of consumers, and they use sophisticated approaches and detailed data from which to develop organizational and marketing strategies. All of this indicates a consumer behavior course is an important component of a business education. In the remainder of this chapter, we discuss the nature of consumer behavior and the parties involved in studying and analyzing it. We also

Consumer behavior involves exchanges such as this one at a Blockbuster Video store.

investigate some relationships between consumer behavior and marketing strategy and the value of this course for a successful career. While this text focuses on consumer behavior and marketing strategy, employees in every business function in a successful company will be involved in serving consumers. Consumer Perspective 1.3 (see page 9) lists some companies that have stayed close to their customers for many years.

WHAT IS CONSUMER BEHAVIOR?

The American Marketing Association defines **consumer behavior** as "the dynamic interaction of affect and cognition, behavior, and environmental events by which human beings conduct the exchange aspects of their lives."[2] There are at least three important ideas in this definition: consumer behavior is dynamic; it involves interaction among affect and cognitions, behaviors, and environmental events; and it involves exchanges.

Consumer behavior is dynamic

First, the definition emphasizes that consumer behavior is *dynamic*. This means individual consumers, consumer groups, and society at large constantly change and evolve. Change has important implications for the study of consumer behavior as well as for developing marketing strategies. One implication is that generalizations about consumer behavior are usually limited to specific time periods, products, and individuals or groups. Thus, students of consumer behavior must be careful not to overgeneralize theories and research findings.

The dynamic nature of consumer behavior implies that one should not expect the same marketing strategy to work all of the time, or across all products, markets, and industries. While this may seem obvious, many companies do not recognize the need to adapt their strategies in different markets. For example, Philip Morris was unable to make 7UP a leading brand despite use of strategies that had been successful in other industries.

Further, a strategy that is successful at one time may fail miserably at another. For example, the American automobile industry had no problem selling automobiles of relatively modest quality—until U.S. consumers learned about the superior quality and value of Japanese cars. This resulted in American manufacturers working hard to improve the quality of their offerings. As health-conscious consumers became aware of the cholesterol problems associated with palm or coconut oil, Kellogg's adapted its marketing strategy by

Companies today can buy or rent a variety of mailing lists to focus their marketing efforts on individual consumers. These mailing lists include the names and addresses of consumers who have demonstrated certain kinds of behavior that might indicate they would be interested in a given company's products. Some of the lists available for sale include:

▶ 26,912 Southern California investors who own at least $100,000 worth of "jumbo" certificates of deposit.

▶ 95,293 people who visited the Basketball Hall of Fame and bought a souvenir at the novelty shop.

▶ 140,426 grandparents who bought Johnson & Johnson child development toys.

▶ 323,050 users of Wordstar, a computer program.

▶ 356,330 contributors to the Democratic National Committee.

▶ 861,345 owners of Apple II computers. A separate list of 253,448 women who bought Apple products.

▶ 2.4 million people who ordered by phone using a credit card.

▶ 11 million people who moved recently. 15 million families with children.

▶ 30 million mail-order shoppers.

Source: Reprinted from "Nearly Everyone's on Somebody's List," by Robert S. Boyd, © 1990 by Knight-Ridder Newspapers, by permission of the Knight-Ridder/Tribune News Service.

removing these oils from its Cracklin' Oat Bran. In sum, the dynamic nature of consumer behavior makes marketing strategy development an exciting, yet challenging, task.

Consumer behavior involves interactions

A second important point that comes out of the definition of consumer behavior is that it involves interactions among affect and cognitions, behaviors, and environmental events. To understand consumers and develop superior marketing strategies, we must understand what they think (cognition) and feel (affect), what they do (behavior), and the things and places (environmental events) that influence and are influenced by what consumers think, feel, and do. We believe it is shortsighted to analyze only the effects of an environmental event on affect, cognitions, or behaviors, as is common in basic research. Instead, whether we are evaluating a single consumer, a target market, or an entire society, analysis of all three elements is useful for understanding and developing marketing strategies.

Consumer behavior involves exchanges

A final point emphasized in the definition of consumer behavior is that it involves exchanges between human beings. Typically, consumers exchange their money for products and services. This definition of consumer behavior is consistent with current definitions of marketing that also emphasize exchange. In fact, the role of marketing is to facilitate exchanges with consumers by formulating and implementing marketing strategies.

WHO IS INTERESTED IN CONSUMER BEHAVIOR?

Two broad groups are interested in consumer behavior—a basic research group and an action-oriented group. The basic research group is mainly academic researchers interested in studying consumer behavior to develop a unique body of knowledge about this aspect of human behavior. These researchers have backgrounds in anthropology, sociology, psychology, economics, and marketing, as well as other fields. The majority of published work on

Some analysts argue that brand names are becoming less important to consumers. Clearly, some companies, however, have stayed close to their customers and kept their brands on top for many years. Some brands have been sales leaders for decades.

| | Leading brand in | |
Category	1923	1991
Cameras	Kodak	No. 1
Canned fruit	Del Monte	No. 1
Chewing gum	Wrigley's	No. 1
Crackers	Nabisco	No. 1
Razors	Gillette	No. 1
Soft drinks	Coca-Cola	No. 1
Soap	Ivory	No. 1
Soup	Campbell	No. 1
Toothpaste	Colgate	No. 2

Source: Mark Landler, Zachary Schiller, and Lois Therrien, "What's in a Name? Less and Less," *Business Week*, July 8, 1991, pp. 66–67.

consumer behavior is basic research, which is the work that forms the foundation for our text. The major thrust of our book is applying this research to marketing problems.

The action-oriented group can be divided into three subgroups as shown in Exhibit 1.1: marketing organizations, government and political organizations, and consumers. Each of these is interested in consumer behavior not just for the sake of knowledge, but for using this knowledge to influence the other subgroups.

Marketing organizations include not only conventional business firms, but also other organizations such as hospitals, museums, law firms, and universities. Thus, marketing organizations include all groups that have a market offering and seek exchanges with consumers. The primary focus of our text is on relationships between marketing strategy and consumers from the perspective of business firms, but the ideas we present can also be applied to other marketing organizations, such as the American Cancer Society or your college or university.

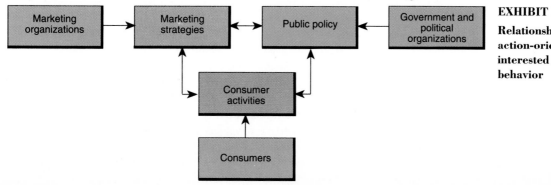

EXHIBIT 1.1

Relationships among action-oriented groups interested in consumer behavior

Nonprofit organizations also use marketing to influence consumer behavior.

The second group, government and political organizations, includes government agencies such as the Federal Trade Commission and the Food and Drug Administration, which are concerned with monitoring and regulating exchanges between marketing organizations and consumers. They do this through the development of public policy, which affects marketing strategies and consumer activities. Political organizations in this subgroup include activists, such as Ralph Nader or the members of Students Against Driving Drunk. While these relationships are not the major concern of our text, they are considered, particularly in Chapter 18.

The third group is consumers, which includes both individual consumers and organizational buyers who exchange resources for various goods and services. Their interest in consumer behavior is primarily to make exchanges that help them achieve their goals. Although the major concern of our text is with ultimate consumers, the logic presented here can be applied in organizational markets. Several examples of organizational buyer behavior are discussed later in the text.

MARKETING IMPLICATIONS

From the viewpoint of marketing organizations, a **marketing strategy** is a plan designed to influence exchanges to achieve organizational objectives. Typically, a marketing strategy is intended to increase the probability or frequency of certain consumer behaviors, such as frequenting particular stores or purchasing particular products. This is accomplished by developing and presenting marketing mixes directed at selected target markets. A marketing mix consists of product, promotion, pricing, and distribution elements.

Exhibit 1.2 presents consumer behavior issues involved in developing various aspects of marketing strategy. Issues such as these can be addressed through formal marketing research, informal discussions with consumers, or thinking about the relationships between consumer behavior and marketing strategy.

Exhibit 1.2 shows that understanding consumers is a critical element in developing marketing strategies. Few—if any—strategy decisions do not involve a consideration of consumer behavior. Analysis of the competition, for example, requires an understanding of what consumers think and feel about competitive brands, which consumers buy these

Marketing Elements	Consumer Issues
Segmentation	▷ Which consumers are the prime prospects for our product? ▷ What consumer characteristics should we use to segment the market for our product?
Product	▷ What products do consumers use now? ▷ What benefits do consumers want from this product?
Promotion	▷ What promotion appeal would influence consumers to purchase and use our product? ▷ What advertising claims would be most effective for our product?
Pricing	▷ How important is price to consumers in various target markets? ▷ What effects will a price change have on purchase behavior?
Distribution	▷ Where do consumers buy this product? ▷ Would a different distribution system change consumers' purchasing behavior?

EXHIBIT 1.2

Examples of consumer issues for marketing

brands and why, and in what situations they buy them. In sum, the more a firm learns about consumers (and approaches to analyzing them), the better its chances for developing successful marketing strategies. Consumer Perspective 1.4 discusses the importance of understanding consumers for developing marketing strategies.

Finally, marketing strategies, particularly as developed and implemented by successful corporations, exert a powerful force on consumers and society at large. Marketing strategies

Successful companies can stay close to their customers by making products their customers can trust.

If ROBIN MILLAGE paid much attention to conventional wisdom, she wouldn't be standing where she is today.

Petersburg, Alaska, is a tiny fishing village on an island off the coast of northern British Columbia. And for Robin Millage, it was nothing more than a vacation destination, until she saw it and decided to stay. You see, Robin's a bit of an adventurer.

Which may be why she recently bought a brand new Saturn, sight unseen, from a retailer in Spokane, Washington, and had it shipped 2500 miles to the village.

According to our records, not a lot of people do that.

But Robin wanted a car she could trust. A car that was easy to service. Plus, a car that wasn't going to leave her alone in the woods. And everything she read pointed to a Saturn.

Of course, Robin's an exception. And we realize that everybody isn't going to just pick up and move to some pristine island in Alaska and buy a Saturn.

So why do you suppose there are two on the island now?

A DIFFERENT KIND *of* COMPANY. A DIFFERENT KIND *of* CAR.
If you'd like to know more about Saturn, and our new sedans and coupe, please call us at 1-800-522-5000.

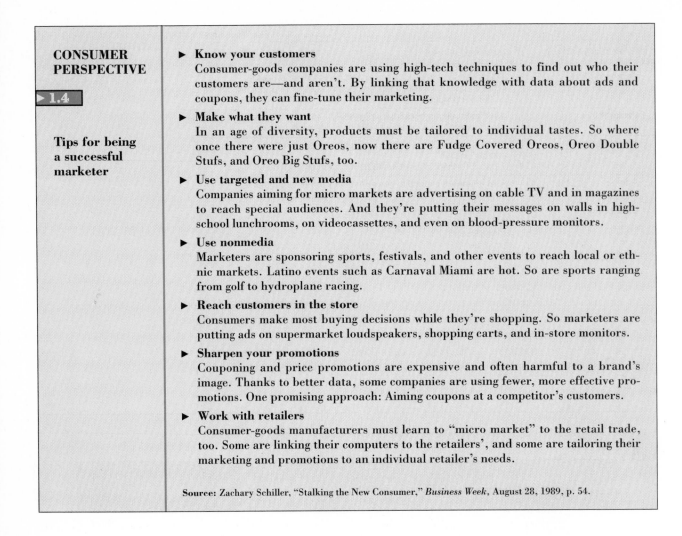

CONSUMER PERSPECTIVE

▶ 1.4

Tips for being a successful marketer

▶ **Know your customers**
Consumer-goods companies are using high-tech techniques to find out who their customers are—and aren't. By linking that knowledge with data about ads and coupons, they can fine-tune their marketing.

▶ **Make what they want**
In an age of diversity, products must be tailored to individual tastes. So where once there were just Oreos, now there are Fudge Covered Oreos, Oreo Double Stufs, and Oreo Big Stufs, too.

▶ **Use targeted and new media**
Companies aiming for micro markets are advertising on cable TV and in magazines to reach special audiences. And they're putting their messages on walls in high-school lunchrooms, on videocassettes, and even on blood-pressure monitors.

▶ **Use nonmedia**
Marketers are sponsoring sports, festivals, and other events to reach local or ethnic markets. Latino events such as Carnaval Miami are hot. So are sports ranging from golf to hydroplane racing.

▶ **Reach customers in the store**
Consumers make most buying decisions while they're shopping. So marketers are putting ads on supermarket loudspeakers, shopping carts, and in-store monitors.

▶ **Sharpen your promotions**
Couponing and price promotions are expensive and often harmful to a brand's image. Thanks to better data, some companies are using fewer, more effective promotions. One promising approach: Aiming coupons at a competitor's customers.

▶ **Work with retailers**
Consumer-goods manufacturers must learn to "micro market" to the retail trade, too. Some are linking their computers to the retailers', and some are tailoring their marketing and promotions to an individual retailer's needs.

Source: Zachary Schiller, "Stalking the New Consumer," *Business Week*, August 28, 1989, p. 54.

not only adapt to consumers, but also change what consumers think and feel about themselves, about various market offerings, and about the appropriate situations for product purchase and use. This does not mean marketing is unethical or devious. At the same time, the power of marketing and the ability of marketing research and consumer analysis to gain insight into consumer behavior should not be underestimated or misused.

▶ SUMMARY

Learning objective 1: *Explain the marketing concept.*
The marketing concept suggests an organization must satisfy consumer needs and wants to make profits. To implement the marketing concept, organizations must understand their customers and stay close to them to provide products and services that consumers will purchase and use appropriately.

Learning objective 2: *Cite three reasons companies today are changing to serve consumers better.*
First, the visible success of Japanese companies such as Toyota and Sony that focus on providing value-laden products has spurred other companies to do the same. Second, a dramatic increase in the quality of consumer and marketing research has made it easier for companies to implement consumer-oriented strategies. Third, consumer behavior

research has developed markedly in recent years, offering more sophisticated views to help companies understand customers.

Learning objective 3: *Define consumer behavior.*

Consumer behavior is the dynamic interaction of affect and cognition, behavior, and environmental events by which human beings conduct the exchange aspects of their lives.

Learning objective 4: *Explain three points emphasized in the definition of consumer behavior.*

First, the definition emphasizes that consumer behavior is dynamic. This means individual consumers, consumer groups, and society at large constantly change and evolve.

Second, the definition emphasizes the interactions between affect and cognitions, behaviors, and environmental events. This means that to understand consumers and develop successful marketing strategies, a firm must understand what consumers feel (affect) and think (cognition), what they do (behavior), and the things and places (environmental events) that influence and are influenced by what consumers feel, think, and do.

Third, the definition emphasizes that consumer behavior involves exchanges between human beings. Typically, consumers exchange their money for products and services.

Learning objective 5: *Explain why three major groups are interested in consumer behavior.*

The three major groups are marketing organizations, government and political organizations, and consumers. Marketing organizations, such as businesses, are interested in consumer behavior primarily because they want to develop marketing strategies to influence consumers to purchase their products. Government and political organizations are interested mainly for purposes of monitoring and regulating exchanges between marketing organizations and consumers. Consumers are interested because they want to make exchanges that satisfy their goals.

Learning objective 6: *List five elements of a marketing strategy for which knowledge of consumer behavior can help make better decisions.*

The five elements are market segmentation, product, promotion, pricing, and distribution. The last four elements are called the marketing mix.

---

marketing concept	consumer behavior	marketing strategy	► **KEY TERMS AND CONCEPTS**

---

1. Why is consumer behavior an important course in business education?
2. Do you think marketing is a powerful force in society? Why or why not?
3. What is the role of consumer analysis in developing marketing strategies?
4. Describe three examples of situations where a marketing strategy influenced your purchase behavior. Why did each succeed over competitive strategies?
5. Using Exhibit 1.2 as a take-off point, discuss other questions and decisions in marketing strategy that could be affected by a study of consumer behavior.
6. Select a market segment of which you are not a member, and, with other students in the class, discuss the kinds of information you would need to develop a strategy aimed at that segment.
7. Using a campus organization of interest (i.e., student government, professional fraternity, political interest group), discuss how a better understanding of the consumer behavior of students could help the organization improve its influence strategies.

► **REVIEW AND DISCUSSION QUESTIONS**

2

The Wheel of Consumer Analysis: A Framework for Understanding Consumers

LEARNING OBJECTIVES

After completing this chapter, you should be able to:

► 1. List the three elements of the Wheel of Consumer Analysis.

► 2. Define affect and cognition, and give an example of each.

► 3. Define behavior, and give an example.

► 4. Define environment, and give an example.

► 5. Explain four points concerning use of the Wheel of Consumer Analysis.

► 6. Describe four levels of consumer analysis.

DR. LINTON BUYS PROTECTION

Dr. Barbara Linton is 37 years old and the mother of two daughters, Joanne and Jenny. She lives in a house in an upscale Chicago suburb with her children. Recently, several burglaries have occurred in her neighborhood. Dr. Linton is worried about her safety and that of her children and is considering buying a gun for protection, although she is concerned about the safety of having a loaded gun in her home with the kids around.

After hearing a news report of yet another burglary, Dr. Linton decides to purchase a handgun. She remembers that there is a gun store on her way to the clinic, and she decides to stop there on her way home the next evening. She does so, and after discussing her situation with the clerk, decides to purchase a Smith & Wesson Model LadySmith® frosted revolver. She also purchases a box of 357 magnum cartridges and a trigger lock so the gun cannot be fired by the children. After taking lessons on how to fire the gun, Dr. Linton now feels much safer in her home.

Although the description of this purchase is brief, it contains all of the major elements of consumer analysis. First, Barbara Linton had feelings of fear and worry for her safety and that of her children. Feelings such as these are called *affect*. Second, Barbara did some planning, remembering, and decision making before she purchased the handgun. Thinking like this is called *cognition*. Third, Barbara listened to a news report, drove to the gun store, discussed her situation with the clerk, and purchased the gun, cartridges, and gun lock. Doing things like this is called *behavior*. Finally, a number of factors influenced her behavior, such as the crime situation in her town, the news reports, the location of the gun store, the information she received from the clerk, and the look and feel of the gun. Such things taken together are called the *environment*. To understand even a simple purchase such as this one, marketers must analyze all of these elements—affect and cognition, behavior, and environment.

To help understand consumer behavior, researchers have borrowed ideas from other fields, including economics, psychology, social psychology, sociology, and cultural anthropology. A number of ideas about consumers also come from marketing experience. Valuable insights have been obtained from all of these areas; but no one approach can completely explain a consumer purchase. In many cases, ideas borrowed from different areas overlap and even compete with each other as useful descriptions of consumers. To date, no one approach is fully accepted. A single, all-encompassing theory of consumer behavior that everyone accepts is unlikely to be devised.

Even though a grand theory of consumer behavior may not be possible, marketers need to have a general framework for studying and understanding consumers. Such a framework should encompass all of the useful ideas and theories in the field. Marketers could use such a general model to guide their analyses of consumers, develop a deeper understanding of consumers, and create more effective marketing strategies.

THE WHEEL OF CONSUMER ANALYSIS

This chapter describes one useful framework for studying, analyzing, and understanding consumers. We call this framework the **Wheel of Consumer Analysis**. Exhibit 2.1 presents the three parts of the Wheel of Consumer Analysis: affect and cognition, behavior, and environment. You saw these components in the story about Dr. Linton's gun purchase. These three categories describe the major concepts and events that marketers must analyze to understand consumers. Each element is the focus of a major section of this book. We believe an analysis of consumers' affect and cognition, behavior, and environment is the foundation for understanding consumers and for developing effective marketing strategies. In this section, we discuss the major elements of the Wheel of Consumer Analysis and how they are related, and we show how to identify these components.

EXHIBIT 2.1

The Wheel of Consumer Analysis

In this text, **affect** and **cognition** refer to two types of internal, psychological reactions that consumers may have in response to objects and events in the external environment or to their own behavior. In simple language, *affect* concerns *feelings*, while *cognition* involves *thinking.*

Affect varies in evaluation and intensity. Some affective feelings are positive and favorable (love, joy, relaxed), while others are negative and unfavorable (boredom, anger, fear). Affect includes relatively intense emotions such as love or anger, less strong feelings such as satisfaction or frustration, diffuse moods such as relaxation or boredom, and rather mild evaluations such as "I like McDonald's french fries."

Cognition refers to the knowledge and thinking processes involved in people's responses to the environment. Cognition includes the knowledge, meanings, and beliefs people have acquired from their experiences and have stored in their memories. Cognition also includes the psychological processes associated with paying attention to and understanding aspects of the environment, remembering past events, forming attitudes, and making purchase decisions. Many cognitive processes are conscious, while others are unconscious and essentially automatic.

Section II explores consumer affect and cognition. Consumer Perspective 2.1 (see page 18) offers a sample of the types of questions marketers might ask about affect and cognition.

Affect and cognition

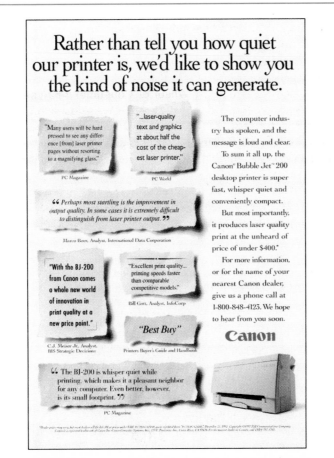

Some ads require considerable cognitive activity.

CONSUMER PERSPECTIVE

▶ 2.1

Some basic questions about consumer affect and cognition

Although many competing theories and ideas about consumer affect and cognitions have been proposed, no single theory completely describes the workings of the consumer's mind. Carefully studying and thinking about the information in Section II of this text should help you develop informed answers to questions about affect and cognition such as:

1. How do consumers interpret information from marketing stimuli such as products, stores, and advertising?
2. How do consumers choose from among alternative product classes, products, and brands?
3. How do consumers form evaluations of products and brands?
4. How does memory affect consumer decision making?
5. How do affect and cognition influence behavior and environments?
6. How do behavior and environments influence affect and cognition?
7. How do consumers interpret the benefits of marketing offerings?
8. Why are consumers more interested in some products or brands than others?
9. How do marketing strategies influence consumers' affective and cognitive responses?
10. How do affective and cognitive responses influence each other?

Behavior

In this text, **behavior** refers to the overt acts of consumers. Examples of behaviors include watching a TV commercial, visiting a store, or buying a product. Thus, while affect and cognition are concerned with what consumers feel and think, behavior deals with what consumers actually *do.* Despite the importance of behavior for developing marketing strategy, little consumer research has been conducted on the topic. Section III discusses ways of analyzing consumers' overt behavior. Consumer Perspective 2.2 illustrates the types of questions marketers might ask in analyzing consumers' behaviors.

Environment

In this text, **environment** refers to all the physical and social characteristics of consumers' external world. The environment includes objects, places, and other people that influence consumers' affect, cognition, and behavior. Section IV explores the physical and social aspects of the environment. Consumer Perspective 2.3 (see page 20) offers a sample of the types of questions marketers might ask about the environment.

The marketing strategies designed by managers create part of the physical and social environment experienced by consumers. For instance, products, packaging, advertisements, presentations by salespeople, price tags, signs, and stores are physical and social stimuli in the environment that marketers create to influence consumers. How marketers use consumer behavior analysis to develop marketing strategy is introduced in Chapter 3 and is discussed throughout the text.

Identifying the wheel components

Marketers can analyze any consumer behavior situation in terms of the three elements of the Wheel of Consumer Analysis—the environment, behavior, and affect and cognition (see Exhibit 2.1). Because these factors interact and influence each other, no one factor can be fully understood in isolation. Understanding consumers requires attention to all three elements. To help you identify the components of the Wheel of Consumer Analysis, we examine an everyday grocery shopping situation.

Like millions of other consumers, Bruce Macklin makes a weekly trip to a local supermarket to buy groceries. On this sunny Saturday morning, Bruce has driven to the Giant

Little attention has been given to studying the overt behavior of consumers, but many behavior influence techniques seem to be commonly used by marketing practitioners. Carefully studying and thinking about the information in Section III of the text should help you develop informed answers to questions about behavior such as:

1. How do behavior approaches differ from affective and cognitive approaches to studying consumer behavior?
2. What is classical conditioning, and how do marketers use it to influence consumer behavior?
3. What is operant conditioning, and how do marketers use it to influence consumer behavior?
4. What is vicarious learning, and how do marketers use it to influence consumer behavior?
5. What consumer behaviors are of interest to marketing managers?
6. How much control does marketing exert on consumers' behavior?
7. How do affect and cognition and environments affect behavior?
8. How does behavior influence affect and cognition and environments?
9. How can marketing managers use behavior theory?
10. How does consumer behavior vary by individuals, products, and situations?

CONSUMER PERSPECTIVE

2.2 ◄

Some basic questions about consumer behavior

supermarket with his three-year-old daughter, Angela. As he walks through the front doors, Bruce enters one of the most complex information environments a consumer can face. The average American grocery store stocks some 10,000 items, but some very large stores may carry as many as 20,000. Most supermarkets offer many alternatives in each product category. For instance, one large store offers 18 brands of mustard in a variety of sizes. Moreover, most product packages show lots of information. The average package of breakfast cereal, for example, provides some 250 pieces of information! During the next 50 minutes (the average time consumers spend in the store on a major shopping trip),

Bed, Bath & Beyond stores stock more than 20,000 items, presenting a complicated shopping environment with many physical and social stimuli compared to the physician's waiting room, which has only a few stimuli.

CONSUMER PERSPECTIVE

▶ **2.3**

Some basic questions about consumer environments

Environmental psychology seeks to extend knowledge about the relationships between environmental stimuli and human behavior. In consumer research, the major environmental factors examined have been concerned with the impact of various societal aspects. Carefully studying and thinking about the information in Section IV should help you develop informed answers to questions about the environment such as:

1. In what physical environments do consumer behaviors occur?
2. How do marketing environments influence consumers' affect, cognition, and behavior?
3. How do consumer affect, cognition, and behavior influence the environment?
4. What influence does culture have on consumers?
5. What influence does subculture have on consumers?
6. What influence does social class have on consumers?
7. What influence do reference groups have on consumers?
8. What influence do families have on consumers?
9. In what ways do people influence each other in consumer environments?
10. How powerful are interpersonal influences on consumer behavior?

Bruce will see much of this information and make numerous purchase decisions. Most of his choices will be made easily and quickly, seemingly with little effort. Some choices, though, will involve noticeable thinking and may require a few seconds. And some of his choices may require many seconds, perhaps even minutes and substantial effort.

Environment

What is the physical and social environment of the supermarket like? On a Saturday morning, the market is likely to be *busy,* with many people *crowding* the aisles. The store is likely to be somewhat *noisy.* Because Bruce is shopping with Angela, her *chatter* adds to the commotion. These social aspects of the environment will influence Bruce's affect, cognition, and overt behavior. The store *layout,* the *width* of the aisles, the special sale *signs* on the shelves, the product *displays* at the ends of the aisles and elsewhere in the store, the *lighting,* and other physical aspects of the supermarket environment may also have an effect. Other environmental factors such as the *temperature,* background *music,* and the *wobbly wheel* on his shopping cart may also influence Bruce's affect, cognition, and behavior.

Much of the in-store environment Bruce experiences is the result of marketing strategy decisions made by the retailer and the manufacturers of the products. A grocery store is a good place to observe marketing strategies in action. The huge number of products sold in such stores requires an equally large number of marketing strategies. For instance, a firm's distribution strategy (place products only in discount stores) determines whether that product is even present in a store. A variety of pricing strategies (reduced price on Oreo cookies) and promotion strategies (free samples of cheese) are evident in a supermarket environment. Package designs (easy-opening milk containers) and specific product characteristics (low-calorie frozen entrée) are also marketing strategies. Finally, specific environmental details such as point-of-purchase displays (a stack of Pepsi six-packs near the store entrance) are important aspects of marketing strategy. All these marketing strategies create changes in the physical and social environment that are intended to influence consumers' affect and cognitions and their behaviors.

Behavior

What behaviors occur on a shopping trip? Bruce is engaged in many behaviors, including *walking* down the aisles, *looking* at products on the shelves, *picking up* and *examining* packages, *talking* to Angela and a friend he meets in the store, *steering* the wobbly cart, and so on. While many of these behaviors may not be of much interest to a marketing manager, some behaviors have important effects on Bruce's affect and cognitions and his eventual purchases. For example, unless Bruce *walks* down the aisle containing breakfast cereals, he cannot *notice* and *buy* a package of Kellogg's Raisin Squares. Typically, marketers are most concerned about purchase behavior. In the supermarket environment, purchase requires several behaviors such as *picking up* a package, *placing* it in the cart, and *paying* for it at the checkout counter.

Affect and cognition

Bruce's affective and cognitive systems are active in the supermarket environment, but only some of this internal activity is conscious. Many affective and cognitive responses occur without much awareness. For instance, Bruce may feel irritated about getting a cart with a wobbly wheel. He also *pays attention* to certain aspects of the store environment and *ignores* other parts. Some products capture his attention, while others do not. He *interprets* a large amount of information in the store environment—from aisle signs to brand names to price tags to nutrition labels. In addition, he *evaluates* some of the products in terms of meeting his needs and those of his family. He *remembers* what products he has at home and what he has run out of and needs to replace. He *chooses* from among some of the 10,000 to 20,000 items available in the store. In addition, he *makes decisions* about other specific behaviors. Should he go down aisle 3 or skip it this week? Should he stock up on canned peaches or buy just one can? Should he give Angela a cookie for being good? Should he take the wobbly cart back and get another one? Should he pay with cash or by check?

Summary

About 45 minutes after entering the Giant supermarket, Bruce emerges with five bags of groceries containing 48 different products. His grocery shopping activities on this Saturday morning are influenced by the social and physical environment of the store (including the marketing strategies found there), his own behaviors, and his affective and cognitive

---

The Wheel of Consumer Analysis gives marketing managers a powerful tool for analyzing and understanding consumers and for developing marketing strategies. Four points need to be emphasized about how marketers should apply this framework.

First, any comprehensive analysis of consumer behavior must consider all three elements of the Wheel of Consumer Analysis. Descriptions of consumer behavior expressed in terms of only one or two of the elements are incomplete. For example, to assume that affect and cognition cause behavior and to ignore the influence of environment underestimates the dynamic nature of consumer behavior and may lead to a less effective marketing strategy.

Second, it is important to understand the relationships among the elements of the Wheel of Consumer Analysis.[1] At any given time, any one of the elements can influence either or both of the other elements. For example, suppose today a consumer is interested in Lynx golf clubs and decides to buy a set. She purchases them, uses them for a week, and then decides she doesn't like them. Expressed in terms of the elements of the Wheel of Consumer Analysis, her initial liking of the clubs and her decision to buy them are affect and cognition; purchasing and using the clubs are behaviors. Initially, her affect and cognitions influenced her behaviors. The behaviors, or purchase and use, however, then

APPLYING THE WHEEL OF CONSUMER ANALYSIS

influenced her affect and cognition and she came to dislike the product. The direction of influence between any of the model elements depends on the particular time and scope of the analysis.

Third, any of the three elements may be the starting point for consumer analysis. In the Lynx golf clubs example, the starting point was the consumer's affect and cognition. But an analysis could begin before this point by determining which environmental events, such as advertisements for Lynx clubs, influenced her feelings and beliefs about Lynx and her decision to purchase. Or the analysis could begin by examining an earlier behavior such as trying a friend's clubs. Fundamentally, marketers are interested in influencing specific behaviors. Therefore, consumer analysis usually begins with a focus on the desired behavior (buying a particular brand, going into a store, entering a sweepstakes contest) and attempts to determine the factors that influence that behavior.

CONSUMER PERSPECTIVE

▶ **2.4**

Rubbermaid Inc.'s Sidekick

Rubbermaid, Inc., introduced a litter-free lunch box known as the Sidekick in the early 1990s. It is a simple, yet catchy-looking (splashy violet and blue-green models with sporty lime-green trim) insulated cooler including three plastic containers for a sandwich, a drink, and one other item. That means no plastic wrapping, no cans, no milk cartons—and presumably no waste. Rubbermaid figured its offering would be a natural for parents concerned about the nation's swelling garbageglut—especially those whose school-age children have read them the environmental riot act.

While regular lunch boxes sell for $5 to $7, the Sidekick sells for $10 or over and has become the rage for many grade-school kids. The higher price was dictated by the 12 to 14 percent return on assets that the company demands for its new products. Consumers have not resisted the higher price, and Rubbermaid hasn't been able to ship the product fast enough to keep up with demand. The company has expanded the line to include six other versions with different colors and additional food containers. One model is a larger version, including a reusable ice pack to keep food chilled, targeted at workers who carry their own lunches.

The Sidekick is a huge success. Rubbermaid doubled its sales in the $35 million lunch box market to roughly 12 percent in its first year. As one buyer from Target Stores put it, "It's both functional and trend-right."

Sources: Jon Berry, "Rubbermaid Packs an Ecological Lunch," *Adweek's Marketing Week*, September 9, 1991, p. 10; "The Art of Rubbermaid," *Adweek's Marketing Week*, March 16, 1992, pp. 22–26; and Zachary Schiller, "At Rubbermaid, Little Things Mean a Lot," *Business Week*, November 11, 1991, p. 126.

Fourth, the Wheel of Consumer Analysis views consumer behavior as a dynamic process of continuous change. A marketer might develop a sound marketing strategy based on careful analysis of the components of the Wheel of Consumer Analysis at a particular time and a good description of consumers. However, any or all of the wheel elements can change, making the original marketing strategy less effective. So, even if consumer analysis leads to an excellent marketing strategy, changes in consumers' affect and cognition, behavior, or environment may necessitate a change in strategy. For example, because many consumers have developed strong values about protecting the environment and begun to use environmentally safe products, businesses have tried to improve their products to meet this market need. Consumer Perspective 2.4 discusses one company that has successfully responded to such changes.

LEVELS OF CONSUMER ANALYSIS

The Wheel of Consumer Analysis is a flexible tool for analyzing and understanding consumers and for developing marketing strategies. It can be used fruitfully by both marketing managers and officials concerned with public policy to understand the dynamics of consumer behavior. The Wheel of Consumer Analysis can be applied at four levels to analyze an entire society, an industry, a market segment, or an individual consumer.

Society

Changes in what a society believes and how its members behave can be analyzed using the Wheel of Consumer Analysis. For example, a long-term trend in our society is increasing concern with health and fitness. How did this change occur? Surely, consumers were always concerned with living long, happy lives. For one thing, the media has widely

Changes in society, such as the health and fitness movement, create opportunities for new products.

CONSUMER
PERSPECTIVE

▶ 2.5

Madonna's
changing
marketing
strategies

Staying in business over the long run is a matter of creating and keeping customers in the face of continuous change. Managers must be able to adapt their marketing strategies to dynamic changes in the three components of the Wheel of Consumer Analysis—consumers' environment, affect and cognition, and behavior. Few marketers have done so as successfully as Madonna Ciccone, the pop music star.

Madonna is a rarity in show business—a star who runs her own business affairs. People who know her (and will talk about her) speak of her business skill in deal-making, financing, and marketing. Throughout the late 1980s and early 1990s, Madonna was one of the top-earning female entertainers in the United States, earning an estimated $39 million in 1990 alone. Since her career began in the early 1980s, Madonna has changed her image and her position in the marketplace several times. How does she do it?

1983:   Madonna's original image was punk and trampy. She dressed in skimpy black clothes showing an exposed navel. She produced upbeat "dance music" with sexy lyrics sung in a girlish voice. Her premier album, "Madonna," sold 9 million copies.

1984:   Madonna's second album hit the stores showing her dressed in a white wedding dress with a belt buckle reading "boy toy." She began wearing underwear as outerwear. Her album, "Like a Virgin," sold 11 million copies.

1986–1988:   Madonna dropped the sex kitten look for a more traditional and feminine appearance. Her singing voice became deeper and more serious. She appeared in a video with honey-blond hair and a demure flowered dress. In 1987, she was on the cover of *Cosmopolitan* as a glamorous blond; she appeared on the cover of *Harper's* in 1988 as a brunette. Her "True Blue" album sold 17 million copies.

1989:   Madonna once again changed her image to a combination of gypsy and hippie. In the video accompanying "Like a Prayer," she flirted with religious symbols. That album sold 11 million copies.

1990:   Madonna went futuristic with her blond hair tied back, a microphone strapped to her head, and wearing a bustier that looked more like armor than underwear.

1992:   Madonna became more sexually explicit in her songs and her behavior. She released the album "Erotica" along with a $50 book titled *Sex* showing nude pictures of herself.

Madonna continually redesigned and updated her product (both her music and herself as a personality) to stimulate new interest in her fans and to appeal to new market segments. Part of her strategy has been to stimulate controversy among some segments

publicized a growing body of medical research indicating people can be healthier and live longer if they eat properly and exercise regularly. This research may have changed some consumers' attitudes about eating and exercise. As these consumers began living more healthful lifestyles, other consumers copied their behavior and developed their own positive values and attitudes toward health. Another factor that may have accelerated the health and fitness movement is that healthy, well-shaped people are considered more attractive in our society and are more prominent in ads, films, and public life. Also, a variety of health-related industries, such as health foods, exercise equipment, and sports apparel, promoted eating right and exercising regularly, which exposed many consumers to these ideas and contributed to adopting an active lifestyle.

Clearly, changes in the environment (medical research reports), cognition and affect (beliefs about how to live longer and healthier), behavior (eating more healthful foods

of the population, usually with a sexual theme, to the delight of her fans. She also tried to expand her appeal by appearing in movies such as *Dick Tracy* and *Body of Evidence*.

One thing Madonna does shy away from is product endorsements. The only U.S. endorsement she has done was for Pepsi, in 1989. For a $5 million fee, Madonna contracted to do three ads and allow Pepsi to sponsor her tour. The expensive ads were to be aired just after the release of her album, "Like a Prayer." But the video for the title song showing her kissing a black saint and dancing provocatively in front of burning crosses caused so much controversy for Pepsi that the company canceled the contract. Madonna still collected her fee along with millions in free publicity.

Although she hates to be described as an astute businesswoman (it isn't consistent with the image she is selling), Madonna is a very successful marketer who adapts her marketing strategies to changing market conditions as suggested by the Wheel of Consumer Analysis.

Source: Adapted from Matthew Schifrin and Peter Newcomb, "A Brain for Sin and a Bod for Business," *Forbes*, October 1, 1990, pp. 162–66. Reprinted by permission of *Forbes* magazine, © Forbes Inc., 1990.

and exercising), and marketing strategies (development and promotion of health food, equipment, and exercise apparel) have interacted to influence this dynamic change in society. Of course, not everyone has been affected by these changes (63 percent of Americans weigh more than is recommended for their height and frame).[2] The Wheel of Consumer Analysis can help marketers think about changes in affect and cognition, behavior, and environment in various societies around the world.

Industry

The Wheel of Consumer Analysis can be used to analyze and understand consumers who purchase products from companies in a specific industry. For example, changing health concerns have influenced beer consumers and companies in the beer industry. Changes in consumer beliefs and behavior about calorie intake influenced Miller Brewing to develop a low-calorie beer, Miller Lite. This marketing strategy, in turn, helped reinforce and spread the changes in consumer beliefs and behaviors. Then, the success of Miller Lite prompted competitors to offer other brands of light beers, further stimulating demand for this product category.

Another change affecting the beer industry is consumers' increasing concern with responsible drinking, which decreases demand for alcohol products in general. This led to the marketing of low-alcohol beer (and other nonalcoholic drink products such as mineral waters, juices, and soft drinks). Consumer groups such as Mothers Against Drunk Driving and Students Against Driving Drunk have also influenced many members of society to reduce their alcohol consumption or abstain from any alcoholic beverage. In fact, while drunken and boisterous behavior was once considered acceptable, many people no longer find drunkenness to be funny. Similarly, smoking was once considered a sign of maturity and sophistication, and today smoking is not tolerated in most public places.

In sum, changes in consumer cognition, affect, and behavior can weaken the appeal of certain products at the industry level. But such changes can also create opportunities for new products more consistent with emerging values and behaviors. Successful marketing strategies depend on analyzing consumers' relationships with your own company's products and those of your competitors, and then creating an advantage over competitive offerings.

Market segment

The Wheel of Consumer Analysis can be used to identify segments of consumers with similar affect and cognitions, behaviors, or environments. Most successful firms divide the total market into segments and try to appeal most strongly to one or more segments. The emphasis on health, for example, has encouraged many consumers to take up sports. In the past, specific shoes were not designed for each particular sport. Today, there are many varieties and styles of shoes for running, bicycling, aerobics, soccer, basketball, and other sports. These shoes vary in design, features, and price ranges to appeal to groups of consumers who are similar in some way.

Reebok, for example, developed its Blacktop shoes for young basketball fans who play on urban, outdoor courts. The shoe is a few ounces heavier than its competitors, moderately priced, and designed for use on asphalt and concrete. The shoe looks good, so it appeals to the 80 percent of consumers who buy athletic shoes solely for fashion, but it is also tough enough to stand up to rugged outdoor play. The shoe sold out in many stores in its first two months and was expected to sell over 2.2 million pairs in its first year, a smashing marketing success.[3] Thus, Reebok developed a successful marketing strategy by understanding the wants and preferences (cognitions and affect) of urban youths (target market) for a good-looking, moderately priced, long-wearing shoe, for regular guys who play basketball (behavior) on outdoor courts (environment).

Marketers can use the Wheel of Consumer Analysis to monitor consumers in various segments. Successful marketers continuously monitor consumers' affect and cognition, behavior, and the environment and are ready to modify their marketing strategies in response to significant changes in these factors. Such changes occur rapidly in some industries (pop music, computer software), and marketers must respond quickly. In other industries, changes occur more slowly (men's suits, home furnishings), and marketers have the luxury of time to develop effective strategies. Consumer Perspective 2.5 describes how Madonna has changed her image and marketing strategies over 10 years to keep her customers (her fans) and attract new customers.

Individual consumer

Finally, the Wheel of Consumer Analysis can be used to analyze a single consumer in a variety of ways. For example, the Wheel of Consumer Analysis could be used to understand the consumption history of an individual by analyzing all the major purchases made in the past five years. The Wheel of Consumer Analysis could also be used to understand a series of purchases an individual makes in a particular product class, such as automobiles. Analyses such as these could give a rich understanding of the consumption dynamics of an individual consumer. Comparing such profiles across consumers in the same and in different cultures could provide insights into the meaning of consumption at different times in history and in different parts of the world.

For marketing purposes, the Wheel of Consumer Analysis can be used to analyze and describe an individual shopping trip, an individual purchase, or some aspect of them. For example, to understand Dr. Linton's purchase of a Smith & Wesson handgun discussed at the beginning of the chapter, we needed to consider her cognitions, affect, behavior, and environments. Bruce Macklin's grocery shopping trip is another example of consumer analysis at the individual level.

Learning objective 1: *List the three elements of the Wheel of Consumer Analysis.*
The three elements of the Wheel of Consumer Analysis are affect and cognition, behavior, and environment.

▶ SUMMARY

Learning objective 2: *Define affect and cognition, and give an example of each.*
Affect refers to feelings the consumer may have. Affect varies in evaluation—positive or negative, favorable or unfavorable. Affect also varies in intensity or level of arousal. Affect includes emotions (joy), feeling states (guilt), moods (bored), and evaluations (liking).

Cognition refers to the knowledge and mental processes involved in thinking responses to the environment. For instance, cognition includes knowledge that people have acquired from their experiences and have stored in their memories. Cognition also includes psychological processes associated with paying attention to and understanding aspects of the environment, remembering past events, forming attitudes, and making purchase decisions.

Learning objective 3: *Define behavior, and give an example.*
Behavior refers to the overt acts or actions of consumers that can be directly observed. It deals with what people actually do rather than what they think or feel.

Learning objective 4: *Define environment, and give an example.*
Environment refers to all the physical and social features of consumers' external world. The environment includes objects (products, store displays), places (factory outlet malls, the checkout area), and other people (friends, relatives, salespeople) that can influence the consumer's affect, cognition, and behavior. An important part of the environment for consumer analysis includes the stimuli that marketers create to influence consumers (products, stores, ads, signs).

Learning objective 5: *Explain four points concerning use of the Wheel of Consumer Analysis.*
To use the Wheel of Consumer Analysis appropriately, analysts should recognize that (1) all elements of the Wheel must be included for a comprehensive analysis; (2) at any given time, any one of the elements can influence the other two elements; (3) any of the elements could be the starting point for a consumer analysis, but behavior is often the best one to start with; (4) the Wheel of Consumer Analysis views consumer behavior as a dynamic process of continuous influences.

Learning objective 6: *Describe four levels of consumer analysis.*
Four levels of consumer analysis include society, industry, market segment, and individual consumer. Societal analysis focuses on the affect and cognition, behavior, and environment of very large groups of consumers in a society. Industry analysis is applied to all consumers who are customers for the products of a particular industry (blue jeans, athletic

shoes, stereo systems). Segment-level analysis focuses on the affect and cognition, behavior, and environment of consumers in a particular market segment. Individual-level analysis is intended to understand the affect and cognition, behavior and environment of a single consumer.

▶ **KEY TERMS AND CONCEPTS**

Wheel of Consumer Analysis	affect	behavior
	cognition	environment

▶ **REVIEW AND DISCUSSION QUESTIONS**

1. Explain the relationship between the environment and marketing strategy.
2. Relate each of the four points the text makes about the use of the Wheel of Consumer Analysis to the impact these issues would have on marketing strategy.
3. The text indicates that analysis can begin with affect and cognition, behavior, or environment. Why not begin with marketing strategy?
4. Offer three examples of changes in a marketing strategy that led to changes in your affect and cognition and behavior.
5. Bring three magazine advertisements to class. Be prepared to explain what effect the ads are intended to have on your affect, cognition, and behavior.
6. List the four levels of consumer analysis, and offer a specific example of a recent change at each level.

3

Using Consumer Analysis: Market Segmentation and the Marketing Mix

LEARNING OBJECTIVES

After completing this chapter, you should be able to:

► 1. Define market segmentation and explain why marketers segment markets.

► 2. List five major types of segmentation and give examples of each.

► 3. Explain psychographic, benefit, and usage situation segmentation.

► 4. List the elements of the marketing mix.

► 5. Offer examples of marketing mix issues for which consumer analysis is important.

► 6. Explain product positioning.

GILLETTE AND THE DRUGSTORE DINOSAURS

Gillette is one of the best marketers of personal-care products for men. The company invented the disposable razor blade and has a history of success involving new styles of razors and blades. In 1990, it hit the jackpot again with the Sensor blade and a razor whose spring mechanism makes for what the company claims is the closest shave ever. With margins of 30 percent or more, Gillette can make profits of over $500 million per year on blades and razors alone. It benefits from loyal customers and dominates the market with a 63 percent share.

For all its marketing success in the male market, however, Gillette has had problems marketing personal-care products to women. Gillette's women's products include Silkience hair conditioner, White Rain shampoo, Dippity-Do hair treatment, Toni home permanent, Aapri facial cleanser, and Deep Magic skin cream. All were hot brands in their day, but young trendsetting women today view them as drugstore dinosaurs. Revitalizing these products has been difficult. For example, a $20 million campaign to re-launch Silkience conditioner did not succeed.

Gillette apparently has done excellent consumer analysis in the case of men's shaving products and understands this market. What Gillette doesn't seem to understand is that women's hair-care products require different marketing strategies. For one thing, fresh, new products tend to do better in the hair-care market. While shaving products for men have reached the stage where they satisfy the bulk of the market, many women are still searching for a shampoo that meets their specific needs. Another factor is that in our culture the appearance of their hair is important to many people. Given the many variables of color, texture, thickness, and style of hair, it is not likely that one shampoo will meet everyone's needs as one type of razor may. In other words, careful consumer analysis is needed to develop products and strategies that are successful in varying target markets.[1]

As we note in Chapter 1, marketing organizations, government and political organizations, and consumers are all interested in understanding consumer behavior. Marketing organizations need to analyze consumers to develop successful marketing plans and strategies. To stay close to its customers, a company needs to carry out consumer analysis to understand consumer affect and cognitions, behaviors, and environments for its products and those of its competitors. This chapter focuses on some ways marketing organizations can use consumer analysis to make marketing decisions.

Marketing managers have two major tasks: selecting target markets, and developing marketing mixes. This chapter discusses consumer analysis in terms of these two tasks. First, we examine the concept of **market segmentation,** that is, dividing consumers into groups that are similar in one or more ways to market to them more effectively. The group or groups a firm seeks to serve is called a **target market.** Second, the chapter discusses some important marketing mix questions that consumer analysis can help answer to develop more effective marketing strategies.

MARKET SEGMENTATION	

MARKET SEGMENTATION

Market segmentation is one of the most important concepts in the consumer behavior and marketing literature. A primary reason for studying consumer behavior is to identify bases for effective segmentation, and a large portion of consumer research is concerned with segmentation. Selecting the appropriate target market is paramount in developing successful marketing strategy.

The logic of market segmentation has a simple basis: a single product usually will not appeal to *all* consumers. People's purchase goals, product knowledge, and purchase behavior vary; and successful marketers often adapt their marketing strategies to appeal to specific consumer groups. Even a simple product such as chewing gum comes in multiple flavors and package sizes and varies in sugar content, calories, consistency, and colors to appeal to different consumers. While a single product seldom appeals to all consumers, it can almost always be attractive to more than one consumer. Thus, there are usually *groups of consumers* to whom a single item will appeal. If a particular group can be reached profitably by a firm, it constitutes a viable market segment or target market. A marketer should then develop a marketing mix to serve that group.

In the past, many marketers focused on target markets in a general, nonpersonal way. As we note in Chapter 1, marketers may have operated with some notion of the general characteristics of their target market, but they could not identify particular consumers who actually purchase and use their products. Today's technology, including scanner and other personal data sources, improved methods of marketing research, and efficient computers to handle large data bases, now gives marketers detailed, personal information on many members of its target market. For example, one tobacco

EXHIBIT 3.1

Tasks involved in market segmentation

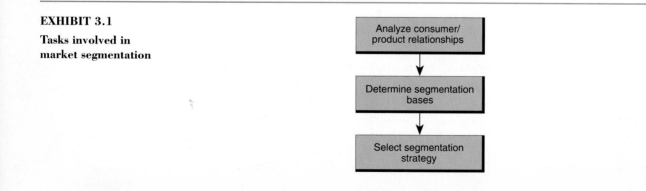

Today a company can combine data from several sources to produce extensive information on its target users and where they shop. Below are examples of the target user profiles for three products and stores in the New York area where these users are most likely to purchase them. Marketers could design special promotions in such stores to enhance the probability of purchase.

Brand	Heavy User Profile	Lifestyle and Media Profile	Top 3 Stories Profile
Peter Pan peanut butter	Households with kids headed by 18- to 54-year-olds, in suburban and rural areas	▶ Heavy video renters ▶ Go to theme parks ▶ Below average TV viewers ▶ Above average radio listeners	Foodtown Super Market Pathmark Supermarket King Kullen Market
Stouffers Red Box frozen entrees	Households headed by people 55 and older, and upscale suburban households headed by 35- to 54-year-olds	▶ Go to gambling casinos ▶ Give parties ▶ Involved in public activities ▶ Travel frequently ▶ Heavy newspaper reader ▶ Above average TV viewers	Dan's Supreme Super Market Food Emporium Waldbaum Super Market
Coors Light beer	Head of household, 21-34, middle to upper income, suburban and urban	▶ Belong to a health club ▶ Buy rock music ▶ Travel by plane ▶ Rent videos ▶ Heavy TV sports viewers	Food Emporium (2 locations) Gristedes Supermarket

Source: Reprinted by permission of *The Wall Street Journal*, © 1991 Dow Jones & Company, Inc. All Rights Reserved Worldwide.

CONSUMER PERSPECTIVE

3.1 ◀

Hitting target markets in the 1990s

company is reported to know the names, addresses, and purchasing patterns of over 30 million smokers. As Consumer Perspective 3.1 shows, some marketers can now identify a product's best customers as well as the stores where they're most likely to shop.

We define *market segmentation* as the process of dividing a market into groups and individuals for the firm to target. We can break the process of market segmentation into three tasks, as shown in Exhibit 3.1. Below we discuss each of the market segmentation tasks shown. While these tasks are related, and firms may approach them in a different order (depending on the firm and the situation), market segmentation analysis can seldom (if ever) be ignored. Even if the final decision is to mass market and not to segment, this decision should be reached only *after* market segmentation analysis has been conducted. Thus, market segmentation analysis is critical for sound marketing strategy development.

The first task involved in segmenting markets is analyzing consumer/product relationships. This entails analysis of the affect and cognitions, behaviors, and environments involved in the purchase/consumption process for a particular product. Managers take three general approaches to this task. First, marketing managers may brainstorm a product concept and consider what types of consumers are likely to purchase and use the product and how

Analyze consumer/product relationships

Marketing attempts to communicate the consumer/product relationship for a target segment of consumers.

they might differ from those less likely to buy. Second, focus group and other types of primary research can be useful for identifying differences in attributes, benefits, and values of various potential markets. Third, secondary research may be used to investigate specific differences in potential target markets, determine the relative sizes of these markets, and develop a better understanding of consumers of this or similar products.

For many established product categories, considerable information is available for analyzing various markets. For product categories such as automobiles, toothpaste, and many food products, various target markets are well established. For example, the automobile buyer category includes luxury, sports, midsize, compact, and subcompact markets. Within each of these markets further analysis may offer insights into market opportunities. One market of great concern to General Motors, for example, is the group that purchases foreign automobiles. Only one in five of these buyers even considers a General Motors car. GM executives believe that if they produce an American car comparable to cars that Honda and Toyota make, they can recapture up to 80 percent of this market. In fact, GM has spent $3.5 billion to produce the Saturn to appeal to this market. Given the fact that many owners of Japanese vehicles are reported to be highly satisfied with their cars, GM's decision would appear to represent a risky strategy unless GM has thoroughly analyzed the affect and cognitions, behaviors, and environments of foreign car buyers and can build an American car these consumers will purchase instead of foreign brands.

For many products, the initial breakdown in markets is between the prestige and mass market. The prestige market seeks the highest-quality (and often the highest-priced)

There are many ways to segment markets.

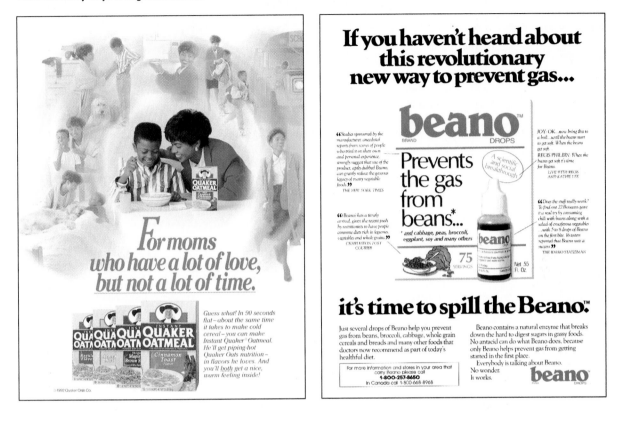

product available. Often, particular products in this market have very important meanings for their purchasers, such as expressions of good taste, expertise, and status. Rolex watches, Mercedes-Benz automobiles, Hartmann luggage, and Gucci handbags are targeted to these consumers. The marketing strategies for these products generally involve selling them in exclusive stores at high prices and promoting them in prestige media. For consumers in this market, affect and cognitions (feelings about and meaning of the product), behaviors (shopping activities), and environments (information and store contact) differ from those of consumers in the mass market. Thus, the initial analysis of consumer/product relationship has important implications for all the subsequent tasks involved in market segmentation and strategy development.

Analysis focusing on differences in consumers is also important when companies seek new target markets. For example, Holiday Inns has saturated the midpriced lodging market with over 265,000 motel rooms. When a survey of Holiday Inns guests revealed that over one third wanted to pay less for a room, management decided to test a smaller facility without lounge or food services. Holiday Inns opened Hampton Inns which charge lower prices and offer fewer services. Here, a difference in consumers' cognitions about lodging prices led to a change in marketing strategy (resegmenting the midpriced market) and the lodging environment (creation of Hampton Inns), which led to a change in consumer behavior (staying at Hampton Inns instead of Holiday Inns). Competitors such as Marriott Corporation also target this market (Fairfield Inns).

Our example demonstrates how analysis of consumer/product relationships led to a successful marketing strategy for Holiday Inns. A number of other tasks, however, occur after an

It starts with a box of free samples left in college dorm rooms. The free magazines soon follow. Concerts beamed into the student lounge include commercials. Wallboards feature ads next to the campus calendar.

Madison Avenue has invaded the Ivory Tower, and advertisers are making increased use of targeted media to stay there. In one recent year, advertisers spent about $100 million trying to sway the shopping choices of 12 million collegians. The group has considerable economic potential. College students have an estimated $20 billion to spend after paying for books, board, and tuition, according to a recent Simmons Market Research study. Other studies estimate the average student has about $200 a month to spend after paying for school-related expenses.

The college segment is a delight for consumer product marketers. Many of its members are away from home for the first time, now making their own decisions on what brands of soap, deodorant, and hair mousse to buy.

But shaping brand loyalties isn't easy. This is a hip, educated audience that grew up in front of the television set and learned to spot even the most casual commercial plug. Even without skepticism about sales pitches, getting a sales message to college students can be difficult. They tend to watch television less frequently, listen to radio less often, and read metropolitan newspapers more rarely than their peers who don't go to college. Traditional advertising vehicles often don't do the job.

As a result, marketers try to latch onto things students seem to pay attention to—college newspapers, college-oriented magazines, programs carried on college television systems, and billboards listing campus events. Market Source Corp. developed a backlit electronic billboard and has placed 1,250 of them on 550 campuses. They have room for an ad, a campus calendar, and an electronic message space. Minimum annual charges for advertising on the billboards run about $200,000.

Both Market Source and Whittle Communication distribute a variety of products and coupons in about 1.2 million sampler boxes each fall. The sampling programs "are the best vehicle we have" to reach college students, said Carole Johnson, a marketing manager for Gillette Co., which spent about $105,000 to include Soft 'N Dri deodorant in 700,000 kits one fall. Thus, while it may be a hard market to reach, many marketers feel it is well worth the effort.

Source: Excerpted from "Advertisers Target College Market," *Marketing News* 21, no. 22 (October 23, 1987), p. 5. Published by the American Marketing Association.

initial analysis of consumer/product relationships and before finalizing marketing strategies. A logical next step is to investigate various bases on which markets could be segmented. Consumer Perspective 3.2 explores a marketing strategy to reach the college market.

Determine segmentation bases

There is no simple way to determine the relevant bases for segmenting markets. In most cases, however, at least some initial dimensions will be obvious from previous research, purchase trends, managerial judgment, and analysis of consumer/product relationships. For example, suppose we wish to segment the market for all-terrain vehicles. Several dimensions come to mind for initial consideration: gender (male); age (18 to 35); lifestyle (outdoors); and income level (perhaps $25,000 to $40,000). At a minimum, these variables should be included in subsequent segmentation research.

Exhibit 3.2 presents five different ways a consumer market could be segmented, with a number of segmentation categories for each. The five types are geographic, demographic, sociocultural, affective/cognitive, and behavioral segmentation. While there are other bases for segmenting markets, they usually represent combinations of the types and bases discussed here.

Segmentation Types/Bases	Illustrative Categories
Geographic Segmentation	
Region	North, south, east, west
City size	Up to 100,000; 100,001 +
Population density	Urban, suburban, rural
Climate	Hot, temperate, cold
Demographic Segmentation	
Age	Up to 12; 13–19; 20–39; 40–59; 60 +
Gender	Female, male
Household size	1, 2, 3, 4 or more persons
Income	Up to $25,000; $25,001 to $50,000; over $50,000
Occupation	Professional, blue-collar, retired, unemployed
Education	High school or less, some college, college graduate
Sociocultural Segmentation	
Culture	American, European, South American
Subculture	
Religion	Baptist, Catholic, Jewish, Mormon
National origin	Italian, French, Canadian
Race	Hispanic, Oriental, African-American
Social class	Upper-class, middle-class, working-class, lower-class Americans
Marital status	Single, married, divorced, widowed
Psychographics	Achievers, strivers, strugglers
Affective and Cognitive Segmentation	
Degree of knowledge	Expert, novice
Benefits sought	Convenience, economy, prestige
Attitude	Positive, neutral, negative
Behavioral Segmentation	
Brand loyalty	None, divided, undivided loyalty
Store loyalty	None, divided, undivided loyalty
Usage rate	Light, medium, heavy
User status	Nonuser, ex-user, current user, potential user
Payment method	Cash, credit card, time payments
Media usage	Newspapers, magazines, TV
Usage situation	Work, home, vacation

EXHIBIT 3.2

Examples of segmentation bases for consumer markets

Geographic segmentation

Geographic segmentation calls for dividing markets on the basis of location. Common bases for segmenting a market geographically include by region, by size of cities, by population density, and by climate. City (and trading area) size is a popular segmentation basis for retailers. For example, when Wal-Mart first set up its discount stores, it intentionally located them in smaller towns capable of supporting only one discount store. This way, it did not have to compete directly with larger chains such as Kmart and could monopolize the trading area. The success of this strategy led the discounter eventually to move into larger trading areas and become the number one retailer in the country.

Demographic segmentation

Demographic segmentation is dividing the market on the basis of a population's characteristics. The most common ones are age, gender, household size, income, occupation, and education. Even if a market is segmented on other bases, it is common for companies also to obtain a demographic profile of customers to help know their market better.

A good example of demographic segmentation can be found in the increased attention many companies are giving to marketing products to women. Smith & Wesson, for example, traditionally marketed its line of handguns exclusively to men. However, recognizing the need to expand its market, the company launched the LadySmith, a line of guns specifically for women. This line was so popular that sales to women jumped from 5 percent to 18 percent of the company's total sales.[2] The Gap clothing store offers four different cuts of jeans for women and three for men, recognizing differences in body shapes both between and within the sexes.

Sociocultural segmentation

Sociocultural segmentation involves dividing markets on the basis of similarities and differences in social and cultural factors, such as religion or marital status. One of the most popular of these is **psychographic segmentation** which groups consumers on the basis of similarities and differences in their lifestyles.

Lifestyles are usually measured by asking consumers about their activities (work, hobbies, vacations), interests (family, job, community) and opinions (about social issues, politics, business). The activity, interest, and opinion **(AIO)** questions in some studies are of a very general nature. In others, at least some of the questions are related to specific products. Psychographic information can be obtained from sources other than company-sponsored research projects, as illustrated in Consumer Perspective 3.3.

Psychographic segmentation studies often include hundreds of questions and provide a tremendous amount of information about consumers. Such segmentation is based on the idea that the more you know and understand about consumers, the more effectively you can communicate and market to them.

However, different psychographic studies reach different conclusions about the number and nature of lifestyle categories, and the validity of psychographic segmentation is sometimes questioned.

One well-known psychographic segmentation was developed at SRI International in California. The original segmentation divided consumers in the United States into nine groups and was called **VALS**™ , which stands for "values and lifestyles." Although commercially successful, this segmentation tended to place the majority of consumers into only one or two groups, and SRI updated VALS™ to reflect changes in society. The new typology is called VALS 2™.[3]

VALS 2 is based on two national surveys of 2,500 consumers who responded to 43 lifestyle questions. The first survey developed the segmentation, and the second validated it and linked it to buying and media behavior. The questionnaire asked consumers to agree or disagree with statements such as "My idea of fun at a national park would be to stay at an expensive lodge and dress up for dinner" and "I could stand to skin a dead animal." Consumers were then clustered into the eight groups described in Exhibit 3.3 (see page 40).

The VALS 2 groups are arranged in a rectangle according to two vertical and horizontal dimensions. The vertical dimension represents resources, which include levels of income, education, self-confidence, health, eagerness to buy, intelligence, and energy level. The horizontal dimension represents self-orientation and includes three different types. *Principle-oriented consumers* are guided by their views of how the world is or should be; *status-oriented consumers* by the actions and opinions of others; and *action-oriented consumers* by a desire for social or physical activity, variety and risk taking.

Here's how marketers get lifestyle information about consumers who use 800 and 900 telephone numbers. Do you have an opinion about their access to this information?

1. **Make a phone call:** You call an 800 or 900 number to buy a product, get information, or express an opinion.

2. **Connect to computer:** In many cases, the call goes to a computer in Omaha, Nebraska, owned by AT&T and American Express. It has 10,000 continuously operating phone lines.

3. **Computer identifies you:** Using your phone number, the computer connects with a marketing service to get your name and address and display it on a salesperson's computer screen. Tens of millions of names can be searched in a second or two.

4. **Do your business:** The salesperson greets you by name, then takes your order, answers questions, or asks for more information.

5. **Instant check on your credit:** If you order something by credit card, the computer checks an electronic credit authorization bureau to make sure your credit is good.

6. **Your call is recorded:** Your name, address, phone number, and the subject of your call are provided electronically to the sponsoring company or organization, which then can use it for targeted mailing lists or marketing campaigns.

7. **Marketers analyze your lifestyle:** The sponsoring company can match this data with information in other data bases—voter lists, magazine subscriptions—to find out even more about your lifestyle.

Source: Reprinted from "How Big Brother Sees Consumers," by Robert S. Boyd, © 1990 by Knight-Ridder Newspapers, by permission of Knight-Ridder/Tribune News Service.

CONSUMER PERSPECTIVE

3.3 ◄

An interesting source of lifestyle information

Each of the VALS 2 groups represents from 9 to 17 percent of the U.S. adult population. Marketers can buy VALS 2 information for a variety of products and can have it tied to a number of other consumer data bases. Depending on the validity of the psychographic approach, VALS 2 could provide a useful basis for segmenting markets.

Affective and cognitive segmentation

Dividing markets on the basis of similarities and differences in consumers' knowledge, beliefs, or other internal psychological states is called **affective and cognitive segmentation**. For example, different hardware and software can be marketed to consumers who have a lot of knowledge about computers from the products sold to those who are just beginning to learn what a keyboard is.

A traditional type of such segmentation is **benefit segmentation.** The assumption underlying this approach is that the *benefits* consumers seek in using a particular product are the basic reasons for differences in true market segments. This approach measures consumer perceptions of various brands in order to understand the benefits they look for in a product class.

Exhibit 3.4 (see page 41) shows three possible benefit segments for blue jeans. Hardy Workers want durable jeans that can be purchased at a price that gives them good value for their money. Casual Wearers want jeans that are comfortable and fit well for shopping and weekend activities. This segment is less price conscious than the Hardy Workers. The third segment is the Trendies, who want expensive brands of jeans that make a statement about

EXHIBIT 3.3 VALS 2™ eight American lifestyles

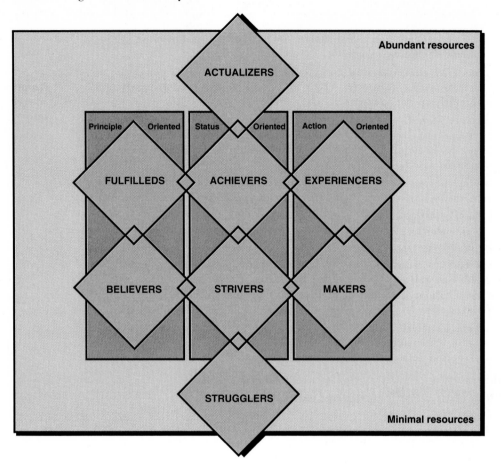

Actualizers. These consumers have the highest incomes and such high self-esteem and abundant resources that they can indulge in any or all self-orientations. They are located above the rectangle. Image is important to them as an expression of their taste, independence, and character. Their consumer choices are directed toward the finer things in life.

Fulfilleds. These consumers are the high resource group of those who are principle-oriented. They are mature, responsible, well-educated professionals. Their leisure activities center on their homes, but they are well-informed about what goes on in the world and they are open to new ideas and social change. They have high incomes but are practical consumers.

Believers. These consumers are the low resource group of those who are principle-oriented. They are conservative and predictable consumers who favor American products and established brands. Their lives are centered on family, church, community, and the nation. They have modest incomes.

Achievers. These consumers are the high-resource group of those who are status-oriented. They are successful, work-oriented people who get their satisfaction from their jobs and families. They are politically conservative and respect authority and the status quo. They favor established products and services that show off their success to their peers.

Strivers. These consumers are the low-resource group of those who are status-oriented. They have values very similar to Achievers but have fewer economic, social, and psychological resources. Style is extremely important to them as they strive to emulate people they admire and wish to be like.

Experiencers. These consumers are the high-resource group of those who are action-oriented. They are the youngest of all the segments with a median age of 25. They have a lot of energy, which they pour into physical exercise and social activities. They are avid consumers, spending heavily on clothing, fast foods, music, and other youthful favorites—with particular emphasis on new products and services.

Makers. These consumers are the low-resource group of those who are action-oriented. They are practical people who value self-sufficiency. They are focused on the familiar—family, work, and physical recreation—and have little interest in the broader world. As consumers, they appreciate practical and functional products.

Strugglers. These consumers have the lowest incomes. They have too few resources to be included in any consumer self-orientation and are thus located below the rectangle. They are the oldest of all the segments with a median age of 61. Within their limited means, they tend to be brand-loyal consumers.

Source: Martha Farnsworth Riche, "Psychographics for the 1990s," *American Demographics*, July 1989, pp. 24–25ff. Reprinted with permission © AMERICAN DEMO-GRAPHICS, July 1988. For subscription information, please call (800) 828-1133.

	Hardy Workers	Casual Wearers	Trendies
Principal benefits sought	Durability, value	Comfort, fit	Social identity
Common demographics	Blue-collar males	Professional women over 30 years of age	Middle- and upper-income family teenagers, young adults
Brands favored	Levi's, Wranglers, Plain Pockets	Lees, Gap, Zena	Guess?, Polo, Girbaud
Usage situations	Daily work and home wear	Shopping, weekend activities	Social events, including school
Lifestyle characteristics	Conservative	Active	Pleasure-seeking

EXHIBIT 3.4

Three benefit segments for blue jeans

them. This segment is the least price conscious and prefers expensive jeans with brand marks identifying them as costly.

These segments differ on a number of criteria, so different marketing approaches are likely to be successful for each. For example, because Hardy Workers shop in stores such as Penneys and Sears, Levi's made a good move in selling its jeans in these outlets several years ago. Different types and sizing of jeans, different packaging and labeling, different advertising appeals and media, and different retail outlets are generally needed to appeal to different benefit segments.

Behavioral segmentation

Dividing markets on the basis of similarities and differences in the overt actions of consumers is called **behavioral segmentation.** An example is a credit-card promotion. Fleet Bank wanted to increase its holders of Visa and MasterCards and decided to offer a promotion giving substantial discounts to people skiing at a number of New England resorts. The bank created the Ski New England Card, which offered $1,000 worth of discounts at 11 New England resorts and no credit-card fees for the first two years. Such a segmentation based on skiing behavior proved successful in achieving its sign-up goal. Of course, people who ski likely have other characteristics that make them good credit-card customers, such as higher incomes. In the saturated credit-card market, however, focusing on a particular behavior turned out to be a successful strategy.[4]

An extension of behavioral segmentation involves segmenting not just on behaviors but also on situations in which the behaviors occur. This is called **usage situation segmentation.** For example, clothing and footware markets are divided not only on the basis of gender and size, but also on the usage situation such as weather conditions (boots), physical activities (basketball shoes), and social events (loafers). As another example, Doulton china is designed for special occasions; Corelle dinnerware is designed for everyday family use. One advocate for this type of segmentation claims, "In practice, the product whose unique selling proposition (quality, features, image, packaging, or merchandising) is not targeted for particular people in particular usage situations is probably the exception rather than the rule."[5]

Usage situation is a more complete approach to segmentation than some others. To use this segmentation technique successfully, marketers have to understand what consumers think and feel about using a product, what actions they take, and what environmental events occur in the condition of use. In other words, marketers have to understand differences in consumer affect and cognitions, behaviors, and environments to target the best markets for their products.

Usage situations can be effective means for segmenting markets.

Select segmentation strategy

Having completed analysis of consumer/product relationships and the bases for segmentation, the appropriate segmentation strategy can now be considered. There are four basic alternatives. First, the firm may decide not to enter the market. Analysis so far may reveal there is no viable market niche for the product, brand, or model. Second, the firm may decide not to segment but to be a mass marketer. This may be the appropriate strategy in at least three situations:

1. When the market is so small that marketing to a portion of it is not profitable.
2. When heavy users make up such a large proportion of the sales volume that they are the only relevant target.
3. When the brand is dominant in the market, and targeting to a few segments would not benefit sales and profits.[6]

Third, the firm may decide to market to only one segment. Fourth, the firm may decide to market to more than one segment and design a separate marketing mix for each.

In any case, marketers must have some criteria on which to base segmentation strategy decisions. Three important criteria are that a viable segment must be measurable, meaningful, and marketable:

1. **Measurable.** For a segment to be selected, marketers must be able to measure its size and characteristics. One of the difficulties with segmenting on the basis of social class is that the concept and its divisions are not clearly measurable. Alternatively, income is much easier to measure.

2. **Meaningful.** A meaningful segment is one that is large enough to have sufficient sales and growth potential to offer long-run profits.

3. **Marketable.** A marketable segment is one that can be reached and served profitably.

Segments that meet these criteria are viable markets for the product. The marketer must now give further attention to the marketing mix.

The **marketing mix** consists of product, price, promotion, and channels of distribution. These are the primary elements marketing managers can control to serve consumers. The aim is to develop a consistent mix where all elements work together to serve the target market or markets the company has selected. Selecting target markets and developing marketing mixes are related tasks.

Companies increasingly recognize that the starting point for making marketing mix decisions is a thorough understanding of consumers in their target markets. Each of the marketing mix elements involves many decisions, and analysis of consumers can help make the decisions more effective for achieving company goals.

MARKETING MIX DECISIONS

Product decisions

A product is any offering made for the purpose of exchange. Marketing questions in this area include such issues as:

▷ What function does this product or service serve for consumers in a target market, and what does it mean to them?

▷ What attributes or features of the product are most important to the target market?

▷ What types of packaging and labeling information would best serve consumers and attract them to purchase the product?

▷ What brand name and trademark for the product would create the appropriate image in the target market?

▷ What kinds of pre- or post-sale service would satisfy consumers in the target market?

▷ How many models, variations, or sizes of the product are needed to satisfy various target markets?

While this list is not exhaustive, it demonstrates that many product decisions depend on understanding consumers in various target markets. Think about tennis rackets, for example. Analysis of this market reveals that most tennis players do not spend the time to practice often and to get into good playing condition. Standard rackets let them enjoy the game but do not give them the power good players have. For many of these players, however, tennis performance is important, and they are willing to pay more for a racket that could improve their game. Weekend players can purchase high-tech, wide-body design graphite rackets that offer exceptional power, yet are lighter, so players can swing them harder than conventional rackets. The names of these expensive rackets—Wilson's Hammer, Prince's Vortex, and Head's Discovery—communicate the idea of superior performance.

In the case of tennis rackets, redesign of a conventional product to serve a particular target market using new technology resulted in a dramatic change in demand. In fact, every top 10 selling racket today is a wide-body model. Wide-bodies account for about 90 percent of the $115 million Americans spend on rackets. Understanding what the target market wanted and how they play the game allowed tennis racket manufacturers to score a huge marketing success.[7]

CONSUMER PERSPECTIVE

▶ 3.4

Increasing consumer prices

Manufacturers can raise the price consumers pay for products in a number of ways. Prices can be increased outright for the same quantity and quality, or maintained for less quantity, less quality, or fewer auxiliary services. Price deals could be reduced or eliminated, or interest rates and charges could be increased. Examples of maintaining the same price but offering less quantity include:

Brand	Product	It Looks Like . . .	You Pay . . .	But You Get . . .
Knorr	Leek soup and recipe mix	**More:** Box is 1/2" deeper	**The same**	**Less:** Makes three 8-oz. servings, reduced from four
StarKist	Canned tuna	**A bit less:** Can is 1/16" less tall	**The same**	**Less:** Weight of tuna reduced by 3/8 oz., or 5.8%
Lipton	Instant lemon-flavored tea	**The same**	**The same**	**Less:** Weight reduced by 7.5%; company claims it contains same number of servings as before
Brim	Decaffeinated coffee	**The same**	**The same**	**Less:** Weight reduced by 4.2%; company claims it contains same number of servings as before

Source: David E. Kalish, "Prices Stable, but Products Are Less Filling," *Wisconsin State Journal*, January 6, 1991, p. 1D. Reprinted by permission of the Associated Press.

Price decisions

Price is what consumers must give up to purchase a product. Marketing issues in this area include such things as:

▷ How much are consumers in a target market willing to pay for a particular product?

▷ At what price would consumers in this market consider this product a good value?

▷ What do specific prices communicate to consumers about the quality of a particular product?

▷ If the price of a product were lowered in the short run, would consumers continue to buy the product when it goes back to full price?

▷ Would consumers stop purchasing the product if the price were increased permanently?

▷ How important is price to consumers in a particular target market?

Whether a company is introducing a new product or planning a short-term or long-term price change, it needs to analyze how consumers will respond to the price variable. For example, consumers view nationally branded motor oil as essentially a commodity, where price is the most important determinant of purchase. In this market, price wars are common among brands such as Pennzoil, Havoline, Valvoline, and Castrol.

Quaker State motor oil, at one time the market leader, tried to avoid competing on the basis of price. The company promoted its long warranty and its new synthetic oil line in an attempt to convince consumers that its products were of superior quality and should command a higher price than other brands. Consumers cannot detect differences in major brands of motor oil, though, and were not willing to pay a higher price for Quaker State. The company's market share dropped from 22 percent to 14 percent, and Pennzoil gained

Buick found the appropriate image and features for its target market.

the market lead. Overall, Quaker State's volume dropped from almost 125 million gallons in the mid-1980s to about 85 million in the early 1990s. Analysis of consumers' beliefs and the way they buy and use motor oil could have saved Quaker State from making this mistake in its pricing strategy. Even so, some companies do find ways of charging higher prices that do not decrease consumer demand, as Consumer Perspective 3.4 shows.

Promotion decisions

Promotion refers to the variety of ways marketers communicate with consumers about products to influence their affect, cognitions, and behaviors. Marketing questions in this area include such things as:

▷ What are the best media for reaching a target market for a particular product?

▷ What message should be communicated to consumers about a product?

▷ What image should advertising try to create about a product?

▷ What types of sales promotions would be most effective for getting consumers to buy a product?

▷ What approach should salespeople use to match consumers' needs and wants with particular products?

▷ What role should publicity play in communicating with consumers about a product?

Decisions about these questions clearly depend on knowing a lot about consumers. For example, Buick, like many American car brands, suffered losses in sales and market share through much of the 1980s. Part of the problem was that it came to ignore its traditional target market and designed and promoted cars for a younger market. The "traditional" Buick buyer has a median income of $42,700, a median age of 61 years, and a high school education.

Gloria Jean's found a way to make coffee appeal to a profitably large market.

To reestablish Buick in its traditional market, GM promoted it as a premium American motorcar. The intended message was that it is a substantial, distinctive, powerful, and mature automobile. Buick ads changed to feature a bit more mature people and emphasized automotive features that consumer analysis indicates this market prefers, such as powerful engines, comfortable ride, and easy control.

While sales of other General Motors brands continued to decline in the early 1990s, Buick division sales increased sharply. In fact, Buick moved ahead of Pontiac and Oldsmobile to rank second only to Chevrolet in General Motors sales. One of the reasons for Buick's success was that it learned to promote the appropriate image and features for its target market.[8]

Channels of distribution decisions

Channels of distribution refer to the system by which products are directed from producers to consumers. Channels for consumer goods often include wholesalers and retailers. Consumers typically purchase from retail stores, but may also buy from mail-order houses, TV home shopping networks, and other sources. Marketing questions in this area include such things as:

▷ Would consumers prefer to purchase a product in stores or from different channels, such as mail-order catalogs or in-home salespeople?

▷ What image do various stores and chains have that might influence consumer preference and purchase behavior for various products?

▷ Do various stores have particular atmospheres that might influence consumer purchase of a product?

▷ How do such things as in-store layout, signs, and displays influence consumer affect, cognition, and behavior toward various products?

▷ Where should service facilities be located to make them readily available for consumers?

▷ What role do in-store salespeople play in educating consumers about various products?

Decisions such as these influence not only the specific retail channels that a manufacturer selects, but also what other intermediaries are involved. For example, a major trend for many manufacturers in recent years is to sell directly to major discount chains and bypass wholesalers.

Distribution decisions can also play an important role in determining what consumers think about various products. For example, Oshkosh B'Gosh Inc. has had an image as

In the 1980s, a number of retailers recognized that the teenage population was shrinking and decided to switch to other markets. There were 30 million teenagers in the United States in 1975, while by 1990, there were only 22.7 million. However, according to one poll, teenage spending doubled in this period to a whopping $57 billion. Merry-Go-Round Enterprises thought there was still a lot of money to be made in selling reasonably priced funky fashions to young adults, especially men. In 1990, sales from the company's three divisions—Merry-Go-Round, Cignal, and Menz (which runs stores under the names DJ's, Dejaiz, and Attivo)—were up 30 percent and earnings rose 69 percent to $37.5 million.

Few other retailers understand the teenage and young-adult market as well as Merry-Go-Round. The company recognizes that over half the men who shop in its stores still live at home and spend the majority of their income on cars, stereos, and clothes. Because there are so few teens, it's easier for them to get jobs, even in a recession. Buyers who select styles and colors for Merry-Go-Round stores keep a careful eye on what's happening in the teenage world and know what musical groups and fashions are hot.

Step inside any of the company's rap-and-rock-music-filled stores and you'll be greeted with "How are you?" rather than "Can I help you?" (You can't answer "no" to the first question.) New salespeople are shown how to select outfits, the proper way to escort a customer to the dressing room, and how to close the sale in a nonoffensive manner. The stores carry brands such as Skidz, Get Used, and Major Damage and quickly discount new items that its computerized merchandise tracking system shows are selling poorly. Apparently, Merry-Go-Round Enterprises understands consumer/store relationships and responds quickly to changes in the teenage and young-adult market.

Source: Reprinted with permission from "If It's Hot, They've Got It," by Caminiti, *Fortune*, © 1991 Time Inc. All rights reserved.

a manufacturer of high-quality, trendy clothes for kids under seven, earned in part by selling only in exclusive department and specialty stores. In the early 1990s, however, the company decided to sell its products in chains such as Sears and JC Penney. Such a move might damage its image, but if the quality of the product remains high, the company could increase sales dramatically by reaching a larger target market of parents and grandparents. The important point, of course, is that the specific stores that sell a product can influence what consumers think about the product.

As another example, consider the coffee market. For the last 30 years, demand for this product has decreased. Coffee consumption dropped from 3.1 cups per day in the early 1960s to 1.75 cups in the early 1990s. Only half of U.S. adults now drink coffee, compared with three fourths of them in the 60s. Sellers of gourmet coffee have managed to thrive in this declining market, all the same. Specialty retail chains sell gourmet coffee beans, brewed gourmet coffee, and related products. Starbuck Coffee Co. and Gloria Jean's Coffee Beans have taken advantage of social trends away from alcoholic beverages to offer an affordable luxury for many consumers. Gloria Jean's sales, for example, went from $18 million in its first year to $50 million by its third year. In this case, offering a specialty product through a unique channel formed the basis for a successful marketing strategy. Consumer Perspective 3.5 offers an example of a clothes retailer that uses unique in-store design to develop a successful marketing strategy and attract a specific target market.

Marketing implications

Marketing mix decisions clearly depend heavily on understanding consumers and selecting appropriate target markets. One way to summarize this process is to consider product positioning. **Product positioning** involves conveying an image in order to influence consumer behavior. To position a product effectively, all four of the marketing mix elements should be

Shimano positioned its Calcutta reel as a prestige product with ads such as this.

SHIMANO CALCUTTA. ONE-PIECE ALUMINUM FRAME. ANODIZED ALUMINUM FINISH. TWIN POWER™ HANDLE FOR SPEED OR POWER. ONE-WAY INFINITE ANTI-REVERSE. IMPROVED, RUGGED PINION GEAR AND ROTARY CLUTCH MECHANISM. CENTRIFUGAL BRAKE SYSTEM. NO MAGNETICS. THUMB SCREWS FOR INTERNAL ACCESS. RECESSED REEL SEAT FOR COMFORT AND CONTROL. QUICKFIRE II SPOOL RELEASE BAR. THREE STAINLESS STEEL BALL BEARINGS. ALUMINUM SPOOL. 5.0:1 GEAR RATIO. 9.7 OUNCES. NO UNNECESSARY KNOBS. NO BUTTONS. NO LEVERS. NO DISTRACTIONS. JUST YOU AND THE FISH.

LEAD WITH US

designed to work toward creating a consistent image. For example, consider the situation facing Shimano American Corp. in the early 1990s. The fishing tackle company had a good reputation for producing quality rods and reels, but other companies such as Daiwa had introduced several more expensive reel models and threatened to take over the market for high-priced, high-quality reels.

Shimano developed an excellent positioning strategy to combat this threat. First, it developed a distinctive bait-casting reel machined very precisely from a single piece of aluminum, with a brushed aluminum finish that makes it stand out from its competition. And the reel sold for $139.95, a good deal more than all but a few other reels.

Shimano advertised the product in specialty fishing magazines and sold the reel only in independent sporting goods shops, where retailers were required to sell the reel at no less than $139.95. If they did sell it for less, retailers would have a hard time getting reorders filled promptly. This strategy was extremely successful in positioning the reels; the company could not keep up with demand for the product.

In this case, each marketing mix element fits with and reinforces the other elements to encourage purchase. The Calcutta 200 reel is clearly positioned as a top-quality product for serious purchasers, promoted only in selected media, and sold only by independent retailers. The fact that the product is unlikely to be discounted reinforces the image of quality, given that most other such reels can be purchased in discount stores at far below suggested retail prices. The high price implies quality. In essence, this company developed a successful positioning strategy that involved all four elements of the marketing mix and was appropriately targeted at a group of consumers. Consumers' affect, cognition, and behaviors changed as a result of this strategy.

Learning objective 1: *Define market segmentation, and explain why marketers segment markets.*

Market segmentation is the process of dividing markets into groups of similar consumers and selecting the most appropriate groups and individuals for the firm to serve. Marketers segment markets because seldom does a single product appeal to all consumers. Consumers vary in terms of product knowledge, involvement, and purchasing behavior. Thus, marketers group consumers who are similar on some dimensions so a particular product will appeal to and satisfy them better.

Learning objective 2: *List five major types of segmentation, and give examples of each.*

Five major types of segmentation include geographic segmentation with bases such as city size and population density; demographic segmentation with bases such as age and income; sociocultural segmentation with bases such as race and social class; affective and cognitive segmentation with bases such as benefits sought and attitudes; and behavioral segmentation with bases such as brand loyalty and usage rate.

Learning objective 3: *Explain psychographic, benefit, and usage situation segmentation.*

Psychographic segmentation involves segmenting consumers on the basis of similarities and differences in their lifestyles. Benefit segmentation involves segmenting consumers on the basis of the benefits they are looking for in purchasing a product. Usage situation segmentation involves segmenting consumers on the basis of the circumstances surrounding their use of a product.

Learning objective 4: *List the elements of the marketing mix.*

The marketing mix includes product, price, promotion, and channels of distribution.

Learning objective 5: *Offer examples of marketing mix issues for which consumer analysis is important.*

Product decisions about product features, packaging, and branding, and the number of models and sizes to be offered can benefit from consumer analysis. Decisions on pricing a new product or making a short-term or long-term price change can benefit from understanding what price means to consumers of a particular product. Promotion decisions concerning appropriate images, messages, and media for advertising and appropriate types of sales promotion can benefit from analyzing consumers. Finally, consumer analysis is useful in channel of distribution decisions such as the effects of store location and in-store stimuli on consumer purchasing behavior.

Learning objective 6: *Explain product positioning.*

Product positioning involves conveying an image of a product to influence consumer behavior. Successful product positioning depends on combining all four of the marketing mix elements to create a consistent image in the minds of consumers.

▶ **SUMMARY**

▶ **KEY TERMS AND CONCEPTS**

market segmentation
target market
geographic segmentation
demographic segmentation
sociocultural segmentation

psychographic segmentation
AIO
VALS™
affective and cognitive segmentation

benefit segmentation
behavioral segmentation
usage situation segmentation
marketing mix
product positioning

► **REVIEW AND DISCUSSION QUESTIONS**

1. Define market segmentation, and describe the management tasks involved in applying the concept.

2. Select a product (not blue jeans) that you know something about, and draw up possible benefit segments following the structure used in Exhibit 3.4.

3. Identify potential advantages and problems associated with marketing to benefit segments.

4. Use the VALS 2 categories to suggest marketing strategies for psychographic segments of buyers for hotel/motel services.

5. Consider usage situation segmentation as a way of viewing the snack-food market. State the needs and objectives of persons in situations for at least three segments that you identify.

6. How does the concept of segmentation relate to positioning strategies?

7. What options might an organization choose after identifying segments in the market? When would each of these options represent a reasonable choice?

8. Are segmentation and positioning decisions different for a small business entrepreneur compared to a large corporation? If so, in what way?

CASES IN CONSUMER BEHAVIOR

CASES

► **CASE I.1**

Toyota

If any one word describes the Toyota company, it is *kaizen,* which means "continuous improvement." While some companies strive for dramatic breakthrough, Toyota keeps doing lots of little things better and better. Consider the subcompact Tercel, the smallest Toyota sold in the United States. While this model contributes only modestly to its profits, Toyota made the 1991 Tercel faster, roomier, and quieter than its predecessor—with less weight, equally good mileage, and, remarkably, the same under-$8,000 price for the basic four-door sedan. It's $100 cheaper than GM's new Saturn and as much as $1,600 less than other competing models.

One consultant calls Toyota's strategy "rapid inch-up": Take enough tiny steps, and pretty soon you outdistance the competition. By introducing six all-new vehicles within 14 months, Toyota grabbed a crushing 43 percent share of car sales in Japan. In the 1990 model year, it sold more than 1 million cars and trucks in the United States and is poised to move up from its number 4 position in the U.S. market; it is the number 3 automaker in the world market. The company, which enjoys the highest operating margins in the world auto industry, is so rich that it makes more money on financial investments than it does on operations. It has over $22 billion in cash and could buy both Ford and Chrysler with nearly $5 billion to spare.

Toyota simply is tops in quality, production, and efficiency. From its factories pour a wide range of cars, built with unequaled precision. Toyota turns out luxury sedans with Mercedes-like quality using *one sixth* the labor Mercedes does. The company originated just-in-time (JIT) production and remains its leading practitioner. It has close relationships with its suppliers and rigorous engineering specifications for the products it purchases.

Toyota pioneered quality circles, which involve workers discussing ways to improve their tasks and avoid what it calls the three Ds: the dangerous, dirty, and demanding aspects of factory work. The company is investing $770 million to improve worker housing, add dining halls, and build new recreational facilities. On the assembly line, quality is defined not as zero defects but, as another Toyota slogan has it, as "building the very best and giving customers what they want." Because workers serve as customers for the process just before theirs, they become quality-control inspectors. If a piece isn't installed properly when it reaches them, they won't accept it.

Toyota's engineering system allows it to take a new car design from concept to showroom in less than four years, compared to more than five years for U.S. companies and seven years for Mercedes-Benz. This cuts costs, allows quicker correction of mistakes, and keeps Toyota more in tune with market trends. Gains from speed feed on themselves. Toyota accomplishes its advanced engineering and design more quickly because, as one manager puts it, "We are closer to the customer and thus have a shorter concept time." New products are the province of a chief engineer who has complete responsibility and authority for the product from design and manufacturing through marketing and has direct contacts with both dealers and consumers. New-model bosses for U.S. companies seldom have such control and almost never have direct contact with dealers or consumers.

In Toyota's manufacturing system, parts and cars don't get built until dealers request them. In placing orders, dealers essentially reserve a portion of factory capacity. The system is so effective that rather than wait several months for a new car, the customer can get a built-to-order car in a week to 10 days.

"We have learned that universal mass production is not enough," says the head of the Toyota's Tokyo Design Center. "In the 21st century, you personalize things more to make them more reflective of individual needs." The winners in carmaking will be those who target narrow customer niches most successfully with specific models.

Discussion Questions

1. In what ways is Toyota's new-product development system designed to serve customers?
2. In what ways is Toyota's manufacturing system designed to serve customers?
3. How does Toyota personalize its cars and trucks to meet individual consumer needs?
4. How do you think the Toyota Tercel stacks up against the competition in its price range?

Source: Reprinted with permission from "Why Toyota Keeps Getting Better and Better and Better," by Alex Taylor III, *Fortune*, © 1990 Time Inc. All rights reserved.

CASE I.2 ◄

Wal-Mart Stores Inc.

For many years, Americans bought more goods from Sears, Roebuck & Co. than from any other retailer. But in fiscal 1991, Wal-Mart became the number one retailer and Sears slipped to third behind Kmart. Although 1991 witnessed one of the worst recessions in recent years, Wal-Mart sales rose 26 percent over 1990 to $32.6 billion. Wal-Mart's phenomenal growth is shown in Exhibit A.

Wal-Mart sells a variety of standard consumer goods ranging from laundry detergent to sporting goods. One factor contributing to the company's success is consumer willingness to travel past nearby stores to shop at a Wal-Mart. Priscilla Patterson, for instance, drove 25 minutes from her Mount Prospect, Illinois, home to a Wal-Mart in Lake Zurich to buy a portable radio for her son. "I thought I could get the best price," she said, remembering a previous purchase she had made at Wal-Mart.

A trip down the aisles of the Lake Zurich Wal-Mart offers some clues to its marketing strategy. Other than a once-a-month full-color advertising circular distributed in newspapers,

---

EXHIBIT A   Wal-Mart's rise to the top

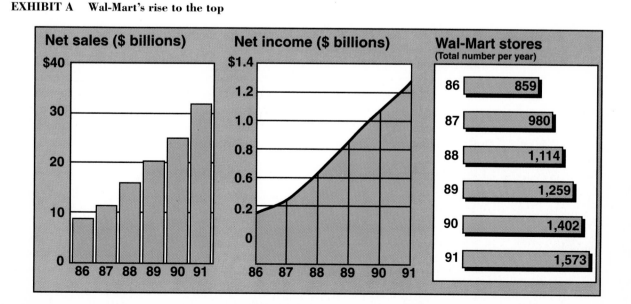

in-store signs are virtually all the advertising Wal-Mart does. Brightly colored signs hang from the ceiling and steer shoppers toward tables offering tantalizing bargains on summer shoes, garden supplies, diapers, and toothpaste. Signs under a hair-care display boast an everyday low price of 97 cents for a 16-ounce bottle of shampoo. A nearby discount health and beauty aids store sells the same bottle for $1.46, or 49 cents more. A popular outdoor barbecue grill sells for $54.94 at Wal-Mart; a leading competitor in a nearby mall sells it for $64.97, a $10.03 difference. If consumers bring in an ad for a product sold by a competitor at a lower price, Wal-Mart lowers its price to match. Department managers and other price-checkers routinely shop other stores to make price comparisons and log the prices that beat theirs into a store computer.

Wal-Mart's expansion strategy was to build stores in trading areas that could support only one large discount store. In this way, it avoided direct competition with other discounters such as Kmart or Target. As Wal-Mart grew and became more profitable, it expanded into larger trading areas. However, it avoided major shopping malls, preferring to locate on the edges of cities where property was less expensive.

Wal-Mart is an expert at holding down overhead costs. Sophisticated warehouse and information systems enable it to keep operating costs down to an enviable 16 percent, the lowest in the industry. Wal-Mart sends checkout-line information on sales of some Procter & Gamble products, such as diapers, directly to P&G at the same time it records the sale in its own computer records. This means P&G has immediate information on sales and can adjust production and shipping schedules to allow efficient replenishment of Wal-Mart's stock. Given that Wal-Mart sells such huge volumes of merchandise, it can demand the best prices from manufacturers such as P&G.

The company also has developed a number of employee programs to promote sales and friendly service. For example, each in-store sales associate selects one piece of merchandise to sponsor for a year. The sales associate builds a display for it and keeps it clean and stocked. In a store with 200 employees, this means someone is watching 200 of the store's products extra carefully. Individual rewards for sponsoring a product are not monetary; workers simply seek recognition for their efforts from fellow employees and bosses—all of whom are on a first-name basis. The best of the merchandising ideas make their way to headquarters, allowing small but good concepts to be adopted nationwide.

About the only unsuccessful Wal-Mart venture has been the development of hypermarts. Wal-Mart built four of these, which sell groceries and everything else in 225,000-square-foot stores, the size of five football fields. Although the hypermarket concept was successful in Europe, Americans apparently do not like searching through such large stores for convenience products. Also, hypermarts often do not have as deep a selection of products as more specialized stores. For example, the hypermart in Arlington, Texas, carries only three brands of videocassette recorders, while electronics stores in the area carry seven brands. Wal-Mart announced it has no plans to build any more hypermarts but will instead focus on stores no larger than 150,000 square feet.

Discussion Questions

1. Based on the case information and your personal experiences, list at least five things you know about Wal-Mart. This list offers you some idea of your *cognitions* about this retail chain.

2. Based on the case information and your personal experiences, list at least five things you like or dislike about Wal-Mart. This list offers you some idea of your *affect* for this retail chain.

3. Based on your personal experiences in shopping at Wal-Mart (or another discount store if you haven't shopped there), list at least five behaviors you have

performed in a shopping trip. This list gives you some idea of the *behaviors* involved in shopping at a discount store.

4. Based on the case information and your personal experiences, list at least five things Wal-Mart has done in the environment to influence consumers to shop there. This list gives you some idea of how enironment influences cognition, affect, and behavior.

5. Write a brief description of a purchase you have made at a Wal-Mart. Did the purchase involve cognition, affect, behavior, and environmental components?

Sources: Kevin Kelly and Amy Dunkin, "Wal-Mart Gets Lost in the Vegetable Aisle," *Business Week*, May 28, 1990, p. 48; Marianne Taylor, "Wal-Mart Prices Its Way to Top of Retail Mountain," *Wisconsin State Journal*, May 5, 1991, p. 1C, 2C.

CASE I.3 ◄

Hershey Chocolate USA

Hershey Chocolate USA, a division of Hershey Foods Corporation, achieved record sales in 1991 despite a difficult economic environment, intense competitive activity, and consumer resistance to price increases. Economic uncertainty led to retailers keeping down inventories of Hershey products. Competitors, such as Mars Candy Company, introduced a variety of new products, brand extensions, and additional pack types. Consumers initially resisted the increases in the price of candy, although it was the first increase in five years.

Record sales were obtained in part by the introduction of a number of new Hershey products, the most significant being Hershey's Kisses with Almonds. This product was introduced in 1990 and became one of the top 20 U.S. candy brands during 1991. By reaching the top 20 in less than one full year of national distribution, Hershey's Kisses with Almonds became the most successful new product introduction in the corporation's history.

In 1991, Hershey Chocolate also received the Equitrend Outstanding Quality Award. This award was based on a national survey that measured how consumers perceived the quality of 190 nationally recognized brand names. Hershey's milk chocolate bar was the highest-rated confectionary brand.

Part of Hershey's strategy is to target to mothers; it reasons that mothers determine children's early taste in candy. In addition, research shows that adults eat more than 55 percent of all candy sold. Bite-size products, such as Hershey's Kisses, Hershey's Miniature chocolate bars, Reese's Miniature peanut butter cups, York peppermint patties, and Rolo caramels, are popular with adult consumers. When wrapped in seasonal colors, these products have tremendous appeal for adults during Christmas and Easter season. Halloween season, however, is more oriented toward candy bars.

Although candy consumption dropped in the late 1980s, due in part to the fitness trend, it rebounded in the early 1990s. The average American consumed 20.7 pounds of confectionary products in 1990, 1.5 pounds more than in 1988.

Discussion Questions

1. What are the advantages of targeting candy to adults rather than to children?
2. Does targeting to adults require a change in image for candy products?
3. Why do you think bite-size candies are so popular with adults?
4. Describe your most recent purchase of a candy bar in terms of relevant affect and cognitions, behaviors, and environments.

Sources: Excerpted from *Hershey Foods Corporation 1991 Annual Report*, pp. 4–6; Jennifer Pellet, "Marketing to America's Sweet Tooth," *Discount Merchandiser*, May 1991, pp. 21–22.

AFFECT AND COGNITION

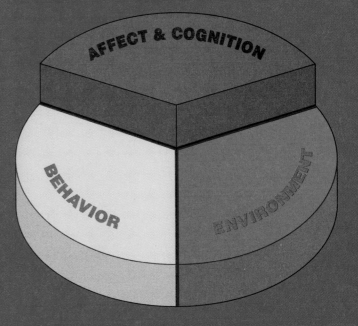

CHAPTER 4

Introduction to Affect and Cognition

LEARNING OBJECTIVES

After completing this chapter, you should be able to:

▶ 1. Describe the affective system, and identify the types of affective responses it produces.

▶ 2. Describe the cognitive system and the types of meanings it creates.

▶ 3. Explain how the affective and cognitive systems influence each other.

▶ 4. Describe the components of the model of consumer decision making.

▶ 5. Explain how knowledge in memory can be activated for use in cognitive processing.

▶ 6. Describe the differences between general and procedural knowledge.

▶ 7. Give examples of associative networks of knowledge in the form of schemas and scripts.

WHAT DOES "RUBBERMAID" MEAN?

Rubbermaid, the housewares company, has cashed in on its well-known brand name in some surprising ways. For example, it has sold feed bins for hogs, cattle, and horses to farmers and now manufactures 25 agricultural products. But an attempt to sell computer workstands for secretaries bombed. Why? Rubbermaid discovered its brand name had a very specific meaning to most consumers. Research revealed Rubbermaid meant "rock solid durability." Durability is a valuable meaning for housewares, feed bins, and office products such as floor mats, but not for computer tables, where ease of use and comfort are more important meanings.

Many companies have learned they need to be careful in extending their valuable brand names to other products. They must ensure that the meanings and feelings associated with the brand name are appropriate for the new product. For instance, Campbell licensed its name and the familiar red-and-white packaging to be used for a line of cooking utensils. This worked because the Campbell's name and logo conjures up emotional images of hearth and home.

Firms such as Landor Associates specialize in determining the hidden meanings and feelings in familiar brands. Landor found that Dole suggests "sunshine foods," which led the company into fruit sorbets, carrots, and snack nuts. Brand names with clear and distinctive meanings cannot be applied to everything, however. Playboy stands for swanky self-indulgence as well as sex, and the Playboy name was used successfully for a line of men's shoes. But a Playboy line of suits didn't work—a college graduate doesn't want to walk into his first job interview with a new haircut and a Playboy suit.[1]

These examples show that marketers need to understand the feelings (affect) and meanings (cognition) that consumers associate with products and brands. In this chapter we begin our examination of affect and cognition. First, we define affect and cognition. Then we explain how consumers' affective and cognitive systems produce affective and cognitive responses. Next, we present a model of consumer decision making that describes the key cognitive processes involved in decision making. Finally, we discuss several types of knowledge stored in memory that consumers can use to make decisions. Our goal is to understand how consumers' affective and cognitive responses to the environment influence their decision making.

AFFECT AND COGNITION AS PSYCHOLOGICAL RESPONSES

Affect and cognition are different types of psychological responses. **Affect** refers to feeling responses; **cognition** is a mental response. Consumers can have both affective and cognitive responses to any element in the Wheel of Consumer Analysis—the environment, behaviors, or other affective and cognitive responses. Affect and cognition are produced by the affective and cognitive systems, respectively. Although the two systems are distinct, they are richly interconnected, and each system can influence and be influenced by the other.[2]

In distinguishing affect from cognition, you can think of affect as something people *are* or something people *feel* (I *am* angry; Linda *is* in a good mood; Joe *feels* bored).[3] Because people experience affect in their bodies, affect seems to be a part of the person at the time they experience it. In contrast, people *have* cognitions (your father *believes* Diet Pepsi is not fattening; Susan *knows* where the grocery store is; you *believe* your interview suit is stylish). Cognitions are mental states; they usually are not felt in the body.

Types of affective responses

People can experience four broad types of affective responses: emotions, specific feelings, moods, and evaluations. Exhibit 4.1 identifies these affective responses and gives examples of each type. Each type of affect can involve positive or negative responses. Feelings, for example, can be favorable (Joan was satisfied with her T-shirt) or unfavorable (John was disgusted with the service he received). Moods can be positive (relaxed) or negative (sad).

The four types of affect differ in the level of bodily arousal or the intensity with which they are experienced.[4] The stronger affective responses, such as emotions, may involve physiological responses such as increased heart rate or blood pressure, perspiration, dry mouth, tears, rushes of adrenaline, or butterflies in the stomach. Specific feelings involve somewhat less intense physiological reactions (Robert was sad when he sold his old Ford Mustang). Moods, which involve lower levels of felt intensity, are rather diffuse affective states (Jennifer was bored by the long shopping trip).[5] Finally, evaluations of products or

EXHIBIT 4.1

Types of affective responses

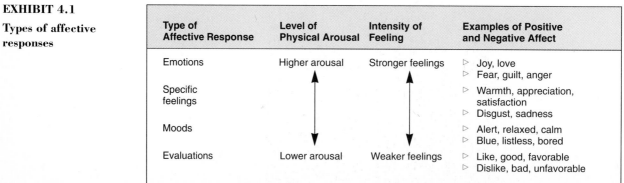

Type of Affective Response	Level of Physical Arousal	Intensity of Feeling	Examples of Positive and Negative Affect
Emotions	Higher arousal	Stronger feelings	▷ Joy, love ▷ Fear, guilt, anger
Specific feelings			▷ Warmth, appreciation, satisfaction ▷ Disgust, sadness
Moods			▷ Alert, relaxed, calm ▷ Blue, listless, bored
Evaluations	Lower arousal	Weaker feelings	▷ Like, good, favorable ▷ Dislike, bad, unfavorable

other concepts (I like Colgate toothpaste) often are rather weak affective responses accompanied by low levels of arousal (one hardly "feels" anything).

Affective responses are produced by the affective system. Although researchers are still studying how the affective system operates, they generally agree on five basic characteristics.[6] One important property is that the affective system is largely reactive in that it cannot plan or purposefully direct its responses toward a goal. Rather, a person's affective system usually responds immediately and automatically to significant aspects of the environment. An obvious example is color. Most people have an immediate positive affective response when they see a favorite color on a car or item of clothing. Consumer Perspective 4.1 discusses how the affective system responds to color.

The affective system

People have little direct control over their affective responses. For instance, if you are insulted by a rude salesclerk, your affective system might immediately and automatically produce feelings of frustration or anger. However, people have indirect control over their affective feelings by changing the behavior that is triggering the affect or moving to another environment. For instance, you might complain about the rude clerk to the manager, which could reduce the negative affect you felt and create a new feeling of satisfaction. Consumers who have negative affective reactions to a crowded clothing shop (feelings of discomfort, frustration, or even anger) might leave the store to shop in a less crowded environment that stimulates more positive affective feelings.[7]

A third feature of the affective system is that affective responses are felt physically in the body. Consider the "butterflies" in the stomach associated with the excitement of making an important purchase, such as a new car or a house. These physical reactions can be powerful feelings for the people experiencing them. Body movements often reflect their affective states (smile when happy, frown when disturbed, clench fists in anger, sit up straight in anticipation, slouch in boredom) and communicate emotional states. Thus, successful salespeople read the body language of their prospects and adapt their sales presentations accordingly.

Fourth, the affective system can respond to virtually any type of stimulus. For instance, consumers can have an evaluative response to a physical object (I *love* my Pioneer stereo

People's affective responses are reflected in their bodies.

All living creatures have certain innate responses to the environment, and the response to color is one of the most important. The first thing people react to in evaluating an object (a product or building) is its color, and their automatic affective response can account for as much as 60 percent of their acceptance of the object. Your affective response to color influences your emotions and feelings, as well as your cognitions and behaviors. Colors can attract or distract you, make you feel good or bad, attract you to other people or repel you, make you want to eat more or less.

A person's affective response to color involves automatic reactions of the eye, optic neurons, parts of the brain, and various glands. Consider the response to red. When the eye sees primary red, the pituitary gland (embedded in the brain) is stimulated to send out a chemical signal to the adrenal medulla (located above the kidneys), which secrete adrenaline that activates and arouses the body. Emotions such as anger or fear are enhanced by this automatic reaction to red—danger signs are usually red. Affective feelings of excitement are generated by red. Thus, cosmetics such as lipstick are based on red. In the presence of red, people tend to eat more, which is why red is a popular color for restaurants.

People have similar automatic reactions to other colors. For instance, a particular shade of vivid pink causes the brain to secrete norepinephrine, a chemical that inhibits the production of epinephrine. Thus, pink is a useful color for places where angry people must be confronted (a principal's office, certain areas of a prison, or the complaint center in a department store).

Yellow is the fastest color for the eye to see because the electrochemical reactions that produce vision work fastest in response to yellow stimulation. Thus, yellow is an excellent color to use to command attention (traffic signs and Post-it Notes are examples). Placing a yellow car in the auto showroom will attract more attention from passing motorists. Although many people think of yellow as cheerful and sunny, the yellow kitchen they often request may increase anxiety and loss of temper.

People's reactions to favorite colors tend to vary by socioeconomic status (income and education level). Lower-income people tend to like primary colors that are pure, simple, and intense. Primary colors can be described in two words, such as

system) or a social situation (I *disliked* talking to the salesperson in the electronics store). People's affective systems can also respond to their own behaviors (I *enjoy* playing my stereo system). Finally, consumers' affective systems can respond to thoughts produced by their cognitive systems (I *like* to think about stereo systems).

Fifth, most affective responses are learned. Only a few basic affective responses such as preferences for sweet tastes or negative reactions to loud, sudden noises seem to be innate. Consumers learn some of their affective responses (evaluations or feelings) through classical conditioning processes (this topic is discussed later in the text). Consumers also acquire many affective responses through early socialization experiences as young children. Because affective responses are learned, they may vary widely across different cultures, subcultures, or other social groups. Thus, people's affective systems are likely to respond in different ways to the same stimulus.

What is cognition?

Human beings have evolved highly sophisticated cognitive systems that support the higher mental processes of thinking, understanding, evaluating, planning, and deciding (see Consumer Perspective 4.2, p. 64). We use the term *cognition* broadly to refer to these mental processes as well as the thoughts and meanings produced by the cognitive system.

sky blue and forest green. Upper-income people tend to prefer more complex colors that require three or more words to describe (a sort of grayed green with a little blue in it). To lower-income people, such colors seem "muddy" or washed out; simple colors that are bright and clean have a higher appeal to this group.

According to the experts, there are sex-based preferences for certain colors, too. The eye sees all colors as having either a yellow base or a blue base. Thus, red can be yellow based (tomato red) or blue based (raspberry). Men inherit a preference for yellow-based reds, while most women like blue-based reds. Thus, when women buy cosmetics that look good to themselves or their female friends, they usually gravitate toward the blue-based reds. However, most men tend to react more favorably to a woman wearing yellow-based red makeup.

Finally, blue is the stated favorite color of 80 percent of Americans. Blue is considered a calming color, but a very strong sky blue is much more calming than other shades. In its presence, the brain sends out some 11 tranquilizing chemicals to calm the body. Some hospitals use this color in the cardiac unit to calm fearful patients. In contrast, a very pale sky blue encourages fantasy, and thus might be a good color for the creative department in an ad agency.

The affective system reacts strongly to certain colors. Red is arousing and exciting.

Source: Adapted from Carlton Wagner, "Color Cues," *Marketing Insights*, Spring 1990, pp. 42–46.

A major function of cognitive systems is to interpret, make sense of, and understand significant aspects of personal experience. To do so, the cognitive system creates symbolic, subjective meanings that represent our personal interpretations of the stimuli we encounter, such as our interpretations of Rubbermaid products. Our cognitive systems can interpret virtually any aspect of the environment. We also can interpret our behaviors (Why did I buy that CD?) and our own affective states (Do I really like this sweater? Why did I get so angry at the salesclerk?). Cognitive interpretations can include the deeper, symbolic meanings of products and behaviors (see Consumer Perspective 4.3, p. 65). Finally, people can interpret the meaning of their own cognitions or beliefs (What does it mean that Hill's Department Store has everyday low prices?). Exhibit 4.2 lists some of the interpretations of cognitive systems.

A second function of our cognitive systems is to "process" (think about) these interpretations or meanings in carrying out cognitive tasks such as identifying goals and objectives, developing and evaluating alternative actions to meet those goals, choosing an action, and carrying out the behaviors. The amount and intensity of cognitive processing varies widely across situations, products, and consumers. Consumers are not always engaged in extensive cognitive activity. In fact, many behaviors and purchase decisions probably involve minimal cognitive processing.

CONSUMER PERSPECTIVE ► **4.2** **"Higher" mental processes**	**What do we mean by higher mental processes?** ► **Understanding**—Interpreting specific aspects of environment, especially determining the meaning of environmental features in terms of their personal relevance. ► **Evaluating**—Judging whether an aspect of the environment, or one's own behavior, is good or bad, positive or negative, or favorable or unfavorable. ► **Planning**—Determining how to achieve a solution to a problem. ► **Deciding**—Comparing alternative solutions to a problem and selecting the best (or a satisfactory) alternative. ► **Thinking**—The cognitive activity that occurs during all these processes. **Source:** Adapted from John R. Anderson, *Cognitive Psychology and Its Implications* (San Francisco: W. H. Freeman, 1985).

How are affect and cognition related?

The relationship between affect and cognition remains an issue in psychology.[8] Several researchers consider the affective and cognitive systems to be (at least somewhat) independent. Others argue that affect is largely influenced by the cognitive system.[9] Still others argue that affect is the dominant system.[10] We believe that some degree of independence is plausible because the affective and cognitive systems appear to involve different parts of the brain. However, the affective and cognitive areas are richly connected by neural pathways, so we also recognize that each system can influence the other.

For understanding consumers, it is more useful to emphasize the interactions between the affective and cognitive systems than to argue about which system is more important or dominant. Exhibit 4.3 (p. 66) presents a simple model to illustrate how the two systems are related. Note that each system can respond independently to aspects of the environment, and each system can respond to the output of the other system. For instance, the affective responses (emotions, feelings, or moods) produced by the affective system in reaction to stimuli in the environment can be interpreted by the cognitive system (I wonder why I am so happy. I don't like the insurance agent because she is too serious). These cognitive interpretations, in turn, might be used to make decisions (I won't buy insurance from this person).

EXHIBIT 4.2

Types of meanings created by the cognitive system

Interpretations of physical stimuli This sweater is made of lambswool. This car gets 28 miles per gallon. **Interpretations of social stimuli** The salesperson was helpful. My friends think Pizza Hut is the best. **Interpretations of affective responses** I love Dove (ice cream) Bars. I feel guilty about not sending Dad a birthday card. I feel mildly excited and interested in a new store. **Interpretations of behaviors** I drink a lot of Diet Pepsi. I am a clever shopper.	**Interpretations of symbolic meanings** This car is sexy. This style of dress is appropriate for older women. Wearing a Rolex watch means you are successful. **Interpretations of sensations** Colors on a box of breakfast cereal. Sound of a soft-drink can being opened and poured. Sweet taste of chocolate chip cookies. Smell of a favorite cologne. Feel of a favorite pair of jeans.

CONSUMER PERSPECTIVE

Symbolic meanings

Most marketers recognize that consumers choose products because of their symbolic meanings as well as their functional utility. In fact, symbolic qualities can be key determinants of product evaluation and purchase. Take food, for example.

Some foods symbolize age and gender differences. Milk and soft mushy foods are appropriate for babies or the elderly. Boys are supposed to prefer chunky peanut butter, while girls like smooth. Hamburgers are for kids; steak or lamb chops are appropriate for adults.

Certain foods are symbols of social status. Everyday American foods such as hot dogs and potato chips symbolize traditional American values. More exotic and expensive foods, such as lobster or caviar, symbolize high status and sophisticated palates. Drinking wine with meals connotes higher status in America, but probably not in France or Italy where wine is expected at most meals.

Eating elsewhere than kitchen or dining room also has symbolic meaning. Eating outdoors, for instance, whether in the backyard, on the deck, or at the beach, symbolizes freedom from convention and a return to more basic ways of cooking (on an open fire) and eating (with fingers). The symbolic meanings of going to a restaurant depend on the type of restaurant. Truck stops, outdoor cafes, bars, and cafeterias have very different symbolic meanings. Fast-food restaurants symbolize youth and unpretentious values. Going to better restaurants involves dressing up and attention to special manners, which helps create a ceremonious atmosphere and contributes to the symbolic meanings of the experience.

The method of food preparation also has symbolic meaning. Elaborate cooking procedures (haute cuisine) signify rarefied and sophisticated tastes. Raw foods tend to symbolize meeting more basic needs, although a few foods that are served uncooked have higher status meanings—caviar, sushi (raw fish and rice), steak tartare (raw ground beef)—perhaps because they symbolize mature or refined tastes.

Sources: Sidney J. Levy, "Interpreting Consumer Mythology: A Structural Approach to Consumer Behavior," *Journal of Marketing,* Summer, 1981, pp. 49–61; and Michael R. Solomon, "The Role of Products as Social Stimuli: A Symbolic Interactionism Perspective," *Journal of Consumer Research,* December 1983, pp. 319–329.

We also know that consumers' affective reactions to the environment can influence their cognitions during decision making. For instance, if you go grocery shopping when you are in a good mood, you might spend more money than if you had been in a bad mood. The affect associated with being in a good mood influences cognitive processes during shopping, so you are more likely to think about the favorable qualities of things to buy. As another example, your cognitive interpretation of a TV commercial can be influenced by your affective reactions to the preceding program material.[11]

In contrast, consumers' cognitive interpretations of information in the environment can trigger affective reactions (Oh, is that a Honda CRX? I like it). We know that people's affective systems can be influenced by their cognitive interpretations of their experiences in a situation.[12] For instance, if you interpret a salesperson's behavior as pushy, you probably will have a negative evaluation of the salesperson. If, on the other hand, you interpret the salesperson's behavior as helpful, you probably will have a favorable affective response.

Marketing implications

Both affect and cognition are important for understanding consumer behavior. Consider, for instance, the cognitive and affective components of brand image.[13] A brand image includes consumer knowledge and beliefs (cognitions) about brand attributes and the consequences of brand use, as well as the evaluations, feelings, and emotions (affect) associated with brand use. Also, marketers need to understand both affective and cognitive responses to marketing strategies such as product design, advertisements, and store

EXHIBIT 4.3

The relationship between the affective and cognitive systems

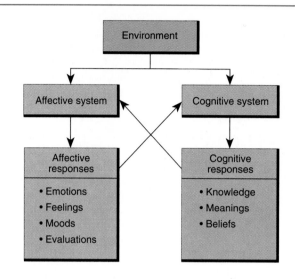

layouts. For some marketing purposes, consumers' affective responses are more important; in other cases, cognitions are key.

Affective responses are especially important for so-called feeling products.[14] These include certain foods (doughnuts, snacks, pizza), beverages (soft drinks, beer, wine), greeting cards, fragrances, skin-care products, and sports cars. For instance, consider consumers' affective responses to ice cream. For most people, eating ice cream is a highly sensory experience, and they associate the product with affective feelings of happiness, fun, and contentment, even sensual pleasure. When Haagen-Dazs, the American maker of superpremium ice cream noted for its high butterfat content and intense flavors, expanded into Europe, the company promoted people's affective, sensual reactions to ice cream.[15] One British ad portrayed a semiclothed couple feeding ice cream to each other. Haagen-Dazs was extremely successful in England, France, and Germany where sales grew from $2 million to $30 million in just two years.

As another example, consumers' initial affective responses to the smell of a cologne may be critical to its purchase. To promote its new scent, Spellbound, Estée Lauder inserted 11 million scent strips in magazines such as *Vanity Fair* and *Vogue*.[16] Once a scent is bought and used, however, consumers' affective responses become influenced by their cognitive interpretations of other people's reactions to the scent. Fragrance advertising may try to convey both affective and cognitive responses. For example, Estée Lauder's ads for Spellbound picture attractive models looking intently into each other's eyes. Apparently, Lauder hopes to communicate both affective and cognitive meanings associated with romance, sensuality, and physical attraction. (Consumer Perspective 4.4 discusses the affective and cognitive aspects of romance.)

COGNITIVE PROCESSES IN CONSUMER DECISION MAKING

The most important aspect of consumer behavior for marketers to understand is how consumers make decisions. Consumers make decisions about a variety of behaviors:

▷ What product or brand should I buy?

▷ Where should I shop?

▷ What TV shows should I watch tonight?

▷ Should I pay for this purchase with cash or credit card?

▷ How much money should I borrow?

▷ Should I read this ad carefully?

▷ Which friend should I consult?

▷ Which salesperson should I buy from?

CONSUMER
PERSPECTIVE

4.4 ◄

**The return of
romance**

Romance as a concept gained ascendancy in American society during the late 1980s and early 1990s, as people sought some refuge from the pressures of work and economic stress. Wedding advertising in Bride magazine portrayed increasingly romantic settings. Sales of romance novels were strong. The growing interest in Victorian furniture and flowery decoration was seen as a nostalgic return to a more romantic time. Advertising showed much more romantic settings and situations for restaurants, vacation locations, and male/female situations in general.

Romance is difficult to define, but it surely involves affective states, including emotions, feelings, and moods. Romance is about relationships, fantasy, imagery, nostalgia, and tradition. The affective responses associated with romantic love are quite different from those associated with more explicit sexual feelings. Look at Calvin Klein cologne ads, for example. To promote Obsession cologne in the mid-1980s, ads pictured nude, interlocked bodies to create an image of intense sexuality. Different advertising imagery was used in 1989 to promote Eternity cologne. Here the goal was to elicit different types of affective responses—romantic emotions and moods, and feelings of commitment and close relationships.

Romance also involves cognitive responses. Romantic love is a whole psychological "package" that combines cognitive beliefs (equality of men and women), ideals (marriage is forever), and expectations (sharing as the most important aspect of marriage) with various affective responses (feelings of "true love" and of closeness, warmth, comfort, and mutual respect).

Interestingly, the trend toward romance may not be limited to U.S. society. The engagement ring, a romantic concept indeed, is a new idea in Japan.

© 1991 Bartle Bogle Hegarty Ltd.

Source: Adapted from Lea Bayers Rapp, "The Return of Romance," *Marketing Insights*, June 1989, pp. 31–39.

Consumers use information to make such decisions. From the consumer's perspective, most aspects of the environment are potential information. In a supermarket, for instance, marketing strategies such as a price tag, a coupon, sale signs in a store window, or a tasting demonstration of a new product provide information. In addition, people's internal affective responses and their own behaviors constitute information that can be interpreted by their cognitive systems. If this information is to influence consumers' decisions, it must be *processed* (taken in, interpreted, and used) by their cognitive systems. To explain how the cognitive system processes information, researchers have developed information processing models.[17] These models identify a sequence of cognitive processes where each process transforms or modifies information and passes it on to the next process where additional operations occur. The decisions that underlie many human actions can be understood in terms of these cognitive processes.

Reduced to its essence, consumer decision making involves three important cognitive processes. First, consumers must *interpret* relevant information in the environment to create personal meanings or knowledge. Second, consumers must combine or *integrate* this knowledge to evaluate products or possible actions and to choose among alternative behaviors. Third, consumers must *retrieve product knowledge in memory* to use in integration and interpretation processes. All three cognitive processes are involved in any decision-making situation.

A model of consumer decision making

Exhibit 4.4 presents a model of consumer decision making that highlights these three cognitive processes of interpretation, integration, and product knowledge in memory. We provide an overview of this decision-making model here, and in subsequent chapters we discuss each element of the model in more detail.

Consumers must interpret or make sense of information in the environment around them. In the process, they create new knowledge, meanings, and beliefs about the environment and their place in it. **Interpretation** involves *exposure* to information and two related cognitive processes—attention and comprehension. *Attention* governs how we select which

EXHIBIT 4.4

Cognitive processes in consumer decision making

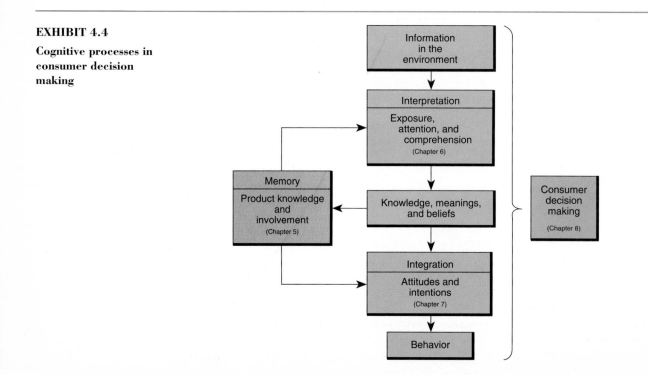

information to interpret and which information to ignore. *Comprehension* refers to how we determine the subjective meanings of information and thus create personal knowledge and beliefs. We discuss exposure, attention, and comprehension processes in Chapter 6.

In this book, we use the terms **knowledge, meanings, and beliefs** interchangeably to refer to the various types of personal or subjective interpretations of information produced by interpretation processes. Exhibit 4.4 shows that knowledge, meanings, and beliefs may be stored in memory as well as used in integration processes.

Integration describes how we combine different types of knowledge (1) to form overall evaluations of products, other objects, and behaviors and (2) to make choices among alternative behaviors, including purchase. In the first instance, consumers combine knowledge and affective feelings about a product or a brand to form an overall evaluation or a *brand attitude* ("I like Breyer's chocolate chip ice cream," or "Wrangler jeans are not as good as Levi's"). We discuss attitudes and intentions in Chapter 7. In the second case, consumers combine knowledge and affective responses to choose a behavior ("Should I go to Ward's or Penneys?"). When consumers choose between different purchase behaviors, they form an *intention or plan* to buy ("I intend to buy a new Bic pen this afternoon"). Integration processes also are used to choose from among other types of behaviors. For instance, a consumer might combine knowledge in deciding when to go on a shopping trip, whether to pay with a check or a credit card, or whether to recommend a movie to a friend.

Product knowledge and involvement describes the various types of knowledge, meanings, and beliefs that are stored in memory. For example, consumers may have product knowledge about the characteristics or attributes of a brand of athletic shoe (gel inserts in the heel), the outcome of using the brand (I can run faster), or the ability of the brand to satisfy important objectives (I will be fit). Product knowledge retrieved from memory can influence interpretation and integration processes. American consumers, for example, need a certain amount of knowledge about nutrition to interpret and understand the many health claims made by food companies. Product involvement refers to consumers' knowledge about the personal relevance of the product in one's life (Nutrition information is important to my health goals). People's level of involvement with health issues influences how much effort they exert in interpreting a nutritional message. We discuss product knowledge and involvement in Chapter 5.

In summary, Exhibit 4.4 shows that consumer decision making involves the cognitive processes of interpretation and integration, as influenced by product knowledge, meanings, and beliefs in memory. In Chapter 8, we discuss how all these factors work together in consumer decision making.

Other characteristics of the cognitive system

Several aspects of the cognitive system influence consumer decision making. *Activation,* for instance, refers to the process by which product knowledge is retrieved from memory for use in interpreting and integrating information. Activation of knowledge in memory is often automatic in that little or no conscious effort is involved.[18] Consumers typically experience activated knowledge as thoughts that "just come to mind." Daydreaming is a good example of activation—various bits of knowledge or meanings surface as a person's mind drifts from one thought to another. Activation also operates when consumers intentionally try to remember certain bits of knowledge. Examples include trying to recall the location of a particular shop in the mall, the salesperson's name, or the price of that black sweater. Remembering such knowledge involves giving ourselves "cues" that might activate the desired knowledge (Let's see, I think her name begins with a B).

The product knowledge in consumers' memories can be activated in various ways. The most common way is by exposure to objects or events in the environment. Seeing something, such as the distinctive BMW grille, can activate various meanings (you might think about sportiness or that this is a rich person's car). People's internal, affective states

The cognitive system interprets this ad to create knowledge, meanings, and beliefs about how the product works.

also can activate knowledge. For instance, positive knowledge and beliefs tend to be activated when a person is in a good mood, while more negative meanings are activated when the same person is in an unpleasant mood. Finally, product knowledge in memory can be activated because it is linked to other activated meanings. Because meanings are associated in memory, activation of one meaning concept may trigger related concepts and activate those meanings as well. Consumers have little control over this process of *spreading activation,* which occurs unconsciously and automatically.[19] For instance, seeing a magazine ad for Jell-O might first activate the Jell-O name and then related knowledge and meanings such as jiggly, tastes sweet, good for a quick dessert, and Bill Cosby likes it. Through spreading activation, various aspects of one's knowledge in memory can spring to mind during decision making.

Another important characteristic of the human cognitive system is its *limited capacity.* Only a small amount of knowledge can be considered consciously at one time. This suggests that the interpretation and integration processes during consumer decision making are fairly simple. For instance, it is unlikely that consumers can consider more than a few characteristics of a brand in forming an attitude or intention to buy the brand. At the same time, we know people are able to handle rather complex tasks such as going to a restaurant because cognitive processes tend to become more *automatic* with experience. That is, over time, cognitive processes gradually require less capacity and conscious control (thinking).[20] Grocery shopping, for instance, is routine and cognitively easy for most consumers because many of the interpretation and integration processes involved in choosing food products have become automatic. Consumer Perspective 4.5 describes a common example of how automatic processes develop.

CONSUMER PERSPECTIVE

4.5

Increasing automatic cognitive processing— learning to drive a car

People who are skilled at doing something can do what seems impossible to both the novice and the theorist. Think about your experience in learning to drive a car. When you first learned to drive, you probably couldn't drive and talk at the same time. The task of driving seemed to require all your concentration. Today, if you are used to driving, you can probably drive in traffic, listen to music on the radio, and carry on a conversation. Could you have done this when you first started driving? Probably then you kept the radio off. If anyone tried to talk to you, you could not pay attention. Of course, even most experienced drivers stop talking if something unfamiliar occurs such as an emergency on the road ahead.

Learning to drive illustrates how cognitive processes (and associated behaviors) become increasingly automatic as they are learned through practice. However, even highly automatic skills such as eating seem to require some "capacity." Perhaps you like to munch on something while you study. You might snack on pretzels or eat an apple while you read this chapter. But if you come on a passage that requires more thought, probably you will stop eating while you interpret the meaning of what you are reading.

Marketing implications

The simple model of consumer decision making that we have described has many implications. Because the next several chapters cover the elements of the model in detail, we mention only a few examples here.

Obviously, it is important for marketers to understand how consumers interpret their marketing strategies. For instance, a store might put a brand on sale because it is overstocked; the consumer, however, might interpret the sale price as an indicator of lower product quality. Marketers need to know the knowledge, meanings, and beliefs that consumers have for their products or brands or stores.

The integration processes involved in forming brand attitudes ("Do I like this brand?") and purchase intentions ("Should I buy this brand?") are critically important for understanding consumer behavior. Marketers need to know what types of product knowledge are used in integration processes and what knowledge is irrelevant. Because the cognitive system has a limited capacity, marketers should recognize that consumers can integrate only small amounts of knowledge when choosing brands to buy or stores to patronize.

Activation of product knowledge has many implications for marketing. The choice of a brand name, for example, can be highly important for the success of the product because a name can activate particular meanings in the consumer's memory. Jaguar is a good name for a sports car because it activates meanings like speedy, agile, exotic, rare, beautiful, powerful, and graceful.[21] Another implication is that marketers need to pay attention to differences between consumers because the same stimulus may activate different meanings for different consumers. The cartoon in Consumer Perspective 4.6 illustrates this point.

KNOWLEDGE STORED IN MEMORY

The model in Exhibit 4.4 shows that knowledge in memory influences the cognitive processes involved when consumers make decisions. We discuss product knowledge and involvement in the next chapter, but here we describe two broad types of knowledge and how this knowledge is organized in memory.

Types of knowledge

The human cognitive system can interpret virtually any type of information and thereby create knowledge, meanings, and beliefs.[22] People can create two types of knowledge: (1) general knowledge about their environments and behaviors, and (2) procedural knowledge about how to do things.[23]

Most activation tends to be automatic and very rapid. Normally, we are not conscious of the activation process that retrieves stored knowledge from memory. The (usually appropriate) meanings just "come to mind."

("The Family Circus" by Bil Keane. Reprinted with special permission of Cowles Syndicate, Inc.)

Source: © 1992 King Features Syndicate, Inc. All Rights Reserved. Reprinted with special permission of King Features Syndicate.

General knowledge concerns people's interpretations of relevant information in their environments. For instance, consumers develop general knowledge about product categories (compact discs, fast-food hamburger restaurants, mutual funds), stores (Sears, Wal-Mart, and Kmart), particular behaviors (shopping in malls, ordering at restaurants, talking to salespeople), other people (one's best friend, the clerk at the 7-Eleven store on the corner, teachers), and even themselves (I am shy, intelligent, and honest).

General knowledge is stored in memory as *propositions* that link or connect two concepts:

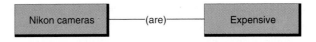

Essentially, every meaning concept in memory is linked to at least one other concept via such propositions. Most propositions are based on a meaningful relationship between the two concepts. For instance, your knowledge that a favorite clothing store is having a sale creates a simple proposition:

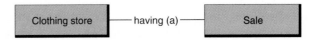

Consumers can have episodic or semantic knowledge.[24] *Episodic knowledge* concerns the specific events that have happened in a person's life. "Yesterday I bought a Snickers candy bar from the vending machine," and "My last bank statement had a mistake," are examples of episodic knowledge. Consumers also have *semantic knowledge* about

These children are using their procedural knowledge to operate their computers.

objects and events in the environment. For instance, the personal meanings and beliefs you have about Snickers candy bars—the peanuts, caramel, and calories it contains; the wrapper design; the aroma or taste—are part of your semantic knowledge. When activated from memory, episodic and semantic knowledge can have important influences on consumers' decision making and behavior.

Consumers also have **procedural knowledge** about how to do things.[25] Procedural knowledge is stored in memory as a *production,* which is a special type of "if . . . , then . . . " proposition that links a concept or an event with the resulting appropriate behavior.

Examples of productions include, "If the phone rings when you are busy, don't answer it," or "If a salesperson presses you for a quick decision, say no and leave."

Over a lifetime of experience, consumers learn a great deal of procedural knowledge, much of which is highly specific to particular situations. When activated from memory, these productions directly and automatically influence a person's overt behavior. For instance, Susan has a production: "If the price on a piece of clothing is reduced by 50 percent or more, I will consider buying it." If this procedural knowledge is activated when Susan sees a half-price sign in the jeans section, she will stop and decide whether now is the time to buy a new pair of jeans.

Like general knowledge, people's procedural knowledge is relevant in many everyday situations. Consider the procedural knowledge consumers need to operate equipment such as computers, videocameras and VCRs, stereo receivers, and televisions. Some people feel such products have become too complex and difficult to operate.[26] For instance, at least one survey found that only 3 percent of total TV viewing time is spent watching shows that have been recorded in advance because many people have not taken the time to acquire the procedural knowledge necessary to use the timed recording

EXHIBIT 4.5

An associative network of knowledge

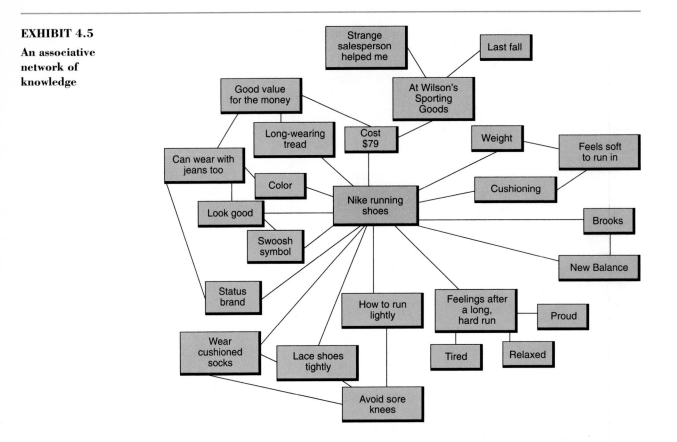

feature on their VCRs.[27] Understanding that relatively few consumers use all the features on their high-tech equipment, some manufacturers are simplifying their products, which reduces the procedural knowledge necessary to use them. For example, Philips, the giant Dutch electronics firm, has developed a group of easy-to-use clock radios, VCRs, and tape players called Easy Line.

Both general knowledge and procedural knowledge can have important influences on consumers' behaviors. Consider the grocery shopping trip described in Chapter 2. Various aspects of Bruce Macklin's general and procedural knowledge were activated as he moved through the grocery store environment. This knowledge affected his interpretation and integration of information as he made his purchase decisions.

Structures of knowledge

Consumers' general and procedural knowledge is organized to form structures of knowledge in memory. Our cognitive systems create networks that organize and link many types of knowledge.[28] Exhibit 4.5 presents an associative network of knowledge for Nike running shoes. In this knowledge structure, the Nike product is connected to various types of general knowledge, including episodic knowledge about past events (shopping at Wilson's) and semantic knowledge about the features of Nike shoes (their appearance, weight, and cushioning). Also included is knowledge of affective responses (memory of one's feelings after a hard run) and the interpretations of those affective feelings (relaxed and proud). This structure of Nike knowledge also contains productions (how to run lightly, when to wear cushioned socks) and related semantic knowledge about the consequences of these behaviors (avoid sore knees).

Parts of this knowledge structure might be activated in certain circumstances. For example, some knowledge could be activated by seeing an athlete on TV wearing Nike shoes, or noticing the Nike swoosh symbol on a billboard. Other knowledge associated with Nike could be activated by experiencing the pleasant affective feelings of satisfaction and relaxation after a hard workout. Finally, some meanings associated with Nike could be activated through spreading activation, as "activation energy" spreads from one meaning concept in the network to related meanings. Whatever element of Nike knowledge is activated during decision making has the potential to influence consumers' interpretation and integration processes at that time.

People's cognitive systems create and use two types of knowledge structures—schemas and scripts. Each structure is an associative network of linked meanings, but schemas include mostly episodic and semantic general knowledge, while scripts contain procedural knowledge. Both schemas and scripts can be activated during decision making, and both can influence cognitive processes. The knowledge structure in Exhibit 4.5 is a schema that represents one consumer's general knowledge about Nike running shoes.[29] Marketers have a vital interest in understanding consumers' schemas about brands, stores, and product categories.

Scripts are organized networks of production knowledge. When consumers experience common situations, they learn what behaviors are appropriate in that situation. This knowledge may be organized as a sequence of if . . . , then . . . productions called a script.[30] Following is an example of a simple script relating to eating in a fast-food restaurant.

Types of knowledge structures

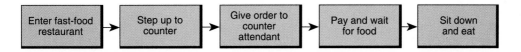

Enter fast-food restaurant → Step up to counter → Give order to counter attendant → Pay and wait for food → Sit down and eat

As another example, consumers who go to auctions develop a generalized script containing production knowledge about how to register with the auctioneer before the sale starts, how to bid, and how to pay for their purchases. When activated at the auction, the script automatically guides and directs many (but not necessarily all) of the consumer's overt behaviors. Thus, consumers who have a well-developed script do not have to make conscious decisions about many auction-related behaviors because those behaviors are controlled by the script. Exhibit 4.6 presents a simplified script for eating in a "fancy" restaurant.

To understand consumers, marketers need to know what product knowledge they have acquired and stored in memory. For instance, a coffee company may want to determine how consumers organize the coffee category into product forms ("Do consumers see ground, freeze-dried, and instant coffee as different forms of coffee?"). Marketers might want to know the contents of consumers' product schemas (associative networks of general knowledge about whole bean coffee) or shopping scripts (associative networks of procedural knowledge about where to shop for whole bean coffee). They also might need to know what types of knowledge are activated by particular marketing strategies. This could require a detailed analysis of the meanings activated when consumers are exposed to a celebrity spokesperson or a certain typeface for a magazine ad. Finally, marketers need to know how consumers' affective systems react to the knowledge, meaning, and beliefs created by their cognitive systems and to the cognitive processes used in decision making. Understanding consumers requires attention to both affect and cognition.

Marketing implications

EXHIBIT 4.6

A hypothetical script of appropriate procedures for dining at a "fancy" restaurant

▷ Enter restaurant.
▷ Give reservation name to maitre d'.
▷ Wait to be shown to table.
▷ Walk to table and sit down.
▷ Order drinks when waiter asks.
▷ Select dinner items from menu.
▷ Order meal when waiter returns.
▷ Drink drinks and talk until first course arrives.
▷ Eat soup or salad when it arrives.
▷ Eat main course when it arrives.
▷ Order dessert when finished with dinner.
▷ Eat dessert when it arrives.
▷ Talk until bill arrives.
▷ Examine bill for accuracy.
▷ Give waiter credit card to pay for bill.
▷ Add tip to credit card form and sign.
▷ Leave restaurant.

Source: Reprinted with permission from "Scripts in Memory for Text," by Gordon H. Bower, John B. Black, and Terrence J. Turner, which appeared in *Cognitive Psychology*, April 1979, pp. 177–220.

▶ **SUMMARY**

Learning objective 1: *Describe the affective system, and identify the types of affective responses it produces.*

The affective system produces affective responses to objects and events in the environment. The affective system also responds to specific behaviors ("I'm pleased with the way I negotiated the price on my new car") and to cognitions ("Thinking about that meal makes me mad"). The affective system is reactive in that it can only respond to things and events; it cannot think or plan. The four types of affective responses vary in intensity and level of physical arousal. Emotions (love, joy, anger) are the most intense and arousing affective responses. Feelings (frustration, interest) are somewhat less intense and arousing. Moods (boredom, calm, blue) are rather diffuse (nonintense) affective states that involve relatively low levels of arousal. Evaluations (judgments of how much you like a product) typically involve relatively low levels of intensity and arousal.

Learning objective 2: *Describe the cognitive system and the types of meanings it creates.*

A primary function of the cognitive system is to interpret and make sense of the environment, one's behaviors, and one's affective responses. The cognitive system creates knowledge and beliefs that represent the personal, subjective meanings of these factors. This knowledge could be about physical objects (a car), social events (a party), affective responses (the reasons for sadness). The cognitive system is capable of creating symbolic meanings ("This type of sunglasses is for kids." "This product is for women, not men"). The cognitive system also interprets physical sensations ("This cookie has too much sugar"). Finally, the cognitive system can interpret one's own overt behaviors ("I bought that CD because my roommate likes it"). Another function of the cognitive system is to integrate or combine knowledge to form attitudes ("I like this textbook") and intentions to behave ("I will go shopping for new shoes").

Learning objective 3: *Explain how the affective and cognitive systems influence each other.*

Because the affective and cognitive systems are highly related, they can influence each other. For instance, people's thoughts can influence their affective responses. Marketers may use nostalgic music from early years to prompt recall of pleasant events in the past and create positive affective feelings and moods. Many affective responses require cognitive interpretation, as when people try to determine the reasons they like a certain sweater. Marketers often want to create a certain mix of affective and cognitive response in consumers. Consider the combined affective and cognitive responses that might be created by ads for cars, cologne, or beer that portray fantasy, romance, and sexual attraction.

Learning objective 4: *Describe the components of the model of consumer decision making.*

The model of consumer decision making (Exhibit 4.4) identifies two major cognitive processes—interpretation and integration. Interpretation involves making sense of information in the environment, as well as one's own behaviors and affective responses. Interpretation processes give rise to knowledge and beliefs that represent the personally relevant meanings of these factors. Interpretation involves exposure to information, attention to selected aspects of the information, and comprehension of the meaning of the information. Integration describes how we combine knowledge (1) to form attitudes toward products, brands, and stores, and (2) to make choices by forming intentions to act ("I want to buy a Big Mac"). The third major component of the model is knowledge and involvement. Involvement refers to consumers' interest and concern with the information. Relevant knowledge that is activated in memory can influence interpretation processes and can be used in integration processes. All of these components are involved in consumer decision making. The outcome of decision making is behavior, such as the purchase of a product.

Learning objective 5: *Explain how knowledge in memory can be activated for use in cognitive processing.*

The knowledge that consumers have acquired and stored in memory must be activated, or retrieved from memory, to influence interpretation and integration processes. Only activated knowledge is available for use in various cognitive processes. Knowledge that is not activated remains stored in memory and cannot influence decision making. Thus, marketers need to understand the factors that can activate desirable knowledge in memory. These factors include exposure to some object or event in the environment. Seeing a picture of the movie star Demi Moore can activate knowledge about her; noticing a can of Green Giant peas may activate knowledge and feelings about the Jolly Green Giant; hearing a song might activate episodic knowledge about special events in your life. Finally, because activation is a kind of "energy" that can spread through a knowledge structure, activation of one knowledge concept can activate related concepts. For example, thinking about the cushioning qualities of Nike Air Jordan basketball shoes might activate recollection of related attributes.

Learning objective 6: *Describe the differences between general and procedural knowledge.*

General knowledge concerns various aspects of the world—the environment, one's own behaviors, and even one's affective responses. There are two types of general world knowledge. Episodic knowledge concerns memory for past events in one's life. Semantic knowledge concerns general knowledge and beliefs about the world. Procedural knowledge is knowledge about how to do things—how to behave and the circumstances in which certain behaviors are appropriate. Both general and procedural knowledge can have important influences on consumer decision making.

Learning objective 7: *Give examples of associative networks of knowledge in the form of schemas and scripts.*

An associative network of knowledge links various meaning concepts to form a network-like structure. The basis for the network organization is the meaningful connections or associations between or among concepts. Associative network structures that contain general knowledge related to some concept or some product are schemas. Marketers are interested in understanding the knowledge contained in consumers' schemas for brands, stores, ads, etc. Exhibit 4.5 gives an example. Associative network structures that include procedural knowledge about how and when to perform certain behaviors are called scripts. A script knowledge structure provides a sequence of behaviors that are appropriate to perform in certain circumstances. See Exhibit 4.6 for an example.

▶ **KEY TERMS AND CONCEPTS**

affect

cognition

interpretation

integration

knowledge, meanings, and beliefs

product knowledge and involvement

general knowledge

procedural knowledge

associative networks of knowledge

schema

script

▶ **REVIEW AND DISCUSSION QUESTIONS**

1. Describe the four broad types of affective responses that are produced by the affective system.

2. How do you distinguish between the cognitive and affective systems? How are they interrelated?

3. Consider a product such as an automobile or a perfume. Describe at least three types of subjective meanings that consumers might construct to represent various aspects of the product, and ways that marketers might try to influence the meaning.

4. Find an advertisement or some other type of marketing information, and assume you are trying to make a decision about this product. Using the model of consumer decision making, describe how a consumer might make a purchase decision. Be sure to describe the cognitive processes of interpretation and integration, and discuss how knowledge in memory might influence these cognitive processes.

5. Give a specific example of how exposure to a marketing strategy could activate certain knowledge and lead to spreading activation within a consumer's associative network of product knowledge.

6. Compare and contrast general and procedural knowledge. Are they related?

7. Discuss the type of knowledge assumed in a script, and describe a simple script that you follow (e.g., going to a bank, buying textbooks, getting up in the morning).

5

Product Knowledge and Involvement

LEARNING OBJECTIVES

After completing this chapter, you should be able to:

▶ 1. List the four categories of product knowledge, and give examples.

▶ 2. Give examples of concrete and abstract attributes, functional and psychosocial consequences, and instrumental and terminal values.

▶ 3. Define benefits and risks.

▶ 4. Describe a means-end chain, and give an example.

▶ 5. Discuss two marketing implications of means-end chains.

▶ 6. Define involvement, and describe how personal and situational sources influence involvement.

▶ 7. Give examples of marketing strategies that can influence personal and situational sources of involvement.

P&G CLEANS UP WITH ULTRA PAMPERS

In the early 1980s, Procter & Gamble's once invincible marketing juggernaut seemed to be stalling as many of its blockbuster brands lost market share.[1] But by the mid-1980s, P&G had stopped chasing the competition with lackluster, me-too products and returned to its original philosophy of producing superior brands. The company scored big gains in diapers, toothpaste, and detergents, product categories that together accounted for about half of profits. A key reason for the turnaround was P&G's renewed commitment to developing products with superior attributes that deliver important benefits to consumers. For instance, P&G's Pampers, although the leading disposable diaper, had lost market share to Kimberly-Clark's Huggies. Then P&G introduced Ultra Pampers, a technically sophisticated product containing a special chemical that turns to a gel when wet to hold moisture away from baby's skin. The result is drier babies and less diaper rash. Drier, nonirritated babies are more comfortable and happier, which makes parents happier. Although introducing Ultra Pampers wasn't cheap (P&G spent more than $500 million to renovate its manufacturing facilities), the payoff was spectacular. P&G's market share skyrocketed to 61 percent, while Kimberly-Clark's share slipped to 28 percent.

Procter & Gamble's experiences illustrate the importance of understanding consumers' reactions to product attributes and benefits. In this chapter, we examine consumers' product knowledge and involvement, two important aspects of the affect and cognition portion of the Wheel of Consumer Analysis. We begin by identifying four types or levels of product knowledge. Then we discuss consumers' knowledge about product attributes as well as the benefits and values provided by the product. Then we show how these attributes, benefits, and values fit in a simple associative network of knowledge called a means-end chain. In the second half of the chapter, we consider consumers' product involvement or feelings of interest and personal relevance. We describe how consumer involvement is influenced by intrinsic (internal) and situational (external) factors. We conclude by discussing how means-end chains can be used to understand the consumer/product relationship and how marketing strategies can influence consumers' product involvement.

LEVELS OF PRODUCT KNOWLEDGE

Consumers have different levels of product knowledge that can be used to interpret new information and make purchase choices. Levels of meaning are formed when people combine separate meaning concepts into larger categories of knowledge.[2] For instance, you might combine knowledge about the braking, acceleration, and cornering ability of an automobile to form a more inclusive concept that you call handling. In a sense, your knowledge of handling "contains" these separate meanings.[3] Another example is the various types of bicycles that make up the overall bike category—racing, mountain, BMX, city bikes. Each of these meaning categories can be separated into more specific knowledge categories (different types of racing bikes or mountain bikes). Thus, a person's knowledge about bikes, mountain bikes, and types of mountain bikes may form a hierarchical structure of bicycle knowledge at different levels.

This idea of related meanings at different levels can help us understand consumers' product knowledge. Consumers can have product knowledge at four levels—the product class, product forms, brands, and models. Exhibit 5.1 gives examples of each level of product knowledge.

Marketers are very interested in consumers' knowledge about *brands.* Most marketing strategies are brand oriented in that they are intended to make consumers aware of a brand, teach them about a brand, and influence them to buy that brand. Most marketing research focuses on consumers' knowledge and beliefs about brands. Likewise, much of our discussion in this text concerns customers' brand knowledge.

For some products, consumers can have knowledge about models, a lower level of product knowledge than brands. A *model* is a specific example of a brand that has one or

EXHIBIT 5.1

Levels of product knowledge

Product Class	Product Form	Brand	Model/Feature
Coffee	Ground	Folgers	1-pound can
	Instant	Maxwell House	8-ounce jar
Automobiles	Sedan	Ford	Taurus with air and power steering
	Sports car	Nissan	300EX with air and 5-speed
	Sports sedan	BMW	Model 325e with air and automatic transmission
Pens	Ballpoint	Bic	$.79 model, regular tip
	Felt tip	Pilot	$.99 model, extra-fine tip
Beer	Imported	Heineken	Dark
	Light	Miller Lite	Kegs
	Low alcohol	Sharps	12-ounce cans

more unique product features or attributes (Exhibit 5.1 gives several examples). For instance Nikon 35mm cameras are available in several different models; Coca-Cola comes in diet, caffeine-free, cherry-flavored, and other versions; and Haagen-Dazs ice cream is sold in different flavors. The 325, 525, and 850 models of BMW automobiles vary in size, price, and exterior design and have distinctive features and options such as air-conditioning, fancy wheels, automatic braking systems, leather seats, and so on.

Going in the other direction from the brand and model levels of knowledge, a *product form* is a broader category that includes several brands similar in some important way. Often, the basis for a product-form category is a physical characteristic the brands share. For instance, freeze-dried, instant, ground, and whole-bean coffee are defined by their physical form. In some cases, certain product forms become so well established in consumers' minds that marketers can treat them as separate markets. Diet soft drinks, sports sedans, fast-food hamburger restaurants, and laptop computers are examples.

The *product class* is the broadest and most inclusive level of product knowledge and may include several product forms. Coffee, cars, and soft drinks are examples. Marketing strategies to promote the entire product class can be effective for brands with a high market share. For example, Frito-Lay might promote consumption of the product class salty chip snacks (various types of potato and flavored chips). Because the company controls as much as a 60 percent market share, any increase in overall consumption of the product class is likely to benefit Frito-Lay more than its competitors.

Marketers need to understand how consumers organize their product knowledge in terms of these different levels, because consumers may make separate purchase decisions at each level of knowledge.[4] For instance, a consumer might choose between alternative product classes ("Should I buy a television or a stereo system?"), different product forms ("Should I purchase a large-screen TV or a portable?"), various brands ("Should I buy an RCA or a Sony TV?"), and alternative models ("Should I choose a 27-inch RCA TV with stereo speakers or a 25-inch RCA set without stereo?"). In sum, all levels of product

The beginning
of real refreshment.

Just for the taste.

diet Coke

NutraSweet

This ad focuses on a key functional consequence of the product.

knowledge are relevant to the marketing manager, and the brand level is of particular importance.

CONSUMERS' PRODUCT KNOWLEDGE

Consumers can have three types of product knowledge—knowledge about product attributes or characteristics, benefits or positive consequences of using the product, and values the product helps to satisfy or achieve. Exhibit 5.2 presents examples of these types of knowledge about Nike running shoes.

Products as bundles of attributes

As the Procter & Gamble example illustrates, decisions about product characteristics or attributes are important elements of marketing strategy. Within the limits imposed by production capabilities and financial resources, marketing managers can add new attributes to a product ("Now, Diet 7UP contains 100% NutraSweet"), remove old attributes ("Caffeine-free Diet Pepsi"), or modify existing attributes (in 1985, Coca-Cola managers modified the century-old secret recipe for Coke). Marketers change brand attributes to make their products more appealing to consumers. For instance, to give Liquid Tide its cleaning power, chemists at Procter & Gamble created a new molecule and included twice as many active ingredients as competitive brands. The 400,000 hours of research and development time

EXHIBIT 5.2

Types of product knowledge

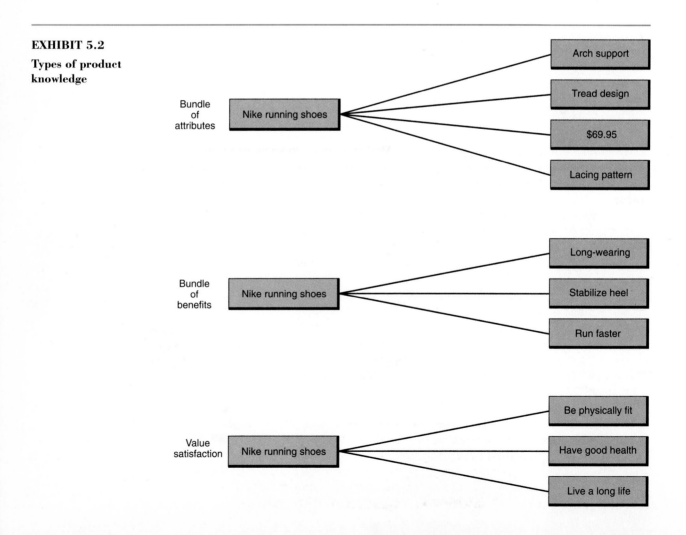

CONSUMER PERSPECTIVE

5.1 ◄

What's in a handle?

The old Pyrex measuring cup made by Corning Glass Works was a kitchen classic. The glass cup with its familiar attributes—a simple volume gauge printed in red on one side, the pouring lip, and the nice big handle—was found in as many as 80 percent of American households. Even though the bulky handle made the three sizes (1-, 2-, and 4-cup) difficult to stack, no one complained. In fact, the cups had not changed much since they had been introduced some 50 years before. Why should marketers change the attributes of a product this successful?

The idea for changing the attributes of the Pyrex measuring cup came about by accident when the handle on a test product sagged during heating. This gave designers the idea of an "open" handle that was attached to the cup at only one end. Besides being cheaper to produce, this handle would make the cups stackable and therefore more convenient to store in a cupboard. Corning also added a second new attribute, making the cup a bit deeper so that foods could be heated in microwave ovens without boiling over. However, the designers kept the familiar red measuring gauge on the side. What was the result of making these simple changes in the attributes of this product? Sales increased 150 percent.

Source: Toni Mack, "What's in a Handle?" *Forbes*, January 25, 1988, p. 87. Reprinted by permission of FORBES magazine. © Forbes 1988.

seemed to pay off, as Liquid Tide's initial sales skyrocketed.[5] Consumer Perspective 5.1 describes another successful change in a product attribute.

Even the simplest products have multiple attributes. Pencils, for example, have different shapes, sizes, and colors as well as varying densities of lead and eraser softness. Many marketers treat products and brands as *bundles of attributes* (see Exhibit 5.2). From a cognitive processing perspective, however, it is not certain that consumers have extensive knowledge about product attributes or that consumers use their attribute knowledge to make purchase decisions. Marketers need to know which product attributes are important to consumers, what those attributes mean to consumers, and how consumers use this knowledge to make purchase decisions about products and brands.

Consumers can have knowledge about the concrete and abstract attributes of products.[6] **Concrete attributes** refer to physical product characteristics such as the type of fiber or thickness of a blanket. The color of a car or its front-seat legroom are also concrete attributes. Concrete attributes have a tangible, physical reality that consumers can experience directly (a high butterfat content in the ice cream is experienced as a rich taste). In contrast, **abstract attributes** are nonmaterial product characteristics such as the warmth and quality of a blanket or the stylishness and comfort of a car. Abstract attributes are intangible in that consumers cannot experience them directly, but must judge them subjectively (you cannot see quality directly, it must be inferred). In addition to abstract and concrete attributes, consumers' product knowledge also may include affective evaluations of each attribute ("I don't like itchy wool blankets." "I love chocolate ice cream").

Products as bundles of benefits

Marketers also recognize that consumers often think about products and brands in terms of their consequences, not their attributes.[7] *Consequences* are outcomes that happen when the product is purchased and used or consumed. For instance, an electric shaver might give a close shave, require repairs, or make the user feel more attractive; a facial cream might cause an allergic reaction or cost too much. Consumers can have knowledge about two types of outcomes—functional and psychosocial consequences.

The *absence* of an attribute (cholesterol) that leads to a negative consequence (heart disease) is promoted as a product benefit.

Functional consequences are the tangible outcomes of product use that consumers usually experience directly and immediately. For instance, functional consequences include the immediate physiological outcomes of product use (eating a Big Mac satisfies your hunger, drinking orange juice quenches your thirst, the tennis racket grip fits your hand). Functional consequences also refer to the tangible performance outcomes of using a product (a hair blower dries your hair quickly, a car gets 26 miles per gallon of gas, a toaster browns bread evenly, an ink pen writes without skipping).

Psychosocial consequences refer to knowledge about the psychological and social outcomes of product use. *Psychological consequences* are internal, personal outcomes about how the product makes you feel. For example, using Nexxus shampoo might make you feel attractive, wearing Benetton sportswear might make you feel stylish, eating an ice cream cone from Baskin-Robbins might make you feel satisfied. Consumers also think about the *social consequences* of product use, the reactions of other people ("My friends will be impressed if I buy this Sony stereo system." "My mother will think I'm a smart shopper if I buy this jacket on sale").

When people experience functional and psychosocial consequences, their affective and cognitive systems produce responses that may be stored as knowledge in memory. For instance, most consumers would feel negative affect (dissatisfaction) if a product needed repairs soon after it was bought. Or a consumer might have positive feelings of pride and self-esteem if other people comment favorably on a new sweater. Beliefs about these functional and psychosocial consequences and related affective reactions are part of consumers' product knowledge in memory. This knowledge may later be activated from memory and used in interpretation or integration processes.

Consumers can think about the positive and negative consequences of product use as possible benefits or potential risks. **Benefits** are the desirable consequences consumers seek when buying and using products and brands ("I want a car with fast acceleration." "I want a car with good mileage"). Benefit knowledge can be described in terms of cognition and affect. Cognitive aspects of benefits include consumers' knowledge of desired functional and psychosocial consequences ("I want my stereo system to have excellent sound reproduction." "People will notice me"). Affective aspects of benefits include positive affective responses associated with the desired consequence ("I feel good when people notice me").

Consumers often think about products and brands as *bundles of benefits* rather than bundles of attributes (see Exhibit 5.2). Thus, marketers can divide consumers into subgroups or segments according to their desire for particular product consequences, a process called *benefit segmentation*.[8] For example, some toothpaste consumers are looking for appearance benefits (whiter teeth), while others are more interested in health benefits (preventing tooth decay).

Perceived risk concerns the undesirable product consequences that consumers try to avoid when buying and using products. Several types of negative consequences might occur. Some consumers worry about the *physical risks* of product consumption (side effects of a cold remedy, injury on a bicycle, electric shock from a hair dryer). Other types of unpleasant consequences include *financial risk* (finding out the warranty doesn't cover fixing your microwave oven; buying new athletic shoes and finding them on sale the next day), *functional risk* (an aspirin product doesn't get rid of headaches very well; a motor oil additive doesn't really reduce engine wear), and *psychosocial risk* (my friends might think these sunglasses look weird on me; I won't feel confident in this suit). As with benefits, perceived risk includes consumers' cognitive knowledge about unfavorable consequences and the negative affective responses associated with these unpleasant consequences (unfavorable evaluations, bad feelings, and negative emotions).

The amount of perceived risk a consumer experiences is influenced by two things: (1) the degree of unpleasantness of the negative consequences and (2) the probability that these negative consequences will occur. In cases where consumers do not know about potential negative consequences (a side effect of a health remedy, a safety defect in a car), perceived risk will be low. In other cases, consumers have unrealistic perceptions of product risks because they overestimate the likelihood of negative physical consequences. Consumer Perspective 5.2 describes marketplace problems created by consumers' misperceptions of risk.

Because consumers are unlikely to purchase products with high perceived risk, marketers should manage consumers' perceptions of the negative consequences of product purchase and use. Lands' End, a highly successful mail-order company, tries to reduce consumers' perceptions of financial and performance risk by offering an unconditional, money-back-if-not-satisfied guarantee. A different marketing strategy is to intentionally activate knowledge about product risk to show how using a particular brand avoids the negative consequences. For instance, AT&T ran advertising campaigns in the late 1980s that were intended to generate doubt and anxiety among business executives by pointing out the negative consequences of not buying AT&T service. In one of these "slice of death" commercials, two young executives meet in the men's room, and one confides he is worried about having selected a telephone system that has become obsolete. He wonders if he too is now "obsolete."

Products as value satisfiers

Consumers also have knowledge about the personal, symbolic values that products and brands help them to satisfy or achieve (see Exhibit 5.2). *Values* are people's broad life goals ("I want to be successful." "I need security"). Values also involve the affect associated with such goals and needs (the feelings and emotions that accompany success).

**CONSUMER
PERSPECTIVE**

▶ 5.2

**Risk: perception
versus reality**

Many Americans seem to believe that consumer products should involve no risk. Moreover, they seem to believe that attaining zero risk is possible. Yet, as we reduce significant risks in our environments, consumers seem to become ever more anxious about the imagined hazards of modern life. Perhaps people are confused about perceived risks of products, because several of the major "hazards" of recent years turned out to be false alarms or were greatly exaggerated.

The Alar scare of 1989 is an example. A series of news stories (including a televised segment on "60 Minutes") reported a study in which rats developed cancers when fed Alar (a growth hormone used on apple trees). Highly publicized estimates of 200 to 900 deaths from cancer per million people created some hysteria. People dumped apple juice down the drain, and apple sales plummeted. Some consumers even called the Environmental Protection Agency (EPA) to ask if the groundwater could be contaminated by discarded apple juice. The original study was discredited when it was found that the rats were fed dosages of Alar over 200,000 times higher than human exposure levels. New studies estimated the risks to be minuscule. In fact, because Alar helps apples stay on the tree, the need for stronger pesticides against apple drop is reduced, which might actually reduce the incidence of cancers.

A similar situation occurred in 1990, when analyses of Perrier (a French brand of mineral water) revealed minute amounts of benzene, a known carcinogen. Benzene is a

Recognizing when a value has been satisfied or a basic life goal has been achieved is rather intangible and subjective ("I feel secure." "I am respected by others." "Am I successful?"). In contrast, functional and psychosocial consequences are more tangible, and it is more obvious when they occur ("Other people noticed me when I wore that silk shirt").

There are many ways to classify values.[9] One useful scheme identifies two types or levels of values—instrumental and terminal. **Instrumental values** are preferred modes of conduct or ways of behaving (having a good time, acting independent, showing self-reliance). **Terminal values,** on the other hand, are preferred states of being or broad psychological states (happy, at peace, successful). Instrumental and terminal values (goals or needs) represent the broadest and most personal consequences that people are trying to achieve in their lives. Exhibit 5.3 lists some of the instrumental and terminal values held by Americans.

Values that are a central aspect of people's self-concept—their knowledge about themselves—are called core values.[10] Because they have a major influence on cognitive processes and behaviors, these core values are of particular interest to marketers. Consumer Perspective 5.3 (p. 90) describes how the core value of protecting the environment has created new marketing opportunities.

Because they represent important, personally relevant consequences, values often are associated with strong affective responses. Satisfying a value usually elicits positive affect (happiness, joy, satisfaction), while blocking a value produces negative affect (frustration, anger, disappointment). For many people, buying their first car satisfies the values of independence and freedom and generates positive affective feelings of pride and satisfaction. On the other hand, your security value is blocked if your new bicycle lock is broken by a thief, which could create substantial negative affect (anger, frustration, fear).

In summary, consumers can have product knowledge about product attributes, consequences of product use, and personal values. Most marketing research focuses on the attribute level of product knowledge, but consequences are studied occasionally (usually benefits rather than risks). Values are examined less frequently. The problem is that marketers have an incomplete understanding of consumers' product knowledge when they study only one type of knowledge.

natural ingredient in the carbon dioxide gas that bubbles up in the springs in France. The benzene usually was removed by filters, but they had not been changed frequently enough. The amount of benzene detected in Perrier was 19 parts per billion, a level that could not have been detected 15 years earlier. This example illuminates a problem in risk assessment. Our technologies for measuring tiny quantities of "harmful" compounds in products have outstripped our ability to make reasonable judgments about the degree of possible harm.

Was Perrier dangerous? That depends on your perceptions of and tolerance for very small risks. The actual risk of developing cancer from drinking Perrier was extremely small. One expert estimated the additional cancer risk from drinking one liter of the "contaminated" Perrier every day for 70 years as somewhere between 1 in 100,000 and 1 in 10 million. This means that if all Americans drank one liter of Perrier every day of their lives, the additional number of cancer deaths might be 200 or so per year. Of course, virtually no one consumes that much mineral water. Yet in the emotional climate of 1990, Perrier thought it had to recall $40 million of essentially harmless product.

Source: Adapted from Warren T. Brookes, "The Wasteful Pursuit of Zero Risk," *Forbes*, April 30, 1990, pp. 161–72. Reprinted with permission of *Forbes* Magazine. © Forbes Inc. 1990.

Instrumental Values (Preferred Modes of Conduct)	Terminal Values (Preferred End States of Being)

Competence
    Ambitious (hardworking)
    Independent (self-reliant)
    Imaginative (creative)
    Capable (competent)
    Logical (rational)
    Courageous
	Social harmony
	    World at peace
	    Equality (brotherhood)
	    Freedom (independence)
	    National security
	    Salvation (eternal life)

Compassion
    Forgiving (pardon others)
    Helpful (work for others)
    Cheerful (joyful)
    Loving (affectionate)
	Personal gratification
	    Social recognition
	    Comfortable life
	    Pleasure (enjoyable life)
	    Sense of accomplishment

Sociality
    Polite (courteous)
    Obedient (dutiful)
    Clean (neat, tidy)
	Self-actualization
	    Beauty (nature and arts)
	    Wisdom (understanding)
	    Inner harmony (no conflict)
	    Self-respect (self-esteem)
	    Sense of accomplishment

Integrity
    Responsible (reliable)
    Honest (sincere)
    Self-controlled
	Security
	    Taking care of family
	    Salvation (eternal life)

	Love and affection
	    Mature love (sexual and spiritual intimacy)
	    True friendship (close companionship)

	Personal contentedness Happiness (contentment)

EXHIBIT 5.3

Instrumental and terminal values

Source: The values are from Milton J. Rokeach, *The Nature of Human Values* (New York: Free Press, 1973). The underlined category labels for groupings of Rokeach's values shown are identified by Donald E. Vinson, J. Michael Munson, and Masao Nakanishi, "An Investigation of the Rokeach Value Survey for Consumer Research Applications," in *Advances in Consumer Research*, vol. 4, ed. W. D. Perreault (Atlanta, Ga.: Association for Consumer Research, 1977), pp. 247–52.

CONSUMER PERSPECTIVE

► 5.3

The value of the environment

More Americans have become "green," environmentally concerned. The media both reflect and stimulate this shift in values. For instance, the network news ran about one environmental story every three nights in 1987, one story every two nights in 1988, and two stories every night in 1989. Most observers see this change as not just a fad, but a long-term trend in values.

But it isn't easy being green—either for Kermit (the Muppet frog) or for marketers. Faced with rapidly shifting legal, political, and social environments, many American manufacturers have frantically relabeled, repackaged, and repositioned their products in an effort to link their products to the growing environmental values in American society. In 1990, 26 percent of all new products introduced made some environmental claim. Yet many of these efforts did not impress American consumers or environmental activists. Nearly half of consumers surveyed in 1990 dismissed environmental claims as "mere gimmickry."

Consider the lowly trash bag. After years of pressure from consumers to make a biodegradable version of its Hefty bag, Mobil did so in June 1989. Package boxes proclaimed the bags were biodegradable, which they were, if left exposed to air and sun. But over 90 percent of trash bags are put into landfills where the lack of light and oxygen halts the degradation. Less than six months after introduction of the bags, the Environmental Defense Fund called for a boycott of the bags, and several state

MEANS-END CHAINS OF PRODUCT KNOWLEDGE

The three levels of product knowledge can be combined to form a simple associative network called a means-end chain. A **means-end chain** is a knowledge structure that connects consumers' meanings about product attributes, consequences, and values.[11]

The means-end perspective suggests that consumers define product attributes in personal, subjective terms—"What is this attribute good for?" or "What does this attribute do for me?" In other words, consumers see a product attribute as a means to some end, which could be a consequence or a value.[12]

A more detailed means-end chain can be created by dividing each of the attribute, consequence, and value levels into two categories:[13]

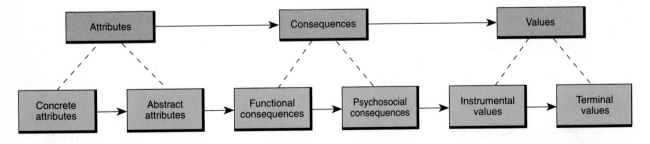

Exhibit 5.4 presents definitions of the six levels in the means-end chain and gives examples of each level. Some of the distinctions between the six levels can be a bit fuzzy. For instance, you might be uncertain whether "being with friends" is a psychosocial consequence or an instrumental value. For the most part, however, marketers don't have to

agencies sued Mobil for deceptive advertising. Mobil, in response, took environmental claims off the boxes.

In late 1990, McDonald's switched from using polystyrene shell containers for hamburgers (adopted in the 1970s at the request of environmentalists) to quilted paper wrappers. But not all environmentalists agree this is a good move. In an attempt to make peace with environmental activists, McDonald's agreed to let the Environmental Defense Fund put together a plan for recycling and cutting waste. They planned to institute some 42 ideas aimed at cutting solid waste volume by 80 percent at the 8,500 U.S. McDonald's restaurants.

Some companies like S.C. Johnson avoid making environmental claims about their products. According to a company spokesperson, "As soon as you go out on a limb and claim you're doing something, a consumer group attacks the validity of your claim." In the face of widespread confusion about environmental claims among consumers, companies, and environmentalists, the Federal Trade Commission has been asked to develop acceptable standards for such environmental terms as *recycled* and *biodegradable*.

Source: Reprinted with permission from "The Big Green Muddle in Green Marketing," by Jaclyn Fierman, *Fortune*, © 1991, Time Inc. All rights reserved.

worry about such issues when using the means-end chain model to develop marketing strategies. The main point of the means-end chain model is that consumers create knowledge structures of linked meanings that connect tangible product attributes to more abstract attributes and consequences, which in turn are associated with more subjective, self-relevant values and goals.

Level of meaning	Explanation	Example	
Terminal values	Preferred end states of being, very abstract consequences of product use.	Self-esteem	**EXHIBIT 5.4** **A means-end chain model of consumers' product knowledge**
Instrumental values	Preferred modes of conduct, abstract consequences of product use.	Being center of attention	
Psychosocial consequences	Psychological (How do I feel?) and social (How do others feel about me?) consequences of product use.	Others see me as special	
Functional consequences	Immediate, tangible consequences of product use. What does the product do? What functions does it perform?	Handles easily	
Abstract attributes	Product characteristic standing for several more concrete attributes. Subjective, not directly measurable or perceived.	Good quality	
Concrete attributes	Knowledge about physical characteristic of product. Directly perceived.	Price	

The means-end chain model is based on the idea that the meaning of a product attribute is given by its consequences.[14] Consider the attributes Gillette designed into its popular Sensor razor—a spring suspension and a lubricating strip. These product attributes probably don't mean much to most consumers until they use the product or learn about its consequences from advertising or other consumers. Some consumers might form the means-end chains below:

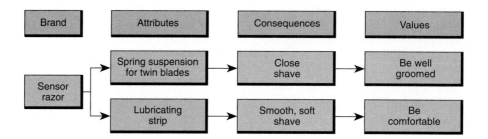

Examples of means-end chains

Exhibit 5.5 presents several means-end chains that represent one consumer's product knowledge for a product class (hair spray), a product form (flavored potato chips), and a brand (Scope mouthwash). This exhibit illustrates four important points about means-end chains. First, actual means-end chains vary considerably in the number and types of meanings they contain. Second, not every means-end chain leads to an instrumental or terminal value. In fact, the end of a means-end chain can be any type of consequence—

EXHIBIT 5.5   Examples of means-end chains

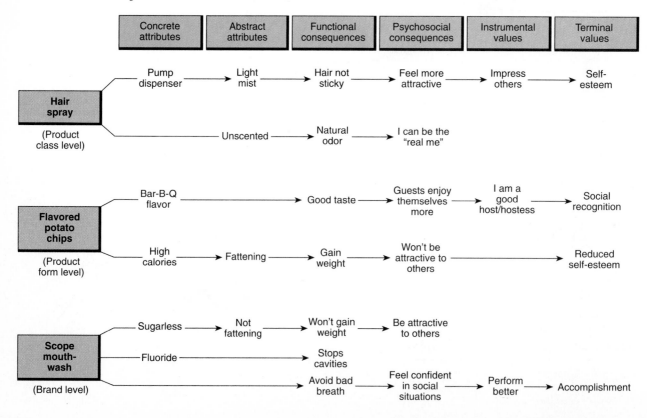

from a functional consequence ("This toothpaste will give me fresh breath"), to a psychosocial consequence ("My friends will like being close to me"), to an instrumental value ("I will be clean"), to a terminal value ("I will be happy"). Third, some of the means-end chains in Exhibit 5.5 are incomplete, with missing levels of meaning. Actual means-end chains do not necessarily include all six levels of product knowledge in the idealized means-end model.

Two other points are not shown in Exhibit 5.5. Some product attributes can have more than one means-end chain. These multiple means-end chains may conflict if they lead to both positive and negative ends (benefits and perceived risks). For example, consider the positive and negative consequences sometimes associated with price for relatively expensive products such as a watch or television:

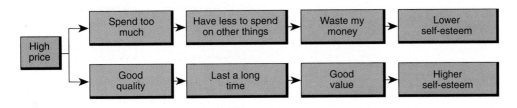

Finally, because consumers create their own personally relevant knowledge structures, their means-end chains are unique. However, consumers in the same market segment often share enough meanings about a product to make it possible to identify a set of common meanings.

Measuring means-end chains

Measuring means-end chains is best accomplished with one-on-one, personal interviews where the researcher tries to understand a consumer's meanings for product attributes and consequences. The process involves two basic steps. First, the researcher must identify the product attributes that are most important to each consumer. One approach is to ask consumers what attributes are most relevant to them when they make decisions about a product. Another approach is for management to specify the attributes of greatest interest. Second, the researcher conducts a *laddering* interview by asking consumers a progression of questions in the format of "why is that important to you?"[15] Exhibit 5.6 shows an example of a laddering interview. By describing why each prior response is important, consumers reveal the connections they make between product attributes, consequences, and values, which is their personal means-end chain.

To summarize, the means-end chain provides a more complete understanding of consumers' product knowledge than methods that focus only on attributes or benefits.[16] For instance, consider the following means-end chain for Ultra Tide laundry detergent:

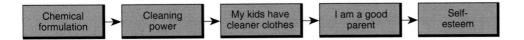

This hypothetical consumer interprets the chemical attributes of Ultra Tide in terms of the more abstract attribute, "cleaning power." Cleaning power, in turn, is seen as providing the functional benefit of "cleaner clothes for the kids," which is seen as helping to achieve the instrumental value of "being a good parent," which finally leads to the terminal value of "feeling good about myself" or "self-esteem."

By identifying the sequence of connections between product-related meanings, marketers can see more clearly what consumers are really communicating when they mention an attribute or a consequence such as "cleaning power." Means-end chain analyses also

EXHIBIT 5.6

An example of a laddering interview

Researcher:	"You said that a shoe's lacing pattern is important to you in deciding what brand to buy. Why is that?"
Consumer:	"A staggered lacing pattern makes the shoe fit more snugly on my foot." [physical attribute and functional consequence]
Researcher:	"Why is it important that the shoe fit more snugly on your foot?"
Consumer:	"Because it gives me better support." [functional consequence]
Researcher:	"Why is better support important to you?"
Consumer:	"So I can run without worrying about injury." [psychosocial consequence]
Researcher:	"Why is it important for you not to worry while running?"
Consumer:	"So I can relax and enjoy the run." [psychosocial consequence]
Researcher:	"Why is it important that you can relax and enjoy the run?"
Consumer:	"Because it gets rid of tension I have built up at work." [psychosocial consequence]
Researcher:	"Why is it important for you to get rid of tension from work?"
Consumer:	"So when I go back to work in the afternoon, I can perform better." [instrumental value—high performance]
Researcher:	"Why is it important that you perform better?"
Consumer:	"I feel better about myself." [terminal value—self-esteem]
Researcher:	"Why is it important that you feel better about yourself?"
Consumer:	"It just is!" [the end!]

identify and help us understand the basic ends (values and goals) consumers are seeking when they buy and use certain products and brands. This gives insights into consumers' purchase motivations. Finally, means-end chains reflect the product/self relationship—that is, they show how consumers relate product attributes to important aspects of their self-concepts. In sum, by providing a more complete understanding of consumers' product knowledge, means-end analysis helps marketers devise more effective advertising, pricing, distribution, and product strategies.

CONSUMERS' PRODUCT INVOLVEMENT

Why do consumers seem to care about some products and brands and not others? Why are some consumers highly motivated to seek information about products, or to buy and use products in certain situations, while other consumers seem to have no interest? Why did some Coke drinkers make such a big fuss when Coca-Cola managers made a minor change in an inexpensive, simple, and seemingly unimportant soft drink (see Consumer Perspective 5.4, p. 96)? These questions concern consumers' involvement, an important concept for understanding consumer behavior.[17]

Involvement is the perceived importance or personal relevance of an object or event.[18] Involvement with a product or brand has both cognitive and affective aspects.[19] Cognitively, consumers feel involved when knowledge about the relevance of a product is activated from memory. This knowledge includes means-end beliefs about important consequences or values produced by the product ("This CD would be fun to play at parties"). Involvement also includes affective states such as product and brand evaluations ("I like David Letterman's show"). If product involvement is high, people may experience stronger affective responses including emotions and strong feelings ("I really love my Mazda").

Marketers often treat consumers' product involvement as either high or low, but involvement can vary from very low (little or no perceived relevance) to moderate (some perceived relevance) to high levels (great perceived relevance). The level of product involvement a consumer experiences during decision making is determined by the type of means-end knowledge activated in that situation.[20] Consumers who believe product attributes are

This ad communicates the key functional consequence of the product—intense fruit taste.

strongly linked to important end goals or values will experience higher levels of involvement with the product. In contrast, consumers who believe the product attributes lead only to functional consequences, or that product attributes are only weakly linked to important values, will experience lower levels of product involvement. Finally, consumers who believe the product attributes are not associated with any relevant consequences will experience little or no involvement with the product.

Involvement is a motivational state that energizes and directs consumers' cognitive processes and behaviors as they make decisions. For instance, consumers who are involved with cameras are motivated to work harder at choosing which brand to buy. They might spend more time and effort shopping for cameras (visiting more stores, talking to more salespeople). They might interpret more product information in the environment (read more ads and brochures). And they might spend more time and effort in integrating this product information to evaluate brands and make a purchase choice. We suspect that in the typical purchase decision, most consumers experience low to moderate levels of involvement for most products and brands.[21]

Consumers do not continually experience feelings of involvement, even for important products such as a car, a home, or special hobby equipment. Rather, people feel involved with such products only on certain occasions when knowledge about the personal relevance of products is activated. As circumstances change, that knowledge is no longer activated, and people's feelings of involvement fade (until another time).

Focus of involvement

Marketers are interested in understanding consumers' involvement with products and brands. But people also may be involved with other *physical objects* such as advertisements. During the 1990s, some people became involved with a series of ads for Taster's Choice coffee that portrayed flirtatious situations between a man and a woman.

In the spring of 1985, the Coca-Cola Company shocked American consumers and other soft-drink manufacturers by announcing it was changing the 99-year-old formula for Coke. The "new" Coke was a bit sweeter, and marketing research showed it was preferred to Pepsi-Cola. The original Coke formula was to be retired to a bank vault and never again produced.

What happened then was the beginning of Coke's lesson in consumer involvement. Outraged U.S. consumers complained bitterly to the Atlanta-based company about the loss of "a great American tradition." In Seattle, a group of strident loyalists calling themselves "Old Coke Drinkers of America" laid plans to file a class-action suit against Coca-Cola. They searched out shop owners, vending-machine owners, and others willing to claim that the company's formula change had cost them business. Then, when June sales didn't pick up as expected, the bottlers also joined in the demand for old Coke's return—and fast.

Although Coca-Cola had spent some $4 million testing the new formula, it had missed one important factor. Millions of consumers had a strong *emotional involvement* with the original Coke. They drank it as kids and still did as adults. Many consumers had a personal attachment to Coke. Says a Coke spokesperson, "We had taken away a little part of them and their past. They [consumers] said, 'You have no right to do that. Bring it back.' "

Coca-Cola had learned a costly lesson. Although consumers preferred the new taste in blind taste tests, Coca-Cola did not measure consumers' emotional reactions to removing the original Coke from the marketplace. Coca-Cola learned that a product is more than a production formula; extra meanings such as emotions and strong connections to self-image may also be present.

Consumers may be involved with other *people*—friends, relatives, lovers, perhaps even salespeople. People can also become involved with certain *environments* (their home or backyard, amusement parks, a lake or the seashore). Some of these may be marketing environments—a clothing store the consumer especially likes, a shopping mall, or a favorite restaurant. People may be involved with specific *activities* or *behaviors* such as playing tennis, working, windsurfing, or reading. Finally, some consumers become involved with marketing-related activities such as collecting coupons, shopping for new clothes, finding the cheapest price in town, or bargaining with vendors at flea markets.

Marketers need to understand the focus of consumers' involvement by identifying exactly what it is that consumers consider to be personally relevant: a product or brand, an object, a behavior, an event, a situation, an environment, or several of these together. In principle, marketers can analyze consumers' involvement with virtually anything, although our main focus here is on products and brands.

Factors influencing involvement

Exhibit 5.7 shows that a person's level of involvement is influenced by two sources—personal and situational.[22] Each source can activate or generate means-end chains that link product attributes to personally relevant consequences and values.

Personal sources of involvement refer to means-end knowledge stored in consumers' memories.[23] Consumers acquire this means-end knowledge through their past experiences with a product. As they use a product (or observe others using it), consumers learn that certain product attributes have relevant consequences that lead to important goals and values. For example, a consumer may learn that various attributes of a stereo

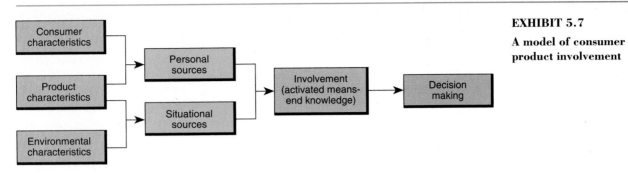

EXHIBIT 5.7

A model of consumer product involvement

Source: Adapted from Richard L. Celsi and Jerry C. Olson, "The Role of Involvement in Attention and Comprehension Processes," *Journal of Consumer Research*, September 1988, pp. 210–24; and Peter H. Bloch and Marsha L. Richins, "A Theoretical Model for the Study of Product Importance Perceptions," *Journal of Marketing*, Summer 1988, pp. 69–81.

system have favorable and unfavorable consequences ("digital readout—This will impress my friends," "remote control—I can be comfortable and relaxed," "programmability—This feature is too much trouble"). This means-end knowledge in memory is a potential source of involvement. To the extent that this knowledge is activated in a decision situation, the consumer will experience feelings of personal relevance or involvement.

Exhibit 5.7 shows the means-end knowledge stored in memory or personal sources of involvement are influenced by characteristics of both the consumer and the product. Consumer characteristics include people's values and life goals. Relevant product characteristics are the concrete and abstract product attributes that lead to important benefits and perceived risks (consumers tend to feel involved in decisions that might have negative consequences). Other product factors that may influence personal sources of involvement include social visibility (Do people know you own the product?) and time commitment (Buying a refrigerator is involving because you are committed to your choice for a long time).

Some people became nvolved with the long-running ad campaign for Taster's Choice.

SHARON: Hi
TONY: Hi.
SHARON: Was it something I said.
TONY: I came over last night
. . . you had company.
SHARON: You mean my brother.
He just loves my coffee.

TONY: Your brother.
ANNCR: Savor the sophisticated taste. of Taster's Choice.
TONY: No just business.
SHARON: How long?
TONY: A month.
SHARON: That's long.

TONY: HI.
SHARON: Don't tell me—you forgot to pack your Taster's Choice.
TONY: Listen, I though you should know i'm going to be in Paris.
SHARON: Paris. How romantic.
TONY: Well, it can be.

Situational sources of involvement are aspects of the immediate physical and social environment that activate important consequences and values and link them to product attributes, thus making products and brands seem self-relevant. For instance, a "50% Off" sign on fishing rods might activate self-relevant thoughts in a person interested in fishing ("I can get a good deal on a new rod"). Because many environmental factors change over time, situational sources often create temporary means-end linkages between a product and important consequences or values. These connections between the product and personal consequences may disappear when the situation changes. For example, the person's involvement with buying a fishing rod might last only as long as the sale continues.

Aspects of the social environment can be situational sources of involvement. For instance, shopping with others could make some consumers more self-conscious than when shopping alone ("I want to impress my friends with my sense of style"). A chance observation in the physical environment can be a situational source of involvement. For example, noticing a window display in a clothing store might activate knowledge about consequences and values that become associated with the clothing in the display ("That sweater would be good for the party next week"). More general aspects of the physical environment can also be situational sources of involvement. The high temperatures on a summer day could activate desirable consequences ("I need to take a break, cool off, or relax") that make buying an ice cream cone or going to an air-conditioned movie theater relevant and involving.

Exhibit 5.7 shows that consumers' overall level of involvement is always determined by a combination of personal and situational sources. Although personal sources have the most influence on involvement in some cases, situational sources have a major influence in many circumstances. Consider the common situation when a consumer's personal source of involvement concerning a product is low (the product is not very important). For instance, most people do not consider hot water heaters to have much self-relevance. But if yours develops a leak, it becomes important to replace it quickly. The negative consequences of showering and washing in cold water are highly self-relevant. This means-end knowledge (which is activated only because your old heater broke) is a situational source of involvement with choosing and buying a new hot water heater. You are likely to feel this involvement and motivation only for the short time it takes to evaluate a few alternatives and make a purchase choice.

Marketers need to understand the *focus* of consumers' involvement and the *sources* that create it. Although most consumers are not personally involved with products such as hot water heaters, they can become temporarily involved with the process of buying the product. Having to replace a broken water heater (a situational source of involvement) makes people think about particular consequences of *purchase* (paying money, taking time and effort to shop, creating stress and hassle) that are important to them. The purchase situation also might activate product knowledge that is important during decision making (purchase price, speed of delivery, ease of installation), but is not relevant later when the product is being used. Involvement declines after the purchase, because most of the involvement consumers experienced concerned the decision process, not the product itself.

This is not an isolated example. Situational sources always combine with consumers' intrinsic or personal sources to create the level of involvement consumers actually experience during the decision making. Therefore, consumers usually experience some level of involvement when making purchase choices, even for relatively unimportant products. Even though personal sources of involvement are low for many everyday consumer products (soap, bread, socks), situational sources are likely to influence the level of involvement consumers feel. This suggests marketers can influence consumers' product involvement by manipulating aspects of the environment that might function as situational sources of involvement.

Rally's has two drive-throughs to speed customers on their way.

A means-end approach to product knowledge and involvement is useful for understanding the critical consumer/product relationship and developing effective marketing strategies. Marketers need a deep understanding of the cognitive and affective factors underlying purchase decisions. Marketers need to develop marketing strategies that will connect their products and services to consumers' goals and values and influence consumers' product involvement.

Marketers can use means-end chain analyses to identify the key attributes and consequences underlying a consumer's product purchase decision. Restaurant choices are a good example. Unlike the people in cultures such as France, many Americans do not feel highly involved with food. Fast-food industry research suggests the three major factors in a decision on where to eat are: (1) time of day, (2) how long the customer wants to spend eating, and (3) price.[24] According to one expert, "We used to eat when the food was ready. Now we eat when we are ready." Speed and convenience are critical consequences, not the food itself.

Rally's, a small chain of 240 restaurants, has developed marketing strategies to provide these desired consequences. The typical Rally's is small enough to be placed anywhere. A Rally's can be built for about $350,000, compared to more than $1 million for the average McDonald's. Rally's offers no seating; food is ordered at walk-up or drive-through windows only. The drive-in line at a Rally's restaurant moves so fast many customers are on their way within 30 seconds, paying only $3 for a cheeseburger, french fries, and a large Coke, about 85 cents less than the nearby McDonald's would charge. Food quality is not a big issue. As one Rally's customer admits, "The food isn't very good here, but it's cheap, quick, and easy." Rally's understanding of what attributes and consequences customers really want led to doubling of sales and tripling of profits from 1989 to 1990, while several competitors experienced decline or stagnant growth. Annual sales at an average Rally's ran about $1,300 per square foot, compared to $400 at McDonald's.

One of the most important concepts in marketing concerns consumers' relationships with products and brands.[25] A good example is the relationships that many Americans have with their cars described in Consumer Perspective 5.5. Marketers need to understand the cognitive and affective aspects of these consumer/product relationships. For instance, teenagers may link the general attributes of cars to important self-relevant consequences

MARKETING IMPLICATIONS

Understanding the key reasons for purchase

Understanding the consumer/product relationship

CONSUMER PERSPECTIVE

▶ 5.5

Consumers' relationships with cars

More than 1 billion automobiles have been sold in this century. Most have been in the United States, where there are two cars for every 3 people, compared to one car for every 3 people in Denmark and one for every 15,000 in China. Car ownership continues to rise worldwide, despite recessions, rising interest rates, and high taxes and gasoline prices. Each year, several million new cars enter crowded U.S. roadways.

Many Americans feel highly involved with their autos, often treating them like pets (stroking, petting, grooming). For some consumers, the product/self relationship reflects a passionate level of intrinsic self-relevance. Such people love their cars and may engage in ritual forms of "worship," such as weekend cleaning and waxing. What self-relevant consequences of owning and driving cars can create such high levels of involvement?

Cars provide numerous opportunities for control and mastery—a sense of domination—which is a desirable value for some consumers. Cars also provide thrills. For instance, a major part of the driving experience involves acceleration, which elicits strong positive affect and arousal responses in many people. For some consumers, these feelings can be intensely pleasurable.

Cars are also a powerful means of self-expression for many consumers. For instance, people can acquire expensive, distinctive automobiles to bolster their social status. Other consumers can buy a reasonable car to establish or express their rational, serious qualities. Some car owners buy personalized license plates, unique gadgets, and other custom products to embellish their cars and further express their self-relevant values.

Source: From *Driving Passion: The Psychology of the Car*, by Peter Marsh and Peter Collett. Copyright © 1986 by Peter Marsh and Peter Collett. Reprinted by permission of Faber and Faber, Inc.

(self-respect, admiration of peers, freedom). A key task of marketing management is to manage this important customer/product relationship.[26] Marketing strategies should be designed to create and maintain meaningful consumer/product relationships and to modify relationships that are not optimal.

There are innumerable examples of the importance of the consumer/product relationship. Consider the huge market for athletic shoes. Americans spent $11.7 billion in 1990 on 393 million pairs of brand-name athletic shoes, and Nike commanded a $2.2 billion

Consumers who are highly involved with a brand tend to be brand loyal.

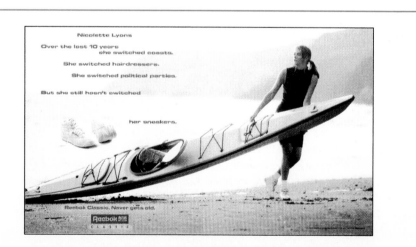

CONSUMER PERSPECTIVE

5.6 ◄

Consumers' relationships with brands

Of the various types of relationships consumers can have with products and brands, brand loyalty is a highly desirable goal for most marketers. Although brand loyalty seems to have eroded considerably over the past 30 years because of increased brand competition and extensive sales promotions (coupons and price reductions), it is not dead. A survey of some 2,000 customers found wide variations in brand loyalty across product classes.

Faithful or Fickle?
Percentage of users of these products who are loyal to one brand

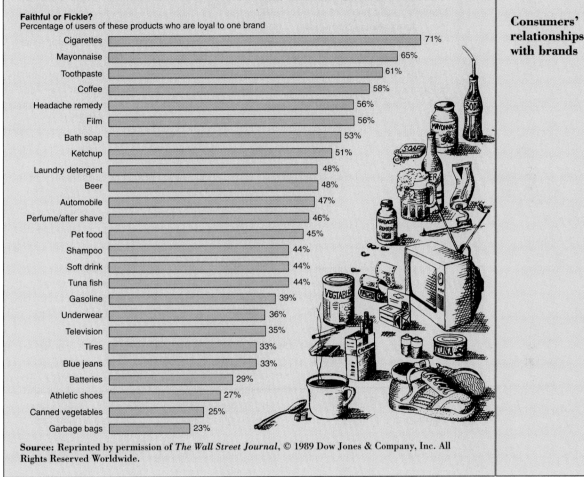

Product	Percentage
Cigarettes	71%
Mayonnaise	65%
Toothpaste	61%
Coffee	58%
Headache remedy	56%
Film	56%
Bath soap	53%
Ketchup	51%
Laundry detergent	48%
Beer	48%
Automobile	47%
Perfume/after shave	46%
Pet food	45%
Shampoo	44%
Soft drink	44%
Tuna fish	44%
Gasoline	39%
Underwear	36%
Television	35%
Tires	33%
Blue jeans	33%
Batteries	29%
Athletic shoes	27%
Canned vegetables	25%
Garbage bags	23%

Source: Reprinted by permission of *The Wall Street Journal*, © 1989 Dow Jones & Company, Inc. All Rights Reserved Worldwide.

share of that market.[27] Nike's revenues soared during the past decade, partly because of the relationships marketing strategies created between fashion-conscious youth and the Nike brand. Muggings, and even murders, have been blamed on kids' desire for a trendy pair of athletic shoes or a jacket—a tragic manifestation of the consumer/product relationship. In the face of such events, Nike was criticized for promoting its expensive basketball shoes to black and Hispanic youths.

If marketers can understand the consumer/product relationship, they may be able to segment consumers in terms of their personal sources of involvement. For instance, some consumers may have positive means-end knowledge about a product category, while others may have favorable beliefs and feelings for a brand. Still other consumers may have favorable means-end knowledge about both the product category and a brand. Consumer Perspective 5.6 gives examples of the varying levels of brand loyalty in different product categories.

We can identify four segments with different personal sources of involvement for the product category and brand.[28] Those with the strongest feelings are brand loyalists and routine brand buyers.

▷ *Brand loyalists* have strong affective ties to one favorite brand they regularly buy. In addition, they perceive the product category in general to provide personally relevant consequences. Their positive means-end knowledge about both the brand and the product category leads them to experience high levels of involvement during decision making. They strive to buy "the best brand" for their needs. For instance, consumers often have strong brand loyalty for sports equipment such as tennis rackets or athletic shoes.

▷ *Routine brand buyers* have low personal sources of involvement for the product category, but they do have a favorite brand they buy regularly (little brand switching). For the most part, their personal sources of involvement with a brand are not based on knowledge about the means-end consequences of product attributes. Instead, these consumers are interested in other types of consequences associated with regular brand purchase ("It's easier to buy Colgate each time I need toothpaste"). These beliefs can lead to consistent purchase, but these consumers are not so interested in getting the "best" brand; a satisfactory one will do.

The other two segments have weaker personal sources of brand involvement. Information seekers and brand switchers do not have especially positive means-end knowledge about a single favorite brand.

▷ *Information seekers* have positive means-end knowledge about the product category, but no particular brand stands out as superior (You may be "into" skis, but know that many ski brands are good choices). These consumers use a lot of information to help them find a "good" brand. Over time, they tend to buy a variety of brands in the product category.

▷ *Brand switchers* have low personal sources of involvement for both the brand and the product category. They do not see that the brand or the product category provides important consequences and have no interest in buying "the best." They have no special relationship with either the product category or specific brands. Such consumers tend to respond to environmental factors such as price deals or other short-term promotions that act as situational sources of involvement.

In sum, different marketing strategies are necessary to address the unique types of product knowledge and involvement of these four segments.

Influencing personal sources of involvement

If marketers can understand the means-end knowledge that makes up consumers' personal sources of involvement, they are better able to design product attributes that consumers will connect to important consequences and values.[29] A good example is P&G's design of Ultra Pampers with a water-retaining gel (mentioned at the beginning of the chapter). Marketers can also try to strengthen consumers' personal sources of involvement with a given brand. Mazda once asked owners of Mazda cars to send in pictures of themselves with their cars, and some of these pictures were included in national magazine ads. This promotion might have enhanced the personal relevance of Mazda cars for their owners.

In the short run, it is difficult to modify consumers' personal sources of involvement for a product or brand. Over longer periods, though, consumers' means-end knowledge can be influenced by various marketing strategies, including advertising.[30] The outcome of this process is not completely predictable, because many factors besides marketing strategy can modify consumers' means-end knowledge. For instance, the direct experience of using a product or brand can have a strong impact on means-end knowledge. If the actual product experience doesn't measure up to the image created by advertising, consumers are not likely to form the desired means-end meanings.

Marketers use many strategies to create, modify, or maintain consumers' situational sources of involvement, usually with the goal of encouraging purchase. Semi-annual clearance sales on summer or winter clothing are situational factors that may temporarily raise consumers' involvement with buying such products. Likewise, premiums such as stickers or small toys in cereal boxes or candy packages may temporarily increase children's involvement with a brand. Special pricing strategies, including rebates on new car models ("Get $1,000 back if you buy in the next two weeks"), may function as situational influences that create a temporary increase in involvement with buying the product.

> **Influencing situational sources of involvement**

Another situational source of involvement is to link a product to a social cause.[31] For instance, American Express once donated 1 cent from every purchase made with an AmEx card to refurbish the Statue of Liberty. In addition to making a total contribution of $1.7 million, American Express reaped lots of publicity and some new card applications. As another example, Johnson & Johnson has promoted Shelter Aid, a program that makes donations to shelters for battered women. Finally, if you bought enough wieners and bologna, Oscar Mayer would donate bats, uniforms, and scoreboards to kids' baseball teams.

▶ **SUMMARY**

Learning objective 1: *List the four categories of product knowledge, and give examples.*
Consumers can have knowledge about a product class or product category (cameras, television, automobiles); various forms of a product (35mm SLR cameras, automatic 35mm cameras, disposable cameras); brands (Nikon, Canon, Olympus, Konika); and models (Olympus Infinity with a zoom lens, Olympus Infinity with a fixed lens).

Learning objective 2: *Give examples of concrete and abstract attributes, functional and psychosocial consequences, and instrumental and terminal values.*
Consumers can have knowledge about the attributes of products, the consequences of product use, and the values that products can satisfy. Concrete attributes are physical characteristics of products that are tangible and can be perceived directly (the type of fabric covering a chair; the amount of padding in the chair). Abstract attributes refer to more intangible product characteristics that cannot be directly perceived (the comfort of a chair; the quality of a pizza). Consequences are the specific outcomes that occur when a product is purchased and used. Functional consequences refer to the relatively immediate and tangible outcomes concerning product performance (the support a chair gives your back; the rich taste of ice cream; the sharpness of a photograph). Psychosocial consequences refer to less tangible and more personal outcomes (feeling relaxed in a chair; feeling proud when driving your car; other people think your new shoes are ridiculous). Values are very intangible and subjective consequences, goals, or ends that consumers are trying to achieve in their lives. Instrumental values are preferred modes of behavior (being comfortable; being the center of attention; acting knowledgeable). Terminal values are desirable end states of being (happiness, achievement, security).

Learning objective 3: *Define benefits and risks.*
Benefits are the desirable functional and psychosocial consequences that people seek when buying and using products and brands ("I want a bike that can handle city potholes; I want a suit that makes me feel confident in myself"). Perceived risks are the undesirable functional and psychosocial consequences that consumers want to avoid when buying and using products and brands ("I don't want to spend too much money for this belt; I don't want people to laugh at me behind my back"). When making purchase decisions, consumers may have to make trade-offs between the benefit and risk consequences of a purchase.

Learning objective 4: *Describe a means-end chain, and give an example.*
Means-end chains are simple knowledge structures that link product attributes to their consequences for the consumer. These consequences, in turn, may be linked to values (which actually are very abstract consequences). For example, the special tread design on an automobile tire (a concrete product attribute) might be seen as providing "good traction in the rain" (a functional consequence), which in turn helps to satisfy the terminal value, "keep my family safe." The links between attributes, consequences, and values are based on meaningful relationships as perceived by the consumer (not the marketer). Essentially, a means-end chain answers the consumer's basic question, "What does this product or brand do for me (mean to me; give me)?" The means-end chain perspective recognizes that consumers tend to see a product attribute as a means to a desirable end.

Learning objective 5: *Discuss two marketing implications of means-end chains.*
Means-end chains can provide marketers with a detailed understanding of consumers' product knowledge (and also their knowledge about services, stores, and behaviors). By showing how concepts are related to each other, means-end chains reveal the meanings of an attribute or a consequence (from the consumer's perspective). Means-end chains reveal what end values, if any, consumers associate with a product. Means-end chains also reflect the important product/self relationship. To develop effective marketing strategies, marketers need to understand how consumers perceive the product and service offered. Knowing consumers' means-end knowledge is a help in designing marketing strategies such as what attributes to add to a product, what product benefits to emphasize in advertising, or how to reduce the perceived risks of a product.

Learning objective 6: *Define involvement, and describe how personal and situational sources influence involvement.*
Involvement refers to consumers' perceptions of personal relevance or feelings of interest and importance for an object, activity, or situation. Product involvement is experienced by consumers as cognitions about product consequences and related affective feelings. Involvement influences consumers' motivation to interpret information and integrate knowledge in decision making, as well as their overt behavior, such as searching for product information in stores. Involvement is influenced by personal and situational sources. Personal sources concern consumers' means-end knowledge about how a product (or some other concept) is related to important end values in their lives. For instance, a sophisticated 35mm camera might be highly involving because it helps satisfy important values of accomplishment. Situational sources are aspects of the environment that create temporary associations between some behavior or product attribute and consumers' valued ends. For instance, a 50-percent-off-sale on camera equipment might be a situational source that increases consumers' involvement with buying a new camera.

Learning objective 7: *Give examples of marketing strategies that can influence personal and situational sources of involvement.*
Typically, consumers form personal sources of involvement over long periods of experience with a product. Marketing strategies can reinforce these means-end associations and encourage the development of new links. During the 1980s, Nike used extensive advertising to generate high levels of involvement for its basketball shoes among young urban males. Many marketing strategies are attempts to create situational sources of involvement. Price deals (two for the price of one), contests and sweepstakes (enter for a chance to win $1,000), and "cause marketing" (buy one and we will donate 25 cents to a charity) may be situational sources that create a level of involvement with buying or trying a product or brand.

▶ **KEY TERMS
AND CONCEPTS**

▶ **REVIEW AND
DISCUSSION
QUESTIONS**

1. Select a product category and identify examples of product forms, brands, and models. Give examples of the attributes, consequences, and values associated with each of these categories.

2. Analyze the possible meanings of mouthwash or deodorant in terms of positive (perceived benefits) and negative (perceived risks) consequences of use. Why are both types of meanings important?

3. Describe the fundamental assumptions underlying means-ends chains. Give examples of how marketing managers can use means-end chains.

4. Define the concept of involvement and illustrate it by discussing products that, for you, would be very low, moderate, and high in involvement.

5. Using the purchase of a personal cassette player as an example, describe how personal and situational sources combine to influence a consumer's involvement with the purchase.

6. Do you agree that the personal sources of involvement for most products are low to moderate for most consumers? Why or why not?

7. Using the concept of means-end chains, discuss why different people might shop for athletic shoes at department stores, specialty athletic footwear shops, and discount stores. Why might the same consumer shop at all these stores on different occasions?

8. Discuss how a marketer of casual clothing for men and women can use consumers' product knowledge (means-end chains) and involvement to understand the consumer/product relationship. What can this marketer do to influence consumers' personal sources of involvement with the product?

9. Identify three ways marketers can influence consumers' situational self-relevance, and discuss how this will affect consumers' overall level of involvement. For what types of products are these strategies most suitable?

6

Exposure, Attention, and Comprehension

LEARNING OBJECTIVES

After completing this chapter, you should be able to:

► 1. Describe the differences between accidental and intentional exposure.

► 2. Define selective exposure, and give an example of how marketers can influence consumers' selective exposure to marketing information.

► 3. Define attention, and identify three factors that influence consumers' attention to marketing information.

► 4. Define comprehension, and describe four ways in which comprehension can vary.

► 5. Define inferences, and give an example.

► 6. Describe how consumers' knowledge (expertise) influences their comprehension of marketing information.

► 7. Describe how comprehension processes can influence consumers' ability to recall marketing information.

TV VIEWERS EXPOSED

On Thursday nights during the mid-1980s, approximately 60 million Americans settled down to watch "The Cosby Show," then the nation's top-rated television program. Advertisers also liked the show, even though they had to pay $350,000 for each 30-second spot in 1987. But how could marketers know if their ads were reaching the audience they were paying for? Researchers have been trying to measure viewer exposure and attention to TV commercials since at least 1952, when a water commissioner in Toledo noticed that huge drops in the city's water pressure (the response to thousands of flushing toilets) coincided with commercial breaks in the popular "I Love Lucy" show.

In the mid-1980s, two rival companies in the United States, A. C. Nielsen and Arbitron, measured TV audiences using electronic meters attached to the TV sets of a sample of 1,500 to 2,000 households. The meters could measure whether the set was on, which channel was selected, and for how long, but they could not tell which, if any, family members watched the program (and presumably the commercials). So Nielsen and Arbitron supplemented the meter data with another, larger sample of households that recorded which programs each family member watched. The diaries were supposed to be filled in each week and mailed in monthly.

This procedure had obvious problems. For one, people could be "watching," but not paying attention. Moreover, filling out diaries describing the TV viewing behavior of an entire family was extremely difficult. Many American homes received multiple TV channels via cable and had multiple TV sets. Who could remember which family member watched what program when? Adding further complexity were VCRs, which can record shows for later viewing, and remote controls, which made switching between channels easy. Little wonder that few advertisers had much faith in the accuracy of people's diaries.

AGB Research, the top ratings company in Europe, had a new idea—a people meter. This remote-controlled device had eight buttons that signaled a small monitor box wired to the set. Each family member was assigned a number to push each time he or she started and stopped watching TV. Data were recorded electronically and sent automatically over telephone lines each night to the company, where it was analyzed and given to broadcasters the next day. A. C. Nielsen Company had installed 2,000 of its people meters by late 1987.

Even people meters, of course, could not tell if anyone was paying attention to the advertising. Some research showed that many people were not. One resourceful researcher mounted a small camera on the sets in about 20 British households to take periodic pictures of the room. He found that approximately equal numbers of "viewers" were paying close attention, some attention, and no attention. The last group included consumers who were sleeping, reading, or kissing instead of watching the commercials.

An even more sophisticated system, designed by R. D. Percy & Company, combines a people meter with a heat sensor that can determine if anyone is in the room. If a viewer left without recording that on the people meter, the system would ask if anyone were there. Without response, it would record that the set played to an empty room. This system could produce separate ratings for the program and for the commercials. In 1992, the so-called passive people meter was still on the horizon, not without questions about whether people would allow such "seeing" devices into their homes.[1]

Consumers' everyday environments contain a great deal of information, much of it created by marketing strategies such as TV commercials. Marketers need to understand how consumers are exposed to marketing information, whether they pay attention to the information, and how they comprehend the information. The opening example illustrates the difficulty in measuring exposure and attention to and comprehension of TV programs and commercials, given multiple-TV households, the proliferation of channels, and remote controls that make changing channels easy.

In this chapter, we consider the interpretation process shown in Exhibit 6.1. Interpretation is a key cognitive process in the general model of consumer decision making. We begin by examining how consumers become exposed to marketing information. Then we discuss attention processes by which consumers focus the cognitive system on certain types of information. Finally, we examine the comprehension processes by which

EXHIBIT 6.1

The interpretation process

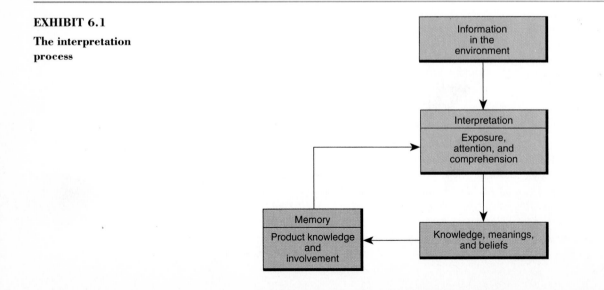

consumers understand the meanings of this information and store that knowledge in memory. We emphasize the effects of existing knowledge, meanings, and beliefs in memory on attention and comprehension. Understanding these aspects of interpretation has implications for developing more effective marketing strategies.

Exposure, defined as contact with information, is the first stage of interpretation. Consumers are continually exposed to information in their environments, including marketing information. Their exposure to marketing information can be accidental or intentional.

EXPOSURE TO INFORMATION

Intentional exposure to marketing information occurs when consumers purposefully search for information relevant to a goal or problem they have. Before buying a camera, for instance, a consumer might read product evaluations of 35mm cameras in *Consumer Reports* or photography magazines. Or a consumer might ask a friend or salesperson for their opinion on which brand of earphones to buy for a Walkman radio. Most investigations of consumer search behavior indicate relatively little intentional exposure to marketing information.[2] For many purchases, buyers visit few stores (often only one) and consult few salespeople or other sources of information. Most consumers already have substantial product-related knowledge stored in memory. If they feel confident in their existing knowledge, or if they feel little involvement with a purchase, consumers have little need or motivation to search for more information. We discuss search behavior more fully in Chapter 8, in the context of consumer decision making.

Most exposures to marketing information are not the result of consumers' intentional search behavior, but happen by chance. **Accidental exposure** occurs when consumers unexpectedly encounter marketing information in their environments. The consumer-oriented environments of most industrialized countries offer many opportunities for accidental exposure to marketing information. We see advertisements in magazines and newspapers, on radio and TV, in direct-mail brochures, and on bus placards and bus-stop shelters. The sheer amount of advertising in the United States is increasing—between 1967 and 1982, the total number of ads doubled, and by 1997 that number is expected to double again.[3] Signs promoting products, services, and retail stores are found everywhere, and nearly all exposures are accidental. Stores provide a great deal of marketing information, including signs, point-of-purchase displays, product demonstrations, and brochures, in addition to the information on packages.

Although some exposures to this information are due to intentional search, many exposures occur accidentally as consumers browse in the retail environments.[4] Some retailers design store environments to maximize the amount of time consumers spend browsing, which increases the likelihood they will be exposed to products and make a purchase. Finally, many exposures to product information in the social environment occur by chance in casual conversations with friends and relatives, salespersons, or even strangers.

Television viewing is a prime example of accidental exposure. Few consumers watch TV to seek information about products and services, yet they are exposed to plenty of commercials during an evening. Such accidental exposure to product information can have powerful effects on behavior. During the Gulf War in early 1991, CNN viewership skyrocketed to twice previous levels (up to 20 times higher in some time periods).[5] Companies that advertised on CNN, such as 1-800-FLOWERS (a New York-based company that delivers flowers anywhere) and Sterling/Range Rover (automobiles), enjoyed higher levels of accidental exposure to their commercials and big increases in sales. For example, the Valentine's Day orders at 800 Flowers increased more than nine times over normal levels to the point where the company couldn't handle all the calls it received.

1-800 FLOWERS uses a commercial with an Easter Bunny to promote sending flowers at Easter time.

Selective exposure

As the amount of marketing information in the environment increases, consumers become more adept at avoiding exposure. Some consumers avoid reading product brochures or talking to salespeople. Others throw all junk mail away unopened. Consider the problems with exposure to TV commercials. People can leave the room as soon as the ads come on or quickly switch to another channel. One simple observation study of family members watching network TV indicated only 47 percent of viewers watched all or almost all of the ads, while about 10 percent left the room. Thanks to remote controls, viewers can easily turn off the sound or switch to another channel during a commercial break. Consumers with videocassette recorders (VCRs) can fast-forward past commercials in programs they have taped. These practices are known as *zapping* and *zipping*.[6] In homes with remote controls, conservative estimates suggest 10 percent of viewers zap the average commercial. About one fifth of households include heavy zappers, who switch channels at the rate of once every two minutes. Advertisers paying media rates based on a full audience of viewers ($100,000 to more than $300,000 for 30 seconds of prime time) worry about getting their money's worth. One strategy to combat zapping is to develop commercials that are so interesting people will want to watch. Pepsi created extravagant ads featuring Michael Jackson that were zapped by only 1 to 2 percent of the audience.[7]

Marketing implications

Because exposure to marketing information is crucial to interpretation and to the success of marketing strategies, marketers need to develop strategies to increase the probability consumers are exposed to product information. There are three ways to do this: facilitate intentional exposure, maximize accidental exposure, and maintain exposure, once begun.

Marketers can *facilitate intentional exposure* by making appropriate marketing information available when and where consumers are intentionally searching for information. This requires that marketers anticipate consumers' needs for product information. IBM trains its retail salespeople to answer technical questions on the spot so consumers don't have to wait while the salesperson looks up the answer. Elaborate product brochures describing the various brands and models are available in most automobile showrooms and audio equipment stores. Home Depot, a successful lumber company, provides numerous in-store seminars on various home building projects such as how to build a masonry wall or install a screen door.

Marketing information should be placed in locations that will *maximize accidental exposure.* For instance, when people park their cars, they see the parking meter for about 14 seconds as they find and deposit the right change.[8] This is plenty of time to be exposed to an ad, and both Campbell Soup Co. and Minolta have placed ads on parking meters in Baltimore. Media planners must carefully select a mix of media (magazines, billboards, radio and TV programming) that increases the chances the target segment of consumers will be exposed to the ads.

The many Au Bon Pain Cafes in downtown Boston maximize the chances consumers will be exposed to the stores and come in to place an order.

Companies also attempt to increase accidental exposure by placing ads in taxicabs, in sports stadiums, and on boats, buses, and blimps. Another strategy is to put four-color ads on grocery store shopping carts.[9] Some 13,000 supermarkets had these rolling billboards in 1990. A big advantage of shopping cart ads is their much lower cost over TV ads—only 50 cents per 1,000 exposures, compared to about $10 to $20 per 1,000 exposures for network television. Advocates also claim this "reminder advertising" reaches consumers at the critical point when they make their purchase choices (an estimated 65 to 80 percent of brand buying decisions occur in the supermarket). Consumer Perspective 6.1 describes another way to expose consumers to marketing information in the grocery store.

Certain types of retail outlets such as convenience stores, ice cream shops, and fast-food restaurants should be placed in locations such as malls and busy intersections where the target group of consumers receives high levels of accidental exposure. Consider the Au Bon Pain cafes, a growing chain selling gourmet sandwiches, freshly squeezed orange juice, and fresh-baked French bread, muffins, and croissants.[10] Using a saturation distribution strategy, Au Bon Pain has packed 16 stores into downtown Boston; some stores are as close as 100 yards. In fact, five outlets are located inside Filene's department store. Besides being highly convenient for regular customers, this saturation strategy maximizes the chances of accidental exposure. The thousands of busy commuters leaving Boston's South Station can hardly avoid walking by a Au Bon Pain cafe. Consumer awareness levels in Boston are high, although the company has never advertised. According to an executive, "It's like having an outdoor billboard in every block; the stores themselves are a substitute for ads." So are the customers carrying the plastic coffee mugs emblazoned with the Au Bon Pain name.

Another strategy to increase accidental exposure is to get a brand into movies or television programs.[11] Sometimes actors will mention actual brand names—Hope, on the show "thirtysomething," once announced she was going out to buy some Junior Mints. Companies usually do not pay for such exposure, which is considered part of the new realism in television and film. In fact, it is illegal for marketers to pay to place a product on TV, unless the payment is disclosed. However, products can be provided free to be used as props—a box of Quaker Oats Squares was seen on "Roseanne" and the secretaries on "L.A. Law" use IBM computers. In other cases, marketers can hire companies that specialize in placing products in movies and on TV in hopes of "accidentally" exposing their brands to millions of viewers.

**CONSUMER
PERSPECTIVE**

▶ 6.1

**Ad exposure at
point of purchase**

After a long day at work, Lisa stops at the supermarket to pick up dinner. As she wheels the grocery cart down the coffee aisle, an ad for Folger's coffee flashes on the liquid-crystal screen attached to her cart's handle. Seeing the ad reminds Lisa that she needs coffee, and she drops a can of Folger's into her cart. Next, she notices on the screen that a coupon for 50 cents off Rice-a-Roni is available with the touch of a button. Provided Lisa buys the product, the 50 cents will be automatically deducted when she arrives at checkout where all purchases are scanned. In the next aisle, VideOcart's "Aisle Features" alerts Lisa that Breyer's Ice Cream is available at a special, reduced price.

It's a marketer's dream to promote items right at the point where consumers make that purchase decision. In April 1988, VideOcart, Inc., unveiled a prototype of the

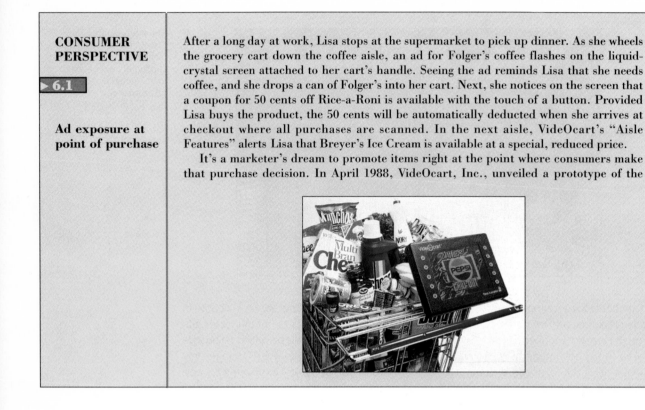

ATTENTION TO INFORMATION

Once consumers are exposed to marketing information, whether accidentally or through their own intentional behavior, the interpretation processes of attention, and then comprehension, begin (see Exhibit 6.1). What does it mean for a consumer to pay attention to marketing information in the environment such as a newspaper ad, a product display in a store, or a clerk's sales pitch? **Attention** involves focusing the cognitive system on information that is relevant to important goals and values.[12] Marketers use many creative strategies to attract consumers' attention to their products and communications.

Attention implies *selection*. Because our cognitive systems have limited capacity, only a portion of information in the environment can be chosen for interpretation; in fact, most information is ignored. In a busy department store, people attend to information selectively—they tend to see and hear what helps them achieve their purchase goals and values. Thus, consumers in a Wal-Mart store might notice signs directing them to a relevant product, grocery shoppers might read ingredient information on the food label, and someone buying a car might consider a deal from a salesperson. At the same time, these consumers can disregard what other shoppers are doing or saying or even ignore product information that doesn't seem relevant at the moment. From a means-end perspective, consumers will selectively attend to information about product attributes and consequences that is perceived as relevant to their goals and values.

Attention varies in *awareness* and *intensity*—from automatic, essentially unconscious levels to controlled, intense levels.[13] In some cases, attention is uncontrolled and unconscious. For instance, you immediately turn your head when someone calls your name, or the word *free* might automatically attract your attention. Even though your attention may be at such a low level of intensity that you are not consciously aware of attending to information, it can still influence your behavior (the bright lights in a jewelry store draw your

VideOcart, a standard grocery cart outfitted with a flat, 6- by-8-inch liquid crystal display mounted on the cart handle. The animated graphics displayed on the screen are created and stored on a personal computer. Once the weekly "show" is finalized and compiled, it is sent to each VideOcart store via high speed network communications and then transferred to the carts via a low-power FM transmitter. VideOcart can customize and change informative messages by market, chain, or individual stores at a moment's notice.

Infrared sensor devices mounted in the ceiling cause these messages to be displayed at the precise moment shoppers pass the products being referenced. The system also can convey other useful information such as an item locator, store map, recipes, and *USA TODAY*'s news, entertainment, and sports features as customers arrive at checkout.

The average supermarket has roughly 100 shopping carts, and in stores using VideOcart, approximately 60 percent of the carts are equipped with the VideOcart unit. Based on the 220 stores using the system in early 1993, nearly four million shoppers weekly are reached in the nation's top U.S. markets.

Test results suggest that VideOcart is a very powerful and effective marketing tool. On average, shoppers pushing VideOcarts spend about $1 more per visit than shoppers using regular carts. Every dollar counts when the average store has 18,000 shoppers per week.

Source: VideOcart, Inc., 1993.

attention to the products). At higher levels of intensity, people consciously focus their attention on marketing information that is relevant to their currently active goals and values. People who are thinking about buying a new bicycle are likely to selectively attend to bike ads, the dieter in a restaurant pays careful attention as the waiter recites the daily specials, or a fan of a heavy metal band listens intently to a radio announcement about a concert.

Consumer reactions to the shopping cart ads described earlier provide some insight into these varying levels of attention. ACTMEDIA, a dominant company in the cart ad business, claims cart ads increase sales of advertised brands by an average of 8 percent, but some research has found rather low levels of attention to the ads.[14] Interviews of shoppers in stores with the ad carts indicated only 60 percent of these consumers were aware of *ever* having seen any cart ads. The remaining 40 percent of shoppers, who were exposed to the ads, did not consciously attend to the ads. Only 13 percent of the shoppers interviewed were aware of seeing any ads on that particular shopping trip, and only 7 percent of the interviewed shoppers could name any brands advertised on the cart they were pushing! Apparently, only a few consumers paid enough attention to the ads to create a memory for the brand. Such results question the effectiveness of shopping cart ads. Perhaps in the crowded information environment of the supermarket, most consumers do not pay much attention to ads, even those on their grocery cart.

Many factors can influence attention to marketing information, including the consumer's general affective state, the consumer's involvement with the information, and the prominence of the information in the environment. Marketers try to influence consumers' attention by developing strategies to address these factors.

Factors influencing attention

What is Avia International, Ltd?

a. A small Italian commuter airline.

b. An up-and-coming courier service.

c. A map exporter specializing in exotic spots.

If you answered "none of the above," you might be among the 4 percent of Americans who know that Avia makes sneakers and sports apparel. According to a company vice president, Avia has a big problem: "There's a whole segment of people who are not buying our shoes because they don't know who we are." In contrast, Nike and Reebok are known by more than 70 percent of U.S. consumers.

The power of a well-known brand name, supported by strong advertising, is so great (and long lasting) that 20 of the top 25 leading brands in 1990 were also among the top 25 70 years ago. But companies find it increasingly difficult to attract the customer's attention and create brand awareness, with the clutter of new products, brands, and advertising in the environment. Today, approximately 90 percent of new products are pulled from the market within two or three years of their introduction. Most of them fail for lack of name recognition—consumers were just not aware of them.

The risks in creating a new brand are so great that many companies instead develop so-called line extensions. Rather than developing a new brand name, marketers

Affective states

A person's affective state influences his attention.[15] For instance, people in a good mood selectively attend to positive information in the environment, while people in a bad mood tend to notice negative information. Shopping when in a good mood stimulates the cognitive system to attend to favorable product attributes and benefits, and positive reasons to buy, while shopping in a bad mood tends to focus attention on negative attributes and risky consequences, and activates reasons not to purchase. A related issue is whether the affective responses created by a TV program (happy, depressed, amused, sad) can influence consumers' attention to (and comprehension of) the commercials placed within that program.[16]

Involvement

Involvement with marketing information is a motivational state that can influence selective attention and the intensity of attention.[17] Consumers who experience high levels of involvement because of an intense need (you desperately need new tires for your spring break trip) tend to focus their attention on marketing information (ads for tires) that seems relevant to their goals. A consumer's level of involvement with product information is determined by the activated means-end beliefs about the relationships between product attributes and relevant goals and values. This means-end knowledge is a function of personal and situational sources (refer back to Exhibit 5.7). Thus, hobby photographers for whom cameras are personally relevant are more likely to notice and attend to ads for photo products. Likewise, the involvement felt by consumers who need to replace a refrigerator influences them to notice and attend to ads and sales announcements.

Environmental prominence

The physical form of marketing information can influence consumers' attention. Because the most prominent information in the environment attracts the most attention, marketers often try to make their information noticeable. For instance, some radio and TV commercials are louder than the surrounding program material to capture consumers' attention.[18] Many apply their existing, well-known brand name to new products. Bud Light, diet Coke, and Liquid Tide are but a few well-known examples.

Building name recognition can be difficult and expensive, especially for small companies. Market leaders often command budgets up to 10 times greater than smaller companies. For instance, Nike spends about $100 million and Reebok $70 million on annual advertising, compared to Avia's $10 million. Coca-Cola and Pepsi-Cola can afford to spend hundreds of millions on extensive advertising campaigns and still commit a small percentage of income. Coke spent about $385 million in 1989, which was only 4 percent of its total sales of $9 billion, while Royal Crown Cola, a smaller competitor, spent upward of 40 percent of its total revenues on advertising and promotion.

Small companies that cannot afford large advertising budgets have used creative marketing strategies to gain exposure for their brands and attract consumer attention. When Nevica, a British manufacturer of high-quality ski clothing, lacked advertising funds, it offered free-lance photographers complimentary ski gear and a fee for every picture of a Nevica-clad skier published in a magazine. A lot of Nevica clothes were pictured, which increased brand awareness.

Sources: William M. Bulkeley, "It Needn't Always Cost a Bundle to Get Consumers to Notice Unknown Brands," *The Wall Street Journal*, February 14, 1991, pp. B1, B4; and Joseph Pereira, "Name of the Game: Brand Awareness," *The Wall Street Journal*, February 14, 1991, pp. B1, B4.

bakeries exhaust the fragrances of baking products onto sidewalks or into malls. Consumer Perspective 6.2 describes how large amounts of advertising can influence consumers' attention and brand awareness.

Many marketing strategies are designed to attract or maintain consumers' attention to marketing information by making the information more prominent in the environment. Other strategies attempt to increase consumers' involvement with marketing information, by addressing personal or situational sources of involvement.

Marketing implications

Personal sources of involvement

In the short run, marketers have little ability to influence consumers' personal sources of involvement for a product. Therefore, the usual approach is to analyze and understand consumers' existing means-end knowledge about the relationships between product attributes and important goals and values. Basically, marketers must identify the goals and values consumers consider most self-relevant. A successful marketing strategy should activate these meanings and link them to product attributes. The involvement thus produced should motivate consumers to attend to this information, comprehend it, and possibly use it in making a purchase decision.

For instance, many marketers of antiperspirants emphasize qualities such as "stops odor" and "stops wetness"—ordinary functional consequences of using the product. The marketers of Sure deodorant, however, identified two more self-relevant and emotionally motivating consequences of using their product—social confidence and avoiding embarrassment. They communicated these psychosocial consequences in a long-running ad campaign "Raise your hand if you're Sure," which showed coatless consumers in social situations raising their arms free of embarrassment by damp spots on their clothing. The marketers of Vaseline Intensive Care lotion identified a similar consequence to invoke the key meaning of many consumers' perceived self-relevance with hand lotion. While brands such as Touch of Sweden discussed their greaseless formula, Vaseline marketers promoted skin restoration. They communicated the implied psychosocial consequence of "looking younger" in ads showing dried-up leaves before and after rejuvenation with Intensive Care lotion.[19]

Situational sources of involvement

All marketing strategies involve creating or modifying aspects of consumers' environments. Some of these environmental stimuli may act as situational sources of involvement by creating a temporary association between a product and important self-relevant consequences. Situational sources of relevance generate higher levels of involvement and motivation to attend to marketing information. Consider consumers who receive a brochure in the mail describing a $1 million sweepstakes contest sponsored by a magazine publisher. This marketing information might generate affective feelings of excitement and personal relevance with the details of the contest. The resulting involvement could motivate consumers to maintain exposure and focus their attention on the marketing offer for magazine subscriptions that accompanies the sweepstakes announcement.

Factors affecting environmental prominence

Marketers attempt to influence the prominence of their marketing information by designing bright, colorful, or unusual packages; by developing novel advertising executions; or by setting unique prices (a sale on small items, all priced at 88 cents). Because they must attract the attention of consumers hurrying by the newsstand, magazine covers often feature objects known to have high attention value—those of celebrities, babies, or dogs, or attractive, seductively clothed models (that old standby, sex).

Vivid images attract consumers' attention and help focus it on the product.[20] Nike, for instance, places powerful graphic portrayals of athletes (wearing Nike shoes, of course) on large billboards. Window displays in retail stores attract the attention (and subsequent interest)

Vivid pictures and unusual images enhance environmental prominence and attract consumers' attention.

Just don't expect it to roar.

ANDERSEN CONSULTING
ARTHUR ANDERSEN & CO. SC

Where we go from here.

of consumers who happen to pass by. Tiffany's (the famous New York jeweler) once used a window display showing construction of a giant doll, four times larger than the figures who were working on it. The doll had nothing to do with jewelry; it was intended to attract the attention of shoppers during the busy Christmas season. Many stores use creative lighting to emphasize selected merchandise and thus attract and focus consumers' attention on their products. Mirrors are used in clothing shops and hair salons to focus consumers' attention on their appearance.

Novel or *unusual* stimuli that don't fit with the consumers' expectations can capture additional attention time to figure out what is happening. For instance, a British ad agency created a dramatic ad to attract attention to the staying qualities of an adhesive called Araldite. The agency attached a car to a billboard placed along a major road into London. The caption read, "It also sticks handles to teapots."

Even a novel placement of an ad on a page can influence consumers' attention. For instance, Sisley, a manufacturer and retailer of trendy clothing owned by Benetton, has run its print ads upside down on the back pages of magazines like *Elle* and *Outdoors.* Other marketers have experimented with ads placed sideways, in the center of a page surrounded by editorial content, or spanning the top half of two adjacent pages.

Marketers must be careful in using novel and unusual stimuli over long periods, though, because prominence due to novelty tends to wear off. Also, novelty is a relative concept. Therefore, placing a black-and-white ad in a magazine where all the other ads are in color will capture consumers' attention only as long as few other black-and-white ads are used.

The strategy of trying to attract consumer attention by making stimuli more prominent sometimes backfires. When many marketers are trying very hard to gain attention at one time and in one place, consumers may tune most of the stimuli out, giving little thought to any of them. Consider the "miracle-mile strips" of fast-food restaurants, gas stations, and discount stores—each with a large sign—that line highways in many American cities. Individually, each sign is large, bright, colorful, and vivid. Together, the signs produce clutter, and none is particularly prominent in the environment. Consumers find it easy to ignore individual signs, and their attention levels are likely to be low. Unfortunately, the typical marketing response is to put up even larger and more garish signs in hope of gaining slightly more environmental prominence. The clutter gets worse, consumer attention decreases further, and communities become outraged and pass ordinances limiting signs.

Sign clutter in Las Vegas makes it difficult for a single sign to attract consumers' attention.

Clutter is also relevant for print and television advertising (too many commercials during program breaks). To avoid the ad clutter found in most magazines, Whittle Communications severely limits the number of ads that can be put into its magazines.[21] Whittle has developed more than 40 magazines targeted at rather narrow audiences, including *GO* (Girls Only) for girls age 11 to 14 and *in View* for college-aged women. Some of these magazines have only one advertiser, thus maximizing possibilities of exposure and attention to that company's marketing messages.

COMPREHENSION OF INFORMATION

Comprehension refers to the cognitive processes by which consumers understand or make sense of their own behaviors and relevant aspects of their environment. As a key aspect of the interpretation stage in consumer decision making (see Exhibit 6.1), comprehension produces knowledge, meanings, and beliefs about concepts, objects, behaviors, and events. When attention is focused on particular information, comprehension of that information is guided and directed by relevant knowledge activated from memory. This means information is interpreted in terms of existing knowledge. The resulting knowledge, meanings, and beliefs from comprehension can be stored in memory and can be activated for use in another interpretation process. The process of creating new meanings and using them to interpret new information is ongoing.

Variations in comprehension

Exhibit 6.2 shows that comprehension processes can vary in four ways: comprehension may be automatic or controlled, produce concrete or abstract meanings, generate few or many meanings, and create weaker or stronger memories.

Automatic processing

Like attention, simple comprehension processes tend to be *automatic.* For instance, most consumers around the world who see a can of Coca-Cola or a McDonald's restaurant immediately comprehend "Coke" or "McDonald's." Direct recognition of familiar products is a simple comprehension process in that exposure to the familiar brand automatically

EXHIBIT 6.2

Variations in comprehension

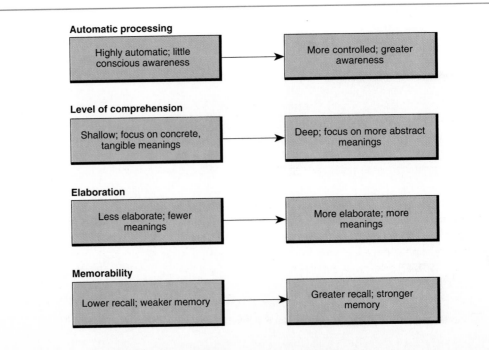

Automatic processing

| Highly automatic; little conscious awareness | → | More controlled; greater awareness |

Level of comprehension

| Shallow; focus on concrete, tangible meanings | → | Deep; focus on more abstract meanings |

Elaboration

| Less elaborate; fewer meanings | → | More elaborate; more meanings |

Memorability

| Lower recall; weaker memory | → | Greater recall; stronger memory |

activates its relevant meanings from memory—perhaps its name and other associated knowledge.

In contrast, comprehending less familiar information usually requires more conscious thought and control. Because consumers do not have well developed knowledge structures for new products or brands, they may have to construct the meanings of such things consciously (or else intentionally ignore them).

Level of comprehension

The specific meanings that consumers construct to represent products and other marketing information in their environment depend on the **level of comprehension** that occurs during interpretation.[22] Comprehension can vary in level from "shallow" to "deep." *Shallow comprehension* produces concrete meanings about tangible things. For example, a consumer could interpret a product in terms of its physical product attributes (these Nike running shoes are black, size 10, and made of leather and nylon).

Deep comprehension produces more abstract meanings that represent broader, more subjective, and more symbolic concepts. For instance, deep comprehension of product information might create meanings about the functional consequences of product use ("I can run faster in these Nike shoes") or the psychosocial and value consequences ("I feel confident when I wear these shoes"). From a means-end perspective, deeper comprehension generates product-related meanings that are more relevant to the consumer, whereas shallow comprehension tends to produce meanings about product attributes. In general, more personal meanings have greater influence in a purchase decision than shallow product meanings.

Elaboration

Comprehension also varies in extensiveness or level of **elaboration**.[23] The degree of elaboration during comprehension determines the amount of knowledge or the number of meanings produced as well as the complexity of the interconnections between those meanings. *Less elaborate (simpler) comprehension* produces few meanings connected by simple relationships, whereas *more elaborate comprehension* produces a greater number of meanings organized into more complex knowledge structures (schemas and scripts).

Memory

Both the level and elaboration of comprehension influence consumers' ability to remember the meanings that are created during comprehension.[24] First, deeper comprehension processes create more abstract, more self-relevant meanings that tend to be remembered better (better recall and recognition) than the more concrete meanings created by shallow comprehension processes. Second, more elaborate comprehension processes create greater numbers of interconnected meanings. This enhances memory because the activation of one meaning can spread and activate other connected meanings.[25] In sum, marketing strategies that stimulate consumers to engage in deeper, more elaborate comprehension processes tend to produce meanings and knowledge that consumers remember better.

Deeper, more elaborate comprehension often produces **inferences**, which are beliefs or knowledge that are not based on information directly present in the environment.[26] Inferences are interpretations that go beyond the information given. For instance, some consumers might infer (form a belief) that a product is of good quality because it is heavily advertised on TV.[27] The quality of the product is not visible in the environment; it is an inference based on other information (the amount of advertising).

Inferences are heavily influenced by consumers' knowledge that is activated during comprehension.[28] For instance, consumers who believe that more expensive brands of

Inferences during comprehension

CONSUMER PERSPECTIVE

▶ 6.3

What's in a name?

A key aspect of the marketing strategy for a new product is the brand name. Consumers can form inferences about important meanings just from the brand name—and those meanings, of course, should be consistent with the intended brand image. For instance, Ford selected a nonword, *Merkur,* for its imported car. Although the word really doesn't mean anything, it is German-sounding and connotes a high-tech image, just the meanings Ford wanted consumers to infer.

A primary function of a brand name is to differentiate the item from the competition. That is, the name should be different from other names and should help create a distinctive image (a unique network of meanings). The dominant image for most fragrances has been romance, so many of the brand names are quite similar—Cie, Ciara, Cerissa, Chimere, Cachet, and Chanel. Marketers of some fragrances have tried to create more distinctive images by using different types of names like Votre, Charlie, Scoundrel, and Babe.

The brand name should describe or connote the key meaning of the product, if possible. Consider how clearly names such as Pudding Pops frozen snacks, Liquid-Plumr drain cleaner, Head and Shoulders shampoo, Easy-Off oven cleaner, and Seduction cologne convey the product's basic function or key benefit.

Finally, a brand name should be memorable and easy to pronounce. Many believe that short names have an advantage here. For instance, the name *Acura* was selected for Honda's luxury car because it was thought to connote precision (as in accuracy), which was Honda's intended meaning. *Acura* also meets other important criteria for a coined word. Because it ends with an "a," it is read as a noun and is obviously the name of something. Also, the word begins and ends with the same letter, making it more memorable. Finally, *Acura* contains three clearly voiced syllables in only five letters, making it easy to pronounce.

In sum, the key consideration in selecting a brand name, whether short or long, is that it conveys a set of distinctive meanings that are consistent with the image intended by the marketing strategy.

Source: Daniel Doeden, "How to Select a Brand Name," *Marketing Communications*, November 1981, pp. 56–61; and Jeffrey A. Trachtenberg, "Name That Brand," *Forbes*, April 8, 1985, pp. 128, 130.

chocolates are higher in quality than cheaper brands are likely to infer that Godiva chocolates are high quality when they learn that they cost up to $20 per pound.[29] As another example, incomplete or missing product information sometimes prompts consumers to "fill in the blanks," by forming inferences based on prior knowledge.[30] For instance, consumers highly knowledgeable about clothing styles may be able to infer the country of origin and even the designer of a suit or dress merely by noticing a few details.

Inferences play a large role in the construction of means-end chains.[31] By making inferences during comprehension, consumers form beliefs about relationships between tangible attributes of a product and its functional consequences and perhaps even the psychosocial and value consequences of product use. In highly familiar products, these inferences may be made automatically without much conscious awareness. For instance, some consumers draw inferences from the color of detergent granules: blue and white seem to be *cues* connoting cleanliness. Packaging cues are another example. Hershey sells a premium-priced candy bar, Golden Almond, wrapped in gold foil, a characteristic that implies quality to many consumers. Finally, as Consumer Perspective 6.3 illustrates, even the brand name of a product can prompt consumer inferences during comprehension.

To stimulate consumers to form inferences, Kellogg's once promoted All-Bran with the headline, "At last, some news about cancer you can live with." The ads repeated the National Cancer Institute's recommendation for increasing levels of fiber in the diet and

CONSUMER
PERSPECTIVE

Cholesterol
inferences

In the 1980s, American consumers discovered cholesterol. Highly publicized research studies created means-end knowledge linking cholesterol content to lifestyle values of good health. Companies trumpeted claims about low levels of cholesterol in their products. Proliferating claims on such products as oils, margarines, and many other processed foods attracted the scrutiny of the Food and Drug Administration. So, Bob Harris, president of a small food processing company in New Jersey, found himself in trouble. In 1991, the FDA ordered him to stop using the labels "no cholesterol" and "lowest in saturated fats" for his oils, cheese substitutes, and corn oil spread. Even worse, he was enjoined from using his "Heart Beat" trademark, a brand name he had invested more than $10 million in developing.

Harris was not alone; many other claims came under FDA scrutiny, including:

Keebler cookies	Package claimed "no cholesterol," but what about saturated fat?
Procter & Gamble's Duncan Hines cake mixes	Contains no cholesterol, but what about the ingredients to be added (eggs)?
Kraft's Parkay margarine	If claims of "no cholesterol" are made, company must also disclose fat content.
Anheuser-Busch's Eagle potato chips	Although chips have no cholesterol, they do contain other forms of fat.

The FDA thought it likely that consumers would make inappropriate and/or incorrect *inferences* about the health qualities of products claiming no cholesterol. In fact, no cholesterol does not mean no fat, and many no-cholesterol products contain high levels of fat, which is not healthy. David Kessler, an FDA commissioner, announced the agency would not tolerate "deceptive claims regarding cholesterol on any products that were high in fat." He further accused American companies of "passing off half-truths to health-minded consumers."

Sources: Adapted from Bruce Ingersoll, "FDA Takes On 'No Cholesterol' Claims," *The Wall Street Journal*, May 15, 1991, pp. B1, B10; and Lois Therrien, John Carey, and Joseph Weber, "The Cholesterol Is in the Fire Now," *Business Week*, June 10, 1991, pp. 34–35.

then stated that "no cereal has more fiber" than All-Bran. Apparently, Kellogg's hoped consumers would make the inference that the product attribute of high fiber leads to the desirable consequence of reduced risk of cancer. Probably, most consumers then made additional inferences that a reduced risk of cancer helps to achieve the universal values of long life, health, and happiness. Consumer Perspective 6.4 describes some other health-related inferences that have come under government scrutiny.

Many factors affect the depth and elaboration of comprehension that occur when consumers interpret marketing information.[32] Three important influences are consumers' existing knowledge in memory, their involvement at the time of exposure, and the nature of their exposure environment. These factors influence consumers' ability to comprehend, motivation to comprehend, and opportunity to comprehend.

Factors influencing comprehension

Knowledge in memory

Consumers' *ability to comprehend* marketing information is determined largely by their knowledge in memory. The particular knowledge, meanings, and beliefs that are activated determine what level of comprehension will occur and what meanings will be produced.

Some people might see radio as the shabby relation to television. But radio delivers high exposure rates to targeted audiences, attracts attention by using offbeat ads at appropriate times of the day, and stimulates comprehension and brand awareness. Best of all, radio is cheap compared to alternative media. An ad on network radio costs only about $2.50 per thousand exposures, while the average costs per thousand are about $8 for magazine ads, $14 for prime-time TV, and $23 for newspapers.

Advertisers are beginning to appreciate radio's ability to reach narrowly targeted audiences better than TV. The most attractive (and most expensive) period for radio advertising is so-called drive time, generally from 6 to 10 A.M. and from 3 to 7 P.M. Ads aired during drive time can achieve high exposure rates because captive commuters have little else to do but listen to the radio, and almost 90 percent of them tune in at least once a week. Moreover, targeting is relatively easy with various stations drawing fairly distinct audiences.

Radio is good for attracting attention because listeners are often in a receptive mood. Burger King, for instance, directs radio spots at drivers who may be only minutes from a Burger King location. Heinz's Ore-Ida french-fried potatoes advertises during evening drive time to target women while they are thinking about dinner plans on their way home from work.

Marketing researchers often discuss consumers' knowledge in terms of expertise or familiarity.[33] *Expert consumers* are quite familiar with a product category, product forms, and specific brands. They tend to have substantial amounts of knowledge about the product. When parts of this knowledge are activated, these expert consumers can comprehend marketing information at relatively deep, elaborate levels.

Novice consumers have little prior experience or familiarity with the product or brand. They tend to have poorly organized knowledge structures, with relatively few, typically shallow meanings and beliefs. When parts of these knowledge structures are activated during exposure to marketing information, novices comprehend the information at shallow and nonelaborate levels that produce a few concrete meanings. They would need more knowledge to comprehend at a deeper, more elaborate level.

Marketers need to understand the knowledge structures of their target audience to develop effective marketing strategies that consumers can comprehend. For instance, the S. C. Johnson Company, manufacturer of Raid and other bug killers, knows that most consumers have limited technical knowledge about how insecticides work.[34] Because the customer wants to see action, the formulation for Raid bug spray allows consumers to comprehend quickly that the product works. Raid attacks bugs' central nervous systems and drives them to race around in circles before they die—a highly satisfying result for the buyer.

Involvement

Consumers' involvement with a product influences their motivation to comprehend information about the product.[35] Consumers with high personal sources of involvement associate the product with values and goals that are central to their self-concept. The involvement experienced when such self-relevant knowledge is activated motivates these consumers to comprehend the information in a deeper and more elaborate way. For instance, a person highly involved in music is likely to construct complex meanings for a new album from a favorite artist. Consumers who experience low levels of involvement when exposed to marketing information will not engage in extensive comprehension and will interpret the information at a relatively shallow, concrete level (this is a pair of socks).

What about comprehension of radio spots? Although people weaned on TV criticize radio's lack of visual cues, this might be its chief advantage. Listeners have to use their imaginations to visualize the action, and these self-generated interpretations may be more powerful than the direct representation of TV ads.

With only $1 million to spend, the Motel 6 chain saw radio as its only way to reach a national audience. Tom Bodett, the corporate spokesperson, delivered a number of folksy messages that positioned Motel 6 as the low-frills alternative to the swankier competition. "You won't find a treadmill or a weight machine like you might at those big fancy motels," he drawled in one spot aimed at business travelers, "but just take a few laps around the parking lot or down the frontage. . . . Now, you're a lean, mean working machine with a few extra bucks in your pocket."

One reason these radio spots worked so well was that listeners couldn't see Tom Bodett, so they had to form their own images of him. Customers of widely differing ages and occupations said they felt Tom was like themselves. This comprehension process created a customer/product relationship based on trust and credibility. Since beginning the radio spots, occupancy levels at Motel 6 rose to a healthy 76 percent.

Source: Reprinted by permission of *Forbes* magazine. © Forbes Inc. 1990.

Exposure environment

Various aspects of the exposure environment can affect consumers' *opportunity to comprehend* marketing information. These include factors such as time pressure, a person's affective state (a good or a bad mood), and distractions (noise, crowds). Consumers who are in a hurry and under a lot of time pressure don't have much opportunity to interpret marketing information, even though they may be motivated to do so (high involvement).[36] In this environment, they are likely to engage in relatively shallow and nonelaborate comprehension. Consumer Perspective 6.5 describes attention and comprehension in the exposure environment for radio advertising.

Savvy marketers consider these environmental factors in designing marketing strategies. Some retailers, for instance, aim for a relaxed, slow-paced environment that encourages people to slow down and comprehend all the information marketers make available. For instance, Ralph Lauren's Polo store in New York City is full of glowing wood, antique furniture, oriental carpets, and warm lighting fixtures—all to simulate an elegant English manor house. This environment helps create the desired images for the casually elegant clothing Lauren designs and sells.

Marketing implications

Marketers need to understand consumer comprehension in order to design marketing information that will be interpreted appropriately. This requires consideration of the characteristics of the target consumers and the environment where consumers are exposed to the information.[37]

Knowledge and involvement

To encourage appropriate comprehension, marketers should design their messages to fit consumers' knowledge structures and involvement (ability and motivation to comprehend). For instance, marketers of high-involvement products such as luxury cars usually want consumers to form abstract, self-relevant meanings about their products. Many of the U.S. print ads for Saab, BMW, or Mercedes-Benz include a great deal of information describing technical attributes and functional aspects of the cars. To comprehend this information at a deep, elaborate level, consumers must have fairly sophisticated knowledge about automobiles and sufficient involvement to motivate extensive interpretation processes.

For other types of products, however, marketers may not want consumers to engage in extensive comprehension processes. Sometimes marketers are interested in creating only simple, nonelaborate meanings about their product. For example, simple products (cologne or beer) are promoted largely through *image advertising,* which is not meant to be comprehended deeply or elaborately.[38] Consider the typical advertising for cigarettes or soft drinks. Often these ads contain virtually no written information beyond a brief slogan such as "Come to Marlboro Country" or "Coke is it." Most consumers probably comprehend such information in a nonelaborate way that produces an overall image and perhaps a general affective reaction, but not detailed means-end chains. Other ads, such as billboards, are reminders intended mainly to activate the brand name and keep it at a high level of "top-of-mind" awareness. In such cases, comprehension might be limited to simple brand recognition.

Remembering

Consumers' ability to recall meanings from memory is important to marketers. Because many purchase decisions are made well after exposure to marketing information, marketers usually want consumers to remember certain key meanings associated with their marketing strategy, particularly the brand name and main attributes and benefits. Retailers want consumers to remember their name and location, the types of merchandise they carry, and the dates of the big sale. Accessible knowledge in memory requires that consumers attend to the information and comprehend it at an appropriate level.

Despite the millions spent each year on advertising and other marketing strategies, much marketing information is not remembered well. For instance, few advertising slogans are accurately recalled from memory. Although some people can remember a slogan, many of them cannot associate it with the right brand name.[39] For instance, 60 percent of consumers recognized the slogan, "Never let them see you sweat," but only 4 percent correctly associated it with Dry Idea deodorant. Although 32 percent recognized "Cars that make sense," only 4 percent associated it with Hyundai. "America's business address" was recognized by 17 percent, but only 3 percent knew it was the slogan for Hilton hotels. Apparently, slogans have to be very heavily advertised to be remembered—a high scorer is General Electric's, "We bring good things to life."

Miscomprehension of marketing information

Research shows that a substantial amount of marketing information is miscomprehended, in that many consumers form inaccurate, confused, or inappropriate interpretations. In fact, all marketing information can be miscomprehended by at least some consumers.[40] Miscomprehension can range from confusion over similar brand names (see Consumer Perspective 6.6) to misinterpreting a product claim by forming an inaccurate means-end chain. It has been estimated that people may miscomprehend an average of 20 to 25 percent of the many different types of information they encounter, whether advertising or news reports.[41] Although unethical marketers may intentionally create deceptive or misleading information, most professional marketers work hard to create marketing information that is understood correctly. For those who don't, the Federal Trade Commission monitors deceptive marketing information and can force a company to correct the false beliefs it creates.[42] For instance, the Food and Drug Administration demanded that P&G's Citrus Hill orange juice stop using "fresh" on its label, when in fact the product is a processed food.[43]

Exposure environment

Many aspects of the environment in which exposure to marketing information occurs can influence consumers' comprehension processes. The type of store, for instance, can affect how consumers comprehend the product and brand sold there. Thus, for some customers, a brand of jeans purchased in a "high-image store" like Saks' or Bloomingdale's may have a

CONSUMER
PERSPECTIVE

6.6 ◄

Confusing
brand names

Marketers guard their brand names jealously. Establishing a brand name in consumers' minds (making it familiar and meaningful) usually requires a large financial investment. When another manufacturer uses the same brand name or a similar one, companies feel that their hard work and creative marketing strategy is being stolen. Lawsuits often result.

For example, Adolph Coors Co., a beer manufacturer in Golden, Colorado, filed a trademark infringement suit against Robert Corr, owner of a small Chicago company, Corr's Natural Beverages, which manufactures an eight-flavor line of "natural sodas."

The two companies reached an out-of-court settlement in which Corr's Natural Beverages agreed to change the name of its product from Corr's to Robert Corr. Corr, who claimed to be happy with the agreement, said, "It is probably better for us not to be associated in consumers' minds with a beer company."

(Photo courtesy R.J. Corr Naturals, Inc.)

Source: Reprinted with permission from AD AGE, © 1984 Crain Communications, Inc. All Rights Reserved.

more positive set of meanings than the same brand bought at Sears or Kmart. Store characteristics such as size, exterior design, or interior decoration can activate networks of meanings that influence consumers' comprehension of the products and brands displayed there.

Another aspect of the exposure environment concerns the actual content and format of the marketing information.[44] Some information may be confusing, unclear, and hard to comprehend. For instance, the volume of nutritional information on food product labels and in advertising claims can be difficult for many consumers to comprehend in a meaningful way.[45]

THE INTERPRETATION PROCESS

Interpretation is an ongoing process of sense-making or meaning creation. Interpretation involves three separate processes of exposure, attention, and comprehension. Exhibit 6.3 shows the relationships among exposure, attention, and comprehension. These interpretation processes are related in a sequence so that what happens later depends on earlier stages. An obvious example is that if exposure does not occur, attention and comprehension are not possible. Exhibit 6.3 also shows the various types and levels of interpretation

EXHIBIT 6.3

Relationships among exposure, attention, and comprehension

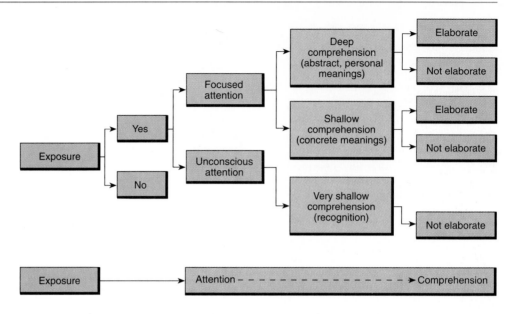

that might occur under different conditions. For instance, deep and elaborate comprehension of marketing information requires focused attention on that information.

Designing and implementing successful marketing strategies—whether price, product, promotion, or distribution—require that marketers consider the flow of effects that occur during interpretation. Marketers must consider three basic issues concerning exposure, attention, and comprehension.

1. How can I *maximize and/or maintain exposure* of the target segment of consumers to my marketing information?
2. How can I *capture and maintain the attention* of the target consumers?
3. How can I influence the target consumers to *comprehend* my marketing information at the *appropriate level of depth and elaboration*?

▶ **SUMMARY**

Learning objective 1: *Describe the differences between accidental and intentional exposure.*
Accidental exposure refers to unintentionally coming in contact with information, essentially at random. A key marketing strategy is to place marketing information in the environment where the chances of accidental exposure are maximized: ads on buses, most television commercials, most ads in magazines, and billboards on highways. Intentional exposure occurs when consumers purposefully seek out marketing information, often to decide on a purchase. An important marketing strategy is to make sure relevant information is available when and where consumers look for it. Examples include placing product brochures in the store to give to interested shoppers or training salespeople to be knowledgeable about the products they are selling.

Learning objective 2: *Define selective exposure, and give an example of how marketers can influence consumers' selective exposure to marketing information.*
Selective exposure occurs when consumers intentionally seek certain types of marketing information. For instance, consumers tend to look for information they think is relevant to a decision. Thus, consumers tend to seek out information that is linked, through means-end chains, to the important goals and values in that situation. Selective exposure also implies

This ad encourages deep, elaborate comprehension of the relationship between product and consumer.

that consumers can intentionally avoid exposure to certain types of marketing information. For instance, some consumers might immediately discard unsolicited catalogs or hang up on telemarketers before hearing the sales pitch. Many marketing strategies can be developed to influence selective exposure, including sending junk mail in an envelope like a telegram so it looks important and won't be thrown away unopened. Advertisers try to capture people's interest in the first few seconds of a TV commercial so they won't look away or leave the room. Another strategy is to place marketing information in places where consumers cannot avoid being exposed and maintaining the exposure. The VideOcart screens on grocery carts (described in the text) are one example. Another example is to show ads on TV monitors placed above the checkout aisles in some grocery stores.

Learning objective 3: *Define attention, and identify three factors that influence consumers' attention to marketing information.*

Attention involves focusing the cognitive system on information that is relevant to one's goals and values. Attention involves selecting certain information for interpretation from the vast array of potential information in the environment. Attention varies in terms of awareness (from unconscious to highly conscious) and intensity (from casual levels to highly focused levels of attention). Attention can be influenced by many factors: consumers' affective states, consumers' involvement with the information, and the prominence of the information in the environment.

Learning objective 4: *Define comprehension, and describe four ways in which comprehension can vary.*

Comprehension refers to the interpretation processes by which consumers make sense of relevant aspects of the environment as well as their own affective responses and behaviors. Comprehension processes can vary in four important ways. First, comprehension varies in the degree of processing from automatic (when a traffic light turns red, the meaning is known immediately) to more controlled comprehension (intentionally trying to figure out what something means). Second, the level of comprehension can vary from shallow to deep, from producing simple, relatively concrete meanings to producing more abstract, self-relevant meanings. Third, comprehension can vary in elaboration: few meanings versus many interrelated meanings. Fourth, comprehension varies in memorability, with lower levels of recall for some meanings and greater recall for others.

Learning objective 5: *Define inferences, and give an example.*

Inferences are beliefs that are based on more than direct information in the environment. Inferences go beyond the information given because they are partially based on consumers' knowledge in memory. For example, consumers might infer the cleaning ability of laundry detergent based on stored (perhaps unconscious) meanings about the scent or the color of the product. Inferences play a major role in the formation of means-end chains of product knowledge. During comprehension, consumers may make inferences about product attributes, consequences of product use, or abstract value outcomes. For instance, some consumers infer the quality of a product from its price or country of origin. Thirty years ago, a made-in-Japan label was interpreted as poor quality, but now most Americans infer that Japanese products are high quality. Consumers' inferences can have important marketing implications. For example, SAS Airlines worries about coffee stains on the seat trays because some consumers might infer from this that engine maintenance is poor if the company can't even keep the plane clean.

Learning objective 6: *Describe how consumers' knowledge (expertise) influences their comprehension of marketing information.*

Consumers vary considerably in their knowledge or expertise concerning products. For example, expert consumers know a great deal about cars, while novice consumers know little. The amount of knowledge affects comprehension processes. More knowledgeable consumers are able to comprehend complex product information at a deeper and more personal level because they understand the means-end connections between product attributes and relevant consequences. In contrast, novice consumers are likely to have difficulty comprehending complex product information. They may be able to form meanings and beliefs only about rather concrete product attributes or simple functional consequences. These variations in consumer expertise suggest that marketers need to understand the type and amount of knowledge their target consumers have about the product category so they can create marketing information that "fits" these knowledge structures and is comprehended appropriately.

Learning objective 7: *Describe how comprehension processes can influence consumers' ability to recall marketing information.*

Typically, marketers want consumers to recall marketing information and use it in making a purchase decision. Consumers' ability to remember marketing information depends on the comprehension processes used to interpret the information. Deeper, more elaborate comprehension tends to create more memorable knowledge, meanings, and beliefs in memory. That is, knowledge that is more related to personal goals and values and is more richly interrelated with other knowledge tends to be easier to call up from memory. Thus, marketers who wish their marketing information to be well remembered should design information that consumers will process at deeper, more elaborate levels.

► **KEY TERMS AND CONCEPTS**

exposure	selective exposure	level of comprehesion
intentional exposure	attention	elaboration
accidental exposure	comprehension	inferences

1. Describe accidental and intentional exposure to marketing information in the context of a retail clothing store. Identify a clothing product such as socks or suits, and discuss effective marketing strategies for both types of exposure.

2. Choose a product (such as breakfast cereal or compact discs), and describe two factors that influence consumers' selective exposure to product information. How can marketers influence consumers' selective exposure to marketing information?

3. Describe two marketing strategies that could influence consumers' attention to marketing information for a product.

4. Consumers may engage in automatic processing during comprehension of marketing information. What are two marketing implications of such automatic processing?

5. Describe the differences in the knowledge, meanings, and beliefs that are produced by varying levels of comprehension. By example, explain when marketers should encourage shallow comprehension of their marketing information. Deep comprehension?

6. Describe the differences in the knowledge, meanings, and beliefs that are produced by more elaborate and less elaborate comprehension processes. By example, explain when marketers should encourage, or when they should discourage elaborate comprehension of their marketing information.

7. Discuss how consumers' existing knowledge structures and their level of involvement can influence their (a) attention to and (b) comprehension of marketing information about the prices (or some other attribute) of brands in a product category.

8. Identify three factors that can affect the inferences formed during comprehension of ads for a packaged food product. Give two examples of marketing strategies that could influence the inferences consumers form.

9. Describe a marketing strategy that you think might result in consumer miscomprehension. Discuss how miscomprehension might occur in this case, and describe how a marketer might reduce the chances of miscomprehension.

10. Discuss how interpretation processes of attention and comprehension can influence consumers' ability to recall marketing information. Give an example of a marketing strategy designed to influence this recall.

▶ REVIEW AND DISCUSSION QUESTIONS

7

Attitudes and Intentions

LEARNING OBJECTIVES

After completing this chapter, you should be able to:

► 1. Define attitude, and give two examples of its relevance for marketers.

► 2. Describe salient beliefs, and give an example of how marketers can influence belief salience.

► 3. Using the multiattribute attitude model as a guide, describe the information integration process by which consumers form an A_o.

► 4. Describe four attitude-change strategies based on the multiattribute attitude model.

► 5. Explain how A_o differs from A_{act}.

► 6. Describe how the components of the theory of reasoned action are combined to create a behavioral intention.

► 7. Identify three factors that can reduce the accuracy of a measure of behavioral intention in predicting the actual behavior.

JAGUAR MAKES THE BIG LEAP

In the early 1980s, Jaguar was in desperate shape. Sales were falling, especially in the United States. Product quality was terrible, and owners had developed increasingly negative attitudes toward the company, the car, and the dealers. Then, almost at the last minute, Jaguar pulled itself back from the brink.

The problem with Jaguar was not that the cars were uninteresting; to the contrary, few automobiles had such passionate owners. But in the early 1980s, these passions were mostly negative. Jokes about Jaguar abounded, such as "Jaguar will soon begin selling its cars in pairs, so you can have one to drive while the other is in the shop." J. D. Power, the market research company that regularly measures consumer attitudes toward automobiles, did not include Jaguar in its studies because so few owners were willing even to discuss owning one. Unfortunately, the beliefs and attitudes of Jaguar owners accurately reflected reality—there were serious quality and reliability problems.

Finally, Jaguar management, factory workers, and dealers set out to save the company. They took drastic measures to improve production quality and dealer service. As these began to work, the company boldly doubled the warranty to two years. Customer beliefs and attitudes started to change, and sales increased dramatically. To learn firsthand what owners felt about their cars, Jaguar management began to track consumer attitudes and hired the J. D. Power research company to interview several hundred buyers each month. Then Power tracked these customers by measuring their attitudes and beliefs after 1, 8, and 18 months.

The early results showed that consumers believed the cars were better. By mid-1983, Jaguar scored about average among all makes on consumer satisfaction, although attitudes toward dealer service were still poor. Jaguar again took strong action to improve service, terminating about 20 percent of its worst dealers. That, combined with continued improvements in production quality and service, produced the single biggest jump in favorable consumer attitudes ever recorded. By 1985, Jaguar had taken fifth place in the United States in favorable consumer attitudes, right behind Honda and ahead of Mazda. In the luxury car market, only Mercedes-Benz topped Jaguar. The turnaround in consumer attitudes had succeeded.[1] Company sources report however, that Jaguar has found the most effective persuasion is good word-of-mouth advertising or independent surveys, such as J. D. Power, rather than hype.

Consumer attitudes are important for understanding consumer behavior. Marketing managers, like those at Jaguar, spend millions of dollars each year researching consumer attitudes toward products and brands. They spend many more millions on advertising, sales promotion, and other sorts of communication to influence those attitudes. By modifying consumer attitudes, marketers hope to influence purchase behavior.

In this chapter, we examine two types of attitude—attitudes toward objects and attitudes toward behaviors. We begin by defining attitude. Then, we describe the integration process by which people combine beliefs to form attitudes toward objects in their environment. Next, we distinguish between attitudes toward objects and behaviors. We then discuss how knowledge is integrated to form attitudes toward behaviors and intentions to perform specific behaviors. Finally, we discuss the relationship between behavioral intentions and actual behaviors. All these attitude issues have implications for marketing strategy.

WHAT IS ATTITUDE?

Attitude has been a key concept in psychology for more than a century, and more than 100 definitions and 500 measures of attitudes have been proposed.[2] Nearly all these conceptions of attitude have one thing in common: they refer to people's evaluations. We define **attitude** as a person's *overall evaluation of a concept*.[3] The concept can be an object (including products, services, or ideas) or a behavior, and the evaluations can be created by both the affective and cognitive systems.

Evaluations created by the affective system are immediate, automatic, positive or negative reactions to simple objects or behaviors. These affective responses are at relatively low levels of intensity and arousal (refer back to Exhibit 4.2) and are produced without conscious, cognitive processing of information. Examples are people's immediate affective responses to the taste of spicy chili or chocolate ice cream, the color of a new car, or another person's appearance. An attitude is formed when these affective evaluatives become associated with a product or brand through the classical conditioning process, which is discussed in Chapter 11.[4]

In this chapter, we treat *attitudes as evaluations produced by the cognitive (not the affective) system*. These **evaluations** take the form of pro/con, favorable/unfavorable, like/dislike judgments of an object or behavior. The model of consumer decision making in Exhibit 7.1 (p. 134) shows that people form an overall evaluation or attitude toward a concept by integrating or combining relevant knowledge, meanings, or beliefs about the concept. The purpose of this **integration process** is to evaluate the concept in terms of its *personal relevance* for the individual consumer. In means-end terms, consumers judge whether the concept has good or bad attributes and favorable or unfavorable consequences—"What does this concept have to do with me? Does this object have positive attributes? Is this a good or bad thing for me? Do I like or dislike this object?"

Exhibit 7.1 shows that the evaluations produced in the integration process may be stored in memory. Once an attitude has been formed and stored in memory, the consumer does not have to repeat the integration process to reconstruct the attitude. Instead, the preformed attitude can be activated from memory and used to interpret new information or be integrated with other knowledge in making a decision.[5] These existing attitudes can have a strong influence on consumers' cognitive processes. This is the reason researchers conduct "blind" taste tests where consumers do not know what brands they are tasting. This approach avoids activating brand attitudes that could bias the taste judgments.

We measure attitudes simply and directly by asking consumers to evaluate the concept of interest. For instance, marketing researchers might ask consumers to indicate their attitudes toward McDonald's french fries on three evaluative scales:

McDonald's French Fries

Extremely Unfavorable	-3	-2	-1	0	$+1$	$+2$	$+3$	Extremely Favorable
Dislike Very Much	-3	-2	-1	0	$+1$	$+2$	$+3$	Like Very Much
Very Bad	-3	-2	-1	0	$+1$	$+2$	$+3$	Very Good

The overall attitude toward McDonald's french fries is measured by the average rating across the evaluative scales. Note that attitudes in this case can vary from *negative* (ratings of -3, -2, -1) through *neutral* (a rating of 0) to *positive* (ratings of $+1$, $+2$, or $+3$). Also note that attitudes are not necessarily intense or extreme. On the contrary, consumers can have essentially neutral evaluations (neither favorable nor unfavorable) toward relatively unimportant, noninvolving concepts. A neutral evaluation is still an attitude, however, although probably a weakly held one. Consumer Perspective 7.1 describes the problems marketers face in dealing with brands toward which consumers hold weak attitudes.

Attitudes toward what?

Attitudes are always *toward* some concept. We can distinguish between two broad types of concepts—objects and behaviors. Consumers can have *attitudes toward objects in the physical and social environment* (A_o) such as products, brands, models, stores, or people (a salesperson at the camera store), as well as aspects of marketing strategy (a rebate offer from General Motors; an ad for Wrigley's chewing gum). Consumers also can have attitudes toward imaginary objects and concepts (an ideal desk chair, a fair price for gasoline, capitalism). Second, consumers can have *attitudes toward their own behaviors or actions* (A_{act}) including their past behaviors (buying that sweater was stupid), current actions (I like talking to this salesperson), and future behaviors (I am looking forward to going to the mall tomorrow afternoon).

Many consumers had positive attitudes toward Absolut vodka in part because of clever ads like these.

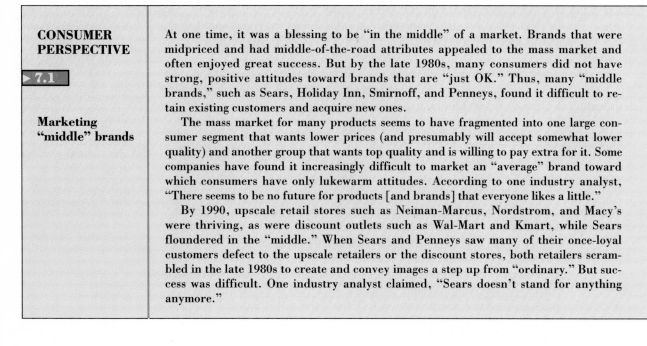

Consumers can have distinct attitudes toward many variations or levels of essentially the same product or brand, and these attitudes may be quite different. Exhibit 7.2 shows several attitude concepts for fast-food restaurants that vary in level of specificity. We can say that Rich has a moderately positive attitude toward fast-food restaurants (the product class), but he has a highly favorable attitude toward hamburger restaurants (one product form). His attitude toward McDonald's, a specific brand of

EXHIBIT 7.1

A model of consumer decision making

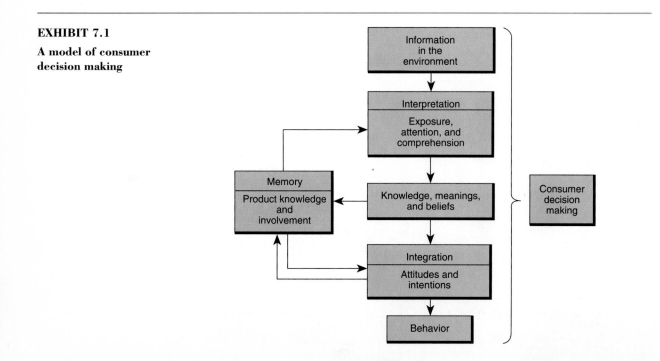

This same phenomenon has occurred in other markets as consumers moved away from acceptable brands with only moderately positive attitudes to brands that generate more excitement and stronger attitudes. Consider the problems of Smirnoff vodka, a middle brand selling for a moderate $6 to $9 a bottle. Although Smirnoff was still the number one brand in the United States in 1990, sales of the higher-priced, imported brands such as Stolichnaya, Finlandia, and Absolut had gained more than 20 percent in the previous year, while sales of Smirnoff were flat. In response, Smirnoff tried to enhance its image and create more positive consumer attitudes by raising prices and running ads with a more upscale look.

As another example, sales of the upscale ice cream brands such as Haagen-Dazs and Ben and Jerry's increased along with those of the cheaper store brands. At the same time, sales for the middle brands were stagnant. Middle brands such as Sealtest tried such marketing strategies as adding a cellophane flap to retard formation of ice crystals and modernizing the package graphics, while maintaining the price at about $3 a half-gallon. Sealtest hoped to convey higher value to the consumer and thereby improve brand attitudes.

Source: Reprinted by permission of *The Wall Street Journal*, © 1990 Dow Jones & Company, Inc. All Rights Reserved Worldwide.

hamburger restaurant, however, is only slightly favorable (he prefers Wendy's). Finally, his attitude toward a particular "model"—the McDonald's on the corner of Grant and Main—is somewhat negative (he had an unpleasant meal there).

Some attitude concepts can be defined in terms of a particular behavior and situation (eating dinner with the kids at the Grant Street McDonald's after a soccer game).

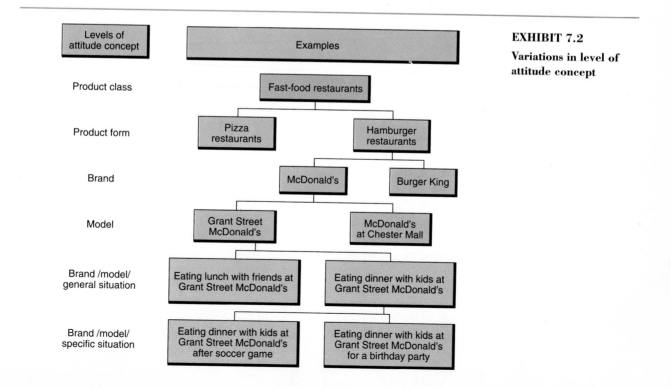

EXHIBIT 7.2

Variations in level of attitude concept

Consumers can have different attitudes toward these concepts that are not necessarily consistent. Rich, for instance, has an unfavorable attitude toward eating lunch with his friends at the Grant Street McDonald's (he'd rather go to a full-service restaurant), but he has a somewhat favorable attitude toward eating dinner there with his kids (it's easy and fast).

Note that although the same McDonald's "object" is present in each of these concepts, Rich's attitudes are toward the *combination* of the object and situation, which is quite a different concept from the object alone.[6] Because consumers can have very different attitudes toward only slightly different attitude concepts, *marketers must precisely identify the attitude concept that is most relevant to the marketing problem of interest.*

Marketing implications

Consumer brand attitudes are the subject of much marketing research. Two application areas are brand equity and attitude tracking studies.

Brand equity

Brand equity refers to the *value* of the brand.[7] Adding the Marriott name to Fairfield Inn, for instance, is estimated to have increased occupancy rates by 15 percent, which can be seen as a tangible indication of the value of the Marriott brand. Hitachi, a Japanese electronics company, and GE once co-owned a factory in England that made identical televisions for both companies.[8] The only differences were the brand name on the set and a $75 higher price for the Hitachi, reflecting its greater brand equity value. From the marketer's perspective, brand equity implies higher profits, more cash flow, and greater market share.

The consumer/brand relationship is the basis for brand equity, and brand attitude is an important aspect of that relationship. Brand equity involves a *positive brand attitude* (a favorable evaluation of the brand) based on favorable meanings and beliefs about the brand. Strong and consistently positive brand attitudes are an important asset for a company. Consumer Perspective 7.2 illustrates the importance of attitudes in brand equity.

Basically, marketers have three ways to get brand equity: they can build it, borrow it, or buy it. Companies can *build brand equity* by ensuring the brand actually delivers relevant consequences and by communicating these important consequences through consistent advertising. Consider the considerable brand equity developed over time by Campbell's soup, Green Giant vegetables, Mercedes-Benz automobiles, and NutraSweet artificial sweetener. When Anheuser-Busch created the Eagle brand of snack foods, it invested heavily in advertising and promotion to create positive consumer attitudes and brand equity.

Companies can *borrow brand equity* by associating a positive brand name with other products. For example, Tide no longer refers to only one type of detergent. When the brand name is extended to other products (Liquid Tide, Ultra Tide), the notion is that some of Tide's original equity is passed along to these new products. Brand extension is an increasingly popular marketing strategy. Coca-Cola once produced a single product, but now the product line includes Coca-Cola Classic, Coke, diet Coke, Caffeine-Free Coke, and Cherry Coke. How brand equity is transferred by brand name extensions is still an issue for research. The success of a brand extension may depend on the key meanings consumers associate with a brand name and whether those meanings are appropriate for the new product.[9]

Finally, a company can *buy brand equity* by purchasing brands that enjoy strong consumer attitudes. The rash of mergers and leveraged buyouts of the 1980s was motivated partially by a desire to buy brands with equity clout. For instance, when Grand

CONSUMER
PERSPECTIVE

7.2

Brand equity
and brand
attitudes

From a means-end perspective, equity is based on the degree to which consumers value the consequences the brand delivers. A key aspect of equity is substitutability. For instance, Suzy and Julie are next-door neighbors who routinely buy Parkay margarine. Each receives an advertisement and coupon for Promise margarine. On their next shopping trips, Julie buys a pound of Promise, but Suzy buys her usual pound of Parkay. These different behaviors are determined by their beliefs and attitudes, or their perceptions of brand equity. Julie believes Promise is essentially the same as Parkay, so she switches brands when offered the small inducement of the coupon. Suzy, however, believes Parkay is the superior product, and she will buy it "no matter what."

People like Suzy are a marketer's dream because they create brand equity. If a brand has high equity, it is less vulnerable to competition. Consumers are less willing to accept substitutes for a brand with high equity, because they want the consequences they believe the brand uniquely provides. Thus, marketers have to spend less money promoting brands with strong equity. This, in turn, makes high-equity brands more profitable.

Source: Gretchen Morgenson, "The Trend Is Not Their Friend," *Forbes*, September 16, 1991, pp. 114–19; and William Moran and Kenneth Longman, "Boosting Profit Potential," *Marketing Insights*, Summer 1991, pp. 24–32.

Metropolitan bought Pillsbury and Philip Morris bought Kraft, they acquired the equity associated with all those brands.

Attitude tracking studies

Large-scale attitude surveys, called *tracking studies,* are conducted to monitor brand attitudes over time. The results of such surveys can indicate the success of marketing

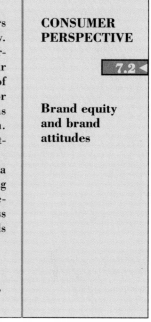

Bristol-Myers Squibb's brands have built up considerable brand equity as reflected by their leadership positions in many product categories.

strategies intended to influence attitudes toward a brand. As these studies identify trends in consumer attitudes, marketers can adjust their marketing strategies, as Jaguar did in the opening example.

An example of a company that failed to track increasingly unfavorable consumer attitudes is Howard Johnson's, one of the original restaurant chains in the United States. During the highway building boom in the 1950s and 1960s, HoJo's was known as a nice place with clean rooms, predictable but wholesome food, and ice cream the kids would like. Consumer attitudes were positive, and Howard Johnson's prospered. But over the next 20 years, HoJo's did not monitor customer attitudes well, nor did it respond effectively to the strategies of competitors passing them by. Howard Johnson's used informal gauges of consumer attitudes, such as comment cards left on restaurant tables, while competitors such as Marriott, Denny's, and McDonald's ran sophisticated market tests that told them what customers liked and didn't like. Marriott bought the once-powerful chain of Howard Johnson's restaurants in 1985.[10]

ATTITUDES TOWARD OBJECTS

Consumers form **attitudes toward objects (A_o)** such as products, brands, and stores by integrating or combining selected product knowledge, meanings, and beliefs to form an overall evaluation of the object (see Exhibit 7.1). The relevant knowledge, meanings, and beliefs that are integrated may be produced by interpretation processes or activated from memory.

Salient beliefs

Consumers acquire many beliefs about products, brands, and other objects in their environments (stores, catalogs, a salesperson) through their past experiences. Exhibit 7.3 presents some of the beliefs a consumer might have about Crest toothpaste. These beliefs are organized in an associative network of linked meanings that is stored in memory. Because the cognitive system has a limited capacity, only a few of all the beliefs in a consumer's memory can be activated and integrated consciously when a person evaluates an object. These few activated beliefs (highlighted in Exhibit 7.3) are called **salient beliefs**, and it is only these beliefs that influence a person's attitude toward a concept.[11] Understanding consumer attitudes requires that marketers understand salient consumer beliefs.

Consumers can have salient beliefs about any level of meaning in a means-end chain, including the attributes of a product (Russell sweatshirts are made of thick material), its functional and psychosocial consequences (Russell sweatshirts keep me warm), and/or the values it might help achieve (I can relax in a Russell sweatshirt). Other beliefs such as the product's country of origin (made in Japan, Taiwan, or Mexico) may be salient in certain circumstances.[12] Consumers also can have salient beliefs about various tactile, olfactory, and visual images (this blouse feels good, these tacos smell spicy, that car looks like a boat). If activated from memory, any type of belief can be salient and influence a consumer's attitude toward a product.

The multiattribute attitude model

The **multiattribute attitude model** attempts to explain how consumers' salient beliefs about the multiple attributes of an object influence their attitudes toward the object. Several versions of the multiattribute attitude model have been proposed, but all take the same basic approach.[13] The key idea is that consumers' overall attitudes toward an object (A_o) are based on two things: the *strength* of their salient beliefs about the attributes of the object and their *evaluation* of those beliefs.[14] Simply put, the multiattribute attitude model proposes that people like objects they believe are associated with "good" characteristics and dislike objects they believe to have "bad" attributes.

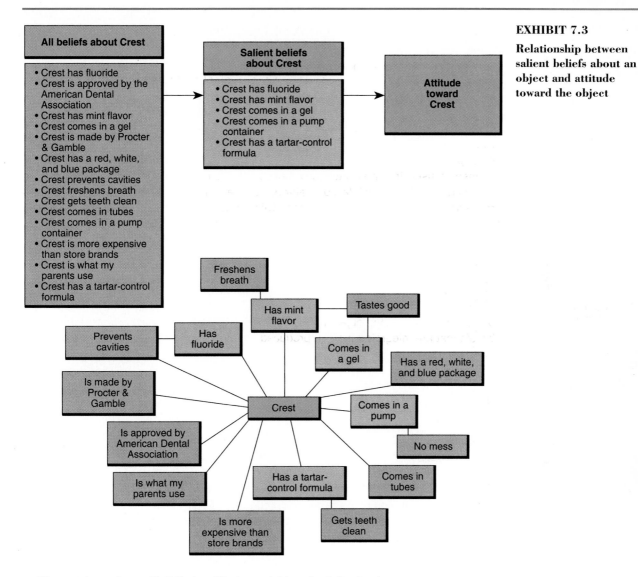

EXHIBIT 7.3

Relationship between salient beliefs about an object and attitude toward the object

The most popular multiattribute attitude model has the following form:

$$A_o = \sum_{i=1}^{n} b_i e_i$$

where

A_o = Attitude toward the object

b_i = The strength of the belief that the object has attribute i

e_i = The evaluation of attribute i

n = The number of salient beliefs about the object

This multiattribute attitude model describes an integration process by which product knowledge (the evaluation and strength of salient beliefs) can be combined to form an overall evaluation or attitude. It is not meant to indicate, however, that consumers mentally multiply belief strength and evaluation when forming attitudes toward objects. Rather, it is designed to

EXHIBIT 7.4

An example of the multiattribute attitude model

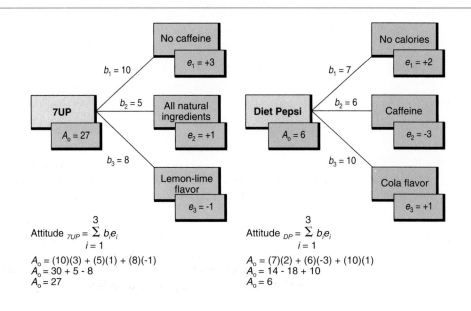

$$\text{Attitude}_{7UP} = \sum_{i=1}^{3} b_i e_i$$

$A_o = (10)(3) + (5)(1) + (8)(-1)$
$A_o = 30 + 5 - 8$
$A_o = 27$

$$\text{Attitude}_{DP} = \sum_{i=1}^{3} b_i e_i$$

$A_o = (7)(2) + (6)(-3) + (10)(1)$
$A_o = 14 - 18 + 10$
$A_o = 6$

predict the attitude produced by the actual integration process. We see the multiattribute model as a useful tool for investigating attitude formation and predicting attitudes.

The typical number of salient beliefs about an attitude object is unlikely to exceed seven to nine.[15] Given the limited capacity of the cognitive system, we might expect even fewer salient beliefs for many objects. In fact, brand attitudes for low-involvement products might be based on very few salient beliefs, perhaps only one or two.

Exhibit 7.4 illustrates how the *strength* and *evaluation* of salient beliefs are combined in the multiattribute model to predict attitudes toward two brands of soft drinks. Note that this hypothetical consumer has salient beliefs about three attributes for each brand. These beliefs differ in content, strength, and evaluation. The multiattribute model predicts this consumer will have a more favorable attitude toward 7UP than toward Diet Pepsi.

Belief strength (b_i) is the perceived probability of association between an object and some relevant attribute. Belief strength can be measured by asking consumers to rate this probability of association for each of their salient beliefs:

"How likely is it that 7UP has no caffeine?"

Extremely unlikely   1 2 3 4 5 6 7 8 9 10   Extremely likely

"How likely is it that 7UP is made from all natural ingredients?"

Extremely unlikely   1 2 3 4 5 6 7 8 9 10   Extremely likely

Consumers who are quite certain that 7UP has no caffeine would indicate a very strong belief strength, perhaps 9 or 10. Consumers who have only a moderately strong belief that 7UP is made from only natural ingredients might rate their belief strength as 5 or 6.

The strength of consumers' product or brand beliefs is affected by their past experiences with the object. Beliefs about product attributes or consequences tend to be stronger when they are based on actual use of the product. Beliefs formed indirectly from mass advertising or conversation with a salesperson tend to be weaker. For instance, consumers are more likely to form a strong belief that "7UP tastes good" if they actually drink some and taste it themselves than if they read a product claim in an advertisement.[16] These stronger beliefs based on direct experience tend to have a greater impact on A_o, so marketers try to give their potential customers actual use experience with their product. They may distribute free samples; sell small, less-expensive trial sizes; offer cents-off coupons; or have a no-obligation trial policy.

The **evaluation (e_i)** associated with each salient belief reflects how favorably the consumer perceives that attribute. Marketers measure the e_i component by having consumers indicate their evaluation of (favorability toward) each salient belief, as shown below.

"Sodas that have no caffeine"

Very bad   −3   −2   −1   0   +1   +2   +3   Very good

"Sodas with all natural ingredients"

Very bad   −3   −2   −1   0   +1   +2   +3   Very good

Exhibit 7.4 shows how the evaluation of each salient belief influences the overall A_o in proportion to the strength of that belief (b_i). Thus, strong beliefs about positive attributes have greater effects on A_o than do weak beliefs about equally positive attributes. Likewise, negative evaluations reduce the favorability of A_o in proportion to their belief strength "weights."

Marketers have been using multiattribute attitude models since the late 1960s to understand consumer behavior. The models are popular because managers find them appealing and relatively easy to use.[17] Three of the many applications of these models are understanding customers, diagnosing marketing strategies, and understanding environmental influences.

Marketing implications

Understanding customers
The multiattribute attitude model is useful for understanding which attributes are the most salient or important to consumers. For instance, airline passengers are loud in complaining about the food served on planes.[18] Yet in a 1988 survey, only 40 percent of passengers rated good food and beverage service as important, while other attributes were seen as much more important, including convenient schedules (over 90 percent), fast check-in (about 80 percent), comfortable seats (about 80 percent), and good on-time performance (about 85 percent). Perhaps airlines use such data to justify not improving the quality of the food they serve (airlines spend only about $4.25 per passenger on food). Of course, the relative importance of different product attributes varies across market segments. For instance, three segments of the airline market—light travelers (1 or 2 trips per year), moderate travelers (3 to 9 trips per year), and frequent travelers (10 or more trips per year)—evaluate some attributes differently. Light travelers have greater concerns about safety and efficient baggage handling, while heavier travelers are more concerned with convenient schedules and the frequent-flyer program.

Diagnosing marketing strategies
Although multiattribute models were developed to predict overall attitudes, marketers often use them to diagnose marketing strategies. By examining the salient beliefs that underlie attitudes toward various brands, marketers can learn whether their strategies are influencing those beliefs and make adjustments to improve their effectiveness. For instance, in the "value conscious" 1990s, marketers found that many consumers were more concerned with price and with the quality and value of products relative to price.[19] It became fashionable to seek a bargain, spend one's money wisely, and not overpay for quality. Many companies adjusted their strategies in light of these beliefs and values. Consider the motto of the world's largest retailer, Wal-Mart, "The low price on the brands you trust." Southwest Airlines combined low fares with friendly, but bare-bones service to enhance consumers' value beliefs and overall attitudes. Taco Bell reduced its operating costs enough to price several items on the menu under $1 and create stronger beliefs about the value provided. Consumer Perspective 7.3 presents another example of marketing strategies directed at consumers' beliefs about value.

CONSUMER PERSPECTIVE

> 7.3

My value is bigger than your value

In focus groups conducted in 1989 and 1990, marketers at MasterCard International recognized changes in consumer beliefs about the importance of quality, value, and thrift. For instance, an ad showing a young woman buying a diamond for herself with a Gold MasterCard was rejected by nearly all participants, although the ad had elicited favorable attitudes only 18 months earlier.

MasterCard changed its marketing strategy accordingly. During the latter 1980s, the motif had been "Master the possibilities," a theme that focused on self-indulgence and buying all the things one wanted. Ads for the 1990s became much more basic, describing such things as how MasterCard can access cash machines at convenient times. The company also ran a holiday season promotion in 1991 called "Master Values," which offered cardholders a 10 to 25 percent discount for purchases made at stores such as Kmart and the Dress Barn.

Sears markets its competitive Discover card using a similar "no-frills" approach, including no annual fee and 1 percent rebate on charges made with the card. Launched in 1986, the Discover Card had gained $19 billion in business by 1990.

All this was serious competition for American Express, which charges annual fees of $55 and up for its card. AmEx continued to follow its established marketing strategy, which is based largely on prestige and status. The immediate response to the Visa challenge was to offer more upscale frills with the prestige Gold Card, including free travel checks by phone or earning points good for a free tennis lesson from Ivan Lendl.

Source: Christopher Power, "Card Wars: My Value Is Bigger Than Your Value," *Business Week*, November 11, 1991, p. 138.

Understanding environmental influences

Finally, marketers can also use the multiattribute attitude model to examine the influence of the product use environment on the relative salience of beliefs about product attributes. The usage environment can vary in many ways, including time of day, presence of others, physical setting, weather, or hundreds of other variables. These environmental factors influence which beliefs are activated from memory, which in turn influences attitudes toward the brands that might be purchased for use in that situation. A study of snack products, for example, found that beliefs about economy and taste were most important in three common snacking situations—for everyday desserts at home, for watching TV in the evening,

Shopping for bargains during a semi-annual sale is consistent with the values held by many consumers.

and for kids' school lunches.[20] However, beliefs about nutrition and convenience were most important in the environmental situation of providing snacks for a children's party. Different salient beliefs in various usage environments can lead to different brand attitudes in those situations.

ATTITUDE-CHANGE STRATEGIES

The multiattribute model is a useful guide for devising **attitude-change strategies**.[21] Basically, a marketer has four ways of changing consumers' attitudes: (1) add a new salient belief about the attitude object—ideally, one with a positive e_i; (2) change the strength of an existing belief; (3) increase the evaluation of a strongly held belief; or (4) make an existing favorable belief more salient.

Add a new salient belief

Adding a new salient belief to the beliefs that consumers already have about a product or brand is probably the most common attitude-change strategy. This strategy may require an actual change in the product. Hasbro Inc. is the biggest and perhaps the most successful toy market in the United States.[22] One of Hasbro's marketing strengths is its ability to manage "old" products effectively, which involves adding new attributes and creating new salient beliefs for these products. In fact, its goal is to achieve 70 percent of revenues from existing products. In 1989, for example, as its G.I. Joe sales dropped, Hasbro discovered that many kids were becoming bored with the figures (attitudes were becoming less favorable). In response, Hasbro redesigned 80 percent of the line by discarding old attributes such as combat fatigues and adding new attributes such as spacesuits, jetpacks, and combat helicopters. Kids loved the new look, and sales jumped back quickly. As another example, when Hasbro acquired the languishing Tonka brand of toy trucks and other vehicles, the company considered adding a salient attribute to the Tonka brand—a lifetime guarantee—to strengthen positive consumer attitudes.

Change strength of salient belief

Marketers can also try to change attitudes by *changing the strength of already salient beliefs.* They can attempt to increase the strength of beliefs about positive attributes and consequences; or they can decrease the strength of beliefs about negative attributes and consequences. Consider the $10 million promotion campaign developed by the Beef Industry Council to develop more favorable attitudes toward beef. Beef consumption had fallen steadily from a high of 94 pounds per capita in 1976 to about 75 pounds in 1985. At the same time, consumption of chicken rose from 43 to 70 pounds per capita. Consumers' attitudes also changed dramatically as the percentage of people who described themselves as meat lovers dropped from 22 percent in 1983 to only 10 percent in 1985. To weaken consumers' negative beliefs that beef is fattening and has high levels of cholesterol, TV and print ads claimed that three ounces of trimmed sirloin has about the same calories and cholesterol as three ounces of chicken breast. To strengthen consumer beliefs that beef is healthful, charts displayed at many supermarket meat counters showed the calorie and cholesterol levels for a cut of beef comparing favorably with the dietary standards recommended by the American Heart Association.

Change evaluation of existing belief

Marketers can try to change consumers' attitudes by *changing evaluations of an existing, strongly held belief* about a salient attribute. They can do this by linking a more positive consequence to that attribute, with the aim of changing the consumer's means-end knowledge. Cereal manufacturers such as Kellogg's, for instance, have tried to enhance consumer attitudes toward cereal brands by linking the food attribute fiber to cancer prevention. Along the same line, consider how evaluations of food attributes have changed (in the United States, at least) as their means-end meanings have changed.[23] Attributes such as butterfat or egg yolks once were seen as favorable because they gave foods a rich, satisfying taste. But by the late 1980s, they were becoming negative attributes, while attributes once seen as rather

This ad attempts to change the strength of consumer beliefs that beef is not as healthful as other meats such as chicken.

undesirable such as low fat or low salt were becoming more highly valued. For instance, Sealtest linked nonfat characteristics of Sealtest Free ice cream to important values such as health and fitness. Likewise, Kraft linked the key attributes of its fat-free line of salad dressings and mayonnaise (egg whites, skim milk, cellulose gel, and various gums) to important health consequences and values (lower risk of heart disease and longer life).

Make existing belief more salient

The final strategy for changing consumer attitudes is to *make an existing favorable belief more salient,* usually by convincing consumers that an attribute is more self-relevant than it once seemed. This strategy is similar to the previous one, in that it attempts to link an

EXHIBIT 7.5

Relationships between beliefs, attitude, and behaviors regarding a specific object

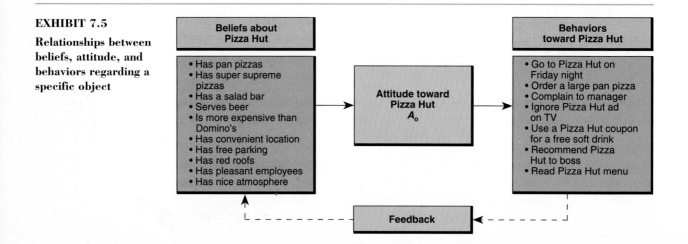

attribute to valued consequences and values. Creating such means-end chains increases both the salience of consumers' beliefs about the attribute as well as the evaluations (e_i) of those beliefs. For example, the marketing strategies of sun lotion manufacturers such as Bain de Soleil and Hawaiian Tropic emphasize the perceived risks of not using products with a sunscreen attribute. By linking the sunscreen attribute to important ends such as lessening the risk of skin cancer and avoiding premature wrinkling, marketers sought to make the sunscreen attribute more salient (more self-relevant) for consumers. Such means-end chains are intended to make sunscreen beliefs more salient and more influential during decision making.

ATTITUDES TOWARD BEHAVIORS

Consumer attitudes toward products and brands have been the subject of extensive research, but it is consumers' actual behaviors in which marketers are most interested, especially their purchasing behaviors. Many managers expect a strong relationship between a consumer's attitude toward an object (A_o) and his or her purchase of that same object. Thus, a marketer might measure consumers' attitudes toward Pizza Hut and use those attitudes to predict whether each person will purchase a pizza at Pizza Hut in the next two weeks. Although this approach might seem reasonable, overall A_o seldom is a good predictor of a specific behavior.[24]

Exhibit 7.5 shows why it is not so simple to relate an overall brand attitude to a single behavior. This exhibit presents the relationships among the beliefs, attitude, and behaviors of one consumer (we'll call her Judy) concerning a particular object—Pizza Hut. Judy has a single attitude, A_o, toward Pizza Hut, which is based on several salient beliefs she has about Pizza Hut. In her case, this is a favorable overall evaluation. Note that Judy can engage in many different behaviors that involve Pizza Hut, some positive and some negative. For instance, she might go to Pizza Hut on Friday night and order a pizza, she might ignore a Pizza Hut ad on television, she might use a Pizza Hut coupon for a free soft drink, or she might complain to the store manager about an improperly cooked pizza.

None of Judy's specific behaviors, however, is necessarily strongly related to or even consistent with her overall A_o, although some might be. This is because a specific behavior is influenced by many factors besides A_o, including various aspects of the physical environment and social pressures from other people. Does this mean attitudes are irrelevant to behaviors? Of course not. Exhibit 7.5 shows that, although Judy's overall attitude is not necessarily related to any specific behavior, her A_o is related to *the entire pattern of her behaviors* involving Pizza Hut (all her behaviors taken together). If someone likes a product, most of her behaviors regarding that product are likely to be positive.

There are many examples of consumers with favorable attitudes toward products that are not purchased. Many consumers have positive attitudes toward fancy cars, diamond jewelry, 45-inch TVs, and vacation homes, but most do not own these products. Favorable attitudes toward products can be expressed in many different behaviors (besides purchase), so it is difficult to predict which behavior will be performed. Consider three consumers who have highly favorable attitudes toward Porsches, although none owns a Porsche. One consumer may read ads and reports about Porsches, while another consumer may go to showrooms to look at Porsches. A third consumer may just daydream about owning a Porsche. Having a generally favorable (or unfavorable) attitude toward a product or brand does not mean the consumer will engage in every possible favorable behavior regarding the product, including purchase. Marketers need a model that identifies the specific attitudinal factors leading to specific behaviors, such as the theory of reasoned action.

The theory of reasoned action

A particular behavior is determined by the consumer's *intention* to perform the behavior, not his or her attitude toward the object of the behavior.[25] Whether you buy a university sweatshirt depends on your intention to take that action, not on your attitude toward the university or the sweatshirt brand. To explain how intentions are formed, researchers extended the basic multiattribute attitude model to create the model shown in Exhibit 7.6.[26] This model is called the **theory of reasoned action** because it assumes that consumers (1) consciously evaluate the consequences of the alternative behaviors they are considering and (2) choose the behavior that is perceived to lead to the most desirable consequences.[27] The theory of reasoned action is not relevant in the case of simple, involuntary behaviors such as sneezing, turning your head at the sound of a telephone, or jumping at a loud sound. Such behaviors are performed automatically, without conscious analysis of their consequences.

Exhibit 7.6 shows the four main components of the theory of reasoned action—behavior (B), intention to behave (BI), attitude toward the behavior (A_{act}), and subjective norm (SN).[28] If you start with a behavior, such as buying a pair of socks, and work backward through the theory of reasoned action, you see that the behavior is determined by a person's intention to perform that behavior. The behavioral intention, in turn, is a function of two factors: the person's *attitude toward the behavior* and the *subjective norm* (or perceived social pressure) to engage in that behavior. A_{act} is based on beliefs about the functional and psychosocial consequences of the behavior, while SN is based on beliefs about what other people expect you to do. Simply stated, the theory of reasoned action proposes that people perform behaviors that are perceived to have desirable consequences and that are favored by other people who are important to them. People are assumed to refrain from behaviors that have unfavorable consequences and are unpopular with others.

All the components of the theory of reasoned action are defined in terms of a specific behavior. **Behavior (B)** is an action directed toward an object for the purpose of achieving one or more goals. Examples of behaviors include driving to the store, buying a swimsuit, drinking a soda, and looking for your lost ink pen. Behavior always occurs *in an*

EXHIBIT 7.6

The theory of reasoned action

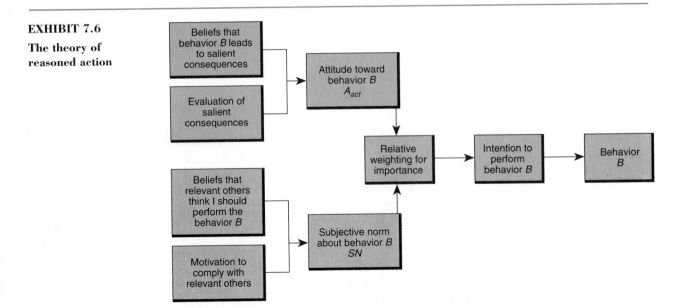

Source: Adapted from Martin Fishbein, "An Overview of the Attitude Construct," in *A Look Back, A Look Ahead*, ed. G. B. Hafer (Chicago: American Marketing Association, 1980), p. 8.

environment or context, at a particular time (reading at home last evening, shopping in the grocery store this afternoon).[29] Marketers have not always been careful in their measures of behavior. To make more accurate measurements of behavior, marketers should specify as precisely as possible the environmental context of the behavior.

The theory of reasoned action proposes that every *voluntary* behavior is determined by a behavioral intention. A **behavioral intention** is a plan to engage in a specific behavior to reach a goal.[30] Behavioral intentions vary in strength, which can be measured with a simple rating scale:

> "All things considered, how likely are you to use newspaper coupons
> when buying groceries this week or next?"
>
> Extremely unlikely   1 2 3 4 5 6 7   Extremely likely

Exhibit 7.6 shows that a behavioral intention is created when consumers integrate or combine two types of information about the behavior: their own attitude toward the behavior or action (A_{act}) and the perceived social pressures from other people to perform that behavior (SN). The relative influence or weight of these two factors depends on the particular behavior that is involved. For example, private behaviors such as what toothpaste you use are determined largely by A_{act}, whereas more social behaviors such as what clothing you wear tends to be influenced by what others think (SN).

Consumers develop an overall evaluation of a behavior or **attitude toward the behavior or action (A_{act})** by integrating their *beliefs* about the salient consequences of the behavior with their *evaluations* of those consequences. For example, if buying a Ford pickup is seen as producing more favorable consequences than buying a Chevy pickup, buying a Ford will have a more favorable A_{act}. Marketers can measure the strengths and evaluations of the salient beliefs about the consequences of a behavior in the same way they measure beliefs about product attributes.

A_{act} can be quite different from A_o because the consequences of a behavior regarding a product often are different from the product attributes. For instance, consider the salient beliefs about the attributes of "Chevrolet" versus the consequences of "buying a Chevrolet next week."

Chevrolet (A_o)	Buying a Chevrolet next week (A_{act})
Moderately priced (+)	Gives me a mode of transportation (+)
Ordinary (−)	Will put me in financial difficulty (−)
Well built (+)	Will lead to high upkeep costs (−)
Dependable (+)	Will cost more now than later (−)
Easily serviced (+)	Will lead to high insurance rates (−)

To the extent that the salient beliefs about the product and about the behavior are evaluated differently, A_o and A_{act} will be different. Also, marketing strategies can have varying effects on A_o and A_{act}.[31] For instance, advertising the advantages of visiting Hallmark stores might influence consumers' attitudes toward shopping in a Hallmark store (A_{act}), but would not necessarily impact their attitudes toward Hallmark greeting cards (A_o).

The **subjective norm (SN)** component reflects the social pressures consumers may feel to perform (or avoid performing) certain behaviors. Exhibit 7.6 shows that the SN component results when a consumer considers his or her beliefs about whether important people want him or her to perform the behavior along with his or her motivation to comply with these people's wishes.[32]

To summarize, the theory of reasoned action proposes an integration process where A_{act} and SN combine to form an intention to behave, which in turn determines the actual behavior. When combined, A_{act} and SN may have different amounts of influence on BI.[33]

CONSUMER PERSPECTIVE

▶ 7.4

Increasing A_{act} and behavioral intentions

Marketers of credit cards have a difficult marketing task to influence specific consumer behaviors. First, they have to get consumers to *accept* the cards; then they have to get consumers to *carry* and *use* the cards. According to the *Nilson Report*, a credit-card newsletter, the average cardholder carries about 7.5 pieces of plastic. Issuers can't make money on cards that aren't used—thus, they need strategies to make A_{act} and *BI* more positive.

Over the years, marketers have tried such inducements as free flight insurance when air travel is charged on an American Express card and discounts on merchandise that most consumers probably wouldn't buy anyway. Neither of these promotions was evaluated very highly, and card usage was not affected very much.

Then, in the mid-1980s, some credit-card marketers finally got serious and began giving away cold, hard cash as an incentive. If you used their card to charge lodging expenses, you could get a 10 percent cash refund. That's what the Bank of New York (TBNY) offered holders of its Visa and MasterCard credit cards. Consumers had to book (in advance) at least $150 worth of hotel expenses and send in a claim with a copy of the credit-card receipt.

Will this marketing strategy work? Well, note that TBNY's strategy adds a belief about a new consequence (getting money back) to the behavior they want consumers to perform more often—using the TBNY credit card. Of course, nearly everyone has a positive evaluation for receiving "free" money. Therefore, we would expect most consumers' attitudes toward using the TBNY card to become more favorable. This, in turn, should increase their intentions to use the card.

By 1990, more credit-card issuers, such as the Sears Discover card, offered cash rebates to consumers for using their card.

Source: Adapted from Mary Kuntz, "Credit Cards as Good as Gold," *Forbes*, November 4, 1985, pp. 234–36.

Some behaviors may be influenced primarily by the *SN* factor. For instance, a person's intention to wear a certain style of clothing to a party is more likely to be determined by beliefs about what others expect than by the functional consequences of wearing those clothes. For other behaviors, normative influences are minimal, and consumers' intentions are largely determined by A_{act}. For example, a consumer's intention to purchase Contac cold remedy is probably due more to A_{act} based on beliefs about the functional consequences of using Contac than on *SN* and beliefs about what other people expect. Marketers need to understand how A_{act} and *SN* are integrated to create *BI* so they can focus their strategies on the dominant influence. Consumer Perspective 7.4 describes a strategy to increase A_{act} and *BI*.

Marketing implications

The environmental context can have powerful influences on consumers' behavioral intentions and their eventual behaviors. Consider Brian, an assistant brand manager for General Foods. Last week, Brian had to decide whether to buy imported or domestic beer in two different contexts. In the first, Brian wanted to have beer on hand at home over the weekend while he watched sports on TV. In the other context, he had a beer after work in a plush bar with a group of his co-workers. The different sets of product-related and social beliefs activated in the two situations created different A_{act} and *SN* components. In the at-home situation, Brian's product beliefs and A_{act} had the dominant effect on his intentions (he bought an inexpensive domestic beer). In the bar, his normative beliefs and *SN* had the stronger influence on his intentions (he bought an expensive imported beer).

To develop effective marketing strategies, marketers need to determine whether the A_{act} or *SN* component has the major influence on behavioral intentions (and thus on behavior). If the primary reason for a behavior (shopping, searching for information, buying a particular brand) is normative (you think others want you to), marketers need to emphasize that the relevant normative influences (friends, family, co-workers) are in favor of the behavior. Often this is done by portraying social influence situations in advertising. Conversely, if intentions are largely influenced by A_{act} factors, the marketing strategy should attempt to create a set of salient beliefs about the positive consequences of the behavior, perhaps by demonstrating those outcomes in an advertisement.

INTENTION AND
BEHAVIOR

Predicting consumers' future behavior, especially their purchase behavior (sales, to marketers), is a critically important aspect of forecasting and marketing planning. According to the theory of reasoned action, predicting purchase behaviors is a matter of measuring consumer intentions to buy just before they make a purchase. In almost all cases, however, this is impractical. Marketing strategies require prediction of consumers' purchase and use behaviors weeks, months, or sometimes years in advance.

Unfortunately, predictions of specific behaviors based on intentions measured well before the behavior occurs may not be very accurate. One survey indicated that only about 60 percent of people who intended to buy a car actually did so within a year.[34] And of those who claimed they did not intend to buy a car, 17 percent ended up buying one. Similar examples could be cited for other product categories (where predictions may be even farther off). This does not mean the theory of reasoned action is wrong in identifying intention as an immediate influence on behavior. Rather, failure to predict the behavior of interest is often due to *when* and *how* intentions are measured.

To accurately predict behavior, marketers should take careful measures of *BI*, being certain to precisely identify the behavior of interest and clearly specify the environmental context. Exhibit 7.7 lists several factors that can weaken the relationship between measured behavioral intention and the observed behavior of interest. In situations where few of these factors operate, measured intentions should predict behavior quite well.

In a broad sense, *time* is the major factor that reduces the predictive accuracy of measured intentions. Intentions, like other cognitive factors, can and do change over time. The longer the intervening time period, the more likely it is that unanticipated circumstances

Some brand choices may be due to A_{act} while others are mostly influenced by the *SN* component.

EXHIBIT 7.7

Factors that reduce or weaken the relationship between intention and behavior

Factor	Examples
Intervening time	As the time between measurement of intention and observation of behavior increases, more factors can occur that act to modify or change the original intention, so that it no longer corresponds to the observed behavior.
Different levels of specificity	The measured intention should be specified at the same level as the observed behavior. Suppose we measure Judy's intentions to wear jeans to class (in general). But we observe her behavior (not wearing jeans) on a day when she made a class presentation and didn't think jeans were appropriate.
Unforeseen event	Sam fully intended to buy Frito chips this afternoon, but the store was sold out. Sam could not carry out his purchase intention. He had to form a new intention on the spot to buy Ripple chips.
Unforeseen environmental context	Sometimes the environmental context the consumer had in mind when the intentions were measured is different from the situation at the time of behavior. In general, Peter has a negative intention to buy Andre champagne. When he decides to prepare a holiday punch calling for eight bottles of champagne, however, Peter formed a positive intention to buy the inexpensive Andre brand.
Degree of voluntary control	Some behaviors are not under complete volitional control. Thus, intentions may not predict the observed behavior very accurately. For instance, Becky intended to go shopping on Saturday when she hoped to be recovered from a bout with the flu, but she was still sick and couldn't go.
Instability of intentions	Some intentions are not stable, if they are founded on only a few, weakly held beliefs that may be easily changed. Such intentions cannot predict actual behavior accurately.
New information	Consumers may receive new information about the salient consequences of their behavior, which leads to changes in their beliefs and attitudes toward the act and/or in the subjective norm. These changes, in turn, change the intention. The original intention is no longer revelant to the behavior and does not predict the eventual behavior accurately.

(such as exposure to competing market strategies) will occur and change consumers' original purchase intentions. Of course, unanticipated events can also occur during very short time periods. An appliance manufacturer once asked consumers entering an appliance store what brand they intended to buy. Of those who specified a brand, only 20 percent came back out with it.[35] Apparently, events occurred in the store to change these consumers' beliefs, attitudes, intentions, and purchase behaviors.

Despite their less-than-perfect accuracy, measures of purchase intentions are often the best way to predict future purchase behavior. For instance, every three months United Air Lines conducts a passenger survey measuring intentions to travel by air during the next three months. Although many events in the ensuing time period can change consumers' beliefs, A_{act}, and *SN* about taking a personal or business trip by airplane, aggregated intentions can provide useful predictions of future airline travel.

Certain behaviors cannot be accurately predicted from beliefs, attitudes, and intentions.[36] Obvious examples include nonvoluntary behaviors such as sneezing or getting sick. It is also difficult to predict purchase behaviors when alternative brands are very similar, and the person has positive attitudes toward several of them. Finally, behaviors about which consumers have little knowledge and low levels of involvement are virtually impossible to predict, because consumers have very few beliefs in memory on which to base attitudes and intentions. In such cases, a consumer's expressed intention may have been created to answer the marketing researcher's question. Such intentions are likely to be unstable and poor predictors of the eventual behavior. In sum, before relying on measures of attitude and intentions to predict future behavior, marketers need to determine whether consumers can reasonably be expected to have well-formed beliefs, attitudes, and intentions toward those behaviors.

Learning objective 1: *Define attitude, and give two examples of its relevance for marketers.*

An attitude is a person's overall evaluation of a concept, whether an object or a behavior. This overall evaluation (pro/con, favorable/unfavorable, positive/negative) develops when people combine or integrate relevant knowledge, meanings, and beliefs about the concept in judging its personal relevance to them. Many marketing strategies (advertising, pricing, product design) are intended to influence consumer attitudes. Marketers often use consumer attitudes toward a brand as criteria for marketing success. Marketers may measure consumers' product or brand attitudes over time to track the performance of a brand or the effectiveness of a marketing strategy.

Learning objective 2: *Describe salient beliefs, and give an example of how marketers can influence belief salience.*

Salient beliefs are the most important or relevant beliefs out of all those in memory that are likely to be activated in a particular situation and used in integration processes. Because the cognitive system has a limited capacity, only a few beliefs can be salient at one time. Marketers hope favorable beliefs about their brand will be salient and activated to influence a purchase decision. Means-end chains are relevant for understanding belief salience. Beliefs about attributes or consequences that are linked to the important goals and values in a situation are most likely to be salient, so marketers can try to influence belief salience by linking product attributes to those important goals or values.

Learning objective 3: *Using the multiattribute attitude model as a guide, describe the information integration process by which consumers form an A_o.*

The multiattribute attitude model describes how consumers form an overall evaluation of a concept by combining salient beliefs about the concept. The model states that a consumer's attitude toward an object (A_o) is a combination of the strengths of a consumer's salient beliefs about product attributes and his or her evaluations of each attribute. The multiattribute attitude model proposes that consumers like objects that have good attributes and dislike objects that have bad attributes. The model represents this integration process by the formula:

$$A_o = \sum_{i=1}^{n} b_i e_i$$

The multiattribute attitude model does not claim that that consumers actually calculate their attitude by multiplying and adding numbers according to this formula. Rather, the formula is an organized way for marketers to predict consumers' attitudes toward products and brands and to identify the salient beliefs that underlie those attitudes.

Learning objective 4: *Describe four attitude-change strategies based on the multiattribute attitude model.*

The multiattribute attitude model suggests four ways to change consumers' attitudes toward a concept (a brand, store, or product category). One strategy is to alter the strength of a salient belief. Marketing strategies that increase the strength of positive beliefs should produce a more positive A_o, while strategies directed at weakening negative beliefs should also increase A_o. Another strategy is to modify the evaluative component of a salient belief. Convincing consumers that a certain belief is more positive or less negative should produce a more positive A_o. The means-end perspective suggests that a more favorable belief can be created by linking a product attribute to desirable end goals or values. A third strategy is to add a new belief about positive attributes to the set of salient beliefs. Commonly, this occurs when a new product attribute is added to a product (Kellogg's now has more fiber). Finally, marketers could try to increase the salience of an existing positive belief. From a means-end chain perspective, this would require making a product attribute more important or personally relevant by linking it to important goals or values.

Learning objective 5: *Explain how A_o differs from A_{act}.*

Attitudes toward an object (A_o) can be quite different from attitudes toward an action involving the same object (A_{act}). This occurs because each type of attitude is based on a different set of salient beliefs. A_o is based on beliefs about product *attributes,* while A_{act} is based on beliefs about the *consequences* of buying and using a product. Although the two are related, they can be rather different. For certain objects and behaviors, there may be little overlap between the salient beliefs. If so, A_o and A_{act} will be quite different. For instance, Joe might like a particular restaurant very much (it has good food, service, and atmosphere), yet have a negative attitude toward eating there on Friday night (it is too far away, too crowded, and hard to find parking).

Learning objective 6: *Describe how the components of the theory of reasoned action are combined to create a behavioral intention.*

The theory of reasoned action claims that behavioral intentions are based on two factors—consumers' attitudes toward the behavior or action (A_{act}) and the subjective norm (SN)—each of which is based on a set of salient beliefs that consumers find relevant. A_{act} is based on consumers' beliefs about the consequences of a behavior (buying a soda from the vending machine is quick and easy, shopping for clothes at Macy's is fun and exciting). The SN component reflects consumers' beliefs about the social pressures to perform a behavior. These beliefs reflect consumers' perceptions about what significant other people want them to do (my mother thinks I should buy the green shorts, my friend wants me to buy the Metallica CD). In a particular situation, A_{act} and SN are integrated, perhaps with different weights, to form a behavioral intention, BI. In some situations, A_{act} may be the dominant influence on BI, while in other cases, SN has the greater effect on intentions.

Learning objective 7: *Identify three factors that can reduce the accuracy of a measure of behavioral intention in predicting the actual behavior.*

In general, measures of behavioral intentions become less accurate as the time increases between BI measurement and the actual behavior. This is because many other things can intervene between the intention and the actual behavior. When the original intention is no longer the relevant determinant of the behavior, the measure is not accurate. Other factors that affect the accuracy of behavioral intentions include consumers' uncertainty about the intention. Sometimes, consumers don't really have a clear intention, yet are asked to indicate what they are likely to do. Sometimes the measure of intention asks consumers about the likelihood they will perform a general behavior, but their actual behavior is constrained by the specific environmental context in which it occurs. To the extent that unanticipated environmental factors influence behavior, the intention measure will be less accurate. Some behaviors are not completely voluntary, and in this case behavioral intentions might not be entirely relevant. Finally, consumers could get new information that leads to changes in their beliefs and eventually creates a new behavioral intention, making the original BI irrele-

---

▶ **KEY TERMS AND CONCEPTS**

attitude

evaluations

integration process

brand equity

attitudes toward objects (A_o)

salient beliefs

multiattribute attitude model

belief strength (b_i)

evaluation (e_i)

attitude-change strategies

theory of reasoned action

behavior (B)

behavioral intention

attitude toward the behavior or action (A_{act})

subjective norm (SN)

1. Define *attitude,* and identify the two main ways consumers can acquire attitudes.

2. How are salient beliefs different from other beliefs? How can marketers attempt to influence belief salience?

3. According to the multiattribute attitude model, how does a consumer integrate beliefs to form an attitude?

4. Consider a product category in which you make regular purchases (such as toothpaste or shampoo). How have your beliefs and evaluations changed over time? Is your attitude accessible in memory?

5. Use an example to describe the key differences between A_o and A_{act}. Under what circumstances would marketers be most interested in each type of attitude?

6. Describe the theory of reasoned action, and discuss the two main factors that are integrated to form a behavioral intention. Describe one marketing strategy implication for each factor.

7. Use the Jaguar example to distinguish between the multiattribute attitude model and the theory of reasoned action. How could each model contribute to the development of a more effective marketing strategy for Jaguar?

8. Discuss the problems in measuring behavioral intentions to (*a*) buy a new car; (*b*) buy a soda from a vending machine; and (*c*) save $250 a month toward the eventual purchase of a house. What factors could occur in each situation to make the measured intentions a poor predictor of actual behavior?

9. How could marketers improve their predictions of behaviors in the situations described in Question 8? Consider both measurement improvements and alternate research or forecasting techniques.

10. Negative attitudes present a special challenge for marketing strategy. Consider how what you have learned about attitudes and intentions could help you to address a consumer who has a brand relationship described as "Doesn't like our brand and buys a competitor's brand."

CHAPTER 8

Consumer Decision Making

LEARNING OBJECTIVES

After completing this chapter, you should be able to:

► 1. Define a decision, and describe why consumer decision making is part of the problem-solving process.

► 2. Describe the six stages of the problem-solving process.

► 3. Define end goals, and discuss the role of end goals in problem solving.

► 4. Define consideration set, discuss how it can be formed, and describe an implication of consideration sets for marketers.

► 5. Define choice criteria, and give examples of how positive and negative choice criteria might be used in problem solving.

► 6. Describe the difference between compensatory and noncompensatory integration processes, and give an example of each.

► 7. Describe three types of heuristics, and give an example of each.

► 8. Describe the three levels of problem-solving effort, and give a marketing implication for each.

THE DINNER PARTY

In mid-September, Barbara decided to have a dinner party for 10 people on October 17. She immediately called and invited all the guests. But now she had a problem: she didn't have enough dishes to serve 10 people. Actually Barbara had two sets of dishes—Wedgwood stoneware and Lenox china—but several pieces of the stoneware had broken over the years, and she had only seven place settings of the china. Barbara decided she had to buy some new dishes. Given her budget restrictions, Barbara decided to replace the missing pieces of stoneware, as she thought the stoneware would be less expensive than the china.

That Friday, Barbara called several department stores, only to discover that none of them had her pattern in stock. In fact, they said it would take from two to six months to get the dishes, and that Wedgwood would probably discontinue the pattern soon. Barbara decided to order the stoneware and borrow dishes for the party. First, though, she would check with her husband.

Barbara's husband was not very enthusiastic. He thought replacing the stoneware might be more expensive than buying a complete set of new dishes, especially with sales at the department stores; and he noted that a six-month wait was also a high cost. Besides, the stoneware they would be matching was chipped and scratched. Barbara might instead add three place settings to the china. Barbara developed a complex plan to take all of these factors into consideration. She decided that if finishing her set of china cost under $200 more than the stoneware replacements, she would buy three place settings of china. If a new set of stoneware cost under $100 more than replacing the missing china, she would buy the new set of stoneware dishes. But if these two alternative actions were more expensive, she would order the replacement pieces for her Wedgwood stoneware.

When she called stores to check sale prices, Barbara learned the sales offered 25 percent off all dishes in stock. She also learned that one store was selling a service for eight of Chinese porcelain for $100. At that price, she could buy two sets (a service for 16) for less than any of her other options would cost. She decided to buy the Chinese porcelain, if she liked it.

Later that Saturday, Barbara's mother-in-law happened to call, and Barbara told her what she was thinking about. Barbara's mother-in-law said to forget the Chinese porcelain because it is too fragile—either bone china or stoneware is much stronger. She also told Barbara about a factory outlet that had a large inventory and very low prices. Barbara decided to go back to her previous plan, but to check out the factory outlet, too.

Barbara began to visit department stores. She learned from one salesperson that porcelain and bone china are equally strong and both are stronger than stoneware. She also discovered that ordering the replacement Wedgwood would cost several hundred dollars and could take up to 12 months. Barbara saw an Imari stoneware pattern she liked that was on sale and within her budget. She decided to check with the factory outlet to see whether it had the Imari pattern, because she might be able to save a lot of money buying at the outlet. If the price was low enough, it might be worth the hour and a half round-trip drive.

Barbara found the number of the outlet and called it. The Imari pattern was out of stock, and an order would take two months, but the outlet had a large number of other patterns. Now, Barbara was in a quandary. She could probably save considerable money by going to the outlet, but it was a long drive and she couldn't go until the weekend. But by then the department store might be sold out of the Imari pattern she liked. And there was a chance that she wouldn't find anything she liked at the outlet. Barbara decided to check out the Chinese porcelain and buy it if she liked it. Otherwise, she would drive to the outlet on the weekend and buy something.

On Wednesday, Barbara went to the department store to look at the Chinese porcelain. Although it was pretty, it came only in a delicate flower pattern, which she did not care for. She decided to drive to the outlet right away. If they didn't have anything she liked, she could go back to the department store and buy the Imari pattern.

Barbara drove 45 minutes to the outlet. It had a huge inventory at much lower prices than the department store, but no stoneware with the Oriental pattern she wanted. So she telephoned the department store to see whether it still had the Imari pattern. It did, but there were no longer 10 place settings left. Perhaps this disappointment led Barbara to ask once again if the outlet had the Imari pattern. She was surprised to find that it did have the pattern in stock, and even better, it was on sale for 25 percent off the already low price. Unfortunately, the dishes were at the warehouse and couldn't be picked up for 7 to 10 days. Barbara was pleased to find a complete set of the dishes she liked best at a great price. Her only worry was that the dinner party was exactly 10 days away. She decided to order the Imari dishes and take the chance that they would be there on time. They were, and Barbara was pleased with her choice.[1]

CONSUMER DECISIONS

Barbara made several decisions during the complex process of buying her new tableware. Each **decision** involved a choice "between two or more alternative actions [or behaviors]."[2] For instance, Barbara had to decide between traveling to the outlet store or buying the tableware at the department store. *Every decision requires a choice between possible behaviors.* For instance, when Joe bought a Snickers candy bar from a vending machine, his actual choice was not among different brands of candy but between the alternative *behaviors of buying Snickers* versus *buying one of the other brands.* When Jill is trying to decide whether to see a particular movie, her choice is really between the behaviors involved in attending the movie versus the behaviors involved in staying home (or going bowling, or whatever other activities she is considering). Marketers are particularly interested in consumers' purchase behaviors, especially their choices of which brands to buy ("Should I get Levi's or Guess? jeans?"). But consumers also make many decisions about behaviors other than brand choice ("Should I go shopping now or wait until after lunch?" "Should I pay with cash or Visa?"). Some of these other behaviors are targets of marketing strategies— "Come down to our store this afternoon for free coffee and doughnuts."

Even though marketers often refer to consumers making decisions about objects (products, brands, or stores), consumers actually choose among alternative behaviors involving those objects. This means the components of the theory of reasoned action—attitude toward the behavior or action (A_{act}), subjective norms (SN), and behavioral intentions (BI)—are relevant for understanding consumer decision making (refer back to Exhibit 7.6).

Exhibit 8.1 shows that each decision a consumer makes involves the cognitive processes of interpretation and integration as influenced by the knowledge, meanings, and beliefs activated from memory. **Integration** is a key process in decision making. During integration, consumers combine salient beliefs about the possible consequences of the behaviors being considered in order to evaluate the alternative behaviors (form A_{act} and SN). By integrating these factors, consumers make a **choice** of which behavior to perform and form a behavioral intention (BI). A behavioral intention ("I am going to buy Wilson tennis balls") can be thought of as a *plan* to engage in the chosen behavior.

We assume that every voluntary behavior is determined by a behavioral intention created by a decision-making process. However, this does not mean people engage in conscious decision making before every behavior.[3] Some voluntary behaviors have become habitual and occur with little or no decision-making effort (Sarah always buys Diet Pepsi when she wants a soft drink). These routine behaviors still are based on intentions that once were produced by a decision-making process, but the intentions or plans are stored in memory. When activated, these behavioral intentions automatically produce the habitual behavior. Conscious decision making is not necessary on each occasion. Also, decision making does not occur for simple involuntary behaviors (sneezing is an example) or for behaviors controlled largely by the environment (the layout of aisles and product displays partly determines consumers' movements through a store).

This chapter treats consumer decision making as part of a problem-solving process. This means consumers evaluate and choose behaviors ("Should I go to Kmart or Wal-Mart?") *in the context of a perceived problem.* During a problem-solving episode such as Barbara's, consumers make many types of decisions. "Where and when should I stop? What products or brands might solve my problem? What product attributes are most relevant to my goals? Who should I consult about this purchase? What brand should I buy? How should I pay for my purchase?" We begin by presenting a general model that identifies several stages of

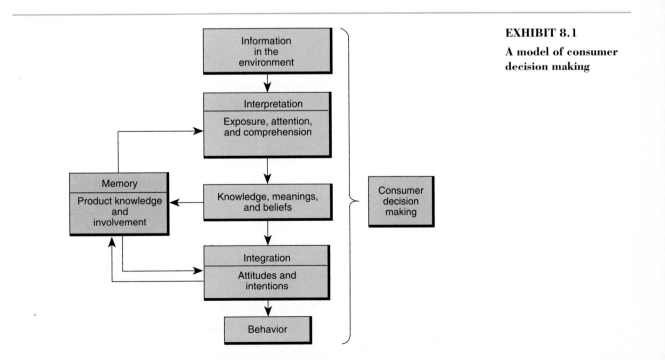

EXHIBIT 8.1

A model of consumer decision making

problem solving, each of which may involve decisions. We discuss each stage of problem solving, along with the decision-making processes of interpretation, integration, and activation of knowledge that may occur. Then, we describe three levels of problem-solving effort and discuss the implications of these levels for marketing strategies.

THE PROBLEM-SOLVING PROCESS

As Barbara's tableware buying experience illustrates, **problem solving** involves a goal-directed sequence of interactions between cognitive and affective responses, behaviors, and environmental factors—the three components of the Wheel of Consumer Analysis.[4] To help understand these complexities, researchers have developed models of problem solving.

Exhibit 8.2 presents a model of six basic stages in problem solving. The first stage is *problem recognition,* where the consumer recognizes that the current situation is not ideal and thus identifies one or more goals. (The upcoming dinner party made Barbara aware of a problem and her goal—she needed a set of nice dishes for 10 people.) In the next stage, consumers *search for relevant information.* (Because Barbara had little relevant knowledge about dishes in memory, she had to search for information by calling and visiting stores, talking to salespeople, and discussing the problem with her husband and mother-in-law.) In the *evaluation of alternatives* stage, the consumer compares alternative behaviors in terms of their potential to achieve the activated goals. (Barbara evaluated the act of buying the different tableware she found during her search in terms of her desired price, delivery, and design criteria.) At the *choice decision* stage, the consumer forms an intention to buy. (Barbara finally decided to buy the Imari pattern at the factory outlet store.) At the *purchase* stage, the purchase intention or plan is carried out. (Barbara ordered the dishes, and a few days later, she returned to pay for the dishes and pick them up.) The final stage of problem solving is *postpurchase use and reevaluation,* where consumers use the purchased product and reconsider their choice decision. (Barbara had her dinner party and was glad to have the new stoneware.)

EXHIBIT 8.2

A model of consumer problem solving

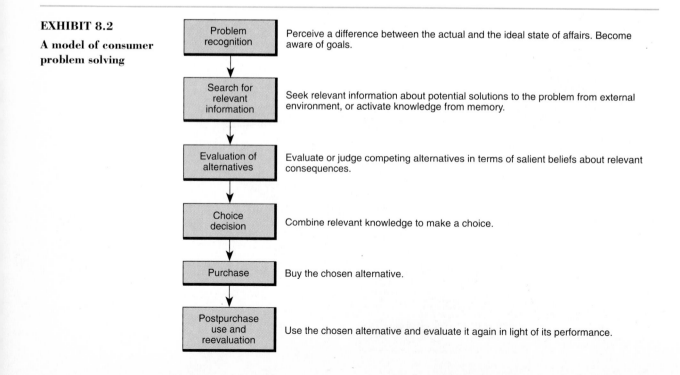

Problem recognition — Perceive a difference between the actual and the ideal state of affairs. Become aware of goals.

Search for relevant information — Seek relevant information about potential solutions to the problem from external environment, or activate knowledge from memory.

Evaluation of alternatives — Evaluate or judge competing alternatives in terms of salient beliefs about relevant consequences.

Choice decision — Combine relevant knowledge to make a choice.

Purchase — Buy the chosen alternative.

Postpurchase use and reevaluation — Use the chosen alternative and evaluate it again in light of its performance.

Understanding consumer problem solving requires a careful analysis of the goals that are activated during problem recognition. A *goal* is a desired consequence or value in a means-end chain. (Dana wants a car that gives her reliable transportation. Steve wants a shampoo that gives his hair extra body. Missy wants to go to a restaurant where her kids won't have to wait.) **Problem recognition** occurs when a consumer notices that the current state of affairs is not the ideal or desired state. At this point, a goal is activated. For instance, a man who notices dandruff on his shoulder recognizes a problem and wants to get rid of the dandruff (a goal). Depending on the perceived importance of the problem, he experiences a certain level of involvement with solving the problem and achieving the goal. This involvement motivates his problem-solving activities and focuses his decision making on reaching the goal.

The most basic consequences or values that consumers want to achieve or satisfy are called **end goals.** They provide a frame that gives a direction and focus to the entire problem-solving process.[5] Some end goals represent concrete, tangible consequences; other end goals are more abstract. For instance, a purchase decision to replace a flashlight bulb involves a concrete end goal of buying a bulb that lights—a simple functional consequence. Other product choices involve more abstract end goals such as desired psychosocial consequences of a product—some people want to serve a wine that indicates their sophisticated taste to their guests. Finally, end goals such as instrumental and terminal values are even more abstract and general—consumers might choose a car that makes them feel sporty or enhances their self-esteem. End goals also vary in evaluation. Some consumer decisions are focused on achieving positive, desirable end goals, while others are focused on negative end goals—distasteful consequences the consumer wishes to avoid.

The particular end goals consumers are striving to achieve have a powerful effect on the problem-solving process and the many decisions that are made. Exhibit 8.3 presents

This ad shows how the product is relevant for solving five different problems.

EXHIBIT 8.3

Types of purchase end goals and related problem-solving motivations

Dominant End Goal	Basic Purchase Motivation	Examples
Optimize satisfaction	Seek maximum positive consequences	Buy dinner at the best restaurant in town
Prevent problem	Avoid potential unpleasant consequences	Buy rust-proofing for a new car
Resolve conflict	Seek satisfactory balance of positive and negative consequences	Buy a moderately expensive car of very good quality
Escape from problem	Reduce or escape from unwanted circumstances	Buy a shampoo to get rid of dandruff
Maintain satisfaction	Maintain satisfaction of basic need with minimal effort	Buy bread at the nearest convenience store

Source: Adapted from Geraldine Fennell, "Motivation Research Revisited," *Journal of Advertising Research*, June 1975, pp. 23–28; and J. Paul Peter and Lawrence X. Tarpey, Sr., "A Comparative Analysis of Three Consumer Decision Strategies," *Journal of Consumer Research*, June 1975, pp. 29–37.

very broad types of end goals that motivate quite different problem-solving processes. For instance, consumers who have an *optimizing* end goal are likely to expend substantial effort searching for the best possible alternative. At the other extreme, consumers with a *satisficing/maintenance* end goal are likely to engage in minimal search behavior. In yet other decisions, consumers may have conflicting end goals that must be resolved during problem solving.

Marketers have relatively little direct influence over consumers' abstract end goals, including values. However, marketers do use promotional strategies to influence more tangible goals, such as desired functional or psychosocial consequences. For instance, an insurance salesperson might try to influence consumers' end goals by convincing them that buying life insurance is a way to guarantee their children's college educations or to maximize the payout from a company pension. The usual strategy is to identify the major goals activated by problem recognition and design product and promotion strategies consistent with those goals.

Search for relevant information

To decide which behavior is likely to satisfy their goals, consumers need knowledge that is relevant to the choice problem. Consumers who have past experience in choosing products to satisfy their goals may have considerable relevant knowledge stored in memory that can be activated for use in interpretation and integration processes. The end goal is a major influence on what product knowledge is activated during decision making.[6] Product attributes and functional consequences that have strong means-end links to the end goal are more likely to be used in making a purchase decision.

Those without suitable knowledge in memory must **search for relevant information** in the environment.[7] Because Barbara had no experience with buying tableware and little relevant knowledge in memory about dishes, prices, and shops, she had to exert considerable effort searching for useful information. In problem-solving situations with less important goals, consumers may engage in casual search behavior. For instance, people can pick up relevant information while browsing in stores or catalogs. Consumer Perspective 8.1 describes how consumers use browsing for casual search and entertainment. Finally, consumers can acquire relevant knowledge through purely accidental exposure to marketing information (learning about a new store through a radio ad).

To make a choice decision, consumers need relevant knowledge about possible solutions to their problem that might achieve their goals. The alternative behaviors consumers consider during decision making are called **choice alternatives.** For purchase decisions, the choice alternatives are different product categories, product forms, brands, or models

CONSUMER PERSPECTIVE

8.1 ◄

Browsing as search and entertainment

Sometimes consumers browse as part of a vague search plan. But frequently, browsing consumers have no specific decision plan in mind. They are shopping for other reasons—recreation, stimulation from store environments, social contact, escape from home or work, or even exercise. In other words, some consumers get satisfaction from shopping/browsing, apart from solving a purchase problem. Browsing, thus, can be both a problem-solving strategy and a form of leisure activity.

One motivation for browsing without a specific decision plan in mind is that the consumer is involved in some way with a particular product class or form and likes to be around it. Consumers who are interested in music may enjoy browsing in record shops. Some consumers are involved with a particular store or set of stores in a mall or a shopping area. Perhaps the atmosphere of these stores is interesting, and this provides part of the attraction. Of course, browsing can and usually does serve multiple goals, needs, and values for different consumers.

Retail stores need to pay attention to browsers, because they can have a major impact on the success of the store, although the retailer may have a serious problem if browsers crowd the store and keep serious customers away. Discouraging browsers is relatively easy—follow them around the store being "helpful." Some clothing stores seem to do this effectively. But driving browsers away can be risky. Many browsers become buyers. If a particular store creates a negative reaction, the browser may make a purchase in a different store.

Some retailers in particular seem to have trouble dealing with browsers. Consider auto dealers. Many people don't like to go into auto showrooms to browse, partly because of the aggressive salespeople who descend on them. One strategy has been to set up regional auto shows in shopping malls, where consumers have more freedom to browse without having to deal with an enthusiastic salesperson.

Another retailing strategy is to develop a store environment that stimulates impulse buying. In-store promotions, displays, and special signs can help convert a browser to a buyer.

Finally, browsers serve to relay information to other consumers. Thus, browsers are doubly important. Not only might they buy something themselves, but they are more likely to spread word-of-mouth information to less well-informed consumers.

Source: Adapted from Peter H. Bloch and Marsha L. Richins, "Shopping without Purchase: An Investigation of Consumer Browsing Behavior," in *Advances in Consumer Research*, 10, ed. R. P. Bagozzi and A. M. Tybout (Ann Arbor, Mich.: Association for Consumer Research, 1983), pp. 389–93.

the consumer is considering buying. For other types of decisions, the choice alternatives might be different stores to visit, times of the day or week to go shopping, or methods of paying (cash, check, or credit card). Given their limited time, energy, and cognitive capacity, consumers seldom consider every possible choice alternative, but instead evaluate a limited subset of all possible alternatives, called the **consideration set.**[8]

Exhibit 8.4 illustrates how a manageable consideration set of brands can be identified during problem solving. Some brands in the consideration set may be activated directly from memory—this group is the *evoked set.*[9] For highly familiar decisions, consumers may not consider any brands beyond those in the evoked set—they are confident they already know the best choice alternatives. In other decisions, choice alternatives may be found through intentional search activities such as reading the results of product tests, talking to knowledgeable friends, or examining brands in a store.[10] Finally, consumers may learn of still other choice alternatives through accidental exposures to information in the environment, such as overhearing others talking about a new brand, a new store, or a sale. Barbara learned about the factory outlet from her mother-in-law, essentially by accident.

EXHIBIT 8.4

Forming a consideration set of brand choice

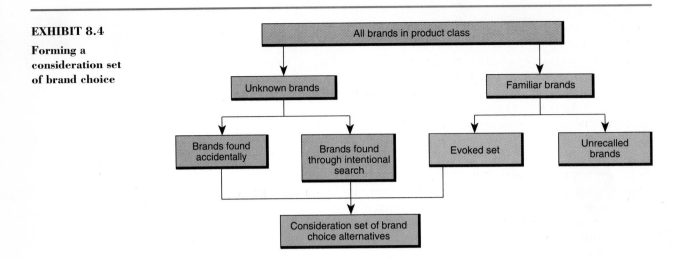

However the choice alternatives are generated, they form a *consideration set* of possible purchase options to be evaluated in decision making.

To be chosen, a brand must be included in the consideration sets of at least some consumers. Marketers therefore develop strategies to increase the likelihood that a brand will be activated from consumers' memories and included in their evoked sets of choice alternatives. The activation potential of a brand, sometimes called its *top-of-mind awareness,* is the result of many factors. One is the amount of past experience consumers have had with the brand. Consumers are much more likely to think of (activate) brands they have used before. For this reason, popular brands with higher market share have a distinct advantage.[11] The more a brand is used, the more likely it is activated, and the greater the probability of its purchase, which, in turn, increases its activation potential, and so on. Unfamiliar and low-market-share brands are at a disadvantage, since they are much less likely to be included in consumers' evoked sets and to be considered choice alternatives.

One marketing strategy to increase the activation potential of a brand is to adopt repetitive (and costly) advertising campaigns such as those promoting cigarettes, beer, soft drinks, and toothpaste.[12] Such heavy expenditures may pay off, because brands with high

Browsing is one way consumers get relevant information about products and brands.

top-of-mind awareness are more likely to be included in the evoked set of choice alternatives that "come to mind" during problem solving.

Finally, a company's distribution strategy can have a critical influence on whether a brand is in the consideration set. Consider food products, where an estimated 65 percent of decisions are made in the store. A key marketing strategy in this case is making sure the product is on the shelf. Availability in the store enhances the likelihood that consumers will encounter the brand at the time of the decision, which increases its chances of entering consumers' consideration sets.

To make purchase decisions, consumers need knowledge about the consequences of the choice alternatives. **Evaluation of alternatives** in the consideration set (forming A_{act}) is based on consumers' beliefs about the consequences of buying and using those products or brands. The specific consequence beliefs a consumer uses to evaluate choice alternatives are called **choice criteria.**[13] Virtually any type of product-related consequence can be a choice criterion in a brand choice decision, including beliefs about functional consequences (product performance), psychosocial consequences (approval of friends), or value consequences (a sense of achievement or self-esteem).

For many common problems, consumers may have some beliefs in memory about the consequences of the choice alternatives in the consideration set. If more knowledge about choice criteria is desired, consumers must search for information by visiting stores, reading *Consumer Reports,* or talking to salespeople. For unfamiliar problems, consumers may not know which product attributes and consequences are appropriate as choice criteria, and they may have to search for relevant information.[14] Barbara spent considerable effort searching for information about what attributes and consequences were appropriate as choice criteria.

Consumers do not necessarily consider a large number of choice criteria in the evaluation integration process. In fact, given their limited cognitive capacity, the number of choice criteria considered at one time may be as few as one or two.[15] The probability that product beliefs will be used as choice criteria (activated and integrated in evaluating choice alternatives) depends on how relevant that knowledge is to the end goal. If the end goal is self-esteem, for instance, then beliefs about product consequences that are linked to self-esteem are likely to be used as choice criteria. The end goal generated by problem recognition is an important influence. Different end goals may be activated in different problem contexts, such as buying a sweater for yourself versus buying one as a gift ("I want to be seen as stylish" versus "I want to be seen as generous"). Different choice criteria (unique design versus looks expensive) may be relevant to these end goals.

Marketers can try to activate certain choice criteria by placing marketing information in prominent places in the decision environment. For instance, special sale signs can activate beliefs about financial consequences (saving money). Prominent labels on food packages, such as "fat free" or "low sodium," enhance the likelihood that the consumer uses these consequences as choice criteria. Finally, salespeople tend to emphasize certain product benefits in their sales pitches, which increases the probability that beliefs about those consequences will be used as choice criteria.

An important influence on choice criteria is the set of product attributes of the choice alternatives in the consideration set.[16] Only *discriminant consequences*—consequences that are perceived to differ across choice alternatives—can be used as choice criteria.[17] If several choice alternatives have a similar consequence, that consequence cannot discriminate between the alternatives and cannot be used as a choice criterion. To present an obvious example, if all the soft drinks in a vending machine contain caffeine, the consequence of stimulation ("I will get a lift") is the same for all alternatives and cannot be used as a choice criterion.

Evaluation of alternatives

Consumers' choice criteria can have varying evaluations. Some choice criteria are desirable consequences that elicit positive affective responses, produce positive A_{act}, and lead to a favorable BI. Other choice criteria, such as price, may have unpleasant consequences and elicit negative affective responses.[18] Over the past decade, for example, many Americans have acquired the negative choice criterion, caffeine content, for soft drinks, as a result of the increasing value of good health. 7UP used this negative choice criterion as the basis for its no-caffeine marketing strategy—"Never had it, never will." Most other soft-drink manufacturers also responded to consumers' increasing negative beliefs about this choice criterion by introducing brands of caffeine-free soft drinks.

Consumers usually see negative choice criteria as perceived risks to be avoided. One strategy to reduce perceived risk is to offer warranties and guarantees of product quality, as Consumer Perspective 8.2 illustrates. Usually, a consumer will reject a choice alternative with negative consequences, unless it also has a number of positive consequences. Consumers who believe a choice alternative has both positive and negative consequences experience a conflict between the perceived benefits and risks of the decision, which may motivate them to search for information to resolve the conflict.[19]

Choice decision

Making a **choice decision** requires that consumers integrate their product knowledge about choice criteria to evaluate the choice alternatives in the consideration set and choose one.[20] Researchers have identified two types of integration processes: *formal integration processes* and simpler procedures called *heuristics.* A key distinction in formal models of the integration process is between compensatory and noncompensatory integration processes.[21]

Compensatory integration processes combine the salient beliefs about choice criteria (perhaps only two or three beliefs) to form an overall attitude (A_{act}) toward each behavioral alternative in the consideration set. The multiattribute attitude model (discussed in

This ad focuses on a discriminant consequence—lower prices—as a choice criterion.

CONSUMER
PERSPECTIVE

Marketing strate-
gies directed at
the negative
consequences
of price

Some people see shopping by mail from catalogs as risky. Direct-mail marketers, therefore, address this perception through their guarantees. A common strategy is to offer consumers "money back with no questions asked." Thus, no financial loss can be incurred (other than postage, and maybe not even that).

The Performance Bicycle Shop, a mail-order company selling high-quality bicycle components, has a somewhat unusual price strategy to give consumers confidence that they are getting the best deal, a powerful desired consequence for many. Note that such a pricing strategy has the added advantage of building shopping loyalty toward the catalog company.

Performance Price Protection Guarantee

We at Performance work hard to provide you with the best values in the cycling market combined with excellent service and the best guarantee you can get on the cycling products you purchase—the "Performance 100% Guarantee."

Occasionally, another company may offer a special sale price on an item which is lower than our current catalog price. The Performance Price Protection Guarantee allows you to buy now from one source the cycling products you want, with the assurance that you received the best value.

This is how the Performance Price Protection Guarantee works: If there is a current nationally advertising special price on the same item you want and you are shopping by telephone, just tell the operator when you are ordering the price and the source where the special is printed. If ordering by mail, send a copy of the ad with your order. This becomes your new Performance Price. That is all there is to it— no more inconvenience of filling out multiple orders or paying multiple shipping charges. And of course, rather than having a limited or no guarantee on these items, you will have bought with the confidence of the "Performance 100% Guarantee"—if any item does not meet your expectations, just send it back for a complete refund, exchange, or credit—your choice. You cannot get a better guarantee on the cycling products you buy. Combined with the Performance Price Protection Guarantee, you can shop in complete confidence that you're getting the best value for your money.

Source: Performance Bicycle Shop.

Chapter 7) is a compensatory process in that a negative consequence (expensive) can be balanced or compensated by a positive consequence (status). Combining a favorable and unfavorable belief leads to a neutral overall attitude. The multiattribute attitude model does not specify how a consumer chooses between the choice alternatives once they have been evaluated, but most researchers assume consumers will select the behavior with the most positive A_{act}.

Noncompensatory integration processes do not combine or consider all the salient beliefs about choice criteria at once. Thus, the positive and negative consequences might not balance or compensate for each other. For instance, Edie might reject a particular model of Reebok aerobic shoe if it has one negative consequence (too expensive), even though it also has several positive consequences (firm support, comfortable, stylish colors).

In another example of a noncompensatory integration process, Tina might evaluate a pair of dress shoes favorably and buy them because they were superior to all the other alternatives on the most important consequence (the color matched her dress). She did not even consider the other product consequences, which were unfavorable (less durable, expensive, and not very comfortable).

Research suggests consumers do not follow any single integration process in evaluating and selecting choice alternatives.[22] Because people do not have enough cognitive capacity to integrate several beliefs about several choice alternatives at once, they probably use a combination of simple integration processes in most problem-solving situations.[23] For instance, a consumer might use a noncompensatory process to reduce the choice alternatives to a manageable number by rejecting all those that fail to meet one or two critical choice criteria. For example, Bill might reject all restaurants that do not have a salad bar. Then, the remaining choice alternatives in the consideration set (perhaps only two or three) could be evaluated on price and atmosphere using a more demanding compensatory integration process. Consumers probably construct most integration processes at the time they are needed, to fit the problem-solving situation. This suggests that most integration processes are rather simple, quite flexible, and easily adaptable to changing problem situations.[24] Such simple integration "rules" are called *heuristics.*

Heuristics are simple "if . . . , then . . . " integration rules that link an event to an appropriate behavior. Because they are applied to only a few bits and pieces of knowledge at a time, heuristics are highly adaptive to the specific problem-solving situation and are not likely to exceed the person's cognitive capacity. Some heuristics may be stored in memory like miniature scripts that are activated and applied automatically in certain situations. Other heuristics may be constructed on the spot in response to information encountered in the environment.

Exhibit 8.5 presents examples of three types of heuristics that consumers use in problem solving. Search heuristics are simple rules for seeking information relevant to a goal. A consumer might have a search heuristic for buying any small appliance—first read the product tests in *Consumer Reports.* Evaluation heuristics are integration procedures for evaluating choice alternatives in light of the end goal. Dieters might have a heuristic that identifies the most important choice criteria for food—low calories or low fat content— which is strongly linked to the problem-solving goal of losing weight. Choice heuristics are simple integration rules for comparing evaluations of alternative behaviors in order to make a choice. A choice heuristic is to select the alternative you bought last time, if you were satisfied.

Purchase

Purchase is determined by a behavioral intention (*BI*) to buy. The integration processes of evaluating choice alternatives and then choosing one produces a **decision plan**, made up of one or more behavioral intentions. Decision plans vary in specificity and complexity.[25] Specific decision plans contain intentions to perform particular behaviors in highly defined situations: This afternoon Jim intends to go to Penney's and buy a blue cotton shirt to go with his new slacks. Other decision plans involve rather general intentions: Paula intends to shop for a new car sometime soon. Some decision plans contain a simple intention to perform a single behavior: Andy intends to buy a large-size tube of Colgate toothpaste. More complex decision plans involve a set of intentions to perform a series of behaviors: Val intends to go to Bloomingdale's and Macy's to browse through their sportswear departments and look for a lightweight jacket.

Although forming a decision plan greatly increases the likelihood that the consumer will perform the intended behavior, not all behavioral intentions are carried out. A purchase intention might be blocked or modified if environmental factors make it difficult to carry out the plan. The problem-solving process might recycle to problem recognition,

Search heuristics	**Examples**
Purchase	If you are buying stereo equipment, always go to Sam's Hi-Fi.
Sources of information	If you want to know which alternatives are worth searching for, read the test reports in *Consumer Reports*.
Source credibility	If a magazine accepts advertisements from the tested products, don't believe its product tests.

Evaluation heuristics	**Examples**
Key criteria	If comparing processed foods, examine sodium content.
Negative criteria	If a salient consequence is negative (high fat content), give this choice criterion extra weight in the integration process.
Insignificant differences	If alternatives are similar on a salient consequence (all low cholesterol), ignore that choice criterion.

Choice heuristics	**Examples**
For familiar, frequently purchased products:	If choosing among familiar products, then . . .
Works best	Choose the product that you think works best—that provides the best level of performance on the most relevant functional consequences.
Affect referral	Choose the alternative you like best over all (select the alternative with the most favorable attitude).
Bought last	Select the alternative you used last, if it was satisfactory.
Important person	Choose the alternative that some "important" person (spouse, child, friend) likes.
Price-based rule	Buy the least-expensive alternative (or buy the most expensive, depending on your beliefs about the relationship of price to product quality).
Promotion rule	Choose an alternative for which you have a coupon or can get at a price reduction (seasonal sale, promotional rebate, special price reduction).
For new, unfamiliar products:	If choosing among unfamiliar products, then . . .
Wait and see	Don't buy any software until someone you know has used it for at least a month and recommends it. Don't buy a new car (computer, etc.) until the second model year.
Expert consultant	Find an expert or more knowledgeable person, have them evaluate the alternatives in terms of your goals, then buy the alternative the expert selects.

EXHIBIT 8.5

Examples of consumer heuristics

new goals might be formed, and a new decision might be made: if Andy finds the store is sold out of large-size tubes of Colgate, he might decide to buy two medium-size tubes. Sometimes unanticipated events bring other choice alternatives to light, or change consumers' beliefs about appropriate choice criteria, which could lead to a revised decision plan. While reading the paper, Val learned Saks was having a 30 percent-off sale on lightweight jackets, so she decided to shop there first instead of Bloomingdale's.

In the **postpurchase use and reevaluation** stage of the problem-solving process, consumers use the purchased product, and they may reevaluate their decision choice— "Am I happy with the purchase choice or not?"[26] The level of **satisfaction/dissatisfaction**

Postpurchase use and reevaluation

Marketers can use consumer complaints to understand their customers and keep them satisfied. But many consumers who are dissatisfied with a product or service do not make a formal complaint. The U.S. Officer of Consumer Affairs estimates that between 37 percent and 45 percent of unhappy people do not complain; they simply go elsewhere. Companies should make it easy for their dissatisfied customers to complain—so the companies can fix the problem and avoid more unhappy customers.

Since they first instituted an 800 number in 1974, Procter & Gamble has been a leader in "consumer services" (their term for the system that allows customers easy access to the company). By 1979, P&G had printed the 800 number on every consumer product they sold in the United States.

In 1983, P&G received 670,000 mail and telephone contacts about its products, and this amount increases nearly every year. P&G employs 75 people in the consumer service department, 30 to answer calls, and the rest to answer letters and analyze the data. As of mid-1984, the system was not computerized; data were tabulated by hand.

According to Gibson Carey, P&G manager for general advertising, the calls fall into three broad categories—requests for information, complaints, and testimonials (praise). P&G uses these data to spot problems and correct them early. Because most consumers call with the package in their hand, and because each package has a

with the purchase choice is a useful concept for understanding consumer behavior.[27] For instance, measures of consumer satisfaction can be used to indicate the success of a company's marketing strategies. Satisfied consumers are more likely to repurchase a product and become brand loyal. They are more likely to tell other people about the product and spread positive word-of-mouth information. Dissatisfaction, on the other hand, can lead to complaints and negative word-of-mouth communications, behaviors with unfavorable consequences for a company.[28] Consumer Perspective 8.3 describes Procter & Gamble's system for handling consumer complaints.

Marketers often study satisfaction and dissatisfaction in terms of the *disconfirmation of consumers' expectations.*[29] *Satisfaction* occurs when the product positively disconfirms consumers' expectations by performing better than expected ("This magazine is more interesting than I thought it would be"). Satisfaction can also occur when the product confirms a consumer's favorable prepurchase expectations ("I thought this would be a great CD, and it is"). *Dissatisfaction* occurs when expectations are negatively disconfirmed, when performance of the product is worse than the consumer anticipated ("This frozen lasagna doesn't taste very good"). The amount of dissatisfaction depends on the extent of disconfirmation and the consumer's level of involvement with the product and the problem-solving process. To avoid disconfirmation and resulting dissatisfaction, marketers should try to manage consumer expectations by not under- or overpromising product performance. When marketing promotions promise more quality or performance than a product can deliver, consumers are more likely to become dissatisfied with the product.

A disconfirmation experience that leads to dissatisfaction also creates a state of cognitive dissonance ("I bought brand X, but X is not very good").[30] *Cognitive dissonance* refers to an inconsistency between two cognitions (beliefs) or attitudes ("I like the $350 one best, but I bought the $200 model"). Consumers who are not sure they made a good decision may experience cognitive dissonance ("I wonder if I could have bought that camera more cheaply somewhere else").

The unpleasant affective feelings associated with cognitive dissonance can motivate the consumer to do something to reduce the dissonance. A consumer might reduce postpurchase dissonance by switching to another brand, returning the product for a refund

code printed on it that identifies the plant, the manufacturing date, and sometimes even the shift and line that made it, P&G can trace a problem to the source and correct it. Based on calls received about various products P&G has:

▶ Included instructions for baking at high altitudes on Duncan Hines brownies packages.

▶ Added a recipe for making a wedding cake to its white cake mix package.

▶ Told users what to do if Downy liquid fabric softener accidentally freezes. (Numerous customers had that problem during a cold spell.)

Carey notes that "we don't look at [consumer service] as a source for new product ideas." Instead, P&G considers the 800 number system as "a distant, early warning signal" of product problems. Without it, "we wouldn't find out about them for weeks or months."

Source: Adapted from "Customers: P&G's Pipeline to Product Problems," July 11, 1984, issue of *Business Week*, by special permission, copyright © 1984 by McGraw-Hill, Inc.; Susan Caminiti, "The New Champs of Retailing," *Fortune*, September 24, 1990, pp. 85–100; and Ivan C. Smith, "Customer Satisfaction Chains Show Where the Weak Links Lie," *Marketing News*, February 4, 1991, pp. 8, 21.

or exchange, telling friends how bad the product is, or throwing the product away. Alternatively, a consumer might rationalize a choice by changing an inconsistent belief or attitude ("This shirt isn't so bad after all; I sort of like it"). Some consumers have reduced their cognitive dissonance by persuading friends to buy the same product or brand, which

Satisfaction with a purchase is influenced by the consumer's perception of value.

validates their product evaluations and supports their choice decision. Other consumers pay selective attention to ads and other positive information about the chosen product or brand in an attempt to convince themselves they made a good decision. A marketing strategy is to send direct-mail information to people who might experience cognitive dissonance, reassuring them about their good choice (Congratulations! Buying your Nikon camera was an excellent decision).

LEVELS OF PROBLEM SOLVING

Consumers put varying amounts of cognitive and behavioral effort into different problem-solving situations. Problem-solving effort ranges from considerable (Barbara's extensive activities in buying new tableware) to very little (buying a soft drink from a vending machine). For convenience, marketers divide problem-solving activity into three levels: extensive, limited, and routine or habitual.[31] Exhibit 8.6 summarizes the major ways these three levels differ.

Extensive problem solving

During **extensive problem solving**, consumers usually put substantial effort into search activities to identify potential choice alternatives and to learn the choice criteria with which to evaluate them. When engaged in extensive problem solving, consumers often make multiple decisions involving significant cognitive effort. For instance, in making a purchase decision, consumers are likely to consider several choice alternatives and carefully evaluate them using choice criteria linked to their personal goals. Extensive problem solving occurs because the important goals activated by problem recognition create high levels of involvement and motivation to engage in problem solving. Extensive problem solving also may occur because consumers do not have enough relevant knowledge in memory to solve the problem. Because consumers care about the consequences of their actions, they may have strong affective responses during problem solving. Extensive problem solving can take a long time, ranging from hours to months. Relatively few consumer purchases require extensive problem solving (buying a house, a car, furniture, a major investment, special items of clothing).

EXHIBIT 8.6

Levels of problem-solving effort

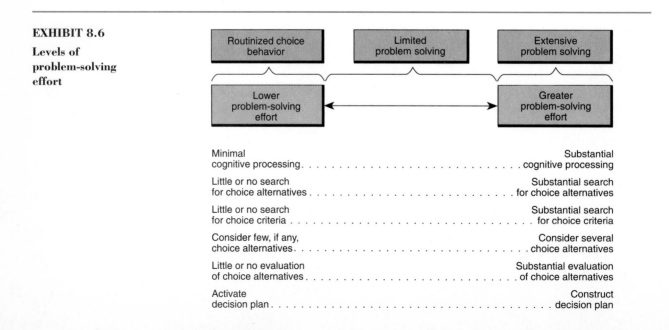

CONSUMER
PERSPECTIVE

8.4

Routinized
choice
behavior

In one study, 120 consumers were observed buying laundry detergent in three chain grocery stores. An observer stationed in the department aisle coded shoppers' activities as they moved down the aisle and picked out the detergent they wanted. The results showed that, for most consumers, laundry detergent choice behavior was quite routinized.

Most consumers examined very few packages of detergent. In fact, 72 percent of the consumers looked at only one package, and only 11 percent looked at more than two. Even fewer packages were physically picked up—83 percent of the consumers picked up only one package, and only 4 percent picked up more than two. Obviously, most of these consumers were not engaged in much in-store problem-solving activity for this product. In fact, hardly any across-brand or within-brand comparisons were made; the vast majority of consumers made none. Finally, consumers took an average of 13 seconds after entering the aisle to make their detergent choice. Given that the laundry detergent section spans an entire aisle and that several seconds are required to walk to the appropriate area, it is obvious that the typical consumer makes an extremely quick choice that involves minimal cognitive and behavioral effort.

The majority of consumers in this study were engaged in routinized choice behavior. They were merely carrying out a simple decision plan: for example, find the large size of Tide and buy it. Are most other grocery store products purchased in such an automatic way?

Source: Adapted with permission of the University of Chicago Press from "An Examination of Consumer Decision Making for a Common Repeat Purchase Product," by Wayne D. Hoyer, in *Journal of Consumer Research*, December 1984, pp. 822–29. © 1984 by the University of Chicago.

Limited problem solving

In **limited problem solving**, consumers exert low to moderate levels of cognitive and behavioral effort. Many common purchase problems tend to activate moderately important end goals, producing low to moderate levels of involvement and motivation. Based on their past experiences with these problems, many consumers have some relevant knowledge in memory that can be activated in evaluating alternatives and making a choice decision. Compared to extensive problem solving, consumers in limited-problem-solving situations conduct fewer search activities, make fewer decisions, consider fewer choice alternatives, and have less complex integration processes. Limited problem solving usually is carried out quickly, requiring only minutes or hours. Limited problem solving is common for many consumer purchases.

Routinized choice behavior

Routinized choice behavior occurs relatively automatically, with minimal effort and little or no decision making. For many simple, everyday purchases, consumers' buying behavior has become habitual or routine—buying another lunchtime Pepsi from the vending machine or always purchasing gum at the grocery checkout counter. Because such purchase problems activate relatively unimportant goals, consumers tend to have low involvement and motivation in the purchase process. Also, because such purchases tend to be made frequently (people buy milk or bread every week), consumers have considerable knowledge in memory to use in making decisions. Given the low involvement and adequate knowledge of routinized choice behavior, consumers perform little or no search for information. In fact, consumers may do little or no conscious decision making (alternative behaviors are not evaluated or compared in terms of their ability to satisfy the problem goals). In most cases, a previously formed decision plan is activated from memory (*BI* to buy a Pepsi) and is carried out automatically to produce the purchase behavior. Consumer Perspective 8.4 describes an example of routinized choice behavior.

Buying breakfast cereals is a routine choice behavior for many consumers.

Changes in problem solving with experience

The amount of effort consumers exert in problem solving tends to decrease with experience.[32] As they make repeated decisions to solve a problem, consumers form means-end chains of product and brand knowledge that is linked to their goals and values. Consumers also learn simple scripts and heuristics regarding the problem that are stored in memory. When activated, these heuristics can automatically direct search and evaluation processes (decisions about what to do are not needed). Consumers also learn which products and brands can successfully solve the problem. This knowledge may be stored in memory as decision plans (*BI*), which can automatically direct purchase behavior when activated. Running down to the convenience store for a loaf of bread or stopping to fill up at a favorite gas station are simple decision plans that require little or no problem solving or decision making to carry out.

The degree to which a problem-solving process becomes routinized depends on the amount of knowledge a consumer has about the problem and the level of the consumer's involvement with the problem. Consumers are more likely to develop habitual choice behavior for frequently purchased, less involving products such as food and personal care items. In contrast, problem-solving processes for higher-involvement, infrequently purchased products (low knowledge in memory) is likely to remain limited (or extensive). Because these products tend to be purchased infrequently, consumers' knowledge in memory may be seen as obsolete, and some search for relevant information is necessary.

Marketing implications

To develop effective marketing strategies, marketers need to know at which level the consumer is making purchase decisions. The level of problem solving has different implications for marketing strategies.

Extensive problem solving

Although relatively few consumer decisions involve extensive problem solving, marketers must recognize and satisfy the special needs of consumers for information when they do engage in extensive decision making. In many extensive-decision-making situations, consumers need information about everything—including which end goals are important, which choice alternatives are relevant, what choice criteria are appropriate, and so on. Marketers should strive to make the necessary information available, in a format and at a level of presentation that consumers can understand and use in the problem-solving process.[33]

Because consumers intentionally seek product information during extensive decision making, interrupting their problem-solving processes is relatively easy. Informational displays at the point of purchase—say, displays of mattresses that are cut apart to show construction details—or presentations by salespeople can be effective sources of information. Complex sales materials such as brochures and product specifications may be effective, along with high-information advertisements. Consumers operating at extensive decision-making levels will attend to relevant information, and they are motivated enough to comprehend it. Marketers may take advantage of the information receptivity of consumers by offering free samples, coupons, or easy trial (take it home and try it for a couple of days) to help consumers gain information about a brand.

Limited problem solving

Most consumer decisions involve limited effort. Because most consumers already have a lot of information about a product from previous experience, the basic marketing strategy here is to make additional pieces of information available to consumers when and where they need them. Advertisements to increase top-of-mind awareness may help to move a brand into the evoked set of choice alternatives at the beginning of the decision process. Such a position is important, because most consumers are not likely to search extensively for other alternatives. Moreover, it is critical that the brand is perceived to possess the few key choice criteria used in the evaluation process. Advertisements that capture the attention of the consumer and communicate favorable beliefs about salient attributes and consequences of the brand may be able to create that knowledge. Marketers may also try to design a store environment that stimulates impulsive purchases, a type of limited decision making.[34]

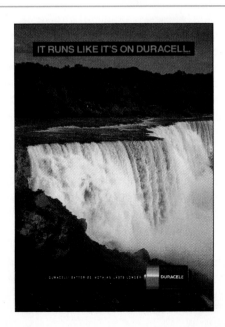

Ads that capture consumers' attention can create knowledge about important product consequences.

The basic purpose of marketing is to create and keep customers. The secret of keeping customers, of course, is to keep them satisfied. One way industrial-goods companies keep their corporate customers satisfied is by routinizing their decision-making processes.

Companies as diverse as Inland Steel, Eastman Kodak, and First Boston Bank put computer terminals connected to the main corporate computer system on their customers' desks, free of charge. The network is called a *channel system*, because it enables customers to simplify the channel of distribution by ordering supplies instantly and directly from the supplying company. Buyers can thus better manage their expensive inventories. Basically, these systems solve many customers' problems. Although the systems are vastly expensive and very tricky to implement successfully, many companies are making the investment, because such systems destroy your customers' interest in competitors' products.

In 1974, American Hospital Supply (AHS) installed one of the pioneer systems in the stockrooms of large hospitals. Instead of having to order from salespeople making regular rounds, purchasing agents and stock clerks could use the terminals to order routine supplies easily and quickly (and directly from AHS). As with most channel

Routinized choice behavior

Much consumer choice behavior is routinized. Consumers may feel they know all they need to about a product category, and they are not motivated to search for new information. Their choice behavior is based on a learned decision plan. In such cases, the appropriate marketing strategy depends on the strength of the brand's position in the market.

In general, the more automatic the choice behavior becomes, the more difficult it is for marketers to interrupt and influence the choice. Marketers of established brands with substantial market share want to maintain their brand in the evoked sets (the choice alternatives activated at the beginning of the problem-solving process) of a significant segment of consumers. When consumers engage in little or no search, marketers have minimal opportunities to propel their brand into consumer consideration sets during problem solving.

Marketers of new brands or brands with a smaller market share must somehow interrupt the automatic problem-solving processes. They could develop strategies of producing prominent environmental stimuli such as large or unusual store displays, creating strong package graphics that stand out on the shelf, giving away free samples, or running sales promotions (buy one, get one free).[35] Such strategies are intended to catch consumers' attention and interrupt their routine choice behavior. The goal of "interrupts" is to prompt a more conscious level of decision making that might persuade the consumer to include the new brand in the consideration set.

Of course, marketers of leading brands such as Doritos snack chips, Snickers candy bars, Budweiser beer, and IBM computers may *want* consumers to follow a routine choice process. Because these brands already have a high market share, they are in the evoked sets of most buyers. Marketers of such products want to avoid marketing-related environmental interrupts such as stockouts, which could push consumers into a limited-decision-making process and lead them to try a competitor's brand. One critical aspect of the overall marketing strategy for high-market-share brands is an efficient distribution system to keep the brands fully stocked and available whenever consumers can make choices. Frito-Lay, the maker of Fritos, Ruffles potato chips, and many popular snack products, has developed a superb distribution system partly for this reason. Consumer Perspective 8.5 shows how several marketers of industrial products attempt to make their buyers' decision-making processes more routine.

systems, customers tend to buy more from the supplier of the system and less from competitors. By making the decision-making process more routine, the company makes it easier than ever to buy from it.

Kodak developed a system called Technet that is targeted at the owners of minilabs (storefront film developers) and that takes routinization to an extreme. Based on an IBM PC, the system does everything but feed the night watchdog. It automatically monitors print quality, offers advice on pricing, and keeps track of sales and complaints. The system also detects when paper and chemicals are running low and automatically reorders from Kodak. To get Technet, the lab must agree to use Kodak paper and chemicals exclusively and to let Kodak monitor its adherence to quality guidelines.

These channel systems and other computerized strategies may be only the early steps toward a time when many (perhaps most) marketing transactions are conducted electronically.

Source: Reprinted with permission, "How to Keep Customers Happy Captives," by Peter Petre, *Fortune*, © 1985 Time Inc. All rights reserved.

Learning objective 1: *Define a decision, and describe why consumer decision making is part of the problem-solving process.*

► SUMMARY

A decision is a choice between two or more possible behaviors or actions. Decisions are always choices between behaviors—what to *do* with an object. In decision making, consumers integrate or combine knowledge about the consequences of alternative actions to evaluate the possible behaviors and choose one. The outcome of this integration process produces attitudes toward a behavior (A_{act}) and the social influences concerning the behavior (SN), which, in turn, are combined to form a behavioral intention—a plan to perform the chosen behavior ("I will buy Colgate toothpaste tomorrow"). Consumer decision making is part of the problem-solving process. Recognizing a problem—"I am thirsty"—activates a goal—"I would like to have a soda." Because the goal is not yet attained, the consumer has a problem to be solved. Solving the problem may involve making multiple decisions. Every decision during problem solving is influenced by the overall goal associated with the problem.

Learning objective 2: *Describe the six stages of the problem-solving process.*

The problem-solving process includes six stages: problem recognition, search for relevant information, evaluation of alternatives, the choice decision, purchase, and postpurchase use and reevaluation. Problem recognition occurs when people become aware of an unsatisfied goal or problem and are motivated to do something to achieve the goal and solve the problem. The search for relevant information involves looking for information that is relevant to the perceived problem, including information about potential choice alternatives (different products or brands) and information about choice criteria. Evaluation of alternatives (forming A_{act}) involves combining salient beliefs about the consequences of each considered behavior. The choice decision involves integrating information to form a decision plan (a behavioral intention to buy one of the alternatives). Purchase involves carrying out the decision plan. The postpurchase stage involves using the chosen alternative and reevaluating it by comparing its performance with one's expectations. Satisfaction with the choice usually results if expectations are confirmed or surpassed, while a negative disconfirmation of expectations creates dissatisfaction.

Learning objective 3: *Define end goals, and discuss the role of end goals in problem solving.*

End goals are the important consequences or values that consumers want to achieve or satisfy (Seth wants to be more popular with his classmates). End goals are a key influence in the problem-solving process. The activated end goals are the basis for involvement, provide the motivation for decision making, and focus consumers' attention on information that is relevant to the perceived problem. End goals can be simple and concrete (Bill wants to buy gas for his car) or more complex and abstract (Mary Lou wants to buy a new dress that makes her feel attractive). We can identify five broad categories of end goals. Consumers who have an end goal of optimizing satisfaction are motivated to find the best possible choice alternative (buy the best tennis racket under $200). Other consumers with a goal of maintaining satisfaction try to find an acceptable (just OK) alternative, while expending little effort (going to the convenience store to buy milk—any brand is OK). Other types of end goals include preventing problems (buying snow tires to avoid the unfavorable consequences of getting stuck in the snow), resolving conflict (buying a moderately expensive brand such as Sony to balance the positive and negative consequences of purchase), and escaping a problem (buy mouthwash to get away from or reduce unpleasant consequences of bad breath).

Learning objective 4: *Define consideration set, discuss how it can be formed, and describe an implication of consideration sets for marketers.*

The consideration set is the various choice alternatives (different behaviors) a consumer evaluates and seriously considers performing during decision making. A purchase consideration set may contain different product categories, product forms, brands, or models. The choice alternatives in a consideration set (different brands, for instance) could be activated from memory, found through intentional search, or "discovered" by accident. If a brand is not in a person's consideration set, it cannot be evaluated or purchased. Brands that are included in many consumers' consideration sets have the potential for a high market share. Thus, marketers may engage in costly marketing strategies (lots of TV advertising and sales promotions, as is the case with Coke and Pepsi) to make it more likely that their brand gets into the consideration set.

Learning objective 5: *Define choice criteria, and give examples of how positive and negative choice criteria might be used in problem solving.*

Choice criteria are the specific consequences used to evaluate different behaviors (buy Sony, buy Panasonic, buy Technics) and to choose among them. Virtually any consequence can be a choice criterion, including salient beliefs about functional and psychosocial consequences as well as values. Some choice criteria are beliefs stored in memory that may be activated during the problem-solving process. In other cases, consumers search for information about choice criteria, which they must interpret and convert into personal beliefs and knowledge. Many choice criteria are benefits or positive consequences consumers wish to achieve. Other choice criteria are perceived risks or negative consequences consumers wish to avoid or escape from.

Learning objective 6: *Describe the difference between compensatory and noncompensatory integration processes, and give an example of each.*

Compensatory and noncompensatory processes describe two ways consumers combine information about choice alternatives to make a purchase decision. In a compensatory integration process, a consumer considers all the salient beliefs about the consequences of the choice alternatives (considered behaviors). That is, a consumer considers all the positive and negative consequences at once so they can "balance" or compensate for each other. Thus, a choice alternative with mostly positive consequences and a few negative consequences will be evaluated less favorably than an alternative with all positive consequences. In a compensatory integration process, consumers do not consider all their salient beliefs about choice criteria at once. Thus, beliefs about consequences are combined in ways that do not balance or compensate for each other. For instance, a choice alternative with one negative consequence (such as high price) might be rejected without considering its several positive consequences (high quality, excellent style, good warranty).

Learning objective 7: *Describe three types of heuristics, and give an example of each.*

Heuristics are simple "if . . . , then . . . " rules that connect an event with an appropriate action—"If you get junk mail, throw it away unopened." Heuristics are simple rules of thumb that can be activated to direct cognitive processes and overt behaviors automatically. Heuristics require consumers to use very little information at a time and, thus, do not exceed the limited capacity of the cognitive system. Heuristics are adaptive in that they are activated and used in specific situations where appropriate. There are three broad categories of heuristics—search, evaluation, and choice heuristics. Search heuristics refer to simple rules about how and where to search for relevant information. For example, some consumers may have a heuristic of seeking advice from a friend with expertise in the problem topic. Evaluation heuristics are procedures for evaluating choice criteria in terms of the current end goal. For instance, some consumers might infer that a product is good quality if it advertises on television. Choice heuristics are rules of thumb for choosing an alternative. For instance, an affect referral heuristic says to buy the product you like the best overall. A wait-and-see heuristic for a new product says to wait several months before buying to make sure it is good.

Learning objective 8: *Describe the three levels of problem-solving effort, and give a marketing implication for each.*

The amount of cognitive and behavioral effort that consumers put into their problem-solving processes is highly variable. Three levels of problem-solving effort have been identified. In extensive problem solving, consumers exert a substantial amount of effort in searching for relevant information and evaluating choice alternatives. Extensive problem solving may require substantial mental and behavioral effort over long periods. For most consumers, buying a car or a new suit for job interviews involves extensive problem solving and considerable decision making. In contrast, routinized choice behavior involves low levels of problem-solving effort and little or no decision making. There may be little or no search for choice alternatives or choice criteria and no consideration of alternative behaviors. Rather, a behavioral intention or decision plan stored in memory is activated and carried out automatically. Between these two extremes of decision-making effort is the moderate amount of effort expended during limited problem solving. Limited problem solving involves a modest amount of searching for relevant information, consideration of a few choice alternatives, and modest amounts of decision making.

▶ **REVIEW AND DISCUSSION QUESTIONS**

1. Discuss what it means to say that decisions are always between alternative behaviors. Illustrate your answer.

2. Why do products or brand not in the consideration set have a low probability of being purchased?

3. Identify three ways that choice alternatives can enter the consideration set. Describe a marketing strategy that could be used to get your brand into consumers' consideration sets for each situation.

4. Discuss why decision making can be treated as a problem-solving process.

5. Think of a purchase decision from your own experience in which you had a well-developed end goal. Describe how it affected your problem-solving process. Then select a decision in which you did not have a well-developed end goal, and describe how it affected your problem-solving process.

6. Assume the role of a product manager for a product about which you (and your management team) have a fairly high level of product knowledge. Consider how each of the formal integration processes would result in different responses to your product, and how you could adjust marketing strategy to deal with these differences.

7. Give at least two examples of how a marketing manager could use routinized choice behavior to increase the likelihood of purchase of his or her new product.

8. Discuss how consumers' involvement and their activated product knowledge might affect the problem-solving processes during purchase decisions for products or services such as new automobiles, an oil change, cold remedies, and health insurance.

9. Relate the examples of decision heuristics shown in Exhibit 8.5 to the concept of involvement. When are these heuristics likely to be useful to the consumer? Under what conditions might they be dysfunctional?

10. Describe the differences between extensive and limited decision making. How should marketing strategies differ for these two types of problem-solving processes?

CHAPTER 9

Communication and Persuasion

LEARNING OBJECTIVES

After completing this chapter, you should be able to:

▶ 1. Describe the four types of promotion communications.

▶ 2. Describe the components of the basic communication model.

▶ 3. Describe the various effects that promotion communications can have on consumers.

▶ 4. Discuss the two routes to persuasion specified by the Elaboration Likelihood Model, and describe the role of attitude toward the ad in persuasion.

▶ 5. Describe how the FCB Grid and vulnerability analysis can be used to understand the consumer/product relationship and help marketers create effective communication strategies.

▶ 6. Describe the MECCAS model of advertising strategy.

▶ 7. Distinguish between lecture and drama advertising.

BARQ'S WINS THE SUPER REGGIE

Each year, the Promotion Marketing Association of America honors the best sales promotions with Reggie Awards (in the form of a cash register that represents increased sales).

In 1992, the most impressive promotion efforts focused on enhancing the value of the brand. Conspicuously absent from the winner's circle were sales promotions based on coupons or other price discounts. Moreover, the winning promotions were integrated across several marketing media such as advertising, packaging, and publicity.

Barq's brand root beer won the Super Reggie Award for the best promotion of the year, called the "Soviet Union Going Out of Business Sale." Consumers were offered Communist memorabilia in exchange for proofs-of-purchase from specially marked 12-packs and 2-liter bottles of Barq's. In addition to extensive free publicity, the promotion was supported by national television and print ads. Barq's created special packaging and point-of-purchase advertising to draw attention to the brand. All aspects of the promotion were integrated to work together.

Another unusual promotion, the "The Talking Can Sweepstakes,'" produced a Reggie for Coors Brewing Company. Here, the product itself delivered the promotion when a light-activated voice chip "spoke" to the consumer if a winning can was opened. The promotion was supported by TV, radio, and magazine advertising and received extensive publicity.

Coors won a second Reggie for "Fishing Hotline" to support its Keystone brand. Coors offered a 900-number consumers could call to receive current, detailed fishing information about specific species.

Other winners included:

▶ Frito-Lay for its D-day promotion, in which over 6 million bags of Nacho Cheese flavor Doritos were distributed in a single day. This was the largest one-day sampling effort ever undertaken by a snack marketer.

▶ Binney & Smith's Crayola brand for a 20-page holiday coloring book.

▶ Emory Worldwide, for "It's Up To You," designed to win back former customers and support Emory's image as the most flexible air freight carrier.[1]

Successful sales promotions illustrate the importance of communication and persuasion in influencing consumer behavior. Marketers develop promotions to *communicate* information about their products and to *persuade* consumers to like and buy them. This chapter discusses four types of marketing promotion communications. Then we present a general model of the communication process that helps us understand how marketing promotions communicate information to consumers. Next, we discuss the persuasion processes by which promotions influence consumers to change their beliefs, attitudes, and behavioral intentions. We conclude by discussing implications for developing and managing promotion strategies.

TYPES OF PROMOTION COMMUNICATIONS

The four types of **promotion communications**—advertising, sales promotions, personal selling, and publicity—constitute a promotion "mix" that marketers try to manage. The most obvious form of promotion communication is advertising, but the other forms can have important influences on consumers.

Advertising

Advertising is any paid, nonpersonal communication about a product, brand, company, or store. Ads may be conveyed via a variety of media including TV, radio, print (magazines and newspapers), billboards, signs, and unusual media such as hot-air balloons and T-shirts. Marketers use advertising to influence consumers' affect and cognitions (feelings, beliefs, attitudes, and intentions). But the vast majority of the hundreds of ads consumers are exposed to each day receive low levels of attention and comprehension.

The broad goal of advertising communication is image management—to create and maintain images and meanings in consumers' minds.[2] For instance, Nike once made a big splash with a series of billboards featuring strong visual images of athletes—Carl Lewis long jumping or Michael Jordan leaping for the basket. Besides the picture, the ads showed only the Nike "swoosh" logo in the corner. At first, viewers probably had to look twice to comprehend what product was being advertised, but the pictures conveyed strong symbolic meanings about Nike products. In markets where the billboards appeared, Nike sales increased 30 percent.[3]

Sales promotions

Sales promotions are communications offering inducements to the consumer to make a purchase. There are many types of sales promotions, including temporary price reductions through coupons and rebates, contests and sweepstakes, trading stamps, free samples, in-store displays, and premiums and gifts. TV advertising might be more glamorous, but more money is spent on sales promotions in the United States. In fact, more than two thirds of the promotion budget is spent on sales promotions versus one third on advertising.[4]

The main objective of sales promotions is to move the product today, not tomorrow. A sales promotion is designed to influence consumers to buy a product immediately by offering them something, such as a premium or price reduction. Dow once designed a back-to-school promotion for its Ziploc sandwich bags that included a 15-cent coupon plus a mail-in offer for free bread with two proofs of purchase. A premium was also included in the package—a set of stickers of the beasties from the movie *Gremlins*. This promotion was intended to get people to stock up on Ziploc products, thereby blocking purchases of competitive brands. Sales volume increased 42 percent, and Ziploc became the number one brand in the category for the first time.[5]

Personal selling

Personal selling involves direct personal communications between a salesperson and a consumer. Personal communications may increase consumers' involvement with the product or the decision, making them more likely to pay attention and comprehend the information presented by the salesperson. Also, the interactive communication situation in personal selling allows the salesperson to adapt the presentation to each potential buyer. Certain products are traditionally promoted through personal selling, such as life insurance, automobiles, and houses. Personal selling in retailing has decreased over the past 20 years as self-service has become more popular. However, some retailers such as Nordstrom have reversed this trend by emphasizing personal selling and customer service. Besides lots of personal attention from a courteous sales staff, customers are wooed by soft piano music and champagne bars.

For other businesses, a form of personal selling by telephone—called *telemarketing*—has become increasingly popular as the costs of a direct sales call increased to between $100 and $200 in 1985.[6] Telemarketing selling differs considerably from face-to-face selling. The telemarketer usually follows a prepared script, never travels, makes 20 to 50 calls per day, which last from one to two minutes, works about four to six hours per day, and is closely supervised. In contrast, a conventional salesperson often travels, usually must improvise the sales presentation to fit the buyer's needs, makes only 2 to 10 sales calls per day that last about 1 hour each, works about 8 to 12 hours per day, and is loosely supervised.[7]

Both Avon and Mary Kay Cosmetics, among the largest U.S. marketers of skin-care products, were built on personal selling. In their earlier days, neither company spent much on advertising or customer sales promotions. Mary Kay, for instance, spent a minuscule $1 million on advertising in 1980 (out of $167 million in sales). Instead, most of its promotion budget was spent on incentives for salespeople: symbolic prizes such as medals, ribbons, and commemorative certificates, and jewelry, calculators, briefcases, and furs. Top sellers receive the use of pink Cadillacs or Buick Regals. Mary Kay also spends heavily on motivational and training programs for sales personnel, which in 1980 numbered some 150,000 women (Mary Kay has virtually no salesmen).

Publicity

Publicity is any unpaid communication about a company, product, or brand. An article in *PC World* comparing various brands of word-processing software is not paid advertising but provides useful product information to consumers at no cost to the marketers of the software. Descriptions of new products or brands; brand comparisons in trade journals, newspapers, or news magazines; or discussions on radio and TV talk shows provide similar product information to consumers.

Nabisco sales representatives are creating an in-store display of Ritz crackers.

Publicity can be positive or negative. Nike received a bonanza of free publicity in the form of favorable news stories about its billboard campaign. In one case, a TV news segment in Los Angeles concluded with a reporter urging viewers to "give a honk for Nike, which has raised the billboard from visual blight to at least camp art."[8] Tylenol, on the other hand, twice received unfavorable publicity when people were poisoned by Tylenol capsules that had been tampered with.

Sometimes publicity can be more effective than advertising, because consumers do not screen out the messages so readily. In addition, publicity communications may be considered more credible because they are not being presented by the marketing organization. Publicity is difficult to manage, however. Marketers sometimes stage "media events" in hopes of garnering free publicity. Procter & Gamble, for example, once held a glitzy news conference at a New York City disco to introduce new Liquid Tide—complete with a 20-foot-high inflatable model of the product. It hoped the media would report the event and perhaps show a picture of the product. P&G had little control over what type of publicity (if any) would result, however.

The promotion mix

Ideally, marketing managers should combine the four types of promotion communications into a coherent overall strategy. The United States in the past two decades has seen major changes in the balance of marketing effort devoted to the four types of promotion. Expenditures for sales promotions have increased much more rapidly than those for advertising. From 1976 to 1986, spending on sales promotions increased about 225 percent (from $30 billion to $107 billion), while ad spending increased about 160 percent (from $22 billion to $58 billion).[9] During the recession of the early 1990s, sales promotions gained even more ground, while advertising expenditures, especially on network TV, decreased (down about 7 percent in 1991 over 1990). Moreover, new forms of promotion communications continue to be developed, such as direct marketing and magazines dedicated to a single advertiser, which allow highly accurate targeting of the desired consumer audience. Despite the attention on advertising and sales promotions, publicity and personal selling remain important promotion communications for certain products such as movies (publicity) and automobiles (personal selling).

Marketers have debated the relative importance of advertising versus personal-selling communications.[10] As would be expected, most advertising agencies argue that advertising is the best way to create a strong relationship between consumers and the brand. Other marketers believe sales promotions can also enhance the consumer/brand relationship while having the advantage of influencing immediate purchase behavior. Some analysts see a long-range trend toward a broader promotion mix where advertising is no longer dominant. The promotion mix of the future may offer many more options, including event sponsoring (Pepsi sponsors rock concerts), sports marketing (Volvo sponsors tennis matches), direct marketing (coupons are sent to purchasers of your competitor's brand), and public relations. Consumer Perspective 9.1 describes an event sponsorship promotion. These "new" promotion communications are valuable developments partly because of the high costs of advertising and partly because marketers need to target customers more precisely than is possible with mass advertising.

THE COMMUNICATION PROCESS

The broad goal of marketing promotions is to communicate a certain set of meanings to consumers.[11] These meanings are intended to create positive beliefs about the product and positive attitudes toward buying (A_{act}) and a positive intention to buy the product (*BI*). Thus, developing successful marketing promotions is a communications issue.

Exhibit 9.1 presents a model that identifies the key factors in the **communication process.** The process begins when the *source* of the promotion communication determines the communication strategy (decides what information to communicate) and creates

More companies have been seeking alternatives to advertising to promote their brands, including sponsoring various events such as rock concerts and tours, bicycle races, and tennis tournaments. Since 1986, the number of companies sponsoring events has doubled to 4,200, and spending has tripled to $2.94 billion. One reason for this change is the spiraling cost of television advertising.

Consider the John Hancock Bowl (once called the Sun Bowl) held in December in El Paso, Texas. For most people, the score of the 1990 game was Michigan State, 17, Southern California, 6. But for John Hancock Financial Services, the sponsor of the event, the score was $5.1 million to $1.6 million. The company laid out about $1.6 million in direct expenditures, but garnered about $5.1 million in equivalent advertising value.

Hancock is serious about documenting the effectiveness of its sponsorship promotions. For instance, it clipped 7,800 newspaper and magazine articles about the John Hancock Bowl, estimating the reach of each story. Converted to equivalent advertising value, the stories were calculated to have a total value of over $1 million in advertising equivalency.

The major value of the sponsorship, however, came from the CBS broadcast of the game, which Hancock estimated to be worth about $3.1 million in advertising equivalence in terms of repeated references to the company, shots of the scoreboard, and visibility of the company logo at midfield and on the uniforms. Tracing the effects of the bowl sponsorship to actual sales of Hancock products, however, would be more difficult. One indirect indicator of behavioral impact is that the proportion of consumers who claimed they would consider buying from Hancock rose from 41 percent to 54 percent. Consumer awareness of the Hancock advertising campaign also increased to 96 percent from 90 percent.

Some companies find the payoffs of event sponsorship to be less impressive. Sunkist, one of the originating sponsors of football bowl games, paid $1.6 million to sponsor the 1991 Fiesta Bowl on New Year's Day, but decided not to be a sponsor in 1992 because it believed the number of companies sponsoring other games had diluted the impact of sponsorship.

In the 1992 Hancock Bowl Game, Baylor beat Arizona 20-15.

CONSUMER PERSPECTIVE

Promotion through event sponsorship

EXHIBIT 9.1   A general model of the communication process

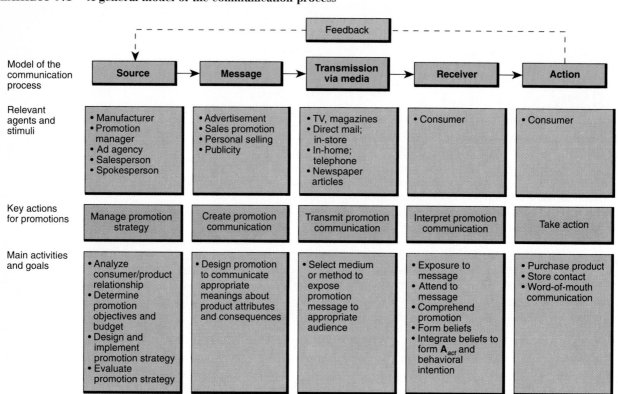

Source: Adapted from Figure 8.1 in Henry Assael, *Consumer Behavior and Marketing Action*, 3rd ed. (Boston: PSW-KENT Publishing Company, 1987), p. 210. © by Wadsworth, Inc. Used by permission of PSW-KENT Publishing Company, a division of Wadsworth, Inc.

the *message* (constructs the communication using appropriate symbols, words, pictures, actions). Then, the message is *transmitted* over some medium such as a television show, direct mail, a billboard, or magazine. The *receiver* or consumer, if exposed to the promotion, must interpret it by attending to it and comprehending its meaning. Then, the consumer might take *action,* which could include going to a store or making a purchase. Two stages are especially critical to the success of promotion strategies: (1) when the marketer creates the promotion message to convey the intended meaning and (2) when consumers are exposed to the promotion and interpret its meaning.[12] Exhibit 9.1 also shows the relevant agents or actors in each stage of the communication process and the key activities at each stage. Next, we discuss some factors that influence each of these stages in the communication process.

Source

The *source* of a promotion message influences its effectiveness.[13] For instance, salespeople whom customers perceive as credible, trustworthy, and similar to themselves tend to be more effective. These can include celebrity spokespersons, who are often hired to appear in ads to serve as the source for promotional messages. After extensive research, AT&T selected actor Cliff Robertson from among 20 potential celebrities to help the company retain its dominance in the $45 billion U.S. long-distance telephone service business against MCI, U.S. Sprint, and other competitors. According to AT&T's director of advertising, "We see Cliff as a solid, reliable, dependable person who will stand up and say directly what he thinks." Robertson accounts for his believability by saying, "I have to say

CONSUMER PERSPECTIVE

Subliminal advertising

Although most advertisers pay little or no attention to the topic, *subliminal persuasion* in advertising just won't go away. Writers like Wilson Key keep turning out widely read books that claim subliminal advertising is all around us. Key claims marketers intentionally embed stimuli such as sexual-objects, symbols, or words, in advertisements. Moreover, he claims these hidden, subliminal stimuli affect us in powerful ways of which we are unaware.

What do we know about the effects of subliminal stimulation? First, it is clear that stimulation below the level of a person's conscious awareness *can* have measurable effects on some aspects of that person's behavior. That is, people can respond to stimuli without realizing the stimuli exist. But these stimuli are not necessarily subliminal—that is, they are not necessarily presented at intensities below our perceptual threshold. They just tend not to be noticed consciously as consumers go about their business; a great deal of cognitive activity occurs automatically. Thus, consumers often are not able to report the existence of a stimulus or an awareness that some cognitive process has occurred.

With regard to Key's claims about sexual symbol embedding, two issues are in question. First, are subliminal embeddings made in advertisements as a matter of course, as Key claims? Virtually no evidence exists that this is so. Certainly, sexual stimuli are found in a great many advertisements, but not in subliminal embeds. Second, could subliminal stimuli affect goal-directed behaviors such as purchase choices?

A key finding in cognitive psychology that is basic to marketing strategy is that the meaning of a stimulus is not inherent in the stimulus itself. Rather, meanings are constructed by consumers in active and sometimes complex ways as they come into contact with the stimulus. Most stimuli have little or no influence on our cognitions or behaviors when presented at a recognizable level. Why, then, should they suddenly have a strong impact when presented subliminally? Key claims that humans have two processing systems, one of which operates on a completely unconscious level and immediately picks up on subliminal embeds. No psychological theories or data support such a system of cognition.

None of this is to say that ads may not have effects on consumers' meanings at a subconscious level—but the stimuli don't have to be subliminal for that to occur.

Sources: Jack Haberstroh, "Can't Ignore Subliminal Ad Charges," *Advertising Age*, September 17, 1984, pp. 3, 42; and Timothy E. Moore, "Subliminal Advertising: What You See Is What You Get," *Journal of Marketing*, Spring 1982, pp. 38–47.

the copy in a way that's effective and that doesn't deter from my beliefs. I don't try to sell. I just try to say it with conviction."[14] But many other celebrity spokespersons don't seem to have this effectiveness.[15]

Message

The effectiveness of a promotion is influenced by the actual information contained in the promotion *message*—the product claim made in a print ad, the value of the coupon or sweepstakes prize, the promises made by the salesperson, or the attractiveness of the premium offer. Marketers work hard to devise effective promotions. For instance, they must trade off making a sales promotion (like those in the opening example) attractive enough to stimulate consumer response and small enough that the costs don't outweigh the benefits.

Most research concerning message effects focuses on advertising. The effects of many message-related factors have been examined—including the use of fear appeals, sexual content, content that produces emotional responses, humor, gender roles, one- versus two-sided messages, evaluative visual material, and explicit versus implicit product

Drama ads such as this tell a story in which the product has an important part.

claims.[16] Some studies have even examined subliminal messages (see Consumer Perspective 9.2).

The results of all this research are mixed, in that a given message characteristic does not always have the same effect on every consumer. This is partly because the effects of any ad message are influenced both by the activated knowledge and involvement of the consumers who receive the ad and by specific features of the environment in which exposure occurs. Thus, the effects of a fear appeal or the use of humor may vary considerably from one situation to another. Because few generalizations can be drawn, marketers usually must research the effects of a new promotion strategy on consumers or rely on their intuition.

The type of information included in an advertising message influences how the ad communicates to consumers. For example, *informational ads* present verbal facts about the product, whereas *image ads* show pictures and visual symbols.[17] Consumers' responses to informational ads are dominated by the cognitive system, which interprets the ad and creates knowledge and beliefs about product attributes and consequences (benefits and risks). Responses to image ads are dominated by the affective system, which produces a range of emotional, feeling, and mood responses.

An ad message can be delivered as a lecture or presented as a drama.[18] A *lecture ad* is like a classroom lecture in that a source offers information about the attributes and functional consequences of a brand. Consider an ad for toothpaste in which a person in a white doctor's coat describes two attributes—tartar-control formula and a special fluoride ingredient. The source claims these attributes reduce cavities and make it less necessary to visit the dentist for teeth cleaning and also presents scientific evidence to support these claims.

Lecture ads communicate product information with the intention of persuading consumers to form positive beliefs about product consequences, a favorable attitude toward

CONSUMER
PERSPECTIVE

A new medium
for transmitting
promotion
communications

Given the difficulty of keeping viewers' attention on 30- or even 15-second commercials, the promotion strategy Toyota used to sell its new minivan, Previa, might be considered a bit risky.

Toyota's ad agency, Saatchi and Saatchi, created an eight-minute videotape commercial for the Previa and mailed it to some 200,000 potential customers. (Toyota assumed these people owned a VCR.) The video had a fragile story line about a woman ad writer assigned to push the new Previa. It portrayed her family (husband and fresh-faced kids) driving around in the car, while she explained its special features. In the background, an orchestra played the Toyota theme song, "I love what you do for me."

The costs of this promotion were estimated at about $1.5 million, including buying the mailing list, producing the video, and mailing the $4 plastic cassettes. Future promotions might use cardboard cassettes, which work for about five plays and cost only about $2. The effectiveness of the Previa tape was hard to determine, but about 2 percent of those who received it visited a Toyota showroom within three months.

The big communications medium issue is would people actually watch such videos? If so, the video surely communicated the Previa name and its special attributes better than any television commercial or print ad.

Source: Reprinted by permission of *Forbes* magazine. © Forbes Inc. 1990.

purchasing the product, and an intention to buy. One possible problem with lecture ads is that consumers may react negatively to the obvious attempt to influence.

In contrast, a message delivered in dramatic form makes few or no explicit product claims. Instead, a *drama ad* tells a story in which the brand has a prominent role. Consider an ad showing a woman executive who has been working late on a cold winter night. As she leaves her office and walks to her car parked on a deserted city street, she wonders whether her car will start. She gets into the car, turns the key, and the engine immediately starts, to her obvious relief. She congratulates herself for buying a DieHard battery.

Such ads are miniature dramas, similar to a play or movie, except much shorter. In contrast to the hard sell of lecture ads, drama ads communicate product information more gently and indirectly. Effective drama ads draw the viewers into the story and encourage them to identify with one or more characters in the story. Consumers who empathize with a character may experience affective feelings and emotions similar to those portrayed by that character.[19]

Transmission via media

Marketing managers must decide what media to use to transmit the promotion message to consumers. For any given promotion, many media choices are available. Advertisements, for example, can be placed in magazines or newspapers, displayed on billboards, aired on television or radio programs, or sent through the mail. Consumer Perspective 9.3 describes a new advertising medium for transmitting product information. Coupons may be placed in magazines or newspapers, delivered by mail, or printed on the product package. Personal-selling messages can be delivered in face-to-face interactions in a store or in the consumer's home, or via telephone in telemarketing.

Because each medium has advantages and disadvantages for communicating with consumers, marketers must give careful attention to media choices for their promotion messages.[20] Clutter is a problem for most media because of the increases in the number of promotion messages over the past decade. In 1989, for instance, over 320,000 commercials were shown on U.S. television.[21] Consumer Perspective 9.4 discusses some

CONSUMER PERSPECTIVE

▶ 9.4

Clutter and the 15-second commercial

At one time, the 60-second commercial was the most common ad on TV, bearing out research data that established benchmarks of effectiveness for ads of this length. Then, in the late 1960s, along came the 30-second commercial. At the time, it was thought that the shorter ads, and the extra "clutter" they would create, would raise havoc with advertising effectiveness and measurement. It didn't happen, and the 30-second ad became the standard.

Enter 15-second ads. What is their effect?

Preliminary evidence provided by a large-scale comparison of 15-second and 30-second ads suggests the new ads won't wreak havoc, either. When the average 30-second commercial scored 100 for communication performance, the average 15-second ad scored 78. The 15-second ads also scored well on a measure of the number of ideas in the ad recalled later by the viewer—2.6 versus 2.9 for the 30-second ads. Finally, both ad lengths scored about the same in terms of the sense of importance of the main idea created by the commercial. Yet the 15-second ad costs only slightly more than half as much money to run.

So, are the 15-second ads a problem? Probably not. It is not the length per se that makes an ad effective or ineffective. If an ad establishes a reason—a reward—for viewing it in the first few seconds, consumers are likely to pay attention and comprehend its meaning, no matter what length it is.

Certain communication goals are more difficult to achieve with 15-second ads: a feeling of newness, a multistep process, a sense of variety, creation of a mood or emotion, and humor. But the very same problems were once issues for the 30-second ads, and we know how that turned out.

Source: Adapted from Robert Parcher, "15-Second TV Commercials Appear to Work 'Quite Well,' " *Marketing News* 20 (January 3, 1986), pp. 1 and 60. Published by the American Marketing Association.

implications of clutter in TV advertising. Sales promotions also suffer from clutter. From 1983 to 1990, the number of coupons distributed to Americans doubled to 260 billion (only 7.2 billion were redeemed).[22] In 1992, 350 billion coupons were distributed. Obviously, getting the consumer's attention with another coupon promotion is difficult in this cluttered environment.

Some supermarkets dispense coupons at the checkout counter based on what products the consumer buys.

Receiver

The effectiveness of a promotion message is influenced by the characteristics of the consumers who receive it. Two key factors are consumers' product knowledge and involvement, which affect their attention and comprehension of the promotion message. Another receiver characteristic is deal proneness—people's general inclination to use sales promotion deals such as coupons, rebates, or buying at reduced sale prices.[23] Some consumers have high personal sources of involvement with using coupons and may even belong to clubs where coupons are traded. Such consumers are much more likely to respond favorably to sales promotions than are consumers who consider coupons a nuisance.

Promotion messages have their initial impact on consumers' affect and cognitions. For a promotion communication to be effective, receivers must be exposed to the message, pay attention to it, and comprehend its meaning. Marketers hope the receiver will form positive beliefs about the consequences of buying and using the product and integrate these beliefs to form a favorable A_{act} and purchase intention (BI). Much research has focused on measuring these affective and cognitive effects of promotion communications, especially advertising.[24] Three indicators of advertising effectiveness have been used— recall, persuasion, and sales.

Consumers' ability to *recall* the promotion message is a simple measure of communication effectiveness. In day-after recall studies, researchers telephone consumers the day after a TV commercial was run and ask them if they remember seeing any ads on TV the day before, and if so, what things they can recall about the ads they remember. Viewers who can remember a visual element or a product claim are counted as having recalled the ad. Recall indicates whether consumers were exposed to the ad and attended to it enough that they can remember seeing it, but recall does not measure whether the ad created appropriate product meanings or elicited the desired affective responses.[25] Exposure and attention to individual ads has decreased due to consumers' use of remote controls to zap ads and sagging loyalty to favorite brands (lower involvement). In 1986, 64 percent of consumers could remember an ad campaign seen in the previous month; this figure plunged to 48 percent in 1990. Recall of single ads has gradually declined from an average of 24 percent in the late 1970s to 21 percent in 1988 (of course, some ads scored higher and lower than this).[26]

A promotion message may have a persuasive effect on the receiver.[27] *Persuasion* occurs when consumers' interpretation of the ad message produces positive beliefs about the attributes and consequences of the product, leading to favorable brand attitudes toward buying the brand (A_{act}) and intentions to purchase (BI). Persuasion also involves creation of means-end chains of product knowledge, linking the brand to important end goals such as terminal and instrumental values.[28]

The basic objective of most promotion communications is to influence *sales* of the brand. But linking sales to a particular promotion message such as a coupon or an ad is difficult because many other factors influence purchase behavior besides the promotion. However, technological advances associated with the scanner devices described in Consumer Perspective 9.5 are moving marketers closer to understanding the relationship between promotions and sales.

Consumer action

Although the key consumer action of interest to marketers is purchase of the promoted product or brand, other behaviors may also be the targets of marketing strategies. For instance, some promotions are intended to generate visits to the store. Some grocery stores offer a "double coupon" strategy (each coupon is worth twice its face value) in an effort to build store traffic.

Other promotions may attempt to stimulate product conversations between customers. Word-of-mouth communications help to spread awareness beyond people who come into direct contact with the promotion. For example, you may call a friend who is looking for tires to say Sears is having a sale. Consumers sometimes recommend that their friends

CONSUMER
PERSPECTIVE

▶ 9.5

Single-source
advertising
research

Information Resources, Inc., knows what Paxton Blackwell of Williamsport, Pennsylvania, eats for breakfast, what television shows he watches, the coupons he uses, where he shops, the products and brands he buys, and which newspapers he reads. He says he doesn't mind the meters on his TV or the frequent surveys he fills out. Blackwell is monitored in an evolving methodology called *single-source research*. This methodology could revolutionize the advertising research business and may be able to show how—or perhaps whether—advertising works to affect brand purchase choices.

Many companies are developing single-source research systems. As they become perfected, marketers will have powerful new methods for determining the effectiveness of advertising. For example, IRI, the pioneer of the methodology, monitors more than 3,000 households in eight small U.S. towns with cable TV service. Microcomputers record when the TV is on and what station it is tuned to. Thus, IRI knows which ads each household receives.

IRI is also able to send special test commercials over the cable channels in place of the regularly scheduled ads. When a member of the household checks out at the supermarket counter, he or she presents an ID card. As the selected items go through the scanner, the brand purchases (including package size, sale price, and number of units bought) are automatically recorded. IRI can then compare what products are bought against the ads the consumer presumably saw. This is the basis for the name "single source"—one method of tracking consumer behavior from ad exposure to brand purchase.

Of course, there are problems with the single-source system, not the least of which is figuring out how to analyze and summarize the mountains of data the system gener-

see a particular salesperson who is especially pleasant or well informed, or who offers good deals on merchandise. Consumers often pass on impressions of a new restaurant or retail store to their friends. Because mention of a product by someone we know is such a powerful form of promotion, marketers design some promotions to encourage word-of-mouth communication (sign up a friend to join the health club, and you get two months' membership free).

EFFECTS OF PROMOTION COMMUNICATIONS

A promotion communication can have five types of effects on consumers, but certain promotion strategies are best suited to produce each effect.[29]

▷ Stimulate a need for the product category or product form.
▷ Create awareness of the brand.
▷ Create a favorable brand attitude.
▷ Form an intention to purchase the brand.
▷ Influence various behaviors that are necessary for brand purchase (traveling to store, finding the brand in the store, talking to salespeople).

Stimulate product need

Before consumers can make a brand purchase, they must recognize a need for the product category or the product form. Problem recognition motivates consumers to consider which product category or product form is most likely to solve their problem and satisfy their end goal. Consumers are said to be "in the market" for the product if they believe the product is relevant to their problem, and they have formed a general intention to purchase it. At any given time, relatively few consumers are in the market for a particular product category (at any moment, perhaps 15 to 20 percent of consumers intend to buy

ates. In addition, single-source research can't tell who, if anyone, in the household actually saw each commercial. Moreover, there are so many other possible influences on purchase besides the advertisement that concluding an ad is solely responsible for a sale usually is not possible. Finally, and most important of all, single-source research does not answer the all-important question of *why* consumers purchase a particular brand.

Despite these drawbacks, however, the single-source systems can be very useful. Consider a demonstration study conducted in Denver by Arbitron Ratings Co., another supplier of single-source research data. Arbitron found that 18 percent of 200 test households had bought General Foods' Post Grape-Nuts cereal in the previous six-months, placing the product fourth behind General Mills' Cheerios and Kellogg's Raisin Bran and Corn Flakes. But a closer look revealed these purchasers bought only 40 ounces of Grape-Nuts out of an average total of 250 ounces bought during the period, well below average. This suggested a new ad strategy. General Foods could try to find current Grape-Nuts buyers and persuade them to buy and use more of the product. To make that possible, Arbitron discovered which television shows Grape-Nuts buyers tended to watch. Then it showed General Foods how to place ads on selected shows to reach many more of the target consumers with no increase in ad budget. With this kind of single-source data, General Foods could spend its promotional budget more effectively and precisely to communicate with the target audience.

Sources: Felix Kessler, "High-Tech Shocks in Ad Research," *Fortune*, July 7, 1986, pp. 58–62; Joanne Lipman, "Learning about Grape-Nuts in Denver," *The Wall Street Journal*, February 16, 1988, p. 36; and Joanne Lipman, "Single-Source Ad Research Heralds Detailed Look at Household Habits," *The Wall Street Journal*, February 16, 1988, p. 36.

laundry detergent, compared to only 1 or 2 percent who intend to buy a new car). This means many consumers are potentially susceptible to communication strategies designed to stimulate a product need.

To stimulate a need for a product, marketers must convince a consumer that using the product category or product form will have desirable consequences that are linked to the consumer's end goal. For instance, having dinner in a nice restaurant could be promoted as enjoyable and relaxing and a deserved reward for working hard. Essentially, marketers must create a positive means-end chain for the product category or form. Marketers often use advertising communications to stimulate a category need, but publicity and personal selling also have an influence.

Because consumers cannot buy a brand unless they know about it, brand awareness is a general communication goal for all promotion strategies. By creating brand awareness, marketers hope the brand will be activated from memory whenever consumers recognize a category need and will be included in the consideration set of choice alternatives.

Create brand awareness

Advertising probably has the greatest influence on brand awareness, and much of the advertising for frequently purchased products such as beer, soda, and cigarettes is designed to create and maintain high levels of brand awareness.[30] But the other types of marketing promotion also can influence brand awareness. Sales personnel generate brand awareness in the store by calling attention to certain brands. Various sales promotion strategies such as colorful price discount signs and in-store displays (a large stack of Ritz cracker packages at the end of the supermarket aisle) draw consumers' attention to brands. The position of brands on the shelf can influence brand awareness (for most products, eye-level placements tend to be noticed more). Finally, prominent displays of brand name signs on stores, buses, and billboards remind consumers of the brand name and help maintain brand awareness.

The level of brand awareness necessary for purchase depends on how and where consumers make their purchase decisions. Many brand choice decisions are made in the store (grocery and personal-care products, clothing items, appliances, and electronic products), so consumers do not need to recall a brand name from memory. They need only to recognize the brand when they see it, which then activates their relevant brand knowledge in memory. Thus, a common communication strategy is to show the brand package in the advertising so consumers can more easily recognize the brand in the store.[31] In other decision contexts, brand awareness must be higher to influence consumers' brand choice. If the purchase decision is made at home where there are few brand-name cues, consumers must recall the brand from memory before it can be included in the consideration set. Restaurant choices are an example. In such cases, knowledge in memory can be more influential than environmental factors.

The appropriate promotion strategy to influence brand awareness depends on how well known the brand name already is. In some cases, the marketing goal is to maintain high levels of brand awareness and make it more likely that the brand is activated during decision making.[32] Much of the advertising for well-known brands such as Coca-Cola, McDonald's, and Anacin serves as a reminder of the brand name. To create brand awareness for less familiar brands, managers may have to spend heavily on advertising.

Create a favorable brand attitude

Every promotion communication has the potential to influence brand attitudes by creating favorable beliefs about the consequences of salient brand attributes.[33] For instance, mint flavor for toothpaste might be associated with the functional consequence "makes my mouth feel fresh," which in turn could connect to a means-end chain of positive consequences, including "eliminate bad breath, avoid offending others, feel confident." These beliefs may be integrated to form an attitude toward buying the brand, which, in turn, could influence an intention to buy the brand. Consumers form positive attitudes toward purchasing a brand if the promotion message creates means-end links between the brand and important consequences and values.

Form an intention to purchase the brand

Most promotion communications are intended to influence the probability that consumers will buy the brand (BI). A purchase intention can be formed through integration processes in decision making ("This T-shirt is such a good deal, I am going to buy it") or activated from memory as a preformed decision plan (When Tammy runs low on mouthwash, she buys Scope).

To design effective promotion communications, marketers need to know *when* most consumers form a brand purchase intention. For instance, only consumers who are actively in the market for the product category are likely to form an intention to buy a brand at the time of exposure to an ad.[34] More typically, consumers form a brand BI well after exposure to advertising, perhaps when they are making a decision in a store (it has been estimated that intentions to buy are formed in the store for about 85 percent of candy purchases, 83 percent of snack purchases, and 45 percent of soft drinks).[35] This delay in forming BI means the consumer must remember advertising information about brand attributes and consequences to activate and use in integration processes during decision making.

Most sales promotions and personal-selling strategies are designed to influence consumers' purchase intentions (and behaviors) *at the time of exposure*.[36] The goal of these promotion communications is to persuade consumers to buy right away. This can happen if the consumer forms beliefs that the brand is connected to important consequences and values and immediately integrates these beliefs to form an A_{act} and a BI to purchase. If a consumer interprets a 25-percent-off sales promotion as leading to "saving money" and "having more money to use for other things," which in turn is linked to the value of "being a careful consumer," that consumer might immediately form a favorable A_{act} and BI and make a purchase on the spot.

Finally, some promotion communication strategies are designed to influence behaviors other than purchase. Consumers often must perform certain behaviors to make a brand purchase. To buy a brand such as Ralph Lauren's Polo, consumers must enter the high-quality clothing shops that carry it, making store choice a critical factor in sales of Polo. All types of promotion communications, including sales promotions, publicity, and personal selling, can influence the probability that consumers will perform these "other" behaviors. For instance, consumers might be invited to an auto dealership for free doughnuts and coffee and a test drive in a new car. Publicity and word-of-mouth communications can influence movie sales or visits to a restaurant. Real estate salespeople might help consumers get a mortgage loan, which greatly increases the probability of their buying a house.

Influence other behaviors

Persuasion refers to changes in beliefs, attitudes, and behavioral intentions caused by a promotion communication. For the most part, marketing researchers have studied the persuasive effects of advertising communications, but sales promotions, personal selling, and publicity also can persuade consumers.

THE PERSUASION PROCESS

The **Elaboration Likelihood Model (ELM)** identifies two cognitive processes by which promotion communications such as advertising can persuade consumers—the central and peripheral routes to persuasion.[37] Exhibit 9.2 shows how these two processes work. Which persuasion process occurs is determined by consumers' level of involvement with the product message. The central route to persuasion is more likely when consumers' involvement is higher; the peripheral route to persuasion is more likely when involvement is

The Elaboration Likelihood Model (ELM)

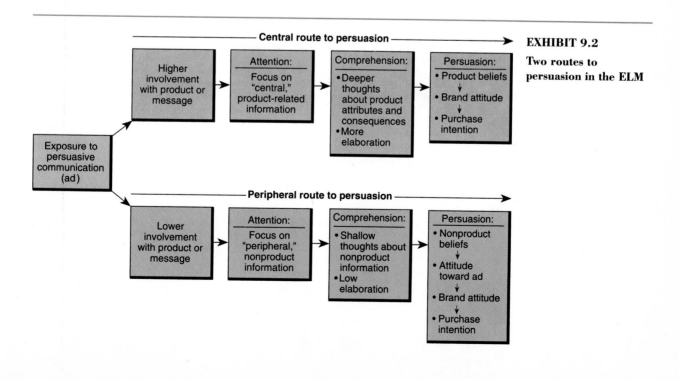

EXHIBIT 9.2

Two routes to persuasion in the ELM

lower. The ELM also distinguishes between two types of information in the promotion communication. Specific claims about product attributes or demonstrations of functional and psychosocial consequences, along with the supporting evidence, are "central" information; information about anything other than the product is "peripheral."

In the *central route to persuasion,* consumers who experience higher levels of involvement with the product or promotion message are motivated to pay attention to the central, product-related information and comprehend it at deeper and more elaborate levels.[38] Consumers' comprehension of the product-related information is indicated by the types of cognitive responses they have to the promotion message.[39] *Support arguments* are positive thoughts about product attributes and the self-relevant consequences of product use—"Head and Shoulders does seem like an effective dandruff shampoo." Support arguments enhance persuasion by leading to favorable product beliefs, positive brand attitudes, and stronger intentions to buy the product. During comprehension, consumers might produce unfavorable thoughts about the product called *counterarguments*—"I don't think that taking this vitamin every day will make a difference in my health." Counterarguing reduces persuasion by leading to unfavorable product beliefs, negative brand attitudes, and weaker intentions or no intention to buy the product.

The *peripheral route to persuasion* is quite different. Consumers who have low involvement with the product message (they are not in the market for the product) have little motivation to attend to and comprehend the central product information in the ad. Therefore, direct persuasion is low because these consumers form few brand beliefs and are unlikely to form brand attitudes or purchase intentions. However, these consumers might pay attention to the peripheral (nonproduct) aspects of the promotion communication such as

Consumers who are involved with cats will tend to pay attention to this ad and engage in central processing of the message.

the pictures in a print ad or the scenery or actors in a TV commercial, perhaps for their entertainment value. For instance, ads for Pepsi featuring entertainers such as Ray Charles might attract such attention. Consumers' affective and cognitive responses to these peripheral features might be integrated to form an attitude toward the ad (A_{ad})—"This is a good ad." Later, if a brand evaluation is called for during decision making, these ad-related meanings could be activated and used to form a brand attitude, since there are no relevant brand beliefs or attitudes in memory. Substantial evidence indicates consumers' affective feelings about an ad (A_{ad}) can influence their brand attitudes and purchase intentions.[40] Thus, the peripheral route to persuasion can persuade consumers to buy, but in an indirect way.

At any given time, relatively few consumers are in the market for a particular product, so much of the advertising consumers are exposed to daily is not particularly relevant to their end goals and values. This suggests that most mass media advertising receives peripheral processing. The low levels of recall for most ads (about 20 percent on average) suggest this is the case. In some cases, marketers might want consumers to engage in peripheral route processes. If a brand is similar to competing brands (soft drinks, beer, and cigarettes are examples), marketers may not be able to make credible claims about unique product attributes or consequences. Promotion strategies, therefore, tend to focus on image advertising for which peripheral processing is appropriate.

In situations where a brand has a distinctive advantage, marketers may want to encourage consumers to engage in central route processing by increasing their involvement with the ad message and the product or brand.[41] Making explicit comparisons with other brands in comparative advertisements tends to make the ad message more interesting and involving.[42] Sending promotion messages directly to consumers who are "in the market" for the product category or product form ensures some level of motivation in the brand information and should stimulate central processing.

MARKETING
IMPLICATIONS

Developing and implementing effective promotion communication strategies can be difficult. Although no single approach or magic formula can guarantee success, the process begins with understanding the consumer/product relationship.

Understanding the consumer/product relationship

Analyzing the relationships between consumers and products or brands begins by identifying the appropriate target market of consumers. Then, marketers should identify the end goals and values of these consumers, their knowledge and beliefs about product attributes and consequences, their involvement with the product and brand, and their current brand attitudes, behavior intentions, and actual behavior. Marketers of established brands may already know a great deal about consumer/product relationships. For new products or brands, marketers may have to conduct considerable marketing research to learn these aspects of the consumer/product relationship. This research could include laddering interviews to identify the dominant means-end chains that reveal how consumers perceive the relationship between the product and their own self-concepts.[43]

The FCB Grid

The **Foote, Cone & Belding (FCB) Grid** model shown in Exhibit 9.3 offers a way to analyze consumer/product relationships.[44] Developed by a major advertising agency to help its clients understand consumers' relationships with products, the FCB Grid is based on two concepts discussed in earlier chapters: consumers' involvement with the product and their dominant mode of psychological response to the product—either cognitive or affective.

Consumers' level of product involvement depends on how closely product attributes are linked, via means-end chains, to self-relevant goals and values. For most products, it is

EXHIBIT 9.3

**The Foote, Cone &
Belding Grid for
analyzing consumer/
product relationships**

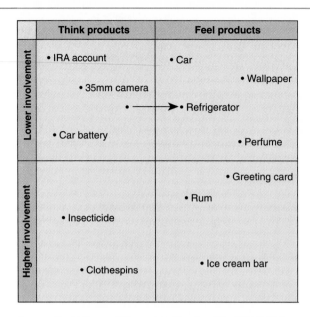

	Think products	Feel products
Lower involvement	• IRA account • 35mm camera • ——▶ • Refrigerator • Car battery	• Car • Wallpaper • Perfume
Higher involvement	 • Insecticide • Clothespins	• Greeting card • Rum • Ice cream bar

Source: David Berger, "Theory into Practice: The FCB Grid,"
European Research, January 1986, p. 35.

possible to identify the typical level of involvement experienced by most consumers. The FCB Grid divides products into two levels—*higher involvement* and *lower involvement.*

Most consumers have a typical mode of psychological response to a product—cognitive or affective. Consumers respond to some products primarily in rational, cognitive meanings, creating beliefs about product attributes and the functional consequences of using the product.[45] These are *think products* in the grid model. Included in this category are such products as financial investments, cameras, and car batteries. Cognitive responses produced by the cognitive system dominate consumer reactions to such products.

The affective system is the dominant mode of psychological response for *feel products.* Consumers react to these products with emotional and feeling responses, and they may form visual or other sensory images of the product.[46] These affective responses may be associated with the psychosocial consequences and value outcomes of product use. Feel products in the FCB Grid are purchased primarily for their sensory qualities (ice cream, soft drinks, cologne) or for their emotional consequences (flowers, jewelry, some types of clothing).

Exhibit 9.3 shows the placement of several products within the FCB Grid, based on extensive consumer research. Because consumers have different types of relationships with products in the four quadrants, the appropriate communication strategy depends on a product's position. For instance, drama or visual advertising that emphasizes emotional, feeling responses and visual images might be appropriate for feel products, but probably not for think products. Lecture ads containing verbal claims about product attributes and consequences would be more appropriate for think products.

Sometimes a product can be moved within the grid by a promotion strategy. This is illustrated in Exhibit 9.3 by the shift of the refrigerator from a think to a feel product. A South American client of FCB presented a problem: 5,000 ugly green refrigerators were not selling. High-involvement products such as refrigerators tend to be marketed as think products and sold in terms of functional consequences, but in this case there was no unique benefit to promote. So FCB designed a promotion strategy to move refrigerators from the think to the feel quadrants. The agency created ads featuring Venezuelan beauty queens and called the refrigerators "another Venezuelan beauty." The 5,000 refrigerators

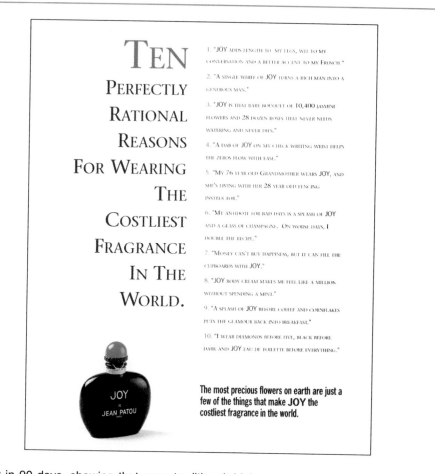

A "think" ad for a "feel" product.

sold out in 90 days, showing that even traditional think products sometimes can be promoted using affective, feel communication strategies. In sum, the FCB Grid can help marketers understand consumer/product relationships to develop more effective promotions.

Vulnerability analysis

Vulnerability analysis is another tool for understanding the consumer/product relationship and developing promotion strategies. By analyzing consumers' attitudes toward its brand and people's past purchases of the brand, a company can identify segments of consumers who vary in their vulnerability to its promotion communications and those of competitors. Exhibit 9.4 provides an example of vulnerability analysis. For instance, people who dislike a brand and never buy it (lower right quadrant) are not likely to be persuaded to buy and can be ignored. Consumers who never buy the brand but have a favorable (or at least neutral) attitude toward it are vulnerable to the company's promotions. Free samples, premiums, contests, or coupons might create an intention to try the brand and move consumers to an occasional user segment.

Occasional purchasers of the brand are vulnerable to the promotion strategies for competing brands. In that situation, marketers might have a promotion objective to encourage repeat purchases of the brand. A purchase plan such as offering a free doughnut after the consumer has bought 12 or a premium for saving proofs of purchase may be effective strategies. Or a firm might try to demonstrate the superiority of its brand over competing brands. For example, Burger King and Pepsi-Cola have used comparative advertising to "prove" their brand is better than McDonald's and Coca-Cola, respectively.[47]

EXHIBIT 9.4

An analysis of consumer vulnerability

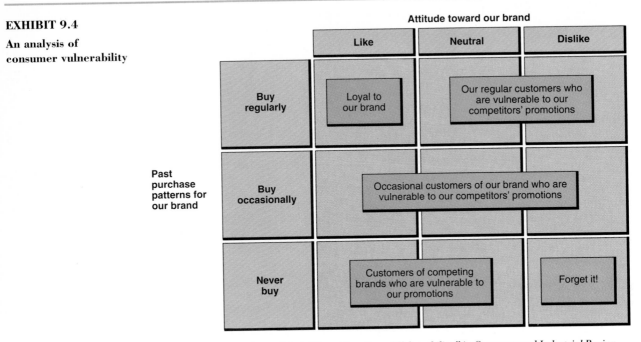

Source: Adapted from Yoram Wind, "Brand Loyalty and Vulnerability," in *Consumer and Industrial Buying Behavior*, ed. A. G. Woodside, J. N. Sheth, and P. D. Bennett (New York: North Holland Publishing, 1977), pp. 313–20. Reprinted by permission of A. G. Woodside.

Finally, brand-loyal consumers who like a company's brand and purchase it consistently can be influenced by promotions designed to keep them happy customers. Frequent flyer programs have been a phenomenally successful promotion to reinforce the attitudes and purchase behavior of airline customers. Consumers rack up mileage on flights taken with the airline and receive free trips when sufficient mileage has been accumulated. The programs are supposed to be limited to frequent flyers, usually defined as those taking 12 or more plane trips per year. By 1984, however, an estimated 7 million Americans had enrolled in frequent-flyer programs, many more than the estimated 1 million frequent flyers. In fact, more than a third of air travelers are enrolled in four such programs—not exactly what the airlines had in mind when the promotion was begun. In any case, these incentive programs have seemed so successful that they are copied by hotels, car rentals firms, restaurants, and other types of companies (see Consumer Perspective 9.6).

Calls by salespeople to "check on how things are going" may reinforce past customers' attitudes and intentions to rebuy when the need arises. Joe Girard, the top car salesperson in the United States for 11 years in a row, sent out over 13,000 cards to his customers each month, wishing them Happy New Year from Joe Girard, Happy St. Patrick's Day, and so on.[48] Finally, promotions can inform current consumers of new uses for existing products. Advertising campaigns promoted Saran Wrap for use in microwave cooking and Static Guard to eliminate static electricity from carpets around computers.

These examples illustrate three important points. First, effective promotion communications depend on the type of relationship consumers have with the product or brand.[49] Second, promotion communications vary in their effectiveness for achieving certain objectives. Personal selling, for example, is usually more effective for closing sales, while advertising is more effective for increasing brand awareness among large groups of consumers. Third, promotion objectives will change over a product's life cycle as changes occur in consumers' relationships with the product.[50] The promotion strategy that worked

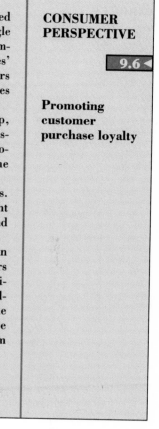

CONSUMER PERSPECTIVE

9.6

Promoting customer purchase loyalty

For airlines, the concept of rewarding loyal customers with free flights has worked like a dream. American Airlines considers its frequent-flyer program "the single most successful marketing tool we've ever had." Now an increasing number of companies from banks to retailers to car rental agencies are trying to mimic the airlines' success with frequent-buyer programs of their own. Under these plans, customers accumulate points, usually based on dollars spent, that can be cashed in for prizes or discounts.

Lester Wunderman, chairman of Young & Rubicam's direct marketing group, finds the trend refreshing. "The history of American marketing has been to breed disloyalty to get someone to try something new," he says. "These frequent-purchase programs are just the opposite. American business is beginning to understand the enormous profit leverage in loyalty."

But these clone programs may not be as successful as the frequent-flyer programs. Airlines can reward free flights at minimal expense because planes often fly with vacant seats. Companies in other industries must devise rewards that tantalize consumers and figure ways of handling the record keeping without breaking the bank.

Neiman-Marcus, the upscale Dallas-based retailer, started its inCircle program in 1984 to differentiate itself from competitors such as Saks Fifth Avenue. Neiman offers relatively modest rewards. For $3,000 in annual purchases, customers receive periodic deliveries of chocolates. They get caviar for spending $12,000. The costs for administering the program are modest, too, because almost all participants use the Neiman charge card and thus are on its computer system. The program seems to be working—more inCircle customers remain high spenders than before the program was instituted.

well when the product was introduced is not likely to be effective at the growth, maturity, or decline stages.

Developing advertising strategy

Marketers should specify advertising strategy in terms of how the product will be related to the consumer. Then ads should be created to communicate the appropriate means-end connections between the product attributes and the consumer's goals and values.[51] The MECCAS model shown in Exhibit 9.5 (see page 202) can help marketers understand the key aspects of ad strategy and make better strategic decisions.[52]

The **MECCAS model** defines four elements of advertising strategy—the driving force, the leverage point, consumer benefits, and message elements—based on analysis of consumers' means-end chains. (MECCAS stands for means-end chain conceptualization of advertising strategy.) The fifth component of the MECCAS model, the executional framework, is part of the creative strategy that must develop the details of the actual advertisement to communicate the ad strategy.

The first step in creating an advertising strategy is to *understand the consumer/product relationship* by measuring consumers' means-end chains for the product category or product form. Then the marketer must select a means-end chain to convert into an advertising strategy. The most important means-end chain in the decision-making process is a likely candidate. Knowing which product attributes are most important for consumers helps marketers decide which information to include as *message elements* in the ad strategy. (Should the ads for Ruffles potato chips emphasize their flavor, their crunchiness, or their ridges?) Knowing what functional consequences are linked to these salient attributes

EXHIBIT 9.5

The MECCAS model

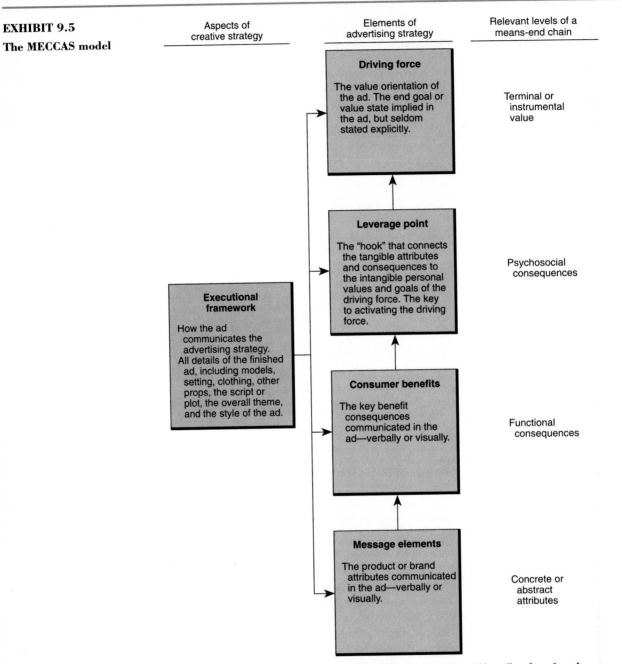

Aspects of creative strategy

Elements of advertising strategy

Relevant levels of a means-end chain

Driving force

The value orientation of the ad. The end goal or value state implied in the ad, but seldom stated explicitly.

Terminal or instrumental value

Leverage point

The "hook" that connects the tangible attributes and consequences to the intangible personal values and goals of the driving force. The key to activating the driving force.

Psychosocial consequences

Executional framework

How the ad communicates the advertising strategy. All details of the finished ad, including models, setting, clothing, other props, the script or plot, the overall theme, and the style of the ad.

Consumer benefits

The key benefit consequences communicated in the ad—verbally or visually.

Functional consequences

Message elements

The product or brand attributes communicated in the ad—verbally or visually.

Concrete or abstract attributes

Source: Adapted with the permission of Lexington Books, an imprint of Macmillan, Inc., from Jerry C. Olson and Thomas R. Reynolds, "Understanding Consumers' Cognitive Structures Implications for Advertising Strategies" (pp. 77–90) in *Advertising and Consumer Psychology* by Larry Percy and Arch G. Woodside, editors. Copyright

helps marketers identify the key *consumer benefits* to be emphasized. (If Ruffles chips are for dipping, focus on the ridges. If Ruffles are an accompaniment for sandwiches, emphasize flavor and crunchiness.)

The *driving force* is the basic value or end goal to be communicated by the ad. The driving force usually is communicated indirectly and in a subtle fashion; values are seldom mentioned explicitly in ads. That would be perceived as heavy-handed by most consumers, who might react negatively to being told what value they should be thinking of. Values and end goals are part of the consumer, not the product, and must be aroused or activated in the consumer. Merely stating a value in an ad does not ensure that it is activated and felt by consumers. Once activated, the emotional and motivational power of the end goals or values provides the driving force for action, including purchase of the brand.

The final component of an ad strategy is the important *leverage point* by which the relatively concrete, tangible message elements and benefits (attributes and functional consequences of the product) are linked to the abstract driving force (values of the consumer). The leverage point can be thought of as a hook that reaches into the consumer and attaches the product to the activated value that is the driving force of the ad strategy. In advertising, the leverage point is often portrayed as a psychosocial consequence of using the brand. Because consumers automatically perceive the values associated with most psychosocial consequences, the leverage point should activate the driving force and form a connection to it. Thus, the ad does not have to explicitly mention the value to communicate the ad strategy.

In sum, an advertising strategy should specify how a brand will be connected to the important ends the consumer wants. The advertising team must then create an ad that will persuasively communicate these meanings and the linkages between them. The *executional framework* refers to the various details of the creative strategy (the type of models, how they are dressed, the setting, what people are saying) that are designed to communicate the ad strategy. In general, an effective advertisement should communicate each of the four means-end levels of meaning in the ad strategy (from message elements to driving force) and the links or connections between the levels.

The MECCAS model is not a foolproof tool to create successful ads; it is a guide to developing advertising strategies and creating effective ads.[53] Marketers still must conduct careful analyses of consumers and use their imaginations. Marketers can use the MECCAS model to translate several means-end chains into possible ad strategies, which can then be evaluated for their competitive advantages. Although any means-end chain can be translated into an advertising strategy using the MECCAS model, not every means-end chain is a viable strategy. Some strategies, for instance, may already be taken by one's competitors. Marketers also can use the MECCAS model as a framework for analyzing the meanings communicated in their current advertising and for considering how these ads could be changed to be more persuasive.[54]

Learning objective 1: *Describe the four types of promotion communications.*   ▶ **SUMMARY**
Marketers use four types of promotions to communicate with consumers and influence them to buy. Advertising is any paid, nonpersonal communication about a product, brand, company, or store. Advertising can be transmitted via many different media, including TV and radio, print ads in magazines and newspapers, billboards and signs, and direct mail. Sales promotions are communications offering inducements to buy a product or brand; they include price reductions, coupons, rebates, premiums and gifts, trading stamps, and sweepstakes contests. Personal selling involves direct personal communications between a salesperson and a potential buyer. Among the forms of personal selling are in-store sales, telemarketing, professional sales to business customers, and door-to-door sales. Publicity is any unpaid communication about a product, brand, company, or store and includes feature stories and news items in popular media, photographs on TV or in newspapers, and discussions on talk shows. Advertising is probably the most noticeable promotion communication, although more marketing dollars are spent on sales promotions than advertising.

Learning objective 2: *Describe the components of the basic communication model.*
The basic communication model identifies the key elements in the communication process. The source (a company, an advertising agency, or a corporate spokesperson) creates a message designed to convey certain meanings. The message could be in the form of an ad, a sales promotion offer, a script for a sales presentation, or a publicity story. The message is transmitted through a medium such as broadcast (TV or radio), print (magazines, newspapers, or mail) signs (billboards), or personal appearance (direct selling). The message is apprehended by a receiver (consumers in the target audience) and comprehended (interpreted). Finally, the receiver initiates some action, perhaps purchase of the product, although other behaviors are possible, such as word-of-mouth discussions with friends, visiting a store, or reading reports of product tests.

Learning objective 3: *Describe the various effects that promotion communications can have on consumers.*
Promotion communications can have at least five types of effects on consumers. Some promotion communications are intended to stimulate a need for the product category or product form by inducing consumers to recognize a problem that the product can solve. Other promotion communications are intended to create or maintain brand awareness. Many promotion communications are designed to persuade consumers by creating positive beliefs about the brand, favorable attitudes toward the brand, and a strong intention to purchase the brand. Finally, some promotion communications are intended to influence other behaviors such as visiting a store or showroom or telling a friend about the brand. Promotion communications can have multiple effects.

Learning objective 4: *Discuss the two routes to persuasion specified by the Elaboration Likelihood Model, and describe the role of attitude toward the ad in persuasion.*
A promotion communication such as an ad transmits two sorts of information—central information about the product or brand being promoted, and peripheral information about all other factors. The Elaboration Likelihood Model describes two cognitive processes or "routes" to persuasion that focus on these types of information. The route taken depends on consumers' involvement. Consumers who are interested in the brand (perhaps because they are in the market for the product) have higher levels of involvement with the product. This motivation focuses their attention on the central product and/or brand information in the message, and these consumers are likely to form brand beliefs and attitudes toward buying the brand. This process is the central route to persuasion.

When involvement with the brand and/or product message is low, consumers are not interested in the central product information in the message and are unlikely to form brand attitudes or purchase intentions. Any attention that occurs is likely to be focused on peripheral aspects of the message, such as the setting or the models used in an ad. Consumers engaged in peripheral processing might form an attitude toward the ad (A_{ad}) instead of toward the product. This peripheral route to persuasion is indirect and based on processing of nonproduct information. In several marketing research studies, A_{ad} has been shown to have an influence on brand attitudes and purchase intentions.

Learning objective 5: *Describe how the FCB Grid and vulnerability analysis can be used to understand the consumer/product relationship and help marketers create effective communication strategies.*
Before they can design effective promotion communication strategies, marketers need to understand the nature of the consumer/product relationship. The text described two models that are useful for developing such an understanding. The FCB Grid combines two

dimensions to categorize products in terms of the types of relationships consumers may have with them: consumer involvement with the product (higher and lower levels of involvement) and think/feel, which refers to the dominant way consumers react to the product—either cognitive or affective. Think products such as laundry detergent, insecticides, and lawn mowers are evaluated in terms of rational, cognitive factors such as product attributes and functional consequences. Feel products such as cologne, ice cream, and beer are evaluated in terms of their affective qualities. The combinations of higher/lower involvement and think/feel describe four broad types of consumer/product relationships.

The vulnerability matrix also describes the relationships consumers may have with a company's brand. The matrix identifies segments of consumers who vary in terms of their attitudes toward the brand (like, neutral to, or dislike the brand) and their past purchasing behavior (buy the brand regularly, occasionally, or never). These groups differ in terms of their vulnerability to the promotion communication strategies of competing companies. The vulnerability matrix also suggests that different types of promotion communications strategies are necessary for each segment. Consumers who like a brand and buy it regularly are loyal and should be rewarded occasionally to keep them satisfied. Consumers who dislike a brand and never buy it are poor targets and probably should be ignored.

Learning objective 6: *Describe the MECCAS model of advertising strategy.*

The MECCAS (means-end chain conceptualization of advertising strategy) model identifies the basic components of advertising strategy. The model is based on the means-end chain approach that identifies the associations consumers make between product attributes, consequences, and value outcomes. According to MECCAS, a fully specified advertising strategy has four elements—message elements, product benefits, the leverage point, and the driving force. The message elements refer to the basic product attributes to be communicated in the ad. The product benefits refer to the functional consequences that are mentioned or shown in the ad. Typically, the leverage point is a psychosocial consequence that is portrayed or implied in the ad. The leverage point helps consumers link the relatively tangible product benefits or functional consequences shown in the ad with the abstract, intangible personal values implied in the ad. The driving force is the end consequence (perhaps a value) that is implied in the ad (most ads do not explicitly mention the value the ad attempts to link the brand with). A good ad strategy should specify the meanings to be communicated at all four levels. The last part of the MECCAS model is the executional framework, which refers to all the details of the ad's creative execution (including the scenes, the dialogue, the models and their clothing, the actions portrayed, the lighting and camera angles).

Learning objective 7: *Distinguish between lecture and drama advertising.*

Lecture and drama advertising are two forms of advertising. They elicit different reactions from consumers and persuade consumers in different ways. Lecture ads resemble a classroom lecture in that the source makes claims about the product and may present evidence to support the claims. Essentially, lecture ads present rational arguments why consumers should buy and use the product. Lecture ads persuade by creating favorable beliefs about product attributes and consequences. Drama ads (sometimes called narrative ads) tell a story in which the product is somehow relevant. A drama ad may not feature any explicit product claims. Drama ads persuade by drawing consumers into the story and encouraging them to identify with the characters. In this way, receivers can vicariously experience some of the product experiences the characters in the drama are portraying and thereby learn about the product. These beliefs in turn may lead to positive attitudes and intentions to buy.

► **KEY TERMS
AND CONCEPTS**

promotion
  communications
advertising
sales promotions
personal selling

publicity
communication process
persuasion
Elaboration Likelihood
  Model (ELM)

Foote, Cone & Belding
  (FCB) Grid
MECCAS model

► **REVIEW AND
DISCUSSION
QUESTIONS**

1. As a consumer of fast-food products, evaluate the effects of promotion communications on your decision processes.

2. Using the soft-drink industry as an example, define and illustrate each of the major types of promotion strategies.

3. Suggest reasons for the growing emphasis on sales promotion in the promotion mix of many marketing organizations.

4. Select an advertisement or sales promotion strategy, and discuss it in terms of the elements in the communication model.

5. Describe the two routes to persuasion in the ELM, and give an implication for developing effective advertising strategies.

6. Use the FCB Grid to describe your consumer/product relationship for two products you recently purchased.

7. Describe how the MECCAS model can be used to develop an effective advertising strategy for a brand of athletic shoe.

8. Discuss the circumstances under which lecture and drama ads might be effective formats.

9. Identify a specific promotion communication, and suggest how marketers could measure its effects.

II

UNDERSTANDING AFFECT AND COGNITION

Ralph Lauren

Ralph Lauren is one of the most successful designers in the United States. He has a unique approach. While other designers create product lines, he first designs lifestyles and then develops a wide range of products to reflect those themes. Lauren creates romantic worlds where handsome families ride to hounds, play lawn tennis with wooden rackets, or dress for dinner on safari. They wear crested blazers and trousers of crisp linen while watching polo matches in Palm Beach. They sip cognac by the fireplace of a chalet, nestled in a Navajo blanket. Phyllis Posnick, executive fashion editor of *Vogue*, says, "He takes an American fantasy of a lifestyle and he creates a Ralph Lauren world—and he does it better than anyone else."

The world where Ralph Lauren grew up was quite different. Born Ralph Lifshitz in a Bronx neighborhood, he was clothes conscious at an early age. He wore canvas jackets and button-down shirts to school in contrast to the typical student who looked like Fonzie in jeans and black leather jackets. At 22, Lauren went to work for a Boston necktie manufacturer, traveling to meet his customers dressed in tweeds and driving a Morgan sports car. His first designs were 4-inch-wide ties to replace the narrow 2 1/2-inch ties then in fashion. Lauren selected the name Polo for his line of ties, because the word connoted to him a lifestyle mood of athletic grace and discreet elegance and an image of men who wore well-tailored, classic clothes with style. Printed on vibrant, Italian silk, his creations were priced at $15 (double the typical price). He sold $500,000 worth in 1967, his first year.

The next year, Lauren began producing an entire menswear line, including wide-collar shirts and wide-lapel suits. He used only the finest fabrics to create the Lauren "look"—distinctive and innovative, but classic and refined at the same time. His suits combined the Ivy League natural shoulder look with the fitted shape and expensive fabrics of the best European custom-tailored clothing. His shirts were all cotton and richly patterned.

Over the years, Ralph Lauren created several product lines targeted at new consumer segments. In 1971, he introduced a line of women's clothing with the image of understated elegance and femininity. Later, he created the Chaps line of men's clothing for executives who wanted a traditional American look at a less expensive price. He introduced Polo University Club line of sportswear for college students and young businessmen who were beginning to form their professional wardrobe. In 1983, he created a collection of home furnishings, including bedding, towels, rugs, and wall coverings. The collection expanded in 1986 to include furniture. All the Lauren furnishings were designed to reflect a lifestyle "look" and were marketed using ads showing entire coordinated rooms. For instance, the "Bride" was a romantic collection in rich cream fabrics, while "Estate" combined the elegance and beauty of white linen with mahogany carved furniture, woven wicker, and bent rattan. In addition, Lauren produces two fragrances—Polo for men and Lauren for women—and he markets a collection of handmade shoes, boots, and moccasins.

By the late 1980s, Ralph Lauren was an international presence in the fashion world. His Polo clothing is distributed in Italy, Japan, Canada, Hong Kong, Singapore, Taiwan, Malaysia, Korea, Panama, Mexico, Germany, Austria, Belgium, Brazil, Uruguay, the Netherlands, Luxembourg, Scandinavia, Switzerland, Spain, England, and France. He has free-standing stores and boutiques in department stores all over the world, but his showcase store is in New York City. In 1987, Lauren converted the Rhinelander mansion on Madison Avenue into the ultimate showcase for the Lauren lifestyle image. He remodeled the five-story limestone structure at a cost of $14 million and fitted it with hand-carved mahogany woodwork, oriental rugs, and fine antique furniture. The clothing displays share space with saddles, trophies, top hats, and billiard cues, making the place feel more like a London club than a retail store. (Ralph Lauren was not the first to use such a

retailing strategy. In 1863, department store magnate A. T. Stewart chose an oriental motif for the interior of a store he built at Broadway and 10th Street in New York City. The store had "luxurious hassocks . . . soft Persian rugs . . . and fairy-like frostings of lace draperies.")

Lauren begins the design process by imagining a lifestyle that he develops like a play, including describing the characters/actors, how and where they live, and the types of clothing they wear. Based on these rich images, his designers create the costumes (clothing products) and the stage sets (retail displays) for the latest dream world. "I want only to make the things I love," Lauren has said repeatedly. "A lot of people have good taste. I have dreams." To make his dreams a reality, he puts great effort into the advertisements and retail displays. Nothing is left to chance. From the furniture to the props to the models who portray the characters, each is carefully chosen to create a very specific look. Each ad and retail display creates a mood and evokes a lifestyle. Every ad invites the reader to share the fantasy and enter the dream world of Ralph Lauren.

Ralph Lauren is a master of mood. His home-furnishing arrangements are opulent and luxurious. A bed might have eight pillows, all with ruffles and contrasting fabrics. The idea is that a customer will want to buy the entire package to acquire the Ralph Lauren look. In the stores, he surrounds his products with loads of charming and inventive "treasures," many of them for sale. Rather than displaying only a blazer or a skirt, he also presents a whole pile of goodies, such as antique tobacco horns and framed pictures of families, that complete the picture and establish the lifestyle mood.

Ralph Lauren creates moods, dreams, and fantasies, and he offers consumers the opportunity to share his dreams and perhaps acquire new identities by purchasing his carefully orchestrated products. No other American designer has created a product range so wide, a retailing network so extensive, and a marketing image so well defined.

By the early 1990s, the Ralph Lauren fashion empire had retail sales approaching $1.5 billion, up over 400 percent since 1981.

Source: Adapted from "A Dream World Labeled Lauren," *Marketing Insights,* June 1989, pp. 91–95; and Valerie Free, "100 Years Ago: Through a Distant Mirror," *Marketing Insights,* Spring 1990, pp. 20–21.

Discussion questions

1. What types of affective responses to the Ralph Lauren advertisements and retail displays might be created by consumers' affective systems? How might the cognitive system interpret these responses?

2. What types of cognitions (knowledge) do Ralph Lauren customers have about Ralph Lauren and Lauren products? What types of schemas might consumers have for the Polo brand?

3. How could consumers' knowledge about Lauren and Polo be activated? How might the affective system react to these cognitive responses? How might this knowledge influence consumers' decision making and contribute to Ralph Lauren's success?

4. How might consumers' affective and cognitive responses influence their decision making and contribute to Ralph Lauren's success?

5. How are consumers' scripts relevant for the marketing of Ralph Lauren products?

▶ **CASE II.2**

Nike

By mid-1985 the signs were becoming clear—after years of mystique and spectacular growth, jogging was puffing into middle age. In 1984, for instance, unit sales of running shoes decreased 17 percent, and dollar sales were off by 15 percent. Nike, the market leader in 1983 with a 31 percent market share, sold about $270 million worth of running shoes. By 1984, Nike's share of the running shoe market was down 26 percent. The decline continued so that by 1987 Nike had only an 18.6 percent share of the market for athletic shoes, a market it had dominated just a few years earlier. What happened?

Nike had become successful as a manufacturer of technically sophisticated shoes for the serious runner, but the market for running shoes had peaked. According to the director of the National Sporting Goods Association, "We've probably reached pretty close to the maximum participation in running." The running shoe market was saturated, as nearly everyone who wanted to run had tried it.

Part of the reason is demographic. During the late 1970s and early 1980s, the large baby boomer group represented the primary market for running gear—ages 25 to 40. But in the mid- to late-1980s, fewer people were entering this age group, thus decreasing overall demand. As the leading age of this group pushed toward 40, lacing up the old shoes for another 5-mile run began to seem less fun that it had at age 24.

The running shoe market had also become highly segmented by the mid-1980s—a sure sign of a mature market. Marketers had to pay even closer attention to consumers' needs, goals, and values and produce product variations for smaller groups of consumers. And, finally, the industry had begun to engage in sporadic price cutting as companies fought to maintain their market share.

Another reason for the drop-off in running concerns consumers' ideas about health. Running develops the legs and cardiovascular system, but little else. Many runners had begun to notice that the rest of their bodies needed conditioning too. Athletically oriented people became increasingly interested in total fitness.

All these changes meant that fewer people were taking up running and that the millions of joggers who were still on the run were doing fewer laps. This translated into fewer replacement shoes sold by Nike, Converse, New Balance, Brooks, and all the others. As the biggest manufacturer in the business, Nike had the most to lose.

From one perspective, makers of running shoes had enjoyed a long run, especially in the sports equipment market, which is often dominated by short-lived fads. Consider tennis, for example. Sales of tennis rackets peaked in 1976 when an estimated 8.6 million rackets were sold. Despite technological innovations and space-age materials such as kevlar, boron, and graphite, the industry sold only about 3.2 million rackets in 1984. Instead, the big boom in 1984 and 1985 was aerobics gear and home gym equipment.

Some commentators believe Nike didn't react quickly enough to these fundamental changes in the consumer markets. One company that did capitalize on these changes was Reebok International. Its sales shot up from $84 million in 1984 to $307 million the next year, with profits increasing sixfold to $39 million. According to Reebok President Paul Fireman, "We go out to consumers and find out what they want. Other companies don't seem to do that."

It seems that what many consumers wanted in the mid-1980s was fashion. Perhaps this would have been evident by simple observation of consumers' product use behaviors. It is estimated that between 70 and 80 percent of the shoes designed for basketball and aerobic exercise are actually used for street wear. These products must have been satisfying some fashion needs or ends.

So when Reebok introduced its first soft-leather Freestyle aerobic shoes in 1983, the brilliant colors and soft leather made them an overnight sensation. Reebok actually expanded the overall market for athletic shoes in attracting women customers from more traditional shoe manufacturers such as Bass. People began to think of this product class as something more than "just sneakers." Reebok's spectacular popularity continued, and by 1986 Nike had lost the number one spot to Reebok.

During 1987 and 1988, Nike worked feverishly (and with some success) to recapture the lead in this expanding and profitable market. In 1987, Nike introduced its Air shoes, headed by the successful basketball shoe Air Jordan, named after Chicago Bulls basketball star Michael Jordan, who wore and promoted the product. Nike spent heavily on TV and print advertising to introduce this innovative product. But perhaps the best strategy was to produce its top-of-the-line models with a transparent "cut-out" in the sole so the consumer could actually see how the air cushioned the impact. In 1988, Nike spent some $34 million on advertising, the highest level yet for the company that once eschewed mass advertising as unnecessary and somewhat demeaning. Of course Reebok, the once-small competitor, wasn't sitting still; it increased its own advertising spending with a substantial amount channeled to TV.

In response to these changes in consumers, Nike expanded its product line beyond running shoes in the mid-1980s. The company began to produce shoes for the aerobic market and other specialty sports activities, including a line of walking shoes to appeal to a submarket that had emerged rapidly in the mid-1980s, perhaps as aging baby boomers found running too stressful on their joints.

And finally, in 1988, Nike introduced a fashion-oriented shoe to compete head-on with arch-rival Reebok. The new shoe was targeted at women, the primary buyers of such shoes, and was called IE. It did not carry the Nike name. Prices were between $25 and $40, somewhat below the price for the average Nike shoe. "With the IE, Nike is attempting to penetrate the very market (the fashion market) where it has been weakest historically," said one industry analyst. The independent brand name seemed a good strategy, as it would not give its core customers (serious and would-be athletes) mixed signals about the meaning of the Nike brand.

Discussion questions

1. Apparently there are two market segments of consumers for many product forms of athletic shoes—those who use them for the designated athletic activity and those who primarily use them for casual wear and seldom engage in the athletic activity.

   a. Discuss the differences between these two segments in means-end chains and especially end goals, needs, and values for running, basketball, aerobics, or tennis shoes.

   b. Draw means-end chains to illustrate your ideas about how these two segments differ.

   c. What types of special difficulties does a marketer face in promoting its products to two segments of consumers who use the product in very different ways?

2. Many manufacturers of athletic shoes promote so-called technological advances such as the "air sole" or the "energy wave." How do consumers make sense of such attributes? Which types of attributes are likely to have a major impact on their purchasing behavior?

3. As the market for athletic shoes has become more segmented, marketers have produced shoes for very specialized purposes. Why? Discuss the special types of means-end chains held by people who buy athletic shoes for particular purposes (walking, tennis, aerobics). Analyze the source of consumers' involvement in these products—personal or situational sources of involvement. How can these analyses help marketers understand the consumer/product relationship and develop more effective marketing strategies?

4. Analyze the changes that have occurred over time in consumers' product/self relationships for running shoes (or some other type of athletic shoe). Consider changes in consumers' affective responses and their product knowledge, as well as their overt behaviors and general environmental factors. How could Nike have kept better track of these changes so that its marketing strategies would have been more effective in the mid-1980s?

Sources: Adapted from Marcy Magiera, "Nike Plans Rebound with Fashion Shoe," *Advertising Age,* January 25, 1988, p. 1; Patrick McGeehan, "Wave Action: Converse Goes Toe-to-Toe with Nike High-Performance," *Advertising Age,* February 22, 1988, p. 76; Richard Phalon, "Out of Breath," *Forbes,* October 22, 1984, pp. 38–40; and Lois Therrien and Amy Borrus, "Reeboks: How Far Can a Fad Run?" *Business Week,* February 24, 1986, pp. 89–90.

► CASE II.3

Black & Decker

At the end of 1985, Black & Decker was about halfway through the biggest brand name swap in marketing history. The company, once best known for its power tools, bought General Electric's small-appliance business in 1984 for $300 million. Black & Decker had until mid-1987 to bring all of GE's 150 or so appliance products under its own logo.

By renaming the GE appliances, B&D did for its competitors something they could not possibly have accomplished by themselves—eliminated the best-known brand name in the small-appliance business. But these other companies—including Sunbeam, Rival, Hamilton Beach, and Norelco—did not show much gratitude. Sensing confusion in the market and weakness in their competitor, they increased their advertising budgets and introduced new products in an attempt to intercept GE customers before they got to Black & Decker. In return, Black & Decker unleashed a new product blitz of its own and began a $100 million advertising and promotion campaign, the largest ever in the small-appliance industry.

For years, GE had been the best-loved name in the appliance game. It still was in 1985. In one survey, consumers were asked to name small-appliance makers: GE came up a remarkable 92 percent of the time. Sunbeam was a distant second at 41 percent, and Black & Decker was mentioned only 12 percent of the time. In fact, another 1985 survey showed that most consumers didn't know GE had left the game.

Kenneth Homa, vice president for marketing, directed the complex Black & Decker strategy to make GE's name its own. The company broke the changeover process for each product into about 140 steps to be completed over 14 months. According to Black & Decker, the process went so smoothly that the timetable was completed by the end of 1986.

Black & Decker decided to launch each product as if it were new. For some products, it made alterations ranging from simple changes in color to major redesigns. For instance, GE's under-the-cabinet Spacemaker products—including a coffee maker, a toaster oven, and a can opener—were remodeled into sleeker units. Black & Decker also doubled the warranty period for every GE product to two years.

One big question for Black & Decker was whether to use its own brand name alongside GE's in the initial promotion and advertising. When research revealed that consumers associate similar reliability and durability qualities with Black & Decker as with GE, Black & Decker tried to keep consumer confusion to a minimum by making a clean switch—the Black & Decker name for GE. For instance, the popular Spacemaker line was remarketed without a reference to GE. TV commercials emphasized the Spacemaker brand name and ended with the tag line "Now by Black & Decker."

Competitors, of course, did not stand still while the brand name switch occurred. In particular, Sunbeam wanted consumers to forget both GE and Black & Decker. It increased its 1985 advertising budget to $42 million, four times what had been planned, to take advantage of the potential for confusion.

Irons are an important part (about 25 percent) of Black & Decker's small-appliance business. Thus, the company delayed conversion until it had experience with other lines. Research showed that 40 percent of customers go into a store intending to buy a particular brand of iron (usually GE). Therefore, Black & Decker modified its "clean switch" strategy and included GE's name next to its own in print ads for irons and in promotional materials in the stores. On TV, however, it was more difficult to explain the switch, so Black & Decker promoted the irons under its own name in television commercials.

The short-run concerns with the name change were not the only problems Black & Decker faced. Most appliance sales are to people replacing worn-out items, rather than to first-time buyers. Therefore, in any given year, only about 10 percent of the small-appliance market turns over. This means most consumers who now own GE products won't buy new ones until after the GE name is long gone from the small-appliance scene. What will they think when they go into the store and find no GE products?

Discussion questions

1. Describe some typical situations where consumers would be (*a*) accidentally and (*b*) intentionally exposed to information about Black & Decker's new line of appliances. What implications would the type of exposure have for Black & Decker's approach to making the name switch from GE?

2. Discuss how consumers' prior knowledge about Black & Decker and GE corporate images could have affected consumers' comprehension of the small appliances now marketed by Black & Decker.

   a. What types of inferences might consumers have drawn when they first became aware that Black & Decker was now selling small appliances?

    b. How would these inferences change over time as consumers became familiar with Black & Decker's appliances?

3. In what ways might consumers become confused with marketing information from Black & Decker? What could Black & Decker do about this?

4. Analyze the pros and cons of Black & Decker's decision not to mention the GE name in its brand changeover. How do you feel about the decision to feature the GE name only on electric irons?

5. What types of strategies could Sunbeam (or some other competitor) have used to try to derail Black & Decker's strategy? How could Black & Decker have countered each of these attacks?

Source: Excerpted from Bill Saporito, "Ganging Up on Black & Decker," *Fortune,* December 23, 1985, pp. 63–72.

▶ **CASE II.4**

Coca-Cola

The past 15 years or so have seen tumultuous changes in the soft-drink industry. After years of slow growth and little product innovation in the 1970s, the 1980s were full of activity. No company exemplifies these changes more than the Coca-Cola Company.

For most of its 100-year history, Coca-Cola has dominated the soft-drink business, largely through sheer size rather than savvy marketing. But Coke's complacency vanished in 1977 when PepsiCo's brand, Pepsi Cola, threatened to become the market leader and take over Coke's role as the top brand in food store sales. Since then Coke has responded with a number of marketing strategies, including some that would have been unthinkable a few years earlier. In the process, the company learned something about American consumers' brand attitudes toward Coke.

In July 1982, Coca-Cola management did the unthinkable: they introduced a diet cola and called it diet Coke. This was the first time in history that the company had allowed the world's best-known trademark to be put on a product other than the flagship Coca-Cola brand. Despite the perceived risks, diet Coke was extremely successful. By 1984, it had become the third best-selling soft drink in the United States, displacing 7UP. Then, in quick succession, Coca-Cola introduced decaffeinated versions of Coke, diet Coke, and Tab.

But these earlier decisions were soon to be overshadowed by another controversial marketing strategy. In the spring of 1985, Chairman Roberto Goizueta announced the introduction of a new Coca-Cola with an improved taste. The 99-year-old secret formula for the original Coke with a secret ingredient (called Merchandise 7X, it was developed by John Styth Pemberton, an Atlanta pharmacist, in a 30-gallon brass kettle in his backyard) was to be locked in a bank vault in Atlanta, never to be used again. The new formula, with ingredient 7X-100, was to replace the old Coca-Cola. Goizueta called the new product "the most significant soft-drink development in the company's history."

Americans got their first taste of the new Coke in late April 1985. In July, less than three months later, the company had reversed its earlier decision. A rather chagrined management announced that the old Coke was coming back under the brand name label Coca-Cola Classic. What happened to Coca-Cola was a classic lesson in consumers' brand attitudes. Some critics thought Coca-Cola had made a giant marketing mistake, and some cynics thought the company had planned the whole thing for publicity value. According to Donald Keough, the president of Coca-Cola, "The truth is that we are not that dumb and we are not that smart."

The positive attitudes and beliefs that keep customers buying the same brand over and over again are called *brand loyalty.* Brand loyalty is an elusive concept. It begins with the customers' positive attitudes and preferences for a brand based on "objective" beliefs about product attributes—the drink is sweeter or more carbonated. The brand name guarantees the customer will receive the same expected attributes and benefits from each product use. But once a product has been around for a while, it can accumulate a variety of emotionally laden meanings and beliefs. Some brands may become linked to consumers' lifestyles and self-images. For example, many consumers associated Coke with fond memories of days gone by.

Apparently these strong affective beliefs about Coke were activated when Coca-Cola announced the old "friend" was gone forever. Consumers inundated Coca-Cola's Atlanta headquarters with protests. A group of brand loyalists in Seattle threatened to sue the company. And when June sales didn't pick up as expected, the independent bottlers demanded to have the old Coca-Cola back.

Interestingly, the decision to retire the old Coke formula was not a casual one. It had been very carefully researched, and managers thought they had covered every angle. For instance, Coca-Cola spent over $4 million on many different taste-tests of the new flavor, involving over 200,000 consumers in some 25 cities. These tests revealed more people liked the new, sweeter flavor than the old (about 55 percent to 45 percent). But apparently this research didn't measure everything. "All the time and money and skill poured into consumer research on the new Coca-Cola could not measure or reveal the deep and abiding emotional attachment to original Coca-Cola," Keough said later.

It is true that understanding consumers' brand loyalties and product attitudes can be difficult. According to John O'Toole, chairman of the Chicago advertising agency Foote, Cone & Belding, one reason is that "you can't get at people's private motivations. In any kind of interview or questionnaire, they want to seem sensible and prudent. They aren't going to tell you how they feel."

A variety of different types of beliefs, not all of them about product attributes, may be salient influences on attitudes. Consumers' attitudes toward the new and old Cokes included more than just their taste and mouth feel—the factors that were measured in the extensive taste-tests. As a company spokesperson said, "We had taken away more than the product Coca-Cola. We had taken away a little part of them and their past. They said, 'You have no right to do that. Bring it back.' " So Coca-Cola did.

Then what happened? When the old Coke returned in the summer of 1985, consumers found six models of Coke on the supermarket shelf—(new) Coke, Coca-Cola Classic, Caffeine-Free Coke, diet Coke, Caffeine-Free diet Coke and Cherry Coke. In 1980, there had been only one brand, Coca-Cola. Some marketing experts thought the company would have a tough time keeping a clear identity for the different brands in consumers' minds. But Roberto Goizueta considered the lineup to be a "megabrand" and a marketing plus.

One advantage of the brand name proliferation involves the environment of the supermarket shelf. Having six brands gives a company a lot more shelf facings, a great advantage in this market. In addition, it may be possible for consumers to have positive attitudes and be loyal to more than one brand in a product class. The phenomenon, known as *brand-cluster loyalty* or *multibrand loyalty,* may be more common than we realize.

Discussion questions

1. Discuss the concept of brand loyalty in terms of consumers' attitudes (both A_o and A_{act}) and purchase intentions. Do you think it is possible for consumers to be loyal to more than one brand of soft drink?

2. How do you think attitudes (and underlying belief structures) differ between the intensely loyal and the less-involved consumers?

3. Is it possible for positive attitudes from one brand to be transferred to a different, but related, brand, perhaps with the same name? What aspects of attitude theory would help marketers develop strategies to do this?

4. According to Morgan Hunter of Marketing Corporation of America, a Connecticut marketing firm, "It is important not to confuse a stated preference with what consumers actually do when they're in the store. They may not actually buy the brand they say they prefer." Do you agree? Justify your position in terms of the theoretical relationships among consumers' attitudes, purchase intentions, and actual behaviors.

Sources: Anne B. Fisher, "Coke's Brand-Loyalty Lesson," *Fortune,* August 5, 1985, pp. 44–46; Carrie Gottlieb, "Products of the Year," *Fortune,* December 9, 1985, pp. 106–12; and Thomas Moore, "He Put the Kick Back into Coke," *Fortune,* October 26, 1987, pp. 46–56.

▶ **CASE II.5**

Hallmark Greeting Cards

It is one of the least likely businesses ever invented. But Hallmark—and its main competitors, American Greetings and Gibson Greetings, plus an assortment of so-called alternative card companies—make a very good living selling sentiment to American consumers. In fact, greeting cards are one of the most profitable things that can be made with paper and ink.

Consider Hallmark's classic pansy card:

Pansies always stand for thoughts—
At least that's what folks say,
So this just comes to show my thoughts
Are there with you today.

Since 1941, Hallmark has sold 22 million of these cards. In 1985, these simple cards cost an estimated 7 cents to manufacture and retailed for about 40 cents. Assuming a 100 percent markup at retail, Hallmark received about 20 cents at wholesale, for almost a 200 percent profit. With these financial numbers, Hallmark has grown at a compounded rate of 17 percent each year for the past 76 years. In 1985, its annual revenues approached $2 billion. Although nearly 50 percent of Hallmark's revenues come from ancillary products such as gift wrap, stuffed animals, and paper plates, greeting cards are still the most profitable line.

The costs of a card reflect not so much the paper or even the artwork, but the organized distribution system. Hallmark produces more than 11 million cards per day, which are sent to some 37,000 outlets, most independently owned. The company has invested millions in computers to keep track of the product. "We know which card is four rows up and five rows over, and how long it's been there," says a company representative. Reorders are shipped from two enormous automated warehouses, according to the past sales of each card. Because 90 percent of the cards are replaced with new designs each year, records must be updated constantly. Currently, Hallmark has some 32,000 card types to track.

Hallmark didn't invent the commercial greeting card. Well-to-do Americans exchanged expensive Christmas cards with friends as long ago as the 1870s. This genteel custom was popularized by two marketing-oriented men—Jacob Sapirstein for American Greetings and Joyce Hall for Hallmark. Between them, they convinced consumers to buy graduation cards, wedding cards, sympathy cards, and cards for many other occasions.

The card business in the United States is treacherous, highly competitive, and huge. In 1988, American consumers spent about $3.7 billion on cards (not including postage!). So popular are the products, in fact, that about 50 percent of all mail between U.S. households is greeting cards.

The market is growing even larger. Packaged Facts of New York estimated a $5.2 billion market in 1992 with the increase largely due to higher sales for alternative cards. Alternative cards are loosely defined as any card with a fresh approach to the market. For instance, there are cards intended for such diverse groups as stepgrandparents, recent divorcees, stressed-out working parents, and gay people. In addition to the traditional birthday, graduation, and Mother's Day cards, cards are being produced for specific occasions such as getting a new job or getting fired from your old one, making up after a romantic tiff, and going on a diet.

There are three main companies in the United States. Hallmark has about 40 percent of the market. American Greetings has 30 to 35 percent, and Gibson Greetings has 10 percent. Hallmark is in the nerve-wracking position of the front runner in a race where the pace of change has been accelerating. Moreover, "alternative" cards (risque or goofy) are becoming a serious threat, accounting for about 17 percent of the market. For instance, Recycled Paper Products, with sales of $100 million in whimsical animal cards, has been growing at a rate of 30 percent a year. Several small companies are thriving by making cards for niche markets that Hallmark leaves alone—such as cards for gays.

"The big segment of the market is what we deal in," says Irvine Hockaday, president of Hallmark. In 1982, Hallmark did introduce a "Lite" line of cards ("A third less serious than regular greeting cards"). More recently, it introduced cards to compete with the alternative lines. While not exactly salacious—"I'd like to tell you how much I love you. Have you got all night?"—these cards are not for staid people.

What is the allure of greeting cards for American consumers? No other society sends so many cards per capita, although the practice is common in Great Britain, where there is a large market. What goals or ends do greeting cards satisfy for the person who sends them? They certainly are not a convenience. "It takes more time to drive down to the store and pick out a card than to write a letter," says a sociology professor. What's wrong with a handwritten note, a telephone call, or a personal visit?

In 1986 to 1987, Hallmark changed its overall marketing strategy to emphasize *place,* in addition to *image.* This strategy recognizes the importance of consumers' store choice in the overall process of selecting a greeting card. Hallmark has a particular interest in store choice because most of its greeting cards are sold in "Hallmark stores" that sell only (or mostly) Hallmark products such as cards, wrapping paper, party goods, toys, and knickknacks. Although most of these stores are privately owned, many are identified as "Hallmark stores" in the store name—e.g., Linda's Hallmark. With this type of distribution system, consumers must first decide to go to a Hallmark store to buy a Hallmark card.

To remind consumers where they should go to buy Hallmark cards, the company added a new phrase, " . . . go to Hallmark," after its familiar slogan. "When you care enough to send the very best . . . ." It also created ads for newspapers and Sunday supplements that list all the local Hallmark retailers and their addresses. American Greetings, whose cards are widely distributed in grocery, department, and discount stores, countered with its own retailer-oriented campaign, "You never have to go out of your way to find American Greetings, because we're in the kinds of stores you shop every day." The battle to influence consumers' store choice was on.

Discussion questions

1. What are evaluative criteria for greeting cards, and what are their dominant overall end goals? How do these factors differ by market segment?

2. It has been estimated that approximately 80 percent of all greeting cards sold in the United States are purchased by women. Do you think there are major differences in the decision-making processes of men and women? What are the implications of these differences for marketing strategies?

3. Contrast the problem-solving process of heavy users of cards (12 or more cards per year, exclusive of Christmas cards) with light users (4 or fewer cards per year) in terms of end goals, product knowledge, and product involvement.

4. How do Hallmark cards get into consumers' consideration sets? Analyze the role of the store choice decision in this process. (How does store choice fit into the overall end goal for the card decision?) Do you think some consumers might become store loyal?

5. What heuristics might consumers develop to simplify their problem-solving processes for buying greeting cards? How could marketers interrupt routine choice behavior to get consumers to consider their brand?

▶ CASE II.6

Promotional battles in the breakfast cereal market

The breakfast cereal market is one of the most fiercely competitive in the United States. Four companies control about 75 percent of this market—Kellogg, General Mills, General Foods (Post cereals), and Quaker Oats. Competition among these firms is characterized by new product development and huge expenditures on various types of promotions, especially advertising. More so than most products, breakfast cereal is "marketing sensitive." That is, dollars spent on mediocre promotions simply fall into the void—they have no noticeable effect on consumers. But the same amount of money spent on a well-designed promotion strategy can dramatically increase sales and produce significant shifts in market shares.

In the early 1980s, Kellogg, the market leader, began to turn up the competitive heat by introducing a stream of new cereal products and substantially increasing promotion expenditures, especially for advertising. This resulted in a 12.2 percent increase in Kellogg's market share from its low of 36.7 percent in 1983 to 41.2 percent in 1988. During this period, the number two company, General Mills, gradually increased its market share from 20 to 21 percent. In contrast, General Food's Post cereal division fared badly in this promotion competition—its market share dropped from 16 percent in 1983 to 13.2 percent in 1988. These changes are not small. By 1988, the ready-to-eat cereal market in the United States was over $5 billion, so each share point was worth about $50 million in sales.

Post/General Foods. In 1983–1984, Post focused most of its advertising promotions on two brands. Fruit & Fiber was successful in attracting adult consumers, but Smurfberry Crunch, a kids' cereal, fizzled despite heavy advertising spending. So when Kellogg began to step up its advertising expenditures (in 1984, for instance, Kellogg outspent Post by a 3-to-1 margin—$160 million to $52 million), Post had limited funds to counter. In addition, Post wasn't able to develop good advertising strategies, so it decided not to spend money to show ineffective ads. Instead, Post focused promotion strategies on cents-off coupons and discounts to grocers. This promotion mix strategy encouraged one-time sales, but did not build brand loyalty the way good advertising can.

In the mid-1980s, Post changed its promotion mix strategy by stepping up advertising promotions of five core brands—Raisin Bran, Grape-Nuts, Fruit & Fiber, Super Golden Crisp, and Pebbles—by over 40 percent. It also developed stronger advertising appeals. For instance, the Grape-Nuts campaign, with its tag line "Are you right for Grape-Nuts?" increased sales by 10 percent, compared to industry growth of only 3 percent. Post also introduced a new cereal, Horizon, based on a trail mix concept of peanuts and grains clumped together (not in flakes). And Post reformulated Raisin Bran by removing preservatives, increasing the fiber, and taking the sugar off the raisins. To promote this "new" product in ads, Post hired singer John Denver, who represents to some people the essence of all that is wholesome.

The odds that these promotion strategies would be successful were not good. Of the dozens of cereal product entries in recent years, only a few brands such as General Mills' Honey Nut Cheerios and Post's Fruit & Fiber have gained a sustainable 1 percent market share. In fact, despite these strong efforts, Post's share of the cereal market continued to decline. Its problems in part were caused by the strong promotion strategies of General Mills, Quaker Oats, and Kellogg, the primary competitors.

General Mills. From 1985 to 1987, General Mills introduced six new cereal products, giving it 28 brands in 1987. Although none was a big hit, only one, Rocky Road, was an outright failure. In contrast, the usual failure rate for new grocery products is about 9 out of 10. In 1987, General Mills introduced a seventh new cereal brand, Total Oatmeal. This product was targeted directly at Quaker Oats, the leading company in the $500 million hot breakfast cereal market with a 68 percent share. General Mills promoted Total Oatmeal with a large budget, including a $12 million, six-month advertising campaign that claimed Total had "more nutrition than any other hot cereal." General Mills also distributed 175 million coupons for the product.

Quaker Oats. Quaker Oats (the fourth-largest cereal company in 1987 with an overall market share of 7.7 percent) countered with its own stepped-up advertising campaign communicating a "sensible nutrition" theme. Ads featured grandfatherly spokesperson Wilford Brimley, who claimed eating Quaker Oats is "the right thing to do." Quaker Oats' promotional strategy also included placing 12.5 million free samples of its instant oatmeal in boxes of its ready-to-eat cold cereal and a game promotion that gave away 1,500 Amana microwave ovens and 5,000 microwave cookbooks.

Kellogg. As the industry leader, Kellogg kept up the competitive pressure during the 1980s. Kellogg's marketing promotions were heavily oriented toward television advertising, although it supplemented the ads with standard sales promotion devices such as coupons and free samples. Most of Kellogg's new products were aimed at the 80 million health-oriented baby boomers (ages 25 to 49, the fastest-growing age segment in the United States). By encouraging these consumers to eat more breakfast cereal, Kellogg upped consumption by 26 percent over 1983 levels. In fact, Kellogg's successful new adult-oriented products and very heavy promotion expenditures had increased the overall market for breakfast cereal to $5 billion by 1988. Do you remember Kellogg's 1984 campaign for Frosted Flakes—"Frosted Flakes have the taste adults have grown to love"? Previously a children's cereal, Frosted Flakes had become the number one U.S. brand in 1988; Cheerios, a General Mills brand, was second.

Consider Kellogg's introduction of Müeslix in 1986. The product consisted of flakes, fruit, and nuts adapted from European-style cereals to appeal to American tastes. Kellogg's introduced Müeslix with a $33 million promotion budget, an industry record. Most of the money was spent on TV advertising, which featured misty morning scenes of rural Europe, and Swedish actor Max Von Sydow touting "the centuries-old balance" of healthy ingredients as "what breakfast was meant to be." The product was an immediate success, garnering about $100 million in sales the first year, even though it costs considerably more per ounce than Corn Flakes.

Further growth in breakfast cereal is likely to come mainly from international markets. Curiously, in terms of breakfast cereal consumption, the United States comes in fourth at 9.6 pounds per person per year (in 1988), after the Irish, British, and Australians. The average breakfaster in the rest of the world eats less than two pounds of cereal per year. To change the cognitions and behaviors of these people, you can be sure U.S. breakfast cereal companies like Kellogg, General Mills, Quaker Oats, and Post will be spending heavily on promotion strategies.

Discussion questions

1. Describe your intuitions about the consumer/product relationship for two key segments of the breakfast cereal market—kids (ages 8 to 16) and maturing baby boomers (ages 25 to 49). If accurate, what implications would your analyses have for designing effective marketing promotions?

2. Find a current print ad for an adult-oriented breakfast cereal. Identify the means-end chains of product knowledge it is trying to communicate. Analyze the advertisement using the MECCAS model described in the text (identify the driving force, message elements, product benefits, leverage point), and critique this promotion strategy.

3. Discuss how the goals and objectives of brand-oriented advertising differ from sales promotion strategies (such as coupons, price reductions, prizes, and premiums) when promoting new brands of breakfast cereal. Under what marketing circumstances would each be appropriate?

4. Use the Wheel of Consumer Analysis to discuss the long-run implications of using these different approaches to promotion. What are relative long-term advantages and disadvantages of weighting advertising or sales promotions more heavily in the promotion mix?

5. Why do you think the breakfast cereal market is so "marketing sensitive"? Why does the market respond to good marketing promotions and not at all to poor promotions?

Sources: Patricia Sellers, "How King Kellogg Beat the Blahs," *Fortune,* August 9, 1988, pp. 54–64; Pamela Sherrid, "Fighting Back at Breakfast," *Forbes,* October 7, 1985, pp. 126–30; and Steve Weiner, "Food Fight," *Forbes,* July 27, 1987, pp. 86–87.

III

BEHAVIOR

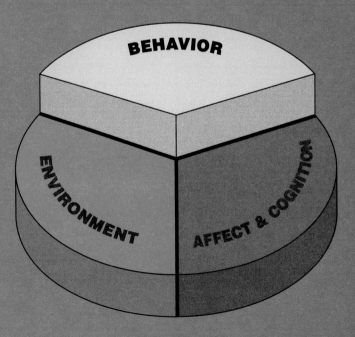

10

Introduction to Behavior

LEARNING OBJECTIVES

After completing this chapter, you should be able to:

▶ 1. Explain some basic differences between behavior and cognitive approaches.

▶ 2. List a number of different types of consumer promotions.

▶ 3. Explain four ways promotions are used to influence consumer behavior.

▶ 4. Explain the uses of behavior approaches in social marketing.

▶ 5. Discuss ethical questions concerning the use of behavior approaches in marketing.

RALSTON-PURINA PROMOTES FREAKIES

▶ Ralston-Purina ran a children's cereals promotion aimed at adults. Inside 11 million boxes of cereal with names like Freakies and Ghostbusters, Ralston-Purina included tiny models of sports cars. Ten of the boxes contained a scale-model red Corvette that could be redeemed for the real thing—a $29,000 Chevrolet Corvette.

▶ Citicorp offered gifts tied to the amount charged on its credit cards. For $500 charged on its Visa card, consumers got free golf balls or a travel clock; for $8,000 in charges, they received a round-trip air ticket for anywhere in the United States.

▶ General Mills inserted a single $1 bill into every 20th box of its Cheerios cereal. The promotion involved giving away a total of $1 million.

▶ Pepsi-Cola offered chances to win cash and prizes in its "Count the Wins" baseball game. If a number printed inside specially marked cans and caps matched the total number of wins by the Milwaukee Brewers on specific dates, the holder qualified for drawings for $10,000 and $30,000. Some instant prizes included $1,000, two tickets to a Brewers game, and two-liter bottles of any Pepsi product. One of Pepsi's more recent promotions offers a $5 rebate on the *Home Alone* video.

▶ American TV of Madison, Wisconsin, offered $100 worth of steak to customers who purchased specially marked items. Even items with prices as low as $69 qualified for the steak bonus.

These promotions run by different companies for different purposes all have something in common: the companies were not trying to change consumers' attitudes or beliefs but trying instead to change consumer behavior. Both Ralston-Purina and General Mills were trying to get consumers to buy their cereals, while Pepsi was trying to get consumers to buy its soft drinks. Citicorp was trying to get consumers to charge more on its credit cards, and American TV was trying to get consumers to come into the store and buy. Such strategies are consistent with the behavior approaches introduced in this chapter.

The previous section of this book presented an in-depth analysis of consumer cognitive and affective processes. Its major focus was on understanding the psychological or mental aspects of consumer behavior. In this section, the focus changes to another element of the Wheel of Consumer Analysis. Our concern here is with attempting to understand overt consumer behavior: behavior that can be directly observed and measured. We focus on what consumers *do* rather than on what they *think* and *feel,* and we delineate some processes by which this behavior can be changed to achieve marketing objectives.

In this chapter, we first compare the *cognitive* and the *behavior* approaches in terms of their basic differences so far as marketing is concerned. We do this so that you can appreciate why there are so few attempts to integrate them. Both cognitive and behavior approaches have value for the study of consumer behavior and for achieving marketing management objectives. We then discuss two areas of consumer research that have recognized the value of behavior approaches: sales promotion and social marketing. The chapter concludes with a discussion of some common misconceptions about behavior approaches.

In Chapter 11, classical and operant conditioning are explained and illustrated with a variety of marketing examples. We then turn to vicarious learning and its value for marketing (Chapter 12). These two chapters provide an overview of the major technology employed in applied behavior analysis. In Chapter 13, the last chapter of this section, we develop a model of overt consumer behavior and a management model for systematically influencing these behaviors.

BEHAVIOR VERSUS COGNITIVE VIEWS

Cognitive approaches, including some aspects of affect, dominate the field of consumer behavior and much of the thinking in marketing. Behavior approaches, which have been an important part of psychology for many years, are relatively new to consumer research and often are not well understood. For this reason, we think it is important to give a brief account of some differences between the two approaches.

There are, of course, many types of cognitive theories and assumptions, as there are a variety of behavior positions. Some cognitive approaches, for example, attempt to apply cognitive theories in explaining overt behavior. Others are concerned only with explaining the mind and mental processes. Some behaviorists view cognitive events as covert behavior to be analyzed in the same way as overt behavior. Other behaviorists see cognitive events as little more than words that may be useful for communication purposes but of no value as scientific explanations. It is unlikely that any discussion of differences between cognitive and behavior perspectives would be accepted by all advocates of either position, but we will attempt to offer representative accounts of them.

The **behavior approach** is based on a view called "applied behavior analysis." The **cognitive approach** is based on current research on topics such as information processing and cognitive science. These two perspectives tend to conflict: they often involve quite different views of the world, with conflicting positions, assumptions, and beliefs about what counts as scientifically important. Most important for our purposes, the behavior and the cognitive approaches often have different implications for designing marketing strategies.

Issues	Behavior Approaches	Cognitive Approaches
Role of the environment	Environment controls consumer behavior	Environment is one of many influences on consumer behavior
Role of cognition	Cognitions may mediate behavior–environment interactions	Cognitions cause and control behavior
Role of behavior	Behavior is the central focus of research and strategy development	Behavior is the result of cognition and is secondary in importance
View of affect	Affect refers to observable behaviors	Affect refers to internal feelings
View of freedom	Consumer behavior is controlled by the environment	Consumers have free will and buy what they need and want

EXHIBIT 10.1

A comparison of behavior and cognitive approaches

Some differences between the two approaches are shown in Exhibit 10.1. Behavior approaches tend to view the environment as the cause of behavior, so behavior approaches focus on the effects of different environmental situations and stimuli on what consumers actually do. For example, setting up a store display for Duracell batteries and observing the effects on consumer purchase behavior would be consistent with the behavior approach. Cognitive approaches, which tend to view mental processes and states as more important, focus instead on what consumers report they think and feel about various aspects of the environment. For example, giving consumers a questionnaire asking them about their attitudes toward Duracell batteries would be consistent with the cognitive approach.

The question of freedom deserves more discussion. Not many people like to think they are controlled or even strongly influenced by the environment. We like to think of ourselves as making free choices and determining our own destiny in a variety of circumstances. Behaviorists look at circumstances from a different perspective. An example will illustrate what behaviorists mean when they argue that the environment controls consumer behavior.

Most adults in our society use products such as deodorant and toothbrushes. In fact, it is socially unacceptable not to use these products, and consumers who do not can be looked down on. Serious health problems can be the result of not brushing one's teeth. In other words, some consequences are connected with use or non-use of these products. In behavior terms, the environment conditions the use of these products by in some way rewarding consumers who use them and punishing consumers who do not.

Given these consequences, how free are we to choose whether to use deodorant or brush our teeth? In fact, our "choice" is influenced to a great extent by the consequences of not engaging in the behaviors. Because behavior is strongly influenced by its consequences, behaviorists argue that consumers are not free to do whatever they want. In this sense, consumer behavior is seen as controlled by the environment.

It is also worth noting that the behavior and the cognitive approach take a different view of affect. So far in the text, we have treated affect as a psychological phenomenon dealing with the way consumers feel. Affect includes such things as consumer attitudes and emotions. To behaviorists, however, affect refers to observable behaviors, not internal states.

The concept of attitude is one example. In cognitive approaches, attitudes deal with what consumers mentally like and dislike. So, a favorable attitude toward a product to a cognitivist means the consumer likes the product a lot. In behavior approaches, the term *attitude* refers instead to the probability of a behavioral response. A favorable attitude toward a product to a behaviorist means the consumer has a higher probability of purchasing the product.

Rebates are often effective at changing purchase probabilities, even for big-ticket items.

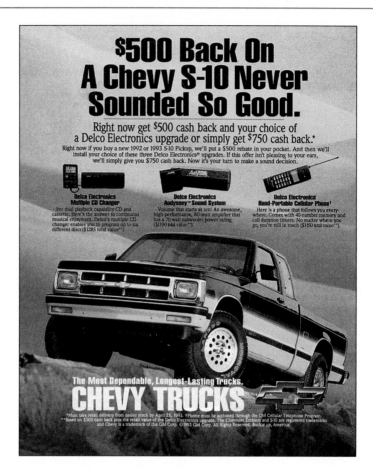

Another example of the difference in cognitive and behavior approaches concerns emotions, such as anger. Cognitivists view anger as an internal feeling. To a behaviorist, anger is a summary statement to describe a set of behaviors, not an internal feeling. For example, if they see a consumer yelling and throwing ice cream at a store clerk, behaviorists would have no problem saying the person appears to be angry. Yet, by "angry" they do not mean what the person feels inside; they refer specifically to the behaviors they are observing. Thus, whether affect is an internal feeling or an observable behavior depends on your view. In this section of the text, we treat affect as observable behaviors.

Exhibit 10.2 offers further comparison of each approach in the ways they tend to view marketing issues. Cognitive approaches assume that the role of marketing action is to satisfy needs at a profit, a theory that requires two further cognitive assumptions. First, it is assumed that consumers have something called "needs," which they attempt to satisfy through purchase and consumption. Second, consumers are somewhat autonomous and rational and largely control their preferences and purchases. Marketing strategies may attempt to change consumer affect and cognitions, such as beliefs and attitudes, the cognitive approach would say, but marketing cannot *create* consumer needs and wants or even modify them very much. Similarly, the question of whether marketing is very effective at changing consumer behavior is seldom addressed by cognitivists.

Behaviorists tend to offer a different account of marketing activity. Marketing is seen as an attempt to achieve organizational objectives by modifying consumer behavior. A main objective typically is to increase profits and/or market share, usually achieved by increasing

Marketing Issues	Behavior Approaches	Cognitive Approaches
Role of marketing	Modify and control consumer behavior to achieve organizational objectives	Satisfy needs of consumers at a profit
Role of marketing/ consumer research	Investigate strategies for predicting and controlling consumer behavior	Investigate strategies for influencing consumer affect and cognitions
View of marketing effectiveness	Recognize the effectiveness of marketing in changing behavior	Often overlook the effectiveness of marketing

EXHIBIT 10.2

A comparison of views of marketing

sales. Two primary methods of increasing sales are: (1) influencing current buyers to buy more of the product, and (2) maintaining current buyers while influencing nonbuyers to become buyers. Both of these involve changing consumer purchase behavior. Many behaviorists would argue that marketing strategies are often effective at changing consumer behavior—and that a variety of current marketing tactics are quite consistent with behavioral principles. Some behaviorists might even suggest that marketers are far more concerned with tactics for making profitable sales than with satisfying consumer needs.

Clearly, the two approaches have considerable differences in marketing and consumer behavior applications. Which approach is "true" or "right" is not at issue. What is important is which approach or combination of approaches is most *useful* in various stages of solving marketing problems and developing marketing strategies.

We believe that a combination of both approaches is superior to either one applied separately. That is, if consideration of consumer needs (cognitive approach) is helpful in the development of successful new products, and if operant conditioning (behavior approach) is helpful in increasing market share for the product, there is no reason to ignore one or the other approach. Consumer Perspective 10.1 illustrates a successful marketing strategy using both approaches.

INFLUENCING OVERT CONSUMER BEHAVIOR

Behavioral principles form the foundation for marketing strategies in several areas. The first of these is sales promotion, an area of increasing interest to consumer researchers and marketing practitioners. A second area deals with social marketing issues. Here the behavior approach is commonly used to develop strategies to influence socially desirable consumer behaviors.

Sales promotion

One area of consumer research that assumes the value of a behavior approach is sales promotion. In fact, leading experts define **sales promotion** as "an action-focused marketing event whose purpose is to have a direct impact on the behavior of a firm's customers."[1] Two points are noteworthy in this definition.

First, the firm's customers may be industry members such as retailers, in which case the promotion is called a **trade promotion.** Companies use trade promotions such as advertising or display allowances to push products through retailers to consumers. The alternative is that the firm's customers are the final consumers, in which case the promotions are called **consumer promotions.** Retailers (and manufacturers) use consumer promotions such as coupons and free samples to encourage consumers to purchase products and pull the product through the distribution channel. In one recent year, overall expenditures on promotion included 44 percent on trade promotions, 31 percent on advertising, and 25 percent on consumer promotions. Consumer Perspective 10.2 (see page 231) shows how much sales promotions have grown in recent years.

CONSUMER
PERSPECTIVE

▶ 10.1

Lifetime Cable
Network

Many marketing practitioners are effective at using a combination of cognitive and behavioral approaches. For example, Lifetime Cable Network conducted cognitive research on why viewers were not watching its programs. This research found that one in five viewers erroneously thought Lifetime was a religious network.

The network set three behavioral objectives: (1) to get more people to "sample" Lifetime's new programming; (2) to get those who may look at Lifetime now to watch a wider variety of programs; and (3) to get people to *keep* watching.

The strategy used to accomplish these objectives featured a "Chance of a Lifetime" game. The game required viewers to match symbols from a game card with symbols shown on the air. The game cards were sent to viewers with their cable bills or could be obtained in *TV Guide* or through requests during on-air promotion. The game was easy to understand and play, lasted long enough to keep people watching, and spread winning symbols over the entire programming day. The $400,000 worth of prizes included stereo systems, personal computers, romantic getaway weekends for two, and many other prizes with universal appeal. There was a game each week for eight weeks, and 200 prizes per week were awarded. A "second chance" drawing offered the grand prize of a $25,000 tour of Europe.

This strategy greatly increased viewer interest and cable system support. For example, on a single day, nearly 1,100 subscribers sent in entries. Tens of thousands of entries for the "second chance" contest were received before the main contest even finished. Thus, by analyzing cognitions to identify the problem, and by devising a unique behavioral intervention to solve the problem, a successful marketing strategy was developed.

Source: Based on "Behind the Lifetime Sweeps," *Promotion Hotline*, Ogilvy & Mather, May 1985, pp. 1–2.

Second, the definition emphasizes "direct impact on the behavior of . . . customers," clearly a behavioral approach. In fact, few consumer promotions provide material designed to change consumer cognitions about a product. Rather, they are designed to influence the probability of purchase or other desired behaviors without necessarily changing any consumer attitudes about a brand. If the promotion is for a new brand, purchase and use may lead to favorable postpurchase attitudes and future purchases. If the promotion is for an existing brand, consumers with a neutral or slightly positive attitude may take advantage of the promotion to reduce their purchase risk and try a brand they do not normally use. For consumers who already purchase a brand, a promotion may be an added incentive to remain loyal to it. The list in Exhibit 10.3 covers the majority of types of consumer promotions.[2] These basic types of consumer promotions are often used in combination to increase the probability of desired behaviors. For example, Procter & Gamble offered a $1 off coupon plus a premium coupon for a free Duncan Hines cake mix for purchasing any size Folgers coffee. Some consumer promotions feature coupons plus a promise to make donations to specific charities for every coupon or refund certificate redeemed. For example, Hartz Mountain offered a $1 coupon on its flea and tick repellent plus a 50-cent donation to the Better Health for Pets Program.

Consumer promotions can be used to influence behavior in a variety of ways. Four particular aspects of behavior that promotions are designed to affect include: purchase probability, purchase quantity, purchase timing, and purchase location.

Purchase probability

Most consumer promotions are designed to increase the probability that consumers will purchase a particular brand or combination of products, although a firm may have a

▷ **Sampling.** Consumers are offered regular or trial sizes of the product either free or at a nominal price. Hershey Foods has handed out 750,000 candy bars on 170 college campuses.

▷ **Price deals.** Consumers are given discounts from the product's regular price. For example, Coke and Pepsi are frequently available at discounted prices.

▷ **Bonus packs.** Bonus packs consist of additional amounts of the product provided in the package or container. For example, Gillette Atra occasionally adds a few extra blades to its blade packs without increasing the price.

▷ **Rebates and refunds.** Consumers, either at purchase or by mail, are given cash reimbursements for purchasing products. For example, consumers are often offered rebates on certain car makes or models.

▷ **Sweepstakes and contests.** Consumers are offered chances to win cash and/or prizes either through chance selection or games of skill. For example, Marriott Hotels teamed with Hertz Rent-A-Car in a scratch-card sweepstakes that offered over $90 million in prizes.

▷ **Premiums.** A premium is a reward or gift that comes from purchasing a product. For example, Procter & Gamble offered a free package of Diaperene baby washcloths with the purchase of any size Pampers.

▷ **Coupons.** Consumers are offered cents-off or added value incentives for purchasing specific products. For example, Lenscrafters offered newspaper coupons for $20 off on the purchase of contact lenses from its stores.

EXHIBIT 10.3

Types of consumer promotions

number of subgoals it hopes to achieve in running a promotion. For a new product, the primary goal may be to get consumers to try a product. For example, Hershey offered a free package of Reese's Crunchy peanut butter cups with the purchase of any other Reese's candy product to encourage trial of the new product. Kellogg's offered a coupon for an 18-ounce box of its popular corn flakes with the purchase of its new Kellogg's Mini Buns. Some car dealers offer special discounts for first-time buyers.

A second subgoal of consumer promotions may be to position a particular brand or company to encourage consumers to purchase and continue to purchase the company's brand. In this case, the promotion is designed to maintain or change both consumer cognition and behavior. One way to do this is to use frequent promotions to offer a competitive price on a brand that is positioned as a high-priced, high-quality product. A lower price in these circumstances has less chance of leading consumers to believe the product is of lower quality than competitive brands. For example, Kellogg's frequently offers coupons and premiums on its market-leading cereals.

Another use of promotions for positioning purposes is seen in the offer to make contributions to charity for each coupon or refund certificate redeemed. This tactic may increase consumer perceptions of the societal commitment of firms. Consumers who are socially and ecologically concerned may then switch to purchasing these companies' brands. Post Alpha Bits offered a 50-cent coupon and promised to make an unspecified donation to Hospitals for Children for each coupon redeemed. Chef Boyardee Pizza Mix offered a 20-cent coupon and promised to make a 25-cent donation to Adam Walsh Resource Centers for each coupon redeemed. Krunchers potato chips offered a 25-cent coupon and promised to make a contribution to the Better Homes Foundation. Procter & Gamble offered a 50-cent refund for a number of its soap products and promised a $1 contribution to Keep America Beautiful, Inc., for each refund certificate redeemed.

Sales promotions such as this price-off strategy are intended to influence consumers' immediate purchase behavior.

A third subgoal of consumer promotions is to effect a brand switch. Consumer promotions result in brand switches by making the purchase of a brand on a deal more attractive than purchasing the usual brand at full price.

A final goal of consumer promotions is to develop brand loyalty. Some consumers may be deal-prone and tend to purchase products on the basis of coupons and other deals, so frequent deals on the brands they use may keep them relatively loyal. Companies such as Kellogg's and Procter & Gamble that have broad product lines and a number of top-selling products frequently offer a variety of forms of consumer promotions for their products. Even deal-prone consumers who have preferred brands may remain loyal through a long succession of coupons and other deals.

Purchase quantity

A number of consumer promotions are designed not only to influence purchase of a brand but also to influence the number of units purchased or size of units purchased. For example, Quaker Oats offered a 70-cent coupon for purchasing two bottles of Gatorade. Best Foods offered a $1 coupon for purchasing two 18-ounce or larger jars of Skippy peanut butter. Procter & Gamble offered $2, $5, and $8 refunds for purchasing one, two, or three gallons of Tide, Cheer, Era, or Solo liquid laundry detergent. A free Mennen Speed Stick deodorant was offered with the purchase of two at the regular price. Such promotions may increase the amount of a company's product sold and may increase brand loyalty, but consumers who already are loyal to particular brands may simply stock up on them during a promotion and wait until the next promotion to purchase again. Some consumers will purchase products only when they can get a deal on them. In fact, U.S. car manufacturers may have unintentionally conditioned many consumers to wait for rebates rather than buy a car without one.

CONSUMER PERSPECTIVE

Trends in sales promotion expenditures

Although advertising remains an important promotion tool, sales promotion expenditures have grown rapidly in recent years. For example:

▶ Combined consumer and trade promotion spending as a percentage of advertising/promotion budgets grew from 58 percent in 1976 to 65 percent in 1987 to 69.4 percent in 1990.

▶ Manufacturers distributed 75 billion coupons in 1977 and over 300 billion in 1990.

▶ More than $1.1 billion was spent on media space to carry coupons in 1990 compared with $979 million in 1989.

Many reasons have been offered for the increase in the use of consumer promotions, including the notion that advertising is becoming less effective, consumers are more price sensitive, and the sales effects of promotions are easier to measure than those of advertising. Perhaps one additional reason is that promotions focus directly on changing consumer behavior, a major goal of marketing.

Source: The comparative statistics are taken from Robert C. Blattberg and Scott A. Neslin, *Sales Promotion: Concepts, Methods, and Strategies* (New York: Prentice Hall, 1990), p. 15; Carrie Goerne, "Marketers Using More Coupons to Fight Recession," *Marketing News*, October 29, 1991, p. 6; and Cyndee Miller, "Trade Promotion Spending in 1990 Hits Record Level," *Marketing News*, October 29, 1991, p. 6.

Purchase timing

Consumer promotions can also influence the time at which consumers purchase. For example, special discounts can be offered to encourage consumers to eat at particular restaurants on nights when business is slow. Pizza Hut often offers discounts and special family prices for Monday or Tuesday nights. Other retail stores have special sales on specific dates to encourage purchases at that time. Services such as airlines and telephone companies offer special rates to encourage consumers to use them at specific times and dates to even out demand. One trend in the use of coupons is to shorten the redemption period to encourage consumers to purchase sooner. Finally, most sweepstakes and contests are relatively short to encourage consumers to enter the contest by purchasing the product promptly.

Purchase location

Consumer promotions can also be used to influence the location or vendor of particular products. Retail stores and retail chains offer their own coupons, contests, and other deals to encourage consumers to shop at their outlets. For example, one grocery chain offered $20 worth of beef if a consumer selected at a specific store was found to have a beef product in the shopping cart. Some retail chains, such as Wal-Mart, have a standing offer to meet any other store's price on a product if the Wal-Mart price is higher. Such promotions and tactics can build store traffic and encourage store loyalty, as discussed in Consumer Perspective 10.3 (see page 233).

Effectiveness of sales promotions

There is little question that promotions are effective in influencing consumer behavior—and this is shown by the growth of sales promotion expenditures, as shown in Consumer Perspective 10.2. Which promotion tools are generally most effective for achieving particular behavioral changes is not fully understood, however. One study compared four consumer promotion tools—coupons, rebates, sweepstakes, and premiums—for their impact

Coupons, too, can be effective at getting consumers to purchase specific products.

on various consumer purchase behaviors.[3] These behaviors included purchasing a product consumers said they didn't need, purchasing a product they had never tried before, purchasing a different brand from their usual brand, purchasing more than usual, purchasing sooner than usual, and purchasing later than usual.

Exhibit 10.4 (see page 234) presents the results of that study. In general, consumers report coupons were the most effective promotions at changing these various behaviors. Over 70 percent of the consumers report they purchased a product they had never tried before because of a coupon; over 75 percent say they purchased a different brand from their usual brand because of a coupon. Of course, of the four promotion tools, coupons are the most commonly available and easiest to use. Rebates and premiums are both shown to be effective in changing consumer behavior in this study but to a lesser extent than coupons. The study found that the bigger the rebate, the more effort consumers would expend to obtain it. Finally, while some consumers also report that sweepstakes influenced them, such promotions were the least effective overall.

The study also finds that changes in behavior varied by the type of product and by characteristics of the consumers. For example, for products such as shampoo, coffee, batteries, toothpaste, and personal appliances, promotions could persuade the majority of consumers to try a different brand. But for products such as alcoholic beverages, automobiles, motor oil, pet food, and floor coverings, consumers report that promotions would not persuade them to switch brands. In terms of consumer characteristics, consumers who are more affluent, educated, and older are more likely to participate in consumer promotions, according to this study.

Amoco Oil Company ran a promotion designed to build store loyalty to Amoco filling stations. The promotion required consumers to fill up (a minimum of 8 gallons) at an Amoco station 10 times and to get a promotion card punched by an attendant. This all had to be done within a specified three-month period. After 10 fill-ups, consumers could mail the card to the "Amoco Fill-Up" address and receive coupons for $1 off on their next five fill-ups.

Consider the possible outcomes of this promotion. If consumers comply with all of the requirements and use the five coupons, then they have made 15 trips to an Amoco station and made 15 purchases of 8 gallons or more. This is a considerable amount of behavior and sales to generate for the company for a relatively small $5 reward. In addition, because Amoco gas is more expensive than gas at discount stations, the consumer may not be saving money. A consumer buying 10 gallons at a time and paying 5 cents more a gallon for Amoco gas in 15 trips spends an additional $7.50 to save $5. Still, Amoco gas is of excellent quality, may give the consumer savings in better gas mileage, and the consumer's car may run better by using it. Thus, the promotion itself could get consumers into the habit of going to an Amoco station and lead to loyalty. The superior product could also contribute to this loyalty.

The promotion card states it will take six to eight weeks to receive the coupons. If the consumer continues to use Amoco in the meantime, the company continues to make full-price sales. If consumers go to other stations in the interim, receipt of the coupons could bring them back to Amoco, giving the company a second chance to develop loyalty.

If consumers do not fill up 10 times in three months, they do not qualify for the promotion, although they might still develop a loyalty to Amoco. In this case, Amoco develops a loyal customer but does not have to pay the promotion value to do so. Overall, this promotion strategy appears to be well designed and capable of building long-term loyal customers.

In sum, promotions can change consumer behavior, although many contingencies can influence their effectiveness. Consistent with behavioral principles, it seems that the greater the reward, the less effort required to obtain it, and the sooner it comes after the behavior, the more likely the promotion will be influential.

Social marketing refers to programs and strategies designed to change behavior in ways deemed good for consumers and society. Much of the research on such programs is in the applied behavior analysis literature rather than in the traditional consumer behavior literature. It focuses on methods of encouraging desired behaviors and discouraging undesired consumer behaviors.

Social marketing

Encourage desired behaviors

Many forms of behavior can be increased through the use of behavior approaches. Research shows, for example, that various incentives increase the probability parents will see that their children get dental and health care. Providing feedback and offering chances to win prizes increases use of seat belts, which could save thousands of lives each year. Small incentives can also increase the use of car pools, which could help save natural resources and reduce air pollution. Providing information in the grocery store about the amount of fat and fiber in products, and offering alternatives, can influence the purchase of particular foods.

Free samples can increase
the probability of trial and
purchase.

Discourage undesired behaviors

Many types of undesired consumer behaviors can also be decreased through applied behavior analysis. For example, various types of interventions can reduce smoking, driving while impaired, dropping out of school, illegal drug use, and teenage pregnancies. While no program has been totally effective, even small advances against such major problems are valuable for both individuals and society in general.[4] Consumer research has contributions to offer to society in exploring better solutions to these problems outside traditional product marketing.

EXHIBIT 10.4

Promotion effects on consumer behavior

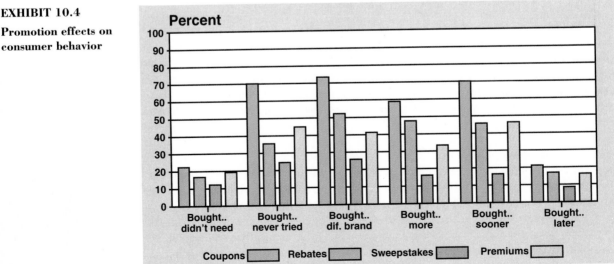

Source: "Study: Some Promotions Change Consumer Behavior," *Marketing News,* October 15, 1990, p. 12.

This ad discourages smoking—an undesired behavior.

This ad encourages healthy eating—a desired behavior.

If applied behavior analysis is a useful approach in sales promotion and social marketing, it may have extensions to other areas of consumer research. In the chapters that follow, we examine behavior technology more fully and suggest how it can be used to help formulate successful marketing strategies.

Sales promotion and social marketing techniques normally do not engender any suspicion about the use of behavior approaches to influence consumers. The application of sales promotion tools is well accepted in our society, and advancing societal goals through social marketing may not seem ethically problematic. Of course, we have not referred to these approaches as *behavior modification,* for this term frequently generates strong negative feelings. A negative reaction may have to do with misconceptions about the nature of behavior modification or applied behavior analysis. Misconceptions center on two major questions concerning the nature of the behavioral approach in general and its application in marketing in particular: (1) Are behavior approaches manipulative and unethical? (2) Do behavior approaches deny that people can think?

There is no question that behavior approaches involve changing behavior. They have been criticized as manipulative and unethical because they attempt to change behavior in a systematic way. In fact, few human interactions are not concerned with people attempting to change the behavior of other people. For example, professors attempt to get students to study, and students attempt to get professors to give them good grades; employers attempt to get employees to work hard, and employees attempt to get employers to pay them more money; parents attempt to get their children to behave well, and children attempt to get parents to give them treats; the government attempts to get people to

MISCONCEPTIONS ABOUT BEHAVIOR APPROACHES

Are behavior approaches manipulative and unethical?

pay taxes and obey laws, while people attempt to get the government to provide municipal services. Behavior approaches should not be singled out as manipulative and unethical solely because they involve systematic methods for doing what most of us are attempting to do anyway.

The ethical question involved in attempts by marketing managers to get consumers to change behavior goes beyond questioning the use of behavior technology. In fact, consumer choice is seen as essential in a competitive, capitalistic system. Firms that survive and prosper in this system are those that are most effective at modifying consumer behavior and encouraging purchase and repurchase of their products and brands.

Even the cognitive approach to marketing and consumer behavior can raise questions of manipulation. The reason we study cognitive variables in marketing and consumer behavior is because they are believed to influence overt behavior. In some cases, marketers try to influence cognitive variables in order to change behavior. In other cases, marketers look at cognitive variables to develop more efficient marketing strategies to change behavior *without* changing the cognitive variable. That is, needs and benefits sought by consumers are often an issue for the purpose of segmenting markets, where the knowledge gained is used to develop products and marketing strategies that reach a particular market segment seeking certain benefits or need satisfactions. In neither case is the cognitive approach of much value unless the firm develops a marketing strategy that effectively changes consumers' behaviors so that they actually purchase a product.

In summary, a major concern of human activity in general and of marketing in particular is to change or maintain overt behavior. Our personal interactions cause this to occur, and society in many cases encourages it. And strategy development in marketing is clearly concerned with influencing overt consumer behavior, whether behavior or cognitive approaches are used. A claim that behavior approaches are unethical and manipulative— but that societal, marketing, and cognitive approaches to marketing are not—does not seem to be logical.

Do behavior approaches deny that people can think?

The conventional wisdom is that behaviorists see people as at the mercy of their surroundings. In fact, while many behaviorists believe behavior is controlled by the environment, few would argue that there is nothing going on in people's brains. Where behaviorists and cognitivists differ is on the ability to analyze cognitive variables "scientifically," what causes cognitive processes, and the importance of thinking versus doing.

Cognitive variables cannot be observed and measured easily and must instead be inferred. Historically, behaviorists have therefore been skeptical of the scientific value of cognitive events; they are not observable directly. To a behaviorist, cognitive events are usually not considered to be explanations of behavior, because they cannot be analyzed scientifically.

Many behaviorists accept self-report measures of cognitive events as supplemental, supporting information, but cognitive information is not a substitute for studying overt behavior. Some marketing professionals agree that it is useful to investigate *what* behaviors consumers perform before acceptance of cognitive theories designed to explain *why* the behaviors are performed.

Even if cognitive processes do mediate behavior, behaviorists see these processes as developed through interactions with the environment. It is interaction with the environment that teaches the individual which behaviors are rewarded and which are punished, and this becomes part of the individual's conditioning history. Cognitivists interpret the process as resulting in interactions that are stored in memory, while behaviorists say the person is changed through the interaction.

Most behaviorists believe that what people *do* is much more important than what they *think.* They believe that what goes on inside people's heads is of less consequence, because results occur only when people actually do something. In this sense, it is unimportant whether consumers need a product, want a product, like a product, plan to purchase a product, or think they would be satisfied with a product, until they engage in some overt behavior, such as telling someone else about the product or actually buying it. For example, we may like a particular presidential candidate, but only by working for and voting for the candidate do we have any impact. Simply liking the candidate makes no difference in the outcome of the election.

In summary, behaviorists view thoughts and feelings as not observable, as caused by the environment, and as less useful for scientific study than behavior. For our purposes, the major limitation of behavior approaches has been their exclusion of cognitive variables from study. At the same time, we acknowledge that a major limitation of marketing and consumer research has been to ignore overt behavior.

Learning objective 1: *Explain some basic differences between behavior and cognitive approaches.*

▶ SUMMARY

Behavior and cognitive approaches differ most strongly on what factors control behavior. Behavior approaches see the environment as controlling, while cognitive approaches view mental processes and states as the controllers. Behavior approaches view marketing as a means to modify and control behavior to achieve organizational objectives; cognitive approaches view marketing as a means of satisfying consumer needs and wants to obtain profits. Behavior approaches investigate strategies to influence behavior; cognitive approaches investigate strategies to influence consumer affect and cognitions. Behavior approaches tend to see marketing as more effective at influencing consumers than do cognitive approaches.

Learning objective 2: *List a number of different types of consumer promotions.*

Consumer promotions include practices such as sampling, price deals, bonus packs, rebates and refunds, sweepstakes and contests, premiums, and coupons.

Learning objective 3: *Explain four ways promotions are used to influence consumer behavior.*

First, promotions are used to influence the probability that consumers will purchase a particular brand or combination of products. Some ways of doing this include offering a premium or coupon on a normally high-priced product or offering to make a charitable contribution based on purchase. Second, promotions can be used to influence the number of units or the size of the package purchased. Some ways of doing this include offering a coupon or premium only for purchasing multiple units or for purchasing the largest size package of the product. Third, promotions are used to influence purchase timing. Some ways of doing this include offering discounts on particular days and dates or limiting the redemption period on coupons. Fourth, promotions can be used to influence purchase location. Some ways of doing this include offering store coupons or offering to meet competitive prices of other stores.

Learning objective 4: *Explain the uses of behavior approaches in social marketing.*

Behavior approaches are used for both encouraging desired behaviors and discouraging undesired behaviors. Behaviors that society values, such as providing medical and dental care for children, using seat belts, carpooling, and purchasing healthier products, can be encouraged using behavioral methods. Behaviors that society does not value, such as smoking, drunken driving, dropping out of school, and using illegal drugs, can be discouraged using behavioral methods.

Learning objective 5: *Discuss ethical questions concerning the use of behavior approaches in marketing.*

Behavior approaches are concerned with changing consumer behavior. So are most of the day-to-day activities we all engage in whether as teachers or students, parents or children, employers or employees. Marketers also use cognitive approaches to find strategies to change consumer affect and cognitions, with the objective of eventually changing behavior. Thus, the ethical question whether influencing and controlling consumer behavior is manipulative requires analysis of more than behavior approaches. Many types of marketing strategies, based on both cognitive and behavior approaches, are acceptable to society.

▶ **KEY TERMS AND CONCEPTS**

| behavior approach | sales promotion | consumer promotions |
| cognitive approach | trade promotion | social marketing |

▶ **REVIEW AND DISCUSSION QUESTIONS**

1. Why have behavior and cognitive approaches not been fully integrated in psychology or consumer research?

2. Explain how behavior and cognitive approaches differ in their views of consumer research.

3. Give examples of purchase decisions where you believe the marketer need take only a behavioral view.

4. In what kinds of purchase decisions would understanding of consumer cognitive processes be superior to a marketing manager's behavioral view?

5. Offer three examples of instances where you have attempted to modify someone else's behavior, or where someone else has attempted to modify your behavior.

6. Do you think behavior modification is ethical or unethical as a marketing tool? Why?

7. Consider a specific occasion, such as dinner at a restaurant. Offer both cognitive and behavioral views of the script you might observe.

8. Assume you want to change the response of restaurant patrons. Suggest strategies (*a*) based on a cognitive view, and (*b*) based on a behavioral view.

9. Find at least two offers for products in magazines or newspapers designed to influence (*a*) purchase probability, (*b*) purchase quantity, (*c*) purchase timing, and (*d*) purchase location.

CHAPTER 11

Classical and Operant Conditioning

LEARNING OBJECTIVES

After completing this chapter, you should be able to:

▶ 1. Define classical conditioning.

▶ 2. Offer examples of how classical conditioning is used to influence consumer behavior.

▶ 3. Define operant conditioning.

▶ 4. Offer examples of discriminative stimuli used to influence consumer behavior.

▶ 5. Explain four types of consequences that can occur after a consumer behavior.

▶ 6. Describe three types of reinforcement schedules that can be used to influence consumer behavior.

▶ 7. Explain shaping, and offer a marketing example of it.

▶ 8. Offer examples of ways operant conditioning is used to influence consumer behavior.

▶ 9. Explain brand loyalty and store loyalty.

LOTTO MANIA

Lotteries are legal in 34 states and the District of Columbia. In one recent year, lotteries sold over 20 billion tickets—that's $109 worth for every man, woman, and child in those states. Consumers often flock to lotteries, particularly when the jackpot has grown. In New York, for example, when the Super Lotto drawing reached $90 million, residents stood in long lines in the bitter January cold to buy tickets. Retailers sold 61 million tickets in 10 days—more than 21,000 per minute toward the drawing hour. When the Florida Lotto prize reached $106 million, mania gripped the state. People who had never dreamed of buying Lotto tickets stood in line with dedicated players—and in the final days before the drawing, retailers sold 44,000 tickets a minute. Apparently, state lotteries have a powerful effect on consumer behavior. Some of the reasons are discussed in this chapter.

This chapter has two major sections. The first explains and illustrates the process of classical conditioning. The second section covers operant conditioning, describing some successful applications along with examples from marketing practice. We treat the two conditioning processes as conceptually distinct, although they overlap in a number of areas.[1] Each of these types of conditioning involves changing the environment to change overt behavior. While the environmental changes may also influence cognition, the focus here is on the behavior element of the Wheel of Consumer Analysis.

CLASSICAL CONDITIONING

You are likely familiar with Pavlov's experiments that conditioned a dog to salivate at the sound of a bell. Pavlov did this by first pairing the sound of a bell with sprays of meat powder for a number of trials. Eventually, he could eliminate the meat powder, and the dog would salivate at the sound of the bell alone. Pavlov's research provides the basis for classical conditioning.

In general, **classical conditioning** can be defined as a process by which a previously neutral stimulus (the bell in Pavlov's experiment), by being paired with an unconditioned stimulus (the meat powder), comes to elicit a conditioned response (salivation) very similar to the response originally elicited by the unconditioned stimulus. In other words, when they are repeatedly paired together, a new stimulus begins to elicit the same behavior as a familiar stimulus. This process is depicted in Exhibit 11.1

Four points are relevant in our discussion. First, classical conditioning can be accomplished not only with unconditioned stimuli but also with previously conditioned stimuli. For example, most of us are previously conditioned to the sound of a doorbell ringing and look in the direction of the sound almost automatically. This previously conditioned stimulus has been used in the beginning of Avon TV commercials to attract consumers' attention.

Second, classically conditioned behaviors are controlled by stimuli that occur *before* the behavior. For example, in Pavlov's experiment the meat powder and the bell were presented before salivation occurred. Consumer Perspective 11.1 discusses the Coca-Cola Company's use of classical conditioning.

Third, the behaviors influenced by classical conditioning are assumed to be under the control of the autonomic nervous system. This system controls the smooth muscles that produce involuntary behavior not under the conscious control of the individual.

Last, and perhaps most important for the purposes of consumer behavior analysis, the behaviors called *emotions* appear to follow the principles of classical conditioning. For example, when a new product for which people have neutral feelings is advertised repeatedly during momentous sports events (such as the Super Bowl), it is possible for the product eventually to generate excitement on its own solely through the repeated pairings with the significant event. Television commercials for lottery games frequently include exuberant past

EXHIBIT 11.1

The process of classical conditioning

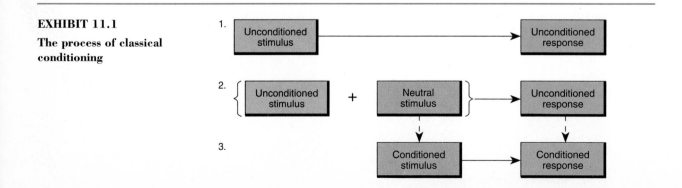

winners who could generate excitement for playing the lottery. Similarly, a political candidate may come to elicit patriotic feelings in voters simply through the effect of the patriotic music constantly playing in the background of political commercials. A number of companies use stimuli in commercials and ads that are designed to generate emotions. These firms include Hallmark, AT&T, and Procter & Gamble, maker of Luvs disposable diapers.

Classical conditioning as a marketing tool

Classical conditioning has important implications for marketing and consumer behavior. It can account for many of the responses that environmental stimuli elicit from individuals. Through classical conditioning, a particular stimulus can come to evoke positive, negative, or neutral feelings. Consequently, classical conditioning can influence an individual to work to obtain, to avoid, or be indifferent to a wide variety of products and services.

Consider product-related stimuli. External stimuli that elicit positive emotions can be paired with a product so that the product itself elicits a positive effect. A response may then be triggered that changes the potential consumer's feelings about the product. That is, if a product elicits positive affect, an individual exposed to it is more apt to behave positively toward it than if negative emotions are elicited. Attending behavior is also apt to be a function of classically conditioned affect. Stimuli that elicit stronger emotional responses (either positive or negative) are apt to receive more attention from a consumer than stimuli that are affectively neutral. To the degree that attending behavior is necessary for product purchase, classical conditioning is influential.

Similarly, stimuli may produce certain learned responses, such as excitement, nostalgia, or some other emotion likely to increase the probability of a desired behavior (such as product purchase). Radio and TV ads often use broadcasters whose voices have been associated for years with big-time sports events. Such repeated association of these voices with an advertised product can result in positive feelings of acceptance of the product. Stimuli that are irrelevant to the specific content of an ad or the function of a product can likewise increase attention paid to the ad itself, as when Michael Jordan was featured in a series of commercials for Gatorade.

CONSUMER PERSPECTIVE

11.1

Coca-Cola turns to Pavlov . . .

Do television commercials make people behave like Pavlov's dogs? The Coca-Cola Company says the answer is yes. In the early 80s, the Atlanta soft-drink company refined an ad-testing procedure based on the behavioral principles developed by the Russian physiologist. It found the new testing system worked remarkably well.

In his classic experiment, Ivan Pavlov discovered he could get dogs to salivate at the ring of a bell by gradually substituting the sound for a spray of meat powder. Coca-Cola says that just as Pavlov's dogs began to associate a new meaning with the bell, advertising is supposed to provide some new image or meaning for a product.

Although the specifics of Coke's test were kept secret, the company said it attempted to evaluate how well a commercial conditions a viewer to accept a positive image that can be transferred to the product. From 1981 to 1984, according to Coca-Cola, ads that scored well in its tests almost always resulted in higher sales of a soft drink.

"We nominate Pavlov as the father of modern advertising," said Joel S. Dubow, communications research manager at Coca-Cola. "Pavlov took a neutral object and, by associating it with a meaningful object, made it a symbol of something else; he imbued it with imagery, he gave it added value. That," said Dubow, "is what we try to do in modern advertising."

Source: Reprinted by permission of *The Wall Street Journal*, © 1984 Dow Jones & Company, Inc. All Rights Reserved Worldwide.

Wrangler attempts to classically condition positive emotional responses to their product by pairing their jeans with a cute dog.

Marketers use stimuli at or near the point of purchase to take advantage of their ability to elicit behaviors. Christmas music in a department store is a good example. Although no data are available to support the point, we suspect that carols are useful in eliciting the feeling labeled the "Christmas spirit." Once these feelings have been elicited, we suspect (and retailers seem to share our suspicions) that people are more apt to purchase a gift for a loved one. In other words, Christmas carols are useful in generating emotions that are compatible with purchasing gifts. Exhibit 11.2 highlights some marketing strategies that use the principle of classical conditioning.

Several points should be noted about classical conditioning as a marketing tool. First, classical conditioning assumes that the presentation of stimuli can elicit certain feelings in the consumer. These stimuli are meant to trigger emotions to increase the probability of certain desired behaviors (as with Christmas music). Second, in many cases, marketers can actually condition responses to stimuli. When promoting political candidates, for example, repeatedly pairing the candidate with the American flag may condition the feelings elicited by the flag to the candidate. After a while, the appearance of the candidate alone may stimulate the same feelings in voters as the flag does. Finally, repetition increases the strength of the association between stimuli.

Consumer research on classical conditioning

Several studies in the marketing/consumer behavior literature demonstrate classical conditioning effects. The first demonstration of these effects in a marketing context is in a study by Gorn.[2] This research investigates the effects of the music used in advertising on consumer choices. Consumers identified one musical selection that they liked and one that they disliked. They also identified two colors of pens toward which they had neutral evaluations (light blue and beige). Together there were four combinations: (1) liked music,

Conditioning Responses to New Stimuli		
Unconditioned or Previously Conditioned Stimulus	**Conditioned Stimulus**	**Examples**
Exciting event	A product or theme song	New product advertised during the Super Bowl
Patriotic events or music	A product or person	Patriotic music as background in political commercial
Use of Familiar Stimuli to Elicit Responses		
Conditioned Stimulus	**Conditioned Response(s)**	**Examples**
Popular music	Relaxation, excitement, "goodwill"	Christmas music in retail stores
Familiar voices	Excitement, attention	Famous sportscaster or movie star narrating a commercial
Sexy voices, bodies	Excitement, attention, arousal	Most soft-drink and beer commericials
Familiar cues	Anticipation, attention	Sirens sounding, telephones or doorbells ringing in commercials
Familiar social cues	Feelings of friendship and love	Television ads depicting calls from family or close friend

EXHIBIT 11.2

Some marketing tactics consistent with classical conditioning principles

light blue pen; (2) liked music, beige pen; (3) disliked music, light blue pen; (4) disliked music, beige pen. Subjects looked at an ad for one of the pens while hearing a tape of one of the types of music and then selected one of the pens to keep.

If classical conditioning were taking place, subjects would select the advertised pen when it was paired with the liked music. Similarly, they would select the other pen when the

Patriotic feelings generated by the flag could be conditioned to Bill Clinton.

advertised pen was paired with the music they didn't like. Exhibit 11.3 shows the results of this experiment. Clearly, the vast majority of subjects appear to have been influenced by the pairing of the unconditioned stimulus (liked and disliked music) with the neutral stimulus (light blue and beige pens) resulting in predicted choice behaviors (pen selection).

A second experiment compared the same pen selections after exposure to advertisements that contained either product information or music. Subjects were either in a decision-making or a nondecision-making situation. It was hypothesized that product information would influence pen choice in the decision-making situation, but music would influence pen choice in the nondecision-making situation. Exhibit 11.4 presents the results of this experiment. Clearly, the majority of subjects appear to be classically conditioned in the no decision-making situation but less so in the decision-making situation. These differences might be explained in terms of involvement—the nondecision-making task may be less involving for subjects. In fact, some researchers have suggested classical conditioning may be most useful in low-involvement situations:

> Consumer involvement is low when the products have only minor quality differences from one another . . . .This is especially the case in saturated markets with mature products. It is exactly in these markets that product differentiation by means of emotional conditioning is the preferred strategy of influencing consumers.[3]

Because a variety of circumstances meet these conditions, classical conditioning should be a useful strategy for low-involvement purchases, although they are also useful in high- involvement situations such as the purchase of a car (see Consumer Perspective 11.2, page 248).

Another study of classical conditioning investigates the effects of a credit card on the amount of money consumers reported they are willing to spend on specific items, including dresses, tents, sweaters, lamps, electric typewriters, and chess sets.[4] In a simulated buying task, consumers consistently reported they would spend more in the "credit-card present" condition. This research suggests credit cards and ads for them may become associated with spending, partly through classical conditioning.

In sum, classical conditioning may account for a wide variety of consumer responses. Advertising and in-store promotions commonly take it for granted, although marketing practitioners perhaps use classical conditioning techniques only intuitively. Further research in this area may clarify conditioning effects on information processing, attitude formation and change, and, most importantly, overt consumer behavior.

OPERANT CONDITIONING

Operant conditioning can be defined as the process of altering the probabilities of behaviors by affecting their consequences. Operant conditioning differs from classical conditioning in two ways. First, the behaviors influenced by operant conditioning are assumed to be voluntary behaviors controlled by the skeletal nervous system. Second, the focus of operant conditioning is on understanding how the consequences that occur after a behavior influence the probability of the behavior occurring again. Exhibit 11.5 (see page 248) identifies the major components in the operant view.

Discriminative stimuli

Discriminative stimuli occur before a behavior, and can influence whether the behavior occurs. The mere presence or absence of a discriminative stimulus can affect the chance that a behavior will follow. For example, if Pizza Hut runs an ad with a coupon for a free quart of Pepsi with every large pizza, this offer may increase the probability of consumers purchasing a large pizza. As the offer occurs before the behavior, and influences the probability of purchase, the offer is considered a discriminative stimulus.

Many marketing stimuli are discriminative. Store signs ("50 percent off sale") and store logos (Wal-Mart's sign, Kmart's big red "K") or distinctive brand marks (the Nike swoosh,

EXHIBIT 11.3

Liked versus disliked music and pen choices

Pen Choice		
Advertised Pen	**Nonadvertised Pen**	
79%	21%	Liked Music
30	70	Disliked Music

EXHIBIT 11.4

Information versus music and pen choices

Decision-Making Situation	Nondecision-Making Situation	
71%	29%	With Information
37	63	With Music

Source: Adapted from Gerald J. Gorn, "The Effects of Music in Advertising on Choice Behavior: A Classical Conditioning Approach," *Journal of Marketing*, Winter 1982, pp. 94–101. Published by the American Marketing Association.

the Levi's red pocket tag, the Polo insignia) are examples of discriminative stimuli. Previous experience may have taught consumers that purchase behavior will be rewarded when the distinctive symbol is present and will not be rewarded when the symbol is absent. For example, many consumers purchase Ralph Lauren shirts, jackets, and shorts with the stitched polo player symbol and avoid other Ralph Lauren apparel without the symbol. A number of competitors have tried to copy the polo player symbol because of its power as a discriminative stimulus. Clearly, much of marketing involves developing effective discriminative stimuli that promote certain behaviors.

Behaviors

Marketers try to influence many types of consumer behavior. They want consumers to read advertisements, watch TV commercials, obtain money to buy products, go to particular malls and stores, purchase products, and tell other consumers good things about the product. These behaviors are discussed in detail in Chapter 13, but at this point it is enough to say that marketers must influence overt consumer behavior to sell products.

Consequences

Marketers can use four basic types of consequences to influence consumer behavior: positive reinforcement, negative reinforcement, extinction, and punishment.

Some events or consequences increase the frequency with which a given behavior is likely to be repeated. For example, if a reward, such as a cash rebate, is given at the time of purchase, it may increase the probability that a shopper will buy something in the same store in the future. In this case, because the reward increases the probability of the

Credit card stimuli can influence consumer behavior.

<table>
<tr><td>

CONSUMER PERSPECTIVE

> 11.2

Can automobile purchases be classically conditioned?

</td><td>

In the early 80s, research by the Young & Rubicam advertising agency revealed awareness of Mercury automobiles to be low among the target audience of people aged 24 to 44. The research also found considerable loyalty of this audience to music from the 1960s.

A series of ads known as the "Big Chill" campaign was developed. The first TV spot from this campaign, called "Reunion," was aired in 1984. The story line of this commercial was a college reunion set to the song "Ain't No Mountain High Enough."

Research conducted after the ad was aired showed the target audience was reading a variety of positive things into the commercial. The audience recalled all kinds of wonderful moments from their college days and attributed those moments to Mercury. Mercury's market share climbed from 4.3 percent in 1983 to 5.1 percent in 1985.

Apparently, featuring Mercury with well-liked music and scenes from a college reunion increased awareness of Mercury and induced feelings of nostalgia. More important, purchase behavior was changed. This example looks like a successful application of classical conditioning.

Chevrolet's "Heartbeat of America" campaign is another example.

Source: Based on "Emotion Sells More than Perfume: It Sells Cars, Too," *Marketing News* 19, no. 24, November 22, 1985, p. 4. Published by the American Marketing Association.

</td></tr>
</table>

behavior being repeated, it is called **positive reinforcement.** Positive reinforcement is the most common type of consequence used by marketers to influence consumer behavior. In general, the greater the amount of the reward and the sooner it is received after the behavior, the more likely it is that the behavior will be reinforced and that similar behavior will occur in the future. For example, a $1 coupon for Tropicana orange juice would likely increase the probability of purchase more than a 50-cent coupon would, and lead to future purchases of this product. Similarly, a coupon redeemable at the time of purchase is likely to be more effective than a mail-in coupon, when the consumer has to wait for the reward.

The frequency of consumer behavior can also be increased by removing aversive stimuli that operate to deter a consumer's purchase. This is called **negative reinforcement.** For example, if purchase of a product gets a salesperson to relax high-pressure techniques, the consumer may be negatively reinforced. That is, performing the behavior of purchasing removes the aversive stimuli (the actions of the pushy salesperson). In the future, operant conditioning predicts that a consumer faced with pushy salespeople will be more likely to purchase again.

Sometimes operant techniques are used to decrease the probability of a response. If the environment is arranged so that a particular response results in neutral consequences, over a period of time that response will diminish in frequency. This process is referred to as **extinction.** The A&P grocery chain, at one time the largest retailer in the world, provides an unwitting example. One mistake it made was to overstock its own brands (which had higher profit margins) and understock nationally branded merchandise. Consumers who were loyal to a number of nationally branded products often could not find them at an A&P store.

EXHIBIT 11.5

Operant conditioning

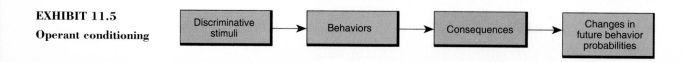

Discriminative stimuli → Behaviors → Consequences → Changes in future behavior probabilities

Eventually, many consumers quit shopping at A&P, partly because they could not obtain their favorite brands. Thus, A&P inadvertently used extinction on its own customers.

If a response is followed by a noxious or unpleasant result, the frequency of that response is also likely to decrease. The term **punishment** is usually used to describe this process. For example, automobile insurance rates may increase if a consumer causes an accident. Punishment is often confused with negative reinforcement, although they are distinctly different concepts. Exhibit 11.6 summarizes these four methods of operant conditioning.

Two other important characteristics of operant conditioning have major implications for designing marketing strategies to influence consumers' behavior: reinforcement schedules and shaping.

Reinforcement schedules refer to how consistently a reward occurs after desired behaviors occur. Three reinforcement schedules used in marketing include continuous, fixed ratio, and variable ratio schedules.

The offer of a reward after every desired behavior is called a **continuous schedule.** Marketers aim to keep the quality of their products constant so that a purchase is continuously reinforced every time it occurs, but this doesn't always happen. Frequent product recalls for automobiles, for example, indicate a failure to maintain product quality. Services such as airlines may not be able to control contingencies such as bad weather, overbooked, canceled, and late flights, and unfriendly employees, which can make flights not reinforcing at all. Sporting events, because they may turn out to be boring or the home team takes a beating, may not be continuously reinforcing for some consumers.

For other products or services, every second, third, or tenth, or so, time a behavior is performed, a reward is given. This is called a **fixed ratio schedule.** Consumer Perspective 11.3 (see page 250) illustrates the way a yogurt chain uses this schedule to increase purchases.

Similarly, it is possible to have a reinforcer follow a desired behavior *on an average* of one half, one third, one tenth, or so, of the time the behavior occurs, but not necessarily every second time or third time. This is a **variable ratio schedule.** A state lottery is an example of rewards occurring on variable ratio schedules.

Variable ratio schedules are of particular interest because they produce high rates of behavior that are reasonably resistant to extinction. Gambling devices are good

Reinforcement schedules

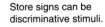

Store signs can be discriminative stimuli.

EXHIBIT 11.6

Operant conditioning methods

Operation Performed after Behavior	Name	Effect
Present positive consequences	Positive reinforcement	Increases the probability of behavior
Remove aversive consequences	Negative reinforcement	Increases the probability of behavior
Neutral consequences occur	Extinction	Decreases the probability of behavior
Present aversive consequences	Punishment	Decreases the probability of behavior

examples. Slot machines are very effective in producing high rates of response, even under conditions that often result in substantial financial losses. This property of the ratio schedule is particularly important for marketers, because it suggests a great deal of desired behavior can be developed and maintained with relatively small, infrequent rewards. One study found that giving a free token for riding a bus on a variable ratio schedule resulted in the same amount of bus riding as when rewards were given on a continuous schedule.[5] Thus, for approximately one third the cost of the continuous schedule, the same amount of behavior could be sustained.

Other examples of variable ratio schedules include sweepstakes, contests, and door prizes, where individuals must behave in a certain way to be eligible for a prize. Consumer Perspective 11.4 (see page 252), discusses the use of variable ratio schedules for selling Pepsi and Mountain Dew products.

Shaping

Another operant conditioning concept with important implications for marketing and consumer behavior is shaping. **Shaping** involves arranging conditions that change the probabilities of certain behaviors *not as ends in themselves, but to increase the probabilities of other behaviors occurring.* Usually, shaping involves the positive reinforcement of successive approximations of a desired behavior or of behaviors that must be performed before the desired response occurs.

Marketing activities that can be described as shaping include loss leaders and other special deals used to reward individuals for coming to a store. Once customers are in the store, the probability that they will make other desired responses (such as purchasing full-priced items) is much greater than when they are not in the store. Shopping centers or auto dealers that hold carnivals in the parking lot are attempting to shape behavior, because consumers are more likely to come in and purchase when they are already in the parking lot drinking the free coffee than when they are at home. Similarly, free trial periods make it more likely for a consumer to have contact with the product and then experience the product's reinforcing properties. Real estate developers that offer free trips to look over resort property are employing a shaping tactic, as are casinos offering free trips to gamblers. In both cases, moving people to the place of purchase or place of gambling increases the probability of these behaviors being performed.

Shaping is not necessarily a one-step process but may affect several stages in a purchase sequence. Suppose a car dealer wants to shape an automobile purchase. Free coffee and doughnuts are offered to anyone who comes to the dealership. Five dollars cash is offered to any licensed driver who will test-drive a car. A $500 rebate is offered to anyone who purchases a car. In this case, operant principles are used in a multistep process to encourage high involvement. Exhibit 11.7 describes a number of marketing tactics applying operant conditioning principles.

Yogurt Express uses a fixed ratio schedule to try to create loyalty to its stores and yogurt products in Madison, Wisconsin. It offers a free 13-ounce yogurt cup after 12 visits and purchases. On each visit the individual or family may make multiple purchases, so the free cup is a relatively small reinforcer. Of course the cost of a free cup to Yogurt Express is much less than the price it charges consumers, so Yogurt Express can influence considerable consumer behavior using a low-cost, infrequent reward.

Because the card has to be punched at the store, consumers need to carry the card with them. Perhaps seeing the card in their wallet or wherever reminds consumers to drop in at Yogurt Express.

CONSUMER PERSPECTIVE

11.3

Developing loyalty to Yogurt Express

Consumer research on operant conditioning

Most of the research on operant conditioning procedures in consumer-related contexts is not reported in the traditional marketing literature. An exception investigates the effects of positive reinforcement on jewelry store customers.[6] The study divides jewelry store charge-account customers into three groups. One group received a telephone call thanking them for their patronage; a second group received a telephone call thanking them and informing them of a special sale; the third group was a control group and received no telephone calls. The study reported a 27 percent increase in sales during the test month over the same month of the previous year, an impressive result because year-to-date sales were down 25 percent. Seventy percent of the increase came from the "thank-you only" group; the remaining 30 percent of the increase came from the "thank-you and sale-notification" group. Purchases made by customers in the control group were unchanged. Positive reinforcement was seen to result in sustained increases in purchases for every month but one in the remainder of the year.

Some operant conditioning research deals with behaviors such as encouraging energy conservation or charitable contributions, or discouraging smoking or littering. One application of operant conditioning concerns punishment in the form of charging telephone customers for local directory assistance, an expensive, labor-intensive service.[7] A study reports the effect of charging 20 cents per local directory-assistance call for more than three calls in a given period. Long-distance directory-assistance calls were not charged. Results show that local directory-assistance calls dropped dramatically. The fact that long-distance directory assistance did not change supports the conclusion that the charge and not some other factor led to the change in consumer behavior.

MARKETING IMPLICATIONS

Classical conditioning is particularly relevant to marketers selecting stimuli for advertisements. Choice of the appropriate stimuli in ads can influence purchase behavior. Classical conditioning is also useful in designing malls and retail stores. Operant conditioning is particularly useful to marketers deciding what types of products, packaging, and sales promotions would be most successful in the marketplace.

Of course, marketers are concerned not merely with influencing consumers to buy a brand one time only or shop at a store one time only. Rather, they want consumers to buy a brand repeatedly or shop at a retail store faithfully. These behaviors are called brand loyalty and store loyalty. Both classical and operant conditioning can be useful for developing such loyalties. If through classical conditioning consumers develop strong affect for a particular product or store, they may continue to buy the brand or shop at the store. If through operant conditioning consumer behavior in buying a particular brand or visiting a particular store is reinforced, the probability that this behavior will continue is increased.

PepsiCo ran its "Unlock the Great Taste and Win" sweepstakes in 1991. The grand prizes in the contest were two Lamborghini sports cars with an estimated retail value of $215,000 each. Other prizes included Kawasaki jet skis, vacations, and sterling silver key chains.

Although consumers could receive two game chances without purchase by writing the company, most game chances were distributed through purchase of Pepsi and Mountain Dew products. Here's how it worked. With purchase of multipacks, that is, 12-, 20-, or 24-can packages, consumers had a chance of receiving a free, inexpensive key chain. Behind the key chain package was notification of any major prize won, although only one out of two multipacks contained the key chain and gave any chance of winning. Thus, *on average*, consumers would have to purchase two multipacks for a chance at the major prizes. PepsiCo thus used a variable ratio schedule to allocate prize chances in order to increase the probability that consumers would purchase several multipacks.

Some bottle caps on 2-liter, 3-liter, and 16-ounce nonreturnable bottles also provided chances to win, but no key chain, and the odds of winning remained better when consumers bought the more expensive multipacks. For example, the odds of winning the grand prizes from a multipack purchase were 1 in 18,444,000 while the odds of winning the grand prizes from a bottle purchase were 1 in 113,118,597. Moreover, only by purchasing multipacks could consumers win the sterling silver key chains valued at $50; the bottle purchases allowed winning only a brass key chain valued at $10. Of course, all prizes were awarded on a variable ratio schedule.

Overall, then, variable ratio schedules were used to allocate the chances to win prizes as well as the prizes themselves. By offering the chances to win and the inexpensive key chain on a variable ratio schedule, PepsiCo increased the probability of consumers making more than one purchase. Costs to the company are another consideration. The cost of the key chain was only half what it would be if every multipack were to contain one. Offering major prizes on a variable ratio schedule is probably the only way expensive products can be used as reinforcers for purchase of inexpensive products and still be profitable.

Brand loyalty

Brand loyalty is defined as repeat purchase intentions and behavior. While we focus mainly on brand loyalty as a behavior, cognitive processes strongly influence the development and maintenance of this behavior. Retaining brand-loyal customers is critical for survival, particularly in today's low-growth and highly competitive marketplace. Retaining customers is often a more efficient strategy than attracting new customers. Indeed, it is estimated the average company spends six times more to attract a new customer than to hold a current one.

Brand loyalty can be viewed on a continuum from undivided brand loyalty to brand indifference. We show this schematically in Exhibit 11.8. Marketers can analyze the market for a particular brand in terms of the number of consumers in each category, as a first step in developing strategies to enhance the brand loyalty of particular groups. In many ways, loyalty categories are somewhat arbitrary, although there are clear degrees of brand loyalty.

Undivided brand loyalty is, of course, an ideal. In some cases, consumers will purchase only a single brand and forgo purchase if that brand is not available. *Brand loyalty with an occasional switch* is likely to be more common, though. Consumers may switch occasionally for a variety of reasons: their usual brand may be out of stock, a new brand may come on the market and is tried once, a competitive brand is offered at a special low price, or a different brand is purchased for a special occasion.

A.   Descriminative Stimuli

Desired Behavior	Reward Signal	Examples
Entry into store	Store signs	50 percent off sale
	Store logos	Kmart's big red "K," McDonald's golden arches
Brand purchase	Distinctive brandmarks	Levi's tag, Ralph Lauren polo player

B.   Continuous Reinforcement Schedules

Desired Behavior	Reward Given following Behavior
Product purchase	Trading stamps, cash bonus or rebate, prizes, coupons

C.   Fixed and Variable Ratio Reinforcement Schedules

Desired Behavior	Reward Given following Behavior
Product purchase	Prize for every second, third, etc., purchase
	Prize to some fraction of people who purchase

D.   Shaping

Approximation of Response	Consequence following Approximation	Final Response Desired
Opening a charge account	Prizes, etc., for opening account	Expenditure of funds
Trip to point of purchase	Loss leaders, entertainment, or event at the shopping center	Purchase of products
Entry into store	Door prize	Purchase of products
Product trial	Free product and/or some bonus for using	Purchase of products

Brand-loyalty switches are a marketing goal in low-growth or declining markets. Competitors in the blue-jean market or the distilled-spirits industry, for example, must encourage brand switches for long-run growth. Switching brand loyalty even within the same firm can be advantageous for the company. Procter & Gamble, for example, sells both Pampers and Luvs disposable diapers. A switch from Pampers to Luvs might be advantageous to P&G in that Luvs are more expensive and may have a higher profit margin.

Divided brand loyalty describes consistent purchase of two or more brands, as might happen in the shampoo market, which has a low level of brand loyalty. One reason is that households may purchase different shampoos for different family members or for different purposes. Johnson's Baby Shampoo may be the choice for youngsters and frequent shampoo users. Other household members may use Head and Shoulders. This household would have loyalty divided between two brands.

Brand indifference refers to purchases showing no apparent repurchase pattern. It is the opposite extreme from undivided brand loyalty. While total brand indifference across the board probably is not common, some consumers of some products may exhibit this pattern. For example, a consumer may make weekly purchases of whatever bread is on sale, regardless of the brand.

Marketers of a particular brand would prefer that consumers have undivided brand loyalty for it. If appropriate reinforcers are used on appropriate schedules, this is a goal that is

EXHIBIT 11.8

Examples of purchase pattern categories and brand purchase sequences

Purchase Pattern Category	Brand Purchase Sequence									
Undivided brand loyalty	A	A	A	A	A	A	A	A	A	A
Brand loyalty/occasional switch	A	A	A	B	A	A	C	A	A	D
Brand loyalty/switch	A	A	A	A	A	B	B	B	B	B
Divided brand loyalty	A	A	B	A	B	B	A	A	B	B
Brand indifference	A	B	C	D	E	F	G	H	I	J

achievable. More consumers in a target market, however, inevitably enjoy something less than undivided brand loyalty, because competitive brands may have marketing strategies that better reinforce consumer behavior. Consider that a $1,000 rebate for a Ford Explorer may influence a consumer who has always bought Chevy trucks to switch brands, at least one time, for one purchase. A major challenge for marketers is to come up with better reinforcers than the competition.

Store loyalty

Most retailers do not look for consumers to come to their stores once and never return: rather, they want repeat patronage. Marketers can influence **store loyalty** (repeat patronage intentions and behavior) by the arrangement of the environment, particularly the reinforcing properties of the retail store. These include such things as friendly salesclerks, good prices, quality merchandise, attractive decor, convenient location, and expeditious service.

Consider one tactic that may be used to develop store loyalty—in-store unadvertised specials. These specials are often marked with an attention-getting sign. Typically, consumers go to a store shopping for a particular product or just to "go shopping." While on their route, they find a favorite brand or a long-sought-after product as an unadvertised special. Such an experience could be quite reinforcing and strongly influence the probability of the consumer returning to the same store, perhaps seeking similar unadvertised specials. Quite likely the consumer would not have to find a suitable unadvertised special on every trip to the store; a variable ratio schedule might be powerful enough to generate a considerable degree of store loyalty. These additional trips to the store allow the consumer to experience other reinforcing properties, such as fast checkout, a pleasant store

Purchase of generics indicates brand indifference.

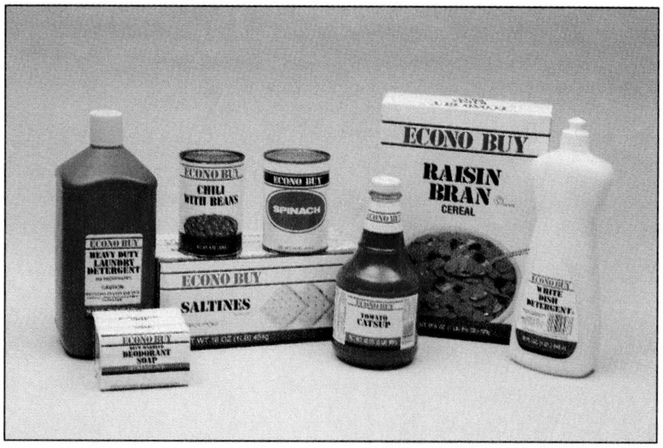

atmosphere, or good-quality merchandise at competitive prices. In sum, reinforcing tactics and positive attributes of the store are used to develop store loyalty.

Store loyalty is a major objective of retail strategy that has an important financial impact. It has been estimated that the loss of a single customer to a supermarket can cost the store about $3,100 per year in sales. Thus, analysis of the store environment and its impact on store loyalty is critical for successful marketing.

Learning objective 1: *Define classical conditioning.*
Classical conditioning is a process by which a previously neutral stimulus (such as a new product) by being paired with an unconditioned stimulus (such as a sexy male or female model) comes to elicit a response (excitement) similar to the response (excitement) originally elicited by the unconditioned stimulus. In other words, when they are repeatedly paired together, a new stimulus begins to elicit the same behaviors as a familiar stimulus.

Learning objective 2: *Offer examples of how classical conditioning is used to influence consumer behavior.*
Advertisements and commercials for products often feature stimuli such as famous people and emotion-generating scenes. Repeated pairing of these stimuli with products could condition affect for the advertised products to be similar to that generated for the conditioned stimuli. Music that generates emotions is also used in ads and in stores. These too could classically condition consumers.

Learning objective 3: *Define operant conditioning.*
Operant conditioning is the process of altering the probabilities of behaviors by affecting their consequences.

Learning objective 4: *Offer examples of discriminative stimuli used to influence consumer behavior.*
Discriminative stimuli are those that occur before a behavior and that can influence whether the behavior occurs. Common examples of discriminative stimuli used to influence consumer behavior include store signs, store logos, and distinctive brand marks.

Learning objective 5: *Explain four types of consequences that can occur after a consumer behavior.*
Four types of consequences include: (1) positive reinforcement, where a reward follows a behavior, to increase the probability of the behavior being repeated; (2) negative reinforcement, where an aversive stimulus is stopped upon engaging in a behavior, also to increase the probability of the behavior being repeated; (3) extinction, where neutral consequences occur after a behavior, again to decrease the probability of the behavior being repeated; and (4) punishment, where aversive consequences occur after a behavior, to decrease the probability of the behavior being repeated.

Learning objective 6: *Describe three types of reinforcement schedules that can be used to influence consumer behavior.*
The first type of reinforcement schedule is a continuous schedule, where a reward is offered every time a desired behavior occurs. The second type is a fixed ratio schedule, where every second, third, or tenth (for example) time the behavior is performed, a reward is given. The third type is a variable ratio schedule, where a reward is offered on an average of one half, one third, one fourth (and so on) of the time the behavior occurs, but not necessarily every second or third or fourth time.

Learning objective 7: *Explain shaping, and offer a marketing example of it.*
Shaping involves arranging conditions that change the probabilities of certain behaviors not as ends in themselves, but to increase the probabilities of other behaviors occurring

A grocery store might offer one product below cost, not just to get consumers to buy it, but to increase the chances of consumers coming to the store and purchasing other full-priced items.

Learning objective 8: *Offer examples of ways operant conditioning is used to influence consumer behavior.*

Marketers use many types of discriminative stimuli, such as store signs, store logos, and brand marks, to influence consumers. Various types of reinforcement schedules, including continuous, fixed ratio, and variable ratio, can be established to try to develop brand and store loyalty. Marketers also use various types of rewards such as trading stamps, bonuses, and premiums to reinforce purchase behavior.

Learning objective 9: *Explain brand loyalty and store loyalty.*

Brand loyalty is defined as repeat purchase intentions and behavior. The degree of brand loyalty varies among consumers from undivided brand loyalty, where consumers always purchase the same brand, to brand indifference, where consumers always purchase different brands. The challenge for marketers is to increase the degree of brand loyalty by offering appropriate reinforcers. Store loyalty is defined as repeat patronage intentions and behavior. Reinforcing properties of a store itself, including store location and in-store stimuli such as fast service and unadvertised specials, can help develop store loyalty.

▶ **KEY TERMS AND CONCEPTS**

classical conditioning	extinction	variable ratio schedule
operant conditioning	punishment	shaping
discriminative stimuli	reinforcement schedules	brand loyalty
positive reinforcement	continuous schedule	store loyalty
negative reinforcement	fixed ratio schedule	

▶ **REVIEW AND DISCUSSION QUESTIONS**

1. Describe classical conditioning, and identify three responses in your own behavior that are the result of classical conditioning.

2. Under what conditions would the use of classical conditioning be likely to produce positive results as part of a marketing strategy?

3. What are two differences between classical and operant conditioning?

4. Describe operant conditioning, and identify three responses in your own behavior that are the result of operant conditioning.

5. Give two marketing examples of positive reinforcement, negative reinforcement, extinction, and punishment.

6. Why are variable ratio reinforcement schedules of greater interest to marketing managers than other types of reinforcement schedules?

7. Define shaping, and explain why it is an essential part of many marketing conditioning strategies.

8. Examine the marketing strategies used in selling fast-food hamburgers and automobiles. Identify specific examples of classical conditioning, operant conditioning, shaping, and discriminative stimuli for each product type.

12

Vicarious Learning and the Diffusion of Innovation

LEARNING OBJECTIVES

After completing this chapter, you should be able to:

► 1. Explain three uses of vicarious learning (modeling).

► 2. Describe three types of modeling.

► 3. Explain three factors that influence the effectiveness of modeling.

► 4. Describe five adopter categories.

► 5. Identify the characteristics that influence the success of new products.

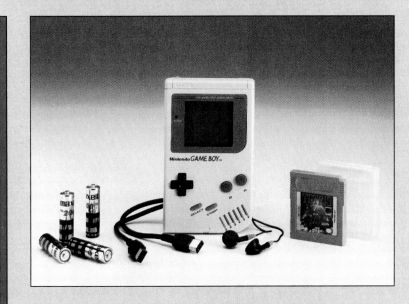

AMERICANS TAKE THE NINTENDO CHALLENGE

In the early 80s, Atari Inc. sold videogames like Pong, a video Ping-Pong game, and rapidly ballooned to $2 billion a year in sales. As children became bored with the games, Atari declined just as fast as it had grown. Nobody thought there was much future for videogames; nobody, that is, except Kyoto, the Japanese company that markets Nintendo games.

Nintendo's first major success was Super Mario Brothers, a full-color videogame in which players manipulate Italian plumbers through a variety of fantasy worlds. Nintendo now has over 200 games, which include challenges from baseball to medieval warfare and sell for about $50. In a departure from the practices in the early 80s, the company produces quality products, repairs damaged games, and provides a hot line for customer problems. One in every four U.S. families owns the Nintendo Entertainment System, a telephone-book-size plastic console that retails for $99 and connects to the back of a TV. Consumers learn to play games like Nintendo by watching how other people behave, which is the subject of this chapter.

Vicarious learning is a deceptively simple idea. Basically, it refers to people changing their behavior because they observe the behavior of others and its consequences. In general, people tend to imitate the behavior of others when they see it leads to positive consequences and avoid performing the behavior of others when they see it leads to negative consequences.

Vicarious learning surprisingly has been almost ignored in published consumer and marketing research, although it has a variety of applications in marketing. In fact, vicarious learning offers a useful approach to developing marketing strategy and consumer education programs. We use the terms *vicarious learning, modeling, observational learning,* and *imitative learning* interchangeably in this chapter, although other writers sometimes draw distinctions among these terms.

We focus first on the most common form of vicarious learning, called "overt modeling," where people actually watch a model perform some activity. Covert modeling involves no demonstration of activity, but rather asks the consumer to imagine one, while verbal modeling merely informs consumers of what other people have done. This chapter discusses how and why these various techniques work in marketing strategies.

USES OF OVERT MODELING

Overt modeling requires that consumers actually observe the model in person, whether a salesperson demonstrating a product (*live modeling*) or TV commercials or in-store videotapes (*symbolic modeling*). Exhibit 12.1 depicts the modeling process. A common example is commercials for cosmetics and grooming aids, which show the model using the product and then becoming sought after by a member of the opposite sex. Clairol commercials frequently show a woman with dull, drab hair (and an equivalent social life) going out with a handsome, well-dressed man after she uses the Clairol product. The modeled behavior (use of the product) is shown to have reinforcing consequences (attention from men).

There are three major uses of overt modeling in marketing. First, modeling can be used to help observers *develop new response patterns* that they did not previously have. Second, modeling can be used *to inhibit undesired responses.* Third, modeling can *facilitate desired responses* whereby observing the behavior of others facilitates the occurrence of previously learned responses.

Developing new responses

Modeling can be used to develop new behavioral responses that were not previously in the consumer's repertoire. It is a common technique used by those selling technically complex organizational and consumer products. Consider, for example, the videocassettes that a variety of stores provide to demonstrate use of a product. Sears has long used

EXHIBIT 12.1

The modeling process

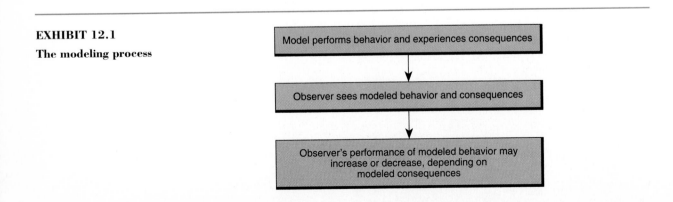

this method to demonstrate the safe use of its chain saws. The appropriate use of Berkeley fishing equipment and of Olt duck calls is also demonstrated in this way. New behaviors also are frequently modeled in TV commercials. Sears used a modeling strategy aimed at this behavior when it began in-store sales of Allstate insurance, a departure from the traditional office or home sales method. A TV commercial shows a family coming to the Sears store and dropping off its old insurance policy for comparisons with Allstate rates. After their shopping trip, the family returns and learns Allstate can give them a better deal, thus modeling the positive consequences of the new behavior. Similarly, Arm & Hammer baking soda ads showed new uses of the product as a carpet and refrigerator freshener and portrayed models being complimented on the freshness of their homes. WD-40 lubricant ads also model new uses of the product.

From these examples we can draw several generalizations about the use of modeling to develop new consumer behaviors. First, overt modeling can be used to develop behaviors that enable potential consumers to use products appropriately. Demonstrating ways to use a product may make purchase more probable, particularly if the models appear to experience positive consequences from using the product. Moreover, repurchase, or influencing one's friends, may become more probable if the consumer has learned to use the product appropriately by watching someone else. Modeling can also be beneficial for consumers because it can help them to develop effective behaviors in the marketplace and to avoid costly errors resulting from poor product purchases or inappropriate uses of a product.

Second, models may be very helpful in developing particular desired purchasing behaviors. Suppose, for example, a firm has a product that is technically superior to those of its competitors. It may be important to teach potential consumers to ask questions about such technical advantages at the point of purchase. Advertisements could show individuals doing this or behaving in other ways that appear to give the product a differential advantage.

Third, it is often necessary (particularly at early stages in the purchase process) to find ways to increase the degree to which potential customers attend to information in ads and

Overt modeling—demonstrating new behaviors.

other messages about a product. Marketers need to pay attention themselves to overt modeling factors such as incentive conditions, the characteristics of the observers, the characteristics of the model, and the characteristics of the modeling cues themselves. In fact, advertising practitioners seem to be sensitive to these issues. Many ads reflect their creators' accurate awareness of salient characteristics of the target audience, of the models in the ad, and of the behaviors exhibited by the model.

Inhibiting undesired responses

Modeling can also be used to decrease the probability of undesired behaviors. Because of the ethical (not to mention practical) problems involved in using punishment to affect consumer behavior, there are not many direct ways of reducing the frequency of undesired responses. Overt modeling, however, lets bad things happen to models rather than to actual consumers.

Modeling research indicates that, under appropriate conditions, observers who see a model experience unpleasant results following a particular action will reduce their tendency to exhibit that behavior. Thus, vicarious learning may be one of the few approaches that can be used to reduce the frequency of unwanted elements in a potential or present consumer's behavior.

Hefty bags, for example, are frequently advertised on TV using a modeling approach. Various family members are shown taking out the trash in "bargain bags." Of course, the bargain bag breaks, and garbage is strewn all over, a visibly annoying experience! The frustrated family member is then told about Hefty bags, uses them successfully, and is socially reinforced for doing so. Head and Shoulders shampoo commercials show people initially found attractive by members of the opposite sex but then rejected when the models scratch their heads, indicating they may have dandruff. Following the use of the advertised product, the model is once again warmly greeted by an attractive member of the opposite sex.

A common use of this type of modeling is in public service advertising. Many behaviors considered socially undesirable can be modeled and shown to have unpleasant consequences. These behaviors include littering, smoking, driving drunk, using drugs, overeating, wasting energy, and polluting. One commercial, for example, showed a drunken driver being caught, taken to court, and given a considerable fine and jail sentence for his behavior.

Facilitating desired responses

Besides use in developing new behaviors and inhibiting undesired ones, modeling can facilitate the occurrence of desired behaviors that the consumer already knows how to do. That is, the modeling not only illustrates uses of a product but also shows what types of people use it and in what settings. Because many of these uses involve behaviors already familiar to the observer, the model's function is merely to *facilitate these responses* by depicting positive consequences for using the product appropriately. For example, Nyquil ads show adult cold sufferers using the product before going to bed and then sleeping comfortably. This is a common technique in advertising for high-status products, where ads do not demonstrate any new behaviors, but show the positive consequences of using the product. A series of ads showing people serving Loëwenbrau beer for very special occasions is a good example.

To the degree that marketers want to encourage positive emotions toward a product, vicarious emotional conditioning may also be useful for the design of effective advertisements. Many emotional behaviors can be acquired through observation of others, as well as through direct respondent conditioning.

Vicarious emotional conditioning results from observing others experience positive or negative emotional effects in conjunction with particular stimulus events. Both direct and vicarious conditioning processes are governed by the same basic principles of associative learning, but they differ in the force of the emotional arousal. In the direct prototype, the learner himself is the

Modeling Employed	Desired Response
Instructor, expert, salesperson using product (in ads or at point of purchase)	Use product in correct, technically competent way
Models in ads asking questions at point of purchase	Ask questions at point of purchase that highlight product advantages
Models in ads receiving positive reinforcement for product purchase or use	Try product; increase product purchase and use
Models in ads receiving no reinforcement or receiving punishment for performing undesired behaviors	Discourage undesired behaviors
Individual or group (similar to target) using product in novel, enjoyable way	Use product in new ways

EXHIBIT 12.2

Some applications of overt modeling principles in marketing

Source: Reprinted from Walter R. Nord and J. Paul Peter, "A Behavior Modification Perspective on Marketing," *Journal of Marketing* 44 (Spring 1980), p. 43. Published by the American Marketing Association.

recipient of pain- or pleasure-producing stimulation, whereas in vicarious forms somebody else experiences the reinforcing stimulation and his affective expressions, in turn, serve as the arousal stimuli for the observer.[1]

Exhibit 12.2 offers a summary of some applications of overt modeling principles in marketing.

COVERT AND VERBAL MODELING

Two other forms of vicarious learning have marketing applications: covert modeling and verbal modeling.

Covert modeling techniques do not show any actual behaviors or consequences. Rather, people are asked to imagine someone behaving in a situation and subject to particular consequences.[2] A radio commercial might conjure up Lance, a construction worker who has just finished work. It's July, it's hot and humid, and Lance has worked for 12 hours pouring concrete. He's driving home; he's tired and thirsty. His mouth is parched and his throat is dry. Imagine how good that first, cold, frosty mug of Oscar's root beer is going to taste!

Covert modeling has received less research attention than overt modeling, but a review of the literature suggests that:

1. Covert modeling can be as effective as overt modeling in modifying behavior.
2. The factors that affect overt modeling should have similar effects on covert modeling.
3. Covert modeling can be tested and shown to be effective.
4. Covert modeling can be more effective if alternative consequences of the model's behavior are described.[3]

While there appears to be no consumer or marketing research on covert modeling, we believe it could be a useful marketing tool.

The **verbal modeling** technique neither demonstrates behaviors nor asks people to imagine a model performing a behavior. Instead, people are *told* how others similar to themselves behaved in a particular situation. Verbal modeling therefore suggests a social norm that may influence behavior. One study, for example, investigated the effects of verbal modeling on contributions to charity.[4] In door-to-door solicitation for donations to the United Way, the solicitor manipulated the percentage of households that had already contributed to the drive: "More than (three fourths/one fourth) of the households that I've contacted in this area have contributed so far." People who were told three fourths of their neighbors had

EXHIBIT 12.3

A comparison of three types of modeling

Type	Description	Example	Useful Media
Overt modeling (live and symbolic)	Consumer observes modeled behavior and consequences	Allstate Insurance commercials demonstrating new method of purchasing insurance	Television, personal selling, in-store video machines
Covert modeling	Consumer is asked to imagine a model (or self) performing behavior and consequences	Airline or travel agency commercial during winter inviting consumers to "imagine you're on the warm sunny beaches of Florida"	Radio, personal selling, possibly print advertising
Verbal modeling	Consumer is given a description of how similar people behave in purchase/use situation	United Way solicitor reporting on gift-giving behavior of neighbors	Personal selling, radio, direct mail, possibly other print advertising

contributed usually donated more. Verbal modeling also outperformed several other strategies, such as social responsibility arguments, arguments for helping less fortunate people, and the amount (not percentage of contributions) people were told others had given. The study concludes that verbal modeling is an effective means of eliciting desired behavior.

Verbal modeling is a natural technique in personal-selling situations. For example, salespeople sometimes tell potential buyers that people like them have purchased a particular product, brand, or model. This may be an effective tactic, but it is not necessarily true or ethical. As in the case of covert modeling, little is known about verbal modeling in consumer behavior contexts.

Exhibit 12.3 compares overt, covert, and verbal modeling and suggests appropriate media for each. Investigations of the effectiveness of these procedures using different media and approaches could provide considerable insight into effective modeling processes and development of marketing strategies.

FACTORS INFLUENCING MODELING EFFECTIVENESS

Watching a model perform a behavior often increases the likelihood that the observer will perform the behavior. It is a well established psychological principle that modeling is effective in changing behavior as Consumer Perspective 12.1 illustrates. Certain factors increase the likelihood that vicarious learning will occur: (1) characteristics of the model and modeled behavior, (2) characteristics of observers, and (3) characteristics of modeled consequences.

Characteristics of the model and the modeled behavior

Several characteristics of the models observed influence the probability that an observer will imitate the modeled behavior.[5] Models found to be attractive may be paid attention to, while less attractive models may be ignored. Models perceived to be credible and successful exert greater influence than those who are not. High-status and competent models are also more influential in determining model success.

The manner in which the modeled behavior is performed is another influence. If the sequence of the modeled behavior is detailed very carefully and vividly, modeling effects tend to increase. Interestingly, models who display a bit of apprehension and difficulty and yet complete the task are more effective than models displaying no struggle or difficulty. A reason for this has been suggested by Manz and Sims:

One mistake zoos used to make was to remove newborn primates from their mothers and family groups. When these primates grew up, they turned out to be poor parents, sometimes beating their own babies and inflicting fatal injuries. Researchers determined that the early social isolation was the leading cause of the abuse and they had to alter the primate's environment if the animals were to thrive. They made sure biological mothers reared infants in spacious group settings, exposed them to play with infants and peers, and introduced older mothers to help with the new mothers' caretaking. They found that inexperienced and even abusive mothers, once given examples of good mothering (modeling) and a chance to play with infants, became competent parents. Today, as few as 2 percent of primate mothers abuse or neglect their babies, compared to about 75 percent in the 1970s.

University researchers tested a similar program for human mothers, where nurses developed relationships with new mothers by regularly visiting them at home. The nurses showed the new mothers how to play with and talk to an infant, much as the older primates had modeled mothering skills. Attempts were made to get new mothers jobs and to obtain benefits to reduce tension at home. In the end, 4 percent of the low-income teen mothers who received the nurse visits neglected or abused their children, compared with 19 percent for those mothers who did not receive the visits. The nurses also succeeded in teaching parents who had been abused as children how to trust in their abilities as nurturing parents.

One important difference was found between the effects of modeling on humans and animals: the animals apparently learned much more quickly. Just two days of contact with newborn infants made primate females more likely to hug and feed their own infants, while the only programs effective for humans required intensive, long-lasting intervention. In this case, humans could have become more human by modeling the behavior of primates.

Source: Based on Art Levine, "The Biological Roots of Good Mothering," *U.S. News & World Report,* February 25, 1991, p. 61. Copyright, February 25, 1991, *U.S. News & World Report.*

It appears that an observer can identify more with a model who struggles and overcomes the difficulties of a threatening task than a model who apparently has no problem. A model who is seen as possessing substantially greater abilities may not be considered a reasonable reference point for the observer. However, experts who display little difficulty in completing a task (e.g., professional athletes) may serve as ideals to be emulated in nonthreatening situations.[6]

Another factor that influences modeling effectiveness is the perceived similarity of the model to the observer. This finding supports the common practice of featuring models similar to members of the target market in commercials, as well as attempts to take advantage of similarities between customers and salespeople in hiring and assigning sales personnel.

Characteristics of the observers

Any number of individual difference variables in observers could be expected to affect successful modeling. For example, individual differences in cognitive processing as well as in physical ability to perform the modeled behavior may affect the process. In covert modeling in particular, people differ in their ability to imagine modeled behavior. Bandura suggests that in many cases observers who are dependent, who lack confidence and self-esteem, and who have been frequently rewarded for imitative behavior are especially prone to adopt the behavior of successful models.[7] Perceptive and confident people readily emulate idealized models who demonstrate highly useful behaviors.

This ad models an appropriate occasion for using a product.

The MCI Card® is easier to use than the AT&T Card. From any hotel room or hotel payphone in the U.S., to virtually any phone in the world.

Unlike the AT&T Card, you never have to read payphone labels, listen for special recordings, or dial differently from different phones. And whether you dial direct or use an operator, you'll never experience hidden charges with MCI.®

The MCI Card guarantees you access to the unsurpassed quality of the MCI network. And savings over AT&T, month after month.

Take the MCI Card. Or take your chances.

Let us show you.®
1-800-888-0800.

The MCI Card. America's Business Card.™

Perhaps most important is the value the observer places on the consequences of the modeled behavior. For example, if consumers value the social approval enjoyed by a model in a Grecian Formula (hair-coloring) commercial, they are more likely to purchase and use the product.

Characteristics of the modeled consequences

Just as operant conditioning places importance on the consequences of behavior, so does vicarious learning. Of course, in vicarious learning, the observer does not experience the consequences directly. Thus, a major advantage of vicarious learning for consumers is that they can learn effective purchase and use behavior while avoiding negative consequences.

Research has demonstrated that positively reinforcing a model's behavior is a key factor in facilitating vicarious learning, although little is known about what types of positive consequences would be most effective to model, in terms of consumer behavior. This is also true for modeling applications that seek to decrease undesired behaviors; the most effective types of negative consequences to model in commercials are unknown. While it has been demonstrated that modeling is useful in deterring smoking, reducing drinking, reducing uncooperative behavior of children, and reducing energy consumption, many other areas of consumer behavior are unexplored. Consumer Perspective 12.2 (see page 269) presents an example of one successful use of modeling, in a business venture.

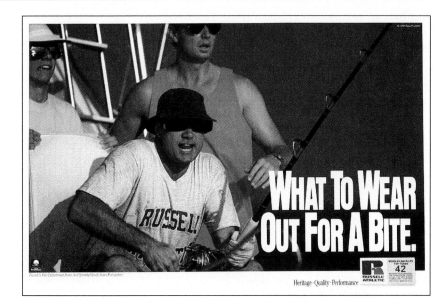

This ad models an appropriate occasion for using (wearing) a product.

MARKETING
IMPLICATIONS

Modeling clearly plays a role in marketing products, particularly in advertising and personal-selling approaches to influencing consumers. Modeling also plays a special role in the diffusion of innovation and the degree to which consumers adopt products.

Diffusion of innovation

Diffusion refers to the way innovations (new products, services, or ideas) are spread throughout society. Successful diffusion of innovations follows a common pattern. First, the innovation is introduced by prominent models. Fred Couples, for example, a leading player on the PGA tour, introduced a new model of Lynx golf clubs in 1992. Next, the innovation is adopted by others at an accelerating rate. Many nonprofessional players purchased Lynx clubs after Couples promoted them and was successful with them. Finally, adoption then either stabilizes or declines, depending on the functional role of the product. Lynx clubs are still selling well.

Modeling affects the diffusion of innovation in several ways. It instructs people about new products and new styles of behavior through social, pictorial, or verbal displays. Some consumers may be reluctant to buy new products until they see the advantages gained by earlier adopters. When Fred Couples won over $500,000 in one of the first tournaments he played with the new Lynx clubs, it may have influenced other golfers at least to try a set of Lynx clubs.

Modeled benefits accelerate diffusion by weakening the resistance of the more cautious consumer. As acceptance spreads, the new users are evidence of further support for the product. Models not only exemplify and legitimize innovations but also serve as advocates for products by encouraging others to adopt them. Even weekend golfers can influence their friends to purchase Lynx clubs either by being observed playing better with them or by offering verbal support for their advantages.

The adoption process

Obviously different types of consumers adopt new products at different stages. A well-known classification of these different types is shown in Exhibit 12.4. This **adoption curve** represents the cumulative percentage of purchasers of a product across time and includes five groups. Traditionally, the five adopter groups are characterized as follows. **Innovators**

EXHIBIT 12.4

The adoption curve

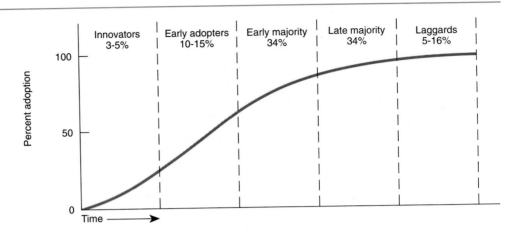

are venturesome and willing to take risks. **Early adopters** are respectable and often influence the early majority. The **early majority** are risk-avoiders and are deliberate in their purchases. The **late majority** are skeptical and cautious about new ideas. **Laggards** are quite traditional and set in their ways.

Marketing managers find innovators particularly important because they influence early adopters, who in turn may influence the early majority to purchase. Thus, a new product's chances of success increase greatly once innovators adopt the product and tell others about it. Modeling is important in this instance because early adopters may be influenced by seeing innovators using a product and being reinforced for doing so.

A major focus of consumer research has been to identify the characteristics of innovators and their differences from other consumers. This research indicates innovators tend to be more highly educated and younger, and to have greater social mobility, more favorable attitudes toward risk (more venturesome), greater social participation, and higher opinion leadership than other consumers.

Innovators also tend to be heavy users of other products within a product class. One study finds that adopters of home computers had greater experience with other technical products—such as programmable pocket calculators and video television games—than did nonadopters.[8] Innovators may have better-developed knowledge structures for particular product categories, which may enable them to understand and evaluate new products more rapidly and thus adopt earlier than other consumers.

The idea that different types of consumers purchase products in different stages of the products' life cycles has important implications for marketing. Marketing strategies must change across time to appeal to different types of consumers.

Characteristics of products

Exhibit 12.5 (see page 270) lists a number of characteristics of new products and brands that influence whether consumers will purchase them. Modeling can play an important role in new product success by demonstrating these characteristics of a product in advertising or in the product's actual use by innovators. Other influences are word-of-mouth communication, including verbal modeling, by innovators, salespeople, and other consumers about these characteristics. Observers are more likely to adopt a new product or brand if these characteristics are easily modeled for them.

Compatibility

Compatibility refers to the degree to which a product is consistent with consumers' current affect, cognitions, and behaviors. Other things being equal, a product that does not require a major change in consumer values and beliefs or their purchase and use behaviors

**CONSUMER
PERSPECTIVE**

**Marketing by
modeling on
videocassettes**

Soloflex Inc., makers of a $495 home exercise machine, provides an impressive example of using modeling on videocassettes as a marketing tool (see page 266). Soloflex's founder and president, Jerry Wilson, couldn't get sales personnel in sporting-goods stores to model the use of his machine properly, so he took it out of retail distribution and started selling it directly to the public.

Then, after purchasing a videocassette recorder for his family, he realized this was the perfect way to market his product. He spent $150,000 to produce a 22-minute demonstration on videotape and began offering it free in magazine and television ads. Each video cost the company about $6.50 for materials, dubbing, packaging, and postage.

After six years in business, the firm was reported to have sold 100,000 units. It had mailed out more than 60,000 free videotapes. It found that up to 40 percent of those who requested the demonstration videotape eventually bought a Soloflex—an astounding sales-conversion percentage compared with only 10 percent conversion of those who did not have a videocassette recorder and were sent only a brochure. Thus, it would appear that modeling the appropriate use of this product on videocassette and the consequences (the well-shaped bodies of the models) was an effective marketing strategy.

Source: Based on Stan Rapp and Tom Collins, "Voluminous Video Enlivens Today's Media Market," *Adweek*, November 17, 1986, p. 43. © 1986 *Adweek*. Used with permission Adweek Marketing Week.

is more likely to be tried by consumers. For example, Chewels chewing gum—the gum with a liquid center—required little change on the part of consumers to try the product.

Trialability

Trialability refers to the degree to which a product can be tried on a limited basis, or divided into small quantities for an inexpensive trial. A product that facilitates a non-purchase trial or a limited-purchase trial is more likely to influence the consumer to try the product. Test-driving a car, trying on a sweater, tasting bite-sized pieces of a new

EXHIBIT 12.5

Characteristics that influence the success of new products

> ▷ **Compatibility:** How well does this product fit consumers' current affect, cognitions, and behaviors?
> ▷ **Trialability:** Can consumers try the product on a limited basis with little risk?
> ▷ **Observability:** Do consumers frequently see or otherwise sense this product?
> ▷ **Speed:** How soon do consumers experience the benefits of the product?
> ▷ **Simplicity:** How easy is it for consumers to understand and use the product?
> ▷ **Relative advantage:** What makes this product better than competitive offerings?
> ▷ **Product symbolism:** What does this product mean to consumers?

frozen pizza, accepting a free trial of a new encyclopedia, or buying a sample-size bottle of a new shampoo are ways consumers can try products on a limited basis and reduce risk.

Observability
Observability refers to the degree to which products or their effects can be perceived by other consumers. New products that are public and frequently discussed are more likely to be adopted rapidly. Many clothing styles, for example, become popular after consumers see movie and recording stars wearing them. Satellite disks are highly observable, a feature that likely influences their purchase.

Speed
Speed refers to how quickly the benefits of the product are experienced by the consumer. Because many consumers are oriented toward immediate rather than delayed gratification, products that can deliver benefits sooner rather than later have a higher probability of at least being tried. For example, weight-loss programs that promise results within the first week are more likely to attract consumers than those that promise results in six months.

Simplicity
Simplicity refers to the degree to which a product is easy for a consumer to understand and use. A product that does not require complicated assembly and extensive training to use has a higher chance of trial. For example, many computer products, such as those made by Apple, are promoted as being "user friendly" to encourage purchase.

Relative advantage
Relative advantage refers to the degree to which an item has a *sustainable, competitive differential advantage* over other product classes, product forms, and brands. There is no question that relative advantage is a most important product characteristic not only for obtaining trial, but also for continued purchase and the development of brand loyalty.

In some cases, a relative advantage may be obtained through technological developments. At the product-class level, for example, RCA introduced the videodisc player, which showed programs on any TV set. The disc player cost half as much as cassette machines, and the discs were cheaper than videocassettes. At the same time, videocassette players had a relative advantage over disc players: they could record programs, and the disc players could not. RCA assumed that recording ability was not an important factor to consumers—and lost more than $500 million finding out otherwise.

At the brand level, however, it is often difficult to maintain a technological relative advantage, because new or improved technology can be quickly copied by competitors. In addition, many brands within product groups are relatively homogeneous in terms of their

A marketing strategy to increase trialability. (See page 269.)

functional benefits for consumers. For these reasons, one of the most important sources of a sustainable relative advantage comes from product symbolism rather than technological change or functional difference in products.

Product symbolism

Product symbolism refers to what the product or brand means to the consumer and what the consumer experiences in purchasing and using it. That is, consumption of some products may depend more on their social and psychological meaning than on their functional utility. For example, the blue-jean market is dominated by major brands such as Levi's, Wrangler, and Lee, which show few clear differences except in pocket design and brand labeling. If these brand names meant nothing to consumers, and blue jeans were purchased only on the basis of product attributes such as materials and styles, it would be difficult to explain differences in market share, given the brand similarity. Obviously jeans brands have different symbolic meanings for consumers. Consumer Perspective 12.3 offers an example of the importance of product symbolism in the car market.

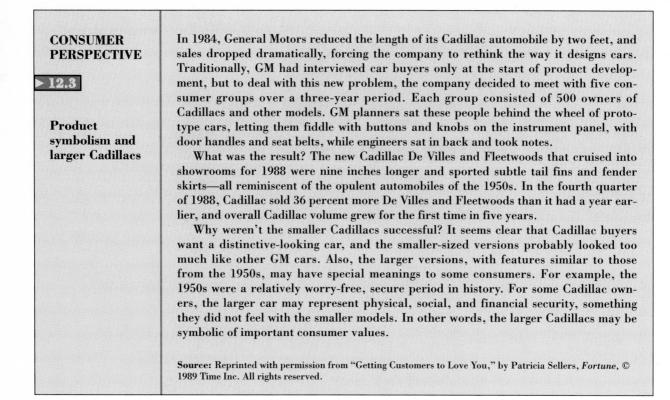

CONSUMER PERSPECTIVE

▶ **12.3**

Product symbolism and larger Cadillacs

In 1984, General Motors reduced the length of its Cadillac automobile by two feet, and sales dropped dramatically, forcing the company to rethink the way it designs cars. Traditionally, GM had interviewed car buyers only at the start of product development, but to deal with this new problem, the company decided to meet with five consumer groups over a three-year period. Each group consisted of 500 owners of Cadillacs and other models. GM planners sat these people behind the wheel of prototype cars, letting them fiddle with buttons and knobs on the instrument panel, with door handles and seat belts, while engineers sat in back and took notes.

What was the result? The new Cadillac De Villes and Fleetwoods that cruised into showrooms for 1988 were nine inches longer and sported subtle tail fins and fender skirts—all reminiscent of the opulent automobiles of the 1950s. In the fourth quarter of 1988, Cadillac sold 36 percent more De Villes and Fleetwoods than it had a year earlier, and overall Cadillac volume grew for the first time in five years.

Why weren't the smaller Cadillacs successful? It seems clear that Cadillac buyers want a distinctive-looking car, and the smaller-sized versions probably looked too much like other GM cars. Also, the larger versions, with features similar to those from the 1950s, may have special meanings to some consumers. For example, the 1950s were a relatively worry-free, secure period in history. For some Cadillac owners, the larger car may represent physical, social, and financial security, something they did not feel with the smaller models. In other words, the larger Cadillacs may be symbolic of important consumer values.

Source: Reprinted with permission from "Getting Customers to Love You," by Patricia Sellers, *Fortune*, © 1989 Time Inc. All rights reserved.

▶ **SUMMARY**

Learning objective 1: *Explain three uses of vicarious learning (modeling).*
First, modeling can be used to help observers acquire new behavioral responses that did not previously exist in their repertoires. In other words, it can help consumers develop new behaviors. Second, modeling can be used to inhibit undesired behaviors. That is, modeling can help decrease incidence of behaviors that are not good for consumers, marketers, or society. Third, modeling can be used to facilitate the occurrence of desired behaviors that are currently in the consumer's repertoire. In other words, it can help consumers engage in behaviors that they already know by showing some appropriate occasions and reinforcement for performing the behaviors.

Learning objective 2: *Describe three types of modeling.*
The three types of modeling are overt, covert, and verbal. In overt modeling, observers actually observe a model either in person (live modeling) or on TV or videotape (symbolic modeling). Covert modeling asks consumers to imagine observing a model behaving in various situations and receiving particular consequences. Verbal modeling techniques call for people to be told how people similar to them behaved in a particular situation.

Learning objective 3: *Explain three factors that influence the effectiveness of modeling.*
First, the characteristics of the model and the modeled behavior influence the effectiveness of modeling. In general, attractive, credible, high-status, competent models are more effective. Modeled behavior that is detailed vividly is also more effective. Second, the characteristics of the observers influence the effectiveness of modeling. Differences in consumers' cognitive processing and physical abilities, as well as factors such as self-confidence, dependence, and self-esteem can influence the success of modeling. Third, the characteristics of the modeled consequences can influence the success of modeling.

In general, presentation of a model receiving positive reinforcement after performing a behavior is a key factor in successful modeling.

Learning objective 4: *Describe five adopter categories.*

Innovators (3 to 5 percent of purchasers) are venturesome and willing to take risks. They are the first group to adopt new products. Early adopters (10 to 15 percent of purchasers) are respectable and often influence the early majority. They follow innovators in purchasing. Members of the early majority (34 percent of purchasers) avoid risks and are deliberate in their purchases. The late majority (34 percent of purchasers) are skeptical and cautious about new ideas. Laggards (5 to 16 percent of purchasers) are traditional and set in their ways. They are the last group to adopt a product.

Learning objective 5: *Identify the characteristics that influence the success of new products.*

Seven major characteristics influence the success of new products. Compatibility refers to the degree to which a product is consistent with consumers' current affect, cognitions, and behaviors. Trialability refers to the degree to which a product can be tried on a limited basis or divided into small quantities for an inexpensive trial. Observability refers to the degree to which products or their effects can be perceived by consumers. Speed refers to how quickly the benefits of the product are experienced by the consumer. Simplicity refers to the degree to which a product is easy for a consumer to understand and use. Relative advantage refers to the degree to which an item has a sustainable, competitive differential advantage over other product classes, product forms, or brands. Product symbolism refers to what the product or brand means to the consumer beyond its strictly functional utility.

► **KEY TERMS AND CONCEPTS**

overt modeling
covert modeling
verbal modeling
diffusion
adoption curve
innovators

early adopters
early majority
late majority
laggards
compatibility
trialability

observability
speed
simplicity
relative advantage
product symbolism

► **REVIEW AND DISCUSSION QUESTIONS**

1. Describe the steps necessary for behavior change in the modeling process.
2. What are the three major uses of modeling in marketing strategy?
3. Why might a marketing organization use symbolic rather than live overt modeling? Give examples to illustrate your points.
4. How are covert and verbal modeling different from overt modeling? How are they similar?
5. Give examples, not already discussed in the text, where you have observed marketing strategies that use each of the types of modeling.
6. In what situations would you recommend that a marketing manager use vicarious learning in advertisements?
7. How could modeling be used to facilitate the introduction of the newest models of lightweight portable personal computers?
8. To which adopter category do you belong in general? Explain.
9. Identify characteristics of new products that would be useful for predicting success and for prescribing effective marketing strategies.
10. Discuss the problems and advantages of appealing to innovators when marketing a new consumer packaged good.

13

Analyzing Consumer Behavior

LEARNING OBJECTIVES

After completing this chapter, you should be able to:

► 1. Describe a sequence of overt consumer behaviors involved in a retail consumer-goods purchase, and explain the behaviors.

► 2. Suggest several tactics marketers could use to influence each of these behaviors.

► 3. Explain a model marketers could use to influence a sequence of consumer behaviors.

WHEN TAKING THE ROAD LESS TRAVELED, BE CAREFUL WHAT YOU DRIVE.

You're going to need a lot more. More interior room. More comfort. More versatility. A powerful 4.0 liter V-6. And, of course, a 4x4 system that lets you shift to 4WD High at the touch of a button. You'll need the one that's first in its class. Explorer. Don't settle for anything less.

FIND YOURSELF IN AN EXPLORER.

FORD EXPLORES THE 4-WHEEL-DRIVE MARKET

Throughout the 1980s, the Jeep Cherokee was the car of choice for many upscale buyers seeking a second car. In fact, common garage-mates for Cherokees were Mercedes-Benzes and BMWs. These consumers wanted a second car with four doors and enough room for the family to pile in for a trip to the beach or the mall. Chrysler, which acquired Jeep in 1987, made from $4,000 to $4,500 profit on each Cherokee it sold during this period.

In 1990, Ford introduced the Explorer, a four-door, four-wheel-drive vehicle that competes directly with the Cherokee. Ford recognized that many more women were buying off-road vehicles or influencing purchase decisions, so they made changes for them as well as for men. As a result, the Explorer has safety features such as front-seat head restraints, rear shoulder belts, and a shift into four-wheel drive that requires simply pushing a button. In just six months, the Explorer outsold the Jeep Cherokee by almost two to one, and Ford's share of the off-road-vehicle market went from 18 to 25 percent while Jeep's dropped from 24 to 20 percent.[1]

Many consumer behaviors are involved in purchasing a new vehicle, as the Cherokee or Explorer example illustrates. There are also many behaviors involved in purchases of simpler, less-expensive products. This chapter investigates the types of consumer behaviors marketers try to influence.

By now you have a general understanding of the major aspects of the behavior approach used in the Wheel of Consumer Analysis. Here we tie this approach more directly to consumer behavior and marketing strategy development. We do this by explaining a model of the behaviors involved in a common purchase situation and how marketers use alternative strategies to change these behaviors.

MODEL OF CONSUMER BEHAVIOR

Traditional models of the purchase or adoption process in marketing treat it as a series of cognitive events followed by a single behavior, usually called *adoption* or *purchase*. These models are consistent with the view that *cognitive variables* (awareness, comprehension, interest, evaluation, conviction) are the main concern of marketing and the primary controllers of behavior. According to this view, the marketing task is to influence these cognitive variables and move consumers through each stage until a purchase is made.

An alternative approach is to analyze adoption or purchase as a *sequence of behaviors.* From this perspective marketing managers want to increase the frequency of a certain behavior, and they design strategies and tactics for doing so. The assumption is that strategies and tactics to change affective and cognitive processes such as attention or attitude may be useful intermediate steps, but they must ultimately change behavior to be profitable for marketers.

Exhibit 13.1 describes a model of a behavior sequence that occurs in the purchase of many consumer goods. While this is a logical sequence, many other combinations of behavior can occur. For example, an unplanned (impulse) purchase of Twix cookie bars could start at the store contact stage. Not every purchase follows the sequence shown in Exhibit 13.1, and not every purchase requires that all of these behaviors be performed. The model is generally useful all the same for categorizing a variety of marketing strategies in terms of the behaviors they are designed to influence.

The model in Exhibit 13.1 is also intended to illustrate only one type of behavior sequence for retail purchases; similar models could be developed for other types of purchases, such as mail-order, telephone, or catalog-showroom exchanges. Further, the sequences involved with other behaviors of interest to consumer analysis, such as voting, physician care, banking, or consumer education, could also be modeled in much the same way. In fact, any attempt to influence behavior should include an analysis of the behavior sequence that is necessary or desired. Unfortunately, many marketing managers do not consider exactly what behaviors are involved in the actions they are attempting to get consumers to perform.

The time it takes for a consumer to perform behaviors in the model depends on a variety of factors. Different products, consumers, and situations may affect not only the total time to complete the process but also the length of time between stages. For example, an avid water-skier purchasing a Mastercraft powerboat likely will spend more time per stage, and more time will elapse between stages, than for a consumer purchasing a Timex watch.

A seller's emphasis on any particular element of the sequence will vary according to the place in the distribution chain for the product or service. Retailers, for example, may be more concerned with increasing store contact than with purchase of a particular brand; manufacturers are less concerned with the particular store patronized, but want to increase brand purchase; credit-card companies may be less concerned with particular store or product contacts so long as their credit card is accepted and used. Store contact, product contact, and transaction method are all common for a retail exchange, however,

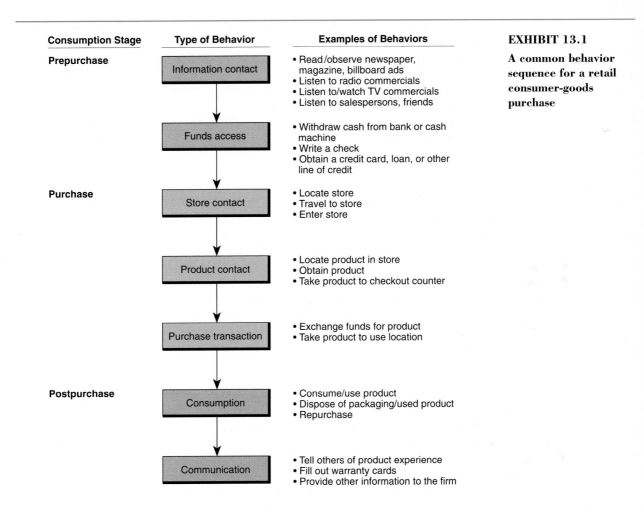

Consumption Stage	Type of Behavior	Examples of Behaviors
Prepurchase	Information contact	• Read/observe newspaper, magazine, billboard ads • Listen to radio commercials • Listen to/watch TV commercials • Listen to salespersons, friends
	Funds access	• Withdraw cash from bank or cash machine • Write a check • Obtain a credit card, loan, or other line of credit
Purchase	Store contact	• Locate store • Travel to store • Enter store
	Product contact	• Locate product in store • Obtain product • Take product to checkout counter
	Purchase transaction	• Exchange funds for product • Take product to use location
Postpurchase	Consumption	• Consume/use product • Dispose of packaging/used product • Repurchase
	Communication	• Tell others of product experience • Fill out warranty cards • Provide other information to the firm

EXHIBIT 13.1

A common behavior sequence for a retail consumer-goods purchase

and all three sellers can benefit from the others' efforts. Consumer Perspective 13.1 (see page 280) discusses a creative strategy for influencing consumers' purchasing behavior that involves a discount card company and restaurants.

Information contact

A common early stage in the purchase sequence, called **information contact**, occurs when consumers come into contact with information about products, stores, or brands. This stage includes behaviors such as reading product information, observing newspaper, magazine, and billboard ads, listening to radio commercials, watching TV commercials, and talking to salespeople and friends. At this point, the practical problem for marketers is to increase the probability that consumers will observe and attend to the information, with the assumption that this will increase the probability of other behaviors.

Marketing managers for brands with low market share usually want to increase overall search behavior, because it may increase the probability of brand switching. High-market-share brands may try to discourage extensive search behaviors, because such behavior may result in a shift to another brand. For example, Heinz currently has a major share of the market for ketchup and does not want most consumers to search for information concerning different brands. Ads showing Heinz as the thicker, richer ketchup while depicting other brands as thin and unsavory may discourage loyal consumers from searching for an alternative. They may also help attract non-Heinz

EXHIBIT 13.2

Factors affecting information search by consumers

Influencing Factor	Increasing the Influencing Factor Causes Search to:
Market characteristics	
Number of alternatives	Increase
Price range	Increase
Store concentration	Increase
Information availability	Increase
Advertising	
Point-of-purchase	
Sales personnel	
Packaging	
Experienced consumers	
Independent sources	
Product characteristics	
Price	Increase
Differentiation	Increase
Positive products	Increase
Consumer characteristics	
Learning and experience	Decrease
Shopping orientation	Mixed
Social status	Increase
Age, gender, and household life cycle	Mixed
Perceived risk	Increase
Situational characteristics	
Time availability	Increase
Purchase for self	Decrease
Pleasant surroundings	Increase
Social surroundings	Mixed
Physical/mental energy	Increase

Source: Del I. Hawkins, Roger Best, Jr., and Kenneth A. Coney, *Consumer Behavior: Implications for Marketing Strategy*, 5th ed. (Homewood, Ill.: Richard D. Irwin, 1992), p. 478.

purchasers by demonstrating the negative consequences of using another brand. The extent of a consumer's search depends on many factors, some of which are listed in Exhibit 13.2.

In general, empirical research has shown:

1. Consumers tend to engage more in search when purchasing higher priced, more visible, and more complex products—i.e., products that intrinsically create greater perceived risk.

2. Search is influenced by individual factors, such as the perceived benefits of search (e.g., enjoyment, self-confidence, role), demographic aspects, and product knowledge already possessed.

3. Search efforts tend to be influenced further by factors in the marketplace (such as store distribution) and by circumstances impinging on the shopper (such as time pressure).[2]

Funds access can occur in a number of ways.

From a public policy standpoint, information search should develop more knowledgeable consumers, although there are differences in the effort required by consumers to obtain information from different sources as well as in the believability of the information.[3] For example, Exhibit 13.3 rates five common sources of information on effort required and believability. Internal sources (stored experiences) and personal sources (friends and relatives) are easiest to access and the most believable. Marketing sources (advertising) are also readily available but not as believable, because advertisers have something to gain from the transaction. Finally, public sources (*Consumer Reports* and other impartial studies) and experiential sources (personally examining or testing the product) are less likely to be used, at least in this early stage, because more effort is required to obtain information from these sources.

Source	Effort Required	Believability
Internal (stored experiences in memory)	Low	High
Personal (friends, relatives)	Low	High
Marketing (advertising)	Low	Low
Public (*Consumer Reports*, other studies)	High	High
Experiential (examining or testing product)	High	High

EXHIBIT 13.3

A comparison of information sources

<table>
<tr>
<td>

CONSUMER PERSPECTIVE

▶ **13.1**

Transmedia's executive savings card

</td>
<td>

Transmedia Network Inc. promotes an innovative strategy to serve consumers profitably with a discount card for restaurant meals. In five years, it attracted 45,000 cardholders, and in 1990 earned $7.5 million in revenues and over $300,000 in net income. The Transmedia Executive Savings Card can be used at over 725 restaurants in parts of New York, New Jersey, Connecticut, and Florida. Here's how it works.

Transmedia makes cash advances to restaurants, which in turn give Transmedia twice the cash amount in credits for meals. For example, Transmedia usually offers $5,000 cash for $10,000 in restaurant credits. It then offers its cardholders a 25 percent discount on meals (before tax and tip) eaten at restaurants that honor its cards. It usually takes about six months for a group of cardholders to use up $10,000 at a particular restaurant. After giving cardholders the 25 percent discount, Transmedia still gets $7,500 for its initial $5,000 cash advance.

Restaurants are willing to deal with Transmedia because they benefit from the quick cash, and the additional business is profitable and helps fill unused capacity. The cards also are a big help to new restaurants trying to build a clientele.

Consumers use the cards because of the large savings, but it has not been easy for Transmedia to attract cardholders. Despite advertising and offers of free cards, consumers have been slow to sign up; they simply didn't believe the company could deliver such good deals. To add more cardholders. Transmedia continues to waive the

</td>
</tr>
</table>

The main marketing task is to increase the probability that the target market comes into contact with product, brand, or store information and pays attention to it. Numerous marketing strategies are directed at encouraging attentive behavior. For example, media scheduling, message content and layout, the use of color and humor in advertising, and repetition all involve presenting stimuli to increase the probability that potential consumers will attend to relevant cues. *Fear appeals* can also be used to bring about attentive behaviors and to stimulate emotions vicariously by exposing the observers to possible distasteful consequences of certain conditions (inadequate insurance, faulty tires and batteries, the absence of smoke alarms, not using dental floss). Strategies such as contests and prizes encourage attentive behavior and promise rewards for engaging in certain behavior that brings the consumer into closer contact with the product or point of purchase. Finally, ads that show models receiving positive reinforcement in the form of social approval and satisfaction for purchasing a product provide stimuli that can move the consumer closer to purchase by stimulating the "buying mood." Consumer Perspective 13.2 (see page 282) discusses a strategy that encourages information contact for magazine subscriptions.

Funds access

Exchange is frequently seen as the key concept for understanding marketing, although relatively little attention has been given to *what consumers exchange* in the marketing process. Beyond time and effort costs, money is the primary medium of consumer exchanges. The consumer must access this medium in one form or another before an exchange can occur, engaging in what is known as **funds access**. The primary marketing issues at this stage are (1) the methods used by consumers to pay for particular purchases, and (2) the marketing strategies to increase the probability that the consumers are able to access funds for purchase.

There are, of course, a variety of ways by which consumers can pay for a product. These include cash in pocket; bank withdrawal of cash; writing a check; using credit cards such as Visa, MasterCard, and American Express; using a store charge account; using debit cards; and drawing on other lines of credit, such as bank loans or GMAC financing.

$50 annual fee for at least the first year and offers cardholders $25 cards for their friends. It offers companies free cards for use by employees on expense accounts. Such a strategy increases the probability of consumers purchasing meals at specific locations and is profitable for both Transmedia and the restaurants.

Access may involve different degrees of effort exerted to obtain the money that is spent or that is used to repay loans. It seems likely that funds obtained from tax refunds, stock sales and dividends, gambling winnings, awards, or regular paychecks are valued differently by the consumer and spent in different ways. A manifestation of this effect is that some retailers encourage the purchase of big-ticket items by offering interest-free loans for a few months while people are waiting for their tax refunds.

A variety of other strategies may increase the probability that consumers can access funds for purchases. For example, Penney's offers a small gift to anyone who fills out a credit-card application. The probability of purchasing at Penney's is increased when a consumer has a credit card, because cash may not always be available. Other strategies include locating cash machines in malls, instituting liberal credit terms and check-cashing policies, and accepting a variety of credit cards. Deferred payment plans and layaway plans that allow the consumer additional time to raise the required funds help stores avoid lost sales. Gift certificates are also used to presell merchandise and to provide some consumers with another source of funds that is restricted for particular purchases. All these strategies have a common goal—to increase the probability of an exchange by increasing the probability of accessing funds.

Other strategies can be employed to increase certain types of purchases. For example, a store could offer a small discount for using cash to avoid the costs of paying credit-card fees. An analysis of the conditions surrounding particular purchases may recommend other successful tactics. Many major home appliances, for example, are purchased only when both husband and wife are present, and a necessary condition is that they can obtain funds. One tactic for an appliance store might be to offer a small gift to any couple who will come to the store with their checkbook or approved credit card. Thus, the appropriate contingencies are prearranged for an appliance sale. Any number of other methods (such as offering rebates) could be used in conjunction with this tactic to increase the probability of purchase. Consumer Perspective 13.3 (see page 284)discusses the strategies used by credit-card issuers to encourage consumers to obtain and use their credit cards for funds access.

<table>
<tr>
<td>

CONSUMER PERSPECTIVE

▶ **13.2**

Encouraging information contact for magazine subscriptions

</td>
<td>

Including subscription cards in magazines is a useful marketing tactic, because the cards are available at the time the magazine is being read and enjoyed. These cards make it convenient for readers of the magazine (the likely target market for future issues) to renew a subscription or start a new one.

Traditionally, magazine marketers have bound subscription cards to the magazines. One drawback to such "bind-in" cards is that readers often simply ignore them. Because the cards are bound to the issue, readers can leaf past them without giving the card (or the idea of starting or renewing a subscription) any consideration.

An alternative method of including subscription cards in magazines is to place them between the pages, unbound. These are called "blow-in" cards. When magazines are open or read, blow-in cards fall out and consumers need to handle them for at least a moment. In other words, the probability of information contact is increased with the use of blow-in rather than bind-in cards. It is not surprising, then, that blow-in cards are more effective than bind-in cards at generating subscription renewals.

</td>
</tr>
</table>

Store contact

Although catalog and telephone-order purchases are important, most consumer-goods purchases are still made in retail stores. Thus, a major task of retailers is to get consumers into the store, where purchase can occur. **Store contact** includes (1) locating the store, (2) traveling to it, and (3) entering it.

One factor that affects the probability of store contact involves how consumers see their roles as shoppers. Some people enjoy shopping and spend many hours looking in stores. To others, shopping is drudgery. Some shoppers are primarily price oriented and favor particular low-price outlets. Others look for a high level of service, or unique products and stores that express their individuality. These differences are important dimensions in design of market segmentation strategies for stores.

Many strategies are designed to increase the probability of store contact. For example, consider the methods used to increase the probability that shoppers will be able to locate a particular outlet. Selecting convenient locations in high-traffic areas with ample parking has been successful for retailers such as 7-Eleven convenience stores and Denny's restaurants. A major advantage for retailers locating in shopping malls is the increase in consumers' ability to find the outlet as well as the additional shopping traffic created by the presence of the other stores. Yellow Pages, newspaper, and other ads frequently include maps and information numbers to aid shoppers in locating an outlet. Outdoor signs and logos (such as the distinctive sign of Domino's Pizza) are well-known discriminative stimuli. One recreational vehicle dealer close to Columbus, Ohio, used an interesting modeling approach to aid potential customers in locating the dealership. Its TV ads reproduced the actual route, landmarks, and road signs people would see when traveling to the dealership. Every turn was shown, as were directional signs on the highway, to help potential customers find the outlet.

Other tactics to encourage store contact include carnivals in mall parking lots, free style shows or other mall entertainments, and visits by Santa Claus, the Easter Bunny, Sesame Street characters, and soap-opera actors. Mall directories and information booths help shoppers find particular stores.

Finally, some tactics are used to get the potential customer physically into the store. Frequently advertised sales, sale signs in store windows, door prizes, loss leaders, sounds (such as popular music), and tempting aromas (such as fresh popcorn) are commonly employed for these purposes.

Manufacturers are concerned primarily with *selective demand* of consumers in stores—purchase of their particular brands and models. Many of the methods employed to accomplish **product contact** involve push strategies such as trade discounts and incentives to enhance the selling effort of retailers. For example, a free case of Tide liquid detergent for every 10 cases the retailer purchases can be a powerful incentive for retailers to feature liquid Tide in newspaper ads, put it in prominent displays, and even sell it at a lower price while maintaining or increasing profit margins. Other approaches involve pull strategies, such as cents-off coupons to encourage the consumer to purchase the manufacturer's brand. In any event, once potential buyers are in the store, three behaviors are usually necessary for a purchase to take place: (1) locating the product or brand in the store, (2) physically obtaining the product or brand, and (3) taking the product or brand to the point of exchange (e.g., the checkout counter).

Product contact

Once consumers are in the store, it is important that they be able to locate products. Store directories, end-of-aisle and other displays, in-store signs, information booths, and store personnel all help consumers move into visual contact with products. While consumers are in the store, their visual contact with the many other available products increases the probability of purchase.

One tactic a major chain uses involves a variation of "blue-light specials." Blue-light specials, pioneered by Kmart, offer shoppers in the store the opportunity to purchase products at special prices when a blue light is flashing at a particular location. Usually, the sale item is one that is low priced and sold at its normal location. A variation involves moving the sale merchandise and the blue light to an area where high-priced or high-margin items are located. This brings the blue-light shoppers to the vicinity of such products and into visual contact with them—which, of course, increases the probability of making these more profitable sales. The tactic has been reported to be quite successful.

Physically coming into contact with a product influences whether a purchase will occur. Attractive, eye-catching packaging and other aspects of product appearance influence the degree to which the consumer pays attention to the product. Trying the product in the store can also affect purchase probabilities, as can the behavior of sales personnel. Salespeople can positively reinforce certain behaviors, extinguish or punish others, influence the stimuli attended to, and model appropriate product usage. Even negative reinforcement can be employed. For example, consider salespeople who are overly aggressive and use high-pressure tactics. One way for consumers to eliminate the pushy treatment is to purchase the product—and some people do this rather than walk away. Thus, the consumer is negatively reinforced to purchase; the probability of this response is likely to be increased in similar situations in the future. Note also that the salesperson is positively reinforced by making the sale using a high-pressure approach, so the salesperson's use of an aggressive selling approach is also likely to persist.

Salespeople can also change the circumstances for purchasing versus not purchasing. Consider this approach to selling furniture to ambivalent customers who state their intention to "go home and think it over." Once the potential buyer leaves the store, of course, the probability of a sale is reduced, so the salesperson can change the contingencies for leaving. Potential buyers who want to think it over are told, "If you buy now, the price is $150. If you go home and come back later, the price will be the original $175." In this way a salesperson can modify the behavior of potential buyers.

There are also a number of tactics for getting potential buyers to the checkout or payment location. Checkout counters are commonly located near the exit, and parking vouchers are usually validated at this location. Also, salespeople frequently escort the buyer to the checkout where they may help arrange financing.

**CONSUMER
PERSPECTIVE**

▶ 13.3

**Heated
competition in
the credit-card
wars**

The credit-card industry is highly competitive and profitable. Banks and retail companies offer different card features in hopes of attracting cardholders and getting them to use their cards frequently. Credit-card issuers make money from fees charged to merchants on purchases consumers make, from annual fees charged consumers, and from interest on credit-card balances.

There have been a number of changes in the credit-card industry as companies vie for market share. Citicorp, the largest issuer of Visa and MasterCards, introduced a program to guarantee its customers the best prices on items they charge. Chemical Bank lowered the interest rate on its cards from a fixed 19.5 percent to a floating rate and offered consumers discounts on meals and telephone bills. American Express attacked Visa and MasterCard's 19+ percent interest charges with its Optima card, which had a 16.25 percent rate. Dean Witter Financial Services Group offers a 1 percent rebate to consumers on purchases charged on its Discover® card. AT&T offered its Universal Visa or MasterCard "free for life" to holders of other companies' Visa or MasterCards. The offer included a 10 percent discount on AT&T long-distance telephone calls.

Why are credit-card companies competing so fiercely for consumer acceptance? The answer is simple: the card company's cost of money is often far less than half the interest rate it charges, making the business very profitable. In one recent year, for example, Citibank made $3.6 billion in credit-card interest and $500 million in card fees! According to one report, Citibank and Chase Manhattan make about 70 percent of their net profits from credit cards, and other banks often make more than 50 percent of their earnings from them.

Consumers use credit cards because they make funds access simple and convenient. When balances are carried over, however, funds access can also become very expensive.

Source: Reprinted with permission from "Melting Point in the Plastic Wars," (1991) and "Who's Winning the Credit Card War?" (1990), by Bill Saporito, © 1990, 1991 Time, Inc. All rights reserved.

**Purchase
transaction**

In a macro sense, *facilitating exchange* is viewed as the primary objective of marketing. In a micro sense, this involves **purchase transactions** where consumers exchange funds for products and services. Many marketing strategies involve removing obstacles to transactions. Credit cards are one example. So are express checkout lanes and electronic scanners that minimize the time consumers must wait in line. (Some consumers will leave stores without making a purchase if checkout lines are too long.) Credit-card companies offer prompt purchase approvals to decrease the chances that a sale will be missed because of a long wait. American Express, for example, spends $300 to $400 million annually to ensure prompt service for its 15 million customers. From its Phoenix computer center, the company approves 250,000 credit-card transactions a day from all over the world in an average of five seconds or less.[4]

Because the behavior of checkout personnel is an important influence on purchase, checkout people are trained to be friendly and efficient. McDonald's personnel frequently offer *prompts* in an attempt to increase the total amount of purchase. Regardless of the food order, prompts for additional food are offered: "Would you like some fresh, hot french fries with that?" or "How about some McDonald's cookies today?" Because these are very low-cost tactics, few incremental sales are required to make them quite profitable.

The positive reinforcers involved are critical elements in encouraging purchase transactions. Tactics such as rebates, friendly treatment and compliments by store personnel, and contest tickets may increase the probability of purchase and repurchase. The reinforcing properties of the product or service itself are also important. These may involve both functional and psychosocial benefits.

(MUSIC UNDER THROUGHOUT)
(SFX: GONG)
AVO: Next time you're dining out.
(SFX: MMMM)

Ponder this:
the Discover Card pays
you a Cashback
Bonus on every meal you charge

Which means you shall soon
(SFX: CHANGE CLINKING)
acquire a small fortune.
It pays to Discover.

Consumption

While **consumption** would seem to be a very simple behavior to delineate, it is not, because of the vast differences in the nature of various products and services. For example, compare typical behaviors involved in the purchase of nondurables such as a fast-food burger and fries versus a durable such as an automobile. The burger and fries are likely to be consumed rather quickly, and the packaging disposed of as directed. Certain strategies can increase the probability that consumption will be rather quick, such as seats in a restaurant that are comfortable for only short periods of time so customers do not take up space for too long. Prompts are often used to encourage proper disposal of packaging, such as "Thank You" signs on refuse containers.

On the other hand, an automobile purchase usually involves several years of consumption or use. In addition, periodic service is required, and additional complementary products such as gas must be purchased. Finally, an automobile may be disposed of in several ways (selling it outright, junking it, or trading it in on another model). At present, little is known about the process by which consumers dispose of durable goods.

Regardless of the type of product, however, a primary marketing concern is to increase the probability of repurchase. For nondurable packaged goods, commonly employed tactics include the use of in- or on-package coupons to encourage the consumer to repurchase the same brand. Many consumers are frequent coupon users who take considerable satisfaction in the money they save. Proof-of-purchase seals are often used to encourage the consumer to purchase the same brand repeatedly to obtain enough seals to receive "free" gifts. Gold Medal flour has long used this tactic, and Pampers diapers ran a promotion in which a

Cents-off coupons
encourage product contact.

coupon for diapers was sent to buyers who mailed in three proof-of-purchase seals. For durable goods, proper instructions on the care and use of the product may be useful, for they help the consumer receive full product benefits. High-quality service and maintenance provided by the seller can similarly help to develop long-term client relationships.

Communication

A final set of behaviors that marketers attempt to encourage involves **communication**. There are two basic audiences with which marketers want consumers to communicate. They want consumers to (1) provide the company with marketing information, and (2) tell other potential consumers about the product and encourage them to purchase it. Of course, consumers can communicate with the company or other consumers about products, brands, or stores any time, not just at the end of the purchase sequence. We describe this behavior as a final step because consumers who have purchased and used a product are likely to be more knowledgeable about it and more influential in telling other consumers about it.

From consumer to marketer

Marketers typically want at least three types of information from consumers. First they want *information about the consumer* to help the company investigate the quality of its marketing strategy and the success of market segmentation. Warranty cards are traditionally used for this purpose. They commonly ask about consumer demographics, what magazines consumers read, where they obtained information about the product, where they purchased it, and what competing brands they own or have tried. Free gifts are sometimes offered to encourage consumers to return warranty cards—as well as subtle threats that the warranty is not in force unless the card is filled out and returned promptly. Of course, legally, companies cannot void warranties for failure to return the cards promptly.

A second type of information sought from consumers is *names of other potential buyers* of the product. Some firms and organizations offer rewards or premiums if the names of several potential buyers are given and then a larger reward if any of these prospects actually make a purchase. Finally, marketers also seek consumer information about *defective products.* Money-back or other guarantees that require the consumer to contact the store or company provide this information and also reduce the risk of loss to the consumer. For example, General Mills offers "a prompt adjustment of equal value" if the consumer is dissatisfied with Cheerios.

Positive consumption experiences may increase the probability of repurchase, such as buying another pair of Avia's.

From consumer to consumer

Marketers also want consumers to tell others about the product. A product that is effective and performs well may encourage this behavior, but other tactics can encourage it as well. Tupperware parties have long been used to take advantage of the fact that consumers respond favorably to information from their friends and to create an environment in which purchase is heavily encouraged. This approach has been so successful that in the first 25 years of its existence Tupperware doubled its sales and earnings every 5 years.

Newly opened bars and lounges frequently offer customers free drinks to encourage them not only to return but also to tell others about the place and to bring their friends. Word-of-mouth communication is the primary way such establishments become popular. Health clubs, such as Elaine Powers and Vic Tanny, often run promotions where members who bring in new customers get special rates for themselves as well as for their friends. One cable TV company ran a promotion offering $10 to any subscriber who got a friend to subscribe. Such tactics increase incidence of other behaviors in the purchase sequence as well.

Managers can analyze consumer behavior and develop marketing programs to increase the probability of consumer behavior that is advantageous to them. This general approach could also be used to develop strategies for discouraging undesired behaviors, although we do not explore such strategies.

Two tasks must be performed to use this analysis model. First, given appropriate marketing objectives, the manager must develop a sequential model of the behaviors that are necessary or desired of the consumer. To develop this sequence, we use the seven-stage model (in Exhibit 13.1), but other models can be developed for various types of purchase/consumption situations.

MARKETING IMPLICATIONS

EXHIBIT 13.4

Examples of methods used to measure consumption behaviors

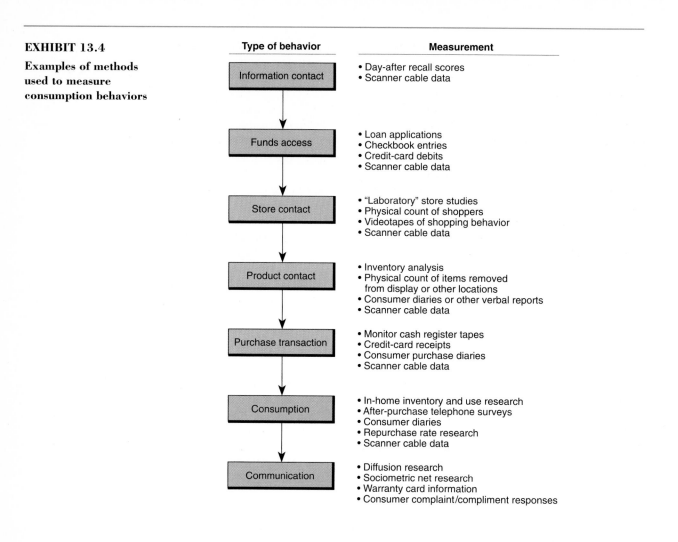

Second, after the behaviors are identified, their frequency must be measured to determine baseline data, or a starting place for comparison. This step is necessary to provide a benchmark for evaluating the effectiveness of the strategy implemented. There are many ways to measure various consumer behaviors; some examples are provided in Exhibit 13.4. These measurement methods are commonly employed in current marketing research, although they are not always used sequentially at every behavior stage.

One approach that does allow monitoring of a number of stages in a purchase sequence is the **scanner cable method** available from research companies such as Information Resources Inc. (IRI) and Nielsen Marketing Research USA. Because this method is consistent with the requirements of a consumer behavior management model, we briefly describe how one such system works.

IRI's research systems are designed to predict which products will be successful and what ads work best to sell them. It has been expanded from grocery stores to include drugstores and mass merchandisers as well. IRI assembles consumer panels in a number of cities and monitors over 60,000 households nationwide. For example, it monitors purchases in 2,700 grocery stores in 66 markets ranging from big cities to small towns. Many leading companies use IRI, including General Foods, Procter & Gamble, General Mills, and Frito-Lay.

Consumer panel members provide demographic information, how many TVs they own, the types of newspapers and magazines they read, and who does most of the shopping. IRI issues a special bar-coded identification card that shoppers present to the cashier when they pay for products in participating supermarkets or drugstores. By passing the card over the scanner or entering the digits manually into the register, the cashier records everything each shopper has purchased. One executive for Frito-Lay, which used IRI's services for the introduction of Sun Chips snacks, concludes, "The beauty of scanner data is that we get a complete description of a household from the panel and can match it with purchasing patterns. We know exactly who's out there buying our product and that helps us design marketing and advertising plans accordingly."[5]

A number of behaviors in the purchase sequence can be monitored and influenced using scanner methods. First, information contact can be influenced because media habits of households are monitored, and commercials can be changed until contact occurs. Funds access can be monitored on the cash register tape by recording prices and the method of payment. Because every purchase in the store is recorded, store contact, product contact, and purchase transaction information is available, along with dates and times of these behaviors. The relative effectiveness of various sales promotions and other marketing strategies on specific consumer behaviors can thereby be determined and successful promotions offered again to encourage store and brand loyalty. The time between purchases can be determined, so information is also available on consumption and usage rates.

Technology allows quite efficient measurement of consumer behaviors, although there presumably are limits to the benefits of extended research on such behavior. While scanner data provide substantial benefits, many firms are not able to bear the costs. Simpler, less expensive methods—such as analysis of advertising expenditures and shipping orders in various markets—may provide useful information about consumer behavior.

Exhibit 13.5 offers a model for managing a sequence of behaviors, which is based on ideas in applied behavior analysis. In its emphasis on the development and maintenance of consumer behavior, the model is fully consistent with the objectives of marketing management and common marketing strategies. It offers a more systematic and efficient approach than many models used in current marketing practice.

Identify problem behavior

Each behavior in the purchase/consumption sequence depends on many factors. In some cases—such as the promotion of a clearly superior product—information contact may be sufficient to drive the entire behavior chain and result in the performance of all the required behaviors. Even a simple comment about a product by a trusted friend may result in the performance of all behaviors in the sequence. In many cases, however, initial consumer behaviors are performed with sufficient frequency that they could lead to the other behaviors—yet the other behaviors do not occur. For example, consumers may go to retail stores where the product is carried and may even look at the product, but not purchase it. In other cases, information contact may not occur, and thus no additional behaviors follow.

The problem or **target behavior** is the earliest behavior in the sequence that is not being performed—or is not being performed appropriately or frequently enough to lead to the next behavior. Such a problem could occur with any behavior in the sequence. The problem behavior is identified by examining the differences in behavior frequencies from one stage to the next. Consumer research can provide information on results at each stage:

1. **Information contact**—90 percent of the target market has been exposed to two commercials per week in the home for the past month. Unaided recall scores are 40 percent; 30 percent of them indicate they like the features of our product.

2. **Funds access**—87 percent of the target market purchases a competitive brand at the same price as ours; 67 percent pays with credit cards.

EXHIBIT 13.5

A model for managing consumer behavior

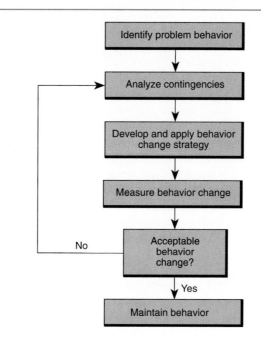

Identify problem behavior

↓

Analyze contingencies

↓

Develop and apply behavior change strategy

↓

Measure behavior change

↓

Acceptable behavior change?

No →

Yes ↓

Maintain behavior

3. **Store contact**—96 percent of the target market shops at least once per week in stores where our brand is carried; 40 percent comes into the physical vicinity of our product once per week.

4. **Product contact**—30 percent of the target market looks at our product; 14 percent picks up the product and inspects it; 2 percent takes our product.

5. **Purchase transaction**—slightly less than 2 percent pays for our product; a few replace it on the shelf.

6. **Consumption**—most purchasers use the product within two weeks of purchase.

7. **Communication**—no indication of significant communication with other consumers; 60 percent of warranty cards are returned in three weeks.

Consumers use a BehaviorScan coded ID card when shopping in markets covered by the scanner network.

Consumer Behaviors	Elements			
	Product	Price	Promotion	Place
Information contact			X	
Funds access		X		
Store contact				X
Product contact	X			X
Purchase transaction	X	X	X	X
Consumption	X			
Communication	X	X	X	X

EXHIBIT 13.6

Primary relationships between consumer behaviors and marketing mix elements

What is the problem behavior in this example? Consumers' information contact, funds access, and store contact are all exceptionally good. Even some phases of product contact are good, but notice how new consumers actually take the product with them. There are a variety of potential ways to deal with any problem behavior in the sequence.

Analyze contingencies

Once the problem behavior is identified, the contingencies or relationships among the behavior and the environment can be analyzed. Among the major contingencies are the effects of competition in maintaining or changing consumer behavior. Many successful firms attempt to interfere with new product test marketing (or other marketing efforts) of their competitors to avoid losing market share and to confound competitors' research results. Other contingencies that require analysis are the nature of the target market and the marketing mix elements, particularly those elements most closely related to the problem behavior. Exhibit 13.6 suggests one way to link the major marketing mix elements with the stages of behaviors.

Analyzing contingencies is an important step because it represents a search for the reasons particular behaviors do not occur. Assessment of affective and cognitive variables as well as behavior environment interactions may also contribute valuable information. Many new products fail because consumers do not perceive a difference in the new product, so research on consumer perceptions and attitudes can be useful for investigating the problem and analyzing contingencies.

Where product contact is the problem behavior, analysis of the contingencies might begin with a comparison of our product and package with those of successful competitors. We could interview consumers to investigate their perceptions of and attitudes toward our product. We might directly investigate other contingencies, such as competitive differences in packaging, labeling, instructions for use, colors, and price.

Develop and apply behavior change strategy

Once the problem behavior is identified and the contingencies surrounding it have been analyzed, a **behavior change strategy** can be developed and applied. Such strategies might include any number of the processes we discussed earlier, such as positive reinforcement, negative reinforcement, shaping, classical conditioning, or modeling, among others. Positive reinforcement is generally recommended for encouraging behavior because it is both effective and flexible. Of course, as with any marketing strategy, the costs and benefits of various procedures must be carefully assessed.

Returning to the example, suppose the analysis of contingencies reveals an important difference between our product and those of successful competitors. Their packaging gives detailed assembly and use instructions, while our package instructions are more sketchy. We might decide to improve the instructions and add pictures of models assembling and using the product. We could also include a toll-free number consumers can call for additional information or help.

Measure behavior change

After implementation of the strategy we remeasure the target behavior to determine whether the problem has been solved. If the behavior has not changed sufficiently, we must reanalyze the contingencies and develop a new intervention strategy.

How much behavior has to change for the strategy to be successful depends on the marketing objectives, the particular behavior, and the situation. For example, if implementation of the strategy results in 3 percent (instead of 2 percent) of those who inspect the product actually purchasing it, this probably would not be considered a successful strategy. In fact, even this 50 percent increase might not cover the cost of the toll-free number. If the majority of those who inspect the product now purchase it, however, we might conclude we have successfully solved the behavior problem.

In some cases, a very small amount of behavior change may be sufficient for a strategy to be successful. For example, Procter & Gamble increased market share for Crest toothpaste from 35 percent to 41 percent by updating its formula, adding a gel version, and sharply increasing advertising and promotion. While a change in toothpaste market share of 6 percentage points may not sound impressive, it translates into additional sales of $42 million.

Maintain behavior

If a new strategy is successful in developing a sufficient amount of behavior, marketers must consider methods of maintaining that behavior. Because much consumer behavior is habitual, maintaining behavior is usually much easier and less expensive than developing it. In fact, one of the major reasons product introductions are so expensive is the promotional cost of developing the behavior. Once a behavior is developed, promotional costs usually can be decreased and behavior can be maintained much more cheaply. As an example, in the most successful cigarette introduction in history, Brown & Williamson gave away free cartons of cigarettes and spent an estimated $150 million to develop use of Barclay cigarettes. Once the company obtained an approximately 2 percent market share—and each share point is worth about $125 million to the manufacturer—it eliminated carton giveaways and reduced promotional spending, while maintaining much of the market share.

If positive reinforcers are used to develop a behavior, very often their frequency and amount can be decreased to maintain the behavior. If continuous schedules of reinforcement were initially employed, it may be possible to switch to ratio schedules and still maintain behavior. Discount coupons of lower value may also be effective; requiring multiunit purchases to receive the same discount may maintain certain behaviors. In fact, encouraging multiunit purchases may not only help develop brand loyalty but also increase use of the product, because additional quantities are then readily available at home.

Different organizations will be concerned with maintaining different behaviors in the purchase-consumption chain. Credit-card companies want to maintain card use or loyalty across a variety of purchase situations; retailers want to maintain store contact or store loyalty; manufacturers want to maintain product contact or brand loyalty. From a behavior viewpoint, these actions are controlled by contingencies in the environment, and loyalty is the degree to which the behaviors are repeated. Consumer Perspective 13.4 offers an example of a coffee chain's tactic to influence loyalty.

If a problem behavior is changed and then maintained, marketers also need to investigate whether the remaining behaviors are now being performed appropriately and frequently enough to achieve the objectives. If not, they identify the new target behavior that is blocking the behavior chain—the next one in the sequence that is not being performed appropriately—and then repeat the stages in the model. This process continues until all of the behaviors are being performed appropriately.

Gloria Jean's Gourmet Coffees uses a simple tactic to try to influence consumer store and brand loyalty. The Frequent Sippers Club gives consumers who purchase 25 cups of Gloria Jean's coffee a quarter pound of coffee. Gloria Jean's stores are located in large shopping malls, and consumers who frequent the mall may be influenced to buy a cup of coffee every time they shop. In fact, the behavior could become habitual. Employees at other stores in the mall who drink coffee regularly are likely to become members of the club because they buy several cups of coffee daily. This tactic may be one reason Gloria Jean's Gourmet Coffees is doing well even though the coffee market in general is stable or declining.

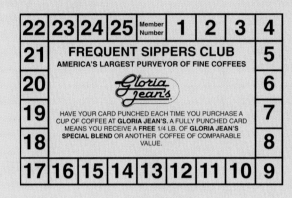

CONSUMER PERSPECTIVE

13.4

Developing loyalty to Gloria Jean's

No matter how successful a particular marketing strategy is, there is always room for improvement. In general, marketing strategies must be monitored continually for more efficient methods of maintaining behavior as well as encouraging it.

Any consumer behavior may decrease in frequency because of changes in the environment (such as more powerful or more frequent reinforcement by a competitor). Thus, while the model in Exhibit 13.5 provides a systematic way to focus directly on consumer behavior, it does not replace analyses such as careful monitoring and responding to competitive strategies. This is part of analyzing contingencies in an ongoing marketing program.

Learning objective 1: *Describe a sequence of overt consumer behaviors involved in a retail consumer-goods purchase, and explain the behaviors.*

▶ **SUMMARY**

A sequence of overt consumer behaviors includes information contact, funds access, store contact, product contact, purchase transaction, consumption, and communication.

Information contact occurs when consumers come into contact with products, stores, or brands. This stage includes behaviors such as reading or observing newspaper, magazine, and billboard ads, listening to radio commercials, watching TV commercials, and talking to salespeople and friends. Marketers encourage information contact, and, in many cases, consumers also search for information.

Funds access involves the consumer behaviors involved in obtaining money for a purchase. These include behaviors such as withdrawing cash from a bank or cash machine, writing a check, opening a store charge account, or using other types of credit.

Store contact concerns the behaviors involved in coming into physical contact with a store. It includes locating, traveling to, and entering the store.

Product contact concerns the behaviors involved in coming into physical contact with products and brands. It includes locating a product in a store, obtaining it, and taking it to the point of exchange.

Purchase transaction refers to the exchange of consumer funds for products and services. It involves behaviors such as handing over payment, receiving change, and taking the product to where it will be used.

Consumption refers to consuming or using a product. It includes disposing of packaging or the used product itself and repurchase.

Communication includes behaviors in which consumers tell others about the product and their experiences with it. It includes communicating both with other consumers and with marketers through such means as warranty cards.

Learning objective 2: *Suggest several tactics marketers could use to influence each of these behaviors.*

Marketers could influence information contact by selecting and scheduling media consistent with the media habits of the target market. Attention-getting advertising features, such as color, humor, and fear appeals, can also be used. Repetition of messages influences the probability of information contact.

Marketers could influence funds access by offering gifts to consumers who fill out credit-card applications, locating cash machines in malls, instituting liberal credit terms and check-cashing policies, and accepting a variety of credit cards.

Marketers could influence store contact by selecting convenient locations in high-traffic areas, using ads with maps and information telephone numbers to aid shoppers, using outdoor signs and logos, featuring carnivals and other entertainment close to the store or mall, offering sales, and using window signs, displays, and other stimuli to attract consumers to enter a store.

Marketers could influence product contact by providing store directories and information booths, using displays and signs, and hiring helpful store personnel. Attractive eye-catching packaging and the presence of salesclerks who escort consumers to product and exchange locations can also influence product contact.

Marketers could influence purchase transactions by having express checkout lanes, fast electronic scanners, and quick credit-card approvals. Prompts and reinforcers such as rebates can also influence purchase transactions.

Marketers could influence consumption by tactics such as providing seats in fast-food restaurants that are comfortable for only short periods and using prompts to encourage disposal of packaging. Repurchase of the same product or brand can be influenced by in- or on-package coupons and offers for bonus merchandise that require multiple purchases.

Marketers could influence communication by offering gifts for returning warranty cards and offering money-back guarantees. Free merchandise or discounts can also be used to reinforce consumers who bring friends to new retail outlets or give their friends' names to sellers of new services.

Learning objective 3: *Explain a model marketers could use to influence a sequence of consumer behaviors.*

The first thing marketers need to do is to identify the problem or target behavior. This is the earliest behavior in a sequence that is not being performed appropriately or frequently enough to lead to the next behavior. The next step is to analyze the contingencies or relationships between the behavior and the environment. Here marketers are looking for things in the environment that both encourage and discourage the behavior. Next marketers can develop and apply a behavior change strategy. This strategy is intended to encourage the target behavior directly or overcome any barrier found in the previous stage that was discouraging it. The amount of behavior change resulting is now measured. If the strategy results in sufficient behavior change, additional strategies can be employed to maintain the behavior. If the strategy fails, the contingencies have to be reanalyzed to find the problem.

Information contact   purchase transactions   scanner cable method
funds access   consumption   target behavior
store contact   communication   behavior change strategy
product contact

1. Describe the differences between traditional cognitive models of the adoption process and the behavior sequence presented in Exhibit 13.1.

2. What advantages do you see in the use of the behavior sequence model for marketing researchers and for marketing managers?

3. Use the behavior sequence model to describe your recent purchases of a product and of a service.

4. Consider the challenge presented by the information contact stage of the behavior sequence for each of the following: (*a*) a leading brand, (*b*) a new brand, and (*c*) an existing low-share brand.

5. Give some examples of marketing strategies aimed at addressing the funds access problems of college seniors.

6. Visit several local supermarkets, and identify strategies used to increase product contact for grocery items.

7. List at least three examples of situations where marketing efforts have been instrumental in changing your consumption or disposal behavior for products you have purchased.

8. Assume the role of a marketing manager for each of the purchases you described in response to Question 3. Which behaviors would you want to change? Using the model in Exhibit 13.5, suggest behavior change strategies you might recommend.

9. Use the model for managing consumer behavior to suggest strategies for decreasing the frequency of post-holiday merchandise returns to a department store.

10. How would the concept of shaping relate to use of the consumer behavior management model?

CASES IN CONSUMER BEHAVIOR

Leslie Wells's recent expedition to the new Cub Foods store in Melrose Park, Illinois, was no ordinary trip to the grocery store. "You go crazy," says Wells, sounding a little shell-shocked. Overwhelmed by Cub's vast selection, tables of samples, and discounts as high as 30 percent, Wells spent $76 on groceries—$36 more than she planned. Wells fell prey to what a Cub executive calls "the wow factor"—a shopping frenzy brought on by low prices and clever marketing. That's the reaction Cub's super warehouse stores strive for—and often get.

Cub Foods has been a leader in shaking up the food industry and forcing many conventional supermarkets to reduce prices, increase services, or—in some cases—go out of business. With Cub and other super warehouse stores springing up across the country, shopping habits are changing, too. Some shoppers drive 50 miles or more to a Cub store instead of going to the nearest neighborhood supermarket, and they bag their own groceries at Cub Foods. Their payoff is that they find almost everything they need under one roof, and most of it is cheaper than at competing supermarkets. Cub's low prices, smart marketing, and sheer size encourage shoppers to spend far more than they do in the average supermarket.

The difference between Cub and most supermarkets is obvious the minute a shopper walks through Cub's doors. The entry aisle, called "power alley" by some, is lined two stories high with specials, such as bean coffee at $2 a pound and half-price apple juice. Above, the ceiling joists and girders are exposed, giving "the subliminal feeling of all the spaciousness up there. It suggests there's massive buying going on that translates in a shopper's mind that there's tremendous savings going on as well," says Paul Suneson, director of marketing research for Cub's parent, Super Valu Stores Inc., the nation's largest food wholesaler.

Cub's wider-than-usual shopping carts, which are supposed to promote expansive buying, fit easily through Cub's wide aisles, which channel shoppers toward high-profit impulse foods. The whole store exudes a seductive, horn-of-plenty feeling. Cub customers typically buy in volume and spend $40 to $50 a trip, four times the supermarket average. The average Cub store has sales of $800,000 to $1 million a week, quadruple the volume of conventional stores.

Cub Foods has a simple approach to grocery retailing: low prices, made possible by rigidly controlled costs and high-volume sales; exceptionally high quality for produce and meats—the items people build shopping trips around; and immense variety. It's all packaged in clean stores that are twice as big as most warehouse outlets and four times as big as most supermarkets. A Cub store stocks as many as 25,000 items, double the selection of conventional stores, mixing staples with luxury, ethnic, and hard-to-find foods. This leads to overwhelming displays—88 kinds of hot dogs and dinner sausages, 12 brands of Mexican food, and fresh meats and produce by the ton.

The store distributes maps to guide shoppers. But without a map or a specific destination, a shopper is guided inevitably by the arrangement of the aisles. The power alley spills into the produce department. From there the aisles lead to highly profitable perimeter departments—meat, fish, bakery, and frozen foods. The deli comes before fresh meat, because Cub wants shoppers to do their impulse buying before they buy the essentials on their lists.

Overall, Cub's gross margin—the difference between what it pays for its goods and what it sells them for—is 14 percent, six to eight points less than most conventional stores. And because Cub relies mostly on word-of-mouth advertising, its ad budgets are 25 percent lower than those of other chains.

Discussion questions

1. List at least five marketing tactics Cub Foods employs in its stores to increase the probability of purchase.

2. What accounts for Cub's success in generating such large sales per customer and per store?

3. Given Cub's lower prices, quality merchandise, excellent location, and superior assortment, what reasons can you offer for why many consumers in its trading areas refuse to shop there?

Source: Excerpted from Steve Weiner and Betsy Morris, "Bigger, Shrewder, and Cheaper Cub Leads Food Stores into the Future," *The Wall Street Journal,* August 26, 1985, p. 17; also see Michael Garry, "Cub Embraces Non-Foods," *Progressive Grocer,* December 1991, pp. 45–48.

▶ **CASE III.2**

Tupperware

In 1958, Justin Dart purchased Tupperware from former Du Pont chemist Earl Tupper for $10 million. From that time until 1980, Tupperware earned an estimated $1.5 billion pretax and had a phenomenal 25-year record of doubling sales and earnings every 5 years. Then in 1983, Tupperware sales slipped 7 percent and operating profits sank 15 percent. In 1992, sales for the second quarter fell 33 percent from the same period a year before. That quarter also saw a 20 percent decline in the number of active U.S. dealers. As shown in the exhibit, changes in families and households contributed to the loss of business.

Traditionally, Tupperware plastic products were sold at in-home parties. Today these parties are held not only in homes but also in offices and other locations convenient for

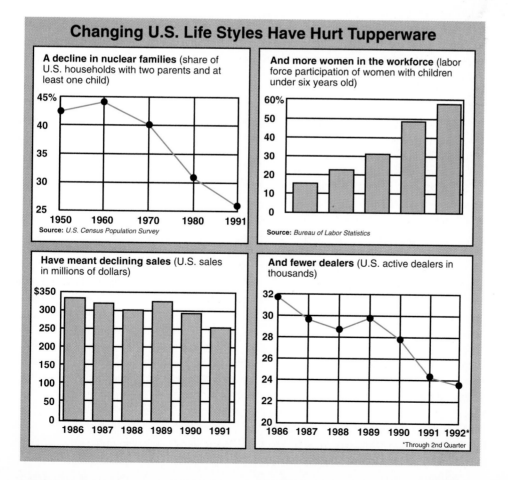

Changing U.S. Life Styles Have Hurt Tupperware

A decline in nuclear families (share of U.S. households with two parents and at least one child)

Source: *U.S. Census Population Survey*

And more women in the workforce (labor force participation of women with children under six years old)

Source: *Bureau of Labor Statistics*

Have meant declining sales (U.S. sales in millions of dollars)

And fewer dealers (U.S. active dealers in thousands)

*Through 2nd Quarter

working people. Tupperware parties consist of a part-time salesperson inviting friends and acquaintances to the location and displaying the many varieties of plastic products. The parties typically include refreshments, a free sample of Tupperware, casual conversation, games in which participants can win pieces of Tupperware, and formal offering of Tupperware products. Customers order at the party and pay for the products on delivery by the salesperson.

To try to curb the decline, Tupperware offered a variety of new products. These included Modular Mates, which defend against cabinet clutter, TupperWave, which microwaves an entire dinner in 30 minutes, and the Earth Pack, a set of containers in a washable green lunch bag.

Tupperware sales are hindered because most women (55 percent by Tupperware's estimate) either have no idea how to find Tupperware or no desire to go to a Tupperware party. Some 40 percent of Tupperware's sales are from people who skip the parties but send orders along with friends who attend.

Tupperware's major competitor, Rubbermaid, reaches consumers by selling in discount stores and supermarkets. Its market share has risen to between 30 and 40 percent of units sold from about 5 to 10 percent in 1984. Tupperware's share has slipped to between 40 and 45 percent from 59 percent of the food-storage container market, according to industry estimates.

Tupperware still isn't considering moving into retail stores, however. Allan R. Nagle, president of Tupperware, said, "To wipe away our existing distribution and replace it would be a pretty traumatic exercise. I don't see a beneficial trade-off."

The company has experimented with a catalog and used television advertising to recruit new dealers. However, the company is hoping the 1990s will see the resurgence of the Tupperware party, which, Nagle predicts, "will become more in vogue than in the 80s because of the greater propensity of women and families to spend more time at home."

Discussion questions

1. Although Tupperware clearly is having problems, it still has between 40 and 45 percent of the food-storage container market. Why do you think Tupperware parties are so effective for selling this merchandise?

2. Considering operant conditioning concepts such as positive reinforcement, variable ratio schedules, and shaping, offer at least five recommendations for Tupperware salespeople to sell products to consumers at a party.

3. What opportunities are there for Tupperware to curb the decline and increase its sales and profits?

Source: Laurie M. Grossman, "Families Have Changed but Tupperware Keeps Holding Its Parties," *The Wall Street Journal*, July 21, 1992, p. A1, A13; and Kerry Hannon, "Party Animal," *Forbes*, November 16, 1987, pp. 262–68.

▶ CASE III.3

Rollerblade Inc.

Rollerblade Inc. introduced its first in-line roller skate in 1980. The company's founder, Scott Olson, was a hockey player with the Winnipeg Jets' farm teams, who envisioned a roller skate with the action of an ice skate, which hockey players and skiers could use to train during the off-season. At first, the plan was to use modern materials to construct a model based on an 18th century design, but Olson discovered a similar in-line skate already on the market and purchased the patent from the Chicago Roller Skate Company. Olson and his brother, Brennan, perfected the design using a plastic molded ski-type boot atop a blade of polyurethane wheels. Their first sales were to Olson's teammates and to a few sporting goods stores. Thus began the sport of blading.

Although they generally cost twice as much as conventional roller skates, in-line skates, which range in price from $79 for regular models to $399 for a racing skate, are purchased for two reasons. First, they are faster and therefore more exciting to use than conventional skates. Second, they require the use of more muscles, providing skaters with a better aerobic workout. It is more difficult to learn how to use in-line skates, however, because they require better balance, and at faster speeds, falls may cause more, and more severe, injuries.

By 1986, wholesale sales of in-line skates had risen to $3.5 million. Recognizing an opportunity to get in on a growing market, a number of companies began producing competitive products in the next several years. First Team Sports Inc., also based in Minneapolis, started manufacturing its Ultra-wheels brand skates, which included the first in-line skates for children. The Roller Derby Skate Corporation in Litchfield, Illinois, a manufacturer of standard roller skates since 1936, produced an in-line skate with a toe-stopper for those accustomed to conventional skates; Rollerblades had a rubber stopper located on the heel. The ice skate manufacturer Bauer entered the market with a skate that has a leather rather than a plastic boot.

Rollerblade Inc.'s sales increased when it expanded its target market. At first, the product was targeted to hockey players, who were 95 percent male and 18 to 25 years old. By broadening the target to include 18-to-35-year-old males and females, sales grew considerably.

By 1990, industry wholesale sales of in-line roller skates were over $50 million, almost as big as the conventional roller skate business. Rollerblade Inc. maintained a 66 percent market share; First Team Sports had a 22 percent share; Bauer had a 5 percent share; Roller Derby had a 3 percent share; other competitors combined shared the remaining 4 percent. Rollerblade likely could have done even better, but it could not fill store orders for several months because it ran out of inventory early in the year.

The fierce industry competition was not limited to product features but included other marketing mix elements as well. Companies rushed to sign celebrities to promote their products. For example, First Team Sports signed Wayne Gretzky, the Los Angeles Kings hockey star, and his wife, Janet Jones Gretzky, to promote its skates. Competitors also moved into new retail markets including discount and department stores. Rollerblade expanded its market by selling to Macy's and Nordstrom.

While the name Rollerblade may become a generic term for this type of skate, the management of the company will have to work hard to maintain its lead in this market. "We have been pioneers and continue to maintain an edge," said a company spokesperson. "You only get one shot at pioneering a new sport, and that's exciting."

Discussion questions

1. What role do you think modeling could have played in the diffusion of this innovation?

2. How could you use live, covert, and verbal modeling to teach a friend how to use Rollerblades?

3. What factors make Wayne and Janet Jones Gretzky good models for Rollerblade's competitor?

4. If you were designing a commercial for Rollerblade to be used for an in-store videotape demonstration, how would you design the commercial to take advantage of your knowledge of modeling?

Source: Based on "Innovator Tries to Protect Its Lead," *New York Times,* August 7, 1990, pp. C1, C6; and Lois Therrian, "Rollerblade Is Skating in Heavier Traffic," *Business Week,* June 24, 1991, pp. 115–16.

Delta Air Lines

In 1982, a market survey revealed that few travelers called Delta Air Lines as their first choice because Delta had acquired a reputation for being high priced in the new deregulated environment. Following this survey, Delta introduced a promotion offering to match any competitor's fare on any of its more than 5,000 routes. Although Delta was successful in attracting passengers, the number of them paying full fare dropped to 8 percent of all seats sold, creating Delta's first annual deficit in 47 years of business. Through 1986, Delta passenger traffic rose only slightly while other airlines made steady inroads into the South, Delta's main market.

However, Delta got moving again in 1986. It acquired Western Air Lines Inc. for $860 million, making it one of the six megacarriers offering service throughout the United States. It also doubled its spending on new planes and facilities to some $1.2 billion annually. By fiscal year 1988, its operating earnings jumped 24 percent to about $500 million on sales of $6.7 billion.

Much of the turnabout for Delta has been the result of savvy marketing. For example, previously Delta was naive about pricing its services. In 1983, when a competitor offered 50 percent discounts on fares to New York, Delta responded with similar cuts. Its competitor, however, was offering these discounts only to passengers who stopped at another city first, while Delta was giving away even nonstop seats at the overly aggressive price. Predictably, Delta lost a great deal of money at that price. Now, Delta is handling its marketing much more carefully, and its revenues are growing. For example, in 1988, it took the offensive by offering frequent flyers a triple-mileage award program in conjunction with American Express. This program captured an additional 250,000 regular business flyers.

As growth in the industry is in the international market, Delta expanded its international operations to compete with larger airlines such as American and United. In 1991, it achieved over $1 billion in overseas revenue but still lagged behind the market leaders. Its profit margin is above these other airlines, however, and its friendly service has developed loyalty among its passengers. Its chairman states, "Our plans are unfolding as we choose to unfold them. We're not striving to be the biggest in the world, just the most profitable."

Discussion questions

1. Develop and describe a sequence of behaviors for purchasing and using airline services. How does this sequence differ from a retail purchase of a product?

2. What are some marketing tactics Delta could use to increase the probability of each of the behaviors you have identified?

Source: Based on Margaret L. Friedman, "Delta Air Lines," in *Marketing Management: Knowledge and Skills,* 3rd ed., J. Paul Peter and James H. Donnelly, Jr. (Homewood, Ill.: Richard D. Irwin, 1992), pp. 572–575; "Why the Folks at Delta Are Walking on Air," *Business Week,* August 1, 1988, pp. 92–93; and Chuck Hawkins et al., "If Delta's Going to Make a Move, 'It's Now or Never,' " *Business Week,* June 3, 1991, pp. 94–98.

THE ENVIRONMENT

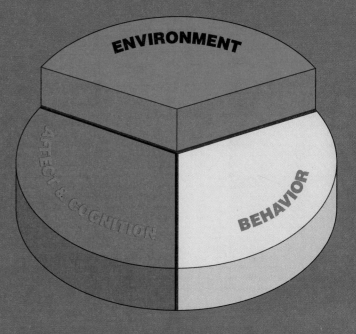

14

Introduction to the Environment

LEARNING OBJECTIVES

After completing this chapter, you should be able to:

► 1. Define the environment and describe the difference between the macro- and microenvironment.

► 2. Define the social environment, identify the types of macro and micro social environments, and describe the flow of influence between the macro- and microenvironments.

► 3. Define the physical environment, and give an example of how the physical environment can influence consumer behavior.

► 4. Give two examples of how a marketing strategy can modify the environment and influence consumer behavior.

► 5. Define a situation, and describe the factors to be examined in a situation analysis.

► 6. Describe the five common consumer situations, and identify behaviors that are important in each situation.

CAESARS LURES ATLANTIC CITY GAMBLERS

A glimpse of the majestic marble lobby with its Roman statues will lure gamblers off Atlantic City's boardwalk and funnel them through carefully placed lights and open space into the casino. Once there, they'll end up enjoying the experience, win or lose. At least that's what interior designer Bob DiLeonardo said would happen when he redesigned Caesars Boardwalk Regency, a 509-room hotel-casino with an art deco decor.

DiLeonardo, who owns the 21-employee DiLeonardo's Interiors Inc. in Cranston, Rhode Island, said his mission at Caesars was "to create an environment that impresses people yet makes them feel comfortable." Achieving this is so complex, however, that he enlisted the aid of an "environmental psychologist"—a relatively new breed of psychologist who studies the impact of the environment on behavior. (They're the ones who put uncomfortable seats in fast-food restaurants to cut down on lingering.)

The consultant and DiLeonardo made several changes in the Caesars environment. Lobby windows, for instance, were replaced by sheets of creamy Italian marble so that "people won't be able to relate to time. Once they step inside, they'll be in an adult Disneyland."

DiLeonardo used materials that "enhance" noise for the casino because "noise creates excitement." Lighting for the blackjack tables extended far enough to envelop the player, but not far enough to include spectators, who "may interrupt (the player's) sense of security."

The high rollers who get complimentary suites experienced the flip side of environmental psychology. DiLeonardo designed their suites in bold contrasting colors with lighting so bright and with noise enhanced to such high levels that the experience represented an escape for the occupants.[1]

THE ENVIRONMENT

The **environment** refers to all the physical and social characteristics of a consumer's external world, including physical objects (products and stores), spatial relationships (location of products and stores in space), and the social behavior of other people (who is around and what are they doing?). As one part of the Wheel of Consumer Analysis (see Exhibit 14.1), the environment can influence a consumer's affective and cognitive responses and behavior. A consumer's cognitive and affective systems will respond to the environment of a new supermarket by interpreting features of this environment and deciding what behaviors to perform to accomplish the shopping goals.

Marketers are especially interested in the *perceived or interpreted environment*, sometimes called the functional environment, because this is what influences consumers' behaviors.[2] Because each consumer draws on a unique set of knowledge, meanings, and beliefs in interpreting any environment, the perceived or functional environment for each consumer will be somewhat different. However, consumers within a society or culture will perceive many parts of the physical and social environment similarly. For example, large groups of American consumers probably have similar perceptions of shopping malls (or credit cards or fast-food restaurants) and therefore use them in similar ways. Marketers need to understand the interpretations of the environment shared by groups of consumers; they are seldom interested in the idiosyncratic perceptions of individual consumers. Fortunately, marketers can usually identify enough consumers who share common interpretations to form a target market segment.

The environment can be analyzed at two levels—macro and micro. Marketers need to determine which level of environment analysis is relevant for a marketing problem and design their research and marketing strategies appropriately. The *macroenvironment* includes large-scale, general environmental factors such as the climate, economic conditions, political system, and general landscape (seashore, mountains, prairie). Macroenvironmental factors have a general influence on behavior as when the state of the economy influences aggregate purchases of homes, automobiles, and stocks. Consumer Perspective 14.1 describes how changes in the macroenvironment can create a marketing opportunity.

The *microenvironment* refers to the more tangible physical and social aspects of someone's immediate surroundings—the dirty floor in a store, a talkative salesperson, the hot weather today, or the people in your family or household. Such small-scale factors can have a direct influence on consumers' specific behaviors and affective and cognitive responses. For instance, people tend not to linger in dirty, crowded stores; consumers might wait until

---

EXHIBIT 14.1

The Wheel of Consumer Analysis

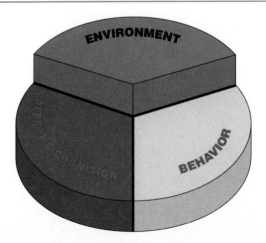

CONSUMER
PERSPECTIVE

Changes in macro-
environment
create market
opportunities

Until the specter of AIDS raised its deadly shadow, the market for condoms in the United States was slack. But in the mid-1980s, the product received an extraordinary amount of free publicity. The surgeon general and the National Academy of Sciences endorsed it. On the news, in classrooms, and in lectures, people were bluntly urged to use condoms. Around college campuses, lighthearted promotions made condoms a more respectable product. Another aspect of the information environment was the increasing negative publicity about other forms of birth control, including birth control pills and IUDs.

This era also marked major changes in the shopping and purchase environments. In years past, one had to buy condoms from behind pharmacy counters or from vending machines that were usually placed in men's rooms. Now most drugstores and supermarkets display the products openly. Women now account for about 50 percent of condom purchases, and many manufacturers have developed promotional campaigns aimed at this large segment.

Before, people seldom talked about such things in public, and most manufacturers never promoted condoms vigorously. Once the only magazines to accept condom ads were the so-called skin magazines, but now many magazines carry the ads. Although condom ads had not appeared on U.S. TV, by 1986 consumers in more sexually open countries like Sweden, Finland, and Denmark had seen TV advertising for condoms.

What were the ramifications of these dramatic environmental changes? In the freewheeling 1970s, few Americans wanted anything to do with condoms, and total sales had shrunk by one half to about $150 million. In 1986, sales grew by 10 percent, and the increase has continued.

Source: Reprinted with permission from "The Rubber Barons," by Colin Leinster, *Fortune*, © 1986 Time Inc. All rights reserved.

evening to go shopping during a heat wave; you get frustrated and angry in a slow-moving checkout line when you want to get home to prepare dinner. Consumer Perspective 14.2 gives an example of how the microenvironment can influence consumers' behavior.

ASPECTS OF THE ENVIRONMENT

The environment has two aspects or dimensions—the social and physical environment. Marketing managers have direct control over some aspects of the social and physical environment, which they form into marketing strategies. But managers have little or no control over large parts of the social and physical environment. Both the controllable and uncontrollable aspects of the social and physical environment can influence consumers' overt behaviors as well as their affective and cognitive responses.

The social environment

Broadly defined, the **social environment** includes all social interactions between and among people. Consumers can interact with other people either directly (you might discuss sports equipment or clothes with a friend, you talk to a salesperson) or vicariously (you watch your father negotiate a car price, you observe the clothing other people are wearing). People can learn from both types of social interactions, direct and vicarious.

It is useful to distinguish between macro and micro levels of the social environment. The *macro social environment* refers to the indirect and vicarious social interactions among very large groups of people. Researchers have studied three macro social environments—culture, subculture, and social class—that have broad and powerful influences on the values, beliefs, attitudes, emotions, and behaviors of individual consumers in those groups. For instance, a marketer might find that consumers in different subcultures or social

CONSUMER
PERSPECTIVE

► 14.2

The
window-shopping
environment

One of the oldest marketing strategies is still one of the most effective. Window displays can have very strong influences on purchasing behavior.

These environmental effects can be clearly seen at the Saks Fifth Avenue store in Manhattan. Saks has 310 feet of prime store frontage along 49th and 50th streets and the famed Fifth Avenue. Each day at lunchtime, more than 3,000 pedestrians walk by the 31 window displays that Saks changes weekly. These microenvironments attract attention. At Christmastime, the elaborately decorated windows draw crowds five people deep.

The displays in these special information and shopping environments can have incredible impacts on sales. One dramatic display was credited with selling armloads of heavy velvet and wool fashions for fall in the middle of a July heat wave. Or consider this example: one year the head of Saks' gift division was worried that a forthcoming move from the ground floor to the ninth floor would seriously reduce sales of her crystal and linen merchandise. Saks estimated that sales might drop as much as 15 percent. But an eyecatching window on Fifth Avenue during the first week of the move upstairs produced a 20 percent increase in sales.

Source: Lisa Gubernick, "Through a Glass, Brightly," Reprinted by permission of *Forbes* magazine, August 11, 1986, © Forbes Inc., 1986.

classes have quite different means-end chains concerning a product, which means they are likely to respond differently to marketing strategies. Such differences make macro social environments useful for market segmentation.

The *micro social environment* includes face-to-face social interactions among smaller groups of people such as families and reference groups. These direct social interactions can have strong influences on consumers' knowledge and feelings about products, stores, or ads and on their consumption behavior. For instance, most people learn acceptable and appropriate behaviors and acquire many of their values, beliefs, and attitudes through direct social interaction with their families and reference groups. The influence of families,

This Japanese family
constitutes a micro social
environment for each person
in the family.

moreover, can continue for years as some adult consumers purchase the same brands, patronize the same stores, and shop in the same way their parents once did.

Families and reference groups are influenced by the macro social environments of culture, subcultures, and social class. Exhibit 14.2 illustrates the flow of influence from the macro social environments of culture, subculture, and social class to the micro social environments of reference groups and family and then on to the individual consumer (and the reverse influence too). We discuss these social influences at length in Chapters 15, 16, and 17.

The hierarchical relationships portrayed in Exhibit 14.2 can help us understand how various levels of the social environment influence consumers. For instance, consumers in different subcultures may have the same cultural value but reflect it in different ways, just as consumers in different social classes may attempt to satisfy a subcultural value in different ways. Consider how people can satisfy the common American value of achievement. A person living in a rural subculture might fulfill this value by going to agriculture school, earning a degree, and becoming an excellent farmer. In an urban subculture, a person with the same achievement value might go to law school after college, earn a degree, and become a successful attorney. Similarly, the social class of an individual can influence the college decision (a local community college, a large state school, or an internationally famous university). In turn, these macro social influences are "filtered" by a person's family situation (parents' expectations and financial support) and reference groups (where one's friends are going to college). In sum, while many individuals may share the same cultural values, their methods of achieving these values may differ considerably, depending on their macro and micro social environments. This means people in different social environments use different means to reach the same ends.

Exhibit 14.2 also identifies other social entities involved in transferring meanings, values, and behavior norms from the macro social environment to individual consumers. These include media such as TV programs, newspapers, and magazines, movies, literature, and music, as well as other organizations such as religious and educational institutions, police and the courts, and government. Organizations also include business firms that develop marketing strategies to influence individual customers.

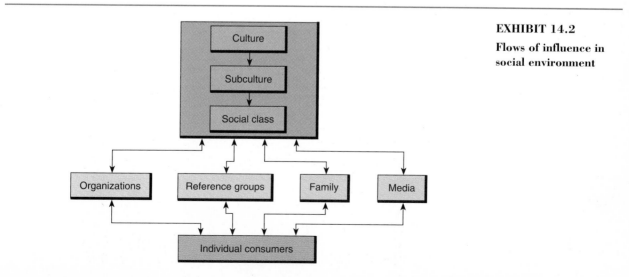

EXHIBIT 14.2

Flows of influence in social environment

Visine reminds consumers of aspects of the physical environment that make the product self-relevant.

Certain products such as iced tea sell best in summertime when the weather is hot.

The physical environment

The **physical environment** includes all the nonhuman, physical aspects of the external world in which behavior occurs. Virtually any aspect of the physical environment can affect consumer behavior. The physical environment can be divided into spatial and nonspatial elements. Spatial elements include physical factors of all types (including products and brands) as well as landscapes, cities, stores, and design elements of the environment. Nonspatial elements include intangible factors such as climate (cold/hot, humid/dry), illumination, noise level, and time. Here we discuss four factors in the nonspatial environment—time, weather, lighting, and color.

Time

Time has a great effect on consumer behavior.[3] For instance, behavior can be influenced by the time of day (stores tend to be more crowded during lunch hour), the day of the week (Mondays often are slow days for restaurants), the day of the month (sales may drop off just before the end of the month and pick up again after the first), and the season of the year (in the pre-Christmas holiday season, people's shopping behaviors are quite different from other times of the year).

In another example of the effect of time, several years ago the Daylight Saving Time Coalition petitioned Congress to increase the period of daylight-saving time by seven weeks per year.[4] Advocates of this change included the management of 7-Eleven convenience stores, who believed that more women would stop at its stores on the way home from work if it were still daylight. The company estimated that this extra daylight would increase sales by $30 million. Another advocate of this change was the Barbeque Industry Association. Reasoning that people would cook out more if it were light during the dinner hour, the trade

The year 1988 will long be remembered in the United States for the searing summer heat that spread over nearly the entire country, accompanied in many places by a prolonged drought. Although the weather wreaked havoc on many of the nation's farmers, it was a blessing for some companies. Sales of products such as water-related toys, fresh cold foods like lettuce and fresh fruit, and bottled water were way up. The Crocodile Mile, a 25-foot plastic water slide that can be used in the backyard, was one of the five hottest selling toys of the year. Production was completely sold out by July. As another example, in a single week during the peak of the hot weather, demand for water sprinklers to soak parched yards (and cool off hot kids) exceeded sales for the previous 12 months combined.

Sales of central air conditioning hit new monthly records for nearly every month in 1988. But consider the market for room air conditioners, which traditionally is even more sensitive to changes in the weather—just a couple of hot days in summer can send people flooding into stores to buy window units, while a few chilly days in summer can cool down demand just as quickly. Room air conditioner sales jumped by 28 percent in June 1988 alone.

What other behaviors are affected by hot weather? Well, people tend to cook less at home when it gets really hot. But they don't flock to full-service restaurants because they don't want to get dressed up, either. Instead, they tend to eat things at home that don't require cooking, pushing up sales of fresh fruits and vegetables (for salads). And so it goes, demonstrating that the physical environment can have very large influences on consumers' purchasing and consumption behaviors.

Source: Reprinted from Ted Knutson, "Sales of Some Products Thrive Due to Heat Wave," *Marketing News* 22, no. 19 (September 12, 1988), pp. 2, 12. Published by the American Marketing Association.

association estimated an increase in sales of charcoal briquettes of 15 percent ($56 million) and increases in sales of starter fluid of 13 percent ($15 million). It is also estimated that golfers would play 4 million more rounds and buy an additional $7 million worth of clubs and balls, and tennis buffs could get in 9.8 million more hours of outdoor play and spend another $7 million on equipment. Thus, what might seem to be a minor change in time could have considerable impact on consumer behavior.

Weather

Many firms have recognized that weather influences consumer behavior.[5] Obviously, ear muffs, gloves, and heavy coats are winter products, and most suntan lotion, air conditioners, and bathing suits are sold during the summer. Some firms pay even daily attention to the weather. For example, Campbell's Soup Company bases some of its spot radio advertising on weather reports. Whenever a storm is forecast, Campbell's ads urge listeners to stock up on soup before the weather worsens; after the storm hits, the ad copy changes to tell people to relax indoors and warm themselves with soup. While research on the relationships between weather and consumer behavior is in its early stages, the weather certainly is an important influence on affect (such as moods), cognitions, and purchase behavior. Consumer Perspective 14.3 presents some examples.

Lighting

There is considerable evidence that lighting affects behavior. In general, it has been found that people work better in brighter rooms, although they find direct overhead lighting unpleasant. In business meetings, people who intend to make themselves heard sit under or near lights, while those who intend to be quiet often sit in darker areas. Intimate candlelight may draw people together; bright floodlights can cause people to hurry past a location. Overall, lighting may affect the way people work and interact with others, their comfort, and even their mental and physical health.

While it seems likely that lighting could affect consumers' moods, anxiety levels, willingness to shop, and purchase behavior, little research directly addresses this topic, although one discussion of lighting in retail stores and malls suggests that specialized lighting systems can increase sales dramatically. Pillowtex Corporation used tiny spotlights attached to glass shelves, rather than overhead lighting, for illumination in its Dallas World Trade Center showroom. The corporation attributed one third of its then $3 million-plus annual sales to this lighting approach.[6]

Color

Color has been shown to have a variety of physical and psychological effects on both humans and animals. A study of the effects of color on consumer perceptions of retail store environment found that while consumers were drawn to warm colors (red and yellow), they felt that warm-color environments were generally unpleasant; cool colors (blue and green) did not draw consumers, but were rated as pleasant.[7] The authors offer these implications of their work for store design:

> Warm-color environments are appropriate for store windows and entrances, as well as for buying situations associated with unplanned impulse purchases. Cool colors may be appropriate where customer deliberations over the purchase decision are necessary. Warm, tense colors in situations where deliberations are common may make shopping unpleasant for consumers and may result in premature termination of the shopping trip. On the other hand, warm colors may produce a quick decision to purchase in cases where lengthy deliberations are not necessary and impulse purchases are common.

Marketing implications

Although much of the environment is uncontrollable by marketing managers, marketers can control certain aspects of the environment. In fact, every marketing strategy created by a marketing manager involves changing some aspect of the social and physical environment. In this sense, marketers can be seen as environmental managers.[8] A marketing strategy alters the social and physical environment in an attempt to influence consumers' affective and cognitive responses and their behaviors. For example, aspects of the physical environment are changed by promotion strategies (a magazine ad, a billboard along the highway), product strategies (a new squeeze bottle for Crest toothpaste, a styling change in the Ford Escort), pricing strategies (a "sale" sign in a window, a price tag on a sweater), and distribution strategies (the location of a Burger King, a product display in a store). Consumer Perspective 14.2 describes how changing a window display, a simple aspect of the physical environment, can influence consumers. Marketing managers may also create marketing strategies that modify aspects of the social environment. For instance, Lexus trains its car salespeople to be less aggressive and less pushy than traditional car salespeople. A health club encourages its members to invite a friend for a free workout. Wal-Mart stations a greeter at the store entrance to smile and welcome customers.

Most environments contain an endless variety of stimuli that could influence consumer affect, cognition, and behavior. For instance, retail stores include social factors such as salespeople and other shoppers, along with physical factors such as store layout, lighting, noise, scents, temperature, shelf space and displays, signs, and the merchandise. We discuss how four of these characteristics—store layout, signs and price information, shelf space and displays, and music—can influence consumers.

Store layout

Store layout can influence how long the consumer stays in the store, how many products the consumer comes into visual contact with, and what routes the consumer travels within the store. These behaviors in turn may affect the products bought and the number of purchases made. Two basic types of store layouts are grid and free-flow.

Exhibit 14.3a presents an example of a *grid layout* common in many grocery and drug stores.[9] Most counters and fixtures are at right angles to each other which create structured channels, with merchandise counters acting as barriers to and guides for traffic flow.

A supermarket grid layout is designed to increase the number of products a consumer comes into visual contact with, thus increasing the probability of purchase. Because produce, meat, and dairy products are typically high-margin items, the grid design is intended to channel consumers toward these more profitable products. In fact, 80 to 90 percent of all consumers shopping in supermarkets pass these three areas. Similarly, the location of frequently purchased items toward the back of the store requires consumers who may be shopping only for these items to pass by many other items. Because the probability of purchasing other items is increased once the consumer comes in visual contact with them, the grid layout can be effective in increasing the number of items purchased.

The grid layout is used in department stores, mass merchandisers, and discount stores to direct customer traffic down the main aisles. Typically, these retailers put highly sought merchandise along the walls to pull customers past slower-moving merchandise. For example, sale merchandise may be placed along the walls not only to draw consumers to these areas, but also to reward consumers for spending more time in the store and shopping carefully. This may increase the probability of consumers returning to the store and following similar traffic patterns on repeat visits.

Exhibit 14.3b also shows a *free-flow layout.* Here, the merchandise and fixtures are grouped into clusters that allow a free flow of customer traffic. Merchandise is identified by fixtures and signs, and customers can see other departments from any place in the

Signs are part of the in-store environment.

EXHIBIT 14.3a

Basic store layouts

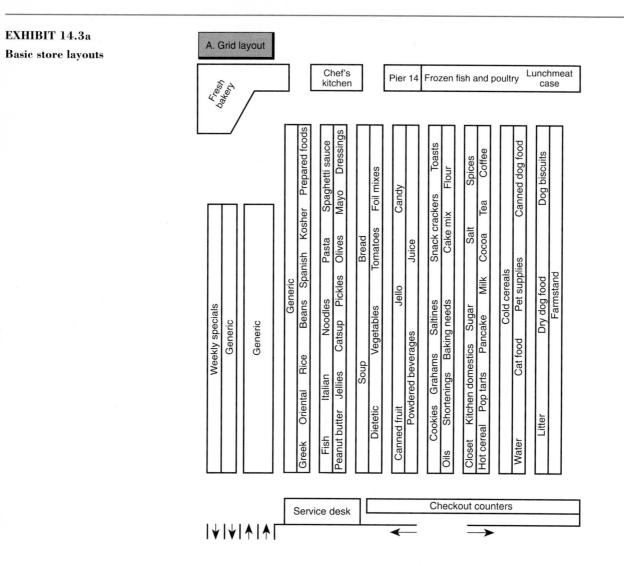

store. The free-flow approach is often used in specialty stores, boutiques, and apparel stores to encourage relaxed shopping, browsing, and impulse purchases. Also, the free-flow layout helps salespeople show consumers different types of merchandise and sell multiple items, such as a shirt and a tie with a suit, or a purse along with a pair of shoes.

Signs

Retail stores often use *signs* to direct consumers to the merchandise and to communicate price information and product benefits. One study investigated how sales of several products were influenced by the type of product information on a sign (price or benefit) and the price on the sign (regular or discounted price).[10] The results presented in Exhibit 14.4 show that (*a*) the price level influenced sales more than the type of information on the sign, (*b*) a price sign does not increase sales at regular prices, but did when the item was on sale, and (*c*) a sign describing product benefits increased sales at both regular and sales prices, but had a greater effect when combined with a discounted price.

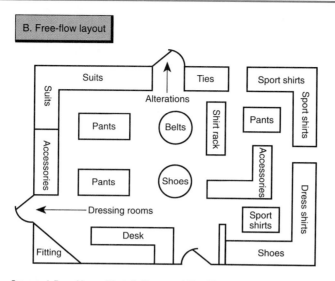

EXHIBIT 14.3b

Basic store layouts

Source: J. Barry Mason, Morris L. Mayer, and Hazel Ezell, *Retailing,* 4th ed. Homewood, Ill.: (Richard D. Irwin, Inc., 1991), pp. 461–62.

Shelf space and displays

Most marketers believe increased *shelf space* and more *in-store displays* capture consumer attention and generate sales.[11] A study compared sales generated by normal shelf space to sales obtained with expanded shelf space (twice the normal shelf space) and special displays (regular shelf space plus special end-of-aisle or within-aisle displays). Exhibit 14.5 (see page 316) shows that manipulating both aspects of the spatial environment increased sales in four product categories, but special displays consistently outperformed expanded shelf space.[12] Consumer Perspective 14.4 (see page 317) presents additional evidence of display effects on purchase behavior.

Music

Considerable research supports the idea that background *music* played in retail stores or restaurants while other activities are being performed influences consumers' affect, cognitions, and behavior.

One study finds that the tempo of such music changes the behavior of supermarket shoppers. No music, slow music, and fast music had different effects on the pace of in-store traffic.[13] Traffic flow was slowest when slow-tempo music was played and fastest under the fast-tempo treatment. Further, the slow-tempo musical selections generated higher sales volumes because consumers spent more time in the store. On average, sales were 38.2 percent greater under the slow-tempo condition than under the fast-tempo condition. Interestingly, when questioned after shopping, consumers showed little awareness of the music that had been playing in the supermarket. Thus, it seems likely that music affected behavior without consumers being totally conscious of it. In terms of marketing strategy, the author suggests that:

> . . . in some retailing situations, the objective may be to slow customer movement, keeping people in the store for as long as possible in an attempt to encourage them to purchase more. However, in other situations, the objective may be the opposite, that is, to move customers along as a way of increasing sales volume. A restaurant, for instance, will most likely want to speed people up, especially during lunch, when the objective is to maximize the "number of

EXHIBIT 14.4

Effects of three types of signs on daily sales

Type of Sign	Units Sold at Regular Price	Units Sold at Sale Price
No sign	7.7	15.4
Price sign	6.1	19.1
Benefit sign	7.8	23.0

Source: Gary F. McKinnon, J. Patrick Kelly, and E. Doyle Robinson, "Sales Effects of Point-of-Purchase In-Store Signing," *Journal of Retailing*, Summer 1981, p. 57.

seats turned" in a very short period of time, normally about two hours or less. Playing slow-tempo music in a restaurant might result in fewer seats turned and lower profit, although it could encourage return visits if customers preferred a relaxed luncheon atmosphere. . . . the music chosen must match the objectives of the business and the specific market situation.[14]

SITUATIONS

Because a huge number of elements make up the social and physical environment, marketers may find it difficult to identify the most important environmental influences on consumers' affect, cognitions, and behaviors. It can be easier to analyze the influences of the environment in the context of a specific situation.[15] A situation is neither the tangible physical environment (a checkout counter, a storefront, your living room, the temperature today, a landscape) nor the objective features of the social environment (the number of people in a store, the time of day).[16] *A situation is determined or defined by a person who is acting in an environment for some purpose.* A situation occurs over a period of time that can be very short (buying a soda in a vending machine), somewhat longer (eating lunch), or protracted (buying a house). The person's goals define the situation's beginning (goal activation or problem recognition), middle (working to achieve the goal), and end (achieving the goal). Thus, a **situation** is described as a *sequence of goal-directed behaviors, along with affective and cognitive responses, and the various environments in which they occur.* For instance, going to the mall to look for a new tape or CD is a shopping situation. This view of situations as a series of goal-directed interactions among the environment, affect and cognitions, and behavior is consistent with the Wheel of Consumer Analysis (see Exhibit 14.1).

Situations vary in *complexity.* Some situations involve simple goals, relatively few behaviors, and few affective and cognitive responses, all of which occur within a single physical and social environment. Examples of relatively simple consumption-related situations include buying a stamp at the post office, bargaining with a salesperson over the price of a stereo system, or discussing a spring break trip with your friends over dinner. Other

EXHIBIT 14.5

Percentage increase in unit sales for expanded shelf space and special display

Product	Expanded Shelf Space	Special Display
Camay soap—bath	39%	243%
Piggly Wiggly pie shells—2 per pkg.	30	185
White House apple juice—32 oz.	16	77
Mahatma rice—1 lb.	27	103

Source: Reprinted from J. B. Wilkinson, J. Barry Mason, and Christine H. Paksoy, "Assessing the Impact of Short-Term Supermarket Strategy Variables," *Journal of Marketing Research* 19 (February 1982), p. 79. Published by the American Marketing Association.

CONSUMER
PERSPECTIVE

Stick by
checkouts, gum
firms find

It pays to have your product near the checkout in supermarkets, a chewing gum company has discovered.

In a survey of 279 stores in 22 states that do $2 billion of business yearly, it was found that the profit per square foot for the checkout-displayed products was nearly four times that of the regular shelf-displayed products.

The survey was commissioned by American Chicle, which produces gums and breath mints.

The survey results showed that checkout items take up 0.26 percent of the store's selling space, but contribute to 1 percent of a store's gross profit.

Since the survey was commissioned by a gum and mint company, it is perhaps not surprising to note that one of the results pointed out in a press release was that "the stores that allocate additional space to confectionary at the checkouts generated disproportionately higher sales and profits."

In other words, "put our stuff near the checkout and we'll both make more money."

consumer situations are more complex. Complex situations may take place in several physical and social environments, involve multiple (perhaps conflicting) goals, and require many different behaviors and cognitive and affective responses. Shopping for a new winter coat or browsing in antique shops on Sunday afternoon are examples of more complex situations.

Other consumer-related situations are common and *recurring*. For instance, American consumers frequently buy gas for their cars, watch TV in the evening, shop for new clothes, rent videos, and go to grocery stores. As their experiences accumulate over time, consumers form clear goals, develop consistent cognitive interpretations of these recurring situations, and learn appropriate behaviors. Thereafter, when the consumer encounters a familiar situation, appropriate knowledge schemas and scripts may be activated from memory, which in turn influence consumers' behavioral, affective, and cognitive responses in that situation. To the extent that people tend to form approximately the same interpretations for common consumer-related situations, their behaviors will also tend to be similar. Consequently, marketers can develop marketing strategies that should affect consumers in a target segment in similar ways.

If consumers do not have clear goals or relevant knowledge when faced with a new or unfamiliar situation, they may have to engage in problem solving (interpretation and integration processes) to determine their goals, identify salient environmental factors, and evaluate alternative behaviors. Marketers should develop strategies to help consumers cope with unfamiliar situations. For instance, life insurance salespeople are trained to help consumers define their goals (college education for kids, retirement planning, pay off mortgage) and identify key environmental considerations (current income and savings, children's ages, time to retirement) before they demonstrate the personal relevance of life insurance.

Analyzing situations

Marketers must identify and analyze important situations to understand the physical and social environment from the perspectives of the consumers who experience them.[17] To analyze a situation, marketers first determine the major goals of their target customers that define the situation. Then they identify the key aspects of the social and physical environments in those situations, including aspects of the marketing environment that might affect consumers. The next step is to understand consumers' affective and cognitive responses to these environmental characteristics. Finally, marketers need to identify the key product-related behaviors in this situation.

EXHIBIT 14.6

Five common situations for consumers

Situation	General Behavior	Specific Behavior and Environment
Information acquisition	Information contact Communication	Reading a billboard while driving Discussing running shoes with a friend at a track meet Watching a TV commercial at home
Shopping	Store contact Product contact	Window shopping in a mall Browsing through an L. L. Bean catalog Comparing brands of shirts in a store
Purchase	Funds access Transaction	Obtaining a Visa card at a bank Going to a checkout counter at Sears Calling in an order to Lands' End from home
Consumption	Use	Eating a taco at Taco Bell Using a refrigerator for 15 years
Disposition	Disposal	Recycling aluminum cans Throwing away a hot-dog wrapper at a hockey game

Marketers can learn a great deal about a consumption situation through detailed observation of consumers' behaviors in that situation. For instance, researchers could develop rich descriptions of ordinary consumer behaviors observed at discount malls, banks, garage sales, or auctions. Another approach is to ask consumers to describe the major occasions when they consume a product. For example, a college student described the following three situations when she ate candy. Each situation occurred in a different environment and involved different goals, affective and cognitive responses, and behaviors. Each consumption situation was defined by the consumer in highly personal terms of her own goals and her environments.

Situation 1. Hungry—in a rush.
   Environment: hectic; many other people around; between classes.
    Goal: satisfy hunger and get energy.
    Affect/cognition: feeling hungry, stressed, anxious.
    Behavior: snack on candy between classes and during class.

Situation 2. Lazy—relaxed.
   Environment: quiet; alone at home in evening.
    Goal: relax so I can concentrate on work.
    Affect/cognition: feeling relaxed and calm, but alert.
    Behavior: snack on candy while reading or studying.

Situation 3. Calm—at lunch.
   Environment: no commotion; alone in kitchen at lunchtime.
   Goal: reward myself.
   Affect/cognition: feeling happy to be home after hectic class
      schedule; starting to calm down.
   Behavior: eat candy for dessert.

Typically, marketers do not base their strategies on an analysis of a single consumer. Marketers are interested in identifying situations experienced similarly by large numbers of consumers. Then, the marketer can develop marketing strategies (special products, prices, or advertising campaigns) for those consumption situations. For instance, consider a study of fast-food restaurants that identified four use situations: lunch on a weekday, a snack during a shopping trip, an evening meal when rushed for time, and an evening meal with family when not rushed for time.[18] The authors found different choice criteria were used in these situations (speed of service was more important at lunch, menu variety was more important in the evening when not rushed). Moreover, certain restaurants (different environments) were considered more appropriate for certain situations. Finally, note that even if the same fast-food restaurant is patronized in these different situations, consumers' behaviors and affective and cognitive reactions in those situations could be quite different (rushed/not rushed, relaxed/not relaxed).

In this section, we consider five common *consumer situations*—information acquisition, shopping, purchase, consumption, and disposition (see Exhibit 14.6). These situations are relevant for most products. Marketers analyze consumers' goals, relevant affect and cognitions, and the key environmental factors in these situations to develop strategies that will change, facilitate, or maintain the key behaviors.

Common consumer situations

Information acquisition

Relevant information may be acquired accidentally, as consumers randomly come across information in their environments, or intentionally, as they consciously seek information related to their current problem-solving goals, such as a brand or store choice. An **information acquisition situation** includes aspects of the social environment (discussions with friends, persuasion attempts by a salesperson), the physical environment (advertisement, prominent signs in a store, labels on the product package), the behaviors involved in exposure to this information, along with the consumer's affective and cognitive responses.

Marketers have considerable control over many aspects of consumers' information environment through the advertising, sales promotion, and personal-selling elements of the promotion mix. Marketers can place signs in stores and on the front windows of shops, send direct-mail material about their products to consumers, and place ads on TV, in magazines, and on billboards.[19] They can add information to packages and labels or provide salespeople with special information to convey to customers.[20] Other aspects of consumers' information environment are not under marketers' direct control—for example, marketers can try to generate publicity and news articles about their product or encourage consumers to tell other people about a product, but they may not be successful in creating this environmental information.

Two especially important behaviors in information acquisition situations are information contact and communication. Because approximately two thirds of retail purchases come from decisions made in the store, *information contact* with relevant product information in a store can have a significant influence on choice. Various marketing strategies are designed to facilitate information contact, including product displays, point-of-purchase information, and signs. An example is the interactive computer display developed for Clarion Cosmetics. After answering a few simple questions, consumers receive information about which Clarion products are best for their skin color and tone.[21] Other strategies include placing ads on shopping carts and printing colored ads on paper grocery bags.[22]

Modern technology enables marketers to make information contact with precisely defined target groups. In some Giant Foods stores on the East Coast, coupon dispensers connected to the checkout scanners can issue different types of coupons, depending on which products and brands a consumer buys. Thus, people purchasing peanut butter might receive a coupon for bread, while customers who buy Folgers coffee might receive a coupon for Maxwell House.

Other marketing strategies focus on *communication,* such as how salespeople communicate with customers. For example, Toyota, manufacturer of the Lexus luxury car, trains its salespeople in all aspects of the car so they spend an average of 90 minutes presenting a car to a potential customer, much more than the industry average.[23] Communication is also relevant in service situations, which is relevant for auto manufacturers and dealers.

CONSUMER PERSPECTIVE

▶ 14.5

Mobile shopping environments

Several companies are experimenting with movable shopping environments. Kentucky Fried Chicken, for example, "rolled out" a new concept in 1991—mobile merchandising. KFC built a restaurant in a 42-foot-long trailer. Towed by a truck, the mobile KFC unit can be set up at fairs, outdoor jazz and rock concerts, and amusement parks to pursue customers wherever they go.

Pizza Hut, considered the innovator in the field, has more than 250 mobile kiosks in place, mostly in airports. Taco Bell hopes to increase the number of its outlets to over 10,000 by the end of the decade; a significant proportion will be mobile units. McDonald's is not involved as yet, and Dairy Queen is studying the use of carts to sell its products.

Why go to the trouble? One reason is that the fast-food industry has already taken most of the best fixed locations on street corners and in malls. With a mobile unit, if customers don't show up, you move the restaurant to another spot. Another advantage is cost. The mobile units are considerably less expensive than a fixed site. A Taco Bell cart in an airport or a countertop merchandiser at a university runs about $30,000, while the larger KFC truck costs about $200,000, compared to about $1 million for a bricks-and-mortar, fast-food restaurant.

Sometimes these unusual shopping environments create interesting consumer behavior problems. For instance, Pizza Hut discovered that some customers didn't believe the pizzas at the mobile airport kiosk were made fresh on site. So the company redesigned the ovens (changed the purchasing environment) so customers could see the pizzas going into the oven.

Consumers' number one complaint with auto service is having to bring the car back because the problem was not fixed properly the first time. Research indicated Lexus buyers saw this as a communication flaw in that their car problem was not adequately explained to the mechanic doing the work. The company modified the service situation so car owners could speak directly to the mechanic who would examine their car. Customers can even stay during the diagnosis to make sure the problem is clearly communicated to the mechanic.

Shopping

The **shopping situation** includes the physical, spatial, and social aspects of places where consumers shop for products and services, as well as shopping behaviors and related affective and cognitive responses. Shopping can occur in a variety of environments, such as boutiques, department and discount stores, factory outlets, malls, pedestrian-only retail areas, in the home via catalogs and television shopping programs, garage sales, auctions, and so on. The shopping situation also includes the merchandise (products and brands) available for sale in those environments. For instance, the shopping environment provided by the auto center, where several franchises are sold under one roof, vastly increases the number of product alternatives. A customer can examine dozens of makes and models on a single shopping trip, much like shopping for a new dress or suit at a large department store.

The shopping environment also includes social factors such as how many salespeople and checkout personnel are in the store, how they act toward consumers, and the types of other customers in the store. Many people dislike going to an auto showroom where aggressive salespeople may pressure them, so at a Lexus dealership, no salespeople are in sight.[24] Instead, consumers are greeted by a receptionist behind a marble desk. They are encouraged to learn more about the Lexus by studying the "media wall" of videos and print materials, without interruption. Only on request will the receptionist call a sales representative to talk to the consumer.

Mobile restaurants must be especially conscious of consumers' consumption environment. In most of these moving restaurants, the range of products available is limited to foods that people can eat while standing. Therefore, KFC sells only chicken nuggets and sandwiches in its mobile restaurant.

KFC places a modular merchandising display in cafeterias at universities, airports, and travel plazas.

Source: Reprinted by permission of *The Wall Street Journal*, © 1991 Dow Jones & Company, Inc. All Rights Reserved Worldwide.

Two general behaviors affected by the shopping environment are of particular importance—store contact and product contact. *Store contact* is critical for retailing success, and many marketing strategies are intended to get consumers to come to the store. Giving away a free cassette tape to the first 100 people to show up at an electronics store on a Saturday morning is an example of such a strategy.

Store location is another critical environmental influence on store contact for many types of stores—for example, fast-food restaurants and convenience food stores need to be located in high-traffic locations. Consumer Perspective 14.5 describes an unusual strategy to increase store contact behavior by changing the location of the store. As another example, consider the location strategy of Sunglass Hut of America, which operates about 200 small kiosks selling high-quality sunglasses costing from $35 to well over $100.[25] Most of their kiosks are placed in well-traveled areas of shopping centers and malls to facilitate store contact. Their marketing strategy also stresses communication with customers. Each Sunglass Hut is staffed with well-trained, knowledgeable salespeople who are able to tell customers why they should pay $80 for a pair of sunglasses (compared to the average price of about $14).

As another example of store contact strategies, the location in a mall of smaller boutiques selling candy, natural foods, or gifts can have a critical effect on store contact behavior. One desirable location is close to the entrance of one of the anchor stores, usually large department stores found at the ends or the middle of the mall. Because these anchor stores draw large numbers of consumers, smaller stores benefit from the traffic flowing past their doors. The importance of location within the mall was clearly shown during the recession of the early 1990s.[26] When retailers Bonwit Teller and B. Altman filed for bankruptcy, The Mall at Short Hills (an upscale mall in New Jersey) lost two of its four anchor stores. Immediately, the

CONSUMER PERSPECTIVE

▶ **14.6**

The store environment as theater

Nike sells a lot of shoes in its hometown store in Portland, Oregon, by creating an exciting in-store environment that makes shopping fun and exciting. The entire store, Nike Town, is a fantasy experience that closely resembles theater. The center of the store is a tranquil town square, with the sounds of birds chirping. Surrounding the square, on two levels, are separate shopping areas for different types of Nike shoes. The basketball area, for instance, has a wooden truss ceiling and a wooden basketball court floor. Speakers beneath the floor fill the space with the hollow bounce of basketballs and the sounds of shoes squeaking on the court. Nike Aqua Gear shoes (for water sports) are displayed surrounded by large vertical tanks containing tropical fish, and several large-screen TVs in the floor show a bed of seaweed swaying among the coral.

To keep the stock from cluttering the fantasy environment, most shoes are stored downstairs. Sales staff use computers to call down for certain models and sizes, and the shoes are sent up through clear plastic tubes via conveyor. Customer response to the store has been so strong that a much bigger store with a five-story town square was opened in Chicago.

Source: Associated Press, "Nike's Vision of the Ultimate Store Includes Fantasy," *Marketing News,* September 16, 1991, p. 9.

smaller stores nearby began having difficulties. Such changes in a mall shopping environment can initiate a sequence of interactions among behaviors, affect and cognitions, and the environment. As more stores depart, a mall accumulates more empty, boarded-up stores, the shopping environment deteriorates further, more consumers become concerned and begin staying away, which continues the process.

Product contact is another important behavior affected by the environmental characteristics of the shopping situation. Consider how the probability of product contact is reduced in very large stores, or if shoppers are discouraged from lingering in a store by overcrowding (too many other shoppers), or if sales personnel are overly aggressive (driving off some customers). Some stores use restful music, warm color schemes, and low-key salespeople to encourage shoppers to linger, thus enhancing the probability of product contact. In large self-service stores, signs are hung from the ceiling to identify product locations. To facilitate product contact, Hallmark recently redesigned its product displays, using colored strips to identify different types of greeting cards and to help customers find the right card quickly.[27]

Certain stores are designed to make the shopping environment more fun and exciting so consumers will spend more time in the store and be more likely to make contact with the merchandise.[28] When a small chain of clothing stores for young women, called "Ups and Downs," redesigned its store interiors, the company added kinetically controlled display racks.[29] This innovation allows customers to spin an entire carousel of clothes with just a light touch. These kinetic displays are intended to facilitate product contact and make the shopping experience more fun. Consumer Perspective 14.6 describes another example of a store environment that makes shopping fun and increases product contact behavior.

Although the retail store environment is certainly important, other types of shopping environments are becoming quite significant. These include shopping at home by telephone or by mail. Consider the great popularity of TV shopping programs and the continued rise of catalog shopping (mail-order sales are currently growing at about 10 percent per year in the United States). Obviously, the environment at home is dramatically different from the in-store shopping environment. Other shopping environments are relevant for some products, including garage sales, flea markets and swap meets, auctions, sidewalk sales, and private sales of merchandise by individuals and street vendors. In some cities, you can even avoid shopping situations altogether, by hiring someone else to shop for you.[30]

Purchasing

The **purchasing situation** includes the social and physical stimuli present in the environment where the consumer actually makes the purchase. Consider, for instance, the differences in the purchasing environment when buying fresh vegetables at a supermarket versus at an outdoor farmers' market. In some cases, the purchasing environment is similar to the shopping environment, but they are seldom identical. In most self-service stores, for instance, consumers pay for the products they have selected at a checkout counter at the front of the store or at various cash register locations scattered around the store. Some purchasing environments are quite distinct from the shopping environment. For instance, the central checkout counter at one trendy music store is designed to look like a giant piano keyboard with black and white keys.

In other retail environments, such as an automobile dealership, the purchasing environment may be a separate room used exclusively for the purchase transaction. This is where the salesperson and the customers retire to negotiate the final details of the purchase. Sometimes the shopping environment intrudes into the purchasing environment. For instance, checkout lines at grocery stores usually include displays of products such as magazines, gum and candy items, and cigarettes to stimulate impulse purchases.

The information acquisition and purchase environments also may overlap. For instance, A&P (a chain of some 1,200 grocery stores) experimented with showing ads on TV monitors placed at the checkout aisle, but many consumers complained that this type of information contact was too intrusive. Besides, few customers wanted to leave the line to get an advertised product.

Marketers are particularly interested in influencing two behaviors in purchasing situations—*funds access* and the *final transaction.* For instance, Sotheby's, the world-famous auction house for fine art, found that the extreme escalation of art prices in the late 1980s had created a funds access problem for its customers. Buyers did not have the large sums of cash (millions, in some cases) necessary to buy fine works of art, so Sotheby's instituted a credit policy allowing a loan of up to half the cost of an artwork, using the purchased painting or other works of art owned by the borrower as collateral. Many grocery stores and other retail stores have streamlined the transaction procedures in the purchasing situation by installing scanner equipment to speed up the checkout process.

Consumption

The **consumption situation** includes the social and physical assets of the environments where consumers actually use or consume the products and services they have bought Obviously, consumption behaviors (and related cognitive and affective processes such as enjoyment, satisfaction, or frustration) are most relevant in such situations. Consider how clean, tidy, well-lighted, and attractively decorated consumption environments in full-service and fast-food restaurants, pubs and bars, nightclubs and discos, and ice cream parlors can enhance consumers' enjoyment of the purchased products. For such businesses, the design of the consumption environment may be critically important to consumers' satisfaction with their purchase.

Consider the consumption environment of two bars at the Minneapolis and Detroit airports.[31] Host International, a division of Marriott Corporation, re-created the Cheers bar from the famous TV show of the same name. The physical environment included Sam's Red Sox jersey framed on the wall, the wooden Indian statue inside the door, the Wurlitzer jukebox, and two familiar patrons perched at the bar—animated, robotic replicas of Norm and Cliff. Up to 46 of these Cheers bars have been planned for U.S. airports.

For other products such as appliances, clothing, cars, and furniture, marketers have almost no direct control over the consumption environment. When purchased, these products are removed from the retail environment and consumed elsewhere. Moreover, for many of these products, the consumption situation involves multiple consumption behaviors over long periods (most people own and use a car or a microwave oven for several years). In some cases, the consumption environment might change during the useful life of the product, which

The West Edmonton Mall is a mixture of shopping and consumption environments, including a Fantasyland amusement park inside the mall.

could affect consumption-related cognitive and affective responses (satisfaction) and behaviors (repairs and service). Perhaps the best marketers can do is to monitor consumer satisfaction levels and behaviors in these consumption situations over the lifetime of the product.

In other cases, however, marketers have a great deal of control over the consumption environment. For instance, many service businesses, such as hair stylists, dentists and doctors, and hotels and motels, have total control over the consumption environment, because consumption of these products and services occurs on the premises of the seller. An obvious example is Disneyland or Disney World (or any other theme or amusement park) where the consumption environment is a major part of the product/service that consumers buy. Disney Enterprises goes to great lengths to ensure the consumption environment meets rigorous standards.

Another instance where design of the consumption environment can be critical is the restaurant industry.[32] The Rainbow Room in New York serves halibut in golden foil to "enhance the theatricality" of the dining experience. Highly decorated theme restaurants are popular in many U.S. cities. A restaurant in Salt Lake City replicates an 18th century French farmhouse, down to ponds with geese and swans, peacocks roaming the grounds, waitresses in period costumes, and dried herbs and flowers hanging from the beamed ceilings. An entrepreneur in Chicago created a series of offbeat restaurants where the consumption environment was as important as the food. They included "R.J. Grunts," which offered a burger and health-food menu served by blue-jeaned waitresses with mystical, new age music in the background. Not all consumption environments are successful, however. A singles-type restaurant called "Not So Great Gritzbe's" had a sign reading "Eat and Get Out." The walls were decorated with Tums and Alka-Seltzer ads, and the food critic awards were grossed out. Although the media were intrigued, consumers did not know what to make of the environment, and the restaurant closed.

Disposition

For certain products, marketers may need to consider other types of environmental situations. For instance, **disposition situations** are highly relevant for some businesses—used car lots and used clothing stores are obvious examples. Here the key behavior of interest is *disposal* of products. Many people simply throw away unwanted products or give them to charity. Others sell their unwanted products at flea markets, garage sales, and swap meets. These situations offer interesting environments for study in and of themselves.[33] Disposition situations are relevant for public policy issues, too.

Consumers in many countries, including the United States, are developing stronger concerns about quality, and cost-consciousness and concern for the natural environment, in turn, are fueling interest in used products and the recycling of waste. The markets for recycled goods and used products (furniture and appliances, clothing, and housewares) are likely to increase in the future, and we can expect entrepreneurs to develop strategies to serve these markets.

Marketing implications

Marketers need to identify the key social and physical environmental features of the information, shopping, purchasing, consumption, and disposition situations for their products. Perhaps some aspects of the particular environment are blocking behaviors crucial for the marketing success of the firm's product. If so, marketing strategies can be developed that modify the environment to stimulate, facilitate, and reinforce the desired behaviors. For instance, if funds access is a problem for consumers, the company might introduce debit cards, accept regular credit cards, or allow charge accounts. If consumers are becoming increasingly discouraged with the shopping environment in many cities (noisy streets, difficult parking, crowded stores), clever marketers are likely to introduce alternative shopping environments, such as home-shopping opportunities through the mail or by telephone. Strong growth for such businesses is forecast for the 1990s.

Learning objective 1: *Define the environment and describe the difference between the macro- and microenvironment.*

The environment refers to all the physical and social characteristics of consumers' external world. The environment includes (*a*) physical objects such as products and stores, (*b*) spatial aspects such as the position of a product in a store or the location of a store in a mall, and (*c*) social aspects associated with other people and their social behaviors. The microenvironment refers to a person's immediate physical and social surroundings (your bedroom, house, or workplace). The macroenvironment refers to the large-scale, broad environmental factors such as the climate or type of landscape where you live, the economic conditions of your region, or whether you live in a large or small city or in a rural environment. Each consumer responds to aspects of the macro- and microenvironment in terms of his or her personal interpretations of those factors. Usually, marketers can identify groups of consumers (possible market segments) with enough common experience that they have similar interpretations of major environmental factors.

Learning objective 2: *Define the social environment, identify the types of macro and micro social environments, and describe the flow of influence between the macro- and microenvironments.*

The social environment includes all social interactions between people. The macro social environment includes the social interactions that occur between very large groups of people. Marketers are interested in three such groups—culture, subculture, and social class. The micro social environment includes the social interactions that occur between small groups of people such as families and reference groups. The macro- and microenvironments have a hierarchical relationship such that the values, norms, and meanings of the overall culture flow to the subcultures within it and on to social class groups. The micro social environments of family and reference groups act as a "filter" in transmitting these influences of the macro social environments to the individual consumer. In turn, the flow of influence can go back "up" the hierarchy as when the behavior of many families can influence the values of a social class or subculture.

Learning objective 3: *Define the physical environment, and give an example of how the physical environment can influence consumer behavior.*

The physical environment includes all the nonhuman, physical aspects of the external world of consumers. The physical environment can be divided into spatial and nonspatial elements. Spatial factors include physical objects such as products, brands, and the layout and design of stores, malls, and cities. Nonspatial aspects of the physical environment include factors such as the weather, time, color, odors, and so on. Any aspect of the physical environment can influence consumer behavior. For example, the availability of parking (an aspect of the spatial environment) will influence consumers' shopping behaviors. As another example, time factors such as the amount of daylight have major effects on behaviors—more sports activities or more shopping during daylight hours.

Learning objective 4: *Give two examples of how a marketing strategy can modify the environment and influence consumer behavior.*

Each marketing strategy modifies some aspect of the social and physical environment. For instance, promotion strategies create physical objects in the environment (ads on TV, billboards, signs in the store) and also may influence the social environment (phone calls from telemarketers, product descriptions by salespeople). These aspects of the environment may attract consumers' attention or persuade them to buy the product. Product strategies may involve physical changes in the product (removing fat from a food product, increasing the horsepower of the Pontiac Grand Am), pricing strategies create small changes in the environment (a sale sign in the store window, a price tag on a blouse), and distribution strategies can change the spatial environment (building a Wal-Mart store, creating a product display in a drugstore). All of these environmental stimuli might influence consumers' affect and cognition and behavior.

Learning objective 5: *Define a situation, and describe the factors to be examined in a situation analysis.*

A "raw" physical environment is not a situation—a shopping mall is not a situation. Rather, a situation is a sequence of goal-directed behaviors that occur in a physical and social environment, accompanied by related affective and cognitive responses. A situation is defined and created by the consumer who is behaving in an environment for some purpose. Thus, going to the mall to buy a sweater is a shopping situation. Situations are like a story in that they have a beginning, a middle, and an end.

To understand the product-related situations that are important to consumers, marketers should analyze the major components of those situations. These factors include the consumers' end goal(s), the major features of the environments in which the situation occurs, the key behaviors involved, and the dominant affective responses and cognitions related to those behaviors.

Learning objective 6: *Describe the five common consumer situations, and identify behaviors that are important in each situation.*

Consumers define particular situations in terms of their own perspectives and goals. However, each culture or society has common or generic situations that most people experience. Five consumer situations are relevant for many marketing problems and most products. To understand each situation, marketers would identify the key behaviors, related affect and cognitive responses, and the major aspects of the physical and social environments in which these behaviors occurred. Marketers are particularly interested in the key behaviors for each situation because they focus their strategies on changing or maintaining these behaviors.

In information acquisition situations, consumers acquire or learn relevant information about products or brands, and two important behaviors are information contact and communication. In shopping situations, people search for appropriate products to solve their problems; two important behaviors are store contact and product contact. In purchasing situations, consumers make the buying exchange, and funds access and the final transaction are important behaviors. In the consumption situation, the product is used or consumed, and consumption behaviors are important. In the disposition situation, consumers discard products; disposition behaviors are important.

---

environment	situation	purchasing situation	▶ **KEY TERMS**
social environment	information acquisition	consumption situation	**AND CONCEPTS**
physical environment	situation	disposition situation	
	shopping situation		

► **REVIEW AND DISCUSSION QUESTIONS**

1. Pick a fast-food restaurant, and identify the social and physical aspects of the marketing environment. Which factors seem most important?

2. Discuss the distinction between the macro- and microenvironment in terms of grocery shopping. How is each level of the environment relevant for developing marketing strategies?

3. Describe how the various levels of the social environment are related and how they affect the individual consumer.

4. Research suggests that about 80 percent of grocery purchase decisions are made while consumers are in the store. What aspects of the physical environment in the store could influence those decisions? (You might choose a product category such as frozen entrées or snack chips to focus your answer.)

5. What is a situation? Using examples from your personal purchasing experience, differentiate situations from the "raw" environment.

6. Describe the key factors in a situation that marketers need to understand, and give an implication for marketing strategy.

7. Consider how you might go about buying a personal cassette player (or another product of your choice). Describe the information acquisition and shopping situations, and identify critical behaviors. What implications for marketing strategies do you see in your analysis?

8. Consider how you might go about buying a personal cassette player (or another product of your choice). Describe the purchase and consumption situations, and identify critical behaviors. What implications for marketing strategies do you see in your analysis?

9. Describe a disposition situation for a personal cassette player (or another product of your choice), and identify critical behaviors. What implications for marketing strategies do you see in your analysis?

15

Cultural and
Cross-Cultural Influences

LEARNING OBJECTIVES

After completing this chapter, you should be able to

► 1. Define culture and cultural meaning.

► 2. Discuss aspects of the content of culture, including core values.

► 3. Describe the cultural process by which cultural meaning is moved from the environment into products and then into consumers.

► 4. Give examples of how rituals move meaning from products into consumers and vice versa.

► 5. Give some examples of important cross-cultural differences.

► 6. Discuss three approaches to developing international marketing strategies.

BIRTH OF THE CONSUMER SOCIETY

Modern consumption cultures are a rather recent historical development. According to one analysis, the birth of the consumer society occurred in England during the late 18th century with several important events. For one, the mass production technologies developed during the Industrial Revolution allowed companies to produce large amounts of standardized goods at relatively low prices. But a *cultural revolution* also occurred about the same time, without which the Industrial Revolution would not have been successful.

During the 18th century, England was gradually transformed from a largely agrarian society into a more urban society. As people moved into towns, their culture changed dramatically. They performed different types of work, established new ways of living, and developed new values. Many people developed an increased desire for material goods, stimulated partly by "new" marketing strategies such as advertising. Increasingly, ordinary citizens (not just the wealthy) became concerned with the symbolic meanings of goods and felt it necessary to buy products that were fashionable and up to date. Owning such things helped satisfy the emerging cultural need for status distinctions, which had become more relevant in the relatively anonymous urban societies where fewer people knew about others' family backgrounds. Thus, people began to see consumption as an acceptable way to convey important social meanings. Finally, more people had disposable income and were willing to spend it to achieve social values.

These cultural changes, combined with the rapidly developing ability of industry to mass produce products of reasonable quality at "low" prices, created a dramatic increase in consumption in 18th century England. Essentially, the same events occurred in France and the United States during the 19th century, and the modern consumer society was born there, too.[1]

This brief summary of the beginnings of the modern consumption society points to the importance of culture in understanding consumer behavior. To develop effective strategies, marketers need to identify important aspects of culture and understand how the cultural environment affects consumers. We begin this chapter by defining culture and examining how culture influences consumers' affect, cognitions, and behaviors. Then, we identify some important characteristics of American culture and discuss the implications of cultural analysis for developing marketing strategies. Next we describe the cultural processes by which cultural meaning is transmitted through marketing strategies from the cultural environment to products and on to consumers who acquire those cultural meanings for themselves. Finally, we discuss cross-cultural (international) differences and their implications for developing global marketing strategies.

WHAT IS CULTURE?

As the all-encompassing aspect of the macro social environment, culture has a strong and pervasive influence on consumers, although the term remains difficult for marketers to understand. Dozens of definitions have confused researchers about what "culture" is or how culture "works" to influence consumers.[2] We define **culture** broadly as *the meanings that are shared by (most) people in a social group.* In establishing a particular vision of the world, each society constructs its cultural view by creating and using meanings that reflect important distinctions in that society. For example, Consumer Perspective 15.1 describes some cultural meanings of the Christmas holiday that are unique to particular societies.

Marketers should consider several issues when analyzing culture. First, cultural meaning can be analyzed at different levels. At the macro level, we would look at the culture of

---

CONSUMER PERSPECTIVE

▶ 15.1

Holiday buying around the world

A witch flies on a broomstick to drop Christmas gifts down Italian chimneys, a kindly old Saint Nicolas leaves gifts at the front doors of Scandinavian homes, a camel does the hauling in southern Syria, and the honorable porter's name is *Santa-san* in Japan. Although the exact method of delivery varies around the world, consumers fill the sacks with presents every holiday season.

Each year, eager shoppers record huge purchases during the Christmas holiday season. For instance, Americans spend more than $450 billion extra during the three-month shopping season from October to New Year's. Most department stores record about one third of their annual sales during this period. Toy vendors from London to Madrid to Los Angeles expect to do about 50 percent of their yearly business in these three months.

Interestingly, shopping for and giving presents at Christmastime has become a worldwide phenomenon. Even in Japan, where less than 1 percent of the population is Christian, Yuletide is widely celebrated with artfully packaged gifts and late-hour partying. West Germany's lively outdoor Christmas markets sell sausages, sweets, and holiday gifts. Shoppers in Rome's oval-shaped plaza Piazza Navona are bathed in light from stalls selling items like books, toys, records, candy, and video games while being entertained by street musicians and magicians. Even the energy shortages and sparsely stocked stores in Eastern Europe cannot extinguish Christmas cheer. Families in Warsaw, Bratislava, and Budapest surrender their bathtubs for a week to give freshwater carp, a holiday delicacy, a place to swim before dinner.

Holiday decorations, especially lights, are popular everywhere. For instance, Christmas trees decorate plazas around the globe (and are found in 75 percent of American homes). In Scandinavia, candles glow from every window to brighten the darkness that arrives by midafternoon. The Stroget, Copenhagen's large pedestrian-

an entire society or country (France or Kenya). Because culture refers to the meanings shared among a group of people of whatever size, marketers can also analyze the cultural meanings of subcultures (African Americans, the elderly, or people who live in New England) or social classes (middle class versus working class). We discuss subcultures and social class in Chapter 16. Marketers also can analyze the shared cultural meanings of smaller groups such as a reference group (people who live on the same dorm floor, members of a sorority or a street gang, or a group of co-workers) or families (people in one's nuclear or extended family). We discuss reference groups and family influences in Chapter 17.

Second, the essence of culture as shared or common meaning is critical to understanding the concept. A meaning is cultural if many people in a social group share the same basic meaning or belief.[3] **Cultural meanings** are usually rather fluid and not rigidly defined in that everyone in a social group does not have precisely the same meaning for any object or activity (an "old" person, an "environmentally safe" product, or a "good" bargain). Fortunately, meanings only have to be "close enough" to be treated as shared or common.

Third, cultural meanings are created by people. Anthropologists often say cultural meanings are constructed or negotiated by people in a group through their social interactions. The construction of cultural meaning is most obvious at the level of smaller groups (consider the social meanings created by college students—what music or clothing look is "in" this semester?). At the level of society, cultural institutions such as governments, religious and educational organizations, and business firms also create cultural meanings.

A fourth issue is that cultural meanings are constantly in motion and can undergo rapid change. In the early days of the consumption society in England, for instance, the cultural changes in people's values, perceptions, and behaviors were so dramatic that

only shopping district, is illuminated by thousands of colored lights and stars. The Via Condotti, Rome's pedestrian-only shopping area, is decorated with hundreds of red poinsettias, called "Christmas stars" in Italian.

For many, the winter weather in the northern hemisphere heightens the holiday mood. But cold weather and lights in the early darkness are not prerequisites for Christmas spirit. South of the equator, the holiday falls in the middle of summer. So when enthusiastic shoppers in Australia and Rio get too hot, they just head for the beach to cool off.

There are differences, of course, between the consumers in various cultures, subcultures, and social classes. Marketers need to identify these factors and understand how they are related to purchasing and consumption behavior. However, there are also similarities between cultures. One example is the generosity and good spirit of the Christmas season. Holiday spending and gift giving seem to be fairly universal in most societies with a well-developed consumption ethic. The details, of course, often differ. The weather (cold and snowy or hot, humid, and rainy), the most desirable gifts (fur coats in Northern Europe, ice cream makers in Brazil), the particular details of the holiday rituals (who brings the gifts), and the religious symbolic meanings may vary considerably. But the core meaning of the holiday, captured by Charles Dickens in *A Christmas Carol*, seems fairly universal. "Christmas," Dickens wrote, "is the only time I know of, in the long calendar year, when men and women seem by one consent to open their shut-up hearts freely." And, we might note, they open their pocketbooks, too.

Source: Adapted with permission from "Christmas Shopping around the World," by Jaclyn Fierman, *Fortune*, © 1987 Time Inc. All rights reserved.

The cultural meanings of products such as clothing are created by advertising and the people who use the products.

one observer felt a kind of "madness" had taken over society. Later in this chapter, we examine the processes by which cultural meanings change and move about in the society, partly through marketing strategies.

Fifth, social groups differ in the amount of freedom their members have to adopt and use certain cultural meanings. North American and European societies afford people a great deal of freedom to select cultural meanings and use them to create a desired self-identity. In many other societies, such as in China, India, or Saudi Arabia, people have less freedom to do so.

Marketers can understand cultural meaning from two useful perspectives. They can examine the *content* of a culture, or they can treat culture as a *process*.[4]

THE CONTENT OF CULTURE

The usual approach in marketing is to analyze culture in terms of its major features or attributes, which is to say its content. Although marketers typically focus on identifying the dominant values of a society, culture is more than values.[5] The **content of culture** includes the beliefs, attitudes, goals, and values that most people in a society hold, as well as the meanings of characteristic behaviors, rules, customs, and norms that most people follow. The content of culture also includes meanings of the significant aspects of the social and physical environment, including the major institutions in a society (governmental bodies, political parties, religions) and the typical physical objects (products, tools, buildings) used by people in a society.

The goal of cultural analysis is to understand the cultural meanings of concepts from the point of view of the people who create and use them.[6] For example, many Americans have similar affective responses to the raising of the American flag (patriotic feelings), to accidentally breaking something in a store (anxiety or guilt), or to a 50-percent-off sale (interest or enthusiasm). Affective responses may vary across cultures. Many Americans and northern Europeans become annoyed if kept waiting for 15 minutes in a checkout line, while people in other cultures might not have a negative reaction.

Culture has a profound effect on how and where people shop for products, as shown in the open-air market in India and a Wal-Mart stor in the United States.

Behaviors also can have important cultural meanings. For instance, the meaning of shaking hands when greeting someone (welcome or friendliness) is shared by many peoples of the world, although in some cultures people bow or kiss instead. Protesters who burn the American flag are communicating scorn through their behavior. Some consumption-related behaviors have a cultural meaning that is unique to particular societies. For instance, the bargaining behaviors that are common (and expected) among shoppers in the open market bazaars of northern Africa indicate a skilled and shrewd buyer. But in the United States, such bargaining behaviors are not appropriate for shopping in Kmart or Wal-Mart and would be considered naive or rude.

Aspects of the social environment can have rich cultural meanings. For instance, the cultural meanings of shopping for a new sweater at a self-service, factory outlet store may be quite different from shopping in an upscale department store with attentive personal service from salespeople. Likewise, the physical or material environment—including the landscape, buildings, and the weather, as well as specific objects such as products—can have significant cultural meaning. For instance, objects such as wedding rings and new cars have cultural meaning for many consumers. All societies have certain objects that symbolize key cultural meanings. Consider the shared meanings that many Americans associate with the flag, the Statue of Liberty, or the bald eagle (pride, freedom, individualism).

Marketing strategies also may have shared meanings. Reactions to advertising, for instance, tend to be culturally specific.[7] In the United States, many advertising appeals are straightforward and direct, while consumers in other societies consider such appeals blunt and even offensive. People in other countries consider many U.S. ads to be overly emotional and sentimental. Thus, a McDonald's ad featuring a young man with Down's syndrome who found a job and acceptance at McDonald's was a tearjerker for Americans, but was booed and jeered at the International Advertising Film Festival in Cannes. The British tend to be embarrassed by a direct sell; their ads are noted for self-deprecating humor. In contrast, the French rarely use humor, but prefer stylish and rather indirect appeals, which Americans may find surrealistic. For example, the best French ad in 1991 (also shown in North America) showed a lion and a tawny-haired woman crawling up opposite sides of a mountain; at the peak the woman outroars the lion for a bottle of Perrier. Most Japanese consumers prefer ads emphasizing affective mood and emotional tone over facts. Although some Japanese ads travel well to other cultures, many are not understood outside Japan.[8] As a final example, marketing strategies such as pricing or distribution have cultural content that can differ across societies. Many U.S. consumers have positive reactions to frequent sales promotions such as discounting, sales, and coupons, but consumers in other cultures may have more negative meanings, wondering whether something is wrong with the product.

Finally, physical objects such as products and brands have cultural meanings that marketers need to understand. For instance, an analysis of beverage products focused on the status and age meanings carried in various beverage products—milk, for example, is seen as weak and appropriate for younger people, while wine is considered to be sophisticated and for mature adults.[9] Consumers look for certain cultural meanings in products and acquire them to create a desirable personal identity.

The core values of American culture

A typical marketing analysis of cultural content begins by identifying the core values of the particular social group. **Core values** describe the *end goals* that people are striving to achieve in their lives. Knowing the core values held by people in a society can help marketers understand the basis for the customer/product relationship for those consumers. For instance, many Americans seem to value mastery and control of their lives and their environment. Their fascination with lawncare (control of nature), TV remote controls (control over entertainment), and time management systems (control over time) reflect this value. Perhaps this value will be held less closely as more people realize that some things (such as nature) cannot be rigidly managed or controlled. Exhibit 15.1 presents several basic, core values that many Americans share.

Changing values in America

The constant changes in American cultural values can affect the success of a company's marketing strategies. As people's values change, their means-end connections with existing products and brands also change, which can change the important consumer/product relationship. Consumer Perspective 15.2 (see page 338) describes several instances where value changes have altered consumers' meanings for products.

Changes in values can create both problems and opportunities for marketers. For instance, after the consumption excesses of the 1980s, many consumers seemed to become less materialistic and more concerned about social issues such as protection of the environment. Certainly, the growth of environmentalism as a cultural value has affected the disposable diaper market dominated by Procter & Gamble and Kimberly-Clark, makers of Pampers and Huggies (with 25 and 32 percent market shares in the United States in 1989).[10] By the late 1980s, an increasing number of consumers began to see disposable diapers as a significant contributor to the solid waste that is overflowing American landfills. Essentially, disposable diapers had become a means to a negative end for some, but not all, consumers. In response to these cultural changes, P&G and other companies claimed that reusable cloth diapers pose about the same environmental impact as disposables after considering the water and energy required to clean and dry them. The major companies also worked to develop a more biodegradable diaper. Consumer Perspective 15.3 (see page 339) presents other examples of corporate responses to changing environmental values.

Changes in cultural values can create new marketing opportunities, too. Chicken products, for instance, have seen significant growth as American consumers turned away from burgers to products seen as more healthful. Increasing health values have led many restaurants to add "healthy or heart-conscious" items (with reduced levels of fat, sugar, and cholesterol) to their menus.

Changes in cultural values are usually accompanied by changes in behavior. For instance, the values of convenience and time-saving led to increases in certain home

Value	General Feature	Relevance to Consumer Behavior
Achievement and success	Hard work is good; success flows from hard work	Acts as a justification for acquisition of goods ("You deserve it ")
Activity	Keeping busy is healthy and natural	Stimulates interest in products that save time and enhance leisure-time activities
Efficiency and practicality	Admiration of things that solve problems (e.g., save time and effort)	Stimulates purchase of products that function well and save time
Progress	People can improve themselves; tomorrow should be better	Stimulates desire for new products that fulfill unsatisfied needs; acceptance of products that claim to be "new" or "improved"
Material comfort	"The good life"	Fosters acceptance of convenience and luxury products that make life more enjoyable
Individualism	Being one's self (e.g., self-reliance, self-interest, and self-esteem)	Stimulates acceptance of customized or unique products that enable a person to "express his or her own personality"
Freedom	Freedom of choice	Fosters interest in wide product lines and differentiated products
External conformity	Uniformity of observable behavior; desire to be accepted	Stimulates interest in products that are used or owned by others in the same social group
Humanitarianism	Caring for others, particularly the underdog	Stimulates patronage of firms that compete with market leaders
Youthfulness	A state of mind that stresses being young at heart or appearing young	Stimulates acceptance of products that provide the illusion of maintaining or fostering youth
Fitness and health	Caring about one's body, including the desire to be physically fit and healthy	Stimulates acceptance of food products, activities, and equipment perceived to maintain or increase physical fitness

EXHIBIT 15.1

Core cultural values in America

Source: Leon G. Schiffman and Leslie Lazar Kanuk, *Consumer Behavior,* 4th ed., p. 424, © 1991. Reprinted by permission of Prentice Hall, Englewood Cliffs, NJ

shopping behaviors, including use of mail-order catalogs and TV shopping channels. Marketers often talk about behavior in terms of lifestyles—ways in which people live their lives to achieve important end goals or values. Exhibit 15.2 (see page 340) lists several important lifestyle trends in American society along with examples of how each may impact marketing strategies. Marketers need to monitor these cultural changes and adjust their marketing strategies as necessary.

CULTURE AS A PROCESS

Understanding the content of culture is important for developing effective marketing strategies, but we can also think about *culture as a process.* Exhibit 15.3 (see page 342) presents a model of the cultural process in a highly developed consumer society.[11] The model shows that cultural meaning is present in three "locations"—in the social and physical environment, in products and services, and in individual consumers. The **cultural process** describes *how this cultural meaning is moved about or transferred among these locations* by the actions of organizations (business, government, religion, education) and by individuals

CONSUMER PERSPECTIVE

▶ **15.2**

Changing cultural meanings of products

No meaning lasts forever. Consider the demise of the so-called yuppies (young urban professionals), perhaps the most prominent symbol of the consumption-oriented 1980s in the United States. By the early 1990s, many "yuppie products" had lost some of their status meaning, as manufacturers desperately tried to distance themselves from the dated yuppie image.

BMW, "The Ultimate Driving Machine," was probably the ultimate yuppie status symbol in the United States during the 1980s. But sales dropped for the Bavarian Motor Works Company in the late 80s and early 90s as people's perceptions and values changed, and the American economy cooled. By 1989, BMW sales in the United States were more than 30 percent below their peak in 1986. In reaction, BMW developed new marketing strategies, actually cutting prices up to 9 percent on some models, and introducing two lower-priced, "entry-level" models.

Few products gained favor faster with the yuppie crowd (and their imitators) than Corona beer, imported from Mexico. The beer developed a distinctive image, partly because it was sold in clear glass bottles rather than brown, and partly because people added a wedge of lime before drinking it, which made the product seem more exotic. Sales surged in the mid-1980s, but then dropped precipitously at the end of the decade as yuppies and their imitators moved on to the next fashion. In 1989, Corona sold about 16 million cases of beer in the United States, a far cry from its U.S. sales of 22.5 million cases two years earlier. Although the company fought back with marketing strategies such as 12-packs, a novelty for imported beer, it seems unlikely that Corona will ever again enjoy the powerful cultural meanings that fueled its early success.

When Swatch introduced its colorful and reasonably priced watches in the United States about 1982, it virtually created the market for fashion timepieces. By 1990, however, many adults considered the watches a bit frivolous. So, the Swiss company introduced new models to attract adults and began to advertise on network television for the first time.

Source: Adapted with permission of *The Wall Street Journal*, © 1990, Dow Jones & Co., Inc. All Rights Reserved Worldwide.

in the society. Meaning is transferred in a consumption-oriented society in two ways. First, marketing strategies are designed to move cultural meanings from the cultural environment into products and services in an attempt to make them attractive to consumers. Second, consumers actively seek to acquire these cultural meanings in products to establish a desirable personal identify or self-concept.

Moving cultural meanings into products

Advertising has been the most closely studied method of transferring cultural meaning from the physical and social environment "into" products.[12] From a cultural process perspective, advertising can be seen as a funnel through which cultural meaning is poured into consumer goods.[13] Essentially, advertisers must decide what cultural meanings they want their products to have and create ads that communicate those cultural meanings, often using symbols (whether words or images) to stand for the desired cultural meanings.[14] For instance, to communicate cool, refreshing, summertime meanings for Nestlé's Nestea instant tea, ads showed people falling, fully clothed, into a cool swimming pool. The long-running "Heartbeat of America" campaign for Chevrolet showed various symbols of small-town American life to represent traditional American values such as simplicity, family, patriotism, and friendship. Animals are seen to have distinctive symbolic meanings that marketers can associate with products (the bull in Merrill Lynch ads, the bald eagle in ads for the U.S.

Many companies are responding to consumers' growing environmental values. Trend watchers think the 1990s will be the decade of environmentalism, and that environmental concern will become an important value for consumers all around the world. Some claim environmentalism is "absolutely the most important issue for business." Among the companies that are reacting:

► Procter & Gamble, along with many other marketers, is trying to cast its products in an environmentally friendly light by using recycled materials for packaging and reformulating some products to reduce pollution.

► Wal-Mart has asked all its suppliers for more recycled or recyclable products, which it then features prominently with in-store signs.

► Du Pont has stated a "zero pollution" goal. Among other initiatives, the company is getting out of a $750 million-per-year business in chlorofluorocarbons, which may damage the earth's ozone layer, and has spent nearly $200 million in developing a safe alternative.

► McDonald's is working to cut the huge waste stream produced daily at 8,500 restaurants in the United States. For instance, it requires suppliers to use corrugated boxes containing at least 35 percent recyclable materials. In 1991, McDonald's was testing a variety of things including reusable salad lids, nonplastic utensils, pump-style containers for condiments, and refillable coffee mugs.

The growing environmental concern of consumers creates not just problems for companies, but also opportunities. Big business is forecast for companies in recycling, pollution control technology, and pollution clean-up. Consider the opportunity to design environmentally friendly packaging for compact discs. CDs now come in a plastic "jewel box" inside a long cardboard box. The long box was developed originally to discourage shoplifting and to fit into existing record racks in stores. Besides requiring near gorilla strength to open, the discarded cardboard created 23 million pounds of garbage in 1990.

Source: Frank Edward Allen, "McDonald's Launches Plan to Cut Waste," *The Wall Street Journal*, April, 17, 1991, pp. B1, B4; Meg Cox, "Music Firms Try Out 'Green' CD Boxes," *The Wall Street Journal*, July 25, 1991, p. B1; and David Kirkpatrick, "Environmentalism: The New Crusade," *Fortune*, February 12, 1990, pp. 44–55.

CONSUMER PERSPECTIVE

 15.3 ◄

Environmental concern: a growing cultural value

Postal Service's Express Mail service, the ram for Dodge "ram tough" trucks). The nude bodies shown in Calvin Klein's ads for Obsession cologne connote obvious meanings about the product. Consumer Perspective 15.4 (see page 342) describes another cultural symbol used in advertising.

Although advertising may be the most obvious marketing mechanism for moving meanings into products, other aspects of marketing strategy are involved as well. Consider pricing strategies. Discount stores such as Kmart and Wal-Mart use low prices to establish the cultural meaning of their stores. For many consumers, high prices may have positive cultural meanings that can be linked to certain products (Mercedes-Benz, Rolex watches, Chivas Regal Scotch, European designer clothing) to convey a deluxe, high-status image of high quality. As for product strategy, Japanese automobile companies intentionally design interior attributes (leather versus cloth seats, analog versus digital gauges, wood versus plastic dash) as well as the location and feeling of the controls to transfer important cultural meanings into the car. Even distribution strategies can influence the transmission of meaning—the limited distribution of Burberry trench coats and similar products in better clothing stores enhances the image of such products.

EXHIBIT 15.2

Lifestyle trends in America

Lifestyle trend	Example
Control of time	Americans increasingly value their time and seek greater control of its use.
Component lifestyles	Consumer behavior is becoming more individualistic because of the wider array of available choices.
The culture of convenience	With the rising number of two-income households, consumers are spending more on services in order to have more free time for themselves.
Growth of home shopping	Consumers want more time for themselves and are frustrated by waiting in checkout lines.
Shopping habits of men and women to converge	Men continue to do more of the shopping, and working women take on many male shopping habits.
Escalation of home entertainment	The VCR is the force behind the boom in home entertainment, which will bring about increased purchases of takeout food and changes in the nature of home furnishings and appliances.
Dressing for success	There has been a widespread return to fashion and concern for one's appearance.
Spread of the diversified diet	Americans are eating differently (e.g., lower beef consumption, greater fish consumption).
Self-imposed prohibition of alcohol	The trend has been toward "lighter" drinks (e.g., vodka, "lite" beer), as well as a decline in the overall consumption of alcohol.
The lightest drink of all—water	Bottled or sparkling water is considered by so-called yuppies to be chic; some people are concerned about the quality of their tap water.
The bifurcation of product markets	There is a growing distance between upscale and downscale markets, and companies caught in the middle may fare poorly.
Product and service quality—more important, if not everything	Products falling below acceptable quality standards will be treated more mercilessly.

Other factors besides marketing strategies can influence the transfer of cultural meaning from the environment to products.[15] For instance, journalists who report the results of product tests of cars or stereo systems, or who review movies, are moving cultural meaning into these products. The fashion world, including designers, reporters, opinion leaders, and celebrities, transfers fashion-related meanings into clothing, cuisine, and home furnishings.[16] Consumer advocates such as Ralph Nader (who convinced people the Chevrolet Corvair was unsafe) or government agencies such as the Consumer Product Safety Commission (which requires warning labels telling people not to step on the top step of a stepladder) also transmit meanings to products through their pronouncements.

Cultural meanings in products

Particular products, stores, and brands do express cultural or symbolic meaning.[17] For instance, Virginia Slims cigarettes are for women, Camels are for men; Rollerblades and T-shirts are for young people, gardening tools and laxatives are for older people. Some products embody cultural meanings, such as the Cooperstown Collection of high-quality reproductions of current and old-time baseball team jerseys, jackets, and hats.[18] Using such products makes their cultural meanings tangible and visible and communicates those meanings to others.

Cultural meanings of products are likely to vary across different societies or cultures. For instance, most societies have favorite foods, which represent important meanings in that culture, but not in others—the Danes love eel, Mexicans love chilies, Irish love

Lifestyle trend	Example
Heightened importance of visuals in advertising marketing	With the VCR revolution, the imperative for advertisers is to make the message seen, not heard.
Fragmentation of media markets	There will be new sources of programming as loyalty to network TV fades.
The return of the family	The family will be seen as something to join, as the baby-boom generation rears its children.
New employee benefits for two-income families	Employers will offer flexible work hours, job sharing, and day-care services.
Growing appeal of work at home	Workers will want to work at home on their own computers.
Older Americans—the next entrepreneurs	Older people want to work past the traditional retirement age and have the resources to invest in their own businesses.
The young American— a new kind of conservative	Although 18- to 29-year-olds are socially liberal, they are economically and politically conservative.
Public relations— tough times ahead for business	Business does not receive the credit it deserves for the creation of new jobs, as people remain suspicious about how business operates.
The nation's mood— the new reality	The euphoric mood of the Reagan administration was divorced from economic realities. Americans are economically more sober today.

EXHIBIT 15.2

Continued

Source: Adapted from "31 Major Trends Shaping the Future of American Business," *The Public Pulse* 2, no. 1 (New York: The Roper Organization, 1988).

Guinness beer, French love cheese, Americans love hamburgers. Not all people in a social group or society, however, perceive a product, brand, or activity to have the same cultural meaning. For example, some teenagers might begin to smoke Marlboros to associate themselves with the positive cultural meanings they perceive to be contained in the act of smoking and in the brand. Others will reject smoking to avoid taking on the negative meanings they perceive in the action.

While some of the cultural meanings in products are obvious to anyone who is familiar with that culture, other meanings are hidden. Nearly everyone would recognize the basic cultural meanings in different styles of clothing (jeans and a sweatshirt compared to a business suit), makes of automobiles (Mercedes-Benz versus Ford versus Honda), types of stores (Penney's versus Wal-Mart versus Nordstrom or Saks). But other, less obvious cultural meanings in products may not be fully recognized by consumers or marketers. This was the case in 1985 when Coca-Cola changed Coke's taste to make it slightly sweeter with less of a bite.[19] When it introduced new Coke, the company was surprised by an immediate flurry of protests from customers. Millions of people had consumed Coca-Cola from childhood and had strong cultural meanings for (and emotional ties to) the original product. These consumers resented its removal from the marketplace and some of them even sued the company. In response, Coca-Cola rather quickly reintroduced the original product under the brand name Coca-Cola Classic.

Finally, many products have *personal meaning,* in addition to cultural meaning. Personal meanings are moved into products by the actions of individual consumers. Although these meanings tend to be highly idiosyncratic and unique to each consumer, they are important as a source of personal relevance that can affect consumers' involvement with the product.

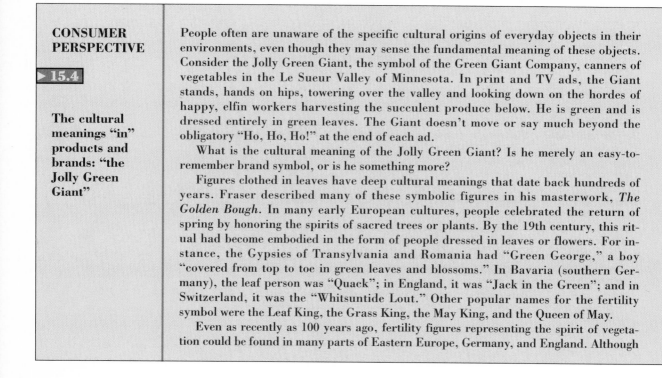

CONSUMER PERSPECTIVE

▶ **15.4**

The cultural meanings "in" products and brands: "the Jolly Green Giant"

People often are unaware of the specific cultural origins of everyday objects in their environments, even though they may sense the fundamental meaning of these objects. Consider the Jolly Green Giant, the symbol of the Green Giant Company, canners of vegetables in the Le Sueur Valley of Minnesota. In print and TV ads, the Giant stands, hands on hips, towering over the valley and looking down on the hordes of happy, elfin workers harvesting the succulent produce below. He is green and is dressed entirely in green leaves. The Giant doesn't move or say much beyond the obligatory "Ho, Ho, Ho!" at the end of each ad.

What is the cultural meaning of the Jolly Green Giant? Is he merely an easy-to-remember brand symbol, or is he something more?

Figures clothed in leaves have deep cultural meanings that date back hundreds of years. Fraser described many of these symbolic figures in his masterwork, *The Golden Bough*. In many early European cultures, people celebrated the return of spring by honoring the spirits of sacred trees or plants. By the 19th century, this ritual had become embodied in the form of people dressed in leaves or flowers. For instance, the Gypsies of Transylvania and Romania had "Green George," a boy "covered from top to toe in green leaves and blossoms." In Bavaria (southern Germany), the leaf person was "Quack"; in England, it was "Jack in the Green"; and in Switzerland, it was the "Whitsuntide Lout." Other popular names for the fertility symbol were the Leaf King, the Grass King, the May King, and the Queen of May.

Even as recently as 100 years ago, fertility figures representing the spirit of vegetation could be found in many parts of Eastern Europe, Germany, and England. Although

Moving meanings from products into consumers

The cultural process model in Exhibit 15.3 identifies rituals as ways of moving cultural meanings from the product to the consumer. A **ritual** is a *symbolic action that people engage in to create, affirm, evoke, or revise certain cultural meanings.*[20] For instance, the consumption ritual performed on Thanksgiving Day by most American families who come

EXHIBIT 15.3

A model of the cultural process

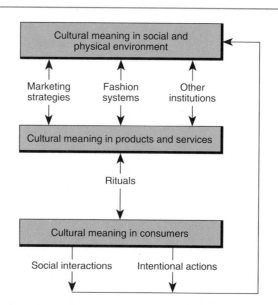

Source: Adapted with permission from the University of Chicago Press from "Culture and Consumption: A Theoretical Account of the Structure and Movement of the Cultural Meaning of Consumer Goods," by Grant McCracken, in *Journal of Consumer Research*, June 1986, pp. 71–84. © 1986 by the University of Chicago.

the details of the costume and the ritual varied from place to place, the overall concept and the representation of the central figure were consistent. A youthful person was dressed with leaves and other vegetation. Sometimes the person was symbolically dunked into a handy pond or stream. Thus were the spirits of fertility and water honored, and the community was assured continued supplies of water and forage.

From a cultural perspective, the Jolly Green Giant can be seen as a 20th century manifestation of these ancient European fertility symbols. Is this just a coincidence, or does the obvious symbolism of such a figure still convey compelling meanings to the sophisticated citizens of the modern world? Did the creative staff at Leo Burnett, Green Giant's ad agency, intentionally appropriate an ancient fertility symbol, or did the idea emerge from their collective unconscious? And, how did the meanings of a giant get added into the equation? Whatever the answers, the Jolly Green Giant seems to represent deep, symbolic cultural meanings that may be partially responsible for the success of the product.

Modern advertising includes other examples of ancient cultural symbols: the Keebler elves, the genie-like Mr. Clean (called Mr. Proper in Germany/Austria), and the white knight of Ajax fame who rode in with lance at the ready and blasted the dirt out of the laundry.

Source: Reproduced by permission of the American F orklore Society from *Journal of American Folklore* 87:343, 1974, pp. 53–65. Not for sale or further reproduction.

together to feast on a big turkey dinner affirms the family's ability to provide abundantly for its needs. Not all rituals involve formal events such as a special dinner, a graduation, or a wedding. Many rituals are actually common actions in everyday life, although people may not recognize their behavior as ritualistic. Here we discuss five specific consumption related rituals involved in the movement of meaning from product to consumer—acquisition, possession, exchange, grooming, and divestment rituals.[21]

Some of the cultural meanings in products are transferred to consumers through specific *acquisition rituals* involved in purchasing and consuming the product. For instance, buying and eating an ice cream cone is necessary to receive the cultural meanings the product conveys (fun, relaxation, a reward for hard work, a "pick-me-up"). Other acquisition behaviors have ritualistic characteristics that are important for meaning transfer. For example, collectors looking for scarce or unique products (antiques, stamps or coins, tools) may perform special *search rituals* when they go out on the hunt, including wearing special lucky clothes.

Another example of acquisition ritual is the *bargaining ritual* involved in negotiating the price of an automobile, stereo system, or something at a garage sale, which can transfer important meanings to the buyer ("I got a good deal"). Consider how an avid antique collector describes the role of bidding rituals at an auction or flea market.

> There's no Alcoholics Anonymous for collectors. You just get bit by the bug and that's it. The beauty and craftsmanship of some of these things is amazing. They were made by people who cared. There's nothing like getting ahold of them for yourself. Especially if you get it for a song and you sing it yourself. It's not just *getting* a great deal, it's *knowing* that you've got a great deal that makes for the thrill. It's even better if you had to bid against someone for it.[22]

Possession rituals are another way consumers acquire the meanings in products. For instance, people moving into a new house or apartment have a housewarming party to show the place off and formally establish its meanings. Many consumers perform similar

These products focus on a lifestyle trend in the United States toward drinking bottled water—the lightest drink of all.

ritualistic displays of new purchases (a car, clothing, stereo system) to solicit the admiration of their friends and gain reassurance that they made a good purchase.

Other possession rituals involve moving personal meaning from the customer "into" the product. For instance, *product nurturing rituals* put personal meaning into the product (washing your car each Saturday; organizing your record or CD collection; tuning your bicycle; tilling your garden).[23] At some point following the nurturing activity, such meanings can be moved back to the consumer, where they may be experienced and enjoyed as satisfaction or pride. Such possession rituals help create strong, involving relationships between products and consumers.

Personalizing rituals serve a similar function. For instance, many people who buy a used car or a house they did not build perform ritualistic actions to remove meanings left over from the previous owner and transfer new meanings of their own into the product. The car owner might purchase special accessories to personalize it (new floor mats, a better radio, different wheels and/or tires, custom stripes). Repainting, wallpapering, or installing new carpeting are rituals that personalize a house.

Certain meanings can be transferred to consumers through *exchange rituals* such as giving gifts.[24] For instance, taking wine or flowers when you go to a dinner party is a ritual that transfers cultural meanings (thanks, courtesy, generosity). People often select gifts for anniversaries, birthdays, or special holidays that contain special cultural meanings to be transferred to the receiver. For instance, giving a nice watch, luggage, or a new car to a college graduate might be intended to convey cultural meanings of achievement, adult status, or independence. Parents often give gifts to their children that are intended to transfer particular cultural meanings (a puppy represents responsibility; a bike represents freedom; a computer conveys the importance of learning and mastery).

Certain cultural meanings consumers acquire tend to fade over time. The central meanings embodied in personal-care products such as shampoo, mouthwash, deodorants, and cosmetics, such as attractiveness, confidence, influence over others, do not become a permanent part of the consumer. Such meanings must be continually renewed by drawing them out of a product each time it is used. *Grooming rituals* describe people's

A study attempted to measure the symbolic, and perhaps largely unconscious, meanings associated with consumers' personal grooming rituals. This research found that hair-care activities dominated the grooming behavior of the young adults (18- to 25-years-old) in the sample. For instance, most of these consumers shampooed their hair nearly every day, and many felt frustrated and emotional about this activity. For instance, one 20-year-old woman said: "Fixing my hair is the most difficult. I spend hours—actually hours—doing my hair. It drives me crazy!"

Because many of the meanings associated with hair care were thought to be relatively unconscious, direct questioning could not be used to tap into these deeper, more symbolic meanings; consumers might just offer rationalizations for their behavior. So the researcher showed male and female consumers pictures of a young man using a blow dryer and a young woman in curlers applying makeup. Each consumer was asked to write a detailed story about the person in the picture. Their stories give some insights into the meanings of those grooming rituals.

For many consumers, hair grooming with the blow-dryer seemed to symbolize an active, take-charge personality who is preparing to go on the "social prowl." For example, one 20-year-old man said, "Jim is supposed to stay home and study tonight, but he's getting ready to go out, anyway. He's hoping to meet some hot chicks, and he wants his hair to look just right."

Symbolic meanings about work and success were prominent in other stories, as the following excerpt from a 21-year-old woman's story illustrates: "Susan is getting ready for her first presentation, and she's very nervous. If it goes well, maybe her boss will help with a down payment on a new car."

Uncovering consumers' deep, symbolic meanings for certain products can be difficult. However, the knowledge may give marketers useful insights into consumers' reactions to their strategies.

Source: Adapted with permission of the University of Chicago Press from "The Ritual Dimension of Consumer Behavior," by Dennis Rook, from *Journal of Consumer Behavior*, December 1985, pp. 251–64. © 1985 by the University of Chicago.

particular ways of using personal-care products that call up these cultural meanings and transfer them to the consumer. Some people engage in elaborate grooming rituals to obtain these important meanings (see Consumer Perspective 15.5).

Consumers perform *divestment rituals* to remove meaning from products. Certain products (clothing, a house, a car or motorcycle, a favorite piece of sports equipment) can embody considerable amounts of personal meaning. Products can acquire such personal meaning through long periods of use, or because they symbolize important meanings (a painting might be a family heirloom that has been handed down through the generations). Often, consumers feel that some of these personal meanings must be removed before such products can be sold or discarded. Thus, for instance, people may wash or dry clean a favorite item of clothing that they plan to give away or donate to charity to remove some of the personal meanings in the product. Others might remove certain highly personal fixtures in a house (a special chandelier), attributes of a car (a special radio), or parts of a motorcycle (a custom seat) before selling it.

In certain cases, the personal meaning in a product is so great that the consumer cannot bear to part with the object. Thus, people hang onto old cars, clothes, or furniture that have sentimental personal meaning. One study found that some people had become highly attached to their Levi's jeans and kept them for years (even more than 20 or 30 years).[25] These consumers associated many salient meanings with Levi's jeans including the self-confidence they felt when wearing the product and the feeling that Levi's were appropriate in many social situations. Other consumers talked as if their Levi's were an old friend who had accompanied them on many adventures, and their jeans were valued for the memories they embodied. If divestment rituals are unable to remove these meanings, consumers may keep such objects practically forever or at least until the personal meanings have faded and become less intense.

Cultural meanings in consumers

Consumers select products as one way to acquire cultural meanings to use in establishing their self-identifies. Consider the sports fan who buys a team hat or jacket. Major League Baseball Properties, a licensing and marketing organization, sells authentic jerseys from the New York Yankees (about $175) and the 1919 Chicago Black Sox ($245) to middle-age fans who want to identify with their favorite teams, present and past. Some people might buy Ben & Jerry's Rain Forest Crunch ice cream (made from nuts grown in the Amazon rain forest) or Tide detergent packaged in recycled materials to express the environmental values embodied in these products. People buy such products to move important cultural meanings into themselves and to communicate these meanings to others.

Americans have a lot of freedom to create different selves, through their choice of lifestyles and environments, as well as products. Personality definition is especially intense during the teenage and young adult years. In trying different social roles and identities, young people often purchase products to gain meanings related to these roles. Thus, teenage rebellion against parental values often involves the purchase of products that symbolize the desired cultural meanings (often clothing). As most people mature, their self-concepts become more stable, and their interest in change lessens. Even so, consumers still use the cultural meanings in products to maintain and fine-tune their current identities.

Although products transfer some useful meanings to consumers, goods cannot provide all the meanings that consumers need to construct a healthy self-concept. People obtain self-relevant meanings from many fundamental sources, including their work, family, religious experience, and various social activities. The meanings gained through these activities are likely to be more basic and more satisfying than those obtained through product consumption. In highly developed consumption societies, however, some people buy products in an attempt to define themselves through possessions. Some marketing strategies encourage this behavior. These consumers may engage in excessive consumption as they desperately seek to acquire cultural meanings with which to construct a satisfactory identity. More often the result is debt and lack of satisfaction.

Most people have favorite possessions that are imbued with significant self-relevant meanings, and they experience high levels of *involvement* with such objects.[26] For instance, older persons tend to feel strong attachments to objects such as photographs and furniture that remind them of past events, while younger consumers tend to value objects that allow them to be active in self-relevant ways (sports or hobby equipment, work-related objects such as books or computers). Marketers who understand these consumer/product relationships can develop more effective marketing strategies.

Moving meanings to the cultural environment

The cultural process model in Exhibit 15.3 shows that the meanings in consumers can be transferred to the social and physical environment through people's social behavior. That is, in a society consisting of many individuals living and working together, culture (shared meaning) literally is created by those people. Much of the movement of meaning to the cultural environment is an automatic consequence of the daily social interactions among people. Sometimes, however, people intentionally try to create new cultural meanings in an attempt to change society. For instance, various interest groups in society (punks, greens or environmental activists, gay rights activists) try to influence others to adopt new cultural meanings.

Consumption rituals or special occasions such as Thanksgiving help create or affirm important cultural meanings.

The cultural process is a continual movement of meanings between and among the physical and social environment, organizations, and individuals in the society. This focuses marketers' attention on the cultural meaning of their brands.[27] The shared cultural meanings of a brand are a large part of its economic value or its *brand equity,*[28] and managing the brand requires that marketers identify these shared brand meanings and monitor any changes. Means-end analysis is useful for this purpose. A marketer might try to maintain positive brand meanings or to create new favorable meanings by selecting appropriate meanings from the cultural environment and transferring them into products and brands by marketing strategies.

Marketing implications

Although marketers usually think their strategies have little effect on culture, marketing strategies do influence the cultural environment in a number of ways. A conspicuous example is the proliferation of marketing information (stores, signs, billboards, ads), which changes cultural meaning of the physical environment. Less obvious is how the huge volume of marketing strategies in a consumption society affects the social environment and thereby the cultural meanings of modern life.[29]

Celebrity endorsers in ads

A popular advertising strategy in North America (and in Japan) for endowing products and brands with cultural meaning is to use celebrities to endorse a product.[30] Among the celebrities appearing in ads in the early 1990s were the actor Michael J. Fox (Pepsi), Cher and the ballet dancer Mikhail Baryshnikov (cologne), CEOs Lee Iacocca (Chrysler) and Victor Kiam (Remington razors), singers Whitney Houston and Michael Jackson and basketball player Michael Jordan (Nike), test pilot Chuck Yeager (car batteries), Tommy LaSorda (diet aid), and politician Tip O'Neill (hotel chain).

From a cultural perspective, celebrities may be seen as cultural objects with specific cultural meanings. Consider, for instance, the meanings associated with James Garner, TV star and spokesperson for the Beef Council, among other products.

Garner plays . . . the generalized James Garner role, the type for which James Garner is always cast—handsome, gentle, bumbling, endearing, a combination of Bret Maverick from "Maverick" and Jim Rockford from "The Rockford Files." The Garner celebrity is capable, but occasionally incompetent and bumbling, forthright but unassuming, and usually the master of his fate, but occasionally up against fate (usually a comic situation).[31]

In developing an effective celebrity endorsement strategy, marketers must be careful to select a celebrity who embodies appropriate meanings that are consistent with the overall marketing strategy (the intended meanings) for the product. For example, celebrities such as Bill Murray, Sylvester Stallone, or Suzanne Sommers convey relatively clear meanings that are based on the types of roles they usually play. Musicians such as Elton John and Sting (for Coke) or Ray Charles (for Pepsi) have distinctive cultural images related to their records, live performances, and video appearances, which enhance their appeal as celebrity spokespersons. Some celebrities such as Madonna have shrewdly re-created their images (and their cultural meanings) over time as the appeal of one set of cultural meanings wanes. Interestingly, celebrities who tend to have been typecast (something actors complain about) are more likely to evoke shared cultural meanings that can be associated with a product. Meryl Streep, for instance, might not be a desirable spokesperson because she has played a wide variety of roles and therefore does not convey a clear set of cultural meanings.

Sometimes the cultural meanings of a celebrity spokesperson are related to their credibility and expertise concerning the product. For instance, Cher and Elizabeth Taylor promote their own perfume brands, while Phil and Steve Mahre, the twin American ski racers, promote K2 skis. In other cases, the person's cultural meanings are not logically linked to the product, but the marketer hopes the general meaning of the celebrity as a credible and trustworthy person will help transfer important meanings to the product. Apparently on this basis, Bill Cosby has been a spokesperson for Jell-O, E. F. Hutton, and Kodak film processing.

Marketers need to understand more about how celebrities transfer meanings to a product. What happens to the cultural meanings of celebrities who are disgraced (Ben Johnson is caught using steroids, Pete Rose is jailed for income tax evasion), or fall from public favor (an actor's performance is panned), or retire from public life (Larry Bird stops playing basketball, Ingmar Bergman stops making films), or return again to fame and favor in some way (Bob Dylan or Mickey Rooney)? How do marketers use such celebrities in transmitting cultural meanings? Do consumers gain the meanings embodied by a celebrity merely by purchasing the endorsed brand, or are ritualistic behaviors necessary? Although it is popular to criticize the North American and Japanese fascination with celebrities as juvenile, celebrities represent important cultural meanings that many consumers find personally relevant. By purchasing and using a product endorsed by a celebrity, consumers can assume some of those meanings and use them in constructing a satisfying identity.

Helping consumers obtain cultural meanings

If they understand the role of rituals in consumer behavior, marketers can devise rituals that serve to transfer important cultural meanings from products to the customer. A real estate firm, for instance, might develop an elaborate purchase ritual, perhaps including an exchange of gifts on the purchase occasion, to symbolize the transfer of the house and its meanings to the buyer. Some upscale clothing stores go through elaborate shopping and buying rituals aimed at their affluent customers, including ushering the customer to a private room, serving coffee or wine, and presenting a selection of clothing. People dining in a fine restaurant participate in many rituals that transfer special meanings, including being seated by the maître d', talking to the wine steward, using different silverware and glasses, eating successive courses, and tipping.

Another example is the strategies Nissan uses to create rituals that help transmit meanings about the luxury car Infinity to consumers.[32] Dealers will gently welcome customers Japanese-style, as "honored guests" (not aggressively descend on the "mooches," as American salespeople sometimes describe naive customers). Tea or coffee is to be offered, served in fine Japanese china. Each Infinity dealership is to have a special shoki-screened contemplation room where consumers can sit quietly with the car, "meditating" about their purchase and the consumer/product relationship. These rituals help reinforce the low-pressure, relaxed meanings Nissan wants to impart to the Infinity experience.

CROSS-CULTURAL INFLUENCES

Foreign markets have become significant for many businesses. In the U.S. film industry, because domestic ticket sales were flat over the past decade (about 1 billion tickets per year), film companies have looked to foreign markets for growth. In 1990, major domestic film studios received about 35 percent of their total revenues from foreign markets (50 percent for smaller companies).[33] Film studios have come under pressure to develop films that would appeal to consumers both in the United States and in foreign markets.

To develop strategies that are effective in multiple cultures, marketers must understand the differences in cultural meanings across societies. **Cross-cultural differences** in meanings create different cultural environments that influence consumers' behaviors, affects and cognition. These cross-cultural differences must be considered in developing international marketing strategies.

Cross-cultural differences do not always coincide with national borders. This is obvious in many countries where the cultural differences between internal social factions can be as great as those between separate nations. Examples include the former Yugoslavia (which was made up of several distinct regions including Slovenia, Croatia, Serbia), Belgium (with two language cultures—Flemish and French), and Canada (with two language cultures—English and French), Switzerland (with German, French, Italian, andRomansch-speaking regions). Understanding the multiple cultural influences in such regions requires an analysis of subcultures, discussed in Chapter 16.

Likewise, national borders do not always demarcate clear cross-cultural differences. For instance, many people living on either side of the long Canadian-U.S. border share similar cultural characteristics (French-speaking Quebec is an exception). Likewise, the people in southern Austria and northern Italy, or northern France and southern Belgium, share many cultural characteristics.

Cross-cultural differences

Marketers must consider cross-cultural differences when developing marketing strategies for foreign markets. We discuss some of these differences here.

Differences in consumption culture

The level of consumption orientation in different markets around the world is an important cross-cultural factor that must be considered in developing international marketing strategies. U.S. society is a highly developed consumer culture, and many other areas of the world—including Canada, most western European countries, and Japan—also have strong consumer cultures. Even in relatively poor countries, significant segments of society may have a developing consumer culture. For instance, India, Mexico, and many South American countries have a large middle class able to consume at significant levels. The Pacific Rim countries have a rapidly growing middle class with substantial spending power. Consumer Perspective 15.6 provides more details on this vast market.

In much of the world, however, the majority of people are unable to participate fully in a consumption culture. For instance, the ordinary citizens of many Eastern European countries, the former Soviet Union, China, India, and most less developed countries do not

CONSUMER PERSPECTIVE

▶ **15.6**

New mass markets develop in Asia

Significant cultural changes in Asia are opening up new marketing opportunities for companies. A number of factors are fueling these massive changes in culture.

People

About 1.7 billion people live in the Asian Pacific Rim region. Although population growth is slowing, there still will be an additional 400 million people in the next 20 years. Thirty percent will be in their 30s and 40s, the prime earning and spending years.

Income

A decade of rising prosperity has spread relative affluence throughout the population. One estimate is that 72 million people in the Pacific Rim (not including Japan) have household incomes of $10,000 or more. To put this into perspective, South Korea and Taiwan, with populations of 42 million and 20 million, will have per capita incomes of $11,000 and $13,000 by the year 2000. These levels are slightly above current incomes in Spain and Ireland.

Cities

As has happened elsewhere, Asian people are moving off the farms and into the cities. For example, in Korea, the population went from 72 percent rural to 73 percent urban in just 30 years. In less developed countries, still largely rural, the urban areas are growing rapidly. As one Asia expert puts it, "When you shift from a rural to an urban lifestyle, from spending 12 to 16 hours a day in a field or rice paddy, to

have sufficient purchasing power to consume at high levels, nor are these societies able to produce goods in sufficient number and variety to meet the consumption needs of their people. A company's marketing strategies must be tailored to the level of consumption culture in the society.

Self-concept

People in different cultures may have strikingly different concepts of themselves and how they should relate to other people.[34] An example is the differences between the independent self-concept typical of North America and Western Europe consumers and the social concept of self as highly interrelated with others that is more common in Japan, India, Africa, and South America. Americans, with their strong individualistic orientation, tend to think of themselves in terms of personal traits and abilities that enable them to achieve their ideal goals of independence, freedom of choice, and personal achievement. The Japanese, by contrast, tend to value an individual who is sensitive to the needs of others, fitting harmoniously into the group and contributing positively to the well-being of the group members. Such cross-cultural differences in self-concept are likely to affect how people in a cultural environment interpret and use products to achieve important ends in their lives.

Materialism

Materialistic values underlie the development of a mass consumption society, and people in different societies vary considerably in their level of materialism. Materialism has been defined as the "importance a consumer attaches to worldly possessions."[35] In fact, **materialism** is a multidimensional value including, for instance, *possessiveness, envy* (jealousy of someone's possessions), and *lack of generosity* (unwillingness to give or

working in a factory for 8 to 10 hours, suddenly things happen to you. Your values and motivations change."

Women
Almost everywhere in Asia, women are staying in school longer, marrying later, and entering the work force in greater numbers.

Families
Families are changing rapidly in Asian countries. Women are having fewer children and later in life, as in the West. The number of people in each household is decreasing, but the number of households is increasing, which creates larger markets for many types of consumer goods (appliances, home furnishings).

Communications
The incredible ability to communicate easily, quickly, and relatively cheaply around the world accelerates cultural changes. Consumers in Taiwan and Hong Kong know what's happening in Japan and the United States. Trends and fads catch on quickly everywhere. For instance, the movie *Dick Tracy* opened in Hong Kong less than one month after it opened in the United States, and with the same T-shirts and toys. Not long ago, the lag might have been two years.

These similarities between cultures help create global markets for many products.

Source: Adapted with permission from "A New Mass Market Emerges," by Ford S. Worthy, *Fortune*, © 1990 Time Inc. All rights reserved.

share possessions). Consumers with this value tend to acquire many possessions that they see as important for achieving happiness, self-esteem, or social recognition (all prominent values in American culture). One study identifies four representations of materialism: possessions are symbols of success or achievement (also prominent American values), a source of pleasure, a source of happiness, and representations of indulgence and luxury.[36]

The United States is usually considered to be the most materialistic culture in the world, although some studies suggest Americans are not more materialistic than some European societies. For instance, one study finds that consumers in the Netherlands have about the same overall level of materialism as American consumers.[37] Interestingly, the Dutch consumers were found to be more possessive than Americans—it may be no accident that the Dutch have no garage sales and few flea markets. U.S. consumers seem to replace old products with new ones fairly easily, but the Dutch seem to form stronger product-self relationships with their possessions.

Similar cross-cultural changes
It is becoming more common to find similar cultural changes occurring in many societies around the world at about the same time. For instance, the social roles for women in North American society have changed considerably over the past 20 years—as more women work outside the home, their values, goals, beliefs, and behaviors have changed.[38] Similar changes are now seen around the world. Modern women in America and Europe, and increasingly in Japan and other countries, want more egalitarian marriages. They want their husbands to share in the housework and nurturing of children, and they want to establish a personal identity outside the family unit. These common cross-cultural changes have created similar marketing opportunities in many societies (particularly for convenience

Celebrity endorsers are used to move cultural meaning into production.

products and time-saving services). For instance, as the Japanese become more consumption oriented and price conscious, the number of malls and discount stores is increasing rapidly.[39]

In developed countries throughout the world, people want more leisure and more free time. Even the world champion workaholics in Japan, where up to 60 percent of workers spend Saturdays on the job, have begun to relax a bit.[40] Although the traditional Japanese values of hard work, dedication, and respect for the established order are still dominant, some Japanese, especially the young, are starting to see certain aspects of Western culture and lifestyle as preferable to their own.

A global culture?

Although some cross-cultural differences can be sharp and distinctive, in other cases people from different cultures may have rather similar values and consumer/product relationships. Some analysts, in fact, see the entire world as moving toward an "Americanized" culture, although this observation is far from accepted. Consumer Perspective 15.7 discusses some examples of the exporting of American popular culture. To the extent that cultural meanings are becoming similar across societies, marketers may be able to develop successful strategies that are indeed global in scope.

Developing international marketing strategies

Cross-cultural differences pose challenges for international marketers. Even translating a brand or model name into another language can cause problems. When Coca-Cola was introduced in China in the 1920s, the translated meaning of the brand name was "bite the wax tadpole"! Sales were not good, and the symbols were later changed to mean "happiness in the mouth." The American Motors Matador model had problems in Puerto Rico because matador means "killer." Ford Motor Company changed the name of the Comet to Caliente when it introduced this car in Mexico, then experienced low sales levels until it discovered that *caliente* is slang for streetwalker. Sunbeam Corporation introduced its mist-producing hair curling iron in the German market under the name Mist-Stick, which translated meant "manure wand."[41]

American companies are not the only ones that have difficulty translating brand names. The Chinese had to find better brand names for several products they hoped to export, including "Double Happiness" bras, "Pansy" men's underwear, and "White Elephant" batteries.[42]

Clearly, cross-cultural differences in language and related meanings can affect the success of a marketing strategy. While differences in cultures can often be identified,

CONSUMER
PERSPECTIVE

15.7

Exporting
American
popular culture

Aspects of American culture are found increasingly around the globe. One can find the icons of American popular culture nearly everywhere. Consider the worldwide presence of Coke and Pepsi, McDonald's and Pizza Hut, Mickey Mouse and Mickey Rourke, cowboys and jazz, American films and Disneyland. The spread of American culture has produced some incongruous scenes of Third World protesters burning the American flag or chanting anti-American slogans, while dressed in T-shirts, Nike shoes, and blue jeans. Although some people consider American culture distasteful, others have adopted many of its forms. Even in anglophobic France, the uniform of young, upper-middle-class Parisian women in 1990 was pure Americana—Calvin Klein jeans, a white button-down oxford shirt, a navy blazer, Bass Weejuns penny loafers, and a Marlboro cigarette.

Clearly, consumers around the world are not attracted to American products solely for their intrinsic physical qualities. People don't buy blue jeans because of some universal aesthetic for denim, nor do Coke or Marlboros or Mickey Mouse have physical attributes that are so special. Rather, these prototypically American products are imbued with meanings that symbolize the United States.

What are these special American meanings? According to a Yale professor, "It's about a dream, a utopian fantasy. Certainly it is about freedom, the freedom of people to create themselves anew, redefining themselves through the products that they buy and use, the clothes they wear, the music they listen to." Blue jeans, perhaps more than any other product, symbolize America and the individualistic meanings it represents to many. Buying blue jeans is a way for consumers to share in the American dream of individualism, personal freedom, and other symbolic characteristics associated with America.

It is important to recognize that American culture is popular partly because it is just that—a *popular culture*, not an elitist culture created by and for the aristocracy in a society. American culture is for the masses. Moreover, it is a *highly democratic culture*, which everyone in the society helps to shape, not just the upper class. Finally, American culture lends itself to export because it is itself a *combination of diverse cultural elements* brought to America by millions of immigrants tumbled together to create something new and desirable. Perhaps this explains why members of the elite social classes in the United States and elsewhere love to turn up their noses at the tawdry popular culture in America. A democratic culture can be threatening for the ruling elites in many societies.

Source: Eric Felten, "Love It or Hate It, America Is King of Pop Culture," *Insight*, March 25, 1991, pp. 14–16.

marketers do not agree on how to treat these differences. There are at least three overall approaches. First, a firm can adapt its marketing strategy to the characteristics of each culture. Second, a firm can standardize its marketing strategy across several cultures. Arguments over which of these is the preferred approach have raged for more then 20 years. Third, a firm can use a marketing strategy to change the culture.

Adapt strategy to culture

The traditional approach to international marketing is to research each local culture to identify important differences from the domestic market. The goal is to understand important differences in consumer needs, wants, preferences, attitudes, and values, as well as in shopping, purchasing, and consumption behaviors. Marketers then tailor a marketing strategy to fit the specific values and behaviors of the culture.

The *adaptation* approach advocates modifying the product, the promotion mix, or any other aspect of marketing strategy to appeal to local cultures.[43] Black & Decker, for

Benetton uses a similar social awareness image strategy across the world.

example, modifies its hand tools because electrical outlets and voltages vary in different parts of the world. Philip Morris had to alter its ads for Marlboro cigarettes in Britain, because the government believed British children are so impressed with American cowboys they might be moved to take up smoking. Nestlé modifies the taste of its Nescafe coffee and the promotions for it in the adjoining countries of France and Switzerland to accommodate different preferences in each nation.[44]

Standardize strategy across cultures

The **global marketing** approach argues for marketing a product in essentially the same way everywhere in the world. Standardizing strategy is not a new idea—Coca-Cola has used this basic approach for over 40 years: "one sight, one sound, one sell." Other companies such as Eastman Kodak, Gillette, and Timex have marketed standard products in essentially the same way for several decades.

Many marketers are beginning to treat the standardized approach more seriously. One of its major advocates, Theodore Levitt, argues that increased world travel and worldwide telecommunications capabilities cause consumers the world over to think and shop increasingly in the same way. Tastes, preferences, and motivations of people in different cultures are becoming more homogeneous, so a common brand name, packaging, and communication strategy can be used successfully for many products.[45] For example, given the international popularity of the "Dallas" TV show, actress Victoria Principal sold Jhirmack shampoo all over the world. Similarly, Victor Kiam sells his Remington shavers using the same pitch in 15 languages. Sales of Remington shavers went up 60 percent in Britain and 140 percent in Australia using this approach. Playtex markets its WoW bra in 12 countries using the same advertising appeal.

One advantage of the standardized approach is that it can be much less expensive in terms of advertising and other marketing costs.[46] Executives at Coca-Cola, for instance, estimate they save more than $8 million a year in the cost of thinking up new imagery. Texas Instruments runs the same ads throughout Europe rather than mounting individual ad campaigns for each country, and it estimates its savings at $30,000 per commercial. Playtex produced standardized ads for 12 countries for $250,000, while the average cost of producing a single Playtex ad for the United States was $100,000.[47]

For some products, a global or standardized marketing approach can work well, although many have severely criticized the global marketing approach.[48] Two issues cloud the debate between adapting versus standardizing international marketing approaches. First is the nature of the product and how standardized the global approach is. For example, advocates of standardizing recognize that Black & Decker had to modify its products to suit local electrical outlets and voltages; yet they would argue the basic meaning and use of such products is becoming similar across cultures. If so, the same type of promotion campaign should work in different cultures.

Second, and perhaps more important, is the question whether advocates of the standardizing approach are identifying a long-term trend toward similarity across cultures or are suggesting that cultures are nearly identical today. If the former is true, this is a trend marketers should be aware of and adapt to when appropriate. Thus, in essence, both sides are arguing for marketers to adapt to cultural trends; there would seem to be little disagreement between the two positions at this level.

Change the culture

The first approach we discussed is to adapt marketing strategy to local cultures. The second approach assumes decreasing cross-cultural differences that, in some cases, can be ignored. Yet a third approach suggests marketing strategies can be developed to influence a culture directly to achieve organizational objectives. As the cultural process model in Exhibit 15.3 shows, marketing does not simply reflect changing cultural values and behaviors of consumers; marketing is an active part of the cultural process of creating and transferring cultural meaning.[49]

Marketing strategies can change cultural values and behaviors. Several years ago, Nestlé marketed vigorously to convince mothers in some Third World countries to change from breast-feeding to baby formula. The campaign was very successful in convincing mothers that breast-feeding was not as healthful for their children as the company's formula, and it dramatically changed their feeding practices. Unfortunately, lack of clean water and improper formula preparation led to an increase in infant mortality. Thus, the preference for and practice of breast-feeding had to be reinstilled in those countries, which was done successfully by Nestlé. This company changed cultural preferences and behaviors—and then changed them back—in a relatively short time.

► SUMMARY

Learning objective 1: *Define culture and cultural meaning.*
Culture is broadly defined as the meanings that are shared by most people in a social group. Those meanings that are similar or common among people in the group are called cultural meanings. Cultural meanings could refer to any component of the Wheel of Consumer Analysis—affect and cognition, behavior, or any aspect of the environment, including marketing strategies. Cultural meanings are created by people in the social group and are in continual flux. Marketers can analyze the cultural meanings of very large groups such as an entire society, a subculture within a society, or quite small groups such as families or reference groups.

Learning objective 2: *Discuss aspects of the content of culture, including core values.*
The content of culture includes the beliefs, attitudes, goals, and values held by most people in a society as well as their emotions and feelings. Culture also refers to the shared meanings of characteristic behaviors, rules, customs, and norms that most people follow.

The content of culture includes shared meanings of the significant aspects of the social and physical environment, including the major social institutions in a society (governmental bodies, political parties, religions) and the typical physical objects (products, tools, buildings) used by people in a society. Core values describe the end goals people are striving to achieve in their lives and are among the most important aspects of culture. An understanding of the core values in a social group is essential for marketers in order to identify how those values are related to products through means-end chains.

Learning objective 3: *Describe the cultural process by which cultural meaning is moved from the environment into products and then into consumers.*

Cultural meaning is present in three locations—in the social and physical environment, in products and services, and in individual consumers. Cultural meaning is moved or transferred between locations through a cultural process effected by organizations (government, business, religion, education) and by individuals in the society. Two forces for meaning transfer in a consumption-oriented society include: (1) Marketing strategies are designed to endow products and services with cultural meaning that makes them attractive to consumers. Advertising is the most obvious marketing strategy for transmitting meaning into products, but in fact all aspects of marketing strategy, including product design, pricing and distribution, are involved. (2) Consumers actively seek the cultural meanings in products to use in establishing a desirable personal identity or self-concept. They engage in ritualistic behaviors to acquire the meanings in products.

Learning objective 4: *Give examples of how rituals move meaning from products into consumers and vice versa.*

Rituals are symbolic actions that people engage in to create, affirm, evoke, or revise certain cultural meanings. Some rituals involve formal ceremonies such as a wedding or a graduation, but rituals also are common behaviors in everyday life. Marketers are especially interested in the rituals consumers perform to transfer meanings from the product to themselves, and vice versa. Acquisition rituals may be important in helping people acquire the cultural meanings of some products. For instance, shopping rituals may be important for consumers who are buying an important suit or special antiques. Bargaining rituals may be part of the acquisition process. Possession rituals such as showing off a new car help establish cultural meanings of ownership and pride. Divestment rituals are actions intended to remove meaning from a product before one disposes of it.

Learning objective 5: *Give some examples of important cross-cultural differences.*

Cross-cultural differences refer to differences in cultural meaning across societies, usually analyzed in terms of national boundaries. Consumers in different societies or countries are likely to have different values, beliefs, emotional responses, and norms of appropriate behavior, as well as different social and physical environments. For instance, people in some societies may be more materialistic than in others. One important cross-cultural difference refers to people's self-concepts—how they see themselves. Such cross-cultural differences can lead to distinctive consumer/product relationships. Cross-cultural differences in consumption behaviors, such as shopping, bargaining, or product use, can be important for marketing. Emotional reactions to marketing strategies (ads, displays, salespeople) may differ across cultures.

Learning objective 6: *Discuss three approaches to developing international marketing strategies.*

First, a company can adapt its marketing strategies to cultural factors found in various societies. This may require a company to develop special product configurations, advertising campaigns, and pricing and distribution strategies for each culture. A second possibility is to develop a standardized marketing strategy to be used in several cultures. A standardized strategy does not mean every tiny detail is identical in every culture, but the

key aspects of the strategy should be the same. A third approach to cross-cultural differences in international marketing is to attempt through marketing and general business
strategies to change cultural values and behaviors in ways advantageous to the company. Most companies follow the first two approaches.

---

culture	core values	cross-cultural differences
cultural meaning	cultural process	materialism
content of culture	ritual	global marketing

► **KEY TERMS
AND CONCEPTS**

---

1. Define culture and describe three issues involved in cultural analysis.
2. Identify a major change in cultural values that seems to be occurring in your society (choose one not discussed in the book). Discuss its likely effects on consumers' affect, cognitions, and behaviors and on the social and physical environment.
3. Discuss two implications of your analysis in Question 2 for developing marketing strategies for a product of your choice.
4. Briefly describe one example of a price, product, and distribution strategy that moves cultural meaning into the product (do not use examples cited in the text).
5. Select a print ad, and analyze it as a mechanism for moving cultural meaning into the product.
6. Choose a popular celebrity endorser, and analyze the meanings that are being transmitted to the product the celebrity is endorsing.
7. Select a holiday in your culture other than Christmas. Discuss the cultural values reflected in this holiday celebration. What rituals does your family perform for this holiday, and how do these actions convey meaning?
8. Think about what you do when getting ready to go to a party or some other social event. Identify a grooming ritual you perform that involves some product (blow dryer, cologne, shampoo, cosmetics). What implications might this ritual have for marketing this product?
9. Describe a personal experience in which you performed a divestment ritual. What personal meanings did you remove through the ritual?
10. Discuss how the three main approaches to dealing with cross-cultural factors in international marketing could be applied to the marketing of a soft drink such as Pepsi-Cola. Describe one problem with each approach. Which approach do you recommend?

► **REVIEW AND
DISCUSSION
QUESTIONS**

16

Subculture and Social Class Influences

LEARNING OBJECTIVES

After completing this chapter, you should be able to

► 1. Define subculture, and discuss the analysis of subcultures.

► 2. Describe a geographic subculture, and give several examples.

► 3. Describe age subcultures, and give some examples.

► 4. Discuss the three major ethnic subcultures in America.

► 5. Define consumer acculturation, and describe the four stages of acculturation.

► 6. Describe the major social classes in America, and discuss how marketers can use social class distinctions.

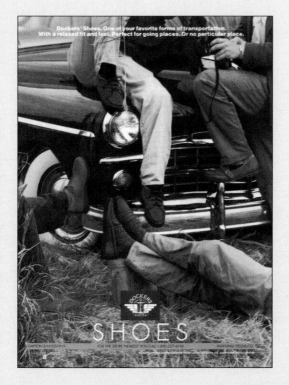

THE BOOMERS MEET THE DOCKERS

The 68 million so-called baby boomers (Americans born between 1946 and 1962) are rapidly becoming middle-aged. The members of this large group will continue to have a disproportionate effect on the culture and economy of the United States, probably even more than they did when they were teenagers and young adults. For instance, by 1997, the number of Americans between 35 and 44 years old will increase by 26 percent and earn an awesome $195 billion. This group will become the nation's biggest spenders. In the 1990s, the number of consumers in the 25 to 34 age group will fall by 9 percent and drop $67 billion in purchasing power.

Many marketers have not understood or appreciated the middle-aged consumer. But confronted with this large a market, advertisers must change their orientation to appeal to these older and more mature consumers. The old approach of portraying baby boomers as an energetic bunch of jeans-wearing, granola-eating, rock music–listening kids doesn't work any more.

The Levi Strauss company has followed the baby boomers for three decades. To promote its new Dockers line of casual slacks, it showed a group of 40-ish men sitting around and jokingly reminiscing about the good old days. The product was not mentioned until the conclusion. According to a Levi's executive, "Real people don't sit around and talk about the brand of clothing they're wearing." The pants were already a hit, but sales accelerated following these ads.

Madison Avenue generally has been late in responding to the aging trend, perhaps because many of the people making creative advertising decisions are themselves pushing 40 and none too happy about it. The apprehension that many Americans have about growing older is a major impediment to creating attractive, imaginative advertising for the not-so-young. As one advertising executive puts it, "Advertisers feel that youth is sexy and glamorous, old age is humorous, but middle age is dreary." This notion will change fast.

People's values and goals tend to change as they age. Younger people like competition, showing off, looking good. Older boomers are starting to care about comfort, convenience, and financial security. Advertisers will have to overcome their obsession with youth and create acceptable mature images that fit the self-concepts, goals, and values of not-so-young consumers.

In 1994, marketing to the 35- to 44-year-old consumer was a strong trend. And, the next few years should witness an avalanche of such marketing strategies as marketers catch up to the demographic changes in this American subculture.[1]

Different age groups represent major subcultures in the United States (and elsewhere). The aging of the baby boomers is one example of how changing demographic characteristics of a subculture can be important to marketers. Subcultures and social class are two aspects of the macro social environment; culture is the third. The key distinction among the three is size. Culture usually is analyzed at the level of a country or an entire society, whereas subcultures are subgroups or segments of a society. Social class is a special type of subculture defined in terms of social status. Subcultures and social classes are cultural groups in that their members share certain cultural meanings; both, however, are part of the larger society and therefore are influenced by the overall culture. Thus, we would not expect middle-class Germans and middle-class Americans to have exactly the same meanings, behaviors, and lifestyles. Marketers use social class and subculture to segment markets, to help understand the shared cultural meanings of large groups of consumers, and to develop targeted marketing strategies.

In this chapter, we define subculture and discuss several subcultures found in the United States (and elsewhere in the world). We also discuss the social classes found in U.S. society. Throughout, we draw implications for marketing strategy.

SUBCULTURES

A **subculture** is a *distinctive group of people in a society who share cultural meanings*. These common cultural meanings may concern affective and cognitive responses (emotional reactions, beliefs, values, and goals), behaviors (customs, scripts and rituals, norms) and environmental factors (living conditions, geographic location, important objects). Although each subculture shares certain cultural meanings with the overall society and other subcultures, some of its meanings are unique and distinctive.

Major demographic changes relating to age and diversity make marketers' analyses of subculture more important than ever. As in most developed countries, the population in the United States is aging (in 2000, the median age will be 36; it was 33 in 1990).[2] Another change is that many societies are becoming more culturally diverse, largely through increased immigration of people from other cultures. About 20 percent of Americans were members of minority groups in the early 1980s; by 2010, this will climb to about 30 percent. These various subcultural groups, each with unique perspectives and cultural meanings, exert considerable influence on the overall culture. To understand this diversity, marketers try to identify and understand subcultures and develop marketing strategies to address their particular needs.

Marketers generally use demographic characteristics to identify subcultures. Exhibit 16.1 lists several examples of subcultures and the demographic characteristics used to classify people into these cultural groups. Subcultures are not mutually exclusive—a person can simultaneously be a Hispanic, middle-class male, with a moderate income, who is a resident of the northwestern United States. Marketers often combine demographic distinctions to identify more precisely defined subcultures (such as affluent, Jewish, middle-aged consumers living in the South).

Demographic Characteristic	Examples of Subcultures
Age	Adolescent, young adult, middle-aged, elderly
Ethnic origin	African, Hispanic, Asian, European
Gender	Female, male
Race	Black, Caucasian, Oriental
Income level	Affluent, middle income, poor, destitute
Nationality	French, Malaysian, Australian, Canadian
Religion	Jewish, Catholic, Mormon, Buddhist, Muslim
Family type	Single parent, divorced/no kids, two parents/kids
Occupation	Mechanic, accountant, priest, professor, clerk
Geographic region	New England, Southwest, Midwest
Community	Rural, small town, suburban, city

EXHIBIT 16.1

Types of subcultures

Marketers can analyze subcultures at different levels. The analysis often is done in stages. First, a general subculture is identified according to some broad demographic characteristic (race: black Americans; age: elderly Japanese; income level: middle-income Italians). Then, depending on the marketing purpose, this broad group is segmented further into sub-subcultures using other demographic characteristics (income: affluent, middle-income, and poor black Americans; physical health: elderly Japanese who are healthy versus those who are ill; community environment: middle-income Italians living in large cities or small towns). If necessary, the segmentation process could continue, creating ever smaller and more narrowly defined subcultures.

Managers must determine the level of subculture analysis that is relevant for the marketing problem (how narrow should the subculture be?) and develop marketing strategies appropriate for consumers at that level. Consider Maybelline's strategy in developing the cosmetic line, Shades of You, for African-American women.[3] The company recognized that black women have a range of skin tones and cannot use the same cosmetics—blacks have at least 35 different skin colors (compared to about 18 for whites). In response, Maybelline

Maybelline created its Shades of You cosmetics product line for women with dark skins.

CONSUMER PERSPECTIVE

▶ 16.1

The average American

The average American is a 32-year-old woman, 5 feet 4 inches, with brown hair (like 69 percent of all Americans), who weighs 143 pounds and is trying to lose weight. She wears glasses or contact lenses.

The average American drives an 8-year-old blue sedan that gets 18 miles per gallon and costs about $3,000 per year to operate. She will drive about 9,000 miles each year, and two other people will own the car before it goes to the junkyard. Some 70 percent of women wear jewelry every day, most of which they buy themselves. Although she hasn't been to church in the past week, the average American believes in God (like 94 percent of Americans) and life after death (69 percent). By age 32, the average American is married and has a child. It will cost $140,000 to raise this child to age 18.

The average American works in a technical, sales, or administrative job, making less than $20,000 per year. The average American spends money as fast as she makes it. She writes 16 checks per month and charges about $2,000 per year on her 10 credit cards. Working women with children buy 37 items of personal clothing a year, while working women without children buy 55 items. Although not rich, the average American carries $104 in her purse along with keys (like 97 percent of women), a comb (80 percent), checks (76 percent), makeup (69 percent), and an address book (69 percent).

Of course, the "average" American does not really exist.

Source: Blayne Cutler, "Meet Jane Doe," *American Demographics*, June 1989, pp. 25–27, 62. Reprinted with permission © *American Demographics*, June 1989. For subscription information, please call (800) 828-1133.

developed a line of cosmetics including 12 shades of liquid makeup and eight blushes appropriate for dark-skinned women. Sold at modest prices in drugstores and supermarkets, the product was almost immediately a hit among black women. Other dark-skinned women, such as Hispanics, have also found the shades appropriate for many of their needs.

The same approach used to understand culture can be used to analyze subcultures. Typically, marketers examine the *content* of a subculture by describing the cultural meanings (especially values and lifestyles) shared by its members. It is much less common for marketers to examine the *process* by which cultural meanings are moved from the physical and social environment of the subculture to products and services and on to the people in the subculture, but this could be done.

Because marketers seek to identify the *typical* characteristics, meanings, and behavioral tendencies shared by people in a subculture, members of a subculture sometimes are characterized in a stereotyped way (blacks are poor ghetto residents, elderly people are weak and ill, yuppies are rich). This can lead to major mistakes when developing marketing strategies. In fact, most subcultures are made up of diverse members who do not respond in the same way to marketing strategies. For example, marketers have identified a subgroup of "young" elderly people, called Opals (old people with active life styles), who think and act younger than their years, have money to spend, and are healthy enough to do so. In fact, it is difficult to identify a "typical" person in a subculture. This should be clear in Consumer Perspective 16.1, which describes some characteristics of the "average" American.

Careful research and thoughtful analysis is necessary to clearly define and understand a subculture. Consider what happened with the group called yuppies (young, urban professionals). Originally, this was a narrow subcultural group, but the term *yuppie* gradually became associated with any upscale, self-centered young person. With the intense media

CONSUMER PERSPECTIVE

16.2 ◄

The "new" elderly

For most people, age is more a state of mind than a physical state. Consider this statement from an 89-year-old woman:

> I might be 89 years old. I feel good. I feel like I could fly the coop. I do. I feel younger, like I'm 45 or 50. I want to doll up, and I like to fuss . . . . I don't know I'm old. I feel like I'm going to live a long time.

This suggests that marketers should analyze subjective or "cognitive age" (the age one thinks of oneself as being) rather than chronological or actual age.

A new subcultural age segment may be emerging—the "new-age elderly." Such people view themselves quite differently from the "traditional" elderly. They perceive themselves as younger and more self-confident, more in control of their lives, less materialistic and concerned with possessions, and more involved with new experiences, challenges, and adventures. They are a good market for concerts and plays, lectures and university courses, and vacation travel to exotic locations.

Source: Leon G. Schiffman and Elaine Sherman, "Value Orientations of New-Age Elderly: The Coming of an Ageless Market," *Journal of Business Research* 22 (1991), pp. 187–94.

---

attention focused on this group through the 1980s, the term became virtually synonymous with the baby boomer generation. In fact, the best estimates counted only about 4 million yuppies, which represents a mere 5 percent of the baby boomer subculture.[4]

Age groups can be treated as subcultures because people of different ages often share distinctive values, meanings, and behaviors. Marketers must be cautious, however, about segmenting consumers on the basis of their actual ages. Many adult American consumers think of themselves as 10 to 15 years younger than they really are.[5] Their behavior, affect, and cognitions are more related to their psychological age than their chronological age (see Consumer Perspective 16.2 for an example). Although many different **age subcultures** can be identified and analyzed, we discuss only three here: teens, baby boomers, and the mature market.

Age subcultures

The teen market

The American teenage market has been gaining in affluence, although it has been shrinking in size.[6] In the mid-1980s, about 26 million persons in the United States were aged 13 to 19. This number decreased to about 23 million in the early 1990s and is expected to increase to about 27 million by the year 2000.

Teenagers are important not only because they have a major influence on household purchases, but also because of their own discretionary purchasing power. The annual Rand Youth Poll estimated that teenagers spend over $45 billion a year and put more than $9 billion into savings. Fully 16 percent of teens own a car, 66 percent own a record player, 34 percent own a television, 86 percent own a camera, 21 percent own a telephone, 12 percent own a home computer, and 14 percent own stocks and bonds.

Several studies have found that teenagers do a considerable amount of grocery shopping for the family: estimates are that from 49 to 61 percent of teenage girls and 26 to 33 percent of teenage boys frequently perform this task. In addition, about 60 percent of teens help make up the supermarket shopping list, and 40 percent select some of the brands to be purchased. It is no wonder that food marketers advertise in magazines such as *Seventeen*.

Brand loyalty has been found to form early among teenage shoppers. In a survey of women ages 20 to 34, at least 30 percent said they made a brand decision as a teenager

CONSUMER PERSPECTIVE

▶ **16.3**

Jeans keep up with the baby boomers

The baby boom generation created the boom market for jeans manufacturers. When the boomers were teens in the 1960s, jeans became the universal emblem of youth and rebellion (as is still the case around the world), and jeans sales increased dramatically.

As the boomers age, manufacturers such as Levi Strauss & Co. have adapted their marketing strategies to keep pace with the changing demographics of their market. Although Levi Strauss & Co.'s key market is still 14-to-24-year-old men, this age group is shrinking, while the huge group of baby boomers is reaching middle age. Thus, Levi Strauss & Co. and other manufacturers have developed products to appeal to the boomers and to fit their changing bodies.

The so-called jeans generation still likes jeans (partly as a symbol of youth), but the style and fit they seek has changed. As waist sizes have increased—more 36s and fewer 32s—Levi Strauss & Co. has introduced new products such as the highly successful Dockers® line made to fit the middle-age man's body. According to John Wyek, director of strategic research at Levi Strauss & Co., "The point is to make products that are relevant. And making relevant products for the me generation hasn't been easy. We have thousands of different products—different styles, colors, silhouettes, sizes, and fabrics—so that our customers have the choice they've become accustomed to."

Levi Strauss & Co. is keeping its eye on other changes in subcultures. For instance, the key market of 18-to-24-year-olds will decline throughout the 1990s, but the number of Hispanics in this age group will increase 40 percent. Levi Strauss & Co. has created a Spanish-language campaign targeted at Hispanics who account for a significant percentage of Levi's annual sales. Levi Strauss & Co. also has produced an ad campaign for 501 button-fly jeans targeted at the core market of 18-to-24-year-old men, which ran on MTV and late-night television programs. Yet another ad campaign was targeted at women. Print ads designed to emphasize the comfort and fit of the Levi's® 500 Group and 900 Series product line showed silhouettes of women in many shapes and sizes.

The marketing trick for Levi Strauss & Co. is to promote its products to all these highly diverse groups in a way that does not erode the overall value or equity of the

and have continued to use the brand to the present. Sixty-four percent said they looked for specific brands when they were teenagers. One reason this market is so important for many products and services is the potential to develop brand loyalty that may last a lifetime!

Baby boomers

Baby boomers are those people born between 1946 and 1962. There are about 68 million people in this group—about a third of the U.S. adult population. This group is in its early 30s to late 40s and entering its prime earning and spending years. The baby boomer market, the largest and most affluent in history, will have a major economic impact for the next 45 years.[7] Over the next decade, baby boomers will account for nearly half of all discretionary spending.

Although the baby boomer subculture is extremely diverse, some general characteristics have been identified. The group is characterized as having a blend of "me-generation" and old-fashioned family values and as strongly influencing the values of other groups.[8] In fact, many people who aren't baby boomers feel as if they were. Baby boomers emphasize health and exercise and have reduced their consumption of cigarettes, coffee, and strong alcoholic beverages. Forty-six percent of this market has completed college, and two thirds of baby boomer wives work, compared with about half the wives in the rest of the population. In terms of products, this group places major emphasis on quality and is less concerned with bargain hunting than their parents were.

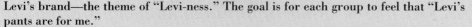

Levi's brand—the theme of "Levi-ness." The goal is for each group to feel that "Levi's pants are for me."

Source: Cyndee Miller, "Jeans Marketers Look for Good Fit with Older Men and Women," *Marketing News*, September 16, 1991, pp. 1, 6; and Bickly Townsend, "Beyond the Boom: An Interview with John Wyek," *American Demographics*, June 1989, pp. 40–41.

Baby boomers have a strong impact on markets for housing, cars, food, clothing and cosmetics, and financial services. For instance, nearly one fourth of boomers are single, creating strong markets for vacations and convenience packaged goods. In addition, although they are having fewer children per household, the sheer size of the group led to an increase in births into the early 1990s—a "baby boom echo."

Boomers who are new parents are especially attractive to marketers. Given the large incomes and small family sizes of this group, spending per child is likely to be the largest in history. Markets for children's products will expand accordingly. Toy sales, for example, are expected to increase more than twice as fast as the population of children for whom they are intended. Other markets, such as child-care services and computer software for tots, may double in the next few years.

The baby boomer market, then, is the most lucrative and challenging marketers have ever seen. It is no wonder many firms are designing new products and redesigning and repositioning old ones for this market. Wheaties used to appeal to kids as "the breakfast of champions"; now it is promoted to adults with slogans such as "what the big boys eat." Commercials for Snickers show adults rather than children eating the candy bar as a snack. Crest and other brands have introduced toothpaste formulas to fight plaque, a distinctly adult problem. Levi Strauss has redesigned its jeans to give a little extra room in the seat to accommodate "booming boomer bodies" (see Consumer Perspective 16.3). Even Clearasil, traditionally an antiacne medication for teenagers, has developed

Clearasil Adult Care to appeal to the growing number of baby boomer adults with skin problems.

The mature market

As America ages (along with other industrialized countries such as Japan and most European nations), marketers have recognized the economic importance of the "mature market," defined as consumers over age 55.[9] The mature market is one of the most rapidly growing age subcultures in American society. In 1987, the over-65 population was 30 million, up from 25.5 million in 1980. In 2000, there will be 35 million consumers over 65. Now, one in four Americans is older than 50; by 2020 over one third will be. Between now and 2020, the number of people aged 50 or older will increase by 74 percent (as baby boomers continue to age), while the population under age 50 will increase by only 1 percent.[10] Nearly 80 percent of the current U.S. population is expected to live until their late 70s.

In 2020, there could be as many as 58 million elderly or as few as 48 million, according to the U.S. Census Bureau. The exact number is hard to predict; it all depends on the mortality rate, especially gains made against diseases such as heart ailments, cancer, and stroke. Because the mature market is diverse, it may be more useful to consider smaller subcultural groups based on narrower age ranges, such as older (55–64), elderly (65–74), aged (75–84), and very old (85 and over).

The next century will see huge increases in demand for products and services for older consumers, including adult day care, home health care, prescriptions and over-the-counter drugs, medical care of all types, and foods low in cholesterol, sugar, salt, and calories. Other nonhealth-related products include vacation travel, restaurants, recreational vehicles, hotels, and motels. Recognizing that extended families will be larger, theme parks such as Six Flags Great America have created packages for grandparents, parents, and grandchildren as a group. Older people will be better educated than previous generations, which will create increased demand for educational programs, books, and news.

Marketers traditionally ignored the mature market, perhaps because it has been assumed to have low purchasing power. However, in addition to its sheer size, the economic character of this market deserves careful consideration.[11] While many of the members of this group no longer work, they often have considerable discretionary income. Unlike younger groups, members of mature markets are usually free of most of the financial burdens associated with child rearing, mortgages, and furnishing a household. Given these differences, per capita discretionary income is higher for the mature group than for any other age group—about 50 percent of the nation's total. In 1980, for example, for those aged 55 to 59 per capita discretionary income was $3,500; for those aged 60 to 64 per capita discretionary income was $3,700; for those aged 65 and over it was the highest of all—$4,100. These figures compare quite favorably with the approximately $2,000 in discretionary income available to people aged 30 to 39.

The mature market is changing. In 1985, only 9 percent of the elderly had a college degree and only 44 percent had graduated from high school. By 1995, the share of older people with college educations will rise to more than 12 percent, and at least one fourth will have had some college. Thus, the mature market is becoming more educated and likely will have even greater incomes. Increases in income are also likely because many of those in tomorrow's mature market will benefit from more generous pension and retirement plans.

Finally, because many people in the mature market subculture are retired, they have more time to enjoy entertainment and leisure activities. Although this market has historically spent more money on food for home consumption than away-from-home consumption, restaurants now cater to them with senior citizen discounts, early bird dinners, and menus designed for the tastes and requirements of older people. The elderly represent a

Go ahead. Get close.

If you've got dental work, there's only one gum you can be confident chewing.

Freedent won't stick to your dental work. And because it also moistens your mouth and keeps your breath really fresh, it's in a class by itself. So go ahead — with Freedent you can get close with confidence.

Non-stick Freedent.
Moistens mouth.
Freshens breath.

Many products are marketed to consumers in the mature market.

significant market for skin-care products, vitamins and minerals, health and beauty aids, and medications that ease pain and promote the performance of everyday activities. In addition, they are a significant market for condominiums in the Sun Belt states, time-share arrangements, travel and vacations, cultural activities, and luxury items given as gifts to their children and grandchildren. Overall, then, the mature market subculture represents an excellent marketing opportunity that will become even better in the future.

Developing marketing strategies that appeal to consumers in the mature market is more difficult than it looks.[12] Few companies are experts at it. Many marketers have inaccurate perceptions of this large and diverse group, including persistent images of frail, cantankerous, and impoverished people who, if not confined to bed, are tottering around on canes. Yet only 5 percent of Americans over 65 are institutionalized. People are staying healthy and active much later into their lives than ever before. Some ads are beginning to use themes and models that older consumers can identify with. No longer depicted as weak and dotty, older people are shown doing the things they do in real life: working, playing tennis, falling in love, and buying cars. McDonald's was a forerunner in this trend with its "Golden Years" spots that showed an elderly man and woman meeting for lunch at McDonald's and an elderly man on his first day of work at McDonald's.

Ethnic subcultures

In the past two decades, the ethnic makeup of the United States has changed dramatically.[13] In 1980, one of every five Americans was a member of a minority group. In 1990, one in four Americans claimed to have either Hispanic, Asian, African, or Native American ancestry. The size of these **ethnic subcultures** increased at unequal rates, due to different immigration patterns and birthrates. For instance, the Asian subculture grew 80 percent during the 1980s, compared to increases of 4.4 percent in the white population, 14 percent for African-Americans, and 39 percent for Hispanics. Increases in these minority

CONSUMER
PERSPECTIVE

▶ 16.4

Cluster 31—
Black
Enterprise

Cluster 31, or "Black Enterprise," is a subcultural group created through statistical analysis by Claritas Corporation. Claritas' PRIZM system groups all the U.S. ZIP codes and census tracks into 40 clusters or segments, on the basis of various demographic characteristics. Claritas ranks the clusters by size and affluence and gives each one a catchy name. Black Enterprise is made up of relatively affluent black consumers. It ranks 11th in affluence and comes closest to describing a black middle class.

In 1988, there were about 420,000 households in cluster 31 neighborhoods around the country. People in this group have several distinctive characteristics. They are more likely to be college educated and hold white-collar jobs. They are more likely than average to sail, drink Scotch, buy classical music, smoke menthol cigarettes, belong to a book club, and travel by rail. These black consumers are quite unlikely to buy country music, a pickup truck, or camping equipment, or to go swimming frequently. Cluster 31 adults spend heavily on clothes, read magazines at above average rates, and watch less television than average. In many cases, these affluent blacks make choices similar to affluent white consumers, including buying station wagons, using Visa cards once a month, and making three or more stock transactions per year.

Source: Brad Edmondson, "Black Enterprise," *American Demographics*, November 1989, pp. 26–27. Reprinted with permission © American Demographics, November 1989. For subscription information, please call (800) 828-1133.

subcultures are expected to continue so that by 2010 more than one third of American children will be African-American, Hispanic, or Asian.

Marketers need to recognize that ethnic subcultures are not distributed equally across the United States.[14] The most ethnically diverse regions in the country are in the Southwest and the South; the least diverse are in the Midwest, where the proportion of whites can exceed 90 percent. The most ethnically diverse county in the nation is San Francisco with approximately equal proportions of whites, blacks, Hispanics, and Asians. New York City and Los Angeles also are highly diverse cities. We discuss the three major ethnic subcultures in the United States—African-American, Hispanic, and Asian.

African-American subculture

The African-American, or black, subculture is the largest ethnic minority group in the United States, with some 31 million people and 7 million families (about 13 percent of the total population).[15] A market worth about $170 billion annually, African-Americans are a highly diverse group. Although many black Americans are poor, two thirds are not. More than 13 percent of black families had incomes exceeding $50,000 in 1988 (up from 8 percent in 1980), but the number of very poor black families (incomes under $5,000) also grew from 10 to 12 percent during this period. The 17 million relatively poor blacks concentrated in densely populated urban centers are more visible in the media, but 8 million blacks live in suburban neighborhoods. Economic conditions for African-Americans vary considerably in different metropolitan areas. For example, about one fourth of blacks in Washington, D.C., are affluent, compared to only 1 in 25 in Miami. In San Francisco, 1 in 10 African-Americans is affluent and more than half are middle class. Middle-class blacks may have more in common with middle-class whites and Asians than they do with lower-class blacks. To deal with the diversity in the African-American subculture, marketers further segment the black market on the basis of factors such as income, social class, or geographic region. Consumer Perspective 16.4 presents an example of such a sub-subculture.

Marketers increasingly are targeting African-Americans with special products and marketing strategies. For example, Tyco, Hasbro, and Mattel are all marketing "ethnically correct" dolls designed for the black market (10 percent of U.S. children under 10 are black).[16] Mattel's dolls, Shani (Swahili for marvelous) and her two friends, Asha and Nicelle, have varying skin tones, hair styles, and facial features that reflect the diversity of black women.

Some marketing strategies directed at the black subculture have been controversial.[17] In 1990, for instance, following intense public pressure, the R. J. Reynolds Tobacco Company withdrew plans to test market a new cigarette, Uptown, that was targeted at black smokers. In 1991, the G. Heileman Brewing Company succumbed to public pressure and canceled plans to market a high-alcohol malt beer, PowerMaster, to low-income, inner-city black consumers.

Hispanic subculture

According to the 1990 census, approximately 23.7 million Hispanics live in the United States (about 8 percent of the total population).[18] Hispanics are people with Spanish-speaking ancestry from such nations as Mexico (by far the largest group in the United States), Puerto Rico, Cuba, and various countries in Central and South America. When combined into a single subculture, Hispanics account for over $70 billion in purchasing power. Hispanics are distributed unequally across the United States, with most living in the border states of Texas, California, Arizona, and New Mexico (each state has a Hispanic population exceeding 500,000). The top six Hispanic U.S. cities are New York (mostly Puerto Ricans and Dominicans); Miami (Cubans); Los Angeles, Houston, and San Antonio (Mexicans); and Chicago (a mix of all). In these regions, the Hispanic subculture has a very significant effect on the overall culture.

The Hispanic subculture is quite diverse, and reaching Hispanic consumers efficiently and effectively can be difficult. Some Hispanics are third- or fourth-generation U.S. citizens and are well assimilated into American culture; they can be reached by traditional U.S. media (TV, radio, and magazines). Other Hispanics retain much of their original culture and may speak mostly or only Spanish. To oversimplify, marketers can identify three broad segments (subgroups) in the Hispanic subculture—only Spanish speaking; bilingual, but favoring Spanish; and bilingual, but favoring English. Using Spanish in advertising can effectively reach all three groups, but the dialect used must be chosen carefully. Although all Hispanics speak Spanish, the Spanish language has several distinctive variations depending on the culture of origin.

Recently developed Spanish-language media (special TV channels, newspapers, and magazines) make it easier than ever to reach the Hispanic market.[19] For instance, Whittle Communications launched a new magazine in late 1990, called *La Familia de Hoy,* targeted at Hispanic women who speak English as a second language and have children at home. Several large companies have placed ads in Spanish in the magazine, including Procter & Gamble, American Airlines, Kraft, AT&T, and Kinney Shoes. Successful advertising campaigns tend to use large and colorful ads that combine images of the American dream with illustrations of the traditional values held by the Hispanic extended family.

Even though U.S. companies spent about $500 million on marketing strategies directed at Hispanic markets in 1987, the largest Hispanic advertiser, Philip Morris, allocated less than 1 percent (about $13 million) of its total ad budget to Hispanic advertising.[20] Many companies would like to develop marketing strategies targeted at the Hispanic market, but find it difficult to get good information about Hispanic needs, values, and perceptions. This situation is rapidly improving as new firms specialize in marketing research on Hispanic consumers. Marketers must decide whether to develop one "global" marketing strategy for all Hispanics or to adapt the strategy for each segment of the Hispanic subculture. Coors, for instance, opts for the adaptive, tailor-made approach, showing ads with a rodeo theme

This magazine is targeted at the Spanish-speaking segment of the Hispanic subculture.

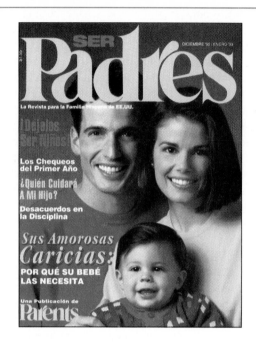

in Houston, but not in Miami. Likewise, Goya Foods sells different products in Miami (Cubans prefer black beans) and New York (Puerto Ricans like red beans).

Marketing to domestic subcultures requires a careful analysis of consumers' affect, cognitions, and behaviors.[21] For example, a telephone company once tried to target the Hispanic market by employing Puerto Rican actors. In the ad, the wife said to her husband, "Run downstairs and phone Mary. Tell her we'll be a little late." The commercial was not successful because it was inconsistent with Hispanic values and behaviors. For one thing, Hispanic wives seldom tell their husbands what to do. For another, few Hispanics would feel it necessary to call if they will be late, because being late is expected. Similarly, Coors ads featuring the slogan "Taste the high country" were not effective with Mexican-Americans, who could not identify with mountain life. The Spanish-language Coors ads were modified to suggest that the mountains were a good source of beer, but that one did not need to live in the mountains to enjoy it. The new slogan in its English translation became "Take the beer from the high country and bring it to your high country—wherever it may be."[22]

Asian subculture

Although they represented less than 3 percent of the population in 1990, Asian-Americans are the most rapidly increasing ethnic group in the United States.[23] The population of people with Asian ancestry increased 80 percent during the 1980s (largely due to increased immigration), growing from 3.8 million in 1980 to about 7 million in 1989. Asian-Americans are concentrated in a few areas of the country, where they have an important influence on the overall culture. Most Asians (56 percent) live in the West, particularly in California (13 percent of Californians will be Asian in the year 2000). Asian-Americans are highly urbanized, with 93 percent living in cities (three quarters of the 3 million Californian Asians live in the Los Angeles basin or the San Francisco Bay area). The Asian subculture in these regions requires special marketing attention for many companies. Grocery stores in LA's Koreatown stock large bags of rice near the checkout counter, where stores in middle America might display the charcoal.

Asian-Americans are a prime market because they are more affluent than any other racial or ethnic group. In 1990, the median income of Asian-American households was $31,500, compared to $28,700 for whites, $20,000 for Hispanics, and $16,000 for blacks. Fully 32 percent of Asian-American households had incomes greater than $50,000 (compared to 29 percent of whites). Asian income levels are high for two reasons: (1) the education level of Asian-Americans is high (35 percent of adults have completed four or more years of college, compared to 22 percent of white Americans), and (2) more Asian-Americans live in married-couple households with two wage earners.

It is tempting to think of Asian-Americans (and other minority subcultures) as a single, homogeneous market, but this is a diverse subculture. Some Asians are well integrated into American culture, while others live in Asian communities and maintain much of their original culture, including their language. Because Asian consumers come from several distinctive cultural backgrounds—Japan, China, Southeast Asia, and the Pacific Islands— many marketers further segment the Asian community into subcultures based on language and/or nationality.[24] Implementing targeted marketing strategies is possible in communities where specialized media (newspapers, magazines, and radio) can reach specific Asian subcultures.

Gender as a subculture

Despite the modern tendency to downplay differences between men and women, there is ample evidence that men and women differ in many respects besides physical characteristics. For instance, women in general seem to be more "generous, more nurturing, and less dominating than men."[25] For some marketing purposes, gender differences may be significant enough to consider the two sexes as separate subcultures with distinctive meanings and behavior norms. For instance, research has found that women treat possessions differently from the way men do. Ownership and possession of products is seen by many men as a way to dominate and exert power over others, distinguish themselves from others (status differentiation), or engage in subtle forms of aggression toward others. Many women, in contrast, tend to value possessions that can enhance interpersonal relationships. Compared to most men, most women seem to value caring over controlling, sharing over selfishness, and cooperating over dominating. Thus, marketers may find it useful to develop different marketing strategies for the male and female subcultures.

Income as a subculture

Marketers can consider level of income as a subculture, because people with similar incomes tend to have similar cultural meanings, values, behaviors, and lifestyles. Income also is used to segment a subculture defined on some other characteristic (age, ethnic group, gender). Many myths and misconceptions about the income distributions in the United States can confuse marketers. For instance, if you think that lower income households are dominated by minorities, you are wrong—most poor Americans are white. Affluence does not necessarily increase with age, either; some people get poorer as they get older.

Marketers often divide American households into three income categories—*downscale* (under $25,000 income per year), *upscale* (over $50,000 per year), and *middle income* (between $25,000 and $50,000 per year).[26] Exhibit 16.2 shows some key demographic characteristics of these income groups. Note the strong relationship between college education and income level—nearly half of the upscale adults have completed four years of college, but only 10 percent of downscale adults have done so. The exhibit also shows that nearly half (46 percent) of American households are downscale. Although the upscale subculture is an excellent market for high-quality, luxury goods, only one in five U.S. households falls into this category. The mass market is definitely downscale. Some American marketers find the downscale market to be very profitable, as the huge success of discount retailers such as Wal-Mart illustrates.

EXHIBIT 16.2

Characteristics of three income subcultures

Selected Characteristics of Households	Total	Income Subcultures		
		Downscale (Less than $25,000)	Middle Income ($25,000 to $49,999)	Upscale ($50,000 and Over)
Total households (in thousands)	92,830	42,569	30,927	19,332
Percent of all households	100.0%	45.9%	33.3%	20.8%
Median household income*	$27,200	$12,900	$35,500	$66,300
Family households	70.9%	56.9%	79.1%	88.7%
Married couples	56.1%	36.6%	66.9%	82.0%
Female-headed families	11.7%	17.5%	8.5%	4.1%
With children under 18	36.1%	29.2%	41.6%	42.7%
One person in household	24.5%	39.5%	15.4%	5.9%
Two or three persons in household	49.8%	44.2%	54.6%	54.6%
Four or more persons in household	25.7%	16.4%	30.0%	39.5%
Median age of householder	49	51	41	42
Percent high school graduates	75.8%	61.0%	85.1%	93.3%
Percent with four or more years of college	22.3%	9.7%	23.7%	47.5%
Black	11.4%	16.4%	8.2%	5.4%
Hispanic	7.1%	8.7%	6.6%	4.4%

*Income figures from the 1989 Current Population Survey are for 1988.

Source: *American Demographics'* tabulation of the Census Bureau's March 1989 Current Population Survey. Reprinted with permission © American Demographics, 1989. For subscription information, please call (800) 828-1133.

Geographic subcultures

Americans like to think of their country as a melting pot, but the "American market" is a myth for many product categories.[27] Different parts of the country have very different physical environments (topography, climate, natural resources) and social environments (economics, population demographics, lifestyles). These factors create **geographic subcultures** of people with shared cultural meanings that can influence their buying behavior.

Many U.S. marketers find it easier to accept Europe or Latin America as different cultural regions than to recognize Arizona, Texas, and Louisiana as separate markets. But in reality, the people of Boston and Houston have cultural characteristics nearly as different as the citizens of Hamburg (Germany) and Milan (Italy). The regions of the United States create a polycultural nation, made up of a mosaic of subcultures and submarkets. For example, product ownership varies widely across the United States.[28] Consumers in California own a much higher percentage of foreign cars than their counterparts in the Midwest or South. Very few brands in any product category enjoy uniform sales across the country. Many national brands get 40 percent to 80 percent of their sales in a core region, but they are a "specialty brand" (with lower market share) in other areas of the country. In the mid-1980s, for instance, Ford pickups were the favorite in a number of northwestern states, while Chevy pickups dominated in many southern states. Wonder bread sells best in New York (for reasons unknown), while snack nuts sell best in Portland, Maine. Seattle leads in sales of "healthy" foods such as Cheerios but is also the top market for Hershey's chocolate bars. To cope with such diversity of demand, marketers must pay attention to regional subcultures.

There are many ways to analyze the geographic subcultures of the United States. One creative approach divided the North American continent into nine subcultural regions

EXHIBIT 16.3   The eight nations of the United States

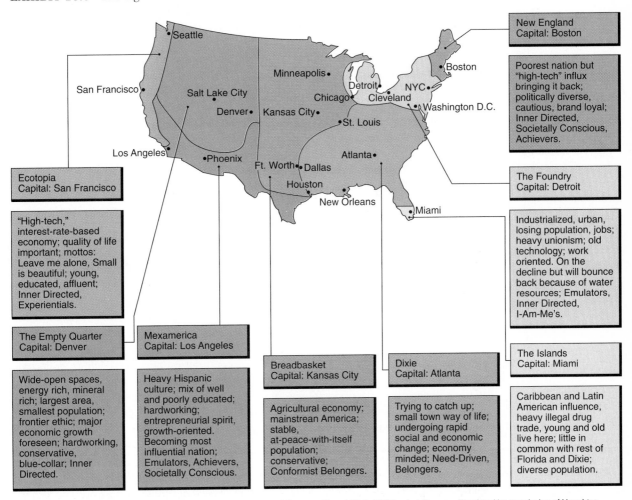

called the "nine nations" of North America based on economic, social, cultural, political, topographical, and natural resource factors.[29] Eight of these regions lie within the U.S. borders, and Exhibit 16.3 summarizes the "personalities" of consumers who live there. Although this framework has been criticized, it offers a fresh way of thinking about the geographic subcultures in the United States.[30]

Marketers must recognize that cultural and subcultural differences do not always coincide with governmental (or other artificial) boundaries. Consider the so-called borderlands along the 2,000-mile border between Mexico and the United States.[31] About 5.2 million people (35 percent are Hispanic) live in the 25 borderland counties in California, New Mexico, Arizona, and Texas; another 3 million people live on the Mexican side of the border. The borderlands have grown about 30 percent since 1980 and constitute a geographic subculture with significant marketing potential.

Consider the area called Los Dos Laredos (the two Laredos)—Laredo, Texas, and Nuevo Laredo, Mexico. Although separated by the Rio Grande River, residents on both sides give little thought to the border as they freely cross the bridges to shop, work, and enjoy themselves. A bank official puts it this way, "We're not the United States and we're not Mexico. We're different. We think we gather the best of both cultures." According to one citizen, "We're more like Minneapolis and Saint Paul than the U.S. and Mexico, because we are the same people."

The borderlands are an important regional market even though the overall demographics are downscale (people have lower than average incomes). The U.S. side swells by thousands of Mexican citizens who cross the border to work and spend their pesos. Although some shopping areas are bordertown tacky, Laredo's new retailing centers provide chain stores like Wal-Mart, Sears, and Penney's. Successful marketing strategies recognize the Hispanic culture as the major influence in borderlands. Many of the signs and store names are in Spanish, prices are often given in both pesos and dollars, and most stores accept either currency. Because Hispanic families tend to be large, grocery stores tend to stock big sizes, including 50-pound sacks of rice.

THE ACCULTURATION PROCESS	A process of acculturation begins when a person moves to a different culture to live and work or becomes a member of a different subculture (gets older, becomes wealthy, changes occupations). **Acculturation** refers to how people in one culture or subculture understand and adapt to the meanings (values, beliefs, behaviors, rituals, lifestyles) of another subculture or culture.[32] *Consumer acculturation* refers to how people acquire the ability and knowledge to be a skilled consumer in a different cultural environment.

Acculturation is common and necessary in the modern world. As many societies experience increasing immigration, they face problems of assimilating people from different cultural backgrounds into the "host culture." This occurred in the United States during the 1980s and 1990s following rapid growth of the Hispanic and Asian subcultures. Acculturation is also important for people who move to different regions within the same country, where they must adapt to a different subcultural environment. One of six Americans moves each year, but for the two thirds who move within the same county (the median distance moved is only six miles), the subcultural changes probably are not great.[33] The 10 percent of Americans moving to a different region of the country, however, are likely to face some acculturation problems as they adapt to a new regional subculture. Finally, acculturation is important for marketing managers, who must try to understand the cultural meanings of consumers in societies and subcultures different from their own.

The degree to which immigrants, people who move, and marketers become acculturated into a new culture or subculture depends on their level of *cultural interpenetration*—the amount and type of social interactions they have with people in the "host" subculture.[34] Social contact with people in other subcultures can be direct, through personal experiences at work, while shopping, or in living arrangements. Other social experiences are indirect or vicarious, as in observing other people from a distance or on television. Perhaps one reason some Americans lack a cultural understanding of people in other societies and subcultures is because much of their social contact with such people has been shallow and indirect. Many Americans learn about other cultures and subcultures largely through vicarious observation in the mass media (movies, television, books, newspapers). When people have the opportunity for deeper cultural interpenetration (through direct working experience or through living in close proximity to other types of people), they tend to become more thoroughly acculturated. Perhaps this is why better educated immigrants tend to become more acculturated—their higher education level leads to greater cultural interpenetration.

When people come into contact with a new culture or subculture, they may go through four **stages of acculturation,** corresponding to four levels of cultural interpenetration.[35] In the *honeymoon stage,* people are fascinated by the new subculture or exotic foreign culture. Because cultural interpenetration is shallow and superficial, little acculturation occurs. Tourists often experience this stage. If cultural interpenetration increases, people may enter a *rejection stage,* where they recognize that many of their established behaviors and meanings that were taken for granted in the "old" subculture are inadequate for acting appropriately in the new subculture. Some people may develop antagonistic attitudes toward the new subculture and reject its key values and meanings. Cultural conflicts are maximum in this stage.

If cultural interpenetration continues and deepens, people may reach the *tolerance stage.* As they come to understand more cultural meanings and behaviors, people may begin to appreciate the "new" subculture, and cultural conflict decreases. Finally, in the *integration stage,* adjustment to the subculture is achieved, although total acculturation may never occur. At this stage, people are able to function satisfactorily in the new culture or subculture, which is viewed as an alternative way of life and is valued for its good qualities.

U.S. marketers must adjust their strategies to the level of acculturation achieved by immigrants who arrive with their own cultural meanings and values and must adapt to the different cultural meanings of American society. One study of immigrants from India finds that "transitional objects" such as Indian clothing, jewelry, special furniture, movies, photographs, and music are highly valued as reminders of the home culture.[36] Many Hispanics maintain their cultural values and traditions, and complete acculturation may take three or four generations. But even long-term resident Hispanic-Americans, Asian-Americans, or African-Americans may never completely incorporate all the values, meanings, and behaviors of American culture.

An important factor in the acculturation of immigrants is proficiency in the language of the new culture. Ability to speak English obviously influences the level of cultural interpenetration an immigrant can achieve in the U.S. society. Hispanic and Asian immigrants who live and work in environments where only their native language is spoken are not likely to penetrate far into American society and may become only partially acculturated. Immigrants with more education are more likely to speak English and can obtain better jobs, which, in turn, allows for greater cultural penetration and more complete acculturation. Interestingly, immigrants who join families already living in the United States tend to be more passive and penetrate less fully into American culture than the more adventurous family members who were the first to come to the United States.

An expert in social class research makes some useful observations about class:

SOCIAL CLASS

> There are no two ways about it: social class is a difficult idea. Sociologists, in whose discipline the concept emerged, are not of one mind about its value and validity. Consumer researchers, to whose field its use has spread, display confusion about when and how to apply it. The American public is noticeably uncomfortable with the realities about life that it reflects. All who try to measure it have trouble. Studying it rigorously and imaginatively can be monstrously expensive. Yet, all these difficulties notwithstanding, the proposition still holds: social class is worth troubling over for the insights it offers on the marketplace behavior of the nation's consumers.[37]

We agree with these observations concerning both the problems and the value of social class analysis. For our purposes in this text, **social class** refers to a status hierarchy by which groups and individuals are distinguished in terms of esteem and prestige. Coleman recommends that four social class groups be used for consumer analysis in the United States—*upper, middle, working,* and *lower class.* Exhibit 16.4 describes these groups and identifies some marketing implications for each.

EXHIBIT 16.4

Social class groups for consumer analysis

Upper Americans (14 percent of population)

This group consists of the upper-upper, lower-upper, and upper-middle classes. They have common goals and are differentiated mainly by income. This group has many different lifestyles, which might be labeled postpreppy, conventional, intellectual, and political, among others. The class remains the segment of our society in which quality merchandise is most prized, special attention is paid to prestige brands, and the self-image ideal is "spending with good taste." Self-expression is more prized than in previous generations, and neighborhood remains important. Depending on income level and values, theater, books, investment in art, European travel, household help, club memberships for tennis, golf, and swimming, and prestige schooling for children remain high consumption priorities.

Middle Class (32 percent of population)

These consumers definitely want to "do the right thing" and buy "what's popular." They have always been concerned with fashion and following recommendations of "experts" in print media. Increased earnings result in better living, which means a "nicer neighborhood on the better side of town with good schools." It also means spending more on "worthwhile experiences" for children, including winter ski trips, college educations, and shopping for better brands of clothes at more expensive stores. Appearance of home is important, because guests may visit and pass judgment. This group emulates upper Americans, which distinguishes it from the working class. It also enjoys trips to Las Vegas and physical activity. Deferred gratification may still be an ideal, but it is not so often practiced.

Working Class (38 percent of population)

Working-class Americans are "family folk" depending heavily on relatives for economic and emotional support, e.g., tips on job opportunities, advice on purchases, help in times of trouble. The emphasis on family ties is only one sign of how much more limited and different working-class horizons are socially, psychologically, and geographically compared to those of the middle class. In almost every respect, a parochial view characterizes this blue-collar world. This group has changed little in values and behaviors despite rising incomes in some cases. For them, "keeping up with the times" focuses on the mechanical and recreational, and, thus, ease of labor and leisure is what they continue to pursue.

Lower Americans (16 percent of population)

The men and women of lower America are no exception to the rule that diversities and uniformities in values and consumption goals are to be found at each social level. Some members of this world, as has been publicized, are prone to every form of instant gratification known to humankind when the money is available. But others are dedicated to resisting worldly temptations as they struggle toward what some believe will be a "heavenly reward" for their earthly sacrifices.

Source: Reprinted by permission of the University of Chicago Press from "The Continuing Significance of Social Class in Marketing," by Richard P. Coleman, in *Journal of Consumer Research*, December 1983, pp. 265–80. © 1983 by the University of Chicago.

Identification with a social class is influenced most strongly by one's level of education and occupation (including income as a measure of work success). But social class is also affected by social skills, status aspirations, community participation, family history, cultural level, recreational habits, physical appearance, and social acceptance by a particular class. Thus, social class is a composite of many personal and social attributes rather than a single characteristic such as income or education. The social classes can be considered as large subcultures because their members share many cultural meanings and behaviors.

Social class and values

Social class is an important source of consumers' beliefs, values, and behaviors.[38] Most of the people an individual interacts with on a day-to-day basis are likely to be members of that person's social class. Family, peer groups, and friends at work, school, and in the neighborhood are all likely to be of the same social class. Association with these people teaches the individual appropriate values for the class as well as behavior norms that are acceptable. This learning process can occur either through direct statement ("You don't have a chance any more unless you go to college") or by example (an individual sees friends going to college, graduating, and purchasing new cars).

Social classes are useful for understanding why consumers develop different beliefs, values, and behavior patterns. For example, the upper class may well be socially secure and not find it necessary or desirable to purchase the most expensive brands to impress other people. Middle-class people, on the other hand, often engage in such conspicuous consumption. As Consumer Perspective 16.5 (see page 378) shows, even homeless people (perhaps the lowest social class in American society) engage in consumption behavior that reflects their values.

Social class and income

Although the members of each social class share distinct values and behavior patterns to some degree, the four major groups can be differentiated even further. There are vast differences in family situations and income totals among subgroups. For instance, families in each social class can be classified further as relatively overprivileged, average, or underprivileged.[39] *Overprivileged* families in each social class are those with incomes usually 25 percent to 30 percent above the median for the class, who therefore have money left over to seek forms of a "better life" preferred by the class. At the same time, because these families continue to share values, behaviors, and associations with other members of the class, they typically do not "move" to a higher social class. The *average* families are those in the middle income range of the class who can afford the kind of house, car, apparel, food, furniture, and appliances expected by their social class peers. Finally, the *underprivileged* families have incomes that fall at least 15 percent below the class midpoint and therefore must scrimp and sacrifice to be able to purchase the proper products for that class.

There has long been disagreement whether social class or income is the better variable for understanding consumer choice for market segmentation. Advocates of each position muster a number of arguments for the superiority of their favorite variable and point out a variety of methodological and conceptual problems with the other one. More recently, consumer researchers have recognized that each variable has its advantages and disadvantages, and the choice between using social class, income, or a combination of the two depends on the product and the situation. Some tentative generalizations come from a study of the issue:[40]

1. Social class is a better predictor than income of areas of consumer behavior that do not involve high dollar expenditures, but do reflect underlying differences in lifestyles or values (drinking imported wines). Social class is superior for understanding the purchase of highly visible, symbolic, and expensive objects such as living room furniture.

2. Income is generally superior for understanding purchases of major kitchen and laundry appliances, and products that require substantial expenditure but are not status symbols within the class.

3. The combination of social class and income is generally superior for understanding purchases of product classes that are highly visible, serve as symbols of social class or status within class, and require either moderate or substantial expenditure (clothing, automobiles, television sets).

Determining whether social class or income or a combination of these or other variables is the dominant factor in a given marketing analysis requires careful examination of the relationship between the product and the consumer.

CONSUMER PERSPECTIVE

▶ 16.5

The homeless— the lowest social class in America?

For a variety of reasons, homeless men and women began to crowd many American cities during the 1980s and early 1990s. Estimates of the homeless population range from over 3 million to a more likely 600,000. Without a home and seldom with a job, the homeless are at the bottom of the social class hierarchy. Despite their very low socioeconomic status, though, homeless people are consumers. In fact, most of them exert considerable physical and cognitive effort to perform various consumption behaviors—finding a place to sleep, getting food to eat, acquiring simple possessions, keeping their meager possessions safe. In a real sense, these consumption activities constitute a full-time job.

One intensive study of the homeless learned a great deal about this distinctive subculture or social class. For instance, most homeless individuals do have a few possessions—a shopping cart is very desirable. Some of their possessions are scavenged from trash cans or abandoned cars and buildings, and some are purchased (hot meals are especially valued). Often individuals will exchange possessions using barter. Some homeless will earn a small income doing odd jobs or, most frequently, by recycling (selling empty bottles or scrap metals). Others may work sporadically as day laborers or as "shiners" and "wipers" washing car windows at city intersections.

The lowest levels of Maslow's need hierarchy identify the basic needs of homeless people—food, water, shelter, and security. By definition, all homeless people lack a house or apartment, but some do have a type of housing of their own. These can range from vacant buildings or abandoned automobiles, to makeshift self-constructed shelters on vacant lots built from abandoned building materials, to partially protected areas such as bridges and tunnels that can provide useful shelter.

Food is the consumer product most often purchased by homeless people, when money is available. But food can also be obtained in shelters or meal programs, by finding road-kill meat, and by scavenging discarded food. Some homeless, for instance, check the dumpsters of fast-food restaurants soon after closing.

Clothing is particularly important in the winter, and homeless people try to accumulate layers of clothing to provide some protection from the cold. Multiple layers of clothing also provide some protection from physical attack. Clothing is often scavenged, although charity distribution centers can be a good source.

▶ **SUMMARY**

Learning objective 1: *Define subculture, and discuss the analysis of subcultures.*
Subcultures are distinctive groups of people in a society that share cultural meanings. These common meanings may concern affective and cognitive responses (emotional reactions, beliefs, values, and goals), behaviors (customs, scripts and rituals, behavioral norms), and environmental factors (living conditions, geographic location, important objects). Subcultures share certain cultural meanings with the overall society and/or other subcultures, but some of a subculture's meanings are unique and distinctive. Subcultures in a society can be analyzed at different levels depending on the marketing purpose—broader groups (middle-age French) or more narrowly defined groups (middle-age French, low income, living in rural areas). Marketers normally analyze a subculture in terms of its content (shared values, lifestyles, or beliefs). Although the people in a subculture have certain cultural meanings in common, analysis of nearly any subculture also reveals great diversity. Marketers must attempt to identify subcultural groups large enough to be useful, without ignoring important differences among people in the group.

Another need is personal hygiene and health care. Satisfying these needs is difficult for homeless people, partly because of their restricted access to water. Homeless people find it hard to wash and clean themselves and their clothes. Shelters are useful for these purposes. Of course, virtually no homeless individuals have health insurance, so they are likely to seek medical attention from emergency rooms or free clinics. Some homeless people deliberately get arrested when depressed or sick, in order to get medical attention in jail.

Finally, tools of various sorts are important possessions for many homeless people. Shopping carts are useful to carry their possessions (to keep them from being stolen). Tools that aid in scavenging parts from cars or buildings are valued (screwdrivers, flashlights, tire irons).

Source: Reprinted by permission of the University of Chicago Press from "The Homeless in America: An Examination of Possessions and Consumption Behavior," by Hill and Stamey, in *Journal of Consumer Research*, December 1990, pp. 303–21. © 1990 by the University of Chicago.

Learning objective 2: *Describe a geographic subculture, and give several examples.*

In any country, groups of people living in different regions have the characteristics of subcultures. That is, consumers in geographic subcultures have different values, behavior norms, beliefs, and lifestyles. These different cultural meanings lead to differences in consumption behavior. In the United States, a state itself or a large city could be analyzed as a geographic subculture. Other geographic subcultures can be identified that do not correspond exactly to governmental boundaries—the mid-Atlantic, New England, South, Midwest, and West Coast regions are commonly considered geographic subcultures. The "eight nations" of the United States divide the country into geographic subcultures based on common cultural meanings.

Learning objective 3: *Describe age subcultures, and give some examples.*

Age subcultures are based on the chronological (or actual) ages of people. Teenagers (13 to 19), baby boomers (mid-30s to mid-40s), and mature market (over age 55) are three age subcultures. Other age subcultures within the mature market include the elderly (65–74), aged (75–84), and very old (85 and over). People in these age categories can be considered subcultures because they share certain cultural meanings (values, beliefs, lifestyles). But as with any other social group, the consumers in any age subculture are also highly diverse (not all elderly feel they are that age).

Learning objective 4: *Discuss the three major ethnic subcultures in America.*

The United States has three major ethnic subcultures—African-American or black, Hispanic, and Asian. With 31 million people of African ancestry, the black subculture is the largest minority group in the United States (about 13 percent of the total population). Taken as a whole, African-Americans are a huge market of about $170 billion per year. However, the black consumers are highly diverse, and marketers usually must further subdivide blacks into more narrowly defined subcultural groups to understand their cultural meanings and develop effective marketing strategies. The Hispanic subculture consists of people of Spanish-speaking ancestry and is also large (about 24 million, or 8 percent of the population). Most Hispanics live in the border states of Texas, California, New Mexico, and Arizona. Again, there is great diversity among Hispanics, and it may be necessary to define Hispanic subcultures more narrowly (Puerto Rican, Mexican, South American, and Central American subcultures). The Asian subculture is much smaller (over 7 million, about 3 percent of the population), but growing rapidly. Like the other subcultures, Asians are highly diverse, including people from numerous Asian countries speaking different languages. Asian-Americans tend to be highly concentrated in certain regions (56 percent live in the West) and most are highly urbanized (93 percent live in cities). Asians have the highest income level of any ethnic group in America.

Learning objective 5: *Define consumer acculturation, and describe the four stages of acculturation.*

Acculturation refers to how people in one culture or subculture come to understand and adapt to the meanings (values, beliefs, behaviors, rituals, lifestyles) of another culture or subculture. Consumer acculturation refers to how people acquire the ability and cultural knowledge to be a skilled consumer in a different culture or subculture. Acculturation is highly relevant for immigrants to a new culture, people who move within a country and experience a new subculture, and marketers who may be managing international marketing strategies in many countries. The degree to which people become acculturated into a new culture or subculture depends on their level of cultural interpenetration—the amount and type of social interactions they have with people in the "host" culture. When people come into contact with a new culture or subculture, they may go through four stages of acculturation corresponding to four levels of cultural interpenetration. In the honeymoon stage, people (often tourists) are fascinated by the exotic foreign culture or subculture, but because their culture interpenetration usually is shallow and superficial, little acculturation occurs. If cultural interpenetration increases, people may enter a rejection stage, develop antagonistic attitudes toward the new subculture, and reject its key values and meanings. If cultural interpenetration continues and deepens, people may reach the tolerance stage where they may begin to appreciate the meanings of the subculture. Finally, in the integration stage, acculturation is adequate for a person to function satisfactorily in the new culture or subculture. Although acculturation may never become total, people view the new culture as an alternative way of life that is valued for its good qualities.

Learning objective 6: *Describe the major social classes in America, and discuss how marketers can use social class distinctions.*

Most of the schemes to subdivide American society into social classes are similar to the four social classes described in the text—the upper, middle, working, and lower classes. Upper-class Americans (about 14 percent) tend to have college educations and professional occupations. They value quality merchandise and self-expression. About 32 percent of Americans are middle class. Middle class people look toward the upper class for inspiration and have a more cosmopolitan outlook than working-class people. Working-class Americans (about 38 percent) have narrower world views and stronger family ties. Lower-class Americans (about 16 percent of the population) are the least educated and have the lowest income levels. Because people in different social classes have rather different beliefs, values, and lifestyles, marketers can use social class as a basis for creating large market segments. As with any subculture, each social class shares certain cultural characteristics but can be diverse in some elements.

subculture	geographic subculture	social class	▶ **KEY TERMS AND CONCEPTS**
age subculture	acculturation		
ethnic subculture	stages of acculturation		

▶ **REVIEW AND DISCUSSION QUESTIONS**

1. Define a subculture. Are college students a subculture? Explain why or why not.

2. Discuss how subcultures (and social class) can influence the way consumers learn cultural meanings (values, behaviors, lifestyles). Give a specific example.

3. What ethical factors should a marketer consider in developing marketing strategies targeted at particular subcultures or social classes? (What is your reaction to selling fortified wine to homeless people, cigarettes to Hispanics, or diet plans to working class people who are overweight?)

4. Identify the age subcultures among members of your own family (or neighborhood). How do these cultural differences affect the consumption behaviors of these people for food, personal-care products, and clothing?

5. Think of three subcultures not discussed in the text and describe them. Discuss one marketing implication for each one. (What product categories would be most relevant?)

6. Discuss the acculturation process by describing what might happen if you come into long-term contact with a different subculture (imagine you move to a different area of the country or city).

7. Discuss the concept of cultural interpenetration in terms of the acculturation of groups of immigrants in your country. What problems and opportunities do you see for marketing strategies?

8. Define the concept of social class and identify the major social class groups in your country. What are the major social class groups in the immediate community where you live? How do you recognize these social class groupings?

9. Select a product class (perhaps a food, beverage, clothing, automobile, or furniture product). How might each of the social classes you have identified above respond to marketing strategies for these products?

17

Reference Groups and Family Influences

LEARNING OBJECTIVES

After completing this chapter, you should be able to

► 1. Define reference groups, and give several examples of types of reference groups.

► 2. Discuss three types of reference group influence on consumers.

► 3. Define household and family, and explain the types of each.

► 4. Describe various roles in family decision making.

► 5. Describe the sources of conflict in family decision making, and discuss how conflict can be handled.

► 6. Discuss consumer socialization, and give an implication for marketing.

► 7. Describe the family life cycle, and discuss several implications of the family life cycle.

TURTLEMANIA AND THE BABY BOOMLET

Max Salvati, age 3, has a bad case of Turtlemania (that's the Teenage Mutant Ninja Turtles, the toy craze of the late 1980s and early 1990s). He sleeps on Ninja Turtle sheets, eats Ninja Turtle cereal, uses a Ninja Turtle cup and plate, wears a Ninja Turtle T-shirt, and has loads of Ninja Turtle toys. Max explains, "I love the Turtles, because they're good and they fight crime."

Spending on children is one of the fastest growing sectors of the American economy. Spending on and by kids age 4 to 12 jumped about 25 percent in 1989 from 1988, to $60 billion, compared to 2 percent growth in overall spending. In 1990, the kids' market was worth about $75 billion, or nearly 2 percent of the U.S. economy.

Fueling this growth are the baby boomers who are having children later in life, creating a baby boomlet. Boomers in their 30s and 40s can afford to indulge their children because their earning power is greater than younger parents, and they already own many of the material things of life. Also, many affluent families have only one or two children, which leaves more money to spend on each child.

These demographic characteristics of American families have affected many markets. For instance, about $1 billion in children's books were sold in 1990. The current generation of boomer parents are concerned about "building a better child," and books are one way to do it. The growth in the kids' market should continue because 4 million children were born in both 1989 and 1990, the highest level since the baby boom peak in the early 1960s.

What do kids buy for themselves? In 1989, children under 12 spent over $10 billion on videogames—$7 billion in arcades and $3 billion for games to play at home. That market was dominated by Nintendo (with about a 90 percent market share), a Japanese company that single-handedly revived the home videogame market.

Sales of traditional toys are also booming. Mattel's Barbie doll brought in about $600 million in worldwide sales in 1990. To keep the interest of the 9-to-12-year-old market, Mattel has expanded the Barbie line to include girls' handbags and trading cards.

Parents can even buy Barbie townhouses and mansions at up to $400. The children's market also has produced phenomenal growth for successful toy retailer Toys 'Я' Us ($4.8 billion in sales in 1989).

Another popular purchase for kids is videocassettes. Eight of the top 10 video movies of all time appeal to kids—*E.T.* and *Bambi* are prime examples. Parents don't mind buying videos for kids, because their children will happily watch a movie dozens of times.

Among other products for kids is Hallmark's new line of greeting cards, "To Kids With Love." These cards are intended to convey affection and encouragement from busy working parents who sometimes are gone before kids get up and return after the kids are in bed.

Today's American child no longer dresses in hand-me-downs from older siblings and cousins. The growing market in children's clothing is evident from the booming sales for companies such as GapKids (now with over 100 stores), Laura Ashley's Mother and Child clothing line (accounting for 13 percent of total sales), Esprit Kids (the company's fastest growing segment with 20 percent of Esprit's $780 million in annual sales). Even adult fashion designers Ralph Lauren and Christian Dior have introduced children's lines.[1]

Evolutionary changes in the social environment of the family influence marketing strategies targeted at children or adults who buy for kids. In making these purchasing decisions, mothers and fathers influence each other's affective responses, cognitions, and behaviors. Parents are also influenced by other people in the social environment, including their relatives, friends, and peers (the latter is highly influential for both kids and adults). In this chapter, we discuss two types of environmental influences—reference groups and family.

Reference groups and family are aspects of a consumer's micro social environment. Social interaction with reference groups and family is often direct and face to face, meaning it can have immediate influence on consumers' cognitive, affective, and behavioral responses to marketing strategies.[2] Reference groups and family are involved in transferring or moving cultural meanings from the overall society, subculture, and social class to individual consumers. For all these reasons, reference groups and family have significant marketing implications.

REFERENCE GROUPS

Individuals may belong to many sorts of groups. A **group** consists of *two or more people who interact with each other to accomplish some goal.* Important groups include families, close personal friends, co-workers, formal organizations (Kiwanis, League of Women Voters, church youth group, professional association), leisure or hobby groups (a bowling team or gourmet diners), and neighbors. Any of these groups may become reference groups.

A **reference group** involves *one or more people that someone uses as a basis for comparison or "point of reference" in forming affective and cognitive responses and performing behaviors.* Reference groups can be of any size (from one person to hundreds of people); they may be tangible (the actual people in your office), or intangible and symbolic (successful business executives or sports heroes you observe from afar). A person's reference group may be from the same or another social class, subculture, or even culture. Reference groups are cultural groups in that members share certain common meanings. For instance, groups of college students tend to develop specific meanings and behavior norms about appropriate clothing, and groups of teenage boys share certain meanings about what types of athletic shoes are "in." Such reference groups can influence the affective and cognitive responses of consumers as well as their purchase and consumption behavior.

Marketers try to determine the *content* of the shared meanings of various reference groups (the common values, beliefs, behavioral norms, lifestyles). Then they select certain reference groups to associate with or promote their products. Marketers seldom examine the *process* by which reference groups move cultural meaning into products and from products into consumers.

Reference groups can have both positive and negative effects on consumers. Social groups that have favorable cultural meanings may become *associative reference groups* that consumers want to emulate or associate with. Other social groups that embody undesirable meanings may serve as a negative point of reference that people want to avoid; they become *dissociative reference groups.*

Exhibit 17.1 lists several types of reference groups and their key distinguishing characteristics. Characteristics may be combined to describe quite specific groups. For example, your immediate co-workers constitute a formal, primary membership group. While these distinctions can be useful, most consumer research focuses on two primary, informal groups—peers and family. The issues that interest marketers about reference groups include:

1. What types of influence do reference groups exert on consumers?
2. How does reference group influence vary across products and brands?
3. How can marketers use their understanding of reference groups to develop more effective marketing strategies?

Type of reference group influence

Most people belong to several primary informal groups and a few formal, membership groups (church, PTA, Chamber of Commerce). Most people could also be associated with many secondary groups, both formal and informal. Why do people use some of these groups as reference groups and not others? And how do these reference groups influence consumers' affect, cognitions, and behaviors? Basically, people identify and affiliate with particular reference groups for three reasons: to gain useful knowledge, to obtain rewards or avoid punishment, and to acquire meanings for constructing, modifying, or maintaining their self-concept. These goals reflect three types of reference group influence—informational, utilitarian, and value-expressive.

Informational reference group influence occurs when a group transmits information to a consumer about other people or about aspects of the physical environment such as products, services, and stores. This information can be conveyed directly, either in words or by direct demonstration. For instance, a consumer thinking about buying running shoes or stereo equipment might ask friends who know about such products. A person learning to play tennis may ask friends to show how to serve or how to hit a backhand shot.

Consumers tend to be influenced by reference groups to the degree that they perceive the information is reliable and relevant to the problem at hand and the information source is trustworthy.[3] Reference sources can be a single person, as when Dave Thomas

EXHIBIT 17.1

Types of reference groups

Type of Reference Group	Key Distinctions and Characteristics
Formal/informal	Formal reference groups have a clearly specified structure; informal groups do not.
Primary/secondary	Primary reference groups involve direct, face-to-face interaction; secondary groups do not.
Membership	People become formal members of membership reference groups.
Aspirational	People want to join or emulate aspirational reference groups.
Dissociative	People avoid or reject dissociative reference groups.

Danskin uses these women athletes with expertise as a credible reference group for product information.

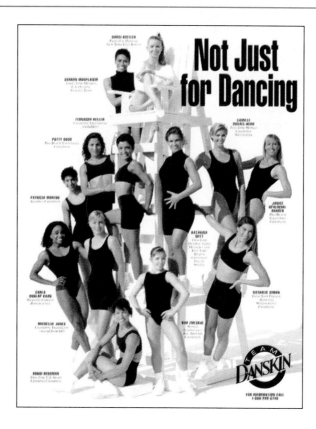

or Frank Perdue extol the merits of Wendy's hamburgers or Perdue chickens. Because highly credible reference groups are more likely to have an informational influence on consumers, marketers may hire recognized experts to endorse a product and tell consumers why it is good (famous extreme skier Scott Schmidt is spokesperson and model for North Face, manufacturer of ski clothing).

Consumers can also obtain information indirectly through vicarious observation of a reference group. People who like fishing will pay attention to the brands of equipment famous bass fishers use in a fishing tournament or on TV fishing shows. This is common behavior; many golfers, skiers, mountain climbers, and other sports enthusiasts engage in similar vicarious observation of the brands used by their reference group. This is why Nike hired basketball star Michael Jordan (obviously an expert) to wear its Air Jordan basketball shoes.

Reference groups can transmit information to consumers in three ways. Sometimes consumers intentionally seek information to reduce the perceived risk of making a decision or to learn how to perform certain behaviors. Thus, most beginning sky divers listen very carefully to their new reference group of experienced skydiving instructors as they explain how to pack a parachute or how to land correctly. Consumers buying a new computer may seek out a reference group of more experienced users who can help them learn how to use the product. In other cases, the reference group may accidentally transmit information; perhaps someone will overhear reference group members talking about a product or happen to observe members of a reference group using a particular brand. A third way information may be transmitted to the consumer is for reference group members to initiate the process. This can occur when enthusiastic reference group members talk up an activity and encourage people to try it. For example, Rollerbladers might try to persuade others to take up the sport. A marketing strategy consistent with informational reference group influence is to encourage current customers to create new customers (bring along a friend for dinner, and get your meal for half-price).

Utilitarian reference group influence on consumers' behaviors and affective and cognitive responses can occur when the reference group is in charge of rewards and punishments that matter to the consumers. Basically, people will comply with the desires of a reference group if (a) they believe the group can control rewards and punishments, (b) the behavior is visible or known to the group, and (c) they are motivated to gain rewards or avoid punishment.

For example, in some work environments (a formal, membership reference group), people are expected to wear business attire. Other work groups may encourage casual dress (jeans and T-shirts in some Silicon Valley companies). The rewards and punishments for compliance with the appropriate form of dress may be tangible (people get raises or bonuses, or they get fired), or more psychological and social consequences may result (approving looks, or disparaging remarks behind your back). Peer groups routinely administer such psychosocial rewards and punishments for adherence to or violation of the reference group code. We all can cite examples of how our own peer reference group influences (even controls) our dressing behavior and attitude. Marketing strategies that use utilitarian reference group appeals include portrayal of social sanctions in TV commercials (people recoiling from someone's offensive body odor or bad breath, or the evidence of dandruff).

Value-expressive reference group influence can affect people's self-concepts. As cultural units, reference groups create and embody cultural meanings (beliefs, values, goals, behavioral norms, lifestyles). As you learned in Chapter 15, people constantly look for desirable cultural meanings to use in constructing, enhancing, or maintaining their self-concepts. When they identify and affiliate with particular reference groups that express these desired meanings, consumers can draw out some of these meanings and use them in their own self-construction.

Consider a group of people who buy Harley-Davidson motorcycles and associated gear—they are largely middle and upper-class professional people, including doctors, dentists, lawyers, and professors. These RUBS (rich urban bikers) or weekend warriors, as the hard-core Harley owners (the tattooed and bearded renegades) refer to them, look to the traditional Harley owners as an aspirational reference group (although very few RUBS will ever become hard-core bikers).[4] The hard-core Harley bikers express several desirable meanings and values for the RUBS, which they can gain through association, and through purchase of Harley-Davidson products, including feelings of freedom from work and family, independence, patriotism (Harleys are built in the United States), and belonging to a special, unique group. Some RUBS even may inspire a bit of the fascination that the hard-core Harley bikers relish from nonbikers or owners of other brands. Value expressive reference group meanings can influence affect, cognitions, and behavior, in this case including purchases of biker clothing and accessories. Harley-Davidson markets a variety of products to satisfy these desires, including black leather jackets, "colors" (clothing with insignias and biker logos), many biking accessories, and even a Harley-Davidson brand of beer.

In summary, reference groups can influence consumers' affect, cognitions, and behaviors in several ways. In fact, all three types of reference group influence can occur through a single reference group. As a reference group for the weekend biker, the hard-core Harley-Davidson bikers can be a source of information (magazine articles and observation), reward or punishment (returning a wave or ignoring the RUBS on the road), and cultural meanings such as values (individualism and independence).

Hard-core Harley bikers such as these members of the Chicago Outlaws are a reference group for some Harley owners.

Reference group influence on product and brand purchase

It is unlikely that reference groups influence all product and brand purchases to the same degree. Research suggests that reference group influence on consumers' purchase decisions varies on at least two dimensions.[5] The first dimension concerns the degree to which the product or brand is a necessity or a luxury. A *necessity* is owned by virtually everyone (a flashlight, a clock, a bed), while a *luxury* is owned only by consumers in particular groups (a sailboat, a camcorder, a tuxedo). The second dimension is the degree to which the object in question is conspicuous or visible to other people.[6] A *public good* is one that other people are aware an individual owns and uses: one for which they can identify the brand with little or no difficulty (a car). A *private good* is used at home or in private so that other people (outside the immediate family) would be unaware of its possession or use (a hair dryer).

Combining these two dimensions produces the matrix shown in Exhibit 17.2. This Exhibit suggests that reference group influence will vary depending on whether the products and brands are public necessities, private necessities, public luxuries, or private luxuries. Consider wristwatches, which are public necessities. Because everyone can see whether a person is wearing a wristwatch, the *brand* may be susceptible to reference group influence. Because this product class is owned and used by most people, however, there is likely to be little reference group influence on whether one should purchase a watch.

Marketing implications

We have seen that reference groups exert an important influence on consumers.[7] Members of primary informal groups affect not only consumer knowledge, attitudes, and values, but also the purchase of specific products and brands—and even the choice of stores in which purchases are made. In some cases, an analysis of primary informal group influences can be used to develop marketing strategies. For example, in industrial marketing, a careful analysis of the group influence dynamics among the various people who have a role in a purchase decision may be useful for determining appropriate marketing approaches.[8] Similarly, peer group influence is a major asset to firms that sell to groups of consumers (perhaps at "parties" in the home), as in the case of Tupperware. In such instances, individuals tend to conform to the norms of the group by purchasing some items.

	Necessity	Luxury

Public	**Public necessities**
	
	Reference group influence
	  Product: Weak
	  Brand: Strong
	
	Examples: Wristwatch, automobile, man's suit
		Public luxuries
		
		Reference group influence
		  Product: Strong
		  Brand: Strong
		
		Examples: Golf clubs, snow skis, sailboat

Private	**Private necessities**
	
	Reference group influence
	  Product: Weak
	  Brand: Weak
	
	Examples: Mattress, floor lamp, refrigerator
		Private luxuries
		
		Reference group influence
		  Product: Strong
		  Brand: Weak
		
		Examples: TV game, trash compactor, ice maker

EXHIBIT 17.2

Effects of public-private and luxury-necessity dimensions on reference group influence for product and brand choice

Source: Adapted with permission of the University of Chicago Press from "Reference Group Influences on Product and Brand Purchase Decisions," by Bearden and Etzel, in *Journal of Consumer Research*, September 1982, p. 185. © 1982 by the University of Chicago.

Occasionally, marketers may try to stimulate reference group influence—a health club might offer you two months' membership free if you get a friend to sign up for a one-year membership.

Salespeople may attempt to create a reference group influence by describing how a customer is similar to previous purchasers of the product—"There was a couple in here last week very much like you. They bought the JVC speakers." Salespeople could describe themselves as a reference group—"Oh, your children go to East High School? My kids go there, too. We bought them an IBM PC to help them with their science projects."

Finally, soliciting experts to aid in the direct sale of products can be a successful strategy for some firms. For example, a consumer's dentist is likely to be a highly influential reference individual, particularly for products related to dental care. Thus, it could be effective for a manufacturer of, say, the Water Pik, to offer gifts to dentists for encouraging patients to use the product. The company could keep track of a dentist's referrals by asking consumers to list their dentist on the warranty card for the product. Of course, experts can also have a negative impact on the sales of a new product if they convey negative information.[9]

For most mass-marketed products, a detailed analysis of the interactions of specific primary informal groups (groups of close friends or co-workers) is impractical. Instead marketers tend to portray both primary informal and aspirational groups in advertising:

Reference group concepts have been used by advertisers in their efforts to persuade consumers to purchase products and brands. Portraying products being consumed in socially pleasant situations, the use of prominent attractive people endorsing products, and the use of obvious group members as spokespersons in advertising are all evidence that marketers and advertisers make substantial use of potential reference group influence on consumer behavior in the development of their communications. . . . Reference groups expose people to behavior and lifestyles, influence self-concept development, contribute to the formation of values and attitudes, and generate pressure for conformity to group norms.[10]

There are many examples of the use of reference group concepts in advertising. Pepsi has featured popular stars such as Ray Charles and Michael Jackson, and popular athletes such as Joe Montana and Dan Marino, with whom many young people may identify. Converse, Puma, Nike, and other running shoe companies for many years spent a large portion of their promotion budget in shoe giveaways to successful athletes, as well as to hire these athletes to wear and recommend their brands. The popular series of Miller Lite advertisements featuring

CONSUMER PERSPECTIVE

> **17.1**

Reference group advertising

Sometimes the reference group is a single person—a referent other. Thus, movie stars such as Meryl Streep or Mickey Rourke (highly popular in France) or musicians such as Madonna or Garth Brooks can serve as a reference group for some people.

American Express has based its advertising on single-person, reference group appeals since the early 1970s, beginning with the classic campaign, "Do You Know Me?" launched in 1974. Each ad featured a person famous for his or her achievements, but whose face was not familiar to the public. In 1987, American Express modified the ad strategy and produced the highly praised "Portraits" campaign with photographs of famous people who had held American Express credit cards for varying periods of time, including Tip O'Neill, John Elway, Willie Shoemaker, and Wilt Chamberlain. The ads were intended to establish the American Express card as the most prestigious card to own. The reference group strategy seems to have worked for American Express, as earnings grew at a 20 percent rate between 1970 and 1990.

The early 1990s ushered in a different era in which prestige and high status no longer seemed so important. Visa had used a different promotion approach since the middle 1980s, developing ads intended to convince consumers that Visa is a more practical card because it is accepted in more places than American Express. The typical ad showed a real place like Rosalie's Restaurant, or the ticket office for the Winter Olympics, accompanied by the same tag line, "If you go to (Rosalie's), be sure to bring your Visa card, because they don't take American Express." Between 1986 and 1991, Visa's worldwide share rose from 44.3 percent to 50.9, while American Express's share fell from 21.7 percent to 16.4. Calculated in dollars, these are huge changes.

In the meantime, American Express rethought its image approach based on reference group celebrities. The 1991 campaign from American Express for its Corporate Card was still based on an aspirational reference group appeal, but not focused on prestige and status. Rather, four different ads portrayed a "real-life" situation in an executive's busy life, such as opening a foreign branch office or starting a small company. The ads briefly described how the American Express Corporate Card and the company's good service gave these executives an advantage in their business. The promotion goal was to form a means-end chain linking the product to the customer.

Source: "American Express Pulls Trigger with New Ads," *Marketing News*, March 4, 1991, p. 6; and Derrick Niederman, "Image Can Be a Fickle Thing," *Investment Vision*, October–November 1991, p. 30.

well-known retired athletes likely appealed to baby boomers who followed the careers of these personalities and considered some of them heroes. Consumer Perspective 17.1 describes the aspirational reference group appeals used by American Express.

FAMILY

In most consumer behavior research, marketers take the individual consumer as the unit of analysis. The usual goal is to describe and understand how individuals make purchase decisions so that marketing strategies can be developed to influence this process most effectively. The area of family research is an exception: it views the family as the unit of analysis.[11]

Actually, marketers are interested in both families and households. The distinction between a family and a household is important.[12] The U.S. Census Bureau defines a housing unit as having its own entrance (inside or outside) and basic living facilities. The people living in the housing unit constitute a **household.** Except for homeless people, most Americans live in households. These households are highly diverse, involving many different living arrangements such as houses, townhouses, apartments and condominiums, college dorm rooms, fraternity houses, and nursing homes. The *householder* is the person who rents or owns the household. Households can be categorized into types on the basis of the relationship of the residents in the household to the householder. Marketers are mainly concerned with two types of households—families and nonfamilies.

Nonfamily households include unrelated people living together, such as college roommates or unmarried couples of the opposite sex or same sex. In 1990, 3 of 10 American households were nonfamilies. A **family** by contrast has at least two people—the householder and someone who is related to the householder by blood, marriage, or adoption. About 70 percent of American households are families. The difference between nuclear and extended families is an important distinction. The *nuclear family* includes one or more parents and one or more children living together in a household. The *extended family* is a nuclear family plus other relatives, usually grandparents, living in one household. Extended families living in one household are more common in Hispanic and Asian subcultures.

Marketers are highly interested in **family decision making**—how family members interact and influence each other when making purchase choices for the household.[13] Research has shown that different people in the family may take on different social roles and perform different behaviors during decision making and consumption.[14] For example, the person who purchases Jif peanut butter for lunchtime sandwiches (the husband) may not be the same person who makes the sandwiches (the mother) or who eats them (the children).

Family decision making

Decision roles and influence

To understand family decision making fully, marketers need to identify which family members take on what roles. Decision-making roles can be described as the following:

▷ *Influencers* provide information to other family members about a product or service (a child tells parents about a new brand of breakfast cereal).

▷ *Gatekeepers* control the flow of information into the family (a mother does not tell her children about a new toy she saw at the store).

▷ *Deciders* have the power to determine whether to obtain a product or service (a husband decides to buy a new snack chip at the grocery store).

▷ *Buyers* actually purchase the product or service (a teenager buys milk for the family at the convenience store).

▷ *Users* consume or use the product or service (the kids eat canned spaghetti that the parents bought).

▷ *Disposers* discard a product or discontinue use of a service (a father throws out a partially eaten pizza; a mother cancels a magazine subscription).

These definitions show how different family members may be involved in particular aspects of the purchase decision and use of the product or service that is bought. From the perspective of the Wheel of Consumer Analysis, each family member and his or her roles and behaviors are part of the social environment for the other family members. Understanding family decision making is a difficult research challenge that requires marketers to study the social interactions and patterns of influence among family members. These interactions and influences will vary for different purchases depending on which family members are involved and how much is at stake.

Some products are purchased for use by the entire family (orange juice), while others are purchased for use by one person in the family (deodorant). Developing successful marketing strategies for selling products to families requires attention to questions such as these:

1. Is the product to be used by one person or several family members?

2. Is the product to be purchased with funds from a single person or family funds?

3. Is the product expensive enough that the purchase requires the family to make trade-offs in buying other items it needs?

4. Do family members disagree about the value of the product? How do they reduce the conflict?

5. If the product is to be used by several people in the family, what product modifications are necessary to accommodate each user?

6. Which family members will influence the product purchase decision? What media and information are used by each influencer?

7. Do different family members prefer different product forms, brands, models, or stores?

Consider the purchase of a car by a family. Answers to these questions will influence the marketing strategies used by car manufacturers and dealers. The appropriate marketing strategies for selling cars will vary if the car is to be used as a second family car for commuting to work, or by a teenager to drive to school, versus if it is the only car in the family.

Because of these variations, relatively few generalizations can be offered about family decision making. Essentially, marketers can expect to find substantial differences in the people involved at each stage of the decision-making process, their roles, and their influences on the decision outcome.[15] This means researchers must analyze the dynamics of family decision making for each marketing problem they face, including identifying which family members are involved, what roles they play, and who has the major influence. These analyses are useful in developing effective marketing strategies targeted at the appropriate family member.

Most research on family decision making has focused on husband/wife roles and influence, while children (and other members of extended families) have not received much attention.[16] Yet we know the children's market is large and important. Children—both younger kids and teenagers—can have major influences on the budget allocation decisions and purchase choices made by the family. The birth of a child, for example, is a major event for a family, which creates demand for a wide variety of products most couples never needed to consider purchasing previously. Consumer Perspective 17.2 describes some of these purchases.

Conflict in family decision making

When more than one person in a family is involved in making a purchase decision, some degree of conflict is likely.[17] **Decision conflict** arises when family members disagree about some aspect of the purchase decision. The means-end chain model provides a useful framework for understanding decision conflict. Family members may disagree about the desired end goals of a purchase. Consider the choice of where to spend a family vacation. The husband might want to go somewhere for lazy relaxation, the wife wants good shopping and nightlife, and the kids want adventure and entertainment. Differences in end goals or values can create major conflict because very different choice alternatives are likely to be related to these incompatible ends. Serious negotiations may be required to resolve the conflict.

In other cases, family members could agree on the desired end goal, yet disagree about the best means to achieve it. For instance, everyone might want to go out to eat or see a movie, but the kids think a fast-food restaurant or an action film is the best choice, while the parents prefer a full-service restaurant or a dramatic film. Again, some means of resolving the conflict is necessary. Often, an alternative (a new means to the end) is chosen as a compromise (everyone goes out for pizza or to see a comedy film). Finally, if either the end or the means is not agreed on, family members are also likely to disagree

CONSUMER PERSPECTIVE

17.2

Bringing up baby

Births in the United States during the late 1980s and early 1990s were at a recent high level of about 4 million per year or about 11,000 new babies each day. This rate should continue into the mid-1990s. Although the number of births is lower than that of the previous high birthrate period (when the baby boomers were born during the late 40s, 50s, and early 1960s), the costs have become much greater. Today, parents spend about twice as much on a baby as they did 30 years ago, even after adjusting for inflation. Careful estimates in 1990 suggest it costs about $5,800 to take care of a baby for the first year. In 1958, *Life* magazine estimated first-year baby expenses at about $800 ($2,900 in 1990 dollars). Why the big difference?

Day care, virtually unavailable in the 50s, is now a necessity for many families, adding $2,200 to the first-year costs. Thirty years ago, kids rode in the car sitting on the seat or in someone's lap. Now many state laws mandate the use of car seats. During the first year, parents need two seats costing about $100—an infant seat for newborns and another one as the baby grows. In the 50s, kids drank cow's milk; now breast-feeding or formula is recommended. Breast milk is free, but formula costs can be $500 in the first year. Cloth diapers were used 30 years ago, but many families today like the convenience of disposable diapers ($570). Food and feeding equipment (high chairs, utensils) cost about $850. Families spend about $350 on clothes, $1,000 on furniture (cribs, dressers, portable cribs, strollers), and another $225 on bedding and bath products.

These first-year expenses are only a sample of what is yet to come. The U.S. Department of Agriculture estimates that raising a child to age 18 costs the average American family about $100,000. Clearly, children create very large markets and many marketing opportunities.

Source: Blayne Cutler, "Rock-A-Buy Baby," *American Demographics*, January 1990, pp. 35–39. Reprinted with permission © *American Demographics*, January 1990. For subscription information, please call (800) 828-1133.

about the choice criteria for evaluating alternatives (in the case of a new car, these could include the appropriate price range, the necessary options, the best color).

When family members disagree about such factors in a purchase situation, conflict may be severe.[18] If so, family members can do several things. Some consumers will procrastinate, ignoring the problem and hoping the situation will improve by itself. Others may try to get their way by attempting to influence other family members. Exhibit 17.3 describes several influence strategies that have been identified in family research.[19] Depending on the product at issue, the family members involved in the decision, the social class and subculture of the family, and the environment, a family member might use any of these strategies to influence other members of the family.

Although serious conflicts can occur in family decision making, many family purchases probably do not involve major conflicts. For one thing, many family purchases are recurring, in that many products and brands are bought repeatedly over a long period. So, even though conflict may have been present at one time, it usually has been resolved. To minimize continual friction, families may develop choice plans to avoid potential conflict. For instance, a family with two children might allow one to choose the breakfast cereal or ice cream flavor one week and the other to choose the next week.

Another reason decision conflict among family members concerning purchase and consumption decisions is not often serious is that many purchases in a household are made by individuals to meet their own personal needs or those of other family members. To the degree that such purchases are reasonably consistent with family values and do not place

EXHIBIT 17.3

Six common types of family influence strategies

Expert
Influence is reflected by a spouse providing specific information concerning the various alternatives. For example, one spouse can try to convince the other that she/he is more knowledgeable concerning the products under consideration by presenting detailed information about various aspects of these products.
Legitimate
Influence deals with one spouse's attempts to draw upon the other's feelings of shared values concerning their role expectations. Therefore, the spouse's influence is based on the shared belief that she/he should make the decision because she/he is the wife/husband. For example, the husband can argue that since he is the "man of the house," he should make a particular decision.
Bargaining
Involves attempts by one spouse to turn the joint decision into an autonomous one in return for some favor granted to the other spouse. For example, in return for autonomy in a particular decision, one spouse may agree to give the other autonomy in another decision when she/he had previously refused to do so. "If you do this, I'll do that" may be the most common type of bargaining attempt.
Reward/referent
Influence is based on a combination of the reward and referent power/influence strategies. Reward influence is based on an individual's ability to reward another by doing something that the other would enjoy. Referent influence is the influence based on the identification or feeling of oneness (or desire for such an identity) of one person with another. Referent influence in marriage stems from the desire of spouses to be like their concepts of the "ideal" husband or wife.
Emotional
Influence attempts involve displaying some emotion-laden reaction. For example, one spouse may get angry at the other. These attempts are often nonverbal techniques. For example, one person may cry or pout, while another may try the "silent treatment."
Impression management
Encompasses premeditated persuasive attempts to enhance one's influence differential in a dyadic relationship. For example, one spouse may claim that the other's preferred brand was "out of stock" when, in fact, it wasn't. The objective is to convince the spouse to attribute the influence attempt to external pressures beyond the influencer's control.

Source: Reprinted by permission of the University of Chicago Press from "Persuasion in Family Decision Making," by Rosann L. Spiro, in *Journal of Consumer Research*, March 1983, p. 394. © 1983 by the University of Chicago.

an undue burden on family resources, there is likely to be little conflict. For instance, we would expect that purchases of books, personal care items, and many food products do not involve much family conflict.

Consumer socialization

It is through socialization processes that families transmit the cultural meanings of society, subculture, and social class to their children, thereby influencing their children's affect, cognitions, and behaviors. **Consumer socialization** refers to the way children acquire knowledge about products and services and various consumption-related skills (how to buy carefully, how to apply for a loan).[20] Younger children acquire much of their consumer knowledge from their parents, but adolescents learn from their peers as well. Both younger and older children absorb consumer knowledge and skills from social institutions such as the media (TV, magazines, movies) and advertising.[21]

Many companies have recognized segments of the family life cycle such as divorced or widowed middle-aged peole.

JAN: Here I am. 40 and dating again.
ANNCR: How Colgate Tartar Control gave Jan her smile back.
JAN: I took a really good look at myself. And my smile didn't look clean.

My dentist removed the tartar and said Colgate Tartar Control helps keep it off.
ANNCR: Colgate fights the tartar that traps bacteria and stains . . . For cleaner teeth.

RANDY: I LOVE TO SEE YOU SMILE.
ANNCR: Colgate Tartar Control. Because your smile was meant to last a lifetime.

Socialization can occur indirectly through observation and modeling or directly through intentional instruction. Indirect socialization occurs when parents take their children on shopping trips or discuss products and brands. In other cases, parents intentionally talk to their children about consumer skills such as how to look for products, find the best price, bargain with salespeople, return unsatisfactory products for a refund, and dispose of products (recycling, holding a garage sale).[22]

The consumer knowledge formed in childhood can influence people in later years. Some adults still use the same brands their parents bought when they were children. A number of long-lived brands may be purchased and used throughout an adult's life (Campbell's soup, Crest or Colgate toothpaste, Heinz ketchup, Tide laundry detergent are examples). Thus, developing early brand awareness and loyalty is an important marketing strategy for many companies. Chrysler, for instance, has sponsored events during spring break at Daytona Beach (including building a 250-foot-long sand sculpture on the beach). Even though teenagers are not often car buyers, they can have a significant influence on their parents' choices, particularly for the second or third car in a household. Chevrolet has advertised on MTV to attract today's teens and tomorrow's new car buyers, and this is a strategy that may be working.[23] One third of all Camaro drivers are under age 25, even though this age group accounts for only about 13 percent of car sales overall.

Socialization is not restricted to the influence of parents on young children. Children can socialize their parents, especially where new products are concerned (teens may introduce their parents to new music styles).[24] In some instances, adult children can influence the consumption behavior of their parents, as in the case of decisions on retirement housing.[25] Finally, consumer socialization occurs throughout life as people continue to learn new consumer skills and acquire product knowledge. Consider the socialization that occurs when people marry or move in together. Each person learns from the other as they adjust to different preferences and consumption behaviors.

Changes in American families

Many cultural and social changes in recent years have influenced the structure of American families (and families elsewhere, too). We briefly discuss four of these changes that are interrelated: women's employment, marriage and divorce, family planning and child-rearing practices, and household composition.

Women's employment

At one time in American society (say, 40 years ago), the typical role of women was as homemakers. Today, over half of all women are in the labor force.[26] Working women are not distributed equally across all age groups, however. Over two thirds of women in their 20s, 30s, and 40s are employed outside the home, but fewer women older than that have outside jobs. Of the women who do work, 45 percent are employed full time the year around, compared to 65 percent of men who work full time all year. More than 50 percent of young women with preschool children are working, up from 30 percent in 1970.

The disposable income of married couple households increases dramatically when both spouses work outside the home. The average household income for dual-earner couples with children was $49,600 in 1990, $9,600 greater than for one-earner households.[27] The total income of this segment is a staggering $890 billion, creating a vast market for many products.

Marriage and divorce

American society has undergone major changes in people's attitudes and behaviors concerning marriage and divorce.[28] Young people are delaying marriage (the median age of first marriage is 23.6 for women and 25.8 for men, a near record). Increasing numbers of Americans may never marry (in 1987, 23 percent of men aged 30 to 35 had never married, compared to 9 percent in 1970; for women, the same statistic is 15 percent never married versus 6 percent in 1970).

In the 1990s, marriage is likely to become even more of an optional lifestyle. Increasing numbers of single women are remaining unmarried and raising children alone. Divorced and widowed people are waiting longer to remarry, and increasing numbers of them will never remarry. And more Americans are living together outside marriage. Some 2.8 million households are unmarried couples (17 percent of unmarried people aged 25 to 29 are cohabiting, and nearly half had cohabited at some time). Although some people claim cohabiting is a way to cut the chance of divorce (because people learn more about a future spouse before marriage), divorce rates actually are higher for couples who cohabit before marriage (53 percent of first marriages that begin with cohabitation end in divorce compared to 28 percent of those where the partners did not live together before marriage).

The net result is that more Americans spend less of their lives married. This change has profound implications for many consumer businesses that may have assumed their market consists of traditional families. Still, most Americans eventually do marry (or remarry), and many of them have children. Current estimates are that 90 percent of American women will marry at some time in their lives. The point is that marketers must consider a greater variety of family types than they once did.

Family planning and child-rearing practices

As more baby boomers begin their families, the number of births has increased to near record levels (4 million births in 1990).[29] The number of births is up because there are more potential parents among the baby boomers, not because families are having more children. In fact, the number of children per family has decreased steadily since the mid-1960s. Women currently bear an average of less than two children, down from nearly three in 1965. Despite the trend toward smaller families, there are still some large families in America. Some 6.4 million families have three or more children (representing 20 percent of families with kids, down from 40 percent in the late 1960s).[30] These relatively larger families constitute significant markets for certain products such as breakfast cereal, milk, toothpaste, and toilet paper. At the same time, because many women marry later and have children later than their mothers did, this changes how they raise their kids and relate to them. Finally, women live many years after the children leave the home. All of these changes together mean people spend less of their lives in child-oriented households than once was the case, which has a strong influence on their consumption behavior.

Household composition

American family and nonfamily households have undergone major demographic changes during the past few decades that have significant implications for marketers. Exhibit 17.4 summarizes some of these changes. First, the number of households grew by 17 percent in the 1980s to 93.9 million households in 1990. The number of households grew faster than the total population (now about 250 million), which means the average household size dropped to 2.6 people in 1990, from 2.8 in 1980.

American families are highly diverse, and the various types of families constitute distinctive markets for many products. Still the most common family is the *married-couple family*—householders who live with their spouse (56 percent of American households). This category grew about 8 percent over the past 10 years. Most of these households are headed by two earners; only 22 percent of married couple households in 1990 included a male breadwinner and a female homemaker, down from 61 percent in 1960.

The so-called *traditional family* has several definitions, but it usually means a married-couple family with children under 18. This category actually declined slightly during the

Nontraditional families, such as single parents with children living at home, are a growing market.

EXHIBIT 17.4

Changes in American family and nonfamily households

	1990		1980		1980–90	
	Households*	Percent Distribution	Households*	Percent Distribution	Change*	Percent Change
All households	93,920	100.0%	80,467	100.0%	13,453	16.7%
Family households	66,542	70.8%	59,190	73.6%	7.352	12.4%
Married couples	52,837	56.3	48,990	60.9	3.847	7.9
Without children <18	28,315	30.1	24,210	30.1	4,105	17.0
With children <18	24,522	26.1	24,780	30.8	−258	−1.0
Other family, female head	11,130	11.9	8,205	10.2	2,925	35.6
Other family, male head	2,575	2.7	1,995	2.5	580	29.1
Nonfamily households	27,378	29.2%	21,277	26.4%	6,101	28.7%
Living alone	22,879	24.4	18,202	22.6	4,677	25.7
Men	9,119	9.7	7,075	8.8	2,044	28.9
Women	13,759	14.7	11,127	13.8	2,632	23.7
Living with nonrelatives	4,500	4.8	3,075	3.8	1,425	46.3
Male householder	2,803	3.0	1,866	2.3	937	50.2
Female householder	1,696	1.8	1,209	1.5	487	40.3

*Households and change in households, in thousands; percent distribution and percent change by household type, 1980–90.

Source: Judith Waldrop and Thomas Exter, "What the 1990 Census Will Show," *American Demographics,* January 1990, p. 27. Reprinted with permission of *American Demographics,* January 1990. For subscription information, please call (800) 828-1133.

1980s and currently stands at 26 percent of all households. Sometimes traditional family means a working husband and homemaker wife, but only 9 percent of households are like this. Finally, if traditional family means a working husband, nonworking wife, and exactly two children, we are talking about only 3 percent of all American households.

So-called *nontraditional families* are also growing in number. Among this type of family, the fastest growing are households with children headed by a woman with no husband present (12 percent of American households, up 36 percent during the 1980s). Only about 3 percent of households with children are headed by single men, but this segment grew 30 percent in the 1980s. Despite this fragmentation into different types of families, the family unit is still America's largest market, accounting for 71 percent of all households. The expectations are that the 1990s will be a family decade, thanks to the large numbers of baby boomers in the middle of their child-rearing years. Three fourths of all boomer households will be families.

Nonfamily households make up 29 percent of all U.S. households and are growing rapidly. They were up 29 percent during the 1980s, compared to a 12 percent gain for families. For instance, households headed by a single, unmarried person constitute nearly 15 percent of all households. Unrelated people living together constitute a rapidly growing proportion (now about 5 percent) of nonfamily households. Nearly 3 million of these households are made up of unmarried couples of both sexes, sometimes called cohabiting couples.

Almost one in four nonfamily households consists of a single person living alone, up 26 percent during the 1980s. Men living alone make up 10 percent of nonfamily households; 15 percent are headed by women. Two factors are behind this surge. First, unprecedented numbers of consumers are not marrying; second, up to 60 percent of those who do will eventually divorce and become single again. These social trends toward living alone create major opportunities for marketers, some of them described in Consumer Perspective 17.3.

CONSUMER PERSPECTIVE

17.3

Home alone

The 1990 census shows that some 23 million Americans live by themselves, up 91 percent for women and 156 percent for men over 1970. Two trends are behind this surge: (1) large numbers of consumers are not marrying or are delaying marriage, and (2) an estimated 60 percent of those who do marry eventually divorce.

These singles, plus college students and young adults living with their parents, constitute a huge market with some $660 billion in annual earnings. It probably comes as no surprise that singles are disproportionate consumers of convenience products, fast-food and regular restaurant meals, and travel.

As with any social segment, there is great diversity among singles, including carefree 21-year-olds, middle-age divorced people, and elderly widows. Some marketers have treated all singles as an "extramarital aberration," which is foolhardy. To be successful, marketers must deal with the diversity in this group.

Consider the ad campaign "Friends and Family" from MCI Telecommunications Corporation. Because singles don't live in a nuclear family, they use the telephone to keep in touch with their families and their friends. The MCI ads show attractive adults of varying ages in nonfamily situations making lists of friends to call. If consumers get their friends and families to join MCI, each party receives a 20 percent discount on calls made to each other. The promotion was quite successful.

Source: Laura Zinn, Heather Keets, and James B. Treece, "Home Alone—With $660 Billion," *Business Week*, July 29, 1991, pp. 76–77; and Blayne Cutler, "Single and Settled," *American Demographics*, May 1991, p. 10.

Analysis of the many demographic changes in family composition and structure can be complicated. To apply an organizing framework, marketers can use the concept of the family life cycle to identify key family segments and develop effective marketing strategies for those households.

Family life cycle

Some 40 years ago, most Americans followed the same life path and went through about the same stages of life. People got married, had children, stayed married, raised their children and sent them on their way, grew old, retired, and eventually died. This sequence of family types delineated by major life events (marriage, birth of children, aging, departure of children, retirement, death) is called the *traditional family life cycle*.[31]

Recent cultural changes in American society such as delayed marriage, childless marriages, working women, and increased divorce rates have rendered the traditional family life cycle somewhat inadequate. Exhibit 17.5 presents a **modern family life cycle** that includes the traditional family life cycle and adds several other family types to describe the more diverse family structures of the 1990s.[32] The modern family life cycle can account for most types of families in American society, including childless couples, divorced persons, and single parents with children.

▷ *Single parents* constitute 9 percent of all households. Most of these are divorced parents, but some women who have never married are raising children. Although income is relatively low ($21,400 average), the growing numbers of such people create a sizable market.

▷ *Young singles* are people under 45 who live by themselves. Currently, they represent 9 million households (9 percent of all households). The tendency to delay marriage, or avoid it, is increasing this segment. Their average income level of $25,000 gives this group significant purchasing power, and their lack of family responsibilities gives them considerable discretion in spending it. This rapidly increasing market is very important for companies that sell products purchased by households (appliances, kitchen utensils, TVs, basic furniture).

EXHIBIT 17.5   A modern family life cycle

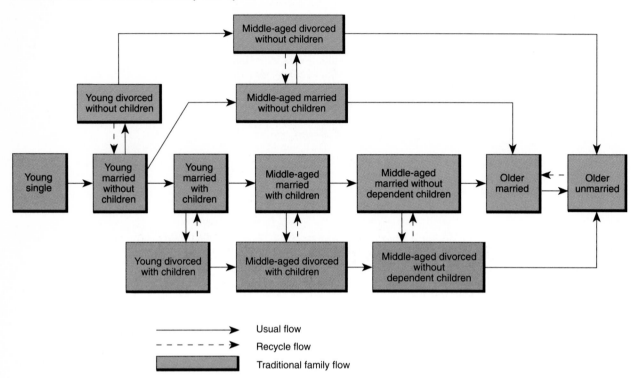

Source: Reprinted by permission of the University of Chicago Press from "A Modernized Family Life Cycle," by Murphy and Staples, in *Journal of Consumer Research,* June 1979, pp. 12–31. © 1979 by the University of Chicago.

▷ *Older singles* are people over 45 who are living alone. They represent 15 million households, or 16 percent of all households. Although their average income is relatively low ($17,500), their large numbers make them a significant market.

▷ *Married couples with children* includes two important subcategories—(1) dual-earner couples and (2) other married couples (usually a working husband and a homemaker wife). The distinction is important for two reasons: average household income is $49,600 for dual-earners versus $40,000 for the others, and lifestyles differ considerably in the different type of households. Life in the dual-earner households is likely to be more fragmented, and parents to be more harassed for time than in other married-couple households.

Television producers seem to cover many of these stages in the family life cycle in creating television situation comedies (see Consumer Perspective 17.4).

Two cautions are worth mentioning about the modern family life cycle in Exhibit 17.5. First, this scheme does not include nonfamily households, which currently represent nearly 30 percent of all American households. This diverse category includes people who remain single and never marry, cohabiting couples, and shared households that include various combinations of unrelated residents. Although these diverse households may be difficult to categorize and target with marketing strategies, the fact that they number 28 million households makes them attractive markets for many products.

Second, the family life cycle framework does not capture every possible change in family status that can occur. For instance, a new life cycle stage may be developing called the "boomerang age."[33] This group refers to the increasing number of young adults (mostly in

Several TV situation comedies in the early 1990s mirror the diversity of the American family structure. Note how these shows represent the various stages of the family life cycle.

Stage in Family Life Cycle	Television Show
Married couple with children, one wage earner	"The Simpsons" "Married With Children"
Married couple with children, two wage earners	"Roseanne"
Married couple with children and related adults	"Family Matters"
Male householder with children and unrelated adults	"Full House"
Nonfamily household	"Perfect Strangers"
Married couple with children from previous marriages	"True Colors" "Step by Step"

Source: Martha Farnsworth Riche, "The Future of the Family," *American Demographics*, March 1991, pp. 44–46. Reprinted with permission, © *American Demographics*, March 1991. For subscription information, please call (800) 828-1133.

CONSUMER PERSPECTIVE

17.4

The family life cycle on TV

their 20s) who left home for work or college but are now returning to live with their parents. Although there were more of these people in 1991 than at any time since the Depression, living with parents past high school and even college is not so unusual. Only one third of young adults (19–24) live independently of their parents (25 percent of men and 38 percent of women). Most young people begin to live independently at ages 22 to 24, but only about 5 percent of these young adults will live alone. Many will live in a nonfamily household of unrelated adults or cohabit with a potential marriage partner. And as many as 40 percent of young adults return to live in their parents' homes at least once. This "boomerang" segment of the family life cycle may offer some marketing opportunities.

Marketers can use the family life cycle to segment the market, analyze market potential, identify target markets, and develop more effective marketing strategies. The family segments identified by the family life cycle include diverse types of people. Each family type is made up of people from every social class and every age, racial, ethnic, and regional subculture in the country.

Marketing implications

Marital status

Consider the young single or bachelor stage of the family life cycle. In 1987, there were 29 million bachelors in the United States, an increase of 21 percent since 1980. About 34 percent of all American men 18 and older were unmarried, and many were living alone. Much of this growth is attributable to the "new" bachelors created by divorce. The number of divorced men (5.6 million) increased nearly twice as fast as the number of never-married men (21 million).

The various types of bachelors constitute rather different markets. For instance, 18-to-24-year-old men in the swinging years (99 percent have never married, but most will someday) are a prime market for tape decks, six-packs, and hot cars. But 35-to-45-year-old unmarried men (51 percent of whom are divorced) are more interested in toys for their kids, living room furniture, and toilet bowl cleaners. Many divorced men are really

Young singles (9 percent of all households) are an important market segment for many products.

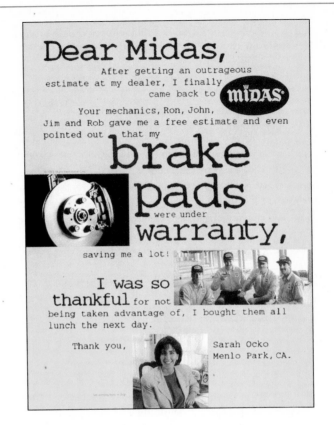

only temporary bachelors, because many will remarry within an average of three years. Finally, approximately 7 percent of bachelors are widowers. With an average age of 61, their behavior resembles that of married men their age more closely than it does that of other bachelors. In sum, developing marketing strategies for this diverse bachelor segment is a real challenge for marketers.

Size of market

Another point to recognize is that some stages in the family life cycle are more important markets than others. For instance, households headed by people age 35 to 54 spend more on every product category (except health care) than other types of families.[34] Consider food. Middle-aged households spent about $4,700 on food in 1988, 22 percent more than average households. The youngest and oldest households spent considerably less than the average ($2,500 and $2,000, respectively). This segment of middle-aged households will become even more important through the 1990s as it grows by 20 percent when all the baby boomers enter this life cycle stage. Most of these boomers will have children and will spend heavily on them.

Effect of time pressure

The family life cycle can help marketers understand how important cultural trends affect family structures and consumption behavior. For example, consider the estimated 43 million "time-starved" consumers in the United States.[35] Time is more precious to many people, as the pace of family and work life becomes more hectic and more families have two wage earners (two thirds of married couples with children are dual-income households) or are headed by a single parent. Millions of people are stressed about time, believe they don't have enough time, and try to conserve time. They are prime candidates for convenience products of all types that can save time, which then can be used for more enjoyable or profitable purposes.

For many of these people, shopping is a painful chore that interferes with their leisure. Fully 63 percent of Americans believe shopping is drudgery. According to one survey, these perceptions are strongest among married-couple families with children, especially if both parents are working. Eleven million of these people do not enjoy shopping, and half believe shopping adds to their stress level. The interest in shopping is gone for many (but not all) Americans.

These attitudes are reflected in various consumption-related behaviors. For instance, in 1988, the average consumer spent 90 minutes on a shopping trip to the mall; in 1990, shopping time was down to 68 minutes. Some consumers develop shopping strategies to save time. For instance, some people shop for clothes only two or three times a year. Some shoppers follow established and regular paths through the store to eliminate duplication of effort. One executive buys a car at a dealer located near the airport, so he can have the car serviced during business trips. In an extreme case, one consumer shops for groceries only on Tuesday from 4:45 to 5:50 p.m. As she rushes through the store virtually on automatic pilot, a new marketing strategy is unlikely to catch her attention.

Although relatively few marketers have done much to reduce shopping time and stress, there are many ways to appeal to the time-stressed shopper. These need not be highly sophisticated strategies—Dayton-Hudson department stores changed to a central-aisle layout to make it easier for customers to find their way. Following are several marketing strategies to help reduce consumers' shopping time and stress.

▷ *Provide useful information.* Marketers who provide useful information to help consumers make the right choices save their customers time and reduce shopping stress. For instance, Blockbuster Video has a computerized data base to help customers find films made by a certain director or starring a particular actor. Computer technology could help consumers make the right choices of color, size, styles for clothing, automobiles, and home furnishings. Coordinated displays of related products such as showing entire ensembles can serve the same purpose.

▷ *Assist in purchase planning.* People often try to cope with time stress by carefully planning their shopping excursions. Marketers who help consumers form purchase plans will help them reduce stress. High-quality sales assistance in the clothing store or appliance showroom can help a time-stressed customer develop a decision plan. Marketers might suggest alternatives when a product is unavailable. Blockbuster Video tries to give customers movie alternatives if their first choice is unavailable.

▷ *Develop out-of-store selling.* Although shopping once may have been a pleasant and enjoyable experience, today many consumers would rather relax at home. This trend creates problems for retailers but also creates new opportunities for selling in the home or at the workplace. Avon, for example, now sells its products to groups of co-workers at the work site.

▷ *Automate transaction processes.* Companies that can automate and thereby speed up transaction processes appeal to time-stressed consumers. At Wegman's, a supermarket chain in Rochester, New York, customers can use a computer to enter their deli orders so they don't have to wait in line to be served; they pick up their deli orders as they leave the store. A&P and Shop Rite are experimenting with automated checkout systems to reduce the waiting time in the checkout line. Some car rental companies such as Hertz and Alamo offer an automated check-in service at major airports. Hand-held computers speed the check-in process so customers receive an invoice on the spot as they leave the car in the parking lot. Customers can speed to the airport with no waiting.

▷ *Improve delivery.* Nothing upsets a time-stressed consumer more than having to wait all day at home for a service person to come to fix the washing machine. For years, GE has made precise appointments for its service calls. Sears now offers repair services six days a week and in the evening. In Pasadena, California, Vons grocery offers drive-up service for 1,400 items. Service courts are being developed where consumers could obtain a variety of services (dry cleaning, shoe repair, small appliance repairs, mailing) in one stop.

▶ **SUMMARY**

Learning objective 1: *Define reference groups, and give several examples of types of reference groups.*

A reference group consists of one or more people that someone uses as a basis for comparison or a point of reference in forming and evaluating his or her affective responses, cognitions, and behaviors. Reference groups can be of any size (from one person to hundreds of people) and may be tangible (actual people) or intangible and symbolic (successful business executives or sports heroes). A person's reference groups may be from the same or different social class, subculture, and culture. Reference groups may be formal or informal (professional associations versus friends), primary or secondary (direct versus no direct social interaction), aspirational or dissociative (want to join or emulate versus want to avoid).

Learning objective 2: *Discuss three types of reference group influence on consumers.*

People identify and associate with reference groups for three basic reasons: to gain useful knowledge, to gain reward or avoid punishment, and to acquire desirable cultural meanings. These goals correspond to three types of influences reference groups can have on consumers' affective responses, cognitions, and behaviors. Informational reference group influence occurs when a group transmits relevant information to consumers about themselves, other people, or aspects of the physical environment such as products, services, and stores. Utilitarian reference group influence can occur when the reference group controls rewards and punishments that are relevant to the consumers. Finally, value-expressive reference group influence can affect people's self-concept. Reference groups are cultural units that embody cultural meanings (beliefs, values, goals, behavioral norms, lifestyles). People constantly look for desirable cultural meanings to construct, enhance, or maintain their self-concepts. By identifying and affiliating with particular reference groups that express these desired meanings, consumers can draw out some of these meanings and use them in their own self-construction.

Learning objective 3: *Define household and family, and explain the types of each.*

A household consists of people living in a housing unit—a dwelling with its own entrance (inside or outside) and basic living facilities. American households are diverse, involving many different living arrangements such as houses, townhouses, apartments and condominiums, college dorm rooms, fraternity houses, and nursing homes. The person who rents or owns the household is the householder. Types of households are defined in terms of the relationship of household residents to the householder. Marketers are concerned with two main types of households—families and nonfamilies. A family consists of at least two people—the householder and someone related to the householder by blood, marriage, or adoption. A nuclear family includes one or more parents and one or more children living together in a household. An extended family is a nuclear family plus other relatives such as grandparents living in one household. In contrast, nonfamily households include unrelated people living together such as college roommates or unmarried couples of the opposite sex or same sex.

Learning objective 4: *Describe various roles in family decision making.*

In family decision making, different people in the family may take on different social roles during the purchase choice process. In these roles, people have varying types and amounts of influence on the final choice outcome. For example, the husband may purchase peanut butter at the store (playing the buyer role). A son or daughter may provide information about choice alternatives (the influencer role). The mother may control which information is considered in the decision process (the gatekeeper role), and she may make the choice of what brand to buy (the decider role). The child might eat a peanut butter sandwich for lunch (the user role) and throw it away half eaten (the disposer role). To understand family decision making, marketers should identify which family members take on which roles and determine how they influence the course of the decision-making process.

Learning objective 5: *Describe the sources of conflict in family decision making, and discuss how conflict can be handled.*

Decision conflict arises when family members disagree about some aspect of the purchase decision. Family members could disagree about the desired end goals of a purchase. Dissimilar end goals can create major conflict because very different choice alternatives are likely to be related to incompatible ends. In other cases, family members may agree on the desired end goal, yet disagree about the best means to achieve it. When either the end or the means is not agreed on, family members are also likely to disagree about the choice criteria for evaluating alternatives. Sometimes, family members try to handle conflict by trying to influence others to change their minds. Their influence might be based on expertise, legitimate role status, or control of rewards. Some family members try to bargain with others to reduce conflict or resort to emotional reactions (anger, tears).

Learning objective 6: *Discuss consumer socialization, and give an implication for marketing.*

Families transmit the cultural meanings of society, subculture, and social class to their children through socialization processes. Consumer socialization describes how children acquire knowledge about products and services and learn various consumption-related skills (how to buy carefully, how to get a loan). Socialization can occur indirectly through observation and modeling or directly through intentional instruction. Indirect socialization occurs when parents take their children on shopping trips or talk about products, brands, and stores. Some socialization occurs when parents intentionally try to teach their children consumer skills such as how to look for products, find the best price, bargain with salespeople, return products for a refund, and dispose of products (recycling, holding a garage sale). The consumer knowledge formed in childhood can influence people in later years. Some adults still use the same brands of products their parents purchased when they were children.

Learning objective 7: *Describe the family life cycle, and discuss several implications of the family life cycle.*

The typical stages in family life are defined by major life events (marriage, birth of children, aging, departure of children, retirement, death). This sequence is called the traditional family life cycle. Marketers use the family life cycle as a basis for segmenting consumers into broad large segments.

Recent cultural changes in American society such as delayed marriage, childless marriages, working women, and increased divorce rates have created new stages not included in the traditional family life cycle. The modern family life cycle includes the stages of the traditional family life cycle, while adding several other family types to describe the more diverse family structures of the 1990s. The modern family life cycle can account for most types of families in American society, including childless couples, divorced persons, and single parents with children.

▶ KEY TERMS
AND CONCEPTS

group
reference group
informational reference
    group influence
utilitarian reference group
    influence

value-expressive refer-
    ence group influence
household
nonfamily households
family
family decision making

decision conflict
consumer socialization
modern family life cycle

▶ REVIEW AND
DISCUSSION
QUESTIONS

1. Identify two reference groups that influence your consumption behavior. Describe each according to the types listed in the text and tell what categories of purchases each influences.

2. From a marketing manager's viewpoint, what are some advantages and problems associated with each type of reference group influence?

3. Describe how public visibility and the distinction between luxury and necessity goods affect reference group influence on choice at the product and brand levels.

4. What is the family life cycle? Discuss how marketers can use it to develop effective marketing strategies.

5. Identify three different family purchases where you have played a role in the decision process. What role did you play? Discuss the interpersonal interactions that were involved in the decisions.

6. Suggest two ways that marketing strategies could influence the decision process in your family or household. How are these different from strategies that might be used to influence individual decisions?

7. Offer examples of conflict in family household decision making that you have experienced or observed. What types of marketing strategies could help to reduce such conflict?

8. Discuss the differences between households and families. Describe how each is important to marketers.

9. How are family influence strategies similar to or different from other reference group influences? Are there marketing implications related to these patterns?

10. Work with another student to identify two different household or family compositions. Assume that each unit has the same level of income. Discuss how the decision processes and conflicts in each household might vary for products such as an automobile, a vacation, and a stereo system.

18

Environmental Influences on Marketing Practices

LEARNING OBJECTIVES

After completing this chapter, you should be able to

► 1. Explain why society needs controls for marketers.

► 2. List the basic rights of consumers.

► 3. Explain four constraints society uses for controlling marketing activities.

McDONALD'S ESCHEWS THE FAT

In the early 1990s, McDonald's Corporation recognized it faced two major problems. First, environmentalists had long criticized the company for the amount of garbage represented by its packaging and leftovers. In the United States alone, McDonald's outlets sent 2 million pounds of garbage per day to incinerators and landfills, much of it polystyrene burger containers and other plastic implements that do not readily decompose. Second, nutritionists were equally critical of McDonald's menu for its high levels of fat and sodium. Millionaire health activist Phil Sokolof bought full-page national newspaper ads headlined: "McDonald's, your hamburgers have too much fat."

To respond to the first criticism, McDonald's instituted a 42-point plan to eliminate 80 percent of the waste from its restaurants. The plan included such changes as replacing polystyrene sandwich boxes with a thin-layered wrap, using new napkins with 21 percent less paper, using brown paper bags made of recycled paper, recycling behind-the-counter cardboard boxes, eliminating plastic cutlery wrappers where allowed by local laws, and trying reusable coffee mugs, reusable coffee filters, and pump-style bulk condiment dispensers instead of individual-serving packages. The Environmental Defense Fund praised McDonald's for these changes.

To improve the nutritional value of its menu, McDonald's made several additional changes. It concocted a new burger, the McLean Deluxe, which is 9 percent fat by weight, compared to 20 percent to 30 percent for most hamburgers. It phased out ice cream, replacing it with frozen yogurt. It replaced animal fat for french-frying with vegetable oil. It test-marketed more healthful foods such as catfish, pasta, and sliced carrots and celery. Organizations like McDonald's are influenced by environmental forces just as consumers are. In this case, political influences led McDonald's to change its operations.

In this text, we have discussed the relationships among consumer affect and cognition, behavior, and the environment. One of our major premises is that marketing is an important and powerful force in society. Properly designed and executed marketing strategies are often effective in changing consumer affect, cognitions, and behaviors in ways that help organizations achieve their objectives.

So far in this section of the text, we have discussed a number of environmental influences on consumers, including the impact of culture, subculture, social class, reference groups, and family. In this last chapter, however, the focus changes. While we are still concerned with environmental influences, we look now at their impact, not on consumers, but on organizations and their marketing strategies. Given that marketing is a powerful force and that marketers can misuse this power, it is important for society to have checks to restrain marketing strategies.

Three points are worth making in our discussion of rights and powers. First, we believe marketing and the free enterprise system offer the best and most effective system of exchange that has ever been developed. This does not mean the system could not be improved. For example, there is still a large group of poor, uneducated, needy people in our society who have little chance of improving their lot.

Second, while marketing may come in for the brunt of society's criticism of business, marketing managers are no more or no less guilty of shortcomings than other business executives. Corporate responsibility to society is a shared responsibility of all business executives, regardless of functional field. Nor are marketing executives any more or any less ethical than most other groups in society. Similarly, while business, particularly big business, is commonly singled out for criticism, there is no question that other fields—including medicine, engineering, and law—also contribute their share of societal problems. And consumers could also be criticized for the billions of dollars of merchandise that is shoplifted annually, as well as for other crimes against businesses and society.

Third, while some critics target marketing practices in general, many abuses are traceable to a relatively small percentage of firms and practices. Exhibit 18.1 presents a list of some of the most commonly cited areas of concern, divided into product, promotion, pricing, and distribution issues. Many of these practices are regulated legally.

THE RIGHTS OF MARKETERS AND CONSUMERS

Both marketers and consumers are granted certain rights by society, and both have a degree of power. Overall, many people believe marketers have considerably more power than consumers. One researcher frames the rights granted to marketers (sellers) as:

1. Sellers have the right to introduce any product in any size, style, color, or whatever, as long as the product meets minimum health and safety requirements.
2. Sellers have the right to price the product as they please so long as they avoid discrimination that is harmful to competition.
3. Sellers have the right to promote the product using any resources, media, or message, in any amount, so long as no deception or fraud is involved.
4. Sellers have the right to introduce any buying schemes they wish, so long as they are not discriminatory.
5. Sellers have the right to alter the product offering at any time.
6. Sellers have the right to distribute the product in any reasonable manner.
7. Sellers have the right to limit the product guarantee or postsale services.[1]

While this list is not exhaustive, it illustrates the considerable latitude marketers have.

Since the Consumer Bill of Rights was proclaimed in the early 1960s, consumers have been assumed to have at least four basic rights. First, consumers have the *right to safety,*

Product Issues	Promotion Issues
Unsafe products	Deceptive advertising
Poor-quality products	Advertising to children
Poor service/repair/maintenance after sale	Bait-and-switch advertising
Deceptive packaging and labeling practices	Anxiety-inducing advertising
Environmental impact of packaging and products	Deceptive personal selling tactics
Pricing Issues	**Distribution Issues**
Deceptive pricing	Sale of counterfeit products and brands
Fraudulent or misleading credit practices	Pyramid selling
Warranty refund problems	Deceptive in-store selling influences

EXHIBIT 18.1

Some problem areas in marketing

which means the right to be protected against products and services that are hazardous to health and life. Second, consumers have the *right to be informed*, which is the right to be protected against fraudulent, deceitful, or misleading advertising or other information that could interfere with making an informed choice. Third, consumers have the *right to choose*—the right to have access to a variety of competitive products that are priced fairly and are of satisfactory quality. Finally, consumers are granted the *right to be heard,* or the right to be ensured that their interests will be fully and fairly considered in the formulation and administration of government policy.

While these rights may appear to provide the consumer considerable protection, note one important weakness: most of these rights depend on the assumption that consumers are both capable of being and willing to be highly involved in purchase and consumption. In fact, however, many consumers are neither. Young children, many elderly people, and the less educated poor often do not have the cognitive abilities to process information well enough to be protected. Furthermore, even those consumers who do have the capacity often are not willing to invest the time, money, cognitive energy, and effort to ensure their rights.

Consumers have the right to choose which products they prefer.

EXHIBIT 18.2

**Major sources of
consumer protection**

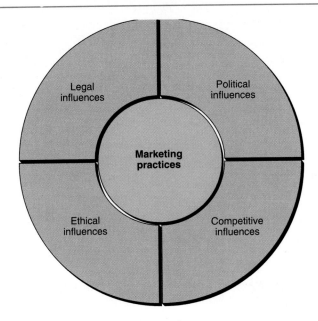

The right to choose is also predicated on the assumption that consumers are rational, autonomous, and knowledgeable decision makers. While we believe most consumers are capable of being so, evidence suggests that consumers often do not behave this way.[2] The right to choose also ignores the power of marketing to influence attitudes, intentions, and behaviors. Consumers' needs, wants, and satisfaction can be shaped through the conditioning and modeling processes that marketers use, for instance. Thus, the assumption of consumer autonomy is not easily supported.

Finally, no matter how much effort consumers exert to ensure they are choosing a good product, they cannot process information that is not available. For example, consumers cannot be aware of product safety risks that are hidden from them.

Overall, then, if there were no other forces operating in society, marketers might well have more rights and power than consumers do. This is not to say consumers cannot exert countercontrol on marketers, or that consumers do not vary in the degree to which they are influenced by marketers. However, as our society and system of government and exchange have evolved, a number of constraints or societal influences on marketing activities have also developed. As shown in Exhibit 18.2, these include legal, political, competitive, and ethical influences.

Legal influences

Legal influences include federal, state, and local legislation and the agencies and processes by which these laws are upheld. Some laws are designed to control practices in specific industries (such as food); others are aimed at controlling functional areas (such as product safety).

A variety of government agencies are involved in enforcing these laws and investigating questionable business practices. In addition to state and local agencies, this includes a number of federal agencies, such as those listed in Exhibit 18.3.

One marketing practice of major interest to the Federal Trade Commission is deceptive advertising—advertising that misleads consumers. One FTC approach to dealing with this problem is **corrective advertising.** Corrective advertising requires firms that have misled consumers to rectify the deception in future ads.[3] Profile bread advertising led consumers to believe it was effective in weight reduction; Domino sugar advertising led consumers to

Agency	Responsibilities
Federal Trade Commission (FTC)	Enforces laws and develops guidelines regarding unfair business practices
Food and Drug Administration (FDA)	Enforces laws and develops regulations to prevent distribution and sale of adulterated or misbranded foods, drugs, cosmetics, and hazardous consumer products
Consumer Product Safety Commission (CPSC)	Enforces the Consumer Product Safety Act, which covers any consumer product not assigned to other regulatory agencies
Interstate Commerce Commission (ICC)	Regulates interstate rail, bus, truck, and water carriers
Federal Communications Commission (FCC)	Regulates interstate wire, radio, and television
Environmental Protection Agency (EPA)	Develops and enforces environmental protection standards
Office of Consumer Affairs (OCA)	Handles consumers' complaints

EXHIBIT 18.3

Some important federal regulatory agencies

Source: E. Jerome McCarthy and William D. Perreault, Jr., *Basic Marketing,* 11th ed. (Homewood, Ill.: Richard D. Irwin, 1993), p. 130.

believe it was a special source of strength, energy, and stamina; Ocean Spray cranberry juice cocktail misled consumers about food energy; and Sugar Information, Inc., misled consumers about sugar benefits. Below are the text and amount of advertising required for correcting these deceptions.

▷ **Profile bread**

"Hi, (celebrity's name) for Profile bread. Like all mothers, I'm concerned about nutrition and balanced meals. So, I'd like to clear up any misunderstanding you may have about Profile bread from its advertising or even its name.

"Does Profile have fewer calories than any other breads? No. Profile has about the same per ounce as other breads. To be exact, Profile has seven fewer calories per slice. That's because Profile is sliced thinner. But eating Profile will not cause you to lose weight. A reduction of seven calories is insignificant. It's total calories and balanced nutrition that count. And Profile can help you achieve a balanced meal because it provides protein and B vitamins as well as other nutrients.

"How does my family feel about Profile? Well, my husband likes Profile toast, the children love Profile sandwiches, and I prefer Profile to any other bread. So you see, at our house, delicious taste makes Profile a family affair."

(To be run in 25% of brand's advertising, for one year.)

▷ **Amstar**

"Do you recall some of our past messages saying that Domino sugar gives you strength, energy, and stamina? Actually, Domino is not a special or unique source of strength, energy, and stamina. No sugar is, because what you need is a balanced diet and plenty of rest and exercise."

(To be run in one of every four ads for one year.)

▷ **Ocean Spray**

"If you've wondered what some of our earlier advertising meant when we said Ocean Spray cranberry juice cocktail has more food energy than orange juice or tomato juice, let us make it clear: we didn't mean vitamins and minerals. Food energy means calories. Nothing more.

EXHIBIT 18.4

Some political groups concerned with consumerism

Broad-Based National Groups	Special-Interest Groups
Consumer Federation of America National Wildlife Federation Common Cause Environmental Defense Fund	Action for Children's Television American Association of Retired Persons Group against Smoking and Pollution
Smaller Multi-Issue Organizations	**Local Groups**
National Consumer's League Ralph Nader's Public Citizen	Public-interest research groups Local consumer protection offices Local broadcast and newspaper consumer "action lines"

"Food energy is important at breakfast since many of us may not get enough calories, or food energy, to get off to a good start. Ocean Spray cranberry juice cocktail helps because it contains more food energy than most other breakfast drinks.

"And Ocean Spray cranberry juice cocktail gives you and your family vitamin C plus a great wake-up taste. It's . . . the other breakfast drink."

(To be run in one of every four ads for one year.)

▷ **Sugar Information, Inc.**

"Do you recall the messages we brought you in the past about sugar? How something with sugar in it before meals could help you curb your appetite? We hope you didn't get the idea that our little diet tip was any magic formula for losing weight. Because there are no tricks or shortcuts; the whole diet subject is very complicated. Research hasn't established that consuming sugar before meals will contribute to weight reduction or even keep you from gaining weight."

(To be run for one insertion in each of seven magazines.)

Legal influences and the power of government agencies to regulate business and marketing practices grew dramatically in the 1970s; but the 1980s witnessed a decrease in many areas of regulation. In fact, deregulation of business was the major thrust in that period, and government agencies considerably reduced their involvement in controlling business practices. It seems likely that the 1990s will witness a resurgence of legal influences at the federal level aimed at consumer and environmental protection.

Political influences

By **political influences** we mean the pressure that various consumer groups can exert to control marketing practices. These groups use a variety of methods to influence marketing practice, such as lobbying with various government agencies to enact legislation or working directly with consumers in redress assistance and education. Exhibit 18.4 lists some organizations established to serve consumer interests. These are but a few examples; one tally found over 100 national organizations and over 600 state and local groups that represent consumers.[4]

Bloom and Greyser argue that "consumerism" has reached the mature stage of its life cycle and that its impact has been fragmented.[5] Yet they believe consumerism will continue to have some impact on business, and they offer three strategies for business to address it. First, businesses can try to accelerate the decline of consumerism by *reducing demand* for it. This could be done by improving product quality, expanding services, lowering prices, and moderating advertising claims. Consumer Perspective 18.1 (see page 416) describes one industry's attempt to reduce demand for consumerism.

Second, businesses can *compete* with consumer groups by establishing active consumer affairs departments that offer redress assistance and consumer education. Alternatively, a business could fund and coordinate activities designed to "sell" deregulation and other probusiness causes. Third, businesses can *cooperate* with consumer groups by providing financial and other support.

Overall, most of these strategies would likely further reduce the impact and importance of political influences. Essentially, to the degree that following these strategies leads business firms to become more socially responsible, the consumer should benefit.

Competitive influences refer to actions of competing firms intended to affect other companies and consumers. These actions can be taken in many ways. For example, one firm might sue another firm or point out what it alleges as fraudulent activities to consumers. Johnson & Johnson frequently took competitors to court to protect its Tylenol brand of pain reliever from being shown in competitive ads. Burger King publicly accused McDonald's of overstating the weight of its hamburgers.

Perhaps the most important consumer protection generated by competition is that it reduces the impact of information from any single firm. In other words, in a marketing environment where there are many active competitors, no single firm can dominate the information flow to consumers. In this sense, conflicting competitive claims, images, information, and offers may insulate consumers from undue influence by a single firm or brand. Conversely, competition may also lead to information overload.

Consumers may also benefit from the development and marketing of better products and services brought about by competitive pressure. Current merger trends and the

Competitive influences

CONSUMER PERSPECTIVE

▶ **18.1**

Political influences: TV network guidelines for advertising to children

Each major television network has its own set of guidelines for children's advertising, although the basics are very similar. A few rules, such as the requirement of a static "island" shot at the end, are written in stone; others, however, occasionally can be negotiated.

Many of the rules below apply specifically to toys. The networks also have special guidelines for kids' food commercials and for kids' commercials that offer premiums.

	ABC	CBS	NBC
Must not overglamorize product	X	X	X
No exhortative language, such as "Ask Mom to buy . . . "	X	X	X
No realistic war settings	X		X
Generally no celebrity endorsements	X	Case-by-case	X
Can't use "only" or "just" in regard to price	X	X	X
Show only two toys per child or maximum of six per commercial	X		X
Five-second "island" showing product against plain background at end of spot	X	X	X (4 to 5)
Animation restricted to one third of commercial	X		X
Generally no comparative or superiority claims	Case-by-case	Handle w/care	X
No costumes or props not available with the toy	X		X
No child or toy can appear in animated segments	X		X
Three-second establishing shot of toy in relation to child	X	X (2.5 to 3)	
No shots under one second in length		X	
Must show distance a toy can travel before stopping on its own		X	

Source: Reprinted by permission of *The Wall Street Journal*, © 1988 Dow Jones & Company, Inc. All Rights Reserved Worldwide.

concentration of various industries may lessen these competitive constraints and societal advantages, however.

Ethical influences

Perhaps the most important constraints on marketing practices are **ethical influences**, which involve self-regulation by marketers. Many firms have consumer affairs offices that seek to ensure the consumer is treated fairly. A number of companies have developed a positive image with consumers through consumer-oriented marketing practices such as offering toll-free lines for information and complaints, promoting unit pricing, and support-ing social causes. Codes of ethics govern practices in many professions; the American Marketing Association's are shown in Consumer Perspective 18.2.

What makes discussing ethical constraints difficult is that there is no single standard by which actions can be judged. Laczniak summarizes five ethical standards proposed by various researchers:

1. **The Golden Rule:** Act in the way you would expect others to act toward you.

2. **The Utilitarian Principle:** Act in the way that results in the greatest good for the greatest number.

3. **Kant's Categorical Imperative:** Act in such a way that the action taken under the circumstances could be a universal law or rule of behavior.

4. **The Professional Ethic:** Act in a way that would be viewed as proper by a dis-interested panel of professional colleagues.

Members of the American Marketing Association (AMA) are committed to ethical professional conduct. They have joined together in subscribing to this Code of Ethics embracing the following topics:

Responsibilities of the Marketer
Marketers must accept responsibility for the consequence of their activities and make every effort to ensure that their decisions, recommendations, and actions function to identify, serve, and satisfy all relevant publics: customers, organizations, and society. Marketers' professional conduct must be guided by:

1. The basic rule of professional ethics: not knowingly to do harm;

2. The adherence to all applicable laws and regulations;

3. The accurate representation of their education, training, and experience; and

4. The active support, practice, and promotion of this Code of Ethics.

Honesty and Fairness
Marketers shall uphold and advance the integrity, honor, and dignity of the marketing profession by:

1. Being honest in serving consumers, clients, employees, suppliers, distributors, and the public;

2. Not knowingly participating in conflict of interest without prior notice to all parties involved; and

3. Establishing equitable fee schedules including the payment or receipt of usual, customary, and/or legal compensation or marketing exchanges.

(continued)

CONSUMER PERSPECTIVE

18.2

Code of Ethics of the American Marketing Association

5. **The TV Test:** Ask: "Would I feel comfortable explaining to a national TV audience why I took this action?"[6]

Following any one of these standards could result in many different interpretations of what is ethical. If you doubt this, consider how you might apply them to the scenarios below.

▷ **Scenario 1**
The Thrifty Supermarket Chain has 12 stores in the city of Gotham, U.S.A. The company's policy is to maintain the same prices for all items at all stores. The distribution manager nevertheless sends the poorest cuts of meat and the lowest quality produce to the store located in the low-income section of town. He justifies this action by the fact that this store has the highest overhead because of factors such as employee turnover, pilferage, and vandalism. *Is the distribution manager's economic rationale sufficient justification for his allocation method?*

▷ **Scenario 2**
The independent Chevy Dealers of Metropolis, U.S.A., have undertaken an advertising campaign headlined by the slogan: "Is your family's life worth 45 MPG?" The ads admit that while Chevy subcompacts are not as fuel efficient as foreign imports and cost more to maintain, they are safer, according to government-sponsored crash tests. The ads imply that responsible parents purchasing a car should trade off fuel efficiency for safety. *Is it ethical for the dealers' association to use this sort of appeal to offset an economic disadvantage?*

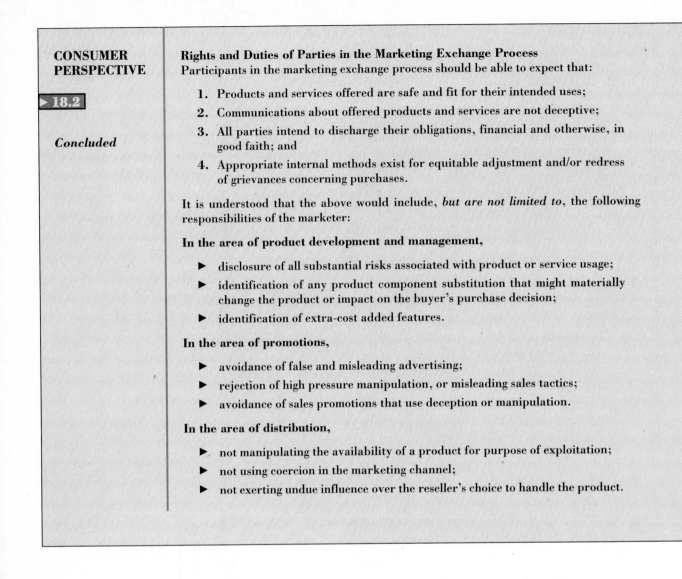

CONSUMER PERSPECTIVE

▶ 18.2

Concluded

Rights and Duties of Parties in the Marketing Exchange Process
Participants in the marketing exchange process should be able to expect that:

1. Products and services offered are safe and fit for their intended uses;
2. Communications about offered products and services are not deceptive;
3. All parties intend to discharge their obligations, financial and otherwise, in good faith; and
4. Appropriate internal methods exist for equitable adjustment and/or redress of grievances concerning purchases.

It is understood that the above would include, *but are not limited to*, the following responsibilities of the marketer:

In the area of product development and management,

▶ disclosure of all substantial risks associated with product or service usage;
▶ identification of any product component substitution that might materially change the product or impact on the buyer's purchase decision;
▶ identification of extra-cost added features.

In the area of promotions,

▶ avoidance of false and misleading advertising;
▶ rejection of high pressure manipulation, or misleading sales tactics;
▶ avoidance of sales promotions that use deception or manipulation.

In the area of distribution,

▶ not manipulating the availability of a product for purpose of exploitation;
▶ not using coercion in the marketing channel;
▶ not exerting undue influence over the reseller's choice to handle the product.

▷ **Scenario 3**
Some studies have linked the presence of the artificial sweetener, subsugural, to incidence of cancer in laboratory rats. While the validity of these findings has been debated by medical experts, the Food and Drug Administration has ordered products containing the ingredient banned from sale in the United States. The Jones Company sends all of its sugar-free J.C. Cola (which contains subsugural) to European supermarkets because the sweetener has not been banned there. *Is it acceptable for the Jones Company to send a possibly unsafe product to another market without waiting for further evidence?*

▷ **Scenario 4**
The Acme Company sells industrial supplies through its own sales force, which calls on company purchasing agents. Acme has found that providing the purchasing agent with small gifts helps cement a cordial relationship and creates goodwill. Acme follows the policy that the bigger the order, the bigger the gift to the purchasing agent. The gifts range from a pair of tickets to a sports event to outboard motors and snowmobiles. Acme does not give gifts to personnel at companies that they know have an explicit policy prohibiting the acceptance of such gifts.

In the area of pricing,

- ▶ not engaging in price fixing;
- ▶ not practicing predatory pricing;
- ▶ disclosing the full price associated with any purchase.

In the area of marketing research,

- ▶ prohibiting selling or fund raising under the guise of conducting research;
- ▶ maintaining research integrity by avoiding misrepresentation and omission of pertinent research data;
- ▶ treating outside clients and suppliers fairly.

Organizational Relationships

Marketers should be aware of how their behavior may influence or impact on the behavior of others in organizational relationships. They should not demand, encourage, or apply coercion to obtain unethical behavior in their relationships with others, such as employees, suppliers, or customers. They should:

1. Apply confidentiality and anonymity in professional relationships with regard to privileged information;

2. Meet their obligations and responsibilities in contracts and mutual agreements in a timely manner.

3. Avoid taking the work of others, in whole, or in part, and representing this work as their own or directly benefiting from it without compensation or consent of the originator or owner;

4. Avoid manipulation to take advantage of situations to maximize personal welfare in a way that unfairly deprives or damages the organization or others.

Any AMA member found to be in violation of any provision of this Code of Ethics may have his or her Association membership suspended or revoked.

Source: The American Marketing Association, Chicago.

Assuming no laws are violated, is Acme's policy of providing gifts to purchasing agents ethically acceptable?

▷ **Scenario 5**

The Buy American Electronics Company has been selling its highly rated System X Color TV sets (21, 19, and 12 inches) for $700, $500, and $300, respectively. These prices have been relatively uncompetitive in the market. After some study, Buy American substitutes several cheaper components (which engineering says may slightly reduce the quality of performance) and passes on the savings to the consumer in the form of a $100 price reduction on each model. Buy American institutes a price-oriented promotional campaign, which neglects to mention that the second-generation System X sets are different from the first. *Is the company's competitive strategy ethical?*

▷ **Scenario 6**

The Smith & Smith Advertising Agency has been struggling financially. Mr. Smith is approached by the representative of a small South American country that is on

As part of self-regulation, marketers can promote responsible use of their products.

good terms with the U.S. Department of State. He wants S&S to create a multi-million-dollar advertising and public relations campaign that will bolster the image of the country and increase the likelihood that it will receive U.S. foreign aid assistance and attract investment capital. Smith knows the country is controlled by a dictatorship that has been accused of numerous human rights violations. *Is it ethical for the Smith & Smith Agency to undertake the proposed campaign?*[7]

What constitutes ethical marketing behavior is a matter of social judgment. Even in areas such as product safety, what constitutes ethical marketing practice is not always clear. While at first blush it might be argued that all products should be either completely safe or not allowed on the market, deeper inspection reveals questions such as "How safe?" and "For whom?" Bicycles, for example, often head the list of the most hazardous products, yet few consumers or marketers would argue that bicycles should not be sold. Much of the problem in determining product safety concerns whether harm attributable to a product results from an inherent lack of product safety or unsafe use by the consumer.

CONCLUSIONS ABOUT CONSUMER BEHAVIOR AND MARKETING PRACTICE

This text presents a comprehensive overview of consumer behavior and demonstrates its importance for marketing and for the success of organizations in general. The first section of the text discusses how successful organizations design and market products and services that consumers want and are willing to purchase. A framework for understanding consumer behavior, called the Wheel of Consumer Analysis, was introduced. This wheel consists of three major elements—affect and cognition, behavior, and environment. The next three sections of the book offer detailed discussions of these three elements and illustrate how analysis of each aids in successful marketing. A consistent theme of the book is that carefully researching and understanding all three parts of the wheel enhances the success of marketing strategies.

Another theme of the book is that marketing is a powerful force and has a strong influence on society and consumers' lives. The ability of marketers to research consumers and understand their affect and cognitions, behaviors, and environments could lead to an organization having too much power in society. For this reason, legal, political, competitive, and ethical influences control the power of marketing organizations. This final chapter of the book discusses these influences in hopes that future marketers will carefully consider their social responsibilities and develop strategies that are good for society and consumers as well as for the organizations for which they work.

▶ **SUMMARY**

Learning objective 1: *Explain why society needs controls for marketers.*
Marketing is a powerful force in society, and power is subject to abuse if marketers misuse it to influence consumer affect, cognitions, and behaviors. Marketers have considerable freedom in designing and executing product strategies, but to keep marketers from becoming unduly influential society exerts some checks.

Learning objective 2: *List the basic rights of consumers.*
Consumers have four basic rights. First, they are entitled to the right to safety, which means the right to be protected against products and services that are hazardous to health and life. Second is the right to be informed, which is the right to be protected against fraudulent, deceitful, or misleading advertising or other information that could interfere with making an informed choice. Third, they have the right to choose—the right to have access to a variety of competitive products that are priced fairly and are of satisfactory quality. Fourth comes the right to be heard, or the right to be ensured that their interests will be fully and fairly considered in the formulation and administration of government policy.

Learning objective 3: *Explain four constraints society uses for controlling marketing activities.*
First, there are legal constraints or influences. These include federal, state, and local legislation and the agencies by which these laws are upheld. Second, there are political influences, which include the pressure that various consumer groups can exert to control marketing practices. Third, there are competitive influences, which means actions of competing firms intended to affect other companies and consumers. Fourth, there are ethical influences, which take the form of various codes and sanctions by which professions regulate their own activities.

▶ **KEY TERMS AND CONCEPTS**

legal influences	political influences	ethical influences
corrective advertising	competitive influences	

▶ **REVIEW AND DISCUSSION QUESTIONS**

1. Compare the rights of marketers and the rights of consumers. Which group do you think has more power?

2. Which of the buyer and seller rights become a problem if we assume consumers are not highly involved in most purchases?

3. Define the four major components of consumer protection. In which of them can the consumer participate?

4. Evaluate the actions in each of the six ethical scenarios in the chapter.

5. Which of the ethical standards proposed in the text do you think would be most useful to you as a marketing manager? Why?

6. In a bait and switch advertisement, the retailer advertises a low price on an item, but either doesn't stock the item or pressures consumers into buying a more expensive item when they come into the store. Evaluate the ethics of this practice.

7. Select three newspaper ads that you consider to be misleading. Tell what elements of the communication are deceptive, and what groups of consumers might be harmed.

8. Discuss with other members of the class the ethics of tobacco or liquor marketing. Could you develop a code of personal ethics to guide you as a promotion manager in these industries?

9. Prepare lists of obligations to complement the lists of rights for marketers and consumers.

IV

UNDERSTANDING THE ENVIRONMENT

CASES

The price of admission to many of America's movie theaters sometimes buys an experience sensible people would pay to avoid. The dingy carpet in the lobby could be a relic from the silent screen era. The $1.25 bucket of popcorn—that's the small size!—holds 10 cents worth of corn tossed with a strange liquid, perhaps derived from petroleum. Beneath the worn-out seats, sticky coats of spilled soda pop varnish the floor. The screen is tiny, the sound tinny, and the audience is rude. Oh, and one more thing—the picture isn't worth seeing.

Many theater owners bought into the business at low prices after 1984, when antitrust rulings forced the major Hollywood studios, which had previously owned the leading theater chains, to give up their movie houses. The new owners got a great deal. They owned the only show in town (sometimes literally), and the studios promoted the movies. As the easy profits rolled in, many exhibitors lost contact with their customers. They milked the business and let their theaters deteriorate.

But the success of videocassette rentals and cable TV converted many moviegoers into stay-at-homers. By 1985, theaters were no longer the only show in town. Attendance dropped 12 percent over 1984 figures. The $5 billion-a-year American movie theater industry was fighting for survival.

This put the theater owners in a bind. To regain their customers, they had to pour money into refurbishing, rebuilding, and restoring the glamour of moviegoing.

To survive, exhibitors developed some temporarily successful strategies. One was to focus on lobby concession stands as a source of revenues. To keep some of their customers, theaters had kept ticket prices fairly low—the average price in 1985 was about $3.50 to $4—prices that lagged behind inflation. Once inside, though, moviegoers were a captive market for the popcorn, soda, and candy sold at stupendous markups of up to 500 percent or more. A well-run concession stand generates at least $1 of sales and as much as 75 cents of profit per ticket buyer.

What brands of candy were in the typical concession stand? Usually, it was a strange mix of oversized boxes that included very few of the best-selling brands in the United States. Theaters tended to stock candy brands like Milk Duds, Sno Caps, and Jujyfruits, hardly big sellers elsewhere. The exception was Snickers, the number one brand in the United States, which was found at most concession stands. Do moviegoers have different tastes from the rest of the population? Of course not. The movie house operators preferred these brands because they were more profitable. With limited space available, the operators stocked the brands with the highest profit margins. Critics claim that by sticking to the most profitable brands, theater owners are missing an opportunity to increase overall candy sales by stocking more popular brands. As it stands now, only about one third of moviegoers buy anything from the concession stand.

The profits from concession sales can be considerable. For instance, in 1985, a tub of popcorn that cost 30 cents was sold for about $2—a markup of 567 percent. A soft drink (often a Coke) that cost the theater 10 cents might have been sold for 75 cents, a 650 percent markup. Candy produces a much smaller profit, with markups of "only" about 180 percent. On average, about 40 percent of the $850 million in annual concession sales came from popcorn, another 40 percent from soft drinks, and only about 20 percent from everything else.

The other strategy was the multiscreen theater. During the 1970s, exhibitors began chopping up their grand old theaters into smaller ones that many moviegoers have come to hate. Individual exhibitors did well though (as long as they owned the only theater in town). A theater with four screens, about the national average, is four times more likely to book a hit picture: the exhibitor then shows the hit in the largest room and lesser movies in the smaller theaters.

But at a macro level, more seats were the last thing the industry needed. In 1985, the total number of tickets sold annually remained constant at about 1 billion, a number that hadn't varied much for 25 years. When the growing population is considered, this translates into a 24 percent per capita decline in moviegoing. As a writer for *Variety* said, "Filmgoing used to be part of the social fabric. Now it is an impulse purchase." During the 1980s, the population began to age and the prime moviegoing segment of the under-30-year-olds to decline. When the damage done by VCRs and cable TV is added . . . well, you get the picture.

To survive into the 1990s, exhibitors must relearn how to woo moviegoers. There is admittedly something special about seeing a terrific film in a great theater with an appreciative audience. And by using technologies such as widescreen 70-millimeter projection and wraparound Dolby sound, theaters can create a sense of spectacle that no TV set can match. Theater owners can make their theaters clean and comfortable again, maybe even palatial. In fact, many exhibitors have remodeled their old elegant theaters and restored them to their former grandeur. New construction is being upgraded. One successful exhibitor coddled customers in specially designed $130 seats, costing twice the national average.

Another exhibitor says, "We have to upgrade the quality of the moviegoing experience." His newest theaters have granite-floored lobbies, muraled walls, spacious auditoriums, and first-rate sound and projection. The higher construction costs paid off in more customers at higher than average ticket prices, and a splendid $1.35 per ticket take at the concession stand. Such theaters are still rare.

As the drama of change pervades the movie exhibition industry, the major beneficiaries may even be the long-suffering moviegoers. When consumers enter the theater of the future, they may not encounter a marvel of technology, but at least they won't stick to the floor.

Discussion questions

1. The VCR is an environmental change that has affected moviegoing behavior in the United States. Compare and contrast the consumption situations of watching a movie in a theater and seeing the same movie at home on your VCR. Discuss the interactions between and among environment, behavior, and cognitive and affective responses. What long-term effects do you think the in-home VCR environments will have on moviegoing? What can movie theaters do to address the situation?

2. What macro environmental factors might affect moviegoing behaviors (both decreases and increases)? Consider their impacts on different market segments. What marketing implications does your analysis have for theater owners or movie companies?

3. Analyze the information, purchasing, and consumption environments of different movie theaters that you know. What recommendations do you have for changing these environments to increase sales?

4. Analyze the effects of the consumption situation at movie theaters on consumers' purchase of snacks at the concession stand. What could theater owners do to change the purchasing and the consumption environment in their theaters to encourage higher levels of snack consumption and greater sales at concession stands?

Source: Alex Ben Block, "Those Peculiar Candies that Star at the Movies," *Forbes,* May 19, 1986, pp. 174–76; and Stratford P. Sherman, "Back to the Future," *Fortune,* January 20, 1986, pp. 909–14.

The Japanese market is the second richest in the world, after the United States. But it is notoriously difficult for foreign companies to succeed in marketing their products in Japan. Yet, in the late 1980s and early 1990s, American companies have better opportunities than ever before to sell in Japan. The Japanese government has relaxed some

▶ **CASE IV.2**

Selling in foreign markets

trade barriers, and the powerful yen and relatively weak dollar have given U.S. firms the best price-cutting opportunity in decades. Recent cultural changes in Japan should increase marketing opportunities. After decades of austerity, Japanese are spending more on consumer goods. Some Japanese, especially young people, have a fondness for American culture.

But succeeding in Japan won't be easy. The Japanese market may just be the toughest on earth. The language is difficult, values and meanings are different, and customs and manners can be baffling to westerners. In addition, attitudes toward foreign products can be frosty. For example, a 1990 survey of Japanese consumers found that 71 percent considered Japanese products to be superior to American. Only 8 percent of Japanese would even consider buying an American car (3 percent would think of buying an American TV). Success requires an extraordinary commitment to quality, a willingness to adjust to cultural differences, a long-range perspective, and patience (lots of patience)—all qualities of the typical Japanese company. Foreign businesses intending to enter the Japanese market might analyze some earlier marketing mistakes to avoid repeating the same blunders. There are plenty of examples to choose from. Consider, for instance, some of the problems that Procter & Gamble had with doing business in Japan.

In 1973, Procter & Gamble charged into Osaka with the marketing strategies that had played so well in Ohio. The results were disastrous. By some accounts, the huge Cincinnati-based company lost about a quarter of a billion dollars over the next decade or so. The gambit started off fairly well. By the late 1970s, P&G's Cheer brand of laundry detergent was the leading brand in Japan with a 10 percent market share, Camay bath soap had 3.5 percent of a very competitive market, and Pampers, with little competition, had 90 percent of the disposable diaper market. But P&G lost ground in all of these markets. Why it happened and what the company did to regain the lost ground provide useful lessons in the importance of understanding cultural factors and their relation to consumer behavior.

In general, the Japanese seem to have learned such lessons better than most American companies. When the Japanese enter a foreign market, they study it carefully. They do not assume that what goes in Japan also goes in the United States. P&G apparently lacked this humility and cross-cultural perspective. As one bitter ex-P&G employee summed up the problem, "They [the company] didn't listen to anybody." Cheer detergent prospered at first because of heavy price discounting. But this strategy partially backfired because it devalued the company's reputation in the eyes of many Japanese consumers. According to one expert, "Unlike Europe and the U.S., once you discount in Japan it is hard to raise prices later." The price-cutting strategy also overlooked several other cultural factors. Because many Japanese do not have a car, they shop in small neighborhood stores where as much as 30 percent of detergents are sold. Owners of these small stores do not like to carry discounted products because they make less money on them.

The advertising also missed the mark. In the late 1970s, Japanese viewers voted Cheer ads the least liked on TV. They were repelled by a typical American hard-sell approach that stressed product benefits and user testimonials. Bad advertising also hurt Camay soap. In one commercial, a man meeting a woman for the first time compared her skin to that of a fine porcelain doll. Although the ad had worked well in the Philippines, South America, and Europe, the Japanese were insulted. Japanese ad executives had warned P&G that women would find the commercial offensive—"For a Japanese man to say something like that to a Japanese woman means he's either unsophisticated or rude"—but their warnings went unheeded.

The worst story was in the disposable diaper market. P&G had literally created the market in 1978 and invested heavily in educating Japanese consumers about the advantages of disposable diapers. By the time a small Japanese manufacturer entered the market in 1981, P&G controlled over 90 percent of a $100 million business. By 1985, it had only about 5 percent. The company had underestimated both the capabilities of the Japanese competitor and the favorable response of Japanese consumers to a higher-quality product.

Unfortunately, there was more to come. P&G stuck too long to its policy of advertising the brand, not the company. In Japan, consumers like to know the company, and they tend to form a personal relationship with it. Most Japanese ads end with a flash of the company's name. But P&G didn't add this to its ads until 1986.

But all was not lost. P&G learned from its very expensive mistakes and is in Japan to stay. Its Ultra Pampers product made inroads into the Japanese market and the advertising is now more in tune with Japanese cultural sensibilities. P&G is gaining back some of its lost market share.

P&G's mistakes should not be taken to imply that Japanese companies are always perfect marketers. They have made some embarrassing blunders of their own in trying to market Japanese products in foreign cultures. But often the Japanese are so determined that they succeed anyway. Their remarkable desire to please the customer is a big factor in their success, according to one P&G executive.

Consider the experience of Shiseido, a giant cosmetics company, in introducing its line of cosmetics into the United States in the mid-1960s. Only after getting its products into more than 800 stores, including Bloomingdale's and Saks, did the company realize how different American women's tastes in cosmetics were from those of their Japanese counterparts. Application of Shiseido's makeup required a lengthy series of steps. Apparently Japanese women didn't mind, but American women balked. The cosmetics flopped, and the company pulled out of more than 600 stores. But Shiseido didn't quit. Instead, it designed a new line of products to meet the needs of American women, beautifully packaged, easy to use, and graced with subtle scents. To promote these products, the company relied less on advertising, as is the typical American approach, and more on the type of extraordinary personal service it gives its customers in Japan. According to an executive of Estée Lauder, a competitor, "The service level in Japan is the highest in the world. It starts with the fact that the store manager and his executives come down to the entrance of the store every morning for 15 or 20 minutes to greet the customers." In the United States, Shiseido trains its saleswomen to treat the customer lavishly, including offering free facial massages at demonstration counters. By 1988, Shiseido's sales were growing at about 25 percent a year, and its products were available in 1,000 stores.

Discussion questions

1. Sometimes even rather subtle cultural factors can make a significant difference in the success of a marketing strategy. Describe several examples of these cultural factors from the case. How can a company learn about these cultural factors? What things should the company consider in deciding whether to adapt its marketing strategies to reflect these cultural factors?

2. Using the model of the cultural process in Exhibit 13.3, discuss the transmission of cultural meaning involved in Shiseido's marketing of cosmetics in the United States.

3. Discuss the stands taken by advocates of global and local marketing strategies in the context of this case. Do you think P&G can sell its household and personal-care products around the world using the same marketing strategies? Defend your answer, and then discuss your position on the debate about global marketing strategies.

4. In 1988, Kao, the large $4 billion-a-year Japanese manufacturer of detergents, diapers, and toothpaste, was making plans to enter the U.S. market. Kao is a direct competitor of P&G in Japan. Many of its U.S. products will probably be introduced under the Jergens name, a company Kao bought in 1988. Identify some of the

more important cultural and subcultural factors that Kao should consider in introducing its shampoo into the U.S. market. What implications do these cultural aspects of the social environment have for devising effective marketing strategies?

Source: Joel Dreyfuss, "How to Beat the Japanese at Home," *Fortune,* August 31, 1987, pp. 80–83; Brian Dumaine, "Japan's Next Push in U.S. Markets," *Fortune,* September 26, 1988, pp. 135–40; Frederick Katayama, "Japan's Prodigal Young Are Dippy about Imports," *Fortune,* May 11, 1987, p. 118; Jeffrey A. Trachtenberg, "They Didn't Listen to Anybody," *Forbes,* December 15, 1986, pp. 168–69; and Carla Rapoport, "How the Japanese Are Changing," *Fortune,* September 24, 1990, pp. 15–22.

▶ CASE IV.3

Hyatt and Marriott build retirement housing for the elderly

As the number of older Americans increases, businesses are beginning to pay more attention to the diversity in this subcultural group. Many companies are rushing to identify the needs of the elderly and to develop products to meet those needs. Both Marriott Corporation and Hyatt Hotels, for example, developed retirement community "products" for the elderly market. Retirement communities combine retirement housing, various services, and nursing care. They offer personal living quarters in apartments of varying sizes, a wide range of activities and entertainment, housekeeping services, food service options (a dining room for some meals, along with one's own kitchen), along with varying levels of on-site health care, including full nursing home services for some people.

The market for retirement communities is immense (over 30 million Americans will be 65 or older by the year 2000), but it is a fallacy to assume everyone over 65 is a potential customer for a retirement community. Actually, the prime customers are in their late 70s or early 80s. Also, it is incorrect that many elderly are feeble and ripe for the nursing home (only 5 percent of Americans over 65 live in such facilities). Contrary to popular belief, not all elderly live alone; many elderly are married (an estimated 8.3 million in 2000). It should be obvious that the "mature market" is quite diverse; only the over-85 subgroup is somewhat homogeneous. The implication is that marketers must analyze the elderly subculture very carefully.

Elderly people differ considerably in how they want to live in retirement. Some would prefer a single-family home, while others want apartments or condominiums. Some want community, social interaction, and recreational amenities, while others prefer solitude and independence.

Both Hyatt and Marriott conducted detailed research using focus groups and telephone and written surveys to understand these needs. One research study identifies three subsubcultures in the elderly subcultures—the "go-go's" (65 to 75, who travel and play golf), the "slow-go's" (75 to 85, still active, but slowing down), and the "no-go's" (85 and older, somewhat active but staying closer to home). The prime target customer for retirement communities is the "slow-go" group. The "go-go's" will be potential customers in another 10 years, while the "no-go's" are potential customers for the more intensive levels of nursing care.

In earlier days, marketing of retirement community products was rather simplistic—some fancy four-color brochures and corporate print ads placed in magazines and newspapers. Early research generally was confined to simple demographic analyses of age, income, and competition. Many marketers did not investigate the elderly market further to understand how its members perceive their own needs. There is a big affective and cognitive problem in marketing retirement communities, for example. Typically, a consumer's first response is "I'm not ready yet." Most elderly people want to stay in their own homes and remain independent until it becomes impossible. Getting consumers to buy into a retirement community requires that they think about the unthinkable (their own mortality and failing health)—not easy for most people. In fact, many elderly, especially those in the affluent subgroup, perceive themselves as younger and more fit than they actually are.

Marriott opened its first two high-rise retirement developments (350 to 400 apartments) in 1988. Its "Jefferson" retirement community, opened in 1992, offered a pool, maid service, and a health club, in addition to 24-hour meals, emergency call buttons in each bathroom and bedroom, a floor with skilled nursing care, and another floor for those who don't require nursing care, but need other types of daily help (in bathing themselves, for example).

One industry consultant has suggested that direct mail is the most effective approach for marketing retirement communities. Every month, a company might send something to potential customers, such as a postcard invitation to an event, a letter describing some service, a newsletter describing people in the retirement community, even recipes. Marriott successfully used a direct-mail promotion to generate early interest in its unbuilt Jefferson retirement community. Brochures and information were mailed to 45,000 affluent elderly residents of the Washington, D.C., area. For a $1,000 deposit, people could reserve a $100,000 to $260,000 apartment in the luxury complex. The mailing generated a phenomenal 4 percent response rate (2 percent or 3 percent is considered good). Over the next several years, Marriott plans to spend more than $1 billion to construct some 150 retirement communities modeled on the Jefferson. Marriott also intends to build another 100 developments that offer only two living options—assisted living and nursing care.

Hyatt developed its retirement community, Classic Residences by Hyatt, in 1990. Classic Residences are upscale apartment complexes that offer a set of services similar to Marriott's. Hyatt's initial research also showed that elderly people have a strong initial negative reaction to retirement communities. Even people living in metropolitan areas who are exposed to a great deal of marketing information about these products think of "retirement communities" as a euphemism for the dreaded nursing home. Thus, Hyatt's marketing promotions tend to emphasize "maintain an active lifestyle" rather than "be taken care of forever."

Hyatt also found that many elderly people believe retirement communities are extremely expensive or that they have to sign away their life savings to get into a retirement community. So Hyatt salespeople explicitly compared the costs of living in one's own home to living in the retirement community. Most people did not factor in how much they were spending to live in their own house, and this discovery had some influence on their conviction that "I'm not ready yet." Marriott, finding the same thing, is experimenting with different pricing strategies, including charging a lower initial payment, with higher monthly rent or fees, so their prospects don't have to use so much of their accumulated savings.

Finally, both Hyatt and Marriott have developed other marketing strategies. Their sales presentations include seminars about retirement planning, health issues, and motivational topics. Open houses often include entertainment to draw in customers. If necessary, incentives are offered to encourage prospects to take that final step, including free rent for a few months, paid moving expenses, free interior decorating advice, or expense-paid vacations.

In sum, developing successful retirement community products and marketing strategies is largely a matter of "listening to the prospects and understanding their needs and interests." Many elderly consumers know what they want, and they respond to the same types of marketing strategies used to sell other services.

Discussion questions

1. Discuss the submarkets (sub-subcultures) within the elderly subculture that are relevant in the case of retirement communities. Discuss how social class can be combined with age subcultures to define the market segments for retirement communities more precisely. What marketing strategies would be necessary to target these different segments of the elderly market?

2. Identify the key target segments for Marriott's new health-care-oriented retirement communities (they offer only some level of health care). For the most attractive segment, identify and analyze the most important behaviors, affective

responses, and cognitions in shopping for, purchasing, and living in such a retirement community.

3. Discuss the marketing strategies that Marriott could use to market its new health-care-oriented retirement units to the key market segments. What different promotional strategies are likely to appeal to these subcultural groups?

4. The customer/product relationship may be a useful way to think about marketing retirement communities. What aspects of this relationship should Marriott and Hyatt consider, and why? Contrast the marketing strategies Marriott and Hyatt could use to develop the customer/product relationship before the purchase with the strategies they might institute after the sale to enhance and maintain this relationship.

Source: Sally Chapralis, "Retirement Community Marketers End Their Retirement," *Marketing News,* July 8, 1991, p. 2; Jame Gollub and Harold Javitz, "Six Ways to Age," *American Demographics,* June 1989, pp. 28–37; and Janet Novack, "Tea, Sympathy, and Direct Mail," *Forbes,* September 18, 1989, pp. 210–11.

► **CASE IV.4**

Hotels and resorts: catering to kids

For years, most of the lodging industry has merely tolerated children, and many upscale hotels and resorts have actively discouraged them. Recently, however, much of the huge travel industry, including some of America's toniest hotels and resorts, have begun to treat kids like important customers.

Major demographic changes in the makeup of American families lie behind this shift in marketing strategy. A baby boomlet occurred in the 1980s, produced when record numbers of baby boomers began having children of their own. According to one travel expert, "Baby boomers are the most widely traveled generation ever. Now as parents, they want to vacation with their kids while still having time to pursue adult activities." Because they had children at a later age and often are dual-income households, many of these families spend substantial amounts on travel and vacations.

Many hotels and resorts now bend over backward to make parents with children feel welcome. Even business-oriented and luxury hotels are adding elaborate day-care programs for kids. For instance, consider San Francisco's luxurious Four Seasons Clift Hotel, where average room rates are $200 per night. In 1986, the Clift realized it needed a strategy for dealing with the children who were showing up with their parents, often for extended stays. "Many people wanted to stay in a luxury hotel and still have their kids with them," said a hotel spokesperson.

Rather than discourage the trend and lose business, the hotel launched its Clift Dweller program. Now, when the hotel takes a reservation for a family, it asks for the names and ages of the children. When the family shows up, the kids are greeted at check-in with a toy or a book appropriate for their age. Infants receive a first-day supply of diapers and formula or baby food at no charge. Children get their own room, connecting to the parents' room, at a discount rate. The Clift Hotel will arrange baby-sitting and escorted trips to museums or the zoo at rates of about $5 per hour. It offers bedtime snacks and 24-hour room service from a children's menu and keeps a pediatrician on call around the clock. The Clift even welcomes youngsters into its fanciest dining room, where the tuxedoed waiters have been trained to deal with small children.

Other hotels and resorts have begun to offer their own versions of programs for kids. For instance, virtually all the Sheraton hotels in Hawaii have added children's programs in recent years. Beginning in 1985 with a casual "day-camp" format, they switched in 1987 to a Thursday-through-Sunday formal program for children 4 to 12 years old. For about $10 per day, parents can sign their kids up for activities ranging from tennis instruction to magic lessons.

Travel agents and vacation planners are responding to the changing market, too. Family-oriented travel agencies, like the California firm Rascals in Paradise, have been doing a good business. There's even a monthly newsletter, "Travel with Your Children," that tracks trends in the family-travel market and has documented the explosion in travel services for kids. In the early 1980s, for example, only about a dozen hotels (apart from the obvious family destinations such as Disney-type theme parks) had special programs for children. By 1988, there were 50 family-friendly hotels and resorts in Hawaii alone.

Even firms that once ignored kids have learned to cater to them. Consider the marketing strategies adopted by Club Med, once the epitome of singles resorts geared to young, swinging baby boomers. Club Med offers fixed price, all-inclusive vacations at its own special resorts around the world, often built on secluded beaches. When the company faced losing its clientele of young baby boomers as they began to marry and have children, Club Med reshaped itself from a free-spirited camp for singles to a leader in the family-vacation market. Now more than half of Club Med's customers are married, and many bring their children. Club Med currently has six "miniclub" resorts that provide day camps and baby-sitting for kids 2 to 11 years old. In 1987, Club Med entertained almost 80,000 children with their parents, up 10 percent from the previous year. In 1988, the company opened its first "baby club" at the Sandpiper Resort in Florida and welcomed over 1,500 kids under 2 in the first year.

The author of a family-travel guidebook believes that these changes in the marketing strategies of the travel industry are only the beginning: "The catalyst is money. These are parents who have waited to have their children. They have money and are already used to a certain style of travel. Places will either start to accommodate them or they simply will go somewhere else."

Discussion questions

1. Discuss how the family decision process for deciding where to go on a family vacation is likely to vary for three types of families—families with young kids (ages under 7 or 8), families with preteens and young teens (ages 9 to 14), and families with older teens (ages 15 to 19). What implications do these differences have for the types of hotels and resorts mentioned in the case?

2. What types of conflict might occur in the three types of family situations listed above? How might that conflict be resolved? What implications does this analysis have for developing marketing strategies for the hotel and resort industry?

3. Discuss how the hotel and resort industry could use the modern family life cycle to help identify potential market segments, and then develop targeted marketing strategies for those segments.

4. Discuss how reference groups could influence a family's vacation decisions. What implications does this analysis have for the hotel and resort industry? What types of strategies could the hotel and resort industry undertake to stimulate favorable reference group influence?

Source: Ken Wells, "Hotels and Resorts Are Catering to Kids; Day Care and Activities Programs Help Welcome Traveling Families," *The Wall Street Journal,* August 11, 1988, p. 25.

▶ **CASE IV.5**

The Tylenol crisis

Pain relievers are a lucrative, $1.2-billion-a-year industry. Until recently, there were no chemical or medicinal differences among brands of nonaspirin pain relievers, so aggressive marketing was the key to gain market share—up to $130 million was spent on advertising for pain relievers in a recent year. Johnson & Johnson, producer of Tylenol analgesic, developed very successful marketing strategies and obtained the largest share of the pain reliever market, 37 percent, in a matter of a few years.

In 1959, Johnson & Johnson acquired McNeil Laboratories, which had introduced the Tylenol brand in 1955 in the form of an elixir for children without the irritating side effects of aspirin. Traditionally, Tylenol was sold "ethically" through physicians and pharmacists and not directly to end-use consumers. It was sold only as a prescription drug until 1960 and then as a nonprescription drug advertised only to doctors and pharmacists, who in turn recommended it to patients.

In 1975 Bristol-Myers introduced its own nonaspirin pain reliever, Datril, successfully marketing it directly to end users. Datril's success spurred Johnson & Johnson to expand its marketing effort to end users. The company cut prices, formed a sales force, and spent $8 million on advertising representing Tylenol as an alternative to aspirin. Tylenol's solid reputation among pharmacists and physicians gave it a definite competitive advantage with end-use consumers as it was perceived as a safe product endorsed by health professionals. In fact, two of every three Tylenol customers started using the product because it was recommended by their doctors.

In 1976, Extra-Strength Tylenol was introduced, the first product to contain 500 milligrams of painkiller per tablet. Market research then indicated that many consumers believed Tylenol was too gentle to be effective. Extra-Strength Tylenol was advertised as the most "potent pain reliever available without a prescription." Tylenol's market share rose from 4 percent to 25 percent in 1979, due largely to the extra-strength version of the brand. In 1982, Tylenol had 37 percent market share, as shown in the Exhibit I.

Competitors frantically tried to defend their brands against Tylenol. Excedrin, Anacin, and Bayer each introduced extra-strength versions with little success. Datril turned out to be a noncontender in the fight for market share because of failure to build a favorable reputation among physicians and pharmacists. Tylenol seemed unbeatable. The product became the largest-selling health and beauty aid, outstripping the 18-year dominance of Procter & Gamble's Crest toothpaste.

Tylenol employed very aggressive competitive tactics to dominate the industry. Litigation became a significant competitive strategy, as Johnson & Johnson took several competitors to court with claims of infringement on Tylenol's trademark and name. Tylenol

EXHIBIT 1

Market shares: pain reliever industry

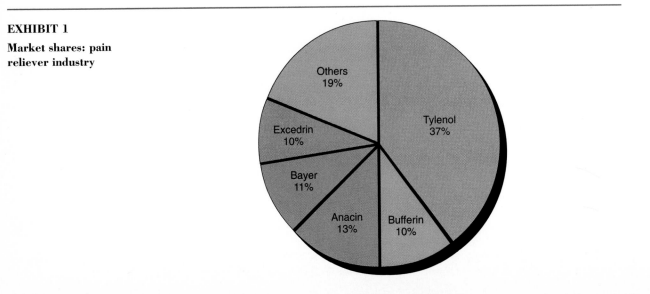

Others 19%
Tylenol 37%
Excedrin 10%
Bayer 11%
Anacin 13%
Bufferin 10%

found that the use of litigation kept competitors from active competition for up to two years. After that time, the competition emerged in a weakened market position and seldom recovered. This strategy was especially effective against Anacin. Tylenol sued Anacin four times, once for trademark infringement and three times for false advertising, winning each time. One marketing expert went so far as to credit Johnson & Johnson with inventing the fifth "P" of marketing—plaintiff.

Then, in the early fall of 1982, a tragedy threatened the company's strong position. Eight Chicago-area consumers of Extra-Strength Tylenol took capsules that had been tampered with and laced with cyanide. The coupling of the Tylenol name with their deaths caused Tylenol's market share to drop from 37 percent to 7 percent overnight.

Research indicated many consumers came away with misconceptions about the poisoning incidents. Many consumers did not learn that (1) the company was absolved of all responsibility by the investigating authorities, (2) Tylenol's production process conformed to all safety standards, (3) only Tylenol capsules were involved, not tablets, and (4) the tragic deaths were confined to that single incident.

Tylenol's competitors benefited greatly from the tragedy. Anacin won about 25 percent of Tylenol's lost business, mainly by aggressively advertising Anacin-3, and Bufferin and Bayer each took 20 percent of Tylenol's business. Most experts predicted the Tylenol brand would never recover. The situation was described as a consumer goods marketer's darkest nightmare.

Very soon after the crisis, Johnson & Johnson made a strategic decision to attempt to save the Tylenol brand that had been so successful and profitable. The company had built up a reservoir of consumer trust and loyalty that management felt could play a key role in the brand's recovery. The company had always tried to live up to the credo set for it in the 1940s by its leader, General Robert Wood Johnson: "We believe our first responsibility is to the doctors, nurses, and patients, to mothers and all others who use our products and services. In meeting their needs, everything we do must be of high quality." Company management interpreted the crisis as a monumental challenge to live up to this credo against overwhelming odds.

Discussion questions

1. What tactics should Johnson & Johnson use to rebuild consumer trust in Tylenol?

2. What lessons are there for marketers of drug products in Tylenol's response to the crisis, which resulted in the recovery of 90 percent of the lost market share in less than one year?

3. Should Johnson & Johnson have abandoned Tylenol and marketed a new brand?

Source: This case was prepared by Margaret L. Friedman, Assistant Professor, School of Business, University of Wisconsin-Whitewater. Used by permission. Based on "Tylenol, the Painkiller, Gives Rivals Headache in Stores and in Court," *The Wall Street Journal,* September 2, 1982; "A Death Blow for Tylenol?" *Business Week,* October 18, 1982, p. 151; "The Fight to Save Tylenol," *Fortune,* November 29, 1982, pp. 44–49; "Rivals Go After Tylenol's Market, but Gains May Be Only Temporary," *The Wall Street Journal,* December 2, 1982, pp. 25ff; and taken from J. Paul Peter and James M. Donnelly, *Marketing Management: Knowledge and Skills* (Homewood, Ill.: Richard D. Irwin, 1989), pp. 573–76.

▼ Notes

Chapter 1

1. The popular business press frequently features articles on the importance of organizations staying close to consumers. For examples, see Terence P. Pare, "Banks Discover the Consumer," *Fortune*, February 12, 1990, pp. 96–104; Stephen Phillips et al., "King Customer," *Business Week*, pp. 88–94; Patricia Sellers, "What Customers Really Want," *Fortune*, June 4, 1990, pp. 58–68; Frank Rose, "Now Quality Means Service Too," *Fortune*, April 22, 1991, pp. 97–108.

2. Peter D. Bennett, *Dictionary of Marketing Terms* (Chicago: American Marketing Association, 1988), p. 40.

Chapter 2

1. See Albert Bandura, "The Self System in Reciprocal Determinism," *American Psychologist*, April 1978, p. 346; also see Albert Bandura, *Social Foundations of Thought and Action: A Social Cognitive Theory* (Englewood Cliffs, N.J.: Prentice Hall, 1986).

2. Chip Walker, "Fat and Happy?" *American Demographics*, January 1993, pp. 52–57.

3. See Keith H. Hammond, "The 'Blacktop' Is Paving Reebok's Road to Recovery," *Business Week*, August 12, 1991, p. 27.

Chapter 3

1. Geoffrey Smith, "Does Gillette Know How to Treat a Lady?" *Business Week*, August 27, 1990, pp. 64–6.

2. Laura Zinn, "This Bud's for You. No. Not You—Her," *Business Week*, November 4, 1991, pp. 86–90.

3. This discussion of VALS 2 is abstracted from Martha Farnsworth Riche, "Psychographics for the 1990s," *American Demographics*, July 1989, pp. 24–26ff.

4. Howard Schlossberg, "How Five Companies Targeted Their Best Prospects," *Marketing News*, February 18, 1991, p. 4.

5. Peter R. Dickson, "Person-Situation: Segmentation's Missing Link," *Journal of Marketing*, Fall 1982, p. 57.

6. Shirley Young, Leland Ott, and Barbara Feigin, "Some Practical Considerations in Market Segmentation," *Journal of Marketing Research*, August 1978, p. 405.

7. David Greising, "Whap! Ace. Point. You Call This Tennis?" *Business Week*, September 9, 1991, p. 71.

8. Alex Taylor III, "How Buick Is Bouncing Back," *Fortune*, May 6, 1991, pp. 83–88.

Chapter 4

1. Joshua Levine, "But in the Office, No," *Forbes*, October 16, 1989, pp. 272–73.

2. C. E. Izard, "Emotion-Cognition Relationships and Human Development," in *Emotions, Cognition, and Behavior*, ed. C. E. Izard, J. Kagan, and R. B. Zajonc (New York: Cambridge University Press, 1984), pp. 17–37; Rom Harre, David Clarke, and Nicola De Carlo, *Motives and Mechanisms: An Introduction to the Psychology of Action* (London: Methuen, 1985), chap. 2, pp. 20–39; Martin L. Hoffman, "Affect, Cognition, and Motivation," in *Handbook of Motivation and Cognition*, ed. R. M. Sorrentino and E. T. Higgins (New York: Guilford Press, 1986), pp. 244–80; and Robert Plutchik, *Emotion: A Psychoevolutionary Synthesis* (New York: Harper & Row, 1980).

3. Rik G. M. Pieters and W. Fred Van Raaij, "Functions and Management of Affect: Applications to Economic Behavior," *Journal of Economic Psychology* 9 (1988), pp. 251–82.

4. Werner Kroeber-Riel, "Activation Research: Psychobiological Approaches in Consumer Research," *Journal of Consumer Research*, March 1979, pp. 240–50.

5. Meryl Paula Gardner, "Mood States and Consumer Behavior: A Critical Review," *Journal of Consumer Research*, December 1985, pp. 281–300.

6. See Harre et al., *Motives and Mechanisms: An Introduction to the Psychology of Action;* Robert B. Zajonc and

Hazel Markus, "Affective and Cognitive Factors in Preferences," *Journal of Consumer Research* 9 (1982), pp. 123–31; Hoffman, "Affect, Cognition, and Motivation," pp. 244–80; Robert B. Zajonc, "On the Primacy of Affect," *American Psychologist* 39 (1984), pp. 117–23; and Richard S. Lazarus, "On the Primacy of Cognition," *American Psychologist* 39 (1984), pp. 124–29.

7. Michael K. Hui and John E. G. Bateson, "Perceived Control and the Effects of Crowding and Consumer Choice on the Service Experience," *Journal of Consumer Research,* September 1991, pp. 174–84.

8. For example, see the exchange between Yehoshua Tsal, "On the Relationship between Cognitive and Affective Processes: A Critique of Zajonc and Markus," *Journal of Consumer Research* 12 (1985), pp. 358–64; Zajonc and Markus, "Affective and Cognitive Factors in Preferences"; and Robert B. Zajonc and Hazel Markus, "Must All Affect Be Mediated by Cognition?" *Journal of Consumer Research* 12 (1985), pp. 363–64.

9. Lazarus, "On the Primacy of Cognition," pp. 124–29; Pieters and Van Raaij, "Functions and Management of Affect: Applications to Economic Behavior," pp. 251–82; and Richard S. Lazarus, "Cognition and Motivation in Emotion," *American Psychologist,* April 1991, pp. 352–67.

10. S. S. Tomkins, "Affect Theory," in *Emotion in the Human Face,* ed. P. Ekman (Cambridge, England: Cambridge University Press, 1983); Robert B. Zajonc, "On the Primacy of Affect," *American Psychologist* 39 (1984), pp. 117–23; and Richard S. Lazarus, "On the Primacy of Cognition," *American Psychologist* 39 (1984), pp. 124–29.

11. For example, see Julie A. Edell and Marian Chapman Burke, "The Power of Feelings in Understanding Advertising Effects," *Journal of Consumer Research,* December 1987, pp. 421–33; William J. Havlena, and Morris B. Holbrook, "The Varieties of Consumption Experience: Comparing Two Typologies of Emotion in Consumer Behavior," *Journal of Consumer Research,* December 1986, pp. 394–404; Morris B. Holbrook and Rajeev Batra, "Assessing the Role of Emotions as Mediators of Consumer Responses to Advertising," *Journal of Consumer Research,* December 1987, pp. 404–20; and Rajeev Batra and Douglas M. Stayman, "The Role of Mood in Advertising Effectiveness," *Journal of Consumer Research,* September 1990, pp. 203–14.

12. For example, see Hoffman, "Affect, Cognition, and Motivation," pp. 244–80.

13. Dawn Dobni and George M. Zinkhan, "In Search of Brand Image: A Foundation Analysis," in *Advances in Consumer Research,* vol. 17, eds. M. Goldberg, G. Gorn, and R. Pollay (Provo, Utah: Association for Consumer Research, 1990), pp. 110–19; and Ernest Dichter, "What's in an Image?" *Journal of Consumer Marketing,* Winter 1985, pp. 75–81.

14. John R. Rossiter, Larry Percy, and Robert J. Donovan, "A Better Advertising Planning Grid," *Journal of Advertising Research,* October–November 1991, pp. 11–21; and Brian Ratchford, "New Insights about the FCB Grid," *Journal of Advertising Research,* August–September 1987, pp. 24–38.

15. Mark Maremont, "They're All Screaming for Haagen-Dazs," *Business Week,* October 14, 1991, p. 121.

16. Kathleen Deveny, "As Lauder's Scent Battles Calvin Klein's, Cosmetics Whiz Finds Herself on the Spot," *The Wall Street Journal,* June 27, 1991, pp. B1, B6.

17. One complex information processing model of consumer decision making is by John Howard and Jagdish Sheth, *The Theory of Buyer Behavior* (New York: John Wiley & Sons, 1969). Another is James R. Bettman, *An Information Processing Model of Consumer Choice* (Reading Mass.: Addison-Wesley, 1979).

18. Alan M. Collins and Elizabeth F. Loftus, "A Spreading Activation Theory of Semantic Memory," *Psychological Review* 82 (1975), pp. 407–28.

19. John R. Anderson, "A Spreading Activation Theory of Memory," *Journal of Verbal Learning and Verbal Behavior* 22 (1983), pp. 261–75; and Collins and Loftus, "A Spreading Activation Theory of Semantic Memory," pp. 407–28.

20. John A. Bargh, "Automatic and Conscious Processing of Social Information," in *Handbook of Social Cognition,* vol. 3, ed. R. S. Wyer and T. K. Srull (Hillsdale, N.J.: Lawrence Erlbaum, 1984), pp. 1–43; and Richard M. Shiffrin and Susan T. Dumais, "The Development of Automatism," in *Cognitive Skills and Their Development,* ed. John R. Anderson (Hillsdale, N.J.: Lawrence Erlbaum, 1981), pp. 111–40.

21. Jeffrey F. Durgee and Robert W. Stuart, "Advertising Symbols and Brand Names that Best Represent Key Product Meanings," *Journal of Advertising,* Summer 1987, pp. 15–24.

22. Wayne A. Wickelgren, "Human Learning and Memory," in *Annual Review of Psychology,* ed. M. R. Rosenzweig and L. W. Porter (Palo Alto, Calif.: Annual Reviews, 1981), pp. 21–52.

23. John R. Anderson, *The Architecture of Cognition* (Cambridge, Mass.: Harvard University Press, 1983); and Terence R. Smith, Andrew A. Mitchell, and Robert Meyer, "A Computational Process Model of Evaluation Based on the Cognitive Structuring of Episodic Knowledge," in *Advances in Consumer Research,* vol. 9, ed. Andrew A. Mitchell (Ann Arbor, Mich.: Association for Consumer Research, 1982), pp. 136–43.

24. Endel Tulving, "Episodic and Semantic Memory," in *Organization of Memory,* ed. Endel Tulving (New York: Academic Press, 1972), pp. 382–404.

25. Merrie Brucks and Andrew Mitchell, "Knowledge Structures, Production Systems, and Decision Strategies," in *Advances in Consumer Research,* vol. 8, ed. Kent B. Monroe (Ann Arbor, Mich.: Association for Consumer Research, 1982).

26. Donald A. Norman, *The Psychology of Everyday Things* (New York: Basic Books, 1988).

27. Bruce Nussbaum and Robert Neff, "I Can't Work This Thing!" *Business Week,* April 29, 1991, pp. 58–66.

28. Although many types of memory structures have been proposed, most can be reduced to the more general associative network model. See James R. Bettman, "Memory Factors in Consumer Choice: A Review," *Journal of Mar-*

keting, Spring 1979, pp. 37–53; Andrew A. Mitchell, "Models of Memory: Implications for Measuring Knowledge Structures," in *Advances in Consumer Research,* vol. 9, ed. Andrew A. Mitchell (Ann Arbor, Mich.: Association for Consumer Research, 1982), pp. 45–51; and Edward Smith, "Theories of Semantic Memory," in *Handbook of Learning and Cognitive Processes,* vol. 6, ed. W. K. Estes (Hillsdale, N.J.: Lawrence Erlbaum, 1978), pp. 1–56.

29. Joseph W. Alba and Lynn Hasher, "Is Memory Schematic?" *Psychological Bulletin,* March 1983, p. 203–31; and Donald E. Rumelhart and Anthony Ortony, "The Representation of Knowledge in Memory," in *Schooling and the Acquisition of Knowledge,* eds. R. C. Anderson, R. J. Spiro, and W. E. Montague (Hillsdale, N.J.: Lawrence Erlbaum, 1977), pp. 99–136.

30. Thomas W. Leigh and Arno J. Rethans, "Experiences with Script Elicitation within Consumer Decision-Making Contexts," in *Advances in Consumer Research,* vol. 10, ed. R. P. Baggozzi and A. M. Tybout (Ann Arbor, Mich.: Association for Consumer Research, 1983), pp. 667–72; and Roger C. Schank and Robert P. Abelson, *Scripts, Plans, Goals, and Understanding: An Inquiry into Human Knowledge Structures* (Hillsdale, N.J.: Lawrence Erlbaum, 1977).

Chapter 5

1. Faye Rice, "The King of Suds Reigns Again," *Fortune,* August 4, 1986, pp. 130–32, 134.

2. Eleanor Rosch, Carolyn B. Mervis, Wayne D. Gray, David M. Johnson, and Penny Boyes-Braem, "Basic Objects in Natural Categories," *Cognitive Psychology,* July 1976, pp. 382–439; Mita Sujan, "Consumer Knowledge: Effects on Evaluation Strategies Mediating Consumer Judgments," *Journal of Consumer Research,* June 1985, pp. 31–46; Joel Cohen and Kunal Basu, "Alternative Models of Categorization: Toward a Contingent Processing Framework," *Journal of Consumer Research,* March 1987, pp. 455–72; Carolyn B. Mervis, "Category Structure and the Development of Categorization," in *Theoretical Issues in Reading Comprehension,* ed. Rand Spiro et al. (Hillsdale, N.J.: Lawrence Erlbaum, 1980), pp. 279–307.

3. For examples, see Joseph W. Alba and Amitava Chattopadhyay, "The Effects of Context and Part-Category Cues on the Recall of Competing Brands," *Journal of Marketing Research,* August 1985, pp. 340–49; Mita Sujan and Christine Dekleva, "Product Categorization and Inference Making: Some Implications for Comparative Advertising," *Journal of Consumer Research,* September 1987, pp. 141–54; Mita Sujan and James R. Bettman, "The Effects of Brand Positioning Strategies on Consumers' Brand and Category Perceptions: Some Insights from Schema Research," *Journal of Marketing Research,* November 1989, pp. 454–67.

4. Michael D. Johnson, "The Differential Processing of Product Category and Noncomparable Choice Alternatives," *Journal of Consumer Research,* December 1989, pp. 300–09.

5. Zachary Schiller and Mark N. Varmmos, "Liquid Tide Looks like Solid Gold," *Business Week,* December 24, 1984, p. 32.

6. For example, Elizabeth C. Hirschman, "Attributes of Attributes and Layers of Meaning," in *Advances in Consumer Research,* vol. 7, ed. Jerry C. Olson (Ann Arbor, Mich.: Association for Consumer Research, 1980), pp. 7–12; and Lyle V. Geistfeld, George B. Sproles, and Susan B. Badenhop, "The Concept and Measurement of a Hierarchy of Product Characteristics," in *Advances in Consumer Research,* vol. 4, ed. H. Keith Hunt (Ann Arbor, Mich.: Association for Consumer Research, 1977), pp. 302–7.

7. Theodore Levitt, "Marketing Myopia," *Harvard Business Review,* July–August 1960, pp. 45–56.

8. Paul E. Green, Yoram Wind, and Arun K. Jain, "Benefit Bundle Analysis," *Journal of Advertising Research,* April 1972, pp. 32–36; and Russell I. Haley, "Benefit Segmentation: A Decision-Oriented Research Tool," *Journal of Marketing,* July 1972, pp. 30–35.

9. For instance, Jonathan Gutman and Donald E. Vinson, "Values Structures and Consumer Behavior," in *Advances in Consumer Research,* vol. 6, ed. William L. Wilkie (Ann Arbor, Mich.: Association for Consumer Research, 1979), pp. 335–39; Janice G. Hanna, "A Typology of Consumer Needs," in *Research in Marketing,* vol. 3, ed. Jagdish N. Sheth (Greenwich, Conn.: JAI Press, 1980), pp. 83–104; and Lynn Kahle, "The Values of Americans: Implications for Consumer Adaptation," in *Personal Values & Consumer Psychology,* ed. Robert E. Pitts, Jr., and Arch G. Woodside (Lexington, Mass.: Lexington Books, 1984), pp. 77–86.

10. Anthony G. Greenwald and Anthony R. Pratkanis, "The Self," in *The Handbook of Social Cognition,* eds. Robert S. Wyer and Thomas K. Srull (Hillsdale, N.J.: Lawrence Erlbaum, 1984), pp. 129–78; Hazel Markus and Paula Nunus, "Possible Selves," *American Psychologist,* September 1986, pp. 954–69; John F. Kihlstrom and Nancy Cantor, "Mental Representations of the Self," in *Advances in Experimental Social Psychology,* 1984, pp. 1–47; Hazel Markus, "Self-Schemata and Processing Information about the Self," *Journal of Personality and Social Psychology,* 1977, pp. 63–78; and Hazel Markus and Keith Sentis, "The Self in Social Information Processing," in *Psychological Perspectives on the Self,* ed. J. Suis (Hillsdale, N.J.: Lawrence Erlbaum, 1982), pp. 41–70.

11. The basic idea of means-end chains can be traced back at least to Edward C. Tolman, *Purposive Behavior in Animals and Men* (New York: Century, 1932). Among the first to suggest its use in marketing was John A. Howard, *Consumer Behavior Application and Theory* (New York: McGraw-Hill, 1977). Jon Gutman and Tom Reynolds have been active proponents of means-end chain models. For example, see Jonathan Gutman and Thomas J. Reynolds, "An Investigation of the Levels of Cognitive Abstraction Utilized by Consumers in Product Differentiation," in *Attitude Research under the Sun,* ed. John Eighmey (Chicago: American Marketing Association, 1979), pp. 125–50; and Jonathan Gutman, "A Means-End Chain Model Based on Consumer Categorization Processes," *Journal of Marketing,* Spring 1982, pp. 60–72.

12. Shirley Young and Barbara Feigen, "Using the Benefit Chair for Improved Strategy Formulation," *Journal of Marketing,* July 1975, pp. 72–74; James H. Myers and Alan D. Schocker, "The Nature of Product-Related Attributes," in *Research in Marketing,* ed. J. N. Sheth (Greenwich, Conn.: JAI Press, 1981), pp. 211–36; Joel B. Cohen, "The Structure of Product Attributes: Defining Attribute Dimensions for Planning and Evaluation," in *Analytic Approaches to Product and Marketing Planning,* ed. A. D. Shocker (Cambridge, Mass.: Marketing Science Institute, 1979), pp. 54–86; Jonathan Gutman, "A Means-End Chain Model Based on Consumer Categorization Processes," *Journal of Marketing,* Spring 1982, pp. 60–72; and Jerry C. Olson, "The Theoretical Foundations of Means-End Chains," *Verbeforschung & Praxis* 5, 1990, pp. 174–78.

13. Jerry C. Olson and Thomas J. Reynolds, "Understanding Consumers' Cognitive Structures: Implications for Marketing Strategy," in *Advertising and Consumer Psychology,* vol. 1, ed. Larry Percy and Arch Woodside (Lexington Mass.: Lexington Books, 1983), pp. 77–90.

14. For a good example, see Sunil Mehrotra and John Palmer, "Relating Product Features to Perceptions of Quality: Appliances," in *Perceived Quality,* ed. Jacob Jacoby and Jerry Olson (Lexington, Mass.: Lexington Books, 1985), pp. 81–96.

15. Thomas J. Reynolds and Jonathan Gutman, "Laddering Theory, Method, Analysis, and Interpretation," *Journal of Advertising Research,* February–March 1988, pp. 11–31; Jonathan Gutman, "Exploring the Nature of Linkages between Consequences and Values," *Journal of Business Research,* 1991, pp. 143–48.

16. For a good example, see Jonathan Gutman and Scott D. Alden, "Adolescents' Cognitive Structures of Retail Stores and Fashion Consumption: A Means-End Chain Analysis of Quality," in *Perceived Quality,* ed. Jacob Jacoby and Jerry Olson (Lexington, Mass.: Lexington Books, 1985), pp. 99–114.

17. One of the first and most influential writers about involvement was Herbert E. Krugman. See Herbert E. Krugman, "The Impact of Television Advertising: Learning without Involvement," *Public Opinion Quarterly,* 1965, pp. 349–56; and Herbert E. Krugman, "The Measurement of Advertising Involvement," *Public Opinion Quarterly*, 1967, pp. 583–96.

18. For instance, see John H. Antil, "Conceptualization and Operationalization of Involvement," in *Advances in Consumer Research,* vol. 11, ed. Thomas C. Kinnear (Ann Arbor, Mich.: Association for Consumer Research, 1984), pp. 203–09; Andrew A. Mitchell, "Involvement: A Potentially Important Mediator of Consumer Behavior," in *Advances in Consumer Research,* vol. 6, ed. William Wilkie (Ann Arbor, Mich.: Association for Consumer Research, 1979), pp. 191–96; Robert N. Stone, "The Marketing Characteristics of Involvement," in *Advances in Consumer Research,* vol. 11, ed. Thomas C. Kinnear (Ann Arbor, Mich.: Association for Consumer Research, 1984), pp. 210–15; Peter N. Bloch, "An Exploration into the Scaling of Consumers' Involvement with a Product Class," in *Advances in Consumer Research,* vol. 8, ed. Kent B. Monroe (Ann Arbor, Mich.: Association for Consumer Research, 1981), pp. 61–65; and Judith Lynne Zaichkowsky, "Measuring the Involvement Construct," *Journal of Consumer Research,* December 1985, pp. 341–52.

19. This section draws on Richard L. Celsi and Jerry C. Olson, "The Role of Involvement in Attention and Comprehension Processes," *Journal of Consumer Research,* September 1988, pp. 210–24; also see Andrew A. Mitchell, "The Dimensions of Advertising Involvement," in *Advances in Consumer Research,* vol. 8, ed. Kent B. Monroe (Ann Arbor, Mich.: Association for Consumer Research, 1981), pp. 25–30; and William L. Moore and Donald R. Lehmann, "Individual Differences in Search Behavior for a Nondurable," *Journal of Consumer Research,* December 1980, pp. 296–307.

20. Beth A. Walker and Jerry C. Olson, "Means-End Chains: Connecting Products with Self," *Journal of Business Research,* 1991, pp. 111–18.

21. Joel B. Cohen, "Involvement and You: 100 Great Ideas," in *Advances in Consumer Research,* vol. 9, ed. Andrew A. Mitchell (Ann Arbor, Mich.: Association for Consumer Research, 1982), pp. 324–27; Harold H. Kassarjian, "Low Involvement—A Second Look," in *Advances in Consumer Research,* vol. 8, ed. Kent B. Monroe (Ann Arbor, Mich.: Association for Consumer Research, 1981), pp. 31–34.

22. Celsi and Olson, "The Role of Involvement in Attention and Comprehension Processes," pp. 210–24. A similar perspective is provided by Peter H. Bloch and Marsha L. Richins, "A Theoretical Model of the Study of Product Importance Perceptions," *Journal of Marketing,* Summer 1983, pp. 69–81. Some researchers treat these two factors as two forms of involvement—enduring and situational involvement, respectively. For instance, see Michael J. Houston and Michael L. Rothschild, "Conceptual and Methodological Perspectives on Involvement," in *1978 Educators Proceedings,* ed. S. C. Jain (Chicago: American Marketing Association, 1978), pp. 184–87. We believe it is clearer to treat these factors as sources of involvement.

23. For a similar proposal, see Peter H. Bloch, "Involvement beyond the Purchase Process: Conceptual Issues and Empirical Investigation," in *Advances in Consumer Research,* vol. 9, ed. Andrew A. Mitchell (Ann Arbor, Mich.: Association for Consumer Research, 1982), pp. 413–17.

24. John Harris, "I Don't Want Good, I Want Fast," *Forbes,* October 1, 1990, p. 186.

25. Russell W. Belk, "Worldly Possessions: Issues and Criticisms," in *Advances in Consumer Research,* vol. 10, ed. Richard P. Baggozzi and Alice M. Tybout (Ann Arbor, Mich.: Association for Consumer Research, 1983), pp. 514–19; and Terence A. Shimp and Thomas J. Madden, "Consumer-Object Relations: A Conceptual Framework Based Analogously on Sternberg's Triangular Theory of Love," in *Advances in Consumer Research,* vol. 15, ed. Michael J. Houston (Ann Arbor, Mich.: Association for Consumer Research, 1988), pp. 163–68.

26. For a similar idea in an advertising context, see Thomas J. Reynolds and Jonathan Gutman, "Advertising Is Image Management," *Journal of Advertising Research,* February–March 1984, pp. 27–37.

27. Bill Brubaker, "Athletic Shoes: Beyond Big Business," *Washington Post,* March 10, 1991, pp. A1, A18.

28. For a detailed description of the perceived personal relevance (involvement) of some consumer researchers, see Donald R. Lehmann, "Pumping Iron III: An Examination of Compulsive Lifting," in *Advances in Consumer Research,* vol. 14, ed. Melanie Wallendorf and Paul Anderson (Ann Arbor, Mich.: Association for Consumer Research, 1987), pp. 129–31; and Debra Scammon, "Breeding, Training, and Riding: The Serious Side of Horsing Around," in *Advances in Consumer Research,* vol. 14, ed. Melanie Wallendorf and Paul Anderson (Ann Arbor, Mich.: Association for Consumer Research, 1987), pp. 125–28.

29. Sunil Mehrotra and John Palmer, "Relating Product Features to Perceptions of Quality: Appliances," in *Perceived Quality,* ed. Jacob Jacoby and Jerry C. Olson (Lexington, Mass.: Lexington Books, 1985), pp. 81–96.

30. Grant McCracken, "Advertising: Meaning or Information," in *Advances in Consumer Research,* vol. 14, ed. Melanie Wallendorf and Paul Anderson (Ann Arbor, Mich.: Association for Consumer Research, 1987), pp. 121–24.

31. Joshua Levine, "I Gave at the Supermarket," *Forbes,* December 25, 1989, pp. 138–40; and Jaclyn Fierman, "The Big Muddle in Green Marketing," *Fortune,* June 3, 1991, pp. 91–101.

Chapter 6

1. This material is adapted from Brian Dumaine, "Who's Gypping Whom in TV Ads?" *Fortune,* July 6, 1987, pp. 78–79; Dennis Kneale, "Using High-Tech Tools to Measure Audience," *The Wall Street Journal,* April 25, 1988, p. 21; Jeffrey A. Tachtenberg, "Anybody Home Out There?" *Forbes,* May 19, 1986, pp. 169–70; Jeffrey A. Tachtenberg, "Diary of a Failure," *Forbes,* September 19, 1988, pp. 168–70; Howard Scholssberg, "Case of Missing TV Viewers," *Marketing News,* September 17, 1990, pp. 1, 7; and Lynn G. Coleman, "People Meter Rerun," *Marketing News,* September 2, 1991, pp. 1, 44.

2. Sharon E. Beatty and Scott M. Smith, "External Search Effort: An Investigation across Several Product Categories," *Journal of Consumer Research,* June 1987, pp. 83–95; Peter H. Bloch, Daniel Sherrell, and Nancy M. Ridgway, "Consumer Search: An Extended Framework," *Journal of Consumer Research,* June 1986, pp. 119–26; Joseph W. Newman, "Consumer External Search: Amount and Determinants," in *Consumer and Industrial Buying Behavior,* ed. A. G. Woodside, J. N. Sheth, and P. D. Bennett (New York: Elsevier-North Holland, 1977), pp. 79–94; and Richard R. Olshavsky and Donald H. Granbois, "Consumer Decision Making—Fact or Fiction," *Journal of Consumer Research,* June 1979, pp. 63–70.

3. Leo Bogart, "Executives Fear Ad Overload Will Lower Effectiveness," *Marketing News,* May 25, 1984, pp. 4–5.

4. Peter H. Bloch and Marsha L. Ritchins, "Shopping without Purchase: An Investigation of Consumer Browsing Behavior," in *Advances in Consumer Research,* vol. 10, ed. R. P. Baggozi and A. M. Tybout (Ann Arbor, Mich.: Association for Consumer Research, 1983), pp. 389–93.

5. Joanne Lipman, "CNN Ads Get Extra Mileage during the War," *The Wall Street Journal,* February 27, 1991, pp. B1, B4.

6. Avery Abernethy and Hubert Rotfield, "Zipping through TV Ads Is Old Tradition—But Viewers Are Getting Better at It," *Marketing News,* January 7, 1991, pp. 6, 14.

7. Dennis Kneale, "Zapping of TV Ads Appears Pervasive," *The Wall Street Journal,* April 25, 1988, p. 21.

8. Christine Dugas, "Ad Space Now Has a Whole New Meaning," *Business Week,* July 29, 1985, p. 52.

9. David W. Schumann, Jennifer Gayson, Johanna Ault, Kerri Hargrove, Lois Hollingsworth, Russell Ruelle, and Sharon Seguin, "The Effectiveness of Shopping Cart Signage: Perceptual Measures Tell a Different Story," *Journal of Advertising Research,* February–March 1991, pp. 17–22.

10. Suzanne Alexander, "Saturating Cities with Stores Can Pay," *The Wall Street Journal,* September 11, 1990, p. B1.

11. Joanne Lipman, "Brand-Name Products Are Popping Up in TV Shows," *The Wall Street Journal,* February 19, 1991, pp. B1, B3.

12. Roy Lachman, Janet L. Lachman, and Earl C. Butterfield, *Cognitive Psychology and Information Processing: An Introduction* (Hillsdale, N.J.: Lawrence Erlbaum, 1979).

13. Daniel Kahneman, *Attention and Effort* (Englewood Cliffs, N.J.: Prentice Hall, 1973); Anthony A. Greenwald and Clark Leavitt, "Audience Involvement in Advertising: Four Levels," *Journal of Consumer Research,* June 1984, pp. 581–92; and Chris Janiszewski, "The Influence of Non-attended Material on the Processing of Advertising Claims," *Journal of Marketing Research,* August 1990, pp. 263–78.

14. Schumann et al., "The Effectiveness of Shopping Cart Signage."

15. David M. Sanbonmatsu and Frank R. Kardes, "The Effects of Physiological Arousal on Information Processing and Persuasion," *Journal of Consumer Research,* December 1988, pp. 379–85; Meryl Paula Gardner, "Mood States and Consumer Behavior," *Journal of Consumer Research,* December 1985, pp. 281–300; and Noel Murray, Harish Sujan, Edward R. Hirt, and Mita Sujan, "The Effects of Mood on Categorization: A Cognitive Flexibility Hypothesis," *Journal of Personality and Social Psychology,* September 1990, pp. 411–25.

16. Marvin E. Goldberg and Gerald J. Gorn, "Happy and Sad TV Programs: How They Affect Reactions to Commercials," *Journal of Consumer Research,* December 1987, pp. 387–403.

17. See Richard L. Celsi and Jerry C. Olson, "The Role of Involvement in Attention and Comprehension Processes," *Journal of Consumer Research,* September 1988, pp. 210–24.

18. Sana Siwolop, "You Can't (Hum) Ignore (Hum) That Ad," *Business Week,* September 21, 1987, p. 56.

19. Both examples are taken from "Intuition: Microstudies, Humanized Research Can Identify Emotions that Motivate Consumers," *Marketing News,* March 19, 1982, p. 11.

20. Ann L. McGill and Punam Anand, "The Effect of Vivid Attributes on the Evaluation of Alternatives: The Role of Differential Attention and Cognitive Elaboration," *Journal of Consumer Research,* September 1989, pp. 188–96.

21. Cathryn Donohoe, "Whittle Zeroes In on His Target," *Insight,* August 14, 1989, pp. 50–52.

22. Fergus I. M. Craik and Robert S. Lockhart, "Levels of Processing: A Framework for Memory Research," *Journal of Verbal Learning and Verbal Behavior,* 1972, pp. 671–89; and Jerry C. Olson, "Encoding Processes: Levels of Processing and Existing Knowledge Structures," in *Advances in Consumer Research,* vol. 7, ed. J. C. Olson (Ann Arbor, Mich.: Association for Consumer Research, 1980), pp. 154–59.

23. John R. Anderson and Lynne M. Reder, "An Elaboration Processing Explanation of Depth of Processing," in *Levels of Processing in Human Memory,* ed. Larry S. Cermak and Fergus I. M. Craik (Hillsdale, N.J.: Lawrence Erlbaum, 1979), pp. 385–404; and Richard E. Petty and John T. Cacioppo, "The Elaboration Likelihood Model of Persuasion," in *Advances in Experimental Social Psychology,* vol. 19, ed. Leonard Berkowitz (New York: Academic Press, 1986), pp. 123–205.

24. Alain d'Astous and Marc Dubuc, "Retrieval Processes in Consumer Evaluative Judgment Making: The Role of Elaborative Processing," in *Advances in Consumer Research,* vol. 13, ed. Richard J. Lutz (Provo, Utah: Association for Consumer Research, 1986), pp. 132–37; Jerry C. Olson, "Encoding Processes: Levels of Processing and Existing Knowledge Structures," in *Advances in Consumer Research,* vol. 7, ed. J. C. Olson (Ann Arbor, Mich.: Association for Consumer Research, 1980), pp. 154–59; and Douglas M. Stayman and Rajeev Batra, "Encoding and Retrieval of Ad Affect in Memory," *Journal of Consumer Research,* May 1991, pp. 232–39.

25. Kevin Lane Keller, "Memory Factors in Advertising: The Effect of Advertising Retrieval Cues on Brand Evaluations," *Journal of Consumer Research,* December 1987, pp. 316–33; and Joan Myers-Levy, "Priming Effects on Product Judgments: A Hemispheric Interpretation," *Journal of Consumer Research,* June 1989, pp. 76–86.

26. Gary T. Ford and Ruth Ann Smith, "Inferential Beliefs in Consumer Evaluations: An Assessment of Alternative Processing Strategies," *Journal of Consumer Research,* December 1987, pp. 363–71; Richard J. Harris, "Inferences in Information Processing," in *The Psychology of Learning and Motivation,* vol. 15, ed. Gordon A. Bower (New York: Academic Press, 1981), pp. 81–128; and Mita Sujan and Christine Dekleva, "Product Categorization and Inference Making: Some Implications for Comparative Advertising," *Journal of Consumer Research,* December 1986, pp. 372–78.

27. Amna Kirmani, "The Effect of Perceived Advertising Costs on Brand Perceptions," *Journal of Consumer Research,* September 1990, pp. 160–71; and Amna Kirmani and Peter Wright, "Money Talks: Perceived Advertising Expense and Expected Product Quality," *Journal of Consumer Research,* December 1989, pp. 344–53.

28. See Joseph W. Alba and J. Wesley Hutchinson, "Dimensions of Consumer Expertise," *Journal of Consumer Research,* March 1987, pp. 411–54; and Jerry C. Olson, "Inferential Belief Formation in the Cue Utilization Process," in *Advances in Consumer Research,* vol. 5, ed. H. Keith Hunt (Ann Arbor, Mich.: Association for Consumer Research, 1978), pp. 706–13.

29. Carl Obermiller, "When Do Consumers Infer Quality from Price?" in *Advances in Consumer Research,* vol. 15, ed. Michael J. Houston (Provo, Utah: Association for Consumer Research, 1988), pp. 304–10; Jerry C. Olson, "Price as an Informational Cue: Effects on Product Evaluations," in *Consumer and Industrial Buying Behavior,* ed. Arch G. Woodside, Jagdish N. Sheth, and Peter D. Bennett (New York: North Holland, 1977), pp. 267–86; and Valarie A. Zeithaml, "Consumer Perceptions of Price, Quality, and Value," *Journal of Marketing,* July 1988, pp. 2–22.

30. Frank R. Kardes, "Spontaneous Inference Processes in Advertising: The Effects of Conclusion Omission and Involvement on Persuasion," *Journal of Consumer Research,* September 1988, pp. 225–33; Richard D. Johnson and Irwin P. Levin, "More than Meets the Eye: The Effect of Missing Information on Purchase Evaluations," *Journal of Consumer Research,* June 1985, pp. 169–77; Carolyn J. Simmons and John G. Lynch, Jr., "Inference Effects with Inference Making? Effects of Missing Information on Discounting and Use of Presented Information," *Journal of Consumer Research,* March 1991, pp. 477–91.

31. For examples of inferring means-end chains, see Zeithaml, "Consumer Perceptions of Price, Quality, and Value," pp. 2–22; and Sunil Mehrotra and John Palmer, "Relating Product Features to Perceptions of Quality: Appliances," in *Perceived Quality,* ed. Jacob Jacoby and Jerry C. Olson (Lexington, Mass.: Lexington Books, 1985), pp. 81–96.

32. Durairaj Maheswaran and Brian Sternthal, "The Effects of Knowledge, Motivation, and Type of Message on Ad Processing and Product Judgments," *Journal of Consumer Research,* June 1990, pp. 66–73.

33. James R. Bettman and Mita Sujan, "Effects of Framing on Evaluation of Comparable and Noncomparable Alternatives by Expert and Novice Consumers," *Journal of Consumer Research,* September 1987, pp. 141–54; Joseph W. Alba and J. Wesley Hutchinson, "Dimensions of Consumer Expertise," *Journal of Consumer Research,* March 1987, pp. 411–54; Eric J. Johnson and J. Edward Russo, "Product Familiarity and Learning New Information," *Journal of Consumer Research,* June 1984, pp. 542–50; Larry J. Marks and Jerry C. Olson, "Toward a Cognitive Structure Conceptualization of Product Familiarity," in *Advances in Consumer Research,* vol. 8, ed. Kent B. Monroe (Ann Arbor, Mich.: Association for Consumer Research, 1981), pp. 145–50; and Mita Sujan, "Consumer Knowledge: Effects on Evaluation Processes Mediating Consumer Judgments," *Journal of Consumer Research,* June 1985, pp. 31–46.

34. Michael O'Neal, "Attack of the Bug Killers," *Business Week,* May 16, 1988, p. 81.

35. Richard E. Petty, John T. Cacioppo, and David Schumann, "Central and Peripheral Routes to Advertising Effectiveness: The Moderating Role of Involvement," *Journal of Consumer Research,* September 1983, pp. 135–44.

36. Peter L. Wright and Barton Weitz, "Time Horizon Effects on Product Evaluation Strategies," *Journal of Marketing Research,* November 1977, pp. 429–43.

37. Christine Moorman, "The Effects of Stimulus and Consumer Characteristics on the Utilization of Nutrition Information," *Journal of Consumer Research,* December 1990, pp. 362–74.

38. Deborah J. MacInnis and Linda L. Price, "The Role of Imagery in Information Processing: Review and Extensions," *Journal of Consumer Research,* March 1987, pp. 473–91; and Elizabeth C. Hirschman, "Point of View: Sacred, Secular, and Mediating Consumption Imagery in Television Commercials," *Journal of Advertising Research,* December–January 1991, pp. 38–43.

39. Ronald Alsop, "Marketing: The Slogan's Familiar, but What's the Brand?" *The Wall Street Journal,* January 8, 1988, p. B1.

40. Jacob Jacoby and Wayne D. Hoyer, "Viewer Miscomprehension of Televised Communication: Selected Findings," *Journal of Marketing,* Fall 1982, pp. 12–26; and Jacob Jacoby and Wayne D. Hoyer, "The Comprehension/Miscomprehension of Print Communication: Selected Findings," *Journal of Consumer Research,* March 1989, pp. 434–43.

41. Some researchers feel these estimates are too high, because there are problems in measuring miscomprehension. See Gary T. Ford and Richard Yalch, "Viewer Miscomprehension of Televised Communication—A Comment," *Journal of Marketing,* Fall 1982, pp. 27–31; and Richard W. Mizerski, "Viewer Miscomprehension Findings Are Measurement Bound," *Journal of Marketing,* Fall 1982, pp. 32–34.

42. Gary T. Ford and John E. Calfee, "Recent Developments in FTC Policy on Deceptions," *Journal of Marketing,* July 1986, pp. 82–103; and Ivan L. Preston and Jef I. Richards, "The Relationship of Miscomprehension to Deceptiveness in FTC Cases," in *Advances in Consumer Research,* vol. 13, ed. Richard J. Lutz (Provo, Utah: Association for Consumer Research, 1986), pp. 138–42.

43. Bruce Ingersoll, "FDA Takes On 'No Cholesterol' Claims," *The Wall Street Journal,* May 15, 1991, pp. B1, B10.

44. Chris Janiszewski, "The Influence of Print Advertisment Organization on Affect toward a Brand Name," *Journal of Consumer Research,* June 1990, pp. 53–65; James M. Munch and Jack L. Swasy, "Rhetorical Questions, Summarization Frequency, and Argument Strength Effects on Recall," *Journal of Consumer Research,* June 1988, pp. 69–76; and Thomas J. Olney, Morris B. Holbrook, and Rajeev Batra, "Consumer Responses to Advertising: The Effects of Ad Content, Emotions, and Attitude toward the Ad on Viewing Time," *Journal of Consumer Research,* March 1991, pp. 440–53.

45. Jacob Jacoby, Robert W. Chestnut, and William Silberman, "Consumer Use and Comprehension of Nutrition Information," *Journal of Consumer Research,* September 1977, pp. 119–28; and Joyce A. Vermeersch and Helene Swenerton, "Interpretations of Nutrition Claims in Food Advertisements by Low-Income Consumers," *Journal of Nutrition Education,* January–March 1980, pp. 19–25; and Moorman, "The Effects of Stimulus."

Chapter 7

1. Adapted from Michael H. Dale, "How We Rebuilt Jaguar in the U.S.," *Fortune,* April 29, 1986, pp. 110–19.

2. Martin Fishbein and Icek Ajzen, *Belief, Attitude, Intention, and Behavior: An Introduction to Theory and Research* (Reading, Mass.: Addison-Wesley, 1975); and Martin Fishbein, "Attitude, Attitude Change, and Behavior: A Theoretical Overview," in *Attitude Research Bridges the Atlantic,* ed. Philip Levine (Chicago: American Marketing Association, 1975), pp. 3–16.

3. Many authors have defined attitudes in this way, including Russell H. Fazio, "How Do Attitudes Guide Behavior?" in *Handbook of Motivation and Cognition: Foundations of Social Behavior,* ed. R. M. Sorrentino and E. T. Higgins (New York: Guilford Press, 1986), pp. 204–43.

4. For an excellent overview, see Elnora W. Stuart, Terence A. Shimp, and Randall W. Engle, "Classical Conditioning of Consumer Attitudes: Four Experiments in an Advertising Context," *Journal of Consumer Research,* December 1987, pp. 334–49; also see Chris T. Allen and Thomas J. Madden, "A Closer Look at Classical Conditioning," *Journal of Consumer Research,* December 1985, pp. 301–15; Terence A. Shimp, Elnora W. Stuart, and Randall W. Engle, "A Program of Classical Conditioning Experiments Testing Variations in the Conditioned Stimulus and Context," *Journal of Consumer Research,* June 1991, pp. 1–12.

5. Alain d'Astous and Marc Dubuc, "Retrieval Processes in Consumer Evaluative Judgment Making: The Role of Elaborative Processing," in *Advances in Consumer Research,* vol. 13, ed. Richard J. Lutz (Provo, Utah: Association for Consumer Research, 1986), pp. 132–37; Paul W. Miniard, Thomas J. Page, April Atwood, and Randall L. Ross, "Representing Attitude Structure: Issues and Evidence," in *Advances in Consumer Research,* vol. 13, ed. Richard J. Lutz (Provo, Utah: Association for Consumer Research, 1986), pp. 72–76; Russell H. Fazio, Martha C. Powell, and Carol J. Williams, "The Role of Attitude Accessibility in the Attitude-to-Behavior Process," *Journal of Consumer Research,* December 1989, pp. 280–88; and Ida E. Berger and Andrew A. Mitchell, "The Effect of Advertising on Attitude Accessibility, Attitude Confidence, and the Attitude-Behavior Relationship," *Journal of Consumer Research,* December 1989, pp. 269–79.

6. Kenneth E. Miller and James L. Ginter, "An Investigation of Situational Variation in Brand Choice Behavior and Attitude," *Journal of Marketing Research,* February 1979, pp. 111–23.

7. This section draws on Peter H. Farquhar, "Managing Brand Equity," *Marketing Research,* September 1989, pp. 24–33.

8. Norman C. Berry, "Revitalizing Brands," *Journal of Consumer Marketing,* Summer 1988, pp. 15–20.

9. David M. Boush and Barbara Loken, "A Process-Tracing Study of Brand Extension Evaluation," *Journal of Marketing Research,* February 1991, pp. 16–28; and C. Whan Park, Sandra Milberg, and Robert Lawson, "Evaluation of Brand Extensions: The Role of Product Feature Similarity and Brand Concept Consistency," *Journal of Consumer Research,* September 1991, pp. 185–93.

10. This example is adapted from John Merwin, "The Sad Case of the Dwindling Orange Roofs," *Forbes,* December 30, 1985, pp. 75–79.

11. Fishbein and Ajzen, *Belief, Attitude, Intention, and Behavior;* and Andrew A. Mitchell and Jerry C. Olson, "Are Product Attributes the Only Mediators of Advertising Effects on Brand Attitude?" *Journal of Marketing Research,* August 1981, pp. 318–32.

12. Susan B. Hester and Mary Yuen, "The Influence of Country of Origin on Consumer Attitudes and Buying Behavior in the United States and Canada," in *Advances in Consumer Research,* vol. 14, ed. Melanie Wallendorf and Paul Anderson (Provo, Utah: Association for Consumer Research, 1987), pp. 538–42; and Sung-Tai Hong and Robert S. Wyer, "Determinants of Product Evaluation: Effects of the Time Interval between Knowledge of a Product's Country of Origin and Information about Its Specific Attributes," *Journal of Consumer Research,* December 1990, pp. 277–88.

13. See William L. Wilkie and Edgar A. Pessemier, "Issues in Marketing's Use of Multiattribute Attitude Models," *Journal of Marketing Research,* November 1973, pp. 428–41. Relatively little work has investigated the integration process itself—see Joel B. Cohen, Paul W. Miniard, and Peter R. Dickson, "Information Integration: An Information Processing Perspective," in *Advances in Consumer Research,* vol. 11, ed. Thomas C. Kinnear (Ann Arbor, Mich.: Association for Consumer Research, 1980), pp. 161–70. Another influential model, particularly in the early days of marketing research on attitudes, was developed by Milton J. Rosenberg, "Cognitive Structure and Attitudinal Affect," *Journal of Abnormal and Social Psychology,* November 1956, pp. 367–72. Although different terminology is used, the structure of Rosenberg's model is quite similar to Fishbein's.

14. Fishbein and Ajzen, *Belief, Attitude, Intention, and Behavior.*

15. Ibid.

16. See Philip A. Dover and Jerry C. Olson, "Dynamic Changes in an Expectancy-Value Attitude Model as a Function of Multiple Exposures to Product Information," in *Contemporary Marketing Thought,* ed. B. A. Greenberg and D. N. Dellenger (Chicago: American Marketing Association, 1977), pp. 455–59; Robert E. Smith and William R. Swinyard, "Information Response Models: An Integrated Approach," *Journal of Marketing,* Winter 1982, pp. 81–93; and Russell H. Fazio and Mark P. Zanna, "Attitudinal Qualities Relating to the Strength of the Attitude-Behavior Relationship," *Journal of Experimental Social Psychology,* 14 (1987), pp. 398–408.

17. Richard J. Lutz and James R. Bettman, "Multiattribute Models in Marketing: A Bicentennial Review," in *Consumer and Industrial Buying Behavior,* ed. A. G. Woodside, J. N. Sheth, and P. D. Bennett (New York: Elsevier-North Holland Publishing, 1977), pp. 137–50.

18. Monci Jo Williams, "Why Is Airline Food So Terrible?" *Fortune,* December 19, 1988, pp. 169–72.

19. Christopher Power, Walecia Konrad, Alice Z. Cuneo, and James B. Treece, "Value Marketing: Quality, Service, and Fair Pricing Are the Keys to Selling in the 90s," *Business Week,* November 11, 1991, pp. 132–40.

20. John B. Palmer and Russ H. Crupnick, "New Dimensions Added to Conjoint Analysis," *Marketing News,* January 3, 1986, p. 62.

21. Richard J. Lutz, "Changing Brand Attitudes through Modification of Cognitive Structure," *Journal of Consumer Research,* March 1975, pp. 49–59; and Andrew A. Mitchell, "The Effect of Verbal and Visual Components of Advertisements on Brand Attitudes and Attitude toward the Advertisement," *Journal of Consumer Research,* June 1986, pp. 12–24.

22. Keith H. Hammonds, "'Has-Beens' Have Been Very Good to Hasbro," *Business Week,* August 5, 1991, pp. 76–77.

23. Frank Rose, "If It Feels Good, It Must Be Bad," *Fortune,* October 21, 1991, pp. 91–108.

24. Martin Fishbein, "An Overview of the Attitude Construct," in *A Look Back, A Look Ahead,* ed. G. B. Hafer (Chicago: American Marketing Association, 1980), p. 3.

25. See Icek Ajzen and Martin Fishbein, "Attitude-Behavior Relations: A Theoretical Analysis and Review of Empirical Research," *Psychological Bulletin,* September 1977, pp. 888–918; and Alan W. Wicker, "Attitudes versus Action: The Relationship of Verbal and Overt Behavioral Responses to Attitude Objects," *Journal of Social Issues* 25 (1969), pp. 41–78.

26. See Fishbein, "An Overview of the Attitude Construct," pp. 1–19; and Fishbein and Ajzen, *Belief, Attitude, Intentions, and Behavior.*

27. Icek Ajzen and Martin Fishbein, *Understanding Attitudes and Predicting Social Behavior* (Englewood Cliffs, N.J.: Prentice Hall, 1980); and Fishbein and Ajzen, *Belief, Attitude, Intention, and Behavior.* Note that choosing behavior with positive consequences is consistent with our means-end chain conceptualization of consumers' product knowledge.

28. For a detailed exposition, see Terence A. Shimp and Alican Kavas, "The Theory of Reasoned Action Applied to Coupon Usage," *Journal of Consumer Research,* December 1984, pp. 795–809.

29. Ajzen and Fishbein, "Attitude-Behavior Relations: A Theoretical Analysis and Review of Empirical Research," pp. 888–918.

30. Richard P. Baggozzi and Paul R. Warshaw, "Trying to Consume," *Journal of Consumer Research,* September 1990, pp. 127–40.

31. Barbara Loken, "Effects of Uniquely Purchase Information on Attitudes toward Objects and Attitudes toward Behaviors," in *Advances in Consumer Research,* vol. 10, ed. R. P. Baggozzi and A. M. Tybout (Ann Arbor, Mich.: Association for Consumer Research, 1983), pp. 88–93.

32. Some researchers have argued that the strong distinction between A_{act} and SN may not be justified. See articles by Paul W. Miniard and Joel B. Cohen, "Isolating Attitudinal and Normative Influences in Behavioral Intentions Models," *Journal of Marketing Research,* February 1979, pp. 102–10; and Paul W. Miniard and Joel B. Cohen, "An Examination of the Fishbein-Ajzen Behavioral Intentions Model's Concepts and Measures," *Journal of Experimental Social Psychology* 17 (1981), pp. 309–39. Alternatively, the underlying salient beliefs for both A_{act} and SN could be considered as one set of activated beliefs that are combined to form a single, global A_{act}. One version of such a model is proposed by Paul W. Miniard and Joel B. Cohen, "Modeling Personal and Normative Influences on Behavior," *Journal of Consumer Research,* September 1983, pp. 169–80. For simplicity, however, we follow the separate approach advocated by the theory of reasoned action.

33. Pat McIntryre, Mark A. Barnett, Richard Harris, James Shanteau, John Skowronski, and Michael Klassen, "Psychological Factors Influencing Decisions to Donate Organs," in *Advances in Consumer Research,* vol. 14, ed. Melanie Wallendorf and Paul Anderson (Provo, Utah: Association for Consumer Research, 1987), pp. 331–34; William O. Bearden and Randall L. Rose, "Attention to Social Comparison Information: An Individual Difference Factor Affecting Consumer Conformity," *Journal of Consumer Research,* March 1990, pp. 461–71.

34. Cited in Kenneth A. Longman, "Promises, Promises," in *Attitude Research on the Rocks,* ed. L. Adler and L. Crespi (Chicago: American Marketing Association, 1968), pp. 28–37.

35. Ibid.

36. For an interesting discussion of this issue, see Gordon R. Foxall, "Consumers' Intentions and Behavior: A Note on Research and a Challenge to Researchers," *Journal of the Market Research Society* 26 (1985), pp. 231–41.

Chapter 8

1. Adapted from Barbara Hayes-Roth, "Opportunism in Consumer Behavior," in *Advances in Consumer Research,* vol. 9, ed. A. A. Mitchell (Ann Arbor, Mich.: Association for Consumer Research, 1982), pp. 132–35.

2. Flemming Hansen, "Psychological Theories of Consumer Choice," *Journal of Consumer Research,* December 1976, pp. 117–42.

3. Richard W. Olshavsky and Donald H. Granbois, "Consumer Decision Making—Fact or Fiction?" *Journal of Consumer Research,* September 1979, pp. 93–100.

4. A similar notion is presented by Girish N. Punj and David W. Stewart, "An Interaction Framework of Consumer Decision Making," *Journal of Consumer Research,* September 1983, pp. 181–96.

5. Daniel Kahneman and Amos Tyersky, "Choices, Values, and Frames," *American Psychologist* 39 (1984), pp. 341–50; Christopher P. Puto, "The Framing of Buying Decisions," *Journal of Consumer Research,* December 1987, pp. 301–15; William J. Qualls and Christopher P. Puto, "Organizational Climate and Decision Framing: An Integrated Approach to Analyzing Industrial Buying Decisions," *Journal of Marketing Research,* May 1989, pp. 179–92; James R. Bettman and Mita Sujan, "Effects of Framing on Evaluation of Comparable and Noncomparable Alternatives by Experts and Novice Consumers," *Journal of Consumer Research,* September 1987, pp. 141–54; Joshua L. Wiener, James W. Gentry, and Ronald K. Miller, "The Framing of the Insurance Purchase Decision," in *Advances in Consumer Research,* vol. 13, ed. Richard J. Lutz (Provo, Utah: Association for Consumer Research, 1986), pp. 257–62; and Peter Wright and Peter D. Rip, "Product Class Advertising Effects on First-Time Buyers' Decision Strategies," *Journal of Consumer Research,* September 1980, pp. 176–88.

6. Lawrence A. Crosby and James R. Taylor, "Effects of Consumer Information and Education in Cognition and Choice," *Journal of Consumer Research,* June 1981, pp. 43–56; John G. Lynch and Thomas K. Srull, "Memory and Attentional Factors in Consumer Choice: Concepts and Research Methods," *Journal of Consumer Research,* June 1982, pp. 18–37; Gabriel Biehal and Dipankar Chakravarti, "Consumers' Use of Memory and External Information in Choice: Macro and Micro Perspectives," *Journal of Consumer Research,* March 1986, pp. 382–405; Gabriel Biehal and Dipankar Chakravarti, "Information Accessibility as a Moderator of Consumer Choice," *Journal of Consumer Research,* June 1983, pp. 1–14; and Valerie S. Folkes, "The Availability Heuristic and Perceived Risk," *Journal of Consumer Research,* June 1988, pp. 13–23.

7. Peter H. Bloch, Daniel L. Sherrell, and Nancy M. Ridgway, "Consumer Search: An Extended Framework," *Journal of Consumer Research,* June 1986, pp. 119–26.

8. David B. Klenosky and Arno J. Rethans, "The Formation of Consumer Choice Sets: A Longitudinal Investigation at the Product Class Level," in *Advances in Consumer Research,* vol. 15, ed. Michael J. Houston (Provo, Utah: Association for Consumer Research, 1988), pp. 13–18; John R. Hauser and Birger Wernerfelt, "An Evaluation Cost Model of Consideration Sets," *Journal of Consumer Research,* March 1990, pp. 393–408; and John H. Roberts and James M. Lattin, "Development and Testing of a Model of Consideration Set Composition," *Journal of Marketing Research,* November 1991, pp. 429–40.

9. John Howard and Jagdish N. Sheth, *The Theory of Buyer Behavior* (New York: John Wiley & Sons, 1969); and Prakash Nedungadi, "Recall and Consumer Consideration Sets: Influencing Choice without Altering Brand Evaluations," *Journal of Consumer Research,* December 1990, pp. 263–76.

10. Sharon E. Beatty and Scott M. Smith, "External Search Effort: An Investigation across Several Product Categories," *Journal of Consumer Research,* June 1987, pp. 83–95.

11. Wayne D. Hoyer and Steven P. Brown, "Effects of Brand Awareness on Choice for a Common, Repeat-Purchase Product," *Journal of Consumer Research,* September 1990, pp. 141–48.

12. William Baker, J. Wesley Hutchinson, Danny Moore, and Prakash Nedungadi, "Brand Familiarity and Advertising: Effects on the Evoked Set and Brand Preference," in *Advances in Consumer Research,* vol. 13, ed. Richard J. Lutz (Provo, Utah: Association for Consumer Research, 1986), pp. 637–42.

13. Kristian E. Moller and Pirjo Karppinen, "Role of Motives and Attributes in Consumer Motion Picture Choice," *Journal of Economic Psychology* 4 (1983), pp. 239–62.

14. Joel E. Urbany, Peter R. Dickson, and William L. Wilkie, "Buyer Uncertainty and Information Search," *Journal of Consumer Research,* September 1989, pp. 208–15.

15. Klaus G. Grunert, "Cognitive Determinants of Attribute Information Usage," *Journal of Economic Psychology* 7 (1986), pp. 95–124; and C. Whan Park and Daniel C. Smith, "Product-Level Choice: A Top-Down or Bottom-Up Process?" *Journal of Consumer Research,* December 1989, pp. 289–99.

16. John U. Farley, Jerrold Katz, and Donald R. Lehmann, "Impact of Different Comparison Sets on Evaluation of a New Subcompact Car Brand," *Journal of Consumer Research,* September 1978, pp. 138–42; Srinivasan Ratneshwar, Allan D. Shocker, and David W. Stewart, "Toward Understanding the Attraction Effect: The Implications of Product Stimulus Meaningfulness and Familiarity," *Journal of Consumer Research,* March 1987, pp. 520–33; Merrie Brucks and Paul H. Shurr, "The Effects of Bargainable Attributes and Attribute Range Knowledge on Consumer Choice Processes," *Journal of Consumer Research,* March 1990, pp. 409–19; Kim P. Corfman, "Comparability and Comparison Levels Used in Choices among Consumer Products," *Journal of Marketing Research,* August 1991, pp. 368–74; Noreen M. Klein and Manjit S. Yadav, "Context Effects on Effort and Accuracy in Choice: An Enquiry into Adaptive Decision Making," *Journal of Consumer Research,* March 1989, pp. 411–21; and Rashi Glazer, Barbara E. Kahn, and William L. Moore, "The Influence of External Constraints on Brand Choice: The Lone Alternative Effect," *Journal of Consumer Research,* June 1991, pp. 119–27.

17. Mark I. Alpert, "Unresolved Issues in Identification of Determinant Attributes," in *Advances in Consumer Research,* vol. 7, ed. Jerry C. Olson (Ann Arbor, Mich.: Association for Consumer Research, 1980), pp. 83–88.

18. Valerie S. Folkes, "The Availability Heuristic and Perceived Risk," *Journal of Consumer Research,* June 1988, pp. 13–23; and John W. Vann, "A Conditional Probability View of the Role of Product Warranties in Reducing Perceived Financial Risk," in *Advances in Consumer Research,* vol. 14, ed. Melanie Wallendorf and Paul Anderson (Provo, Utah: Association for Consumer Research, 1987), pp. 421–25.

19. Narasimhan Srinivasan and Brian T. Ratchford, "An Empirical Test of a Model of External Search for Automobiles," *Journal of Consumer Research,* September 1991, pp. 233–42; and Keith B. Murray, "A Test of Services Marketing Theory: Consumer Information Acquisition Activities," *Journal of Marketing,* January 1991, pp. 10–25.

20. Robert S. Billings and Lisa L. Scherer, "The Effects of Response Mode and Importance on Decision-Making Strategies: Judgment versus Choice," *Organizational Behavior and Human Decision-Processes* 41 (1988), pp. 1–19; and Peter Wright, "Consumer Choice Strategies: Simplifying versus Optimizing," *Journal of Marketing Research,* February 1975, pp. 60–67.

21. James R. Bettman and C. Whan Park, "Effects of Prior Knowledge and Experience and Phase of the Choice Process on Consumer Decision Processes: A Protocol Analysis," *Journal of Consumer Research,* December 1980, pp. 234–48; Joel B. Cohen, Paul W. Miniard, and Peter Dickson, "Information Integration: An Information Processing Perspective," in *Advances in Consumer Research,* vol. 7, ed. Jerry C. Olson (Ann Arbor, Mich.: Association for Consumer Research, 1980), pp. 161–70; Wayne D. Hoyer, "An Examination of Consumer Decision Making for a Common Repeat Purchase Product," *Journal of Consumer Research,* December 1984, pp. 822–29; and David J. Curry, Michael B. Menasco, and James W. Van Ark, "Multiattribute Dyadic Choice: Models and Tests," *Journal of Marketing Research,* August 1991, pp. 259–67.

22. James R. Bettman, *An Information Processing Theory of Consumer Choice* (Reading, Mass.: Addison-Wesley, 1979); Denis A. Lussier and Richard W. Olshavsky, "Task Complexity and Contingent Processing in Brand Choice," *Journal of Consumer Research,* September 1979, pp. 154–65; and Merrie Brucks and Andrew A. Mitchell, "Knowledge Structures, Production Systems and Decision Strategies," in *Advances in Consumer Research,* vol. 8, ed. Kent B. Monroe (Ann Arbor, Mich.: Association for Consumer Research, 1981).

23. Bettman and Park, "Effects of Prior Knowledge," pp. 234–48; and Hoyer, "An Examination of Consumer Decision Making for a Common Repeat Purchase Product," pp. 822–29.

24. James R. Bettman, "Presidential Address: Processes of Adaptivity in Decision Making," in *Advances in Consumer Research,* vol. 15, ed. Michael J. Houston (Provo, Utah: Association for Consumer Research, 1988), pp. 1–4; Surjit Chabra and Richard W. Olshavsky, "Some Evidence for Additional Types of Choice Strategies," in *Advances in Consumer Research,* vol. 13, ed. Richard J. Lutz (Provo, Utah: Association for Consumer Research, 1986), pp. 12–16; Wayne D. Hoyer, "Variations in Choice Strategies across Decision Contexts: An Examination of Contingent Factors," in *Advances in Consumer Research,* vol. 13, ed. Richard J. Lutz (Provo, Utah: Association for Consumer Research, 1986), pp. 32–36; James R. Bettman and Michel A. Zins, "Constructive Processes in Consumer Choice," *Journal of Consumer Research,* September 1977, pp. 75–85; Bettman and Park, "Effects of Prior Knowledge," 234–48; Hoyer, "Examination of Consumer Decision Making," pp. 822–29; John Payne, "Task Complexity and Contingent Processing in Decision Making," *Organizational Behavior and Human Performance* 16 (1976), pp. 366–87; and David Grether and Louis Wilde, "An Analysis of Conjunctive Choice: Theory and Experiments," *Journal of Consumer Research,* March 1984, pp. 373–85.

25. C. Whan Park and Richard J. Lutz, "Decision Plans and Consumer Choice Dynamics," *Journal of Marketing Research,* February 1982, pp. 108–15.

26. David K. Tse, Franco M. Nicosia, and Peter C. Wilton, "Consumer Satisfaction as a Process," *Psychology & Marketing,* Fall 1990, pp. 177–93.

27. Reviews of the literature on consumer satisfaction include Stephen A. Latour and Nancy C. Peat, "Conceptual and Methodological Issues in Consumer Satisfaction Research," in *Advances in Consumer Research,* vol. 6, ed. W. L. Wilkie (Ann Arbor, Mich.: Association for Consumer Research, 1979), pp. 431–37; and Denise T. Smart, "Consumer Satisfaction Research: A Review," in *Consumer Behavior: Classical and Contemporary Dimensions,* ed. J. U. McNeal and Stephen W. McDaniel (Boston: Little Brown, 1982), pp. 286–306.

28. See Marsha L. Richins, "Negative Word-of-Mouth by Dissatisfied Consumers: A Pilot Study," *Journal of Marketing,* Winter 1983, pp. 69–78; and Jagdip Singh, "Consumer Complaint Intentions and Behavior: Definitional and Taxonomical Issues," *Journal of Marketing,* January 1988, pp. 93–107.

29. See Richard L. Oliver, "A Cognitive Model of the Antecedents and Consequences of Satisfaction Decisions," *Journal of Marketing Research,* November 1980, pp. 460–69; Richard L. Oliver and Wayne S. DeSarbo, "Response Determination in Satisfaction Judgments," *Journal of Consumer Research,* March 1988, pp. 495–507; and Priscilla A. LaBarbara and David Mazursky, "A Longitudinal Assessment of Consumer Satisfaction/Dissatisfaction: The Dynamic Aspect of the Cognitive Process," *Journal of Marketing Research,* November 1983, pp. 393–404.

30. There are many sources on cognitive dissonance, stemming from the original work by Leon Festinger, *A Theory of Cognitive Dissonance,* (Stanford, Calif.: Stanford University Press, 1957).

31. This terminology comes from John Howard, *Consumer Behavior: Applications of Theory* (New York: McGraw-Hill, 1979).

32. Robert J. Meyer, "The Learning of Multiattribute Judgment Policies," *Journal of Consumer Research,* September 1987, pp. 155–73; and Lawrence W. Barsalou and J. Wesley Hutchinson, "Schema-Based Planning of Events in Consumer Contexts," in *Advances in Consumer Research,* vol. 14, ed. Melanie Wallendorf and Paul Anderson (Provo, Utah: Association for Consumer Research, 1987), pp. 114–18.

33. Kevin Lane Keller and Richard Staelin, "Effects of Quality and Quantity of Information on Decision Effectiveness," *Journal of Consumer Research,* September 1987, pp. 200–13.

34. Dennis W. Rook, "The Buying Impulse," *Journal of Consumer Research,* September 1987, pp. 189–99.

35. Interrupts are discussed by Bettman, *An Information Processing Theory of Consumer Choice*; also see Robert M. Schlinder, Michael Berbaum, and Donna R. Weinzimer, "How an Attention Getting Device Can Affect Choice among Similar Alternatives," in *Advances in Consumer Research,* vol. 14, ed. Melanie Wallendorf and Paul

Anderson (Provo, Utah: Association for Consumer Research, 1987), pp. 505–09.

Chapter 9

1. News release, "Reggie Winners Score Big on Brand Strategy," Promotion Marketing Association of America, 322 Eighth Avenue, Suite 1201, New York, NY, March 16, 1993.

2. C. Whan Park, Bernard J. Jaworski, and Deborah J. MacInnis, "Strategic Brand Concept Image Management," *Journal of Marketing,* October 1986, pp. 135–45; and Thomas J. Reynolds and Jonathan Gutman, "Advertising Is Image Management," *Journal of Advertising Research,* February–March 1984, pp. 27–37.

3. Kevin Higgins, "Billboards Put Nike Back in the Running," *Marketing News,* June 7, 1985, p. 7.

4. Felix Kessler, "The Costly Coupon Craze," *Fortune,* June 9, 1986, pp. 83–84; and Richard Gibson, "Recession Feeds the Coupon Habit," *The Wall Street Journal,* February 20, 1991, p. B1.

5. "McDonald's Olympic Promotion Gets the Gold."

6. Mary Ann Falzone, "Survey Highlights Lower Costs, Higher Productivity of Telemarketing," *Telemarketing Insider's Report* (Special Report, 1985), pp. 1–2.

7. Stewart W. Cross, "Can You Turn a 1985 Salesperson into a TSR?" *Telemarketing Insider's Report,* April 1985, p. 2.

8. Higgins, "Billboards Put Nike Back in the Running," p. 7.

9. Michael Wahl, "Eye POPping Persuasion," *Marketing Insights,* 1989, pp. 130–34.

10. W. E. Philips, "Continuous Sales (Price) Promotion Destroys Brands: Yes," *Marketing News,* January 16, 1989, pp. 4, 8; Bill Robinson, "Continuous Sales (Price) Promotion Destroys Brands: No," *Marketing News,* January 16, 1989, pp. 4, 8; Chris Sutherland, "Promoting Sales Out of a Slump," *Marketing Insights,* Winter 1990, pp. 41–43; and Wahl, "Eye POPping Persuasion."

11. Deborah J. MacInnis and Bernard J. Jaworski, "Information Processing from Advertisements: Toward an Integrative Framework," *Journal of Marketing,* October 1989, pp. 1–24.

12. Alan J. Bush and Gregory W. Boller, "Rethinking the Role of Television Advertising During Health Crises: A Rhetorical Analysis of the Federal AIDS Campaigns," *Journal of Advertising* 20, no. 1 (1991), pp. 28–37.

13. Brian Sternthal, Ruby Dholakia, and Clark Leavitt, "The Persuasive Effect of Source Credibility: Tests of Cognitive Response," *Journal of Consumer Research,* March 1978, pp. 252–60.

14. Jennifer Pendleton, "Robertson Believe-Ability: Star Presenter Oozes Honesty," *Advertising Age,* May 2, 1985, pp. 5, 49.

15. Lynn R. Kahle and Pamela M. Homer, "Physical Attractiveness of the Celebrity Endorser: A Social Adaptation Perspective," *Journal of Consumer Research,* March 1985, pp. 954–61; and John C. Mowen and Stephen W. Brown, "On Explaining and Predicting the Effectiveness of

Celebrity Endorsers," in *Advances in Consumer Research,* vol. 8, ed. Kent B. Monroe (Ann Arbor, Mich.: Association for Consumer Research, 1981), pp. 437–41.

16. David A. Aaker, Douglas M. Stayman, and Michael R. Hagerty, "Warmth in Advertising: Measurement, Impact, and Sequence Effects," *Journal of Consumer Research,* March 1986, pp. 365–81; Calvin P. Duncan, James E. Nelson, and Nancy T. Frontczak, "The Effect of Humor on Advertising Comprehension," in *Advances in Consumer Research,* vol. 11, ed. Thomas C. Kinnear (Ann Arbor, Mich.: Association for Consumer Research, 1984), pp. 432–37; Mary C. Gilly, "Sex Roles in Advertising: A Comparison of Television Advertisements in Australia, Mexico, and the United States," *Journal of Marketing,* April 1988, pp. 75–85; Michael A. Kamins and Henry Assael, "Two-Sided versus One-Sided Appeals: A Cognitive Perspective on Argumentation, Source Derogation, and the Effect of Disconfirming Trial on Belief Change," *Journal of Marketing Research,* February 1987, pp. 29–39; Leo Bogart and Charles Lehman, "The Case of the 30-Second Commercial," *Journal of Advertising Research,* February–March 1983, pp. 11–20; Morris B. Holbrook and Rajeev Batra, "Assessing the Role of Emotions as Mediators of Consumer Responses to Advertising," *Journal of Consumer Research,* December 1987, pp. 404–20; and George M. Zinkhan and Claude R. Martin, Jr., "Message Characteristics and Audience Characteristics: Predictors of Advertising Response," in *Advances in Consumer Research,* vol. 10, ed. Richard P. Baggozzi and Alice M. Tybout (Ann Arbor, Mich.: Association for Consumer Research, 1983), pp. 27–31.

17. Terry L. Childers, Michael J. Houston, and Susan E. Heckler, "Measurement of Individual Differences in Visual versus Verbal Information Processing," *Journal of Consumer Research,* September 1985, pp. 125–34; Julie A. Edell and Richard Staelin, "The Information Processing of Pictures in Print Advertisements," *Journal of Consumer Research,* June 1983, pp. 45–61; Andrew A. Mitchell, "The Effect of Verbal and Visual Components of Advertisements on Brand Attitudes and Attitude toward the Advertisement," *Journal of Consumer Research,* June 1986, pp. 12–24; and Deborah J. MacInnis and Linda L. Price, "The Role of Imagery in Information Processing: Review and Extensions," *Journal of Consumer Research,* March 1987, pp. 473–91.

18. John Deighton, Daniel Romer, and Josh McQueen, "Using Drama to Persuade," *Journal of Consumer Research,* December 1989, pp. 335–43.

19. Gregory W. Boller and Jerry C. Olson, "Experiencing Ad Meanings: Crucial Aspects of Narrative/Drama Processing," in *Advances in Consumer Research,* vol. 18, ed. R. Holman and M. Solomon (Provo, Utah: Association for Consumer Research, 1991), pp. 172–75.

20. Scott S. Liu and Patricia A. Stout, "Effects of Message Modality and Appeal on Advertising Acceptance," *Psychology and Marketing* 3 (1987), pp. 167–87.

21. See Peter H. Webb and Michael L. Ray, "Effects of TV Clutter," *Journal of Advertising Research,* June 1979, pp. 7–12; and Joanne Lipman, "Ads on TV: Out of Sight, Out of Mind," *The Wall Street Journal,* May 14, 1991, pp. B1, B8.

22. Scott Hume, "Coupon Use Jumps 10% as Distribution Soars," *Advertising Age,* October 5, 1992, pp. 3, 44.

23. Kapil Bawa and Robert W. Shoemaker, "The Effects of a Direct Mail Coupon on Brand Choice Behavior," *Journal of Marketing Research,* November 1987, pp. 370–76; P. S. Raju and Manoj Hastak, "Consumer Response to Deals: A Discussion of Theoretical Perspective," in *Advances in Consumer Research,* vol. 7, ed. Jerry C. Olson (Ann Arbor, Mich.: Association for Consumer Research, 1980), pp. 296–301; and Robert Blattberg, Thomas Biesing, Peter Peacock, and Subrata Sen, "Identifying the Deal Prone Segment," *Journal of Marketing Research,* August 1978, pp. 369–97.

24. For a review of various measures of advertising effectiveness, see David W. Stewart, Connie Pechmann, Srinivasan Ratneshwar, John Stroud, and Beverly Bryant, "Advertising Evaluation: A Review of Measures," in *Marketing Communications—Theory and Research,* ed. Michael J. Houston and Richard J. Lutz (Chicago: American Marketing Association, 1985), pp. 3–6. For a discussion of copy testing, see Benjamin Lipstein and James P. Neelankavil, "Television Advertising Copy Research: A Critical Review of the State of the Art," *Journal of Advertising Research,* April–May 1984, pp. 19–25; Joseph T. Plummer, "The Role of Copy Research in Multinational Advertising," *Journal of Advertising Research,* October–November 1986, pp. 11–15; and Harold M. Spielman, "Copy Research: Facts and Fictions," *European Research,* November 1987, pp. 226–31.

25. Lawrence D. Gibson, "Not Recall," *Journal of Advertising Research,* February–March 1983, pp. 39–46; Herbert E. Krugman, "Low Recall and High Recognition of Advertising," *Journal of Advertising Research,* February–March 1986, pp. 79–86; and Jan Stapel, "Viva Recall: Viva Persuasion," *European Research,* November 1987, pp. 222–25.

26. Jeffrey A. Trachtenberg, "Viewer Fatigue?" *Forbes,* December 26, 1988, pp. 120, 122.

27. Marvin E. Goldberg and Jon Hartwick, "The Effects of Advertiser Reputation and Extremity of Advertising Claim on Advertising Effectiveness," *Journal of Consumer Research,* September 1990, pp. 172–79; Jerry C. Olson, Daniel R. Toy, and Philip A. Dover, "Do Cognitive Responses Mediate the Effects of Advertising Content on Cognitive Structure?" *Journal of Consumer Research,* December 1982, pp. 245–62; Arno J. Rethans, John L. Swasy, and Lawrence J. Marks, "Effects of Television Commercial Repetition, Receiver Knowledge, and Commercial Length: A Test of the Two-Factor Model," *Journal of Marketing Research,* February 1986, pp. 50–61; and Daniel R. Toy, "Monitoring Communication Effects: A Cognitive Structure Cognitive Response Approach," *Journal of Consumer Research,* June 1982, pp. 66–76.

28. Jon Gutman and Thomas J. Reynolds, "Coordinating Assessment to Strategy Development: An Advertising Assessment Paradigm Based on the MECCAS Approach," in *Advertising and Consumer Psychology,* vol. 3, ed. Jerry Olson and Keith Sentis (New York: Praeger, 1987).

29. This section is adapted from John R. Rossiter and Larry Percy, *Advertising and Promotion Management* (New York: McGraw-Hill, 1987), pp. 129–64.

30. William T. Moran, "Brand Presence and the Perceptual Frame," *Journal of Advertising Research,* October–November 1990, pp. 9–16; and H. Rao Unnava and Robert E. Burnkrant, "Effects of Repeating Varied Ad Executions on Brand Name Memory," *Journal of Marketing Research,* November 1991, pp. 406–16.

31. Kevin Lane Keller, "Memory and Evaluation Effects in Competitive Advertising Environments," *Journal of Consumer Research,* March 1991, pp. 463–76.

32. Punam Anand and Brian Sternthal, "Ease of Message Processing as a Moderator of Repetition Effects in Advertising," *Journal of Marketing Research,* August 1990, pp. 345–53.

33. Banwari Mittal, "The Relative Roles of Brand Beliefs and Attitude toward the Ad as Mediators of Brand Attitude: A Second Look," *Journal of Marketing Research,* May 1990, pp. 209–19.

34. Cornelia Pechmann and David W. Stewart, "The Effects of Comparative Advertising on Attention, Memory, and Purchase Intentions," *Journal of Consumer Research,* September 1990, pp. 180–91.

35. Wahl, "Eye POPping Persuasion."

36. Aradhna Krishna, "Effect of Dealing Patterns on Consumer Perceptions of Deal Frequency and Willingness to Pay," *Journal of Marketing Research,* November 1991, pp. 441–51.

37. Richard E. Petty, John T. Cacioppo, and David Schumann, "Central and Peripheral Routes to Advertising Effectiveness: The Moderating Role of Involvement," *Journal of Consumer Research,* September 1983, pp. 135–46.

38. Richard L Celsi and Jerry C. Olson, "The Role of Involvement in Attention and Comprehension Processes," *Journal of Consumer Research,* September 1988, pp. 201–24; Deborah J. MacInnis and C. Whan Park, "The Differential Role of Characteristics of Music on High- and Low-Involvement Consumers' Processing of Ads," *Journal of Consumer Research,* September 1991, pp. 161–73; David W. Schumann, Richard E. Petty, and D. Scott Clemons, "Predicting the Effectiveness of Different Strategies of Advertising Variation: A Test of the Repetition-Variation Hypotheses," *Journal of Consumer Research,* September 1990, pp. 192–202; H. Rao Unnava and Robert E. Burnkrant, "An Imagery-Processing View of the Role of Pictures in Print Advertisements," *Journal of Marketing Research,* May 1991, pp. 226–31.

39. Manoj Hastak and Jerry C. Olson, "Assessing the Role of Brand-Related Cognitive Responses as Mediators of Communication Effects on Cognitive Structure," *Journal of Consumer Research,* March 1989, pp. 444–56; and John L. Swasy and James M. Munch, "Examining the Target of Receiver Elaborations: Rhetorical Question Effects on Source Processing and Persuasion," *Journal of Consumer Research,* March 11, 1985, pp. 877–86.

40. Andrew A. Mitchell and Jerry C. Olson, "Are Product Attribute Beliefs the Only Mediator of Advertising Effects on Brand Attitude?" *Journal of Marketing Research,* August 1981, pp. 318–32; Meryl Paula Gardner, "Does Attitude toward the Ad Affect Brand Attitude under a Brand Evaluation Set?" *Journal of Marketing Research,* May 1985, pp. 192–98; Thomas J. Olney, Morris B. Holbrook, and Rajeev Batra, "Consumer Responses to Advertising: The Effects of Ad Content, Emotions, and Attitude toward the Ad on Viewing Time," *Journal of Consumer Research,* March 1991, pp. 440–53; Scott B. MacKenzie, Richard J. Lutz, and George E. Belch, "The Role of Attitude toward the Ad as a Mediator of Advertising Effectiveness: A Test of Competing Explanations," *Journal of Marketing Research,* May 1986, pp. 130–43; Andrew A. Mitchell, "The Effect of Verbal and Visual Components of Advertisements on Brand Attitudes and Attitude toward the Advertisement," *Journal of Consumer Research,* June 1986, pp. 12–24; Pamela M. Homer, "The Mediating Role of Attitude toward the Ad: Some Additional Evidence," *Journal of Marketing Research,* February 1990, pp. 78–86; and Douglas M. Stayman and Rajeev Batra, "Encoding and Retrieval of Ad Affect in Memory," *Journal of Consumer Research,* May 1991, pp. 232–39.

41. Celsi and Olson, "The Role of Involvement," pp. 210–24; Hastak and Olson, "Assessing the Role of Brand-Related Cognitive Responses," pp. 444–56; and Deborah J. MacInnis, Christine Moorman, and Bernard J. Jaworski, "Enhancing and Measuring Consumers' Motivation, Opportunity, and Ability to Process Brand Information from Ads," *Journal of Marketing,* October 1991, pp. 32–53.

42. George E. Belch, "An Examination of Comparative and Noncomparative Television Commercials: The Effects of Claim Variation and Repetition on Cognitive Response and Message Acceptance," *Journal of Marketing Research,* August 1981, pp. 333–49; and Cornelia Droge and Rene Y. Darmon, "Associative Positioning Strategies through Comparative Advertising: Attribute versus Overall Similarity Approaches," *Journal of Marketing Research,* November 1987, pp. 377–88; Cornelia Pechmann and S. Ratneshwar, "The Use of Comparative Advertising for Brand Positioning: Association versus Differentiation," *Journal of Consumer Research,* September 1991, pp. 145–60; and Cornelia Droge, "Shaping the Route to Attitude Change: Central versus Peripheral Processing Through Comparative versus Noncomparative Advertising," *Journal of Marketing Research,* May 1989, pp. 193–204.

43. Jon Gutman, "Analyzing Consumer Orientations toward Beverages through Means-End Chain Analysis," *Psychology and Marketing* 3/4 (1984), pp. 23–43.

44. See David Berger, "Theory into Practice: The FCB Grid," *European Research,* January 1986, pp. 35–46; Richard Vaughn, "How Advertising Works: A Planning Model," *Journal of Advertising Research,* October 1980, pp. 27–33; and Richard Vaughn, "How Advertising Works: A Planning Model Revisited," *Journal of Advertising Research,* February–March 1986, pp. 57–66.

45. Roberto Friedman and V. Parker Lessig, "A Framework of Psychological Meaning of Products," in *Advances in Consumer Research,* vol. 13, ed. Richard J. Lutz (Provo, Utah: Association for Consumer Research, 1986), pp. 338–42.

46. Julie A. Edell, "Nonverbal Effects in Ads: A Review and Synthesis," in *Nonverbal Communication in Advertising,* ed. David Stewart and Sidney Hecker (Lexington, Mass.: Lexington Books, 1988); Werner Kroeber-Riel, "Emotional

Product Differentiation by Classical Conditioning," in *Advances in Consumer Research,* vol. 11, ed. Thomas C. Kinnear (Ann Arbor, Mich.: Association for Consumer Research, 1984), pp. 538–43; and Marian Chapman Burke and Julie A. Edell, "The Impact of Feelings on Ad-Based Affect and Cognition," *Journal of Marketing Research,* February 1989, pp. 69–83.

47. Belch, "An Examination of Comparative and Noncomparative Television Commercials," pp. 333–49; and William L. Wilkie and Paul W. Farris, "Comparison Advertising Problems and Potential," *Journal of Marketing,* October 1975, pp. 7–15.

48. Thomas J. Peters and Robert H. Waterman, Jr., *In Search of Excellence: Lessons from America's Best-Run Companies* (New York: Warner Books, 1982), p. 158.

49. Celsi and Olson, "The Role of Involvement," pp. 210–24; and C. Whan Park and S. Mark Young, "Consumer Response to Television Commercials: The Impact of Involvement and Background Music on Brand Attitude Formation," *Journal of Marketing Research,* February 1986, pp. 11–24.

50. Marian C. Burke and Julie A. Edell, "Ad Reactions over Time: Capturing Changes in the Real World," *Journal of Consumer Research,* June 1986, pp. 114–18.

51. Thomas J. Reynolds and John P. Rochon, "Means-End Based Advertising Research: Copy Testing Is Not Strategy Assessment," *Journal of Business Research* 22 (1991), pp. 131–42.

52. Material for this section is derived from Jerry C. Olson and Thomas J. Reynolds, "Understanding Consumers' Cognitive Structures: Implications for Advertising Strategies," in *Advertising and Consumer Psychology,* ed. Larry Percy and Arch Woodside (Lexington, Mass.: Lexington Books, 1983), pp. 77–90.

53. Thomas J. Reynolds and Alyce Byrd Craddock, "The Application of the MECCAS Model to the Development and Assessment of Advertising Strategy: A Case Study," *Journal of Advertising Research,* April–May 1988, pp. 43–54.

54. Thomas J. Reynolds and Charles Gengler, "A Strategic Framework for Assessing Advertising: The Animatic vs. Finished Issue," *Journal of Advertising Research,* June–July 1991, pp. 61–71.

Chapter 10

1. Robert C. Blattberg and Scott A. Neslin, *Sales Promotion: Concepts, Methods, and Strategies* (Englewood Cliffs, N.J.: Prentice Hall, 1990), p. 3.

2. J. Paul Peter and James H. Donnelly, Jr., *A Preface to Marketing Management,* 5th ed. (Homewood, Ill.: Richard D. Irwin, 1990), p. 151.

3. "Study: Some Promotions Change Consumer Behavior," *Marketing News,* October 15, 1990, p. 12.

4. For further discussion and examples of research, see Alan E. Kazdin, *Behavior Modification in Applied Settings,* 4th

ed. (Pacific Grove, Calif.: Brooks/Cole Publishing, 1989); and Lee Smith, "Getting Junkies to Clean Up," *Fortune,* May 6, 1991, pp. 103–8. Also, see recent issues of the *Journal of Applied Behavior Analysis.* For example, the Spring 1991 issue has a series of articles on improving safe driving.

Chapter 11

1. Much of the material in this chapter is based on Walter R. Nord and J. Paul Peter, "A Behavior Modification Perspective on Marketing," *Journal of Marketing,* Spring 1980, pp. 36–47; and J. Paul Peter and Walter R. Nord, "A Clarification and Extension of Operant Conditioning Principles in Marketing," *Journal of Marketing,* Summer 1982, pp. 102–7.

2. Gerald J. Gorn, "The Effects of Music in Advertising on Choice Behavior: A Classical Conditioning Approach," *Journal of Marketing,* Winter 1982, pp. 94–101.

3. Werner Kroeber-Riel, "Emotional Product Differentiation by Classical Conditioning," in *Advances in Consumer Research,* vol. 11, ed. Thomas C. Kinnear (Provo, Utah: Association for Consumer Research, 1984), pp. 538–43.

4. Richard A. Feinberg, "Classical Conditioning of Credit Cards: Credit Cards May Facilitate Spending," in *Proceedings of the American Psychological Association, Division of Consumer Psychology,* ed. Michael B. Mazis (Washington, D.C.: American Psychological Association, 1982), pp. 28–30; also see Richard A. Feinberg, "Credit Cards as Spending Facilitating Stimuli: A Conditioning Interpretation," *Journal of Consumer Research,* December 1986, pp. 348–56.

5. B. C. Deslauriers and P. B. Everett, "The Effects of Intermittent and Continuous Token Reinforcement on Bus Ridership," *Journal of Applied Psychology,* August 1977, pp. 369–75.

6. J. Ronald Carey, Stephen H. Clicque, Barbara A. Leighton, and Frank Milton, "A Test of Positive Reinforcement of Customers," *Journal of Marketing,* October 1976, pp. 98–100.

7. A. J. McSweeney, "Effects of Response Cost on the Behavior of a Million Persons: Charging for Directory Assistance in Cincinnati," *Journal of Applied Behavioral Analysis,* Spring 1978, pp. 47–51.

Chapter 12

1. Albert Bandura, *Principles of Behavior Modification* (New York: Holt, Rinehart & Winston, 1979), p. 167.

2. See Joseph R. Cautela, "The Present Status of Covert Modeling," *Journal of Behavior Therapy and Experimental Psychiatry,* December 1976, pp. 323–26.

3. Cautela, "Present Status," pp. 323–26.

4. Viola Catt and Peter L. Benson, "Effect of Verbal Modeling on Contributions to Charity," *Journal of Applied Psychology,* February 1977, pp. 81–85.

5. See Charles C. Manz and Henry P. Sims, "Vicarious Learning: The Influence of Modeling on Organizational Behavior," *Academy of Management Review,* January 1981, pp. 105–13. For discussions of model characteristics in advertising, see Michael J. Baker and Gilbert A. Churchill, Jr., "The Impact of Physically Attractive Models on Advertising Evaluations," *Journal of Marketing Research,* November 1977, pp. 538–55; "Models' Clothing Speaks to Ad Market: Study," *Marketing News,* November 22, 1985, p. 16; and Lynn R. Kahle and Pamela M. Homer, "Physical Attractiveness of the Celebrity Endorser: A Social Adaptation Perspective," *Journal of Consumer Research,* March 1985, pp. 954–61.

6. Manz and Sims, "Vicarious Learning," p. 107.

7. Albert Bandura, *Social Learning Theory* (Englewood Cliffs, N.J.: Prentice Hall, 1977), p. 89.

8. Mary Dee Dickerson and James W. Gentry, "Characteristics of Adopters and Nonadopters of Home Computers," *Journal of Consumer Research,* September 1983, pp. 225–35. Also see William E. Warren, C. L. Abercrombie, and Robert L. Berl, "Characteristics of Adopters and Nonadopters of Alternative Residential Long-Distance Telephone Services," in *Advances in Consumer Research,* vol. 15, ed. Michael J. Houston (Provo, Utah: Association for Consumer Research, 1987), pp. 292–98.

Chapter 13

1. James B. Treece and Mark Landler, "Beep, Beep! There Goes Ford's Explorer," *Business Week,* January 28, 1991, pp. 60–61.

2. Sharon E. Beatty and Scott M. Smith, "External Search Effort: An Investigation across Several Product Categories," *Journal of Consumer Research,* June 1987, p. 84.

3. For a complete discussion of these issues, see Howard Beales, Michael B. Mazis, Steven Salop, and Richard Staelin, "Consumer Search and Public Policy," *Journal of Consumer Research,* June 1981, pp. 11–22.

4. "American Express Plays Its Trump Card," *Business Week,* October 24, 1983, p. 62; also see "Credit Cards: The U.S. Is Taking Its Time Getting 'Smart,'" *Business Week,* February 9, 1987, pp. 88–89.

5. Susan Caminiti, "What the Scanner Knows about You," *Fortune,* December 3, 1990, pp. 51–52; also see Jeffrey Rothfeder et al., "How Software Is Making Food Sales a Piece of Cake," *Business Week,* July 2, 1990, pp. 54–55; Dom Del Prete, "Advances in Scanner Research Yield Better Data Quicker," *Marketing News,* January 7, 1991, p. 54; and Howard Schlossberg, "IRI Expands Sales Tracking to Drugstores, Mass Merchandisers," *Marketing News,* May 27, 1991, pp. 1, 10.

Chapter 14

1. Adapted from Stephen P. Morin, "Interior Designer Sets Out to Make Casino that Relaxes Your Morality," *The Wall Street Journal,* January 10, 1983, p. 21.

2. Adapted from Jack Block and Jeanne H. Block, "Studying Situational Dimensions: A Grand Perspective and Some Limited Empiricism," in *Toward a Psychology of Situations: An Interactional Perspective,* ed. David Magnusson (Hillsdale, N.J.: Lawrence Erlbaum, 1981), pp. 85–102.

3. For example, see Robert J. Graham, "The Role of Perception of Time in Consumer Research," *Journal of Consumer Research,* March 1981, pp. 335–42; Laurence P. Feldman and Jacob Hornik, "The Use of Time: An Integrated Conceptual Model," *Journal of Consumer Research,* March 1981, pp. 408–19; Jacob Hornik, "Situational Effects on the Consumption of Time," *Journal of Marketing,* Fall 1982, pp. 44–55; and Jacob Hornik, "Subjective versus Objective Time Measures: A Note on the Perception of Time in Consumer Behavior," *Journal of Consumer Research,* June 1984, pp. 615–18.

4. See Fern Schumer Chapman, "Business's Push for More Daylight Time," *Fortune,* November 12, 1984, pp. 149–62.

5. See Debra A. Michal's, "Pitching Products by the Barometer," *Business Week,* July 8, 1985, p. 45; Ronald Alsop, "Companies Look to Weather to Find Best Climate for Ads," *The Wall Street Journal,* January 19, 1985, p. 27; and Fred Ward, "Weather, Behavior Correlated in New Market Test," *Marketing News,* June 7, 1985, p. 9.

6. See Mark Harris, "Evaluate Lighting Systems as a Marketing Device, Not Overhead," *Marketing News,* October 26, 1984, p. 1.

7. Joseph A. Bellizzi, Ayn E. Crowley, and Ronald W. Hasty, The Effects of Color in Store Design," *Journal of Retailing,* Spring 1983, pp. 21–45. Also see J. Edward Russo, Richard Staelin, Catherine A. Nolan, Gary J. Russell, and Barbara L. Metcalf, "Nutrition Information in the Supermarket," *Journal of Consumer Research,* June 1986, pp. 48–70.

8. Carl P. Zeithaml and Valarie A. Zeithaml, "Environmental Management: Revising the Marketing Perspective," *Journal of Marketing,* Spring 1984, pp. 46–53.

9. The figures and part of the discussion of store layout are based on J. Barry Mason, Morris L. Mayer, and Hazel F. Ezell, *Retailing,* 3rd ed. (Plano, Texas: Business Publications, Inc., 1988), pp. 244–77.

10. Gary F. McKinnon, J. Patrick Kelly, and E. Doyle Robinson, "Sales Effects of Point-of-Purchase In-Store Signing," *Journal of Retailing,* Summer 1981, pp. 49–63.

11. See Rockney G. Walters and Scott B. MacKenzie, "A Structural Equations Analysis of the Impact of Price Promotions on Store Performance," *Journal of Marketing Research,* February 1988, pp. 51–63; and V. Kumar and Robert P. Leone, "Measuring the Effect of Retail Store Promotions on Brand and Store Substitution," *Journal of Marketing Research,* May 1988, pp. 178–85.

12. J. B. Wilkinson, J. Barry Mason, and Christie H. Paksoy, "Assessing the Impact of Short-Term Supermarket Strategy Variables," *Journal of Marketing Research,* February 1982, pp. 72–86.

13. Ronald E. Milliman, "Using Background Music to Affect the Behavior of Supermarket Shoppers," *Journal of Marketing,* Summer 1982, pp. 86–91.

14. Ibid., p. 91. For additional support for these ideas, see Ronald E. Milliman, "The Influence of Background Music on the Behavior of Restaurant Patrons," *Journal of Consumer Research,* September 1986, pp. 286–89.

15. See James H. Leigh and Claude R. Martin, "A Review of Situational Influence Paradigms and Research," in *Review of Marketing* (1981), ed. Ben M. Enis and Kenneth J. Reering (Chicago: American Marketing Association, 1981), pp. 57–74; Pradeep Kakkar and Richard J. Lutz, "Situational Influences on Consumer Behavior," in *Perspectives in Consumer Behavior,* 3rd ed., ed. Harold H. Kassarjian and Thomas S. Robertson (Glenview, Ill.: Scott, Foresman, 1981), pp. 204–15; and Joseph A. Cote, Jr., "Situational Variables in Consumer Research: A Review," Working Paper, Washington State University, 1985.

16. See Russell W. Belk, "The Objective Situation as a Determinant of Consumer Behavior," in *Advances in Consumer Research,* vol. 2, ed. Mary J. Schlinger (Chicago: Association for Consumer Research, 1975), pp. 427–38; and Richard J. Lutz and Pradeep K. Kakkar, "The Psychological Situation as a Determinant of Consumer Behavior, in *Advances in Consumer Research,* vol. 2, ed. Mary J. Schlinger (Chicago: Association for Consumer Research, 1975), pp. 439–54.

17. Geraldine Fennell, "Consumers' Perceptions of the Product Use Situation," *Journal of Marketing,* April 1978, pp. 38–47; Russell W. Belk, "Situational Variables and Consumer Behavior," *Journal of Consumer Research,* December 1976, pp. 156–64; Kenneth E. Miller and James L. Ginter, "An Investigation of Situational Variation in Brand Choice Behavior and Attitude," *Journal of Marketing Research,* February 1979, pp. 111–23.

18. Kenneth E. Miller and James L. Ginter, "An Investigation of Situational Variation in Brand Choice Behavior and Attitude," *Journal of Marketing Research,* February 1979, pp. 111–23.

19. J. Edward Russo, Richard Staelin, Catherine A. Nolan, Gary J. Russell, and Barbara L. Metcalf, "Nutrition Information in the Supermarket," *Journal of Consumer Research,* June 1986, pp. 48–70.

20. Dennis L. McNeill and William L. Wilkie, "Public Policy and Consumer Information: Impact on the New Energy Labels," *Journal of Consumer Research,* June 1979, pp. 1–11.

21. These examples come from Skip Wollenberg, "P-O-P Campaigns Increase as Profile of Shoppers Change," *Marketing News,* April 11, 1988, p. 25.

22. Joe Agnew, "P-O-P Displays Are Becoming a Matter of Convenience," *Marketing News,* October 9, 1987, pp. 14, 16.

23. J. Davis Illingworth, "The Personal Plus," *Marketing Insights,* Winter 1991, pp. 31–33, 45.

24. Illingworth, "The Personal Plus."

25. Antonio Fins, "Sunglass Huts: Thriving in Nooks and Crannies," *Business Week,* July 27, 1987.

26. Jeffrey A. Trachtenberg, "When a Mall's Biggest Retailers Fall, Surviving Shops Get an Unpleasant Jolt," *The Wall Street Journal,* October 25, 1990, p. B1, B8.

27. "Hallmark Now Marketing by Color," *Marketing News,* June 6, 1988, p. 18.

28. Meryl P. Gardner and George J. Siomkos, "Toward Methodology for Assessing Effects of In-Store Atmospherics," in *Advances in Consumer Research,* vol. 13, ed. Richard J. Lutz (Provo, Utah: Association for Consumer Research, 1986), pp. 27–31; and Robert J. Donovan and John R. Rossiter, "Store Atmosphere: An Environmental Psychology Approach, *Journal of Retailing,* Spring 1982, pp. 34–37.

29. Diane Schneidman, "Visual Aura, Kinetics Help Stabilize Store Image," *Marketing News,* October 23, 1987, p. 4.

30. Michael Solomon, "The Missing Link: Surrogate Consumers in the Marketing Chain," *Journal of Marketing,* October 1986, pp. 208–18.

31. Patricia Strnad, "Bars Tap 'Cheers' Name," *Advertising Age,* March 11, 1991, p. 16.

32. Elizabeth Ames and Geraldine Fabrikant, "Rich Melman: The Hot Dog of the Restaurant Business," *Business Week,* February 11, 1985, pp. 73–77; and Howard Riell, "Slumping Restaurant Industry Seeks New Marketing Ideas," *Marketing News,* February 18, 1991, pp. 2, 5.

33. Russell W. Belk, John Sherry, and Melanie Wallendorf, "A Naturalistic Inquiry into Buyer and Seller Behavior at a Swap Meet," *Journal of Consumer Research,* March 1988, pp. 449–70.

Chapter 15

1. Adapted from Grant McCracken, *Culture and Consumption: New Approaches to the Symbolic Character of Consumer Goods and Activities* (Bloomington, Ind.: Indiana University Press, 1988), chap. 1; and Janeen A. Costa, "Toward an Understanding of Social and World Systemic Processes in the Spread of Consumer Culture: An Anthropological Case Study," in *Advances in Consumer Research,* 17, ed. (Provo, Utah: Association for Consumer Research, 1991), pp. 826–32.

2. Over 160 definitions of culture are reported in Frederick D. Sturdivant, "Subculture Theory: Poverty, Minorities, and Marketing," in *Consumer Behavior: Theoretical Sources,* ed. Scott Ward and Thomas S. Robertson (Englewood Cliffs, N.J.: Prentice Hall, 1973), pp. 469–520.

3. McCracken, *Culture and Consumption.*

4. John F. Sherry, "The Cultural Perspective in Consumer Research," in *Advances in Consumer Research,* vol. 13, ed. Richard J. Lutz (Provo, Utah: Association for Consumer Research, 1986), pp. 573–75.

5. Ann Swidler, "Culture in Action: Symbols and Strategies," *American Sociological Review,* April 1986, pp. 273–86. Most consumer behavior textbooks focus on the content of culture, describing the values and lifestyles of consumers in different cultures. For example, see Leon G. Shiffman and Leslie Lazar Kanuk, *Consumer Behavior,* 4th ed. (Englewood Cliffs, N.J.: Prentice Hall, 1991); and William L. Wilkie, *Consumer Behavior,* 2nd ed. (New York: John Wiley & Sons, 1990).

6. Craig J. Thompson, William B. Locander, and Howard R. Pollio, "Putting Consumer Experience Back into Consumer Research: The Philosophy and Method of Existential-Phenomenology," *Journal of Consumer Research*, September 1989, pp. 133–47; and Craig J. Thompson, William B. Locander, Howard R. Pollio, "The Lived Meaning of Free Choice: An Existential-Phenomenological Description of Everyday Consumer Experiences of Contemporary Married Women," *Journal of Consumer Research,* December 1990, pp. 346–61.

7. Margot Hornblower, "Advertising Spoken Here," *Time,* July 15, 1991, pp. 71–72.

8. David Kilburn, "Japan's Sun Rises," *Advertising Age*, August 3, 1987, p. 42.

9. Sidney J. Levy, "Interpreting Consumer Mythology: A Structural Approach to Consumer Behavior," *Journal of Marketing,* Summer 1981, pp. 49–61.

10. Laurie Freeman, "Diaper Image Damaged: Poll," *Advertising Age,* June 11, 1990, pp. 1, 57.

11. This model is an adaptation and extension of the cultural process described by Grant McCracken, in *Culture and Consumption,* focusing on how cultural meanings are first transferred to products and then passed on to individuals.

12. Grant McCracken, "Culture and Consumption: A Theoretical Account of the Structure and Movement of the Cultural Meaning of Consumer Goods," *Journal of Consumer Research,* June 1986, pp. 71–84.

13. McCracken, *Culture and Consumption*, p. 79.

14. Jeffrey F. Durgee and Robert W. Stuart, "Advertising Symbols and Brand Names that Best Represent Key Product Meanings," *Journal of Advertising,* Summer 1987, pp. 15–24.

15. Elizabeth C. Hirschman, "The Creation of Product Symbolism," in *Advances in Consumer Research,* vol. 13, ed. R. J. Lutz (Provo, Utah: Association for Consumer Research, 1986), pp. 327–31.

16. For a brief discussion of the meaning transfer aspects of the fashion system see McCracken, "Culture and Consumption."

17. Mihaly Csikszentmihalyi and Eugene Rochberg-Halton, *The Meaning of Things: Domestic Symbols and the Self* (Cambridge: Cambridge University Press, 1981); Sidney J. Levy, "Interpreting Consumer Mythology: A Structural Approach to Consumer Behavior," *Journal of Marketing,* 1981, pp. 49–61. Michael Solomon, "The Role of Products as Social Stimuli: A Symbolic Interactionism Perspective," *Journal of Consumer Research,* December 1983, pp. 319–29.

18. Seth Lubove, "Going, Going, Sold!" *Forbes,* October 14, 1991, pp. 180–81.

19. Anne B. Fisher, "Coke's Brand-Loyalty Lesson," *Fortune,* August 5, 1985, pp. 44–46.

20. McCracken, *Culture and Consumption;* and Dennis W. Rook, "The Ritual Dimension of Consumer Behavior," *Journal of Consumer Research,* December 1985, pp. 251–64.

21. The last four rituals are described in McCracken, "Culture and Consumption," pp. 71–84.

22. John F. Sherry, Jr., "A Sociocultural Analysis of a Midwestern American Flea Market," *Journal of Consumer Research,* June, pp. 13–30.

23. Peter H. Bloch, "Product Enthusiasm: Many Questions, A Few Answers," in *Advances in Consumer Research,* vol. 13, ed. R. J. Lutz (Provo, Utah: Association for Consumer Research, 1986), pp. 61–65.

24. Russell W. Belk, "Gift-Giving Behavior," in *Research in Marketing,* vol. 2, ed. Jagdish Sheth (Greenwich, Conn.: JAI Press, 1979), pp. 95–126.

25. Michael R. Solomon, "Deep-Seated Materialism: The Case of Levi's 501 Jeans," in *Advances in Consumer Research,* vol. 13, ed. R. J. Lutz (Provo, Utah: Association for Consumer Research, 1986), pp. 619–22.

26. Edmund Sherman and Evelyn S. Newman, "The Meaning of Cherished Personal Possessions for the Elderly," *Journal of Aging and Human Development* 8, no. 2 (1977–78), pp. 181–92; and Terence A. Shimp and Thomas J. Madden, "Consumer-Object Relations: A Conceptual Framework Based Analogously on Sternberg's Triangular Theory of Love," in *Advances in Consumer Research,* vol. 15, ed. M. Houston (Provo, Utah: Association for Consumer Research, 1988), pp. 163–68.

27. Thomas Reynolds and Jonathan Gutman, "Advertising Is Image Management," *Journal of Advertising Research*, 1984, 24(1), pp. 27–36; for a similar viewpoint, see C. Whan Park, Bernard J. Jaworski, and Deborah J. MacInnis, "Strategic Brand Concept-Image Management," *Journal of Marketing,* October 1986, pp. 135–45.

28. Peter H. Farquhar, "Managing Brand Equity," *Marketing Research,* September 1989, pp. 24–33.

29. Russell W. Belk, "ACR Presidential Address: Happy Thought," in *Advances in Consumer Research,* vol. 14, ed. M. Wallendorf and P. Anderson (Provo, Utah: Association for Consumer Research, 1986), pp. 1–4.

30. This section is adapted from Grant McCracken, "Who Is the Celebrity Endorser? Cultural Foundations of the Endorsement Process," *Journal of Consumer Research,* December 1989, pp. 310–21.

31. Michael Schudson, *Advertising: The Uneasy Persuasion* (Chicago: University of Chicago Press, 1984), p. 212.

32. Joshua Levine, "The Sound of No Dealers Selling," *Forbes,* February 19, 1990, pp. 122–24.

33. Some foreign markets are not growing because of competition from television and home videos (box office receipts in Finland were down about 15 percent in 1990, for example). See Kathleen A. Hughes, "You Don't Need Subtitles to Know Foreign Film Folk Have the Blues," *The Wall Street Journal,* March 5, 1991, p. B1.

34. Hazel Rose Markus and Shinobu Kitayama, "Culture and Self: Implications for Cognition, Emotion, and Motivation," *Psychological Review* 98, no. 2 (1991), pp. 224–53.

35. Russell W. Belk, "Materialism: Trait Aspects of Living in the Material World," *Journal of Consumer Research,* December 1985, pp. 265–79.

36. Marsha L. Richins and Scott Dawson, "Measuring Material Values: A Preliminary Report of Scale Development," in *Advances in Consumer Research,* 17, eds. M. Goldberg, G. Gorn, and R. Pollay (Provo, Utah: Association for Consumer Research, 1990), pp. 169–75.

37. Scott Dawson and Gary Bamossy, "Isolating the Effect of Non-Economic Factors on the Development of a Consumer Culture: A Comparison of Materialism in the Netherlands and the United States," in *Advances in Consumer Research,* vol. 17, eds. (Provo, Utah: Association for Consumer Research, 1990), pp. 182–85.

38. Thompson et al., "The Lived Meaning of Free Choice."

39. Carla Rapoport, "How the Japanese Are Changing," *Fortune,* September 24, 1990, pp. 15–22.

40. Laurel Anderson and Marsha Wadkins, "Japan—A Culture of Consumption?" in *Advances in Consumer Research,* vol. 18, eds. R. Holman and M. Solomon (Provo, Utah: Association for Consumer Research, 1991), pp. 129–34; and Yumiko Ono, "Japan Becomes Land of the Rising Mall," *The Wall Street Journal,* February 11, 1991, pp. B1, B6.

41. For further discussion of these and many other examples, see David A. Ricks, *Big Business Blunders: Mistakes in Multinational Marketing* (Homewood, Ill.: Dow Jones-Irwin, 1983).

42. Lynne Reaves, "China's Domestic Ad Scene: A Paradox," *Advertising Age,* September 16, 1985, p. 76.

43. "Global Advertisers Should Pay Heed to Contextual Variations," *Marketing News,* February 13, 1987, p. 18.

44. See Anne B. Fisher, "The Ad Biz Gloms onto 'Global,'" *Fortune,* November 12, 1984, pp. 77–80. The examples in this section are taken from this article. Also see Bill Saporito, "Black & Decker's Gamble on 'Globalization,'" *Fortune,* May 14, 1984, pp. 40–48.

45. For example, see "Levitt: Global Companies to Replace Dying Multinationals," *Marketing News,* March 15, 1985, p. 15; Theodore Levitt, *The Marketing Imagination* (New York: The Free Press, 1983), chap. 2; and Theodore Levitt, "The Globalization of Markets," *Harvard Business Review,* May–June 1983, pp. 92–102.

46. Subrata N. Chakravarty, "The Croissant Comes to Harvard Square," *Forbes,* July 14, 1986, p. 69.

47. Christine Dugas and Marilyn A. Harris, "Playtex Kicks Off a One-Ad-Fits-All Campaign," *Business Week,* December 16, 1985, pp. 48–49.

48. Julie Skur Hill and Joseph M. Winski, "Good-bye Global Ads: Global Village Is Fantasy Land for Big Marketers," *Advertising Age,* November 16, 1987, pp. 22–36; and Joanne Lipman, "Marketers Turn Sour on Global Sales Pitch Harvard Guru Makes," *The Wall Street Journal,* May 12, 1988, pp. 1, 10.

49. McCracken, "Culture and Consumption," pp. 71–84.

Chapter 16

1. Fay Rice, "Wooing Aging Baby-Boomers," *Fortune,* February 1, 1988, pp. 67–77; and Susan B. Garland, "Those Aging Baby-Boomers," *Business Week,* May 20, 1991, pp. 106–12.

2. Alecia Swasy, "Changing Times," *The Wall Street Journal,* March 22, 1991, p. B6.

3. Gretchen Morgenson, "Where Can I Buy Some," *Forbes,* June 24, 1991, pp. 82–86.

4. Diane Crispell, "Guppies, Minks, and Ticks," *American Demographics,* June 1990, pp. 50–51.

5. Associated Press, "Survey: Age Is Not Good Indicator of Consumer Need," *Marketing News,* November 21, 1988, p. 6.

6. This discussion is based on Doris L. Walsh, "Targeting Teens," *American Demographics,* February 1985, pp. 20–25.

7. This discussion is based on Geoffrey Calvin, "What the Baby-Boomers Will Buy Next," *Fortune,* October 15, 1984, pp. 28–34.

8. Russell W. Belk, "Yuppies as Arbiters of the Emerging Consumption Style," in *Advances in Consumer Research,* vol. 13, ed. Richard J. Lutz (Provo, Utah: Association for Consumer Research, 1986), pp. 514–19.

9. This discussion is based on William Lazer, "Inside the Mature Market," *American Demographics,* March 1985, pp. 23–25.

10. Thomas Exter, "How Big Will the Older Market Be?" *American Demographics,* June 1990, pp. 30–32, 36.

11. Janet Neiman, "The Elusive Mature Market," *Ad Week,* April 6, 1987, p. 16; For a complete work on this market, see Charles D. Schewe, *The Elderly Market: Selected Readings* (Chicago: American Marketing Association, 1985). Also see Eleanor Johnson Tracy, "The Gold in the Gray," *Fortune,* October 14, 1985, pp. 137–38.

12. For example, see Janice Castro, "Is That You on TV, Grandpa?" *Time,* March 6, 1989, p. 53.

13. Joe Szczesny and Richard Woodbury, "A Nation on the Move," *Time,* April 29, 1991, pp. 30–31; and Jon Schwartz and Thomas Exter, "All Our Children," *American Demographics,* May 1989, pp. 34–37.

14. James P. Allen and Eugene Turner, "Where Diversity Reigns," *American Demographics,* August 1990, pp. 34–38.

15. Judith Waldrop, "Shades of Black," *American Demographics,* September 1990, pp. 30–34.

16. Cyndee Miller, "Toy Companies Release 'Ethnically Correct' Dolls," *Marketing News,* September 30, 1991, pp. 1, 2.

17. James R. Shiffman, "Uptown's Fall Bodes Ill for Niche Brands," *The Wall Street Journal,* January 22, 1990, pp. B1, B5; Alix M. Feedman, "Heileman, under Pressure, Scuttles PowerMaster Malt," *The Wall Street Journal,* July 5, 1991, pp. B1, B4.

18. Sigredo A. Hernandez and Carol J. Kaufman, "Marketing Research in Hispanic Barrios: A Guide to Survey Research," *Marketing Research,* March 1990, pp. 11–27.

19. Cyndee Miller, "Hispanic Media Expand; TV Has Strongest Appeal," *Marketing News,* January 21, 1991, pp. 1, 10.

20. This section is derived from Ed Fitch, "Is the Red Carpet Treatment Plush Enough?" *Advertising Age,* February 8, 1988, pp. S-1, S-15, 16.

21. Rohit Deshpande, Wayne D. Hoyer, and Naveen Donthu, "The Intensity of Ethnic Affiliation: A Study of the Sociology of Hispanic Consumption," *Journal of Consumer Research,* September 1986, pp. 214–20.

22. David A. Ricks, *Big Business Blunders: Mistakes in Multinational Marketing* (Homewood, Ill.: Dow Jones-Irwin, 1983), p. 70. Also see Edward C. Baig, "Buenos Dias, Consumers," *Fortune,* December 23, 1985, pp. 79–80.

23. The information in this section is from William O'Hare, "A New Look at Asian Americans," *American Demographics,* October 1990, pp. 26–31.

24. Dan Frost, "California's Asian Market," *American Demographics,* October 1990, pp. 34–37.

25. Joan Myers-Levy and Durairaj Maheswaran, "Exploring Differences in Males' and Females' Processing Strategies," *Journal of Consumer Research,* June 1991, pp. 63–70; and Floyd W. Rudmin, "German and Canadian Data on Motivations for Ownership: Was Pythagoras Right?" in *Advances in Consumer Research,* vol. 17, eds. M. Goldberg, G. Gorn, and R. Pollay (Provo, Utah: Association for Consumer Research, 1990), pp. 176–81.

26. Judith Waldrop, "Up and Down the Income Scale," *American Demographics,* July 1990, pp. 24–27, 30.

27. Thomas W. Osborne, "An American Mosaic," *Marketing Insights,* June 1989, pp. 76–83; and James W. Gentry, Patriya Tansuhaj, and Joby John, "Do Geographic Subcultures Vary Culturally," in *Advances in Consumer Research,* vol. 15, ed. Michael J. Houston (Provo, Utah: Association for Consumer Research, 1988), pp. 411–17.

28. Thomas Moore, "Different Folks, Different Strokes," *Fortune,* September 16, 1985, pp. 65–72.

29. Joel Garreau, *The Nine Nations of North America* (Boston: Houghton Mifflin, 1981).

30. For a critical perspective on this approach, see Lynn R. Kahle, "The Nine Nations of North America and the Value Basis of Geographic Segmentation," *Journal of Marketing,* April 1986, pp. 37–47. For a more detailed discussion, see Del I. Hawkins, Don Roupe, and Kenneth A. Coney, "The Influence of Geographic Subcultures in the United States," in *Advances in Consumer Research,* vol. 8, ed. Kent B. Monroe (Ann Arbor, Mich.: Association for Consumer Research, 1981), pp. 713–17.

31. Blayne Cutler, "Welcome to the Borderlands," *American Demographics,* February 1991, pp. 44–49, 57.

32. Ronald J. Faber, Thomas C. O'Guinn, and John A. McCarty, "Ethnicity, Acculturation, and the Importance of Product Attributes," *Psychology & Marketing,* Summer 1987, pp. 121–34; and Lisa N. Penaloza, "Immigrant Consumer Acculturation," in *Advances in Consumer Research,* 16, (Provo, Utah: Association for Consumer Research, 1989), pp. 110–18.

33. Larry Long, "Americans on the Move," *American Demographics,* June 1990, pp. 46–49.

34. Alan R. Andreasen, "Cultural Interpenetration: A Critical Consumer Research Issue for the 1990s," in *Advances in Consumer Research,* vol. 17, eds. M. Goldberg, G. Gorn, and R. Pollay (Provo, Utah: Association for Consumer Research, 1990), pp. 847–49.

35. Kalervo Oberg, "Cultural Shock: Adjustment to New Cultural Environments," *Practical Anthropologist* 7 (1960), pp. 177–82.

36. Raj Mehta and Russell W. Belk, "Artifacts, Identity, and Transition: Favorite Possessions of Indians and Indian Immigrants to the United States," *Journal of Consumer Research,* March 1991, pp. 398–411.

37. Richard P. Coleman, "The Continuing Significance of Social Class to Marketing," *Journal of Consumer Research,* December 1983, pp. 265–80. Much of the discussion in this part of the chapter is based on Coleman's view of social class as described in this article.

38. Ibid.

39. James E. Fisher, "Social Class and Consumer Behavior: The Relevance of Class and Status," in *Advances in Consumer Research,* vol. 14, ed. Melanie Wallendorf and Paul Anderson (Provo, Utah: Association for Consumer Research, 1987), pp. 492–96.

40. Adapted from Charles M. Schaninger, "Social Class versus Income Revisited: An Empirical Investigation," *Journal of Marketing Research,* May 1981, pp. 192–208.

Chapter 17

1. Peter Newcomb, "Hey, Dude, Let's Consume," *Forbes,* June 11, 1990, pp. 126–31.

2. Lakshman Krishnamurthi, "The Salience of Relevant Others and Its Effects on Individual and Joint Preferences: An Experimental Investigation," *Journal of Consumer Research,* June 1983, pp. 62–72.

3. C. Whan Park and V. Parker Lessig, "Students and Housewives: Differences in Susceptibility to Reference Group Influences," *Journal of Consumer Research,* September 1977, pp. 102–10; and William O. Bearden, Richard G. Netemeyer, and Jesse E. Teel, "Measurement of Consumer Susceptibility to Interpersonal Influence," *Journal of Consumer Research,* March 1989, pp. 473–81.

4. John W. Schouten and James H. Alexander, "Hog Heaven: The Structure, Ethos, and Market Impact of a Consumption Culture," a paper presented at the Annual Conference of the Association for Consumer Research, Chicago, October 1991.

5. William O. Bearden and Michael J. Etzel, "Reference Group Influences on Product and Brand Purchase Decision," *Journal of Consumer Research,* September 1982, pp. 183–94. The discussion in this section relies heavily on this excellent work.

6. David Brinberg and Linda Plimpton, "Self-Monitoring and Product Conspicuousness in Reference Group Influence,"

in *Advances in Consumer Research,* vol. 13, ed. Richard J. Lutz (Provo, Utah: Association for Consumer Research, 1986), pp. 297–300.

7. For further discussion and an alternative approach to studying reference group influences, see Peter H. Reingen, Brian L. Foster, Jacqueline Johnson Brown, and Stephen B. Seidman, "Brand Congruence in Interpersonal Relations: A Social Network Analysis," *Journal of Consumer Research,* December 1984, pp. 771–83.

8. Julia M. Bristor, "Coalitions in Organizational Purchasing: An Application of Network Analysis," in *Advances in Consumer Research,* vol. 15, ed. Michael J. Houston (Provo, Utah: Association for Consumer Research, 1988), pp. 563–68; Jacqueline Johnson Brown and Peter H. Reingen, "Social Ties and Word-of-Mouth Referral Behavior," *Journal of Consumer Research,* December 1987, pp. 350–62; and Peter H. Reingen, "A Word-of-Mouth Network," in *Advances in Consumer Research,* vol. 14, ed. Melanie Wallendorf and Paul Anderson (Provo, Utah: Association for Consumer Research, 1987), pp. 213–17.

9. Dorothy Leonard-Barton, "Experts as Negative Opinion Leaders in the Diffusion of a Technological Innovation," *Journal of Consumer Research,* March 1985, pp. 914–26.

10. Bearden and Etzel, "Reference Group Influences," p. 184.

11. Joel Rudd, "The Household as a Consuming Unit," in *Advances in Consumer Research,* vol. 14, ed. Melanie Wallendorf and Paul Anderson (Provo, Utah: Association for Consumer Research, 1987), pp. 451–52.

12. This section is adapted from Diane Crispell, "How to Avoid Big Mistakes," *American Demographics,* March 1991, pp. 48–50.

13. Sunil Gupta, Michael R. Hagerty, and John G. Myers, "New Directions in Family Decision Making Research," in *Advances in Consumer Research,* vol. 10, ed. Richard P. Baggozzi and Alice M. Tybout (Ann Arbor, Mich.: Association for Consumer Research, 1983), pp. 445–50; and Jagdish N. Sheth, "A Theory of Family Buying Decisions," in *Modes of Buyer Behavior, Conceptual, Quantitative, and Empirical,* ed. J. N. Sheth (New York: Harper and Row, 1974), pp. 17–33.

14. Dennis L. Rosen and Donald H. Granbois, "Determinants of Role Structure in Family Financial Management," *Journal of Consumer Research,* September 1983, pp. 253–85; and Irene Raj Foster and Richard W. Olshavsky, "An Exploratory Study of Family Decision Making Using a New Taxonomy of Family Role Structure," in *Advances in Consumer Research,* vol. 16, ed. T. K. Srull (Provo, Utah: Association for Consumer Research, 1989), pp. 665–70.

15. William J. Quails, "Household Decision Behavior: The Impact of Husbands' and Wives' Sex Role Orientation," *Journal of Consumer Research,* September 1987, pp. 264–79; Rosen and Granbois, "Determinants of Role Structure in Family Financial Management," Charles M. Schaninger, W. Christian Buss, and Rajiv Grover, "The Effect of Sex Roles on Family Economic Handling and Decision Influence," in *Advances in Consumer Research,* vol. 9, ed. Andrew A. Mitchell (Ann Arbor, Mich.: Association for Consumer Research, 1982), pp. 43–47; Daniel Seymour and Greg

Lessne, "Spousal Conflict Arousal: Scale Development," *Journal of Consumer Research,* December 1984, pp. 810–21; Harry L. Davis, "Decision Making within the Household," *Journal of Consumer Research,* March 1976, pp. 241–60; and George P. Moschis and Linda G. Mitchell, "Television Advertising and Interpersonal Influences on Teenagers' Participation in Family Consumer Decisions," in *Advances in Consumer Research,* vol. 13, ed. Richard J. Lutz (Provo, Utah: Association for Consumer Research, 1986), pp. 181–86.

16. George E. Belch, Michael A. Belch, and Gayle Ceresino, "Parental and Teenage Child Influences in Family Decision Making," *Journal of Business Research* 13 (1985), pp. 163–76; and Ellen R. Foxman, Patriya S. Tansuhaj, and Karin M. Ekstrom, "Family Members' Perceptions of Adolescents' Influence in Family Decision Making," *Journal of Consumer Research,* March 1989, pp. 482–91.

17. Alvin Burns and Donald Granbois, "Factors Moderating the Resolution of Preference Conflict in Family Automobile Purchasing," *Journal of Marketing Research,* February 1977, pp. 68–77; Alvin C. Burns and Jo Anne Hopper, "An Analysis of the Presence, Stability, and Antecedents of Husband and Wife Purchase Decision Making Influence Assessment and Disagreement," in *Advances in Consumer Research,* vol. 13, ed. Richard J. Lutz (Provo, Utah: Association for Consumer Research, 1986), pp. 175–80; Margaret C. Nelson, "The Resolution of Conflict in Joint Purchase Decisions by Husbands and Wives: A Review and Empirical Test," in *Advances in Consumer Research,* vol. 15, ed. Michael J. Houston (Provo, Utah: Association for Consumer Research, 1988), pp. 436–41; and William J. Quails, "Toward Understanding the Dynamics of Household Decision Conflict Behavior," in *Advances in Consumer Research,* vol. 15, ed. Michael J. Houston (Provo, Utah: Association for Consumer Research, 1988), pp. 442–48.

18. Kim P. Corfman and Donald R. Lehmann, "Models of Cooperative Group Decision-Making and Relative Influence: An Experimental Investigation of Family Purchase Decisions," *Journal of Consumer Research,* June 1987, pp. 1–13; Burns and Granbois, "Factors Moderating the Resolution of Preference Conflict," pp. 68–77; and Pierre Filiatrauit and J. R. Brent Ritchie, "Joint Purchasing Decisions: A Comparison of Influence Structure in Family and Couple Decision-Making Units," *Journal of Consumer Research,* September 1980, pp. 131–40; and Dennis L. Rosen and Richard W. Olshavsky, "The Dual Role of Informational Social Influence: Implications for Marketing Management," *Journal of Business Research* 15 (1987), pp. 123–44.

19. Rosann L. Spiro, "Persuasion in Family Decision Making," *Journal of Consumer Research,* March 1983, pp. 393–402.

20. Scott Ward, Donna M. Klees, and Daniel B. Wackman, "Consumer Socialization Research: Content Analysis of Post-1980 Studies, and Some Implications for Future Work," in *Advances in Consumer Research,* vol. 17, ed. M. E. Goldberg and G. Gorn (Provo, Utah: Association for Consumer Research, 1990), pp. 798–803; and George P. Moschis, "The Role of Family Communication in Consumer Socialization of Children and Adolescents," *Journal of Consumer Research,* March 1985, pp. 898–913.

21. Gilbert A. Churchill, Jr., and George P. Moschis, "Television and Interpersonal Influences on Adolescent Consumer Learning," *Journal of Consumer Research,* June 1979, pp. 23–35.

22. Sanford Grossbart, Les Carlson, and Ann Walsh, "Consumer Socialization Motives for Shopping with Children," *AMA Summer Educators' Proceedings* (Chicago: American Marketing Association, 1988); Bonnie B. Reece, Sevgin Eroglu, and Nora J. Rifon, "Parents Teaching Children to Shop: How, What, and Who?" *AMA Summer Educators' Proceedings* (Chicago: American Marketing Association, 1988), pp. 274–278; and Les Carlson and Sanford Grossbart, "Parental Style and Consumer Socialization of Children," *Journal of Consumer Research,* June 1988, pp. 77–94.

23. Ellen Graham, "Children's Hour: As Kids Gain Power of Purse, Marketing Takes Aim at Them," *The Wall Street Journal,* January 10, 1988, pp. 1, 24.

24. Karin M. Ekstrom, Patriya S. Tansuhaj, and Ellen Foxman, "Children's Influence in Family Decisions and Consumer Socialization: A Reciprocal View," in *Advances in Consumer Research,* vol. 14, ed. Melanie Wallendorf and Paul Anderson (Provo, Utah: Association for Consumer Research, 1987), pp. 283–87; Elizabeth S. Moore-Shay and Richard J. Lutz, "Intergenerational Influences in the Formation of Consumer Attitudes and Beliefs about the Marketplace: Mothers and Daughters," in *Advances in Consumer Research,* vol. 15, ed. Michael J. Houston (Provo, Utah: Association for Consumer Research, 1988), pp. 461–67; and Scott Ward, Thomas S. Robertson, Donna M. Klees, and Hubert Gatignon, "Children's Purchase Requests and Parental Yielding: A Cross-National Study," in *Advances in Consumer Research,* vol. 13, ed. Richard J. Lutz (Provo, Utah: Association for Consumer Research, 1986), pp. 629–32.

25. Susan E. Heckler, Terry L. Childers, and Ramesh Arunachalam, "Intergenerational Influences in Adult Buying Behaviors: An Examination of Moderating Factors," in *Advances in Consumer Research,* 16, ed. T. Srull (Provo, Utah: Association for Consumer Research, 1990), pp. 276–84; Patricia Sorce, Lynette Loomis, and Philip R. Tyler, "Intergenerational Influence on Consumer Decision Making," in *Advances in Consumer Research,* vol. 16, ed. T. Srull (Provo, Utah: Association for Consumer Research, 1990), pp. 271–75; and George P. Moschis, "Methodological Issues in Studying Intergenerational Influences on Consumer Behavior," in *Advances in Consumer Research,* vol. 15, ed. Michael J. Houston (Provo, Utah: Association for Consumer Research, 1988), pp. 569–73.

26. For a review of these issues, see Michael D. Reilly, "Working Wives and Convenience Consumption," *Journal of Consumer Research,* March 1982, pp. 407–18. Also see Charles M. Schaninger and Chris T. Allen, "Wife's Occupational Status as a Consumer Behavior Construct," *Journal of Consumer Research,* September 1981, pp. 189–96; and Charles B. Weinberg and Russell S. Winer, "Working Wives and Major Family Expenditures: Replication and Extension," *Journal of Consumer Research,* September 1983, pp. 259–63.

27. Gordon Green and Edward Welniak, "The Nine Household Markets," *American Demographics,* October 1991, pp. 36–40.

28. This section draws from Martha Farnsworth Riche, "The Postmarital Society," *American Demographics,* November 1988, pp. 22–26, 60.

29. Martha Farnsworth Riche, "The Future of the Family," *American Demographics,* March 1991, pp. 44–46.

30. Diane Crispell, "Three's a Crowd," *American Demographics,* January 1989, pp. 34–38.

31. For a review, see Patrick E. Murphy and William A. Staples, "A Modernized Family Life Cycle," *Journal of Consumer Research,* June 1979, pp. 12–22.

32. Ibid. For other approaches and discussion, see Frederick W. Derrick and Alane K. Lehfeld, "The Family Life Cycle: An Alternative Approach," *Journal of Consumer Research,* September 1980, pp. 214–17; Mary C. Gilly and Ben M. Enis, "Recycling the Family Life Cycle: A Proposal for Redefinition," in *Advances in Consumer Research,* vol. 8, ed. Andrew Mitchell (Ann Arbor, Mich.: Association for Consumer Research, 1982), pp. 271–76; Janet Wagner and Sherman Hanna, "The Effectiveness of Family Life Cycle Variables in Consumer Expenditure Research," *Journal of Consumer Research,* December 1983, pp. 281–91.

33. Martha Farnsworth Riche, "The Boomerang Age," *American Demographics,* May 1990, pp. 25–27, 30, 52.

34. Margaret Ambry, "The Age of Spending," *American Demographics,* November 1990, pp. 16–23, 52.

35. This section is adapted from Eugene H. Fram, "The Time Compressed Shopper," *Marketing Insights,* Summer 1991, pp. 34–39; and Eugene H. Fram and Joel Axelrod, "The Distressed Shopper," *American Demographics,* October 1990, pp. 44–45.

Chapter 18

1. Philip Kotler, "What Consumerism Means for Marketers," *Harvard Business Review,* May–June 1972, pp. 48–57. Also see Joseph V. Anderson, "Power Marketing: Its Past, Present, and Future," *Journal of Consumer Marketing,* Summer 1987, pp. 5–13.

2. For example, see Richard W. Olshavsky and Donald H. Granbois, "Consumer Decision Making: Fact or Fiction?" *Journal of Consumer Research,* September 1979, pp. 93–100.

3. For an excellent, comprehensive discussion of corrective advertising, see William L. Wilkie, Dennis L. McNeill, and Michael B. Mazis, "Marketing's 'Scarlet Letter': The Theory and Practice of Corrective Advertising," *Journal of Marketing,* Spring 1984, pp. 11–31.

4. Ann P. Harvey, *Contacts in Consumerism: 1980–1981* (Washington, D. C.: Fraiser/Associates, 1980).

5. Paul N. Bloom and Stephen A. Greyser, "The Maturing of Consumerism," *Harvard Business Review,* November–December 1981, pp. 130–39.

6. Gene R. Laczniak, "Framework for Analyzing Marketing Ethics," *Journal of Macromarketing,* Spring 1983, pp. 7–18.

7. Ibid.

▼ Credits and Acknowledgments

Chapter 1

p. 3 Grateful Dead's Jerry Garcia: Wide World Photo; **p. 6** Beta Research ad: Courtesy Beta Research Corporation; **p. 7** Blockbuster Video store: Courtesy Blockbuster Entertainment Corporation; **p. 10** Nonprofit ad: Courtesy American Cancer Society; **p. 11** Saturn ad: Courtesy Saturn Corporation.

Chapter 2

p. 15 Smith & Wesson ad: Courtesy Smith & Wesson; **p. 17** Canon ad: Courtesy Canon; **p. 19** Bed & Bath store: Frederick Charles; doctor's waiting room: Custom Medical Stock Photo/Chicago; **p. 23** Litterless™ Lunch Kits: Courtesy Rubbermaid Incorporated; **p. 24** Power Bar ad: Courtesy Power Food Inc.; **p. 25** Madonna 1984: Michael Putland/Retina Ltd.; Madonna 1990: Mark Allan/Globe Photos, Inc.

Chapter 3

p. 31 Woman buying shampoo: Melanie Carr/Zephyr Pictures; **p. 34** Rolex ad: Courtesy Rolex Watch USA, Inc.; **p. 35** Quaker Oats ad: Courtesy Quaker Oats Co.; Beano ad: Courtesy Beano; **p. 42** Lunchables ad: Courtesy of Oscar Mayer Foods Corporation. The Oscar Mayer rhombold and Lunchables are trademarks of Oscar Mayer Foods Corporation, Madison, Wisconsin; **p. 45** Buick ad: Featured with permission of Buick Motor Division; **p. 46** Gloria Jean's store: Courtesy Gloria Jean's Gourmet Coffees; **p. 48** Shimano ad: Courtesy Shimano American Corporation.

Chapter 4

p. 59 Rubbermaid products: Courtesy Rubbermaid Inc.; **p. 61** High school students: Roy Morsch/The Stock Market; **p. 63** Samsara ad: Courtesy Guerlain, Inc.; **p. 67** Haagen-Dazs ad: © 1991 Bartle Bogle Hegarty Ltd.; Agency: Bartle Bogle Hegarty; Copywriter: Larry Barker; Art Director: Rooney Carruthers; Photographer: Jeanloup Sieff; **p. 70** Norelco ad: © 1992 Norelco Consumer Products Company; **p. 73** Kids on Computers: Charles Gupton/The Stock Market.

Chapter 5

p. 81 Ultra Pampers: Michael J. Hruby; **p. 83** diet Coke ad: "diet Coke" is a registered trademark of the Coca-Cola Company and is used with permission; **p. 86** Dannon Yogurt ad: Courtesy The Dannon Company, Inc.; **p. 95** Jolly Rancher ad: Courtesy Leaf, Inc./Agency: Ayer Chicago; **p. 97** Taster's Choice: Courtesy McCann-Erickson Worldwide; **p. 99** Rally's restaurant: Michael J. Hruby; **p. 100** Reebok ad: Courtesy Reebok International Ltd.

Chapter 6

p. 107 People meter on TV: Courtesy A.C. Nielson Co.; **p. 110** 1-800-Flowers: Courtesy 800 FLOWERS; **p. 111** Au Bon Pain Cafe: Courtesy Au Bon Pain Co., Inc.; **p. 112** VideOcart photo: Courtesy VideOcart; **p. 116** Andersen bunny ad: Reprinted with permission of Andersen Consulting; **p. 117** Las Vegas signs: James Blank/Zephyr Pictures; **p. 125** Coors/Coor's cans: Courtesy R.J. Coor Naturals, Inc.; **p. 127** Nike forest ad: Courtesy Nike, Inc.

Chapter 7

p. 131 Jaguar ad: Courtesy Jaguar, Inc.; **p. 133** Absolut Vodka ads: Courtesy Carillon Importers, Ltd.; **p. 137** Bristol-Myers products: Courtesy Bristol-Myers Squibb Company; **p. 142** Store sale: Stock Imagery; **p. 144** Beef Council ad: Courtesy National Live Stock & Meat Board; **p. 149** Buying beer: Melanie Carr/Zephyr Pictures.

Chapter 8

p. 155 Looking at china: Melanie Carr/Zephyr Pictures; **p. 159** Bayer Select ad: © Sterling Winthrop Inc. Reprinted with permission of Sterling Winthrop Inc.; **p. 162** Supercomputer store: © Larry Ford; **p. 164** Southwest Airlines ad: Courtesy Southwest Airlines; **p. 169** Toyota Tercel ad: Courtesy Toyota Motor Sales USA, Inc.; **p. 172** Buying cereals: © Steve Winter/Black Star; **p. 173** Duracell ad: Courtesy Ogilvy & Mather.

Chapter 9

p. 181 Reggie awards: Courtesy Promotion Marketing Association of America; **p. 183** Nabisco display; Mike Clemmer/Picture Group; **p. 185** John Hancock Bowl: Otto Gruele Jr./AllSport USA; **p. 188** Suzuki ad: Courtesy American Suzuki Motor Corporation; **p. 190** Dispensing coupons: Courtesy Catalina Marketing; **p. 196** Cat food ad: Courtesy IAMS Company; **p. 199** Jean Patou ad: Courtesy Jean Patou.

Chapter 10

p. 223 Pepsi promotion: Courtesy: The Pepsi-Cola Company; **p. 226** Chevy truck ad: Courtesy General Motors Corporation; **p. 230** Circuit City tv sale: © Michael Grecco; **p. 232** Jewel ad: Courtesy Jewel Food Stores; **p. 234** Smartfood promotion: © 1993 Seth Resnick; **p. 235** Adopt a smoker and food choice ads: Courtesy American Cancer Society.

Chapter 11

p. 241 Buying lottery tickets: Rob Daemmrich/Stock Boston; **p. 244** Wrangler ad: Courtesy Wrangler/Agency: The Martin Agency; **p. 245** Candidate Clinton campaigning: Wide World Photos; **p. 247** Credit cards: Martha Bates/Stock Boston; **p. 249** Wal-Mart sign: Courtesy Wal-Mart Stores, Inc.; **p. 254** Generic items: Michael J. Hruby.

Chapter 12

p. 259 Nintendo: Courtesy Nintendo of America; **p. 261** Product demonstration: Ken Kerbs/Dot Pictures; **p. 266** MCI card ad: © MCI Communications Corporation, 1989; **p. 267** Russell shirt ad: Courtesy Russell Corporation; **p. 269** Soloflex ad: Courtesy Soloflex, Inc.; **p. 271** 3M ad: Courtesy 3M.

Chapter 13

p. 275 Explorer ad: Courtesy Ford Motor Co.; **p. 279** Paying by check: T. Collicot/Zephyr Pictures; Automated teller machine: Michael Krasowitz/FPG; Using credit card: Michael

Keller/FPG;   **p. 281** Transmedia card: Courtesy Transmedia Network Inc.; **p. 285** Discover storyboard: Courtesy Discover Card;   **p. 286** Coupons: © Joe Jacobson;   **p. 287** Avia ad: Courtesy Avia; **p. 290** BehaviorScan photo: Courtesy Information Resources Inc.   **p. 293** Gloria Jean's coupon: Courtesy Gloria Jean's Gourmet Coffees.

Chapter 14

p. 305 Caesar's: Courtesy Boardwalk Regency Corporation;   **p. 308** Japanese family: Brian Lovell/Nawrocki; **p. 310** Visine ad: Courtesy Pfizer, Inc. photo: David Langley; Lipton Iced Tea ad: Reprinted with permission of the Thomas J. Lipton Company;   **p. 313** In-store signage: Courtesy Albertson's;   **p. 321** KFC modular merchandising: Courtesy Kentucky Fried Chicken;   **p. 322** Nike Town store: Courtesy Nike, Inc.; photo by Strode Eckert ; **p. 324** West Edmonton Mall: Courtesy West Edmonton Mall.

Chapter 15

p. 331 Early consumerism: The Bettmann Archive;   **p. 334** Levi's ad: Courtesy Levi Strauss & Co.;   **p. 335** Open-air market in India: John Elk/Stock Boston; Wal-Mart Store: Courtesy Wal-Mart Stores, Inc.; **p. 344** Bottled waters: Michael J. Hruby; **p. 347** Family at Thanksgiving dinner: Mug Shots/The Stock Market;   **p. 352** Gatorade ad: Courtesy Quaker Oats;   **p. 354** Benetton ad: Courtesy Benetton Cosmetics.

Chapter 16

p. 359 Dockers ad: Courtesy Levi Strauss & Co.;   **p. 361** Shades of You ad: Courtesy Maybelline, Inc.;   **p. 365** Spanish Levi's ad: Courtesy Levi Strauss & Co.;   **p. 367** Freedent ad: Reprinted courtesy of the Wm. Wrigley Jr. Company;   **p. 370** *Padres* magazine: Courtesy Ser Padres;   **p. 379** Work for food: Leo Gradinger/Zephyr Pictures.

Chapter 17

p. 383 Turtlemania: Steve Vidler/Nawrocki Stock Photos;   **p. 386** Danskin ad: Courtesy Danskin;   **p. 388** Bikers: Michael Brohm/Nawrocki Stock Photos; **p. 395** Colgate storyboard: Courtesy Colgate-Palmolive Company;   **p. 397** Hispanic family: Mary Elenz Tranter;   **p. 402** Midas ad: Courtesy Midas International Corporation.

Chapter 18

p. 409 McDonald's CEO: Michael L. Abramson;   **p. 411** Buying microwaves: Bob Daemmrich/Stock Boston; **p. 415** AARP ad: Reprinted with permission AARP;   **p. 420** Miller ad: Courtesy Miller Brewing Company.

Glossary of Consumer Behavior Terms

abstract attributes   Intangible, subjective characteristics of the product, such as the quality of a blanket or the stylishness of a car.

accessibility   The probability that a meaning concept will be (or can be) activated from memory. Highly related to top-of-mind awareness and salience.

accidental exposure   Occurs when consumers come in contact with marketing information in the environment that they haven't deliberately sought out. Compare with *intentional exposure.*

acculturation   The process by which people in one culture or subculture learn to understand and adapt to the meanings, values, lifestyles, and behaviors of another culture or subculture.

activation   The essentially automatic process by which knowledge, meanings, and beliefs are retrieved from memory and made available for use by cognitive processes.

adopter categories   A classification of consumers based on the time of initial purchase of a new product. Typically, five groups are considered—Innovators, Early Adopters, Early Majority, Late Majority, and Laggards.

adoption curve   A visual representation of the cumulative percentage of persons who adopt a new product across time.

adoption process   An ambiguous term sometimes used to refer to a model of stages in the purchase process ranging from awareness to knowledge, evaluation, trial, and adoption. In other cases, it is used as a synonym for the diffusion process.

advertising   Any paid, nonpersonal presentation of information about a product, brand, company, or store.

affect   A basic mode of psychological response that involves a general positive/negative feeling and varying levels of activation or arousal of the physiological system that consumers experience in their bodies. Compare with *cognition.* See also *affective responses.*

affective and cognitive segmentation   Identifying groups of consumers based on similarities in their knowledge, meanings, and beliefs and affective responses.

affective responses   Consumers can experience four types of affective responses—emotions, specific feelings, moods, and evaluations—that vary in level of intensity and arousal.

age subcultures   Groups of people defined in terms of age

categories (teens, elderly) with distinctive behaviors, values, beliefs, and lifestyles.

AIO   An acronym standing for activities, interest, and opinions. AIO measures are the primary method for investigating consumer lifestyles and forming psychographic segments.

aspirational group   A reference group an individual consumer wants to join or be similar to.

associative network of knowledge   An organized structure of knowledge, meanings, and beliefs about some concept such as a brand. Each meaning concept is linked to other concepts to form a network of associations.

attention   The process by which consumers select information in the environment to interpret. Also the point at which consumers become conscious or aware of certain stimuli.

attitude   A person's overall evaluation of a concept. An attitude is an affective response at a low level of intensity and arousal. General feelings of favorability or liking.

attitude models   See *multiattribute attitude models.*

attitude toward objects (A_o)   Consumers' overall evaluation (like/dislike) of an object such as a product or store. May be formed in two different ways: a cognitive process that involves relatively controlled and conscious integration of information about the object, and a largely automatic and unconscious response of the affective system linked to an object through classical conditioning.

attitude toward the ad (A_{ad})   Consumers' affective evaluations of the advertisement, not the product or brand being promoted.

attitude toward the behavior or action (A_{act})   The consumer's overall evaluation of a specific behavior.

automatic processing   Cognitive processes tend to become more automatic—to require less conscious control and less cognitive capacity—as they become more practiced and familiar.

baseline   The frequency of the problem behavior before an intervention strategy.

behavior   Overt acts or actions that can be directly observed.

behavior approach   An approach to studying consumer behavior that focuses on the relationship between overt behavior and the environment.

behavior change strategy   A strategy developed to change the frequency or quality of a problem behavior.

behavior effort   The effort consumers expend when making a purchase.

behavioral intention (*BI***)**   A plan to perform an action—"I intend to go shopping this afternoon." Intentions are produced when beliefs about the behavioral consequences of the action and social normative beliefs are considered and integrated to evaluate alternative behaviors and select among them.

behavioral segmentation   Grouping consumers on the basis of similarities in their overt behavior.

behaviors   Specific overt actions of consumers.

belief evaluation (*e***$_i$)**   The degree of liking or favorability a consumer feels for an attribute or consequence associated with a product.

belief strength (*b***$_i$)**   The perceived strength of association between an object and its relevant attributes or consequences.

beliefs   The perceived association between two concepts. May be stored in memory as a proposition. Beliefs about products often concern their attributes or functional consequences. For example, after trying a new brand of toothpaste, a consumer may form a belief that it has a minty taste. Beliefs are synonymous with knowledge and meaning in that each term refers to consumers' interpretations of important concepts.

benefits   Desirable consequences or outcomes that consumers seek when purchasing and using products and services.

benefit segmentation   The process of grouping consumers on the basis of the benefits they seek from the product. For example, the toothpaste market may include one segment seeking cosmetic benefits such as white teeth and another seeking health benefits such as decay prevention.

brand choice   The selection of one brand to purchase from a consideration set of alternative brands.

brand equity   The value of a brand. From the consumer's perspective, brand equity is reflected by the brand attitude based on beliefs about positive product attributes and favorable consequences of brand use.

brand indifference   A purchasing pattern characterized by a low degree of brand loyalty.

brand loyalty   The degree to which a consumer consistently purchases the same brand within a product class.

brand switching   A purchasing pattern characterized by a change from one brand to another.

central route to persuasion   One of two types of cognitive processes by which persuasion occurs. In the central route, consumers focus on the product messages in the ad, interpret them, form beliefs about product attributes and consequences, and integrate these meanings to form brand attitudes and purchase intentions. See *peripheral route to persuasion.*

choice   Choice involves evaluating alternative actions or behaviors and forming a behavioral intention or plan to engage in the selected behavior. The outcome of the integration processes involved in consumer decision making. See also *behavioral intention.*

choice alternatives   The different product classes, product forms, brands, or models considered for purchase.

choice criteria   The specific product attributes or consequences used by consumers to evaluate and choose from a set of alternatives.

choice decision   Requires that consumers integrate their product knowledge about choice criteria to evaluate the choice alternatives in the consideration set and choose one.

classical conditioning   A process through which a previously neutral stimulus, by being paired with an unconditioned stimulus, comes to elicit a response very similar to the response originally elicited by the unconditioned stimulus.

cognition   The mental processes of interpretation and integration, and the thoughts and meanings they produce.

cognitive activity   The mental thought and effort involved in interpreting and integrating information, as in a purchase decision. Often considered as a cost.

cognitive approach   An approach to studying consumer behavior based on current research on topics such as information processing and cognitive science.

cognitive dissonance   A psychologically uncomfortable condition brought about by an imbalance in thoughts, beliefs, attitudes, or behavior. For example, behaving in a way that is inconsistent with one's beliefs creates cognitive dissonance and a motivation to reduce the inconsistency.

cognitive processes   The mental activities (both conscious and unconscious) by which external information in the environment is transformed into meanings and combined to form evaluations of objects and choices about behavior.

cognitive response   The thoughts one has in response to a persuasive message such as support arguments or acceptance thoughts, counterarguments, and curiosity thoughts.

communication   A type of behavior that marketers attempt to increase, involving two basic audiences: consumers who can provide the company with marketing information and consumers who can tell other potential consumers about the product and encourage them to buy it.

communication model   A simple representation of the communication process that focuses on characteristics of the source, message, medium, and receiver.

communication process   The broad goal of marketing communications is to communicate or convey a set of meanings to consumers. See *communication model.*

compatibility   The degree to which a product is consistent with consumers' current cognitions and behaviors.

compensatory integration processes   In decision making, the combination of all the salient beliefs about the consequences of the choice alternatives to form an overall evaluation or attitude (A_{act}) toward each behavioral alternative. In evaluating alternatives, a consumer will select the alternative with the highest overall evaluation on a set of criteria. Criteria evaluations are done separately and combined such that positive evaluations can offset (or compensate for) negative evaluations. This term is also called compensatory rule and compensatory model. See also *noncompensatory integration processes.*

competitive influences   Actions of competing firms intended to affect each other and consumers.

comprehension   The cognitive processes involved in interpreting, understanding, and making sense of concepts, events, objects, and persons in the environment and behavior.

concrete attributes   Tangible, physical characteristics of a product such as the type of fiber in a blanket or the front-seat legroom in a car.

confirmation In consumer satisfaction theory, confirmation refers to a situation in which a product performs exactly as it was expected to (i.e., prepurchase expectations are confirmed).

consideration set A set of alternatives that the consumer evaluates in making a decision. Compare with *evoked set*.

consumer acculturation The process by which people acquire the ability and cultural knowledge to be a skilled consumer in a different culture or subculture.

consumer behavior (1) The dynamic interaction of cognition, behavior, and environmental events by which human beings conduct the exchange aspects of their lives; (2) a field of study concerned with (1) above; (3) a college course concerned with (1) above; and (4) the overt actions of consumers.

consumer behavior management model Based on ideas in applied behavior analysis, this model is concerned with developing and maintaining consumer behavior.

consumer decision making The cognitive processes by which consumers interpret product information and integrate that knowledge to make choices among alternatives.

consumer information processing The cognitive processes by which consumers interpret and integrate information from the environment.

consumer/product relationship The relationship between target consumers and the product or brand of interest. How consumers perceive the product as relating to their goals and values. Important to consider in developing all phases of a marketing strategy. See also *means-end chain*.

consumer satisfaction The degree to which a consumer's prepurchase expectations are fulfilled or surpassed by a product.

consumer socialization How children or adults acquire knowledge about products and services and various consumption-related skills.

consumption Use of a product.

consumption situation The social and physical aspects of the environments where consumers actually use and consume the products and services they have bought.

content of culture All the beliefs, attitudes, goals, and values shared by most people in a society, as well as the typical behaviors, rules, customs, and norms that most people follow, plus characteristic aspects of the physical and social environment.

continuous reinforcement schedule A schedule of reinforcement that provides a reward after every occurrence of the desired behavior.

core values The abstract, broad, general end goals that people are trying to achieve in their lives.

corrective advertising Ads that are mandated by the Federal Trade Commission to correct the false beliefs created by previous misleading or deceptive advertising.

covert modeling In this type of modeling, no actual behaviors or consequences are demonstrated; instead, subjects are told to imagine observing a model behaving in various situations and receiving particular consequences.

cross-cultural differences How the content of culture (meanings, values, norms) differs between different cultures.

cross-cultural research Studies in which marketers seek to identify the differences and similarities in the cultural meaning systems of consumers living in different societies.

cultural interpenetration The amount and type of social interaction between newcomers to a culture (immigrants) and people in the host culture. Influences the degree of acculturation the newcomers can attain. See also *acculturation*.

cultural meanings The shared or similar knowledge, meanings, and beliefs by which people in a social system represent significant aspects of their environments.

cultural process The process by which cultural meaning is moved or transferred between three locations in a society—the social and physical environment, products and services, and individual consumers.

culture The complex of learned meanings, values, and behavioral patterns shared by a society.

deal proneness A consumer's general inclination to use promotional deals such as buying on sale or using coupons.

decision A choice between two or more alternative actions or behaviors. See also *choice* and *behavioral intention*.

decision conflict Arises when family members disagree about various aspects of the purchase decision such as goals and appropriate choice criteria.

decision making See *consumer decision making*.

decision plan The sequence of behavioral intentions produced when consumers engage in problem solving during the decision-making process. See also *behavioral intention*.

demographic segmentation Dividing a market by demographic characteristics such as age, income, family size, sex.

diffusion The process by which new ideas and products become accepted by a society. See also *adopter categories*.

disconfirmation In consumer satisfaction theory, disconfirmation refers to a situation in which a product performs differently than expected. See also *negative disconfirmation* and *positive disconfirmation*.

discriminant consequences Only those consequences that differ across a set of alternatives that may be used as choice criteria.

discriminative stimulus A stimulus that by its mere presence or absence changes the probability of a behavior. For example, a "50 percent off" sign in a store window could be a discriminative stimulus.

disposition situation The physical and social aspects of the environments in which consumers dispose of products, as well as consumers' goals, values, beliefs, feelings, and behaviors while in those environments.

dissatisfaction Occurs when prepurchase expectations are negatively confirmed (when the product performs worse than expected).

dissociative reference group A reference group with undesirable meanings that an individual does not want to join or be similar to.

early adopters The second group of adopters of a new product.

early majority The third group of adopters of a new product.

elaboration The extensiveness of comprehension processes; the degree of elaboration determines the amount of knowledge or the number of meanings produced during comprehension as well as the richness of the interconnections between those meanings.

Elaboration Likelihood Model (ELM)   Identifies two cognitive processes by which promotion communications can persuade consumers—central and peripheral routes.

end goal   The most abstract or most basic consequence, need, or value a consumer wants to achieve or satisfy in a given problem-solving situation.

enduring involvement   The personal sources of relevance or involvement of a product or activity. Compare with *situational sources of involvement.*

environment   The complex set of physical and social stimuli in consumers' external world.

environmental prominence   The marketing strategy of making certain stimuli obvious or prominent in the environment to attract consumers' attention.

episodic knowledge   Cognitive representations of specific events in a person's life. Compare with *semantic knowledge.*

ethical influences   Basic values concerning right and wrong that constrain marketing practices.

ethnic subcultures   Large social groups based on consumers' ethnic background. In the United States, the important ethnic subcultures include African-Americans or blacks, Hispanics, Asians, and Native Americans.

evaluation   An overall judgment of favorable/unfavorable, pro/con, or like/dislike. An attitude toward an object such as a brand, an ad, or a behavioral act.

evoked set   The set of choice alternatives activated directly from memory.

expertise   Occurs when consumers are quite familiar with a product category and specific brands, possessing substantial amounts of general and procedural knowledge organized in schemas and scripts.

exposure   Occurs when consumers come into contact with information in the environment, sometimes through their own intentional behaviors and sometimes by accident.

extensive problem solving   A choice involving substantial cognitive and behavioral effort, as compared to limited decision making and routine choice behavior.

extinction   The process of arranging the environment so that a particular response results in neutral consequences, thus diminishing the frequency of the behavior response over time.

family   A group of at least two people in a household formed on the basis of marriage, cohabitation, blood relationships, or adoption. Families often serve as a basis for various types of consumer analysis.

family decision making   The processes, interactions, and roles of family members involved in making decisions as a group.

family life cycle   A sociological concept that describes changes in families across time. Emphasis is placed on the effects of marriage, births, aging, and deaths on families and the changes in income and consumption through various family stages.

fixed ratio schedule   A type of reinforcement schedule where every second, third, tenth, etc., response is reinforced.

focal attention   A controlled, conscious level of attention that focuses cognitive processes on relevant or prominent stimuli in the environment.

Foote, Cone & Belding (FCB) Grid   A two-by-two grid developed by the Foote, Cone & Belding advertising agency for analyzing consumers and products. The FCB Grid categorizes products based on consumers' level of involvement (high or low) and on whether consumers' dominant response to the product is cognitive or affective (think or feel).

four stages of acculturation   Four levels of acculturation a newcomer to a culture could achieve, depending on the level of cultural interpenetration: honeymoon, rejection, tolerance, and integration stages.

free-flow layout   A store layout that permits consumers to move freely rather than being constrained to movement up and down specific aisles.

functional consequences   The immediate tangible outcomes of product use that can be directly experienced by consumers. For instance, a toothpaste may get your teeth white.

funds access   The behaviors by which consumers obtain money for their purchases. Primary marketing issues include the methods consumers use to pay for particular purchases and the marketing strategies used to increase the probability that consumers are able to access their funds for purchase.

general knowledge   The meanings that consumers construct to represent important informational stimuli they encounter in the environment. Sometimes called declarative knowledge. Compare with *procedural knowledge.*

geographic segmentation   Dividing a market by geographic characteristics such as regions in a country or areas of a city.

geographic subculture   Large social groups defined in geographic terms. For instance, people living in different parts of a country may exhibit differences in cultural meanings.

global marketing   An approach that argues for marketing a product in essentially the same way everywhere in the world.

goal hierarchy   The end goal and the subgoals that are involved in achieving it.

grid layout   A store layout where all counters and fixtures are at right angles to each other, with merchandise counters acting as barriers and guides to traffic flow.

group   Two or more people who interact with each other to accomplish some goal. Examples include families, co-workers, bowling teams, and church members.

heuristics   Propositions connecting an event with an action. Heuristics simplify problem solving. For example, "buy the cheapest brand" could be a choice heuristic that would simplify purchase choice.

hierarchy of effects model   An early model that depicted consumer response to advertising as a series of stages including awareness, knowledge, liking, preference, conviction, and pu chase.

hierarchy of needs   See *Maslow's need hierarchy.*

high involvement   See *involvement.*

household   The people living in a housing unit—a dwelling with its own entrance and basic facilities.

ideal self-concept   The ideas, attitudes, and meanings people have about themselves concerning what they would be like if they were perfect or ideal. Compare with *self-concept.*

impulse purchase   A purchase choice typically made quickly in-store with little decision-making effort.

inferences   Meanings or beliefs that consumers construct to represent the relationships between concepts that are not based only on explicit information in the environment, but on consumers' prior knowledge.

information acquisition situation   Includes physical and social aspects of environments where consumers acquire information relevant to a problem-solving goal, such as a store choice or a decision to buy a particular brand.

information contact   A common early stage in the purchase sequence that occurs when consumers come into contact with information about the product or brand. This often occurs in promotions, where such contact can be intentional (consumers search newspapers for coupons) or accidental (a consumer just happens to come into contact with a promotion while engaging in some other behavior). See also *exposure.*

information processing   See *consumer information processing.*

information-processing model   Used to divide complex cognitive processes into a series of simpler subprocesses that are more easily measured and understood.

information search   Consumers' deliberate search for relevant information in the external environment.

informational reference group influence   Information from a group that is accepted if the consumer believes it will help achieve a goal.

innovativeness   A personality trait to account for the degree to which a consumer accepts and purchases new products and services.

innovators   The first group of consumers to adopt a new product.

instrumental conditioning   See *operant conditioning.*

instrumental values   One of two major types of values proposed by Milton Rokeach. Instrumental values represent preferred modes of conduct or preferred patterns of behavior. See *terminal values.*

integration process   The process by which consumers combine knowledge to make two types of judgments. Attitude formation concerns how different types of knowledge are combined to form overall evaluations of products or brands. Decision making concerns how knowledge is combined to make choices about what behaviors to perform.

intentional exposure   Occurs when consumers are exposed to marketing information due to their own intentional, goal-directed behavior. Compare with *accidental exposure.*

interpretation processes   The processes by which consumers make sense of or determine the meaning of important aspects of the physical and social environment as well as their own behaviors and internal affective states.

interrupts   Stimuli that interrupt or stop the problem-solving process, such as unexpected information encountered in the environment.

involvement   The degree of personal relevance a product, brand, object, or behavior has for a consumer. Experienced as feelings of interest and importance. A *high-involvement* product is one a consumer believes has important personal consequences or will help achieve important personal goals. A *low-involvement* product is one that is not strongly linked to important consequences or goals. Determined by personal and situational sources of involvement.

knowledge   Meanings and beliefs about products, brands, and other aspects of the environment that are stored in memory. See *meanings* and *beliefs.*

laggards   The last group to adopt a new product.

late majority   The next-to-last group to adopt a new product.

legal influences   Federal, state, and local legislation and the agencies and processes by which these laws are upheld.

level of competition   A key aspect of the promotion environment for a product category—as competition heats up, marketers' use of promotions usually increases.

level of comprehension   Refers to the different types of meanings that consumers construct during interpretation processes. Shallow meanings concern physical attributes and functional consequences; deeper meanings concern psychosocial consequences and values.

levels of abstraction   Consumers have product knowledge at different levels of abstraction from concrete attributes to more abstract functional consequences to very abstract value outcomes.

lifestyle   The manner in which people conduct their lives, including their activities, interests, and opinions.

limited capacity   The notion that the amount of knowledge that can be activated and thought about at one time is limited and quite small.

limited problem solving   A choice process involving a moderate degree of cognitive and behavioral effort. See also *extensive problem solving.*

macro social environment   The broad, pervasive aspects of the social environment that affect the entire society or at least large portions of it; including culture, subculture, and social class.

market segmentation   The process of dividing a market into groups of similar consumers and selecting the most appropriate group(s) for the firm to serve.

marketing concept   A business philosophy that argues organizations should satisfy consumer needs and wants to make profits.

marketing mix   The various elements of marketing strategy, including product, price, promotion, and channels of distribution. The goal of marketing management is to develop an effective mix of these elements so they all work together to serve the target market.

marketing strategy   A plan designed to influence exchanges to achieve organizational objectives usually focused on consumers' behaviors; includes product, price, promotion, and channels of distribution; a part of the environment consisting of a variety of physical and social stimuli.

Maslow's need hierarchy   A popular theory of human needs developed by Abraham Maslow. The theory suggests humans satisfy their needs in a sequential order starting with physiological needs (food, water, sex), and ranging through safety needs (protection from harm), belongingness and love needs (companionship), esteem needs (prestige, respect of others), and, finally, self-actualization needs (self-fulfillment).

materialism   A multidimensional value held by many consumers in developed countries. Materialism includes possessiveness, envy of other people's possessions, and nongenerosity.

meanings   People's personal interpretations of stimuli in the environment. See *knowledge* or *beliefs.*

means-end chain   A simple knowledge structure that links product attributes to functional and social consequences and perhaps to high-level consumer values. Means-end chains organize consumers' product knowledge in terms of its self-relevance.

MECCAS model   Attempts to simplify the difficult task of developing effective advertising strategies by identifying five key factors; stands for means-end chain conceptualization of advertising strategy.

micro social environment   Important aspects of consumers' immediate social environment, especially reference groups and family.

modeling   See *vicarious learning.*

modern family life cycle   The various life stages for modern American families, including the stages of the traditional family life cycle, plus other stages found in modern culture such as divorce, single (never married), and single parents.

multiattribute attitude models   Models designed to predict consumers' attitudes toward objects (such as brands) or behaviors (such as buying a brand) based on their beliefs about and evaluations of associated attributes or expected consequences.

multiple-baseline design   Commonly used in applied behavior analysis, these designs demonstrate the effect of an intervention across several different behaviors, individuals, or situations at different times.

negative disconfirmation   In consumer satisfaction theory, negative disconfirmation refers to a situation in which a product performs worse than expected.

negative reinforcement   Occurs when the frequency of a given behavior is increased by removing an aversive stimulus. See also *reinforcement.*

noncompensatory integration processes   Choice strategies in which the positive and negative consequences of the choice alternatives do not balance or compensate for each other. Compare with *compensatory integration processes.* In evaluating alternatives using noncompensatory rules, positive and negative consequences of alternatives do not compensate for each other. Included among the types of noncompensatory integration processes are conjunctive, disjunctive, and lexicographics. The *conjunctive rule* suggests consumers establish a minimum acceptable level for each choice criterion and accept an alternative only if it equals or exceeds the minimum cutoff level for every criterion. The *disjunctive rule* suggests consumers establish acceptable standards for each criterion and accept an alternative if it exceeds the standard on at least one criterion. The *lexicographic rule* suggests consumers rank choice criteria from most to least important and choose the best alternative on the most important criterion.

nonfamily households   Unrelated people living together in same household—about 30 percent of American households.

observability   The degree to which products or their effects can be perceived or observed by other consumers.

operant conditioning   The process of altering the probability of a behavior being emitted by changing the consequences of the behavior.

opportunity to process   The extent to which consumers have the chance to attend to and comprehend marketing information; can be affected by factors such as time pressure, consumers' affective states, and distractions.

overt modeling   The most common form of vicarious learning, this requires that consumers actually observe the model performing the behavior.

penetration price policy   A pricing strategy that includes a plan to sequentially raise prices after introduction of a new product at a relatively low price.

perceived environment   Those parts of the environment that are attended to and interpreted by a particular consumer on a particular occasion.

perceived risk   The expected negative consequences of performing an action such as purchasing a product.

peripheral route to persuasion   One of two types of cognitive processes by which persuasion occurs. In the peripheral route, the consumer does not focus on the product message in an ad but on "peripheral" stimuli such as an attractive, well-known celebrity or popular music. Consumers' feelings about these other stimuli may indirectly influence beliefs and attitude about the product by first influencing attitude toward the ad. Compare with *central route to persuasion.*

personal selling   Direct personal interactions between a salesperson and a potential buyer.

personal sources of involvement   A consumer's personal level of self-relevance for a product. Represented in memory by the means-end chains of product/self relationships that consumers have learned through experience. Compare with *situational sources of involvement.*

personality   The general, relatively consistent pattern of responses to the environment exhibited by an individual.

persuasion   Refers to the cognitive and affective processes by which consumers' beliefs and attitudes are changed by promotion communications.

physical environment   The collection of nonhuman, physical, tangible elements that comprises the field in which consumer behavior occurs. Compare with *social environment.*

place utility   Occurs when goods and services are made available where the consumer wants to purchase them.

political influences   The pressure exerted to control marketing practices by various consumer groups.

positioning   See *product positioning.*

positive disconfirmation   In consumer satisfaction theory, positive disconfirmation refers to a situation in which a product performs better than expected.

positive reinforcement   Occurs when rewards are given to increase the frequency with which a given behavior is likely to occur. See also *reinforcement.*

prepurchase expectations   Beliefs about anticipated performance of a product.

problem recognition   Occurs when consumer notices the current state of affairs is not the ideal or desired state. Involves activation of a goal and a certain level of involvement.

problem solving   A general approach to understanding consumer decision making. Focuses on consumers' perception of the decision as a problem. Important aspects of the problem representation include end goals, subgoals, and relevant knowledge. Consumers construct a decision plan by integrating knowledge within the constraints of the problem representation.

procedural knowledge   Consumers' knowledge or beliefs about how to perform behaviors. See also *script*.

product contact   Occurs when a consumer comes into physical contact with a product.

product positioning   Designing and executing a marketing strategy to form a particular mental representation of a product or brand in consumers' minds. Typically, the goal is to position the product in some favorable way relative to competitive offerings.

product symbolism   The various abstract meanings of a product to a consumer and what the consumer experiences in purchasing and using it.

promotion clutter   The growing number of competitive promotion strategies in the environment.

promotion communications   See *promotion strategies*.

promotion strategies   Used by marketers to help achieve their promotion objectives, these include advertising, sales promotions, personal selling, and publicity.

promotions   Information that marketers develop to communicate meanings about their products and persuade consumers to buy them.

psychographic segmentation   Dividing markets into segments on the basis of consumer lifestyles, attitudes, and interests.

psychosocial consequences   This term refers to two types of outcomes or consequences of product use: Psychological consequences (I feel good about myself) and social consequences (Other people are making fun of me).

publicity   Any unpaid form of communication about the marketer's company, products, or brand.

pull strategies   Ways to encourage the consumer to purchase the manufacturer's brand, such as cents-off coupons.

punishment   A term used to describe the process of a response being followed by a noxious or aversive event, thus decreasing the frequency of the response.

purchase intentions   A decision plan or intention to buy a particular product or brand. See also *behavioral intention*.

purchase transactions   Behaviors involving the exchange of funds for products and services.

purchasing situation   Includes the physical and social stimuli that are present in the environment where the consumer actually makes the purchase.

push strategies   Ways to influence the selling efforts of retailers, such as trade discounts.

rate of usage   The rate at which a consumer uses or consumes a product.

reference group   People who serve as a point of reference and who influence an individual's affect, cognitions, and behaviors.

reinforcement   A consequence that occurs after a behavior that increases the probability of future behavior of the same type.

reinforcement schedule   The rate at which rewards or reinforcements are offered in attempts to operantly condition behavior. See *reinforcement*.

relative advantage   Refers to the degree to which an item has a sustainable, competitive differential advantage over other product classes, product forms, and brands.

relevant knowledge   Appropriate or useful knowledge that is activated from memory in the context of a decision or interpretation situation.

respondent conditioning   See *classical conditioning*.

response hierarchy   The total list of behaviors a consumer could perform at any given time arranged from most probable to least probable.

reversal design   In this approach, the problem behavior of a subject or group of subjects is first assessed to determine baseline performance. After a stable rate of behavior is determined, the intervention is introduced until behavior changes. The intervention is then withdrawn and then reintroduced to determine if it is influencing the behavior.

rituals   Actions or behaviors performed by consumers to create, affirm, evoke, revise, or obtain desired symbolic cultural meanings.

routinized choice behavior   A purchase involving little cognitive and behavioral effort and perhaps no decision. Purchase could be merely carrying out an existing decision plan. Compare with *limited* and *extensive problem solving*.

sales promotions   Direct inducements to the consumer to make a purchase, such as coupons or cents-off deals.

salient beliefs   The set of beliefs activated in a particular situation; may be represented as an associative network of linked meanings.

satisfaction/dissatisfaction   Useful concept for understanding consumer behavior; refers to the consumer's affective and cognitive reactions to the chosen product after purchase.

scanner cable method   A method of monitoring a number of stages in a purchase sequence. One such system, BehaviorScan, is designed to predict which products will be successful and which ads will work best to sell them.

schema   An associative network of interrelated meanings that represents a person's general knowledge about some concept. Compare with *script*.

script   A sequence of productions or knowledge about the appropriate actions associated with particular events. Consumers often form scripts to organize their knowledge about behaviors to perform in familiar situations. Compare with *schema*.

segmentation   See *market segmentation*.

segmentation strategy   The general approach marketers use to approach markets such as mass marketing, or marketing to one or more segments.

selective exposure   A process by which people selectively come into contact with information in their environment. For instance, consumers may avoid marketing information by leaving the room while commercials are on TV or not opening junk mail.

self-concept   The ideas, meanings, attitudes, and knowledge people have about themselves.

self-regulation   A form of ethical influence employed by marketers; many professions have codes of ethics and many firms have their own consumer affairs offices that seek to ensure the consumer is treated fairly.

semantic knowledge   The general meanings and beliefs people have acquired about their world. Compare with *episodic knowledge*.

shaping   A process of reinforcing successive approximations of a desired behavior, or of other required behaviors, to increase the probability of the desired response.

shopping situation   The physical and spatial characteristics of the environments where consumers shop for products and services.

simplicity   The degree to which a product is easy for a consumer to understand and use.

situation   The ongoing stream of interactions between goal-directed behaviors, affective and cognitive responses, and environmental factors that occur over a defined period of time. Situations have a purpose and a beginning, middle, and end.

situational sources of involvement   Temporary interest or concern with a product or a behavior brought about by the situational context. Aspects of the immediate physical and social environment that activate important consequences and values and link them to product attributes, thus making products and brands seem self-relevant. For example, consumers may become situationally involved with buying a hot water heater if their old one breaks. Compare with *personal sources of involvement*.

social class   A status hierarchy by which groups and individuals are categorized on the basis of esteem and prestige. For example, one classification divides American society into upper class (14 percent of the population), middle class (32 percent of the population), working class (38 percent of the population), and lower class (16 percent of the population).

social environment   Includes all human activities in social interactions, direct or indirect.

socialization   The processes by which an individual learns the values and appropriate behavior patterns of a group, institution, or culture. Socialization is strongly influenced by family, reference groups, and social class.

social marketing   Programs and strategies designed to change behavior in ways that are deemed good for consumers and for society.

social stratification   See *social class*.

sociocultural segmentation   Dividing a market by social and cultural characteristics (ethnicity, country of origin, social class).

speed   Refers to how fast the benefits of the product are experienced by the consumer.

spreading activation   Through this usually unconscious process, interrelated parts of a knowledge structure may be activated during interpretation and integration processes (or even daydreaming).

stages of acculturation   Four stages of acculturation are: honeymoon stage, rejection stage, tolerance stage, integration stage.

store atmosphere   Affective and cognitive states that consumers experience in a store environment but may not be fully conscious of while shopping.

store contact   An important set of behaviors for most consumer-goods purchases, this includes locating the outlet, traveling to the outlet, and entering the outlet.

store image   The set of meanings consumers associate with a particular store.

store layout   The basic floor plan and display of merchandise within a store. At a basic level, this influences such factors as how long the consumer stays in the store, how many products the consumer comes into visual contact with, and what routes the consumer travels within the store. Two basic types are *grid* and *free-flow layouts*.

store location   Where a store is situated in a specific geographic area; influences the ease of store contact.

store loyalty   The degree to which a consumer consistently patronizes the same store when shopping for particular types of products.

store patronage   The degree to which a consumer shops at a particular store relative to competitive outlets.

subcultures   Segments within a culture that share a set of distinguishing meanings, values, and patterns of behavior that differ in certain respects from those of the overall culture.

subjective or social norms (*SN***)**   Consumers' perceptions of what other people want them to do; influences behavioral intentions.

subliminal perception   A psychological view that suggests attitudes and behaviors can be changed by stimuli that are not consciously perceived.

symbolic meaning   The set of psychological and social meanings products have for consumers. More abstract meanings than physical attributes and functional consequences.

target behavior   The earliest behavior in a purchase sequence not being performed, or not being performed appropriately or frequently enough to lead to the next behavior. Also known as *problem behavior*.

target market   Group of consumers selected as potential customers for product or service; the consumers targeted to receive marketing strategies.

terminal values   One of two major types of values proposed by Milton Rokeach. Terminal values represent preferred end states of being or abstract, global goals that consumers are trying to achieve in their lives. Compare with *instrumental values*.

theory of reasoned action   Assumes consumers consciously consider the consequences of alternative behaviors and choose the one that leads to the most desirable outcomes. The theory states behavior is strongly influenced by behavioral intentions, which in turn are determined by attitudes toward performing the behavior and social normative beliefs about the behavior.

trade promotion   Marketing tactics, such as advertising or display allowances, designed to get channel members to provide special support for products or services.

traditional family life cycle   The typical stages of life followed by most American families some 30 to 40 years ago. Each stage is distinguished by a major life event: marriage, birth of children, aging, retirement, and death.

transactions   The exchanges of funds, time, cognitive activity, and behavior effort for products and services. In a micro sense, the primary objective of marketing, where consumers' funds are exchanged for products and services.

trialability   The degree to which a product can be tried on a limited basis or divided into small quantities for an inexpensive trial.

usage situation segmentation   Group consumers on the basis of product usage situations (buying ice cream for an after-dinner dessert versus as an afternoon snack).

utilitarian reference group influence   Compliance of an individual with perceived expectations of others to obtain rewards or avoid punishments.

VALS   An acronym standing for Values And Life-Styles. VALS and VALS 2 are well-known psychographic segmentation schemes marketed by SRI International.

value-expressive reference group influence   An individual's use of groups to enhance or support his or her self-concept.

values   The cognitive representations of important, abstract life goals that consumers are trying to achieve. See *terminal* and *instrumental values.*

variable ratio schedule   Occurs when a reinforcer follows a desired consequence on an average of one half, one third, one fourth, etc., of the time the behavior occurs, but not necessarily every second or third time, etc.

verbal modeling   In this type of modeling, behaviors are not demonstrated and people are not asked to imagine a model performing a behavior; instead, people are told how others similar to themselves behaved in a particular situation.

vicarious learning   Changes in an individual's behavior brought about by observing the actions of others and the consequences of those actions.

Wheel of Consumer Analysis   A simple model of the key factors in understanding consumer behavior and guiding marketing strategy. Consists of four parts: affect and cognition, behavior, environment, and marketing strategy.

WOM   An acronym standing for word-of-mouth communication.

word-of-mouth communication   Occurs when consumers share information with friends about products and/or promotions (good deals on particular products, a valuable coupon in the newspaper, or a sale at a retail store).

Subject Index

$$\frac{1}{4} + \frac{1}{5} = \frac{9}{20}$$

$\frac{1}{1}$